**Capital Market
Equilibrium and
Efficiency**

Capital Market Equilibrium and Efficiency

Implications for Accounting, Financial, and Portfolio Decision Making

Edited by
James L. Bicksler
Rutgers University

Lexington Books
D.C. Heath and Company
Lexington, Massachusetts
Toronto

Library of Congress Cataloging in Publication Data

Main entry under title:

Capital market equilibrium and efficiency.

    CONTENTS: Fama, E.F. Efficient capital markets.—Samuelson, P.A. Proof that properly discounted present values of assets vibrate randomly.—Hess, P. and Bicksler, J. Capital asset prices versus time series models as predictors of inflation. [etc.]
    1. Capital—Addresses, essays, lectures. 2. Investments—Addresses, essays, lectures. 3. Capital assets pricing model—Addresses, essays, lectures. 4. Finance—Addresses, essays, lectures.
I. Bicksler, James L.
HG4539.C36   332'.041   75–21829
ISBN 0–669–86660–1

International Standard Book Number: 0–669–86660–1

Library of Congress Catalog Card Number: 75–21829

To
Conchita, John, and Katherine
for Their Love, Support, and Encouragement

Far better it is to dare mighty things to win glorious triumphs, even though checkered with failure, than to take rank with those poor spirits who neither enjoy much nor suffer much because they live in the grey twilight that knows not victory nor defeat.

Theodore Roosevelt

Contents

Foreword

How often at deans' receptions or publishers' cocktail parties have we heard the sneering put-down: "If you people really believe that the capital markets are so efficient, what on earth can you teach for a whole semester?" The answer is "plenty!" as the Contents of this book will make clear. And this selection, of course, is intended only as a sample and an introduction, not an exhaustive survey. A glance through the leading journals in finance will show that the efficient markets doctrine is fast becoming the dominant stream in academic research in finance.

The phrase "fast becoming" can be replaced by "has become" [the dominant stream] if we broaden the term "efficient markets doctrine" to include, as I believe we should, the parallel stream of research under the rubric of the capital asset pricing model (CAPM) of Sharpe and Lintner (or perhaps of Treynor-Sharpe-Lintner-Mossin-Fama and Black, to name one of the precursors and some of the major subsequent contributors to the model in its present-day form). It is no accident that these two streams have developed in tandem and that they are intertwined in so many of the papers in this book. The efficient markets principle (henceforth the EMP) really tells us only that we may treat the observed prices of securities as *equilibrium prices*. To exploit the principle to test propositions about valuation, we must usually invoke a specific model of equilibrium. The CAPM (also referred to in some of the papers as the two-parameter model, risk-return model, or two-fund model) has served effectively in that role.

Of the two streams, the EMP and the CAPM, the success achieved by the former could surely have been predicted 10 years ago. The only surprising thing really has been how long its hegemony was resisted by those coming into finance by way of economics. From the accounting wing, such resistance might well have been expected, of course, since the EMP is a direct challenge to that profession's obsessive concern with the form and language to be used in reporting a business's past history. If the EMP were valid, then it would have to be concluded that the thousands of hours that are devoted annually by accounting practitioners, academics, and regulatory bodies to such disputes as that over flow-through versus deferral of accelerated depreciation or over pooling versus purchase accounting of acquisitions are largely a pointless charade. The studies of Kaplan and Roll and Dopuch and Gonedes in Part II provide tests of this conclusion about the impact of accounting conventions on market valuations with results that are thoroughly consistent with EMP predictions.

But while we can understand the reaction of accountants to this threatened breaking of their rice bowl, how are we to account for the hostility to EMP on the part of so many economists? Economics, after all, had long had a major stake in the notions of market equilibrium and rational economic calculation.

ix

The answer may well lie with the profession's preoccupation with a particular kind of macroeconomics during the late 1950s and early 1960s. The macromodels of that era, whether of the monetarist or Keynesian persuasion, did not
merely fail to exploit the EMP, but were fundamentally incompatible with it.
Virtually without exception they pictured interest rates, bond prices, stock
prices, and the prices of assets generally as lagging systematically and pre-
dictably behind changes in directly observable monetary and fiscal variables.
As long as such models, with their built-in irrationalities and seemingly un-
exploited profit opportunities, held center stage in economics, the EMP was
bound to strike those economists and finance specialists who were aware of it
as little more than the minor heresy of a small cult at the University of Chicago.

The tide began to turn toward EMP in economics in the late 1960s and
early 1970s, partly in response to the accumulating body of successful research
results in finance and partly in response to the general disillusionment with the
traditional macromodels and especially their failure to deliver the promised
superior forecasting performance. Those failures were emphasized in a very
painful way in those economics departments whose members so gleefully had
formed syndicates to speculate on the "inevitable" rise in long-term bond prices
during the recession of 1969–70. Further disenchantment set in as word spread
about the studies by Michael Rozeff (Chapter 17 in this book) and by Richard
V.L. Cooper on the relation between money and stock prices. But the decisive
factor was perhaps the rediscovery by the profession of the classic paper on
rational expectations by Muth, published in 1961. Here, at last, was a line of
argument that expressed the EMP in a vocabulary more familiar to economists
than that of finance and which may therefore have made its implications for
economics somewhat easier to see. (Muth himself, for example, specifically
called attention to the ineffectuality of "public predictions" or forecasts as well
as to the inadequacy of the standard "cobweb" analysis—an analysis with close
family resemblance to many of the standard macromodels of business fluctuations.) At the time of this writing (March 1976) it seems safe to predict that
the rational-expectations/EMP doctrine will eventually come to dominate in
research economics as it has in finance.

The success achieved by the CAPM in the past decade was a good deal less
predictable than that of the EMP. Two parameters would have struck most
specialists as being too few to capture the essentials of the equilibrium of asset
markets under uncertainty. By the standard of these early doubts, the subsequent accomplishments have been doubly remarkable. The empirical record is
reviewed in great detail in the article by Jensen (Chapter 19). The papers by
Hamada and Rubinstein (Chapters 10 and 13, respectively) show how effective
the model has been even when applied to the class of normative issues that has
become central to the field of corporate finance.

But there are signs even in the chapters of this book that the role of the
CAPM as virtually the exclusive model of equilibrium in finance is about to

change. This is not to suggest that it will be supplanted; it has proved to be far too good a first approximation for that, and, in any event, there are no serious rivals in sight. Rather, we are likely to see it supplemented and extended. The CAPM, for example, can be given a multiperiod interpretation only under very restrictive conditions. It requires us to assume that investors face an unchanging opportunity set (or, if it changes, that the changes are stochastically independent of returns on securities). Chapter 3, by Hess and Bicksler, suggests that the assumption of an unchanging opportunity set may be a weaker reed than we had previously suspected.

It is hard to say at this time what forms the supplements and extensions of the CAPM will take. One likely candidate is a multifund model of the kind derived by Robert Merton and described by Jensen in Chapter 4. More recently there has been a revival of interest in time-and-state preference models. The search for a convenient multiperiod framework may well move in that direction if ways of measuring or estimating implicit prices of state-contingent claims can be developed.

No account of the impact of the EMP and CAPM on finance would be complete without some reference to security analysis and investment management, long the mainstays of business school curricula in finance. Students in these courses were routinely set to writing up elaborate projections of future stock market performance for specific firms and industries based entirely on widely available public information. By the middle 1960s, thanks to the computer, the process of fishing through long-published data had even been mechanized. Students were led to believe that spinning the Compustat tapes would somehow unlock the secrets of the future. Clearly, these days are over. The sneer, in fact, is now on the other lip: "If you don't accept the efficient markets principle, what on earth *can* you teach for a whole semester?"

Preface

Two of the most exciting developments in microfinance and capital markets have been the efficient markets hypothesis and the capital asset pricing model. These conceptual frameworks and the subsequent empirical testing provide important apparatuses for structuring one's thought processes about real-world financial market phenomena, normative strategies for corporate resource allocation, and individual portfolio choice under uncertainty. This book attempts to communicate the central ideas, results, and implications of both the efficient markets and capital asset pricing models. The book is intended to be neither self-contained nor a complete guide to the historical development or the present state of knowledge of either of these topics. Recent and on-going research on both these frameworks, as well as in closely allied areas, would make any such claim pretenious.

My grateful appreciation is extended to numerous friends and academic colleagues for an untold number of helpful suggestions regarding the book. Amir Barnea, Fred Grygiel, Jack Lucken, Philip Malter, and Giles Mellon, in particular, deserve a word of acknowledgment in this regard. Patrick J. Hess made, as usual, a number of penetrating comments. Joint work with him in the last few years has undoubtedly carried over and enriched this book. Dean Horace J. De Podwin and Associate Dean David W. Blakeslee of Rutgers University, Graduate School of Business, gave encouragement and administrative support. A special word of thanks is due Merton H. Miller for both the Foreword and his valuable contributions on technical matters. Betty Patterson and Mike McCarroll have not only done their usual outstanding job in the editorial phase but have exhibited infinite patience. Mrs. Genoble King and Ms. Willa Stewart provided their usual superb secretarial assistance. My wife assisted in countless ways and for this I express my deepest gratitude.

**Capital Market
Equilibrium and
Efficiency**

An Introductory Survey

This introduction previews the central ideas in the chapters of this book as well as their implications for the decision-making process for financial economists, academics, capital market practitioners, accountants, and corporate executives.

Part I, Market Efficiency and Equilibrium, consists of four chapters. In efficient markets, prices "fully reflect" all relevant information. The sufficient conditions ensuring efficient markets are: (1) there are no trading costs; (2) decision information is costless and available to all investors at the margin; and (3) there is concurrence by all investors at the margin regarding the implications of current information for the current price and distribution of future prices for each individual security.[1]

Although the above conditions are sufficient, they are not necessary to ensure market efficiency. Empirical tests of the efficient market do not take the form of inference about the "truth" or validity of the assumptions, but instead focus on the consistency of the implications of the "fair game" model or the submartingale model with the evidence.

The submartingale model states that

$$E(p_{j,\ t+1}|\Phi_t) \geqslant p_{j,t}$$

or identically

$$E(\tilde{r}_{j,\ t+1}|\Phi_t) \geqslant 0$$

where E is the expected value, $p_{j,\ t}$ is the price of security j at time t, Φ_t is the set of information assumed to be "fully reflected" at time t, and $r_{j,\ t+1}$ is the one-period equilibrium expected return, and $\tilde{\ }$ is a tilde that indicates a random variable.

The above is a statement that the series of prices for security j follows a submartingale. This means that trading rules based on information in Φ_t cannot have greater profits than a buy-and-hold policy for the given investor period.[a]

Tests of capital market efficiency are usually classified into three different information sets (e.g., weak, semistrong, and strong tests). In the weak form of the efficient markets test, the information set is the sequence of past prices. Most of the empirical work in this domain focuses on the random walk. The random walk is an extension of the submartingale. The random walk hypothesis

---

[a]Formally, this statement should deal with expected profits above the equilibrium profit level. That is, efficient markets do not rule out the possibility of a portfolio comprised of cash and a single security having returns that are greater than a security having an equilibrium expected return that is negative.

states that the changes in stock market prices (or returns) are independent and identically distributed.[2]

The evidence from Bachelier in 1900 to the tests of serial covariance of returns by Cootner, Moore, Godfrey, Granger, and Morgenstern, and Granger and Morgenstern, the trading rules based on filtering techniques by Alexander and Fama and Blume, and tests using the residuals of the market model and two-parameter model all indicate that historical price or return sequences cannot be used profitably when transaction costs, etc., are taken in account.[3] "Thus, the efficient market model and its sub-martingale formulation share the most fundamental result of the random walk model; viz., in a world conforming to the model, chartist techniques and other mechanistic trading rules will not work."[4] Stated differently, implications of the random walk are that reading the tape (analyzing the past price history of a stock) is of absolutely no value or usefulness in predicting the future price behavior of a security. It is thus no surprise that so many "board watchers" and "tape readers" have holes in their shoes.[5]

In the semistrong form of the efficient market hypothesis, prices and yields are tested to determine whether they fully reflect all available information. Empirical tests utilizing information regarding stock splits, earnings announcements, Federal Reserve discount rate changes, and secondary offerings of common stock indicate that "the available semi-strong form evidence on the effect of various sorts of public announcements of common stock returns is all consistent with the efficient markets model. The strong point of the evidence, however, is its consistency rather than its quantity."[6]

Hypotheses tests of the strong form are limited in number. Two empirical tests are those of Niederhoffer and Osborne and Scholes. Both test the essence of the strong-form version as to whether there is a "profitable" advantage accruing from monopolistic access to information. The Niederhoffer and Osborne study shows that specialists of major security exchanges have access to monopolistic information and use this to generate monopolistic profits.[7] In summary, investors should view the world as having efficient capital markets. More specifically, information, except that possessed by inside investors, should be regarded as already impounded into the present stock price.[8]

Eugene Fama's "Efficient Capital Markets: A Review of Theory and Empirical Work" presents a superb overview of these issues, including the Samuelson and Mandelbrot fair-game model, the submartingale and random walk models that are used as rationales of market efficiency, along with empirical evidence of each of the three forms of tests.[b] Fama concludes that

The evidence in support of the efficient markets model is extensive, and (somewhat uniquely in economics) contradictory evidence is sparse. Nevertheless, we

---

[b]Since Fama's review article, the testing procedures have become more sophisticated. This is a result of there being a more developed framework of capital market equilibrium. That

certainly do not want to leave the impression that all issues are closed. The old saw, much remains to be done, is certainly relevant here. Indeed, as is often the case in successful scientific research, now that we know where we have been in the past, we are able to pose and, hopefully, to answer an even more interesting set of questions for the future. In this case the most pressing field of future endeavor is the development and testing of models of market equilibrium under uncertainty. When the processes generating equilibrium expected returns are better understood, we will have a better framework for more sophisticated test of market efficiency.[9]

Paul Samuelson's Proof That Properly Discounted Present Values of Assets Vibrate Randomly (Chapter 2) demonstrates that, under a given stochastic process generating future dividends, the time series of changes in the present price of a company's stock adjusted for dividends constitutes a random walk (e.g., exhibits white noise).[10] It is also shown that in a world of random walk stock price behavior, it is possible for a subset of investors to have portfolio performance appreciably better than the market. Hence, the fundamentalist valuation model can be compatible with random walk stock price behavior.

Eugene Fama recently investigated the relationship between nominal interest rates and inflation.[11] His time-series analysis using default-free bonds was consistent with the joint hypothesis that the expected real rate of interest (return) on treasury bills was constant and that capital market yields reflect all relevant information about historical inflation rates (i.e., capital markets are efficient).

In Chapter 3, Capital Asset Prices versus Time Series Models as Predictors of Inflation: The Expected Real Rate of Interest and Market Efficiency, Patrick Hess and James Bicksler investigate the behavior of nominal interest rates under conditions of uncertain inflation. Specifically, the joint hypothesis that the expected real rate of return is constant and that the capital markets are efficient is investigated. The evidence is consistent with a rejection of this joint hypothesis. This result appears to be due to the lack of empirical robustness of the constant expected real rate of return proposition. When the empirical tests are modified to account for temporal changes in the expected real rate of return, the results are generally consistent with the efficient markets model. Chapter 3 represents both a methodological and empirical challenge and extension of Eugene Fama's results.[12]

The theory of finance has—or should have—two basic objectives. On the one hand, the theory should be able to explain and interpret phenomena in financial markets. On the other hand, the theory should assist management in making the best decisions with respect to the company's investment and financing decisions by providing useful analytical tools within a realistic theoretical framework.

---

is, since any test of market efficiency implies simultaneously a framework of market equilibrium, a more detailed view of the latter is consistent with more detailed tests of the former. Empirical results of market efficiency using the two-parameter model are discussed later in Chapters 16 and 11, by Jaffe and Mandelker.

Everyone would agree that these two aspects of the theory of finance are closely related. The reason is very simple. The most general and universally acceptable formulation of company objectives is maximization of the market value of the company's equity. Through its actions management can influence the market value, but is clearly unable to determine it completely. The market value is determined by the simultaneous interplay of supply and demand in the capital markets, where other companies also participate as suppliers of securities and where various investors participate in the demand for these securities. No theory of finance can give a satisfactory explanation of security valuation or investment behavior if it fails to take into account the relationships that exist with individual investors' portfolio decisions. This means that all the investment alternatives open to the investor must be taken into account if we want to understand his evaluation of any one of them. Market values are determined by the demand by all investors, and this leads us to establish a theory of general equilibrium in capital markets. For without such a model, management is unable to foresee the effects of alternative investment and financing decisions.[13]

Mossin further states that

in view of the fundamental theoretical role that the analysis of capital markets should play for the study of the corporate decisions, it is remarkable to what limited extent such an analysis has been brought explicitly into existing financial literature. Even in modern and reputable introductions to the theory of finance, the market plays a highly indirect role. A number of hypotheses are advanced concerning the way in which the market evaluates and reacts (e.g., with respect to discounting for time and uncertainty), but these hypotheses are entirely ad hoc and quite arbitrary, since they are not derived from any fundamental assumptions describing market equilibrium.[14]

In sum, a framework of the equilibrium structure of capital assets lies at the core of investment and microfinance knowledge.

The Sharpe-Lintner-Mossin capital asset pricing model was the first equilibrium model of capital market security phenomena that was sufficiently tractable for operational hypothesis testing.[15] The basic assumptions underlying the market equilibrium relationship of security prices in a mean-variance world are:

1. All investors are risk-averse and choose portfolios in a manner consistent with maximizing expected utility of single-period terminal wealth.
2. Portfolio investment opportunities can be described solely in terms of means and variances (or standard deviations) of the *ex ante* distribution of one-period portfolio returns.
3. Investors have homogeneous expectations regarding means, variances, and covariances of returns for all securities in the investment opportunity set; in addition, all investors have identical investment opportunity sets.
4. Capital markets are efficient in the sense that borrowing and lending rates

are equal. There are no restrictions to short sales, no taxes, and no transactions costs. Capital assets are perfectly divisible, etc.

5. The supply of all capital assets is given.

Under these and other less restrictive conditions, equilibrium relationships
for risky capital assets have been derived. The fundamental result of risk,
return, and market equilibrium at the level of the individual asset or security is:

$$E(\tilde{R}_i) = R_f + \beta_i[E(\tilde{R}_m) - R_f]$$

where $E(\tilde{R}_i)$ is the expected return on the individual security for the single
period being considered, $E(\tilde{R}_m)$ is the expected return on the market portfolio,
R_f is the riskless rate of return, and β_i is the systematic risk of the ith security.
This equation says that the equilibrium expected return on an asset equals the
riskless rate of return (the rate of time preference) plus a risk premium.

The beta of a security or capital asset measures the marginal contribution
of that individual risky asset on the dispersion or variance of the expected
return distribution of the market portfolio, $\tilde{R}_m$. Formally, beta,[c] or the marginal
risk of an asset, is

$$\beta_i = \frac{\text{cov}(\tilde{R}_i, R_m)}{o^2(\tilde{R}_m)}$$

From the above, it can be shown that:

$$E(\tilde{R}_i) = R_f + \frac{E(\tilde{R}_m) - R_f}{o^2(\tilde{R}_m)} \text{cov}(\tilde{R}_i, \tilde{R}_m)$$

This is equivalent to saying that the equilibrium expected return for a risky
asset is equal to the riskless rate of interest plus a linear risk premium equal to
the product of the risk premium per unit of risk, commonly called the *proportionality factor*, or $[E(\tilde{R}_m) - R_f/o^2(\tilde{R}_m)]$, and the asset's covariance with the
market portfolio, or $\text{cov}(\tilde{R}_i \tilde{R}_m)$.

This linear expected return-risk relationship for securities was derived from
a market scenario in which investors choose only Tobin efficient portfolios and
market conditions imply a set of clearing prices for all assets in the investment
opportunity set. Under these conditions, the expected return-risk market
equilibrium relationship can be described by the capital market line:

$$E(\tilde{R}_p) = R_f + \lambda[o(\tilde{R}_p)]$$

---

[c]In the abstract, the magnitude of a security's beta could range from plus infinity to minus
infinity. In reality, there are few securities that have negative betas.

where $o(\tilde{R}_p)$ is the standard deviation of the expected return distribution for the Tobin efficient portfolios and λ is the price of risk reduction for Tobin portfolios and is equal to:

$$\frac{E(\tilde{R}_p) - \tilde{R}_f}{o(\tilde{R}_m)}$$

The empirical cross-sectional tests of Douglas, Lintner, Miller and Scholes, and Friend and Blume and the time-series tests of Black, Jensen, and Scholes indicated that the simple version does not provide an entirely adequate description of the structure of security returns.[16, 17]

Because the simple version of the capital asset pricing model has not been entirely adequate, there have been proposed recently some exciting single-period extensions such as the two-factor model of Black, Vasicek, Brennan and Ross and an intemporal (N-factor) model by Merton. These approaches suggest that the simple form of the CAPM model is tractable to extensions and can be generalized to more complicated capital market conditions that offer useful insights.[18,19]

The two-factor model proposed independently by Black, Vasicek, and Ross and empirically tested by Black, Jensen, and Scholes may be expressed as:[20]

$$E(\tilde{R}_i) = E(\tilde{R}_z)(1 - \beta_i) + E(\tilde{R}_m)\beta_i$$

It postulates that in a world in which there is no borrowing or lending of the riskless asset as well as no restrictions on short selling, capital market equilibrium relationships for risky assets can be described as if investors held a linear combination of two funds or portfolios.[21] These two funds are the market portfolio, m, and the minimum-variance zero-beta portfolio, z. The product $E(\tilde{R}_z)(1 - \beta_i)$ represents the expected return on a riskless security which in this context is the zero-beta minimum-variance portfolio. The expected return on a risky asset is still a linear function of its beta risk. The expected equilibrium return on a risky asset is an average of the returns on the two portfolios weighted proportionally to the fractions of portfolio wealth invested.

Capital Markets: Theory and Evidence (Chapter 4) by Michael Jensen is a survey of the literature of the two-parameter mean-variance capital asset pricing model. Within this topic, Jensen explores various extensions of the capital asset pricing model emanating from the dropping of selective restrictive assumptions. These include contributions by Brennan and Vasicek on differential borrowing and lending rates, Mayers on the existence of nonmarketable assets, and Lintner on heterogeneous expectations.[22] Jensen concludes that "we now have substantial empirical documentation of the process generating the returns on assets and at least several potential theoretical explanations of these empirical results."[23] And "while we do not yet have a complete solution to the asset pricing problem, in the recent past we have obtained a much better understanding of the nature of the process generating the returns on assets and it seems likely that the rate of increase in our knowledge in this area will continue at least into the near future."[24] Indeed, Fama argues that "the important basis for the conclusion that the two-parameter model is useful is that it does well, relative to any other capital market model of which I am aware in describing return date."[25]

Implications for Accounting is the title of Part II. It contains three chapters. Capital Market Equilibrium, Information Production, and Selecting Accounting Techniques: Theoretical Framework and Review of Empirical Work (Chapter 5), by Nicholas Gonedes and Nicholas Dopuch, is a broad review that considers some of the fundamental questions and methodological issues of accounting. Among these are the following two questions dealing with capital market efficiency and alternative accounting procedures:

1. Capital market efficiency is a sufficient condition or justification for using equity prices (rates of return) to assess the desirability of alternative accounting procedures.
2. Capital market efficiency is a sufficient condition or justification for using equity prices (rates of return) to assess the effects of alternative accounting procedures.

Gonedes and Dopuch argue that the selection of accounting techniques is basically an information-production decision. Further, the market share price maximization rule does not necessarily lead to optimal information-production decisions because there is no guarantee of correspondence between individual wealth maximization and utility maximization under the "exclusion of non-purchasers" condition. That is, individual utility may be maximized concomitantly with a decrease in equilibrium prices, and therefore the market value maximization rule is an ambiguous criterion for optimal information-production decisions.[26]

The justification of the proposition that the effects of alternative accounting procedures can be assessed via equity share prices (rates of return) is set forth by Gonedes and Dopuch. They argue that capital market efficiency is a sufficient condition for the validity of this proposition. The framework used to examine the effects of accounting procedures is the two-parameter capital asset pricing model. Specifically, the distribution of residuals conditional upon the information set (e.g., a change in accounting technique) is examined to ascertain whether empirically there is informational content in accounting numbers. The hypothesis test is that if $F(e_{it} \, Q_{it}) \neq F(e_{it})$, then there is informational value impounded into the accounting change. Several nuances necessary for a valid test (such as determining whether the sample systematic risk changed) are delineated along with associated problems. In this connection,

several of the more important empirical investigations of the effects of accounting reporting changes, such as Ball, Archibald, Bentson, and Sunder, are reviewed
and examined for insights into test methodology.[27]

A number of other topics are also discussed. One such topic is the ad hoc
nature under conditions of uncertainty of the dividends (earnings) valuation
model. This model's treatment of the risk premium and investors' expectations
is basically unsatisfactory inasmuch as prices and returns are not derived from
a market equilibrium framework.[28] The inappropriateness of nonprice frameworks, such as laboratory and field studies, questionnaires, studies of time-
series properties, and consistency studies, is delineated. The authors argue that
the fundamental theoretical deficiencies of these approaches in reflecting capital
market phenomena under uncertainty limit their usefulness in deriving systematic and meaningful normative and empirical inferences.

Chapter 6, The Association between Market Determined and Accounting
Determined Risk Measures, by William Beaver, Paul Kettler, and Myron Scholes
investigates whether accounting variables can serve as surrogates for systematic
market risk. Specifically, the joint hypothesis that accounting data reflect
information about the risk of capital assets and that the risk of these assets is
impounded into their market price is investigated. The test consists of determining whether the accounting measures are highly correlated with the market
beta. The seven accounting variables used are the payout, growth, leverage,
liquidity, size, earnings variability, and accounting beta. Table 1 reports these
correlations that have been calculated on a portfolio basis. It shows that the
strongest association is via earnings variability, followed by the payout and the
accounting beta. These correlations are consistent with the view that accounting
information is impounded into the market estimate of systematic risk and can
be used with some success as a surrogate of this market risk measure. Also, a
test was conducted to determine the predictive content of accounting measures
in forecasting the market risk in a future period. Beaver, Kettler, and Scholes
argue that an instrumental variable model based on the accounting variables of
dividend payout, growth, and earnings variability is superior to a naive forecasting model that postulates that next period's beta will be equal to this
period's beta.

To conclude, understanding the determinants of beta and predicting its
future behavior are important questions. The study by Beaver, Kettler, and
Scholes was probably the earliest seminal study in this arena. It still contains a
number of useful methodological and modeling implications for practitioners
in this research domain. Unfortunately, while there have been a score of subsequent studies investigating the determinants of beta risk, equation specification
is still somewhat of an ad hoc task.[29] Myers suggests that "the missing link
seems to be a dynamic model of a firm's earnings behavior, growth, and market
valuation."[30] Thus at present we still have a rather elementary understanding
of the stochastic process generating beta. Of course, as our empirical knowledge

Table 1

Contemporaneous Association between Market-Determined Measure of Risk and Seven Accounting Risk Measures[a]

Variable	Period 1 (1947–56) Portfolio[b] Level	Period 2 (1957–65) Portfolio[b] Level
Payout	−0.79 (−0.77)	−0.50 (−0.45)
Growth	0.56 (0.51)	0.02 (0.07)
Leverage	0.41 (0.45)	0.48 (0.56)
Liquidity	−0.35 (−0.44)	0.04 (−0.01)
Size	−0.09 (−0.13)	−0.30 (−0.30)
Earnings Variability	0.90 (0.77)	0.82 (0.62)
Accounting Beta (B_i)	0.68 (0.67)	0.46 (0.46)

[a]Rank correlation coefficients appear in the top row, and product-moment correlations appear in parentheses in the bottom row.
[b]The portfolio correlations are based upon 61 portfolios of five securities each.
Source: William Beaver, Paul Kettler, and Myron Scholes, "The Association between Market Determined and Accounting Determined Risk Measures," *The Accounting Review*, 1970, p. 669.

of the determinants of beta increases, we may want to incorporate our assessments of the probability distributions of these underlying and causal factors into a Bayesian forecast of the beta of the relevant asset, security portfolio, or project.[31]

Investor Evaluation of Accounting Information: Some Empirical Evidence, Chapter 7, by Robert Kaplan and Richard Roll investigates the effect of accounting changes on security prices. Specifically, the impact of a changeover of such accounting procedures as the flow-through investment credit method rather than the previous existing 48–52 method and the use of accelerated depreciation rather than straight-line depreciation is examined. The market model is used to estimate the residuals for each security in order to estimate whether there are any abnormal returns.[32] The disturbance term for 30 weeks on each side of the earnings announcement data is estimated for the groups of firms having made the respective accounting changes. An analysis of the plots of the mean abnormal returns shows that there is positive average abnormal returns in the 10 weeks surrounding the earnings announcements for the investment-credit change case. However, these abnormal returns largely disappear during weeks 39 to 53. As to the effect of depreciation changes, examination of the cumulative abnormal returns indicates that there is a short-lived positive effect coinciding around the earnings announcement date, but the returns also indicate that companies doing earnings manipulation a la depreciation changes are generally characterized by poor performance. To conclude, Kaplan and Roll's empirical evidence is consistent with the hypothesis that earnings manipulation does not permanently affect stock prices.[33]

Part III, Implications for Finance, contains six selections within the area of managerial finance. In Chapter 8 Richard Stapelton attempts to derive, within a portfolio context, normative capital budgeting rules under conditions of uncertainty and perfect capital markets. Three different corporate valuation approaches and derivative capital budgeting frameworks are examined. They are: (1) the certainty equivalent of the normal probability distributions of dividends, (2) the discounted value of the risk-adjusted expected earnings, and (3) the certainty equivalent of time-discounted dividends. Equations (1), (2), and (3) represent respectively these three valuation approaches:

$$P_0 = \sum_{t=1}^{n} C(d_t)(1 + i)^{-t} \tag{1}$$

$$P_0 = \sum_{t=1}^{n} E(d_t)(1 + \bar{r}_t)^{-t} \tag{2}$$

$$P_0 = C(DV_d) \tag{3}$$

where P_0 is the market price of the stock at time 0, $C(d_t)$ is the certainty equivalent of the normal probability distribution of dividends, i is the return on a riskless security, $\bar{r}$ is a discount rate incorprating both time and risk dimensions, and DV_d is the time-discounted value of dividends.

Approaches (1) and (3) separate the time and risk dimensions whereas approach (2) aggregates these components into a single discount rate, $\bar{r}_0$.[34] The conceptual specification of the certainty equivalent is the expected value of the benefit stream, however defined, net of the product of the price of risk reduction (e.g., the slope of the Sharpe-Lintner capital market line) and the relevant measure of risk (e.g., the undiversifiable risk of the project).

Stapelton prescribes the certainty equivalent of the stream of time-discounted dividends as the recommended capital budgeting approach. The reasons are that (1) it presumably avoids the conceptual problems of specifying risk-adjusted discount rates and (2) it circumvents the need to assess period-by-period probability distributions of discounted value of future dividends. Thus, according to Stapelton, "by forming the probability distribution of the discounted value of dividends, the risk-valuation problem becomes equivalent to finding the certainty equivalent of a single immediate dividend from the probability distribution."[35] However, as Brennan notes, Stapelton

while purporting to develop a theory of stock valuation using a multi-period portfolio model, actually employs a single-period certainty-equivalent approach in which it is assumed that the joint probability distribution of all the future dividend payments on a share can be reduced to a probability distribution on the present values at the end of one period of all possible future dividend streams. The probability distribution of these deferred present values is then valued using the single-period capital asset pricing model. This procedure would be legitimate only if, at the end of one period, the investor were to know with certainty the precise pattern of dividend payments over the remainder of the horizon; this of course is highly unrealistic and ignores the fact that information about future dividends becomes available only gradually through time.[36]

Michael Brennan, in Chapter 9, An Approach to the Valuation of Uncertain Income Streams, presents a multiperiod framework for the corporate valuation problem under uncertainty. The substantial progress on the formulation of multiperiod stochastic investment-consumption strategies has provided the foundations for the development of a multiperiod theory of capital market equilibrium.[37] Specifically, Brennan utilizes the Merton multiperiod model of lifetime portfolio selection as the basis for individual investor equilibrium.[38] Specifically, given assumptions of the absence of labor income and transactions costs, a deterministic life span, and the existence of the Tobin-Lintner mutual fund separation theorem, the maximization of expected utility problem can be viewed as

$$E[S_t^h \, e^{-ps} \, U(C_s) \, ds + \beta(W_h)]$$

where $U(C_s)$ is the individual's utility function, C_s is the individual's instantneous rate of consumption, H is the date of death, p is the rate of time preference, and $\beta(W_h)$ is the incremental utility of having net worth W_h at time H. The investor is characterized by risk aversion, implying that both U and β are strictly concave.

Market clearing conditions equating the vectors of the demand and supply for all risky assets, given homogeneous expectations on the joint probability distribution of assets, imply the following market equilibrium:

$$a_{jt} - r + \beta_{jt}(u_t - r) \qquad j = 1, \ldots, m$$

where a is the vector of expected instantaneous risk asset yields, r is the price of time, β is the instantaneous slope of the regression of the yield on asset j

at time t with the yield on the market portfolio of risky assets, and u_t is the instantaneous expected yield on the market portfolio of risky assets. This equation states that in equilibrium the expected risk premium on an asset equals its expected instantaneous return minus the risk-free rate of return. This, in turn, equals the more familiar instantaneous covariance risk of the asset times the risk premium on the market portfolio.

A differential equation solution to corporate project valuation is solved having as the boundary condition an expectations generator implying consistency with the diagonal model of security returns and nonstationary betas. The derived valuation equation views the investment decision for the firm under uncertainty as

$$V_t(\tilde{C}_{jT}) = t_{jt}^a e^{-r(T-t)} + b_{jT} \tilde{I}_t e^{-u(T-t)}$$

The above expression says that the net present value for any given project can be calculated given assessments of the expected return on the market risky portfolio, u, and index-independent and index-dependent components, t_{jt}^a and b_{jt}, of project returns. The project decision is based on the incremental effect upon shareholder wealth. The above differential equation also points out the important and intricate role that index-independent and index-dependent components play in capital budgeting along with the complex nature of the cost of capital (discount rate).

In Chapter 10 Robert Hamada investigates the effects of a firm's capital structure on the systematic risk of common stocks, along with providing a test of the Modigliani-Miller cost of capital hypotheses. The following four market models are tested, using data of 304 firms for the years 1948 to 1967:

$$R_{Ait} = {}_A\alpha_i + {}_A\beta_i R_{mt} + {}_A\epsilon_{it} \tag{4}$$

$$R_{Bit} = {}_B\alpha_2 + {}_B\beta_i R_{mt} + {}_B\epsilon_{it} \tag{5}$$

$$\ln(1 + R_{Ait}) = {}_{AC}\alpha_1 + {}_{AC}\beta_i \ln(1 + R_{mt}) + {}_{AC}\epsilon_{it} \tag{6}$$

$$\ln(1 + R_{Bit}) = {}_{BC}\alpha_1 + {}_{BC}\beta_i \ln(1 + R_{mt}) + {}_{BC}\epsilon_{it} \tag{7}$$

$$i = 1, 2, \ldots, 304 \qquad t = 1948 \text{ to } 1967$$

where R_{it} is the return on company i in time t, α_i and β_i are regression constants for each firm, A^β and B^β are the nonleveraged systematic risk and common stock leveraged systematic risk respectively, R_{mt} is the market rate of return including dividends on the New York Stock Exchange index, and ϵ_{it} is the disturbance term having the standard econometric properties. Inasmuch as

$$A\hat{^\beta} < B\hat{^\beta} \qquad \text{and} \qquad AC\hat{^\beta} < BC\hat{^\beta}$$

Hamada argues that leverage via debt and preferred stock accounts for the observed differences in mean systematic risk. Specifically, Hamada states that "leverage has explained as much as, roughly, 21 to 24 per cent of the value of the mean B."[39] This result is consistent with Modegliani-Miller theory. However, since conventional capital structure theory postulates that reasonably moderate amounts of leverage cannot be discerned by the market, it is questionable whether traditional theory is consistent with the above mean-beta comparison.[40]

Three alternative hypothesis tests are utilized to discriminate between the validity of the Modegliani-Miller and the traditional capital structure theories. First, the standard deviation of the unbiased nonlevered beta estimates of a homogeneous risk class is compared to the standard deviation of the unbiased levered beta estimates for the same groups of firms. The standard deviation of the nonlevered betas is significantly less than the standard errors of the levered betas in eight out of nine risk classes. This is consistent with the Modegliani-Miller theory which postulates that (1) firms in a given risk class should have identical nonlevered betas and (2) the levered betas of a risk class should increase with higher debt-equity proportions. Conventional capital structure theory, however, argues that debt-equity ratio changes are imperceptible to the market over a range and thus the levered betas of firms not reaching the critical leverage point would be identical to the nonlevered betas regardless of differences in leverage.

Second, a chi-square test on distributions of beta obtained via a ranking-grouping procedure for betas generated from each of the four market models indicates that the null hypothesis that nonlevered (levered) betas come from the same distribution as all betas must be rejected (accepted) at the 90% significance level. Further, the nonlevered betas are more highly clustered than the levered betas. This again is (not necessarily) consistent with the Modegliani-Miller (traditional) theory.

Third, an analysis of variance test indicates that the F statistic (estimated variance between industry betas from the market model to the estimated variance within the industry betas) is higher for the unlevered than for the levered beta. This finding can be interpreted as being more consistent with Modegliani-Miller than with traditional capital structure theory. Thus, the results of the standard deviation of unbiased beta estimates in homogeneous risk classes, chi-square, and analysis of variance tests support the claim that the Modegliani-Miller framework is empirically more robust than traditional theory in explaining capital structure valuation relationships in a world of the two-parameter model.[41]

As an aside, Hamada's study has a number of important implications for regulatory rate of return testimony. The Hope decision specified that the fair rate of return that should be allowed to a utility is the rate of return for unregulated firms of the same risk class. Most regulatory testimony takes firms of the same product line as the sample risk class. Hamada's study shows that as a first approximation, this ad hoc procedure is rather unappealing. Further, for "double-levered" companies (e.g., public utility holding companies that own 100 percent of utility operating companies) the systematic risk of the holding company is likely a poor surrogate for the systematic risk of the operating company. Thus, the use of AT&T market data for deriving estimates of the systematic risk and subsequently the equilibrium rate of return for a subsidiary (e.g., Illinois Bell) involves complications and requires adjustments. Otherwise, an upward-biased estimate will be derived.[42]

Gershon Mandelker's "Risk and Return on Stocks of Merging Firms" investigates the ex post performance of conglomerate mergers. This genre of query has a substantial, though largely ad hoc, theoretical and empirical literature.[43] The underlying framework utilized by Mandelker is the Black-Vasicek two-factor equilibrium model. Sixty months of return data are used to estimate the systematic risk for sample companies having (1) purchased over 50 percent of the equity of the acquired company and (2) firm data available on the CRSP file. Firms are ranked according to the magnitudes of their estimated betas and allocated by ranks to twenty portfolios of equal size. The next 60 months of return data are used to reestimate the betas of the firms. The beta estimates of these firms are then used, via an equally weighted scheme, to compute the estimate of beta for each of the twenty portfolios. The beta estimates of the firms, etc., are recomputed annually. The parameters of the following equation are then estimated, using as inputs the returns and betas of the twenty portfolios:

$$R_{pt} = \tilde{V}_{0t} + \tilde{V}_{1t}\tilde{\beta}_{p,t-1} + \tilde{U}_{pt} \quad p = 1, 2, \ldots, 20$$

where R_{pt} are the monthly returns, $\tilde{\beta}_{p,t-1}$ is the beta estimate, $\tilde{U}$ is the residual, and $\tilde{V}_{0t}$ and $\tilde{V}_{1t}$ are the parameter estimates of the expected rate of return on the riskless asset and the expected risk premium on the market portfolio.

Using the parameters $\tilde{V}_{0t}$ and $\tilde{V}_{1t}$, the abnormal performance of stock j is estimated via

$$\hat{e} = R_{jt} - \tilde{V}_{0t} - \tilde{V}_{1t}\tilde{\beta}_{jt}$$

where e_t is the residual or abnormal performance of stock j in month t. The residual term captures firm-specific events rather than market-related changes. The cumulative average residual (CAR) is a weighted average residual across firms for a period relative to the merger.

Two major hypotheses are tested via the CAR procedure.[44] First, are abnormal returns associated with mergers? Second, does the capital market impound information about mergers in a manner consistent with the efficient markets hypothesis? Among the conclusions suggested by inspection of the CAR are:

1. For acquiring firms, the CAR increases 5.1 percent during the period (–40 to 0).
2. For acquired firms, the CAR increases 2 percent per month for the 7 months prior to the merger. That is, the CAR increases 14 percent in the last months prior to the merger. This is a substantial increase.
3. Using a standardized residual approach applied to portfolios, the t statistics indicate that there are no abnormal postmerger returns that accrue to shareholders.[d]

Thus the results of Mandelker's study imply that (1) stockholders of the acquired (acquiring) firm do (not) earn abnormal returns and (2) the market impounds information about merger activity into the price of the acquiring firm before the effective date of the merger.

As to why the gains from mergers go to the acquired firm, Fama argues that "one possible explanation is that the synergy in a merger is in many cases improved management of the acquired firm. If the acquisition market for poorly managed firms is perfectly competitive, competition among acquiring firms will cause all the gains from the merger (removal of the poor management of the acquired firm) to be passed on to the shareholders of the acquired firm."[45]

Chapter 12, Imperfections in International Financial Markets: Implications for Risk Premia and the Cost of Capital to Firms, by Richard Cohn and John Pringle is a theoretical investigation of the effects of international diversification on equilibrium security pricing. It is shown that if additional securities are added to an investment opportunity set via diversification across national boundaries and that if such securities have low correlation or covariance with the prior market portfolio of risky securities, then there are two different effects on security pricing relationships. First, the systematic risk of securities in the prior market portfolio will probably decline.[46] That is, the beta or systematic risk for most securities regressed on the augmented or posterior market portfolio will likely be less than the beta or systematic risk regressed on the prior market portfolio. This is simply a result of the prior and posterior market portfolios differing due to the addition of securities having low correlation with the prior market portfolio. Second, according to Cohn and Pringle, the slope of the capital market line will decline for security market scenarios where investors are postulated to have either logarithmic or exponential utility functions.[47] The product of (1) a likely reduction in the beta of securities of the prior market portfolio and (2) a decrease in the price of risk reduction (e.g., a smaller slope for the capital market line) is that the risk premia component of the cost of

---

[d]Mandelker uses a variant of the standardized residuals technique to estimate the likelihood that the residuals are due to chance. For a more complete discussion, see Mandelker's appendix (Chapter 11).

capital (e.g., the equilibrium structure of the price of risk for securities) is lowered.

In Chapter 13, A Mean-Variance Synthesis of Corporate Financial Theory, Mark Rubenstein treats the corporate financial problems of security valuation, capital budgeting, and capital structure.[48] The Sharpe-Lintner mean-variance market equilibrium framework is used to analyze these issues.

The mean-variance valuation theorem for the expected return of the individual firm or security is:

$$E(\tilde{R}_j) = R_f + \lambda \text{ cov}(\tilde{R}_j, \tilde{R}_m)$$

where

$\tilde{R}_j$ = the expected rate of return on security j

R_f = the risk-free rate of return

$\tilde{R}_m$ = the expected rate of return on the market portfolio

λ = a positive constant

This theorem can be translated into the more familiar risk-adjusted discount and certainty equivalent frameworks. Let $\tilde{R}_j = \tilde{P}_j/P_j$ where P_j is the present price of security j and $\tilde{P}_j$ is the expected change in the price of security j. The risk-adjusted valuation framework can be represented as

$$P_j = \frac{E(\tilde{P}_j)}{R_f + \lambda \text{ cov}(\tilde{R}_j, \tilde{R}_m)}$$

It states that the present price of a security or a project equals the future price discounted at a rate that takes into account both futurity and uncertainty.

Alternatively, the certainty equivalent valuation framework, which separates futurity from uncertainty (e.g., the risk premium for the individual security) into separate discount dimensions, is:

$$\frac{E(\tilde{P}_j) - \lambda \text{ cov}(\tilde{P}_j, \tilde{R}_m)}{R_f}$$

Both the risk-adjusted discounted and the certainty equivalent valuation frameworks, as traditionally expressed, represent mere definitions. The risk premium and price of time estimates that can be derived a la Sharpe-Lintner and the extended version of the capital asset pricing model make possible the operationality of both these models.

The asset expansion discussion includes, among other topics, decision rules

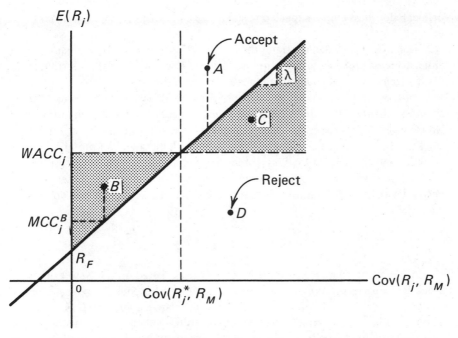

Source: M. Rubenstein, "A Mean-Variance Synthesis of Corporate Financial Theory," *Journal of Finance,* March, 1973, pp. 172.
Figure 1.

for mutually exclusive projects, capital rationing, and mutually interdependent projects. The normative capital budgeting decision rule is to accept (reject) a project if its internal rate of return is greater (less) than the project's risk-adjusted discount rate. Figure 1 illustrates this principle. Acceptable projects plot above the security market line (SML) while unacceptable projects fall below the SML.[49] The theoretically appropriate risk-adjusted discount rate that should be utilized for a project equals the expected return for an individual security of similar risk. This specification of the appropriate risk-adjusted discount rate contrasts with the still popular and previously standard view, which is incorrect, that stipulates that the risk-adjusted discount rate should be the firm's average cost of capital.

The normative capital budgeting rule for the mutually exclusive and capital-rationing cases is to maximize the highest excess expected internal rate of return weighted by its cost. The only footnote stipulation, according to Rubenstein, is that a capital constraint is stipulated for the capital-rationing case.[50] In the mutually interdependent investment scenario, the joint projects should be considered as a single project and analyzed according to the above delineated highest excess expected internal rate of return weighted by its cost rule.

Rubenstein also demonstrates that financial leverage can conceptually either increase or decrease the expected yield on a security as well as setting forth a framework for examining the effect of operating leverage.

Part IV, Implications for Investment Portfolio Management, consists of six chapters. Chapter 14 by John Bildersee, Some Aspects of the Performance of Non-Convertible Preferred Stocks, examines the risk-return behavior of preferred stocks.[51] Instead of the conventional wisdom which dictates that preferred stock is a hybrid security that has neither the income participation possibilities of common stock nor the default protection advantages of debt,[52] Bildersee postulates that the risk-return behavior of preferred stocks is described via the market model.

$$\tilde{R}_{jt} = a_j + \beta_j \tilde{R}_{mt} + \tilde{e}_{jt}$$

A sample of 72 nonconvertible preferred stocks listed on the New York Stock Exchange is used to estimate beta via the market model. Three separate market indices are used. They are the Fisher link relative common stock index, a bond index,[53] and a market index comprised of 65 percent common stocks, 5 percent preferred stocks, and 30 percent government bonds.

When beta was estimated via the market model using the Fisher index as the surrogate of the market index, an examination of the betas showed that in every case the common stock beta was higher than the same firm's preferred stock beta. Further, the mean beta for preferred stocks was significantly less than the mean beta for common stocks. Also, the distribution of betas of preferred stocks has much less dispersion than the distribution of betas for common stocks. A comparison of these distributions indicates that they overlap (e.g., preferred stocks of some companies have higher betas than common stock of other companies). Bildersee devises a grouping procedure based on the beta for the low end of the common-stock category to classify preferred stocks in high- and low-quality rankings. An inspection of the variance-covariance and the correlation matrices for the high- and low-quality preferred and the common stock groupings indicates that low-quality preferreds are more similar to common stocks than to high-quality preferreds. Experimentation with a bond index shows that it is more closely related to the index of high-quality preferreds than to low-quality preferreds. Several of these results are detailed in Tables 2, 3, 4, and 5. To conclude, Bildersee's study

provided us with further tests of the consistency of the market model and of the applicability of that model to an additional class of securities. In particular, the preferred stock sample enabled us to observe the consistency of the relationship between different classes of equity securities by the same firm and among equivalent securities issued by the same firm. In addition, it appears that

Table 2

Distributions of Beta from Regressions on the Common Stock Index

Sample	Obser-vations	Mean	Standard Deviation	Average R^2
Preferreds	72	0.198	0.262	0.061
SCCS–(Same Company's Common Stock)	60^{17}	0.999	0.383	0.284

	Ranges of Beta		
Sample	Inter-Quartile	Extremes	Range of R^2 Extremes
Preferreds	0.053–0.211	–0.029–+1.538	0.0^34–0.334
SCCS	0.693–1.216	+0.356–+2.025	0.071–0.532

Source: J. Bildersee, "Some Aspects of the Performance of Non-Convertible Preferred Stocks," *Journal of Finance*, December 1973, p. 1191.

preferreds with low betas relative to the common stock index perform primarily like bonds in the market while preferreds with higher betas perform primarily like common stocks in the market.[54]

In Chapter 15, Futures Trading and Investor Returns: An Investigation of Commodity Market Risk Premiums, Katherine Dusak examines the historically controversial query of risk premiums on commodity futures. The a priori position taken is that the risk-return behavior of commodities, like that of other investment opportunities, should be in conformity with the CAPM. This contrasts with the well-known Keynesian backwardation thesis, which postulates that an appropriate measure of commodity risk is return variability.

Risk-return relationships are estimated for wheat, corn, and soybeans for the 15-year period 1952 through 1967. The price relatives utilized are future prices rather than spot prices.[55, 56] Also presented are serial correlation coeffi-

Table 3

Variance-Covariance Matrix for Chosen Indexes

Index	High Quality Preferreds	Low Quality Preferreds	Common Stocks
High Quality Preferreds	1.778	1.209	1.249
Low Quality Preferreds		3.589	5.379
Common Stocks			13.854

Source: J. Bildersee, "Some Aspects of the Performance of Non-Convertible Preferred Stocks," *Journal of Finance*, December 1973, p. 1193.

Table 4
Correlation Matrix for Chosen Indexes

	High Quality Preferreds	Low Quality Preferreds	Common Stocks
High Quality Preferreds	1.0	0.518	0.252
Low Quality Preferreds		1.0	0.763
Common Stocks			1.0

Source: J. Bildersee, "Some Aspects of the Performance of Non-Convertible Preferred Stocks," *Journal of Finance*, December 1973, p. 1194.

cients for the time series of returns. They indicate that there is no consistent and pervasive pattern of price dependence.

The beta estimates for these commodities (see Table 6) indicate that their systematic risk is indeed low (e.g., close to zero). Further, since the risk premiums are close to zero, the risk-return relationship is consistent with Sharpe-Lintner theory. On the other hand, because the Keynesian thesis implies that the variance of commodity returns is approximately as large as the variability of the returns on a diversified equity portfolio, the risk premium of commodities and the market index should be approximately the same. However, the returns on the Standard and Poor Index for 1952 to 1967 were 0.0029 (without dividends) per semimonthly period and 0.0046 (with dividends). This is in striking contrast to the point estimates of the truncated means of commodity returns, which are negative or close to zero. In short, risk-return relationships for commodities are consistent with Sharpe-Lintner theory but inconsistent with the Keynesian theory of normal backwardation.[57]

There has been an abundance of studies purporting to investigate the value of inside information for portfolio choice. Most of the prior investigations had important theoretical or empirical limitations, such as the absence of a satisfactory treatment of risk, transactions costs, and market movements. Jeffrey Jaffe,

Table 5
Correlation Matrix for Chosen Indexes

	Government Bonds	High Quality Preferreds	Low Quality Preferreds
Government Bonds	1.0	0.538	−0.016
High Quality Preferreds		1.0	0.518
Low Quality Preferreds			1.0

Source: J. Bildersee, "Some Aspects of the Performance of Non-Convertible Preferred Stocks," *Journal of Finance*, December 1973, p. 1196.

Table 6
Regression Parameters for Wheat, Corn, and Soybeans

Commodity*	$\hat{\alpha}'_i$	$SE(\hat{\alpha}'_i)$	$\hat{\beta}i$	$SE(\hat{\beta}i)$	R^2	Auto-correlation Coefficient of Residuals
Wheat:			-			
July (302)	−.020	.001	.048	.051	.003	.148
March (302)	.000	.001	.098	.049	.013	.080
May (302	−.000	.001	.028	.051	.001	.163
Sept. (319)	−.002	.001	.068	.051	.006	.149
Dec. (319)	−.000	.001	.059	.048	.005	.163
Corn:						
July (301)	−.001	.001	.038	.046	.002	−.041
March (301)	−.003	.001	−.009	.050	.000	.015
May (301)	−.002	.001	−.027	.048	.001	.032
Sept. (320)	−.002	.001	.032	.048	.001	.100
Dec. (320)	−.001	.001	.007	.047	.000	.017
Soybeans (287 all contracts):						
Jan.	.002	.001	.019	.058	.000	.015
March	.003	.002	.100	.065	.008	.018
May	.003	.002	.119	.068	.011	.071
July	.002	.002	.080	.076	.004	.083
Sept.	.001	.001	.077	.065	.005	.060
Nov.	.002	.001	.043	.058	.002	.023

*Numbers of observations are given in parentheses.
Source: K. Dusak, "Futures Trading and Investor Returns: An Investigation of Commodity Market Risk Premiums," *Journal of Political Economy*, November–December 1973, p. 1402.

in Chapter 16, Special Information and Insider Trading, estimates the profitability of insider trading and information about insider transactions using the ingenious standardized portfolio residual methodology. The sample data include all companies on the CRSP tape having net buying or selling trading activity for selected time intervals. Jaffe's tests include net activity, large transactions, and intensive trading samples.[58] A partial list of some of the empirical results that are inferred from an analysis of the standardized residuals is:

1. The CAR during period 15 after the intensive trading activity increases approximately 0.5 percent. Most of this increase is in the first few months. This suggests that forecasts of residuals are more accurate for short rather than long time periods and that the informational value of wider trading activity is impounded quickly into share prices.
2. The profitability of inside trading is not a function of the intensity of trading activity inasmuch as the CAR was not a function of the number of net purchasers.

3.   Appreciable gross profits seem to have been realized in each of the trading
      samples.

   Jaffe's evidence is rather impressive, and it rigorously supports the proposition that insiders have information that is not impounded into security prices.
Furthermore, the study suggests that not all the data contained in the *Official
Summary* at its publication date are impounded as of then into the prices of
the securities. Indeed, Fama notes: "as far as I know, Jaffe's is the only test of
market efficiency that finds that the market ignores some obviously publicly
available information in setting prices."[59]
   Empirical investigations of the impact of money supply changes on stock
prices have been extensive without being definitive. Many of these empirical
studies have reached the conclusion that stock prices lag monetary policy and
that therefore there are profitable trading rules. In most of these studies, there
has been a lack of recognition that the investigation implied a hypothesis about
whether information is impounded into the prices and yields of securities in a
manner consistent with the theory of efficient markets. Cooper's study was one
of the first to recognize this deficiency and attempt to design a hypothesis that
integrated the efficient markets hypothesis.[60] A test, however, providing
stronger empirical results than that of Cooper is found in Chapter 17 by Michael
Rozeff, Money and Stock Prices: Market Efficiency and the Lag in Effect of
Monetary Policy.
   Rozeff's empirical tests consisted of (1) stock price regression models on
monetary policy and (2) investment trading rules. The regression of stock
returns on monetary change data should result in an estimated relationship
exhibiting no systematic lagged effect of money on stock returns. The regression
equation estimated is:

$$R_t = c_0 + \sum_{i=1}^{N} a_{t-1}\left(g_{t-i} - g_{t-i-1}\right) + e_t$$

where R_t equals stock returns, g_t equals the growth rate of money supply, and
N is either 17 or 20. The empirical estimates quite strongly support the efficient
market hypothesis that there is no lag in monetary policy effects being impounded into stock returns.
   The test of alternative trading rules must clearly differentiate between
operational and nonoperational rules. Various trading rules are tested to
determine whether their performance, taking into account transactions costs, is
superior to buy-and-hold rules. Rozeff concludes that the evidence is inconsistent with the predictive form of the monetary portfolio model and consistent
with the efficient market model. Stock returns do not lag behind growth rates
of the money supply, nor would we expect them to do so in an efficient

market. Further, changes in stock prices are related to monetary variables, as the nonpredictive form of the monetary portfolio model suggests. A substantial fraction of current stock price change can be linked to current monetary policy. In addition, an important part of current stock price change appears to reflect stock market anticipations of future monetary growth. This result is expected in an efficient market.

Rozeff's article also includes a superb critical review of past studies of monetary changes and stock returns. Among such studies reviewed are those conducted by Sprinkel, Palmer, Reilly and Lewis, Keran, Hamburger and Kochin, Homa and Jaffe and Cooper.[61,62,63]

How to Use Security Analysis to Improve Portfolio Selection (Chapter 18) by Jack Treynor and Fischer Black links security assessment and portfolio selection.[64] The stipulated scenario is one in which an investor has insights into which securities are overpriced or underpriced (e.g., where the residuals of the CAPM are nonzero) but has no expertise at macroforecasting. The normative portfolio strategy is a three-stage process consisting of blending:[e]

1.   An active portfolio whereby the appraisal ratio is maximized.[f]
2.   A passive portfolio which is a suitable proxy of the market portfolio and which is mixed with the active portfolio to maximize the Sharpe ratio.[65]
3.   A riskless asset which is mixed with both the active and passive portfolios to maximize the expected utility of the investor.

The market portfolio or a reasonable surrogate should be achieved at minimum cost. It is to be mixed with the active portfolio to maximize the Sharpe ratio. The mix of the active and passive or market portfolio is independent of the investor's risk preferences. Only at stage 3 does the investor's utility function affect portfolio blending. Step 3 is combining the portfolio that maximizes the Sharpe ratio with borrowing or lending to derive the optimal portfolio that maximizes investor utility.

To conclude, if the analyst has no assessments that indicate that any individual securities are in disequilibrium, then the derived set of portfolios will be efficient and will include the market portfolio as a principal component. If the analyst has assessments of disequilibrium-priced securities, then the final portfolio will be superefficient (lie above the traditional efficiency locus) and will represent a mix of both the active and passive. The Treynor and Black security analysis model is a premier attempt to integrate underpriced or over-

---

[e]Treynor and Black also postulate that the unsystematic parts of the returns on securities are uncorrelated.

[f]The appraisal ratio is $\sum_{i=1}^{n} u_i^2/\sigma_i^2$, where u equals the disequilibrium returns on security i and σ^2 equals the variance of returns on security i.

priced securities, viewed in a capital market equilibrium context, within the framework of modern portfolio theory.

Michael Jensen, in Chapter 19, Optimal Utilization of Market Forecasts and the Evaluation of Investment Performance, uses the Sharpe-Lintner framework to derive portfolio performance measures under conditions in which the portfolio manager engages in security analysis.[66] Specifically, if the security analyst is "successful," this implies that he is able to consistently forecast individual financial securities that have abnormal risk premiums or equivalently positive $\tilde{e}_{jt}$ from the market model. Alternatively, if the interecept is not constrained to pass through the origin, then a positive intercept a_j would indicate superior security selection

$$\tilde{R}_{jt} = a_j + \beta_j \tilde{R}_{mt} + \tilde{u}_{jt}$$

If we presume that the portfolio manager makes no assessments about the behavior of individual securities but does forecast market movements, then the risk level of his portfolio is a function of the uncertainty of his forecast of the market and the slope of his utility function. The magnitude of the change in the risk level of the portfolio will vary inversely with both the uncertainty of the market forecast and individual investor risk aversion.

An evaluation of the usefulness of the portfolio manager's stock selection and market forecasting tasks requires estimates of the returns attributable to both these tasks. Such estimates require, among other things, a time series of the correlation between predicted and actual unanticipated market returns and presume that the portfolio decision and forecasting periods are identical to the interval over which returns are calculated. If these requirements cannot be met, precise estimates of the separate dimensions of portfolio management cannot be made. However, approximations can be generated of the aggregate performance of the portfolio manager, providing the return measurement period is large relative to the forecast period. The above qualitative implications of Sharpe-Lintner theory for ex post portfolio evaluation can also be derived from the two-factor model of Black.

Conclusions

There are a number of important implications that permeate the book. First, the efficient markets and the two-parameter capital asset pricing models are exceedingly useful approximations for describing and predicting behavior of the capital markets. Their robustness in describing real-world capital market relationships results in numerous policy implications for decision makers.

Investment portfolio decision making has historically focused on choosing individual securities that are underpriced. Many Wall Street institutions have built large staffs who process reams of statistics and information on the economy, industries, and firms in the hope that a pattern will emerge whereby undervalued or overvalued securities can be detected. Indeed, in the not too distant past, many academics used the Compustat tapes in somewhat similar data-dredging exercises. There is, however, extensive evidence that the capital markets are efficient in processing relevant information (e.g., it uses all available information in assessing the joint distribution of future security returns which is the basis for current equilibrium returns).[67] This means that there is little conceptual or empirical justification for the chartist or fundamental approaches to security selection. Stated differently, except for inside information, on the average the processing of public information is an activity that yields no abnormal returns. Thus, a risk-averse mean-variance utility maximizer is indifferent between choosing the optimal portfolio from a set of $(n + 1)$ securities and blending two mutual funds, provided that the investor's expectations are similar to those used in forming the optimal risky portfolio. More specifically, given an efficient market and securities priced in accord with the Black two-factor model, all efficient portfolios may be represented as combinations of the minimum-variance zero-beta portfolio and the market portfolio. Portfolio choice under these conditions is simply blending the optimal proportions of these two assets to derive the desired mean variance of the expected return on the portfolio.[g]

As an aside, modern portfolio theory, given efficient capital markets and securities priced in a manner consistent with the Black two-factor model (e.g., this rules out the scenario in which the Treynor-Black security model is applicable), says nothing about optimizing subportions of an individual's portfolio. Since, for example, pension fund assets represent but a fraction of an individual's portfolio wealth, it would appear that it is not crucial that (1) all the unsystematic risk be eliminated and (2) preferences (e.g., one's utility function) be integrated into the resulting choice framework. Modern finance also provides a framework to evaluate the performance of security analysts and market forecasters as well as to appraise the overall investment performance of a portfolio. This latter test provides a means of determining whether professional money managers have superior, inferior, or average performance according to some well-defined concepts of market equilibrium.

The implications of the efficient markets model for accountants is that, neglecting information costs, debate over appropriate accounting treatment of income, expense, and asset items is rarely of any meaningful consequence to the users of such information. That is, investors are able to perceive the "true" economic situation of the firm despite alternative accounting reporting systems (e.g., different accounting treatment does not lead to systematic differences in investor behavior).[68]

Likewise, the CAPM has relevant implications for corporate decision makers involved in capital budgeting. Specifically, they should use as the

---

[g]Similarly, this implies that performing a Markowitz portfolio analysis is not a recommended prescription for normative choice.

appropriate discount rate or cost of capital the equilibrium rate of return for the systematic risk of the project being considered. Contrary to much prior academic writing, the appropriate cutoff rate or cost of capital should not be measured by the price (e.g., cost of capital) of the supply of funds (e.g., a weighted average of debt and equity). Instead the investment decision of the firm is a determination of whether the new project should represent a portion of the market value of all capital assets (e.g., the market portfolio). In this sense, corporate investment choices are decisions as to whether new securities should be issued where these securities are viewed as claims to possible returns— covariances from the projects being considered. The CAPM suggests that beta is a necessary variable in specifying the magnitude of the risk premium. This contrasts markedly to traditional analysis in which the cutoff rate represents some variant on the cost of the various sources of funds (e.g., the price of the components of the capital structure). Indeed, Mossin argues that "any concept of cost of capital resembling the traditional one is, in general, meaningless, or, even if it can be construed, is probably going to have properties quite different from those of the traditional view."[69]

The CAPM has numerous implications for regulatory rate of return testimony. Inasmuch as the Hope Natural Gas case [*Federal Power Commission v. Hope Natural Gas Company*, 320 U.S. 591, 88L. Ed. 33 (1944)] stipulates that the legal standard for "fair" is that "the return to the equity owner should be commensurate with returns on investments in other enterprises having corresponding risk," it is imperative that a well-specified and operational definition of risk be stated. Alternatively stated, rate of return testimony that does not specify the nature of risk is incapable of dealing with the task as delineated by the Hope decision. The standard approaches in rate of return regulation have been comparative earnings and DCF (discounted cash flow). Neither approach is conceptually appealing for estimating the fair rate of return inasmuch as they imply no specific behavior for any of the microdecision units of a capital market scenario.

This means that an independent referree or commissioner cannot replicate the empirical risk and return structure and implications implicit in such testimony. In the lingo of economists, since no well-defined operational hypotheses of risk and return behavior can be specified, it is impossible to conduct rate of return testimony as an exercise in positive economics a la DCF and comparative earnings.

Both the capital asset pricing and the efficient markets models should be judged in terms of their usefulness to explain and predict financial relationships of the capital markets. Both models, while admittedly not exact descriptions of the real world, are quite robust in explaining, predicting, and giving insights into capital market behavior.[70] Of course, the future will see extensions in both the efficient markets and capital asset pricing model literature. The former, likely, will incorporate Muthian concepts in which the economic structure of financial markets will allow more rigorous concepts of rational expectations so that investors draw upon a more complete and larger information set than the usual unbiased extrapolative method, which uses a recent time series of the variable in question.[71] Similarly, both the economics and econometrics of capital asset pricing models are likely to see new "twists" in the hope of deriving a conceptually more appealing and an empirically more robust explanatory framework. One possibility, though this is only a conjecture, is deriving an empirical counterpart to the theory of financial contingent claims via time-state preference theory.[72] However, problems in this domain are quite formidable and represent a challenge and an opportunity to the best minds in the profession.

Notes

1. See E. Fama, "Efficient Capital Markets: A Review of Theory and Empirical Work," *Journal of Finance*, May 1970, pp. 383–417. Also see C. Granger, "Empirical Studies of Capital Markets: A Survey," in G. Ezego and K. Shell (eds.), *Mathematical Methods in Investment and Finance*, North-Holland Publishing Company, Amsterdam, Netherlands, 1972, pp. 469–519. A somewhat shortened and updated version of the Granger paper appears in E. Elton and M. Gruber, *International Capital Markets*, North-Holland/American Elsevier, 1975, pp. 3–36.

2. Technically, security prices are random walks with a drift inasmuch as expected security price changes or yields are nonzero. For insights into the statistical record of common stock returns, see L. Fisher and J. Lorie, "Rates of Return on Investments in Common Stocks," *Journal of Business*, January 1964, pp. 1–21; and L. Fisher and J. Lorie, "Rates of Return on Investments in Common Stock: The Year-by-Year Record, 1926-65," *Journal of Business*, July 1968, pp. 291–316.

3. L. Bachelier, *Theorie de la Spéculation*, Gauthier-Villars, Paris, 1900; P. Cootner, "Stock Prices: Random versus Systematic Changes," *Industrial Management Review*, Spring 1962, pp. 231–252; M. Kendall, "The Analysis of Economic Time Series," *Journal of the Royal Statistical Society*, 1953, pp. 11–25; A. Moore, "A Statistical Analysis of Common Stock Prices," Ph.D. dissertation, University of Chicago, Chicago, Ill., 1962; M. Godfrey, C. Granger, and O. Morgenstern, "The Random Walk Hypothesis of Stock Market Behavior," *Kyklos*, 1964, pp. 1–30; C. Granger and O. Morgenstern, "Spectral Analysis of New York Stock Market Prices," *Kyklos*, 1963, pp. 162–187; S. Alexander, "Price Movements in Speculative Markets: Trends or Random Walks," *Industrial Management Review*, 1964, pp. 199–218; and E. Fama and M. Blume, "Filter Rules and Stock Market Trading Profits," *Journal of Business*, Special Supplement, 1966, pp. 1–21.

4. R. Roll, "The Behavior of Interest Rates: The Application of the Efficient Market to U.S. Treasury Bill Rates," Ph.D. dissertation, University of Chicago, Chicago, Ill., 1968.

5. For a lucid presentation of the razzmatazz and mysticism of the cult of technicians, see John W. Schulz, "How to Forecast Stock Market Action with Charts," Forbes Reprint Series, New York, n.d. Mr. Schulz comes advertised as "one of the Street's most erudite and respected technicians" and an individual who is "no ivory tower theoretician."

6. Fama, "Efficient Capital Markets," p. 409.

7. V. Niederhoffer and M. Osborne, "Market Making and Reversal on the Stock Exchanges," *Journal of the American Statistical Association*, December 1966, pp. 897–916.

8. For other studies showing that inside investors may possess information not yet impounded into security prices, see the studies by Scholes, Lorie and Neiderhoffer, and Jaffe. M. Scholes, "The Market for Securities: Substitution versus Price Pressure and the Effects of Information on Share Prices," *Journal of Business* Volume XLV, April, 1972, pp. 179–211. M. Scholes, "A Test of the Competitive Market Hypothesis: The Market for New Issues and Secondary Offerings," Ph.D. dissertation, University of Chicago, Chicago, Ill., 1969; J. Lorie and V. Niederhoffer, "Predictive and Statistical Properties of Insider Trading," *Journal of Law and Economics*, April 1968, pp. 35–54; J. Jaffe, "The Effect of Regulation Changes on Insider Trading," *Bell Journal of Economics and Management Science*, Spring 1974, pp. 93–121.

9. Fama, "Efficient Capital Market," p. 416.

10. Stone has extended the Samuelson framework for the scenario "when the appropriate fair-return in any given future time period is itself a random variable." See B. Stone, "The Conformity of Stock Values Based on Discounted Dividends to a Fair-Return Process," *Bell Journal of Economics*, Autumn 1975, pp. 698–702.

11. E. Fama, "Short-Term Interest Rates as Predictors of Inflation," *American Economic Review*, June 1975, pp. 269–282.

12. With regard to appropriate test methodology, also see C. Nelson and G. Schwert, "On Testing the Hypothesis That the Real Rate of Interest Is Constant," Center for Mathematical Studies in Business and Economics, Report 7522, University of Chicago, Chicago, Ill., 1975. Note the contrast in the Nelson-Schwert methodology and that implicit in E. Fama, "Inflation Uncertainty and Expected Returns on Treasury Bills," European Institute for Advanced Studies in Management, Working Paper, Brussels, Belgium, September 1975. Nelson and Schwert's empirical findings corroborate those of Hess and Bicksler and lead to the rejection of Fama's joint hypothesis. In this latter paper, Fama concludes that uncertainty about the future inflation rate does not result in variation over time in the expected real rate of return on Treasury bills.

13. J. Mossin, "Security Pricing and Investment Criteria in Competitive Markets," *American Economic Review*, December 1969, p. 749.

14. Ibid.

15. The Sharpe-Lintner-Mossin two-parameter model of capital market equilibrium derived one of its generic names from its originators. See W. Sharpe, "Capital Asset Prices: A Theory of Market Equilibrium under Conditions of Risk," *Journal of Finance*, September 1964, pp. 425–442; J. Lintner, "The Valuation of Risk Assets and the Selection of Risky Investments in Stock Portfolios and Capital Budgets," *Review of Economics and Statistics*, February 1965, pp. 13–37; and J. Mossin, "Equilibrium in a Capital Asset Market," *Econometrica*, October 1966, pp. 768–783.

16. G. Douglas, "Risk in the Equity Markets: An Empirical Appraisal of Market Efficiency," *Yale Economic Essays*, Spring 1969, pp. 3–45; J. Lintner, "Security Prices and Risk: The Theory and a Comparative Analysis of A.T.&T. and Leading Industrials," a paper presented at the Conference on the Economics of Regulated Public Utilities, June 24, 1965, Chicago, as cited by G. Douglas; M. Miller and M. Scholes, "Rates of Return in Relation to Risk: A Re-examination of Some Recent Findings," in M. Jensen (ed.), *Studies in the Theory of Capital Markets*, Praeger Publishing Company, New York, 1972; and F. Black, M. Jensen, and M. Scholes, "The Capital Asset Pricing Model: Some Empirical Tests," in M. Jensen (ed.), *Studies in the Theory of Capital Markets*, Praeger Publishing Company, New York, 1972.

17. Note Fama's comment that "on the basis of tests similar to those of Fama and MacBeth, Black, Jensen, and Scholes and Friend and Blume likewise come to a negative conclusion with respect to the Sharpe-Lintner hypothesis." See E. Fama, *Portfolios Decisions and Security Prices*, Basic Books, Inc., New York, forthcoming.

18. F. Black, "Capital Market Equilibrium with Restricted Borrowing," *Journal of Business*, July 1972; O. Vasicek, "Capital Market Equilibrium with No Riskless Borrowing," unpublished manuscript, 1972; S. Ross, "Portfolio and Capital Market Theory with Arbitrary Preferences and Distributions—The General Validity the Mean-Variance Approach in Large Markets," Rodney L. White Center for Financial Research, University of Pennsylvania, Philadelphia, 1971; R. Merton, "An Intertemporal Capital Asset Pricing Model," *Econometrica*, 1973, pp. 867–887.

19. See R. Merton, "A Reexamination of the Capital Asset Pricing Model," in I. Friend and J. Bicksler (eds.), *Risk and Return in Finance*, Ballinger Publishing Company, Cambridge, Mass., in press.

20. Black, Jensen, and Scholes, "Capital Asset Pricing Model," pp. 79–121.

21. Black's assumptions are identical to those enumerated previously except that there is no riskless asset and hence no riskless borrowing or lending. See Black, "Capital Market Equilibrium with Restricted Borrowing," pp. 446.

22. M. Brennan, "Capital Market Equilibrium with Divergent Borrowing and Lending Rates," *Journal of Financial and Quantitative Analysis*, December 1971, pp. 1197-1205; O. Vasicek, "Capital Market Equilibrium with No Riskless Borrowing"; D. Mayers, "Non-Marketable Assets and Capital Market Equilibrium under Uncertainty," in M. Jensen (ed.), *Studies in the Theory of Capital Markets*, Praeger Publishing Company, New York, 1972; and J. Lintner, "The Aggregation of Investors' Diverse Judgement and Preferences in Purely Competitive Securities Markets," *Journal of Financial and Quantitative Analysis*, December 1969, pp. 347-400.

23. M. Jensen, "Capital Markets: Theory and Evidence," *Bell Journal of Economics and Management Science*, Autumn 1972, pp. 392.

24. Ibid. Also see R. Roll, "A Difficulty with Two-factor Models of Asset Returns," European Institute for Advanced Studies in Management, Working Paper, Brussels, Belgium, March 1975.

25. E. Fama, "Risk, Return, and Portfolio Analysis; Reply," *Journal of Political Economy*, May–June 1973, pp. 753-755.

26. There is now an extensive literature that shows that production-investment decisions by value-maximizing firms do not lead to Pareto optimal stock market allocations. See, for example, E. Fama, "Perfect Competition and Optimal Production Decisions under Uncertainty," *Bell Journal of Economics and Management Science*, Autumn 1972, pp. 509-530; M. Jensen and J. Long, "Corporate Investment under Uncertainty and Pareto Optimality in the Capital Markets," *Bell Journal of Economics and Management Science*, Spring 1972, pp. 151-174; H. Leland, "Production Theory and the Stock Market," *Bell Journal of Economics and Management Science*, Spring 1974, pp. 125-144; and R. Merton and M. Subrahmanyam, "The Optimality of a Competitive Stock Market," *Bell Journal of Economics and Management Science*, Spring 1974, pp. 145-170. A useful survey of Pareto optimal conditions of capital market allocative efficiency is J. Mossin, "Capital Market Efficiency: An Introductory Survey," N.Y.U. Working Paper, 1973.

27. R. Ball, "Risk, Return and Disequilibrium: An Application to Changes in Accounting Techniques," *Journal of Finance*, May 1972, pp. 343-354; T. Archibald, "Stock Market Reaction to the Depreciation Switch-Back," *Accounting Review*, January 1972, pp. 22-30; G. Benston, "Required Disclosure and the Stock Market: An Evaluation of the Securities Exchange Act of 1934," *American Economic Review*, March 1973, pp. 132-155; and S. Sunder, "Relationships between Accounting Changes and Stock Prices: Problems of Measurement and Some Empirical Evidence," *Empirical Research in Accounting: Selected Studies*, 1973, Supplement to *Journal of Accounting Research*, 1973.

28. This idea (e.g., the trivality of a nonmarket equilibrium scenario having no testable risk-return propositions) has, of course, been noted in the literature many times. For example, Haley and Schall comment on the usefulness of the

risk-adjusted discount model: "For theoretical purposes the model is much less appealing because there is no direct means of determining r_y. It must be considered a derived quantity resulting from some unspecified process. . . . The theoretical issue is how equilibrium prices (or rates of return) are determined." C. Haley and L. Schall, *The Theory of Financial Decisions*, McGraw-Hill Book Company, New York, p. 187. Also see Mossin, "Equilibrium in a Capital Asset Market," *Econometrica*, October, 1966, pp. 768–783.

29. For insights into the present state of empirical knowledge about beta, see the studies by Breen and Lerner, Hamada, Petit and Westerfield, Rosenberg and McKibben, and White. W. Breen and E. Lerner, "Corporation Financial Strategies and Market Measures of Risk and Return," *Journal of Finance*, May 1973; R. Hamada, "The Effect of the Firm's Capital Structure on the Systematic Risk of Common Stocks," *Journal of Finance*, May 1972, pp. 435–452 and reprinted as Chapter 10 in this book; R. Petit and R. Westerfield, "A Model of Capital Market Risk," *Journal of Finance and Quantitative Analysis*, March 1972, pp. 1649–1668; B. Rosenberg and W. McKibben, "The Prediction of Systematic and Specific Risk in Common Stocks," *Journal of Finance and Quantitative Analysis*, March 1973, pp. 317–324; and R. White, "On the Measurement of Systematic Risk," Ph.D. dissertation, M.I.T., Cambridge, Mass., 1972.

30. S. Myers, "The Relation between Book and Market Measures of Risk and Return," paper presented to the AT&T Seminar on Risk and Return, Vail, Colorado, August 1973. Reprinted in I. Friend and J. Bicksler, *Risk and Return in Finance*, Ballenger Publishing Company, Cambridge, Mass., forthcoming.

31. For insights into the methods and techniques for deriving subjective probability distributions, for Bayesian analysis, see R. Winkler, "The Assessment of Prior Distributions in Bayesian Analysis," *Journal of the American Statistical Association*, 1967, pp. 776–800; and L. Savage, "The Elicitation of Personal Probabilities and Expectations," *Journal of the American Statistical Association*, March 1971, pp. 783–801.

32. For a description of the mechanics of the market model residual approach for testing market efficiency, see E. Fama, *Portfolio Decisions and Security Prices*, Basic Books, Inc., New York, forthcoming, chapter 5. In essence, the residuals of the market model capture the effect of new information specific to the firm. Hence, an examination of the residuals or, more precisely, the estimates of the residuals can be used to determine whether the prices of the firm's securities adjust to this new information in a manner consistent with market efficiency or market inefficiency (e.g., market adjustment with a lag). The pioneering study using the residuals approach is E. Fama, L. Fisher, M. Jensen, and R. Roll, "The Adjustment of Stock Prices to New Information," *International Economic Review*, February 1969, pp. 1–21. An examination of the market model's underpinning of stationary Gaussian return distributions and

its implications for a wider set of econometric and economic issues are contained in M. Hinrich and R. Roll, "Measuring Non-Stationarity in the Stochastic Process of Asset Returns," European Institute for Advanced Studies in Management, Working Paper, Brussels, Belgium, 1975. Others studies using the market model residual approach included R. Ball and P. Brown, "An Empirical Evaluation of Accounting Income Numbers," *Journal of Accounting Research*, Autumn 1968, pp. 159–178; and Scholes, "The Market for Securities: Substitution Versus Price Pressure and the Effects of Information on Share Prices," *Journal of Business*, April, 1972, pp. 179–211. 1972.

   33. Because their estimates of dispersion were upward-biased due to cross-sectional correlation in errors, Kaplan and Roll's results are even more consistent with the null hypothesis than they were reported. See N. Gonedes and N. Dopuch, "Capital Market Equilibrium, Information Production, and Selecting Accounting Techniques," *Studies on Financial Accounting Objectives*, University of Chicago, p. 88.

   34. It is generally recognized that the two central issues in finance are the proper treatment of time and risk. In this regard, Merton states that "the two ingredients which make finance a non-trivial subject are *time* and *uncertainty*." See R. Merton, *Finance Theory I*, M.I.T., Cambridge, Mass., 1975.

   35. R. Stapleton, "Portfolio Analysis, Stock Valuation and Capital Budgeting Decision Rules for Risky Projects," *Journal of Finance*, March 1971, p. 99.

   36. M. Brennan, "An Approach to the Valuation of Uncertain Income Streams" *Journal of Finance*, June 1973, pp. 661–662. This approach of Stapelton has a number of conceptual limitations with regard to treating time and uncertainty, and it does not rule out inconsistent choices. For an elaboration, see J. Mossin, "Review of Hillier's Budgeting Interrelated Activities," *Journal of Economic Literature*, 1971, p. 866. However, there has been some confusion over whether the Stapelton framework postulated that the firm's cash flows and investment project's cash flows are perfectly correlated. In this regard, see H. Bierman and J. Hass, "Capital Budgeting under Uncertainty: A Reformulation," *Journal of Finance*, March 1973; R. Stapelton, "Capital Budgeting under Uncertainty: A Reformation: Comment," *Journal of Finance*, December 1974, pp. 1583–1584; and H. Bierman and J. Hass, "Reply," *Journal of Finance*, December 1974, p. 1585.

   37. See R. Hamada, "Multiperiod Capital Asset Prices in an Efficient and Perfect Market: A Valuation or Present Value Model under Two Parameters," unpublished paper presented to the Western Finance Association Meetings, 1974; and R. Merton, "An Intertemporal Capital Asset Pricing Model," *Econometrica*, 1973, pp. 373–413.

   38. R. Merton, "Lifetime Portfolio Selection under Uncertainty: The

Continuous-Time Case," *Review of Economics and Statistics*, 1969, pp. 247–257.

39. R. Hamada, "The Effect of the Firm's Capital Structure on the Systematic Risk of Common Stocks," *Journal of Finance*, May 1972, p. 442. In this regard, Hamada's study likely provides the most definitive findings regarding the impact of a corporate financial variable on beta.

40. Statements of the conventional theory (e.g., non-Modigliani-Miller theory) of the effect of leverage on risk are detailed in D. Durand, "Costs of Debt and Equity Funds for Business: Trends and Problems of Measurement," *Conference on Research in Business Finance*, N.B.E.R., New York, 1952, pp. 225–237; B. Graham and D. Dodd, *Security Analysis*, 3d ed., New York, 1951, pp. 464–466; and E. Solomon, *The Theory of Financial Management*, Columbia University Press, New York, 1963.

41. An alternative interpretation of Hamada's empirical results is W. Sharpe, "Discussion," *Journal of Finance*, May 1972, pp. 456–458. Also see J. Lintner, "Discussion," *Journal of Finance*, May 1972, pp. 453–456.

42. An elaboration and extension of this along with a delineation of the implications of the two-parameter model for regulatory rate of return are detailed in J. Bicksler and P. Hess, "Some Practical Suggestions for Improving Rate of Return Testimony," a paper presented to the National Association of Regulatory Utility Commissioners, Boston, Mass., November 1975. Also see, as illustrative testimony in this regard, Northwestern Bell Telephone Company, Docket No. U–479, State of Iowa, Prepared Direct Testimony by James L. Bicksler, 1973; Southern Central Bell, Docket No. U–3065, State of Mississippi, Prepared Direct Testimony by James L. Bicksler, 1976; and Mississippi Power Company, Docket No. U–3064, State of Mississippi, Prepared Direct Testimony by James L. Bicksler, 1976.

43. Among the rationales are the "abnormal gains" hypothesis, the "chain letter" hypothesis, and the growth maximization hypothesis. See, among others, W. Lewellen, "A Pure Financial Rationale for the Conglomerate Merger, *Journal of Finance*, May 1971; J. Lintner, "Expectations, Mergers, and Equilibrium in Purely Competitive Securities Markets," *American Economic Review*, 1971, pp. 101–111; and D. Mueller, "A Theory of Conglomerate Mergers," *Quarterly Journal of Economics*, 1969, pp. 643–660.

44. The procedure is to examine the behavior of the average and the cumulative average residual from the two-factor model. Thus, this test is similar, in many respects, to the market model residuals test. If the residuals do not depart significantly from zero, then the market is consistent with market efficiency with regard to the company-specific information parameters. Other studies, besides Jaffe, Mandelker, and Rozeff, investigating market efficiency using the two-factor market residuals approach include those by Ball and

Ibbotson. See R. Ball, "Risk, Return, and Disequilibrium: An Application to Changes in Accounting Techniques," *Journal of Finance*, May 1972, pp. 343–354; and R. Ibbotson, "Price Performance of Common Stocks," Ph.D. dissertation, University of Chicago, Chicago, Ill., 1974.

45. Fama, *Portfolio Decisions and Security Prices*, forthcoming. Mandelker also offers this explanation.

46. The rationale for this "likely" result is that the correlation of returns on securities within the prior market portfolio and the returns on the "new" securities is likely to be low. Hence, the covariance of returns on a given security and the "new" market portfolio is likely to be less than the covariance of the returns on the given security and the "old" market portfolio. However, to this reviewer, this rationale seems a bit ad hoc. Since the weighted average of the betas for all securities with the market portfolio must equal 1, it would depend on whether the new securities have above- or below-average betas. In this regard, Subrahmanyam argues that stronger conditions are required for this result to hold and that, hence, Cohn and Pringle are wrong on this point. See M. Subrahmanyam, "International Capital Market Equilibrium and Investor Welfare with Unequal Interest Rates," in E. Elton and M. Gruber (eds.), *International Capital Markets*, North-Holland/American Elsevier, 1975, p. 224. Cohn and Pringle note two possible exceptions. They are where the returns of a given firm are (1) more closely related to the foreign companies than to domestic companies and (2) negatively related to the prior portfolio.

47. For a discussion of the properties of the logarithmic and exponential utility functions, see J. Mossin, *Theory of Financial Markets*, Prentice-Hall, Inc., Englewood Cliffs, N.J., 1973, p. 113.
The effect on the slope of the capital market line for the scenario in which investors have quadratic utility functions is ambiguous. See R. Cohn and J. Pringle, "Imperfections in International Financial Markets: Implications for Risk Premia and the Cost of Capital to Firms," *Journal of Finance*, March 1973, n. 8, p. 63.

48. An elementary exposition of much of the same material in Rubenstein is J. Weston, "Investment Decisions Using the Capital Asset Pricing Model," *Financial Management*, Spring 1973, pp. 25–43. For some cogent insights into capital budgeting of multiperiod projects using Sharpe-Lintner dimensions, see M. Bogue and R. Roll, "Capital Budgeting of Risky Projects with 'Imperfect' Markets for Physical Capital," *Journal of Finance*, May 1974, pp. 601–613.

49. Strictly speaking, "it is incorrect to think of a security as overpriced if it plots below the security market line (or underpriced if it plots above it)." Presumably, an equilibrium relationship postulates that (1) equilibrium does exist, (2) it is unique, and (3) it is stable. See W. Sharpe, *Portfolio Theory and Capital Markets*, McGraw-Hill Book Company, New York, 1970, pp. 98 and 103. However, the availability of disequilibrium returns on new production projects is consistent with equilibrium in the financial markets.

50. The optimal investment criterion for the capital-rationing case appears to be dubious. Specifically, if there are financial constraints, then capital markets are imperfect and ergo the use of market value maximization rule is inappropriate. If capital markets are perfect, then the financial constraints are arbitrary stipulations by management. For a discussion of this and related issues, see E. Fama and M. Miller, *The Theory of Finance*, Holt, Rinehart, and Winston, New York, 1972, pp. 136–137.

51. For a recent unpublished investigation of another financial instrument (e.g., corporate bonds) see M. Weinstein, "The Structure of the Corporate Bond Market: Empirical Tests," Ph.D. dissertation draft, University of Chicago, Chicago, Ill., October 1975. Weinstein's investigation is somewhat different than the Bildersee study inasmuch as it focused on testing the segmentation seasoning hypothesis and estimating the properties of bond returns.

52. For a traditional discussion of the hybrid nature of preferred stocks, see B. Graham, D. Dodd, and S. Cottle, *Security Analysis*, McGraw-Hill Book Company, New York, 1962, p. 375.

53. A description of the bond index which is comprised of a cross-section of U.S. Government bonds of the same maturity is detailed in J. Bildersee, "Some New Bond Indexes," *Journal of Business*, October 1975, pp. 506–525. Similar information on the Fisher index is detailed in L. Fisher, "Some New Stock Market Indexes," *Journal of Business*, January 1966.

54. J. Bildersee, "Some Aspects of the Performance of Non-Convertible Preferred Stocks," *Journal of Finance*, December 1973, p. 1201.

55. The use of future rather than spot prices was simply a matter of computational convenience.

The investment is the futures price and not the margin. The margin payment is simply a good-faith deposit. An investigation of commodity rates of returns which is invalid for this specific reason is N. Shrock, "The Theory of Asset Choice: Simultaneous Holding of Short and Long Positions in the Futures Market," *Journal of Political Economy*, March–April 1971, pp. 270–293.

56. Dusak also estimates the characteristic exponents of the return distributions for commodities. The estimates range from 1.44 to 1.84, and half are below 1.56. While our knowledge about the shape of distribution is not yet definitive, the empirical evidence would strongly suggest that it is not a stationary Gaussian distribution. The two major alternatives are a stationary non-Gaussian distribution (e.g., a stable distribution) and a nonstationary Gaussian distribution. See B. Mandelbrot, "The Variation of Certain Speculative Prices," *Journal of Business*, October 1963, pp. 394–419; E. Fama, "The Behavior of Stock Market Prices," *Journal of Business*, January 1965, pp. 34–105; R. Roll, *The Behavior of Interest Rates*, Basic Books, Inc., New York, 1970; S.J. Press, "A Compound Events Model for Security Prices," *Journal of Business*, July 1967, pp. 317–335; R. Officer, "The Distribution of Stock Returns," *Journal of the American Statistical Association*, December 1972, pp. 807–812; P. Clark,

"A Subordinated Stochastic Process Model with Finite Variance for Speculative Prices," *Econometrica*, January 1973, pp. 135-155; and R. Blattberg and N. Gonedes, "A Comparison of Stable and Student Disturbances as Statistical Models for Stock Prices," *Journal of Business*, April 1974, pp. 244-280.

57. J. Keynes, *A Treatise on Money*, vol. 2, Macmillan, London, 1930, pp. 135-144.

58. Jaffe makes an important contribution in developing the testing procedure for estimating information "profitability" via the standardized residual approach. This technique enables one to estimate whether the portfolio residuals following a given event could have resulted from chance. For a discussion of the technique specifics see Jaffe, "The Effect of Regulation Changes on Insider Trading," pp. 416-418.

59. Fama, *Portfolio Decisions and Security Prices*, forthcoming.

60. The first studies recognizing the inconsistency of a money supply trading rule with efficient markets were J. Bicksler, "A Cross-Spectral Analysis of the Lead-Lag Structure of Money Supply-Stock Prices," in J. Bicksler (ed.), *Methodology in Finance—Investments*, Lexington, Mass., Lexington Books, D.C. Heath and Company, 1972, pp. 229-243; and R. Cooper, "Efficient Capital Markets and the Quantity Theory of Money," *Journal of Finance*, June 1974, pp. 887-908.

61. B. Sprinkel, *Money and Stock Prices*, Richard D. Irwin, Homewood, Ill., 1964; B. Sprinkel, *Money and Markets: A Monetarist View*, Richard D. Irwin, Homewood, Ill., 1971; M. Palmer, "Money Supply, Portfolio Adjustments and Stock Prices," *Financial Analysts Journal*, July–August 1970; F. Reilly and J. Lewis, "Monetary Variables and Stock Prices," Working Paper, University of Kansas, Lawrence, Kansas, 1971; M. Keran, "Expectations, Money and the Stock Market," *Federal Reserve Bank of St. Louis Review*, January 1971; M. Hamburger and L. Kochin, "Money and Stock Prices," *Journal of Finance*, May 1972; K. Homa and D. Jaffe, "The Supply of Money and Common Stock Prices," *Journal of Finance*, December 1971; and R. Cooper, "Efficient Capital Markets and the Quantity Theory of Money," *Journal of Finance*, June 1974, pp. 887-908.

62. Two quasijournalistic synopses of the Rozeff article are M. Rozeff, "The Money Supply and the Stock Market: The Demise of a Leading Indicator," *Financial Analysts Journal*, September–October 1975, pp. 18-26; and A. Ehrbar, "How the Money Supply Drives the Stock Market," *Fortune*, October 1975.

63. A criticism of Rozeff's study is R. Rogalski and J. Vinso, "Stock Returns, Money Supply and the Direction of Causality," University of Pennsylvania, Rodney L. White Center for Financial Research, Working Paper No. 7-75, Philadelphia, Pa., 1975.

64. An insightful analysis and perspective of Treynor-Black are provided in R. Merton, *Finance Theory I*, 1975, pp. 135–147.

65. See W. Sharpe, "Mutual Fund Performance," *Journal of Business*, January 1966, pp. 119–138.

66. This article is similar in many respects to E. Fama, "Components of Investment Performance," *Journal of Finance*, June 1972, pp. 551–567.

67. A qualifying proviso should be added. Specifically, selected insiders may have useful inside information that is not impounded into stock prices. See, for example, the studies by Scholes, Lorie, and Niederhoffer, Niederhoffer and Osborne, and Jaffe referred to earlier.

68. This, of course, does not imply that accounting data may not be useful in certain decision scenarios. One example is the Beaver, Kettler, and Scholes article that was discussed earlier in this book. Also, see the literature on prediction of corporate bankruptcy and corporate bond ratings. W. Beaver, "Financial Ratios as Predictors of Failure," *Empirical Research in Accounting: Selected Studies*, 1966, pp. 71–127; W. Beaver, "Market Prices, Financial Ratios, and the Prediction of Failure," *Journal of Accounting Research*, Autumn 1968, pp. 179–192; E. Altman, "Financial Ratios, Discriminant Analysis and the Prediction of Corporate Bankruptcy," *Journal of Finance*, September 1968, pp. 589–609; and R. West, "An Alternative Approach to Predicting Corporate Bond Ratings," *Journal of Accounting Research*, Spring 1970.

For a somewhat different presentation of the implications of efficient markets and two-parameter security market equilibrium, see B. Lev, *Financial Statement Analysis: A New Approach*, Prentice-Hall Inc., Englewood Cliffs, N.J., 1974; and T. Dyckman, D. Downes, and R. Magee, *Efficient Capital Markets and Accounting: A Critical Analysis*, Prentice-Hall Inc., Englewood Cliffs, N.J., 1975.

69. For a discussion of the fallacies of traditional cost of capital analysis, see J. Mossin, *Security Pricing Theory and Its Implications for Corporate Investment Decisions*, General Learning Press, Morristown, N.J., 1972; and J. Mossin, *Theory of Financial Markets*, p. 136.

70. Note Fama's comment that "the important basis for the conclusion that the two-parameter model is useful is that it does well, relative to any other capital market model of which I am aware, in describing actual return data. Although there is some disagreement on matters of detail, the implications of the model for the measurement of risk and the relationship between risk and average return seem to stand up well in the empirical tests of Friend and Blume, and Black, Jensen, and Scholes, and in the test of Fama and Mac Beth. . . ." See E. Fama, "Risk, Return and Portfolio Analysis," *Journal of Political Economy*, May–June 1973, p. 754.

71. As Nelson notes, "The concept of rational expectations put forward

by J. Muth in 1961 is perhaps one of the most profound in economic theory."
See J. Muth, "Rational Expectations and the Theory of Price Movements,"
Econometrica, July 1961, pp. 315-335; and C. Nelson, "Rational Expectations
and the Predictive Efficiency of Economic Models," *Journal of Business*, 1975,
pp. 331-343. Nelson's article is a seminal article having important implications
for finance in general and for efficient markets specifically.

72. For a unified state-contingent framework of asset valuation, see
J. Ingersoll, "A Theoretical and Empirical Investigation of the Dual Purpose
Funds: An Application of Contingent Claims Analysis," *Journal of Financial
Economics*, March 1973, pp. 83-123; R. Merton, "Theory of Rational Option
Pricing," *Bell Journal of Economics and Management Science*, 1973, pp. 373-
413; R. Merton, "On the Pricing of Corporate Debt: The Risk Structure of
Interest Rates," *Journal of Finance*, May 1974, pp. 449-470; and J. Ingersoll,
"A Contingent Claims Valuation of Convertible Bonds," University of Chicago
Working Paper, Chicago, Ill., February 1976. Ingersoll shows that the use of
contingent claim analysis is robust in explaining the price fluctuations of dual-
purpose funds. However, the analytical solutions for optimal conversions and
call strategies for convertible bonds that are derived by contingent claims
analysis seem to be contradicted by casual empiricism.

Part I
Market Efficiency
and Equilibrium

1

Efficient Capital Markets: A Review of Theory and Empirical Work

Eugene F. Fama

I. Introduction

The primary role of the capital market is allocation of ownership of the economy's capital stock. In general terms, the ideal is a market in which prices provide accurate signals for resource allocation: that is, a market in which firms can make production-investment decisions, and investors can choose among the securities that represent ownership of firms' activities under the assumption that security prices at any time "fully reflect" all available information. A market in which prices always "fully reflect" available information is called "efficient."

This paper reviews the theoretical and empirical literature on the efficient markets model. After a discussion of the theory, empirical work concerned with the adjustment of security prices to three relevant information subsets is considered. First, *weak form* tests, in which the information set is just historical prices, are discussed. Then *semi-strong form* tests, in which the concern is whether prices efficiently adjust to other information that is obviously publicly available (e.g., announcements of annual earnings, stock splits, etc.) are considered. Finally, *strong form* tests concerned with whether given investors or groups have monopolistic access to any information relevant for price formation are reviewed.[1] We shall conclude that, with but a few exceptions, the efficient markets model stands up well.

Though we proceed from theory to empirical work, to keep the proper historical perspective we should note to a large extent the empirical work in this area preceded the development of the theory. The theory is presented first here in order to more easily judge which of the empirical results are most relevant from the viewpoint of the theory. The empirical work itself, however, will then be reviewed in more or less historical sequence.

Reprinted with permission of the author and publisher from *The Journal of Finance* Vol no   May 1970, pp. 383–417.

Research on this project was supported by a grant from the National Science Foundation. I am indebted to Arthur Laffer, Robert Aliber, Ray Ball, Michael Jensen, James Lorie, Merton Miller, Charles Nelson, Richard Roll, William Taylor, and Ross Watts for their helpful comments.

[1] The distinction between weak and strong form tests was first suggested by Harry Roberts.

Finally, the perceptive reader will surely recognize instances in this paper where relevant studies are not specifically discussed. In such cases my apologies should be taken for granted. The area is so bountiful that some such injustices are unavoidable. But the primary goal here will have been accomplished if a coherent picture of the main lines of the work on efficient markets is presented, along with an accurate picture of the current state of the arts.

II. The Theory of Efficient Markets

A. *Expected Return or "Fair Game" Models*

The definitional statement that in an efficient market prices "fully reflect" available information is so general that it has no empirically testable implications. To make the model testable, the process of price formation must be specified in more detail. In essence we must define somewhat more exactly what is meant by the term "fully reflect."

One possibility would be to posit that equilibrium prices (or expected returns) on securities are generated as in the "two parameter" Sharpe [40] - Lintner [24, 25] world. In general, however, the theoretical models and especially the empirical tests of capital market efficiency have not been this specific. Most of the available work is based only on the assumption that the conditions of market equilibrium can (somehow) be stated in terms of expected returns. In general terms, like the two parameter model such theories would posit that conditional on some relevant information set, the equilibrium expected return on a security is a function of its "risk." And different theories would differ primarily in how "risk" is defined.

All members of the class of such "expected return theories" can, however, be described notationally as follows:

$$E(\tilde{p}_{j,\,t+1}\,|\Phi_t) = [1 + E(\tilde{r}_{j,\,t+1}|\Phi_t)]p_{jt} \qquad (1)$$

where E is the expected value operator; p_{jt} is the price of security j at time t; $p_{j,\,t+1}$ is its price at $t + 1$ (with reinvestment of any intermediate cash income from the security); $r_{j,\,t+1}$ is the one-period percentage return $(p_{j,\,t+1} - p_{jt})/p_{jt}$; Φ_t is a general symbol for whatever set of information is assumed to be "fully reflected" in the price at t; and the tildes indicate that $p_{j,\,t+1}$ and $r_{j,\,t+1}$ are random variables at t.

The value of the equilibrium expected return $E(\tilde{r}_{j,\,t+1}|\Phi_t)$ projected on the basis of the information Φ_t would be determined from the particular expected return theory at hand. The conditional expectation notation of (1) is meant to imply, however, that whatever expected return model is assumed to apply, the information in Φ_t is fully utilized in determining equilibrium expected returns. And this is the sense in which Φ_t is "fully reflected" in the formation of the price p_{jt}.

But we should note right off that, simple as it is, the assumption that the conditions of market equilibrium can be stated in terms of expected returns elevates the purely mathematical concept of expected value to a status not necessarily implied by the general notion of market efficiency. The expected value is just one of many possible summary measures of a distribution of returns, and market efficiency per se (i.e., the general notion that prices "fully reflect" available information) does not imbue it with any special importance. Thus, the results of tests based on this assumption depend to some extent on its validity as well as on the efficiency of the market. But some such assumption is the unavoidable price one must pay to give the theory of efficient markets empirical content.

The assumptions that the conditions of market equilibrium can be stated in terms of expected returns and that equilibrium expected returns are formed on the basis of (and thus "fully reflect") the information set Φ_t have a major empirical implication—they rule out the possibility of trading systems based only on information in Φ_t that have expected profits or returns in excess of equilibrium expected profits or returns. Thus let

$$x_{j,\,t+1} = p_{j,\,t+1} - E(p_{j,\,t+1} | \Phi_t) \tag{2}$$

Then

$$E(\tilde{x}_{j,\,t+1} | \Phi_t) = 0 \tag{3}$$

which, by definition, says that the sequence $\{x_{jt}\}$ is a "fair game" with respect to the information sequence $\{\phi_t\}$. Or, equivalently, let

$$z_{j,\,t+1} = r_{j,\,t+1} - E(\tilde{r}_{j,\,t+1} | \Phi_t) \tag{4}$$

then

$$E(\tilde{z}_{j,\,t+1} | \Phi_t) = 0 \tag{5}$$

so that the sequence $\{z_{jt}\}$ is also a "fair game" with respect to the information sequence $\{\Phi\}$.

In economic terms, $x_{j,\,t+1}$ is the excess market value of security j at time $t + 1$: it is the difference between the observed price and the expected value of the price that was projected at t on the basis of the information Φ_t. And similarly, $z_{j,\,t+1}$ is the return at $t + 1$ in excess of the equilibrium expected return projected at t. Let

$$\alpha(\Phi_t) = [\alpha_1(\Phi_t), \alpha_2(\Phi_t), \ldots, \alpha_n(\Phi_t)]$$

be any trading system based on Φ_t which tells the investor the amounts $\alpha_j(\Phi_t)$ of funds available at t that are to be invested in each of the n available securities. The total excess market value at $t + 1$ that will be generated by such a system is

$$V_{t+1} = \sum_{j=1}^{n} \alpha_j(\Phi_t)[r_{j, t+1} - E(\tilde{r}_{j, t+1}|\Phi_t)]$$

which, from the "fair game" property of (5) has expectation,

$$E(\tilde{V}_{t+1}|\Phi_t) = \sum_{j=1}^{n} \alpha_j(\Phi_t)E(\tilde{z}_{j, t+1}|\Phi_t = 0$$

The expected return or "fair game" efficient markets model[2] has other important testable implications, but these are better saved for the later discussion of the empirical work. Now we turn to two special cases of the model, the submartingale and the random walk, that (as we shall see later) play an important role in the empirical literature.

B. *The Submartingale Model*

Suppose we assume in (1) that for all t and Φ_t

$$E(\tilde{p}_{j, t+1}|\Phi_t) \geqslant p_{jt} \quad \text{or equivalently,} \quad E(\tilde{r}_{j, t+1}|\Phi_t) \geqslant 0 \qquad (6)$$

This is a statement that the price sequence $\{p_{jt}\}$ for security j follows a submartingale with respect to the information sequence $\{\Phi_t\}$, which is to say nothing more than that the expected value of next period's price, as projected on the basis of the information Φ_t, is equal to or greater than the current price. If (6) holds as an equality (so that expected returns and price changes are zero), then the price sequence follows a martingale.

A submartingale in prices has one important empirical implication. Consider

---

[2]Though we shall sometimes refer to the model summarized by (1) as the "fair game" model, keep in mind that the "fair game" properties of the model are *implications* of the assumptions that (i) the conditions of market equilibrium can be stated in terms of expected returns, and (ii) the information Φ_t is fully utilized by the market in forming equilibrium expected returns and thus current prices.

The role of "fair game" models in the theory of efficient markets was first recognized and studied rigorously by Mandelbrot [27] and Samuelson [38]. Their work will be discussed in more detail later.

the set of "one security and cash" mechanical trading rules by which we mean systems that concentrate on individual securities and that define the conditions under which the investor would hold a given security, sell it short, or simply hold cash at any time t. Then the assumption of (6) that expected returns conditional on Φ_t are non-negative directly implies that such trading rules based only on the information in Φ_t cannot have greater expected profits than a policy of always buying-and-holding the security during the future period in question. Tests of such rules will be an important part of the empirical evidence on the efficient markets model. [3]

C. *The Random Walk Model*

In the early treatments of the efficient markets model, the statement that the current price of a security "fully reflects" available information was assumed to imply that successive price changes (or more usually, successive one-period returns) are independent. In addition, it was usually assumed that successive changes (or returns) are identically distributed. Together the two hypotheses constitute the random walk model. Formally, the model says

$$f(r_{j,\,t+1} | \Phi_t) = f(r_{j,\,t+1}) \tag{7}$$

which is the usual statement that the conditional and marginal probability distributions of an independent random variable are identical. In addition, the density function f must be the same for all t.[4]

Expression (7) of course says much more than the general expected return

---

[3]Note that the expected profitability of "one security and cash" trading systems vis-à-vis buy-and-hold is not ruled out by the general expected return or "fair game" efficient markets model. The latter rules out systems with expected profits in excess of equilibrium expected returns, but since in principle it allows equilibrium expected returns to be negative, holding cash (which always has zero actual and thus expected return) may have higher expected return than holding some security.

And negative equilibrium expected returns for some securities are quite possible. For example, in the Sharpe [40]-Lintner [24, 25] model (which is in turn a natural extension of the portfolio models of Markowitz [30] and Tobin [43]) the equilibrium expected return on a security depends on the extent to which the dispersion in the security's return distribution is related to dispersion in the returns on all other securities. A security whose returns on average move opposite to the general market is particularly valuable in reducing dispersion of portfolio returns, and so its equilibrium expected return may well be negative.

[4]The terminology is loose. Prices will only follow a random walk if price changes are independent, identically distributed; and even then we should say "random walk with drift" since expected price changes can be non-zero. If one-period returns are independent, identically distributed, prices will not follow a random walk since the distribution of price changes will depend on the price level. But though rigorous terminology is usually desirable, our loose use of terms should not cause confusion; and our usage follows that of the efficient markets literature.

Note also that in the random walk literature, the information set Φ_t in (7) is usually assumed to include only the past return history, $r_{j,\,t}, r_{j,\,t-1}, \cdots$

model summarized by (1). For example, if we restrict (1) by assuming that the expected return on security j is constant over time, then we have

$$E(\tilde{r}_{j,\,t+1} | \Phi_t) = E(\tilde{r}_{j,\,t+1}) \qquad (8)$$

This says that the mean of the distribution of $r_{j,\,t+1}$ is independent of the information available at t, Φ_t, whereas the random walk model of (7) in addition says that the entire distribution is independent of Φ_t.[5]

We argue later that it is best to regard the random walk model as an extension of the general expected return or "fair game" efficient markets model in the sense of making a more detailed statement about the economic environment. The "fair game" model just says that the conditions of market equilibrium can be stated in terms of expected returns, and thus it says little about the details of the stochastic process generating returns. A random walk arises within the context of such a model when the environment is (fortuitously) such that the evolution of investor tastes and the process generating new information combine to produce equilibria in which return distributions repeat themselves through time.

Thus it is not surprising that empirical tests of the "random walk" model that are in fact tests of "fair game" properties are more strongly in support of the model than tests of the additional (and, from the viewpoint of expected return market efficiency, superfluous) pure independence assumption. (But it is perhaps equally surprising that, as we shall soon see, the evidence against the independence of returns over time is as weak as it is.)

D. *Market Conditions Consistent with Efficiency*

Before turning to the empirical work, however, a few words about the market conditions that might help or hinder efficient adjustment of prices to information are in order. First, it is easy to determine *sufficient* conditions for capital market efficiency. For example, consider a market in which (i) there are no transactions costs in trading securities, (ii) all available information is costlessly available to all market participants, and (iii) all agree on the implications of current information for the current price and distributions of future prices of each security. In such a market, the current price of a security obviously "fully reflects" all available information.

But a frictionless market in which all information is freely available and

---

[5]The random walk model does not say, however, that past information is of no value in *assessing* distributions of future returns. Indeed since return distributions are assumed to be stationary through time, past returns are the best source of such information. The random walk model does say, however, that the *sequence* (or the order) of the past returns is of no consequence in assessing distributions of future returns.

investors agree on its implications is, of course, not descriptive of markets met in practice. Fortunately, these conditions are sufficient for market efficiency, but not necessary. For example, as long as transactors take account of all available information, even large transactions costs that inhibit the flow of transactions do not in themselves imply that when transactions do take place, prices will not "fully reflect" available information. Similarly (and speaking, as above, somewhat loosely), the market may be efficient if "sufficient numbers" of investors have ready access to available information. And disagreement among investors about the implications of given information does not in itself imply market inefficiency unless there are investors who can consistently make better evaluations of available information than are implicit in market prices.

But though transactions costs, information that is not freely available to all investors, and disagreement among investors about the implications of given information are not necessarily sources of market inefficiency, they are potential sources. And all three exist to some extent in real world markets. Measuring their effects on the process of price formation is, of course, the major goal of empirical work in this area.

III. The Evidence

All the empirical research on the theory of efficient markets has been concerned with whether prices "fully reflect" particular subsets of available information. Historically, the empirical work evolved more or less as follows. The initial studies were concerned with what we call *weak form* tests in which the information subset of interest is just past price (or return) histories. Most of the results here come from the random walk literature. When extensive tests seemed to support the efficiency hypothesis at this level, attention was turned to *semi-strong form* tests in which the concern is the speed of price adjustment to other obviously publicly available information (e.g., announcements of stock splits, annual reports, new security issues, etc.). Finally, *strong form* tests in which the concern is whether any investor or groups (e.g., managements of mutual funds) have monopolistic access to any information relevant for the formation of prices have recently appeared. We review the empirical research in more or less this historical sequence.

First, however, we should note that what we have called *the* efficient markets model in the discussions of earlier sections is the hypothesis that security prices at any point in time "fully reflect" *all* available information. Though we shall argue that the model stands up rather well to the data, it is obviously an extreme null hypothesis. And, like any other extreme null hypothesis, we do not expect it to be literally true. The categorization of the tests into weak, semi-strong, and strong form will serve the useful purpose of allowing us to pinpoint the level of information at which the hypothesis breaks down. And we shall contend that there is no important evidence against the hypothesis in the weak and semi-strong form tests (i.e., prices seem to efficiently adjust to obviously publicly available information), and only limited evidence against the hypothesis in the strong form tests (i.e., monopolistic access to information about prices does not seem to be a prevalent phenomenon in the investment community).

A. *Weak Form Tests of the Efficient Markets Model*

1. Random Walks and Fair Games: A Little Historical Background. As noted earlier, all of the empirical work on efficient markets can be considered within the context of the general expected return or "fair game" model, and much of the evidence bears directly on the special submartingale expected return model of (6). Indeed, in the early literature, discussions of the efficient markets model were phrased in terms of the even more special random walk model, though we shall argue that most of the early authors were in fact concerned with more general versions of the "fair game" model.

Some of the confusion in the early random walk writings is understandable. Research on security prices did not begin with the development of a theory of price formation which was then subjected to empirical tests. Rather, the impetus for the development of a theory came from the accumulation of evidence in the middle 1950's and early 1960's that the behavior of common stock and other speculative prices could be well approximated by a random walk. Faced with the evidence, economists felt compelled to offer some rationalization. What resulted was a theory of efficient markets stated in terms of random walks, but usually implying some more general "fair game" model.

It was not until the work of Samuelson [38] and Mandelbrot [27] in 1965 and 1966 that the role of "fair game" expected return models in the theory of efficient markets and the relationships between these models and the theory of random walks were rigorously studied.[6] And these papers came somewhat after the major empirical work on random walks. In the earlier work, "theoretical"

---

[6]Basing their analyses on futures contracts in commodity markets, Mandelbrot and Samuelson show that if the price of such a contract at time t is the expected value at t (given information Φ_t) of the spot price at the termination of the contract, then the futures price will follow a martingale with respect to the information sequence $\{\Phi_t\}$; that is, the expected price change from period to period will be zero, and the price changes will be a "fair game." If the equilibrium expected return is not assumed to be zero, our more general "fair game" model, summarized by (1), is obtained.

But though the Mandelbrot-Samuelson approach certainly illuminates the process of price formation in commodity markets, we have seen that "fair game" expected return models can be derived in much simpler fashion. In particular, (1) is just a formalization of the assumptions that the conditions of market equilibrium can be stated in terms of expected returns and that the information Φ_t is used in forming market prices at t.

discussions, though usually intuitively appealing, were always lacking in rigor and often either vague or *ad hoc*. In short, until the Mandelbrot-Samuelson models appeared, there existed a large body of empirical results in search of a rigorous theory.

Thus, though his contributions were ignored for sixty years, the first statement and test of the random walk model was that of Bachelier [3] in 1900. But his "fundamental principle" for the behavior of prices was that speculation should be a "fair game"; in particular, the expected profits to the speculator should be zero. With the benefit of the modern theory of stochastic processes, we know now that the process implied by this fundamental principle is a martingale.

After Bachelier, research on the behavior of security prices lagged until the coming of the computer. In 1953 Kendall [21] examined the behavior of weekly changes in nineteen indices of British industrial share prices and in spot prices for cotton (New York) and wheat (Chicago). After extensive analysis of serial correlations, he suggests, in quite graphic terms:

The series looks like a wandering one, almost as if once a week the Demon of Chance drew a random number from a symetrical population of fixed dispersion and added it to the current price to determine the next week's price [21, p. 13].

Kendall's conclusion had in fact been suggested earlier by Working [47], though his suggestion lacked the force provided by Kendall's empirical results. And the implications of the conclusion for stock market research and financial analysis were later underlined by Roberts [36].

But the suggestion by Kendall, Working, and Roberts that series of speculative prices may be well described by random walks was based on observation. None of these authors attempted to provide much economic rationale for the hypothesis, and indeed, Kendall felt that economists would generally reject it. Osborne [33] suggested market conditions, similar to those assumed by Bachelier, that would lead to a random walk. But in his model, independence of successive price changes derives from the assumption that the decisions of investors in an individual security are independent from transaction to transaction—which is little in the way of an economic model.

Whenever economists (prior to Mandelbrot and Samuelson) tried to provide economic justification for the random walk, their arguments usually implied a "fair game." For example, Alexander [8, p. 200] states:

If one were to start out with the assumption that a stock or commodity speculation is a "fair game" with equal expectation of gain or loss or, more accurately, with an expectation of zero gain, one would be well on the way to picturing the behavior of speculative prices as a random walk.

There is an awareness here that the "fair game" assumption is not sufficient to lead to a random walk, but Alexander never expands on the comment. Similarly, Cootner [8, p. 232] states:

If any substantial group of buyers thought prices were too low, their buying would force up the prices. The reverse would be true for sellers. Except for appreciation due to earnings retention, the conditional expectation of tomorrow's price, given today's price, is today's price.

In such a world, the only price changes that would occur are those that result from new information. Since there is no reason to expect that information to be non-random in appearance, the period-to-period price changes of a stock should be random movements, statistically independent of one another.

Though somewhat imprecise, the last sentence of the first paragraph seems to point to a "fair game" model rather than a random walk.[7] In this light, the second paragraph can be viewed as an attempt to describe environmental conditions that would reduce a "fair game" to a random walk. But the specification imposed on the information generating process is insufficient for this purpose; one would, for example, also have to say something about investor tastes. Finally, lest I be accused of criticizing others too severely for ambiguity, lack of rigor and incorrect conclusions,

By contrast, the stock market trader has a much more practical criterion for judging what constitutes important dependence in successive price changes. For his purposes the random walk model is valid as long as knowledge of the past behavior of the series of price changes cannot be used to increase expected gains. More specifically, the independence assumption is an adequate description of reality as long as the actual degree of dependence in the series of price changes is not sufficient to allow the past history of the series to be used to predict the future in a way which makes expected profits greater than they would be under a naive buy-and hold model [10, p 35].

We know now, of course, that this last condition hardly requires a random walk. It will in fact be met by the submartingale model of (6).

But one should not be too hard on the theoretical efforts of the early empirical random walk literature. The arguments were usually appealing; where they fell short was in awareness of developments in the theory of stochastic processes. Moreover, we shall now see that most of the empirical evidence in the random walk literature can easily be interpreted as tests of more general expected return or "fair game" models.[8]

2. Tests of Market Efficiency in the Random Walk Literature. As discussed

---

[7]The appropriate conditioning statement would be "Given the sequence of historical prices."

[8]Our brief historical review is meant only to provide perspective, and it is, of course, somewhat incomplete. For example, we have ignored the important contributions to the early random walk literature in studies of warrants and other options by Sprenkle, Kruizenga, Boness, and others. Much of this early work on options is summarized in [8].

earlier, "fair game" models imply the "impossibility" of various sorts of trading systems. Some of the random walk literature has been concerned with testing the profitability of such systems. More of the literature has, however, been concerned with tests of serial covariances of returns. We shall now show that, like a random walk, the serial covariances of a "fair game" are zero, so that these tests are also relevant for the expected return models.

If x_t is a "fair game," its unconditional expectation is zero and its serial covariance can be written in general form as:

$$E(\tilde{x}_{t+\tau}\tilde{x}_t) = \int_{x_t} x_t E(\tilde{x}_{t+\tau}|x_t)f(x_t)dx_t$$

where f indicates a density function. But if x_t is a "fair game,"

$$E(\tilde{x}_{t+\tau}|x_t) = 0^9$$

From this it follows that for all lags, the serial covariances between lagged values of a "fair game" variable are zero. Thus, observations of a "fair game" variable are linearly independent.[10]

---

[9]More generally, if the sequence $\{x_t\}$ is a fair game with respect to the information sequence $\{\Phi_t\}$, (i.e., $E(\tilde{x}_{t+1}|\Phi_t') = 0$ for all Φ_t); then x_t is a fair game with respect to any Φ_t' that is a subset of Φ_t (i.e., $E(\tilde{x}_{t+1}|\Phi_t') = 0$ for all Φ_t'). To show this, let $\Phi_t = (\Phi_t', \Phi_t'')$. Then, using Stieltjes integrals and the symbol F to denote cumulative distinction functions, the conditional expectation

$$E(\tilde{x}_{t+1}|\Phi_t' = \int_{\Phi_t''}\int_{x_{t+1}} x_{t+1}dF(x_{t+1}, \Phi_t''|\Phi_t')$$

$$= \int_{\Phi_t''}\left[\int_{x_{t+1}} x_{t+1}dF(x_{t+1}|\Phi_t', \Phi_t'')\right]dF(\Phi_t'|\Phi_t')$$

But the integral in brackets is just $E(\tilde{x}_{t+1}|\Phi_t)$ which by the "fair game" assumption is 0, so that

$$E(x_{t+1}|\Phi_t') = 0 \quad \text{for all } \Phi_t' \subset \Phi_t$$

[10]But though zero serial covariances are consistent with a "fair game," they do not imply such a process. A "fair game" also rules out many types of non-linear dependence. Thus using arguments similar to those above, it can be shown that if x is a "fair game," $E(\tilde{x}_t\tilde{x}_{t+1} \ldots \tilde{x}_{t+\tau}) = 0$ for all τ, which is not implied by $E(\tilde{x}_t\tilde{x}_{t+\tau}) = 0$ for all τ. For example, consider a three-period case where x must be either ± 1. Suppose the process is $x_{t+2} = \text{sign}(x_t x_{t+1})$, i.e.,

x_t	x_{t+1}	$\rightarrow$	x_{t+2}
+	+	$\rightarrow$	+
+	−	$\rightarrow$	−
−	+	$\rightarrow$	−
−	−	$\rightarrow$	+

But the "fair game" model does not necessarily imply that the serial co-variances of *one-period returns* are zero. In the weak form tests of this model the "fair game" variable is

$$z_{j,t} = r_{j,t} - E(\tilde{r}_{j,t} | r_{j,t-1}, r_{j,t-2}, \ldots) \quad \text{(Cf. fn. 9)} \quad (9)$$

But the covariance between, for example, r_{jt} and $r_{j,t+1}$ is

$$E([\tilde{r}_{j,t+1} - E(\tilde{r}_{j,t+1})] \; [\tilde{r}_{jt} - E(\tilde{r}_{jt})])$$

$$= \int_{r_{jt}} [r_{jt} - E(\tilde{r}_{jt})] \; [E(\tilde{r}_{j,t+1} | r_{jt}) - E(\tilde{r}_{j,t+1})] f(r_{jt}) dr_{jt}$$

and (9) does not imply that $E(\tilde{r}_{j,t+1} | r_{jt}) = E(\tilde{r}_{j,t+1})$: In the "fair game" efficient markets model, the deviation of the return for $t + 1$ from its conditional expectation is a "fair game" variable but the conditional expectation itself can depend on the return observed for t.[11]

In the random walk literature, this problem is not recognized, since it is assumed that the expected return (and indeed the entire distribution of returns) is stationary through time. In practice, this implies estimating serial covariances by taking cross products of deviations of observed returns from the overall sample mean return. It is somewhat fortuitous, then, that this procedure, which represents a rather gross approximation from the viewpoint of the general expected return efficient markets model, does not seem to greatly affect the results of the covariance tests, at least for common stocks.[12]

For example, Table 1 (taken from [10]) shows the serial correlations between successive changes in the natural log of price for each of the thirty

---

If probabilities are uniformly distributed across events,

$$E(\tilde{x}_{t+2} | x_{t+1}) = E(\tilde{x}_{t+2} | x_t) = E(\tilde{x}_{t+1} | x_t) = E(\tilde{x}_{t+2}) = E(\tilde{x}_{t+1}) = E(\tilde{x}_t) = 0$$

so that all pairwise serial covariances are zero. But the process is not a "fair game," since $E(\tilde{x}_{t+2} | x_{t+1}, x_t) \neq 0$, and knowledge of (x_{t+1}, x_t) can be used as the basis of a simple "system" with positive expected profit.

[11]For example, suppose the level of one-period returns follows a martingale so that

$$E(\tilde{r}_{j,t+1} | r_{jt}, r_{j,t-1} \ldots) = r_{jt}$$

Then covariances between successive returns will be nonzero (though in this special case first differences of returns will be uncorrelated).

[12]The reason is probably that for stocks, changes in equilibrium expected returns for the common differencing intervals of a day, a week, or a month, are trivial relative to other sources of variation in returns. Later, when we consider Roll's work [37], we shall see that this is not true for one week returns on U.S. Government Treasury Bills.

Table 1 (from [10])
First-order Serial Correlation Coefficients for One-, Four-, Nine-, and Sixteen-Day Changes in Log$_e$ Price

| Stock | Differencing Interval (Days) | | | |
	One	Four	Nine	Sixteen
Allied Chemical	.017	.029	−.091	−.118
Alcoa	.118*	.095	−.112	−.044
American Can	−.087*	−.124*	−.060	.031
A. T. & T.	−.039	−.010	−.009	−.003
American Tobacco	.111*	−.175*	.033	.007
Anaconda	.067*	−.068	−.125	.202
Bethlehem Steel	.013	−.122	−.148	.112
Chrysler	.012	.060	−.026	.040
Du Pont	.013	.069	−.043	−.055
Eastman Kodak	.025	−.006	−.053	−.023
General Electric	.011	.020	−.004	.000
General Foods	.061*	−.005	−.140	−.098
General Motors	−.004	−.128*	.009	−.028
Goodyear	−.123*	.001	−.037	.033
International Harvester	−.017	−.068	−.244*	.116
International Nickel	.096*	.038	.124	.041
International Paper	.046	.060	−.004	−.010
Johns Manville	.006	−.068	−.002	.002
Owens Illinois	−.021	−.006	.003	−.022
Procter & Gamble	.099*	−.006	.098	.076
Sears	.097*	−.070	−.113	.041
Standard Oil (Calif.)	.025	−.143*	−.046	.040
Standard Oil (N.J.)	.008	−.109	−.082	−.121
Swift & Co.	−.004	−.072	.118	−.197
Texaco	.094*	−.053	−.047	−.178
Union Carbide	.107*	.049	−.101	.124
United Aircraft	.014	−.190*	−.192*	−.040
U.S. Steel	.040	−.006	−.056	.236*
Westinghouse	−.027	−.097	−.137	.067
Woolworth	.028	−.033	−.112	.040

*Coefficient is twice its computed standard error.

stocks of the Dow Jones Industrial Average, for time periods that vary slightly from stock to stock, but usually run from about the end of 1957 to September 26, 1962. The serial correlations of successive changes in log$_e$ price are shown for differencing intervals of one, four, nine, and sixteen days.[13]

[13] The use of changes in log$_e$ price as the measure of return is common in the random walk literature. It can be justified in several ways. But for current purposes, it is sufficient to note that for price changes less than fifteen per cent, the change in log$_e$ price is approximately the percentage price change or one-period return. And for differencing intervals shorter than one month, returns in excess of fifteen per cent are unusual. Thus [10] reports that for the data of Table 1, tests carried out on percentage or one-period returns yielded results essentially identical to the tests based on changes in log$_e$ price.

The results in Table 1 are typical of those reported by others for tests based on serial covariances. (Cf. Kendall [21] , Moore [31] , Alexander [1] , and the results of Granger and Morgenstern [17] and Godfrey, Granger and Morgenstern [16] obtained by means of spectral analysis.) Specifically, there is no evidence of substantial linear dependence between lagged price changes or returns. In absolute terms the measured serial correlations are always close to zero.

Looking hard, though, one can probably find evidence of statistically "significant" linear dependence in Table 1 (and again this is true of results reported by others). For the daily returns eleven of the serial correlations are more than twice their computed standard errors, and twenty-two out of thirty are positive. On the other hand, twenty-one and twenty-four of the coefficients for the four and nine day differences are negative. But with samples of the size underlying Table 1 ($N = 1200$–1700 observations per stock on a daily basis) statistically "significant" deviations from zero covariance are not necessarily a basis for rejecting the efficient markets model. For the results in Table 1, the standard errors of the serial correlations were approximated as $(1/(N - 1))^{\frac{1}{2}}$, which for the daily data implies that a correlation as small as .06 is more than twice its standard error. But a coefficient this size implies that a linear relationship with the lagged price change can be used to explain about .36% of the variation in the current price change, which is probably insignificant from an economic viewpoint. In particular, it is unlikely that the small absolute levels of serial correlation that are always observed can be used as the basis of substantially profitable trading systems.[14]

It is, of course, difficult to judge what degree of serial correlation would imply the existence of trading rules with substantial expected profits. (And indeed we shall soon have to be a little more precise about what is implied by "substantial" profits.) Moreover, zero serial covariances are consistent with a "fair game" model, but as noted earlier (fn. 10), there are types of nonlinear dependence that imply the existence of profitable trading systems, and yet do not imply nonzero serial covariances. Thus, for many reasons it is desirable to directly test the profitability of various trading rules.

The first major evidence on trading rules was Alexander's [1, 2]. He tests a variety of systems, but the most thoroughly examined can be described as

---

[14]Given the evidence of Kendall [21] , Mandelbrot [28] , Fama [10] and others that large price changes occur much more frequently than would be expected if the generating process were Gaussian, the expression $(1/N - 1))^{\frac{1}{2}}$ understates the sampling dispersion of the serial correlation coefficient, and thus leads to an overstatement of significance levels. In addition, the fact that sample serial correlations are predominantly of one sign or the other is not in itself evidence of linear dependence. If, as the work of King [23] and Blume [7] indicates, there is a market factor whose behavior affects the returns on all securities, the sample behavior of this market factor may lead to a predominance of signs of one type in the serial correlations for individual securities, even though the population serial correlations for both the market factor and the returns on individual securities are zero. For a more extensive analysis of these issues see [10] .

follows: If the price of a security moves up at least $y\%$, buy and hold the security until its price moves down at least $y\%$ from a subsequent high, at which time simultaneously sell and go short. The short position is maintained until the price rises at least $y\%$ above a subsequent low, at which time one covers the short position and buys. Moves less than $y\%$ in either direction are ignored. Such a system is called a $y\%$ filter. It is obviously a "one security and cash" trading rule, so that the results it produces are relevant for the submartingale expected return model of (6).

After extensive tests using daily data on price indices from 1897 to 1959 and filters from one to fifty per cent, and after correcting some incorrect presumptions in the initial results of [1] (see fn. 25), in his final paper on the subject, Alexander concludes:

In fact, at this point I should advise any reader who is interested only in practical results, and who is not a floor trader and so must pay commissions, to turn to other sources on how to beat buy and hold. The rest of this article is devoted principally to a theoretical consideration of whether the observed results are consistent with a random walk hypothesis [8], p. 351).

Later in the paper Alexander concludes that there is some evidence in his results against the independence assumption of the random walk model. But market efficiency does not require a random walk, and from the viewpoint of the sub-martingale model of (6), the conclusion that the filters cannot beat buy-and-hold is support for the efficient markets hypothesis. Further support is provided by Fama and Blume [13] who compare the profitability of various filters to buy-and-hold for the individual stocks of the Dow-Jones Industrial Average. (The data are those underlying Table 1.)

But again, looking hard one can find evidence in the filter tests of both Alexander and Fama-Blume that is inconsistent with the submartingale efficient markets model, if that model is interpreted in a strict sense. In particular, the results for very small filters (1 per cent in Alexander's tests and .5, 1.0, and 1.5 per cent in the tests of Fama-Blume) indicate that it is possible to devise trading schemes based on very short-term (preferably intra-day but at most daily) price swings that will on average outperform buy-and-hold. The average profits on individual transactions from such schemes are miniscule, but they generate transactions so frequently that over longer periods and ignoring commissions they outperform buy-and-hold by a substantial margin. These results are evidence of persistence or positive dependence in very short-term price movements. And, interestingly, this is consistent with the evidence for slight positive linear dependence in successive daily price changes produced by the serial correlations.[15]

_____

[15]Though strictly speaking, such tests of pure independence are not directly relevant for expected return models, it is interesting that the conclusion that very short-term swings in prices persist slightly longer than would be expected under the martingale hypothesis is also supported by the results of non-parametric runs tests applied to the daily data of Table 1.

But when one takes account of even the minimum trading costs that would be generated by small filters, their advantage over buy-and-hold disappears. For example, even a floor trader (i.e., a person who owns a seat) on the New York Stock Exchange must pay clearinghouse fees on his trades that amount to about .1 per cent per turnaround transaction (i.e., sales plus purchase). Fama-Blume show that because small filters produce such frequent trades, these minimum trading costs are sufficient to wipe out their advantage over buy-and-hold.

Thus the filter tests, like the serial correlations, produce empirically noticeable departures from the strict implications of the efficient markets model. But, in spite of any statistical significance they might have, from an economic viewpoint the departures are so small that it seems hardly justified to use them to declare the market inefficient.

3. Other Tests of Independence in the Random Walk Literature. It is probably best to regard the random walk model as a special case of the more general expected return model in the sense of making a more detailed specification of the economic environment. That is, the basic model of market equilibrium is the "fair game" expected return model, with a random walk arising when additional environmental conditions are such that distributions of one-period returns repeat themselves through time. From this viewpoint violations of the pure independence assumption of the random walk model are to be expected. But when judged relative to the benchmark provided by the random walk model, these violations can provide insights into the nature of the market environment.

For example, one departure from the pure independence assumption of the random walk model has been noted by Osborne [34], Fama ([10], Table 17 and Figure 8), and others. In particular, large daily price changes tend to be

---

(See [10], Tables 12–15.) For the daily price changes, the actual number of runs of price changes of the same sign is less than the expected number for 26 out of 30 stocks. Moreover, of the eight stocks for which the actual number of runs is more than two standard errors less than the expected number, five of the same stocks have positive daily, first order serial correlations in Table 1 that are more than twice their standard errors. But in both cases the statistical "significance" of the results is largely a reflection of the large sample sizes. Just as the serial correlations are small in absolute terms (the average is .026), the differences between the expected and actual number of runs on average are only three per cent of the total expected number.

On the other hand, it is also interesting that the runs tests do not support the suggestion of slight negative dependence in four and nine day changes that appeared in the serial correlations. In the runs tests such negative dependence would appear as a tendency for the actual number of runs to exceed the expected number. In fact, for the four and nine day price changes, for 17 and 18 of the 30 stocks in Table 1 the actual number of runs is less than the expected number. Indeed, runs tests in general show no consistent evidence of dependence for any differencing interval longer than a day, which seems especially pertinent in light of the comments in footnote 14.

followed by large daily changes. The signs of the successor changes are apparently
random, however, which indicates that the phenomenon represents a denial of
the random walk model but not of the market efficiency hypothesis. Nevertheless, it is interesting to speculate why the phenomenon might arise. It may be
that when important new information comes into the market it cannot always
be immediately evaluated precisely. Thus, sometimes the initial price will over-
adjust to the information, and other times it will underadjust. But since the
evidence indicates that the price changes on days following the initial large
change are random in sign, the initial large change at least represents an unbiased
adjustment to the ultimate price effects of the information, and this is sufficient
for the expected return efficient markets model.

Niederhoffer and Osborne [32] document two departures from complete
randomness in common stock price changes from transaction to transaction.
First, their data indicate that reversals (pairs of consecutive price changes of
opposite sign) are from two to three times as likely as continuations (pairs of
consecutive price changes of the same sign). Second, a continuation is slightly
more frequent after a preceding continuation than after a reversal. That is, let
$(+|++)$ indicate the occurrence of a positive price change, given two preceding
positive changes. Then the events $(+|++)$ and $(-|--)$ are slightly more frequent
than $(+|+-)$ or $(-|-+)$[16]

Niederhoffer and Osborne offer explanations for these phenomena based
on the market structure of the New York Stock Exchange (N.Y.S.E.). In
particular, there are three major types of orders that an investor might place in
a given stock: (a) buy limit (buy at a specified price or lower), (b) sell limit
(sell at a specified price or higher), and (c) buy or sell at market (at the lowest
selling or highest buying price of another investor). A book of unexecuted limit
orders in a given stock is kept by the specialist in that stock on the floor of the
exchange. Unexecuted sell limit orders are, of course, at higher prices than
unexecuted buy limit orders. On both exchanges, the smallest non-zero price
change allowed is 1/8 point.

Suppose now that there is more than one unexecuted sell limit order at the
lowest price of any such order. A transaction at this price (initiated by an order
to buy at market[17]) can only be followed either by a transaction at the same
price (if the next market order is to buy) or by a transaction at a lower price
(if the next market order is to sell). Consecutive price increases can usually only
occur when consecutive market orders to buy exhaust the sell limit orders at a

---

[16]On a transaction to transaction basis, positive and negative price changes are about
equally likely. Thus, under the assumption that price changes are random, any pair of non-
zero changes should be as likely as any other, and likewise for triplets of consecutive non-
zero changes.

[17]A buy limit order for a price equal to or greater than the lowest available sell limit price
is effectively an order to buy at market, and is treated as such by the broker.

given price.[18] In short, the excessive tendency toward reversal for consecutive non-zero price changes could result from bunching of unexecuted buy and sell limit orders.

The tendency for the events (+|++) and (−|− −) to occur slightly more frequently than (+|+ −) and (−|− +) requires a more involved explanation which we shall not attempt to reproduce in full here. In brief, Niederhoffer and Osborne contend that the higher frequency of (+|+ +) relative to (+|+ −) arises from a tendency for limit orders "to be concentrated at integers (26, 43), halves (26½, 43½), quarters and odd eighths in descending order of preference."[19] The frequency of the event (+|++), which usually requires that sell limit orders be exhausted at at least two consecutively higher prices (the last of which is relatively more frequently at an odd eighth), more heavily reflects the absence of sell limit orders at odd eighths than the event (+|+ −), which implies that sell limit orders at only one price have been exhausted and so more or less reflects the average bunching of limit orders at all eighths.

But though Niederhoffer and Osborne present convincing evidence of statistically significant departures from independence in price changes from transaction to transaction, and though their analysis of their findings presents interesting insights into the process of market making on the major exchanges, the types of dependence uncovered do not imply market inefficiency. The best documented source of dependence, the tendency toward excessive reversals in pairs of non-zero price changes, seems to be a direct result of the ability of investors to place limit orders as well as orders at market, and this negative dependence in itself does not imply the existence of profitable trading rules. Similarly, the apparent tendency for observed transactions (and, by implication, limit orders) to be concentrated at integers, halves, even eighths and odd eighths in descending order is an interesting fact about investor behavior, but in itself is not a basis on which to conclude that the market is inefficient.[20]

---

[18]The exception is when there is a gap of more than 1/8 between the highest unexecuted buy limit and the lowest unexecuted sell limit order, so that market orders (and new limit orders) can be crossed at intermediate prices.

[19]Their empirical documentation for this claim is a few samples of specialists' books for selected days, plus the observation [34] that actual trading prices, at least for volatile high priced stocks, seem to be concentrated at integers, halves, quarters and odd eighths in descending order.

[20]Niederhoffer and Osborne offer little to refute this conclusion. For example ([32], p. 914):

Although the specific properties reported in this study have a significance from a statistical point of view, the reader may well ask whether or not they are helpful in a practical sense. Certain trading rules emerge as a result of our analysis. One is that limit and stop orders should be placed at odd eights, preferably at 7/8 for sell orders and at 1/8 for buy orders. Another is to buy when a stock advances through a barrier and to sell when it sinks through a barrier.

The Niederhoffer-Osborne analysis of market making does, however, point clearly to the existence of market inefficiency, but with respect to strong form tests of the efficient markets model. In particular, the list of unexecuted buy and sell limit orders in the specialist's book is important information about the likely future behavior of prices, and this information is only available to the specialist. When the specialist is asked for a quote, he gives the prices and can give the quantities of the highest buy limit and lowest sell limit orders on his book, but he is prevented by law from divulging the book's full contents. The interested reader can easily imagine situations where the structure of limit orders in the book could be used as the basis of a profitable trading rule.[21] But the record seems to speak for itself:

It should not be assumed that these transactions undertaken by the specialist, and in which he is involved as buyer or seller in 24 per cent of all market volume, are necessarily a burden to him. Typically, the specialist sells above his last purchase on 83 per cent of all his sales, and buys below his last sale on 81 per cent of all his purchases ([32], p. 908).

Thus it seems that the specialist has monopoly power over an important block of information, and, not unexpectedly, uses his monopoly to turn a profit. And this, of course, is evidence of market inefficiency in the strong form sense. The important economic question, of course, is whether the market making function of the specialist could be fulfilled more economically by some non-monopolistic mechanism.[22]

4. Distributional Evidence. At this date the weight of the empirical evidence is such that economists would generally agree that whatever dependence exists in series of historical returns cannot be used to make profitable predictions of the future. Indeed, for returns that cover periods of a day or longer, there is little in

---

The first "trading rule" tells the investor to resist his innate inclination to place orders at integers, but rather to place sell orders 1/8 below an integer and buy orders 1/8 above. Successful execution of the orders is then more likely, since the congestion of orders that occur at integers is avoided. But the cost of this success is apparent. The second "trading rule" seems no more promising, if indeed it can even be translated into a concrete prescription for action.

[21] See, for example, ([32], p. 908). But it is unlikely that anyone but the specialist could earn substantial profits from knowledge of the structure of unexpected limit orders on the book. The specialist makes trading profits by engaging in many transactions, each of which has a small average profit; but for any other trader, including those with seats on the exchange, these profits would be eaten up by commissions to the specialist.

[22] With modern computers, it is hard to believe that a more competitive and economical system would not be feasible. It does not seem technologically impossible to replace the entire floor of the N.Y.S.E. with a computer, fed by many remote consoles, that kept all the books now kept by the specialists, that could easily make the entire book on any stock available to anybody (so that interested individuals could then compete to "make a market" in a stock) and that carried out transactions automatically.

the evidence that would cause rejection of the stronger random walk model, at least as a good first approximation.

Rather, the last burning issue of the random walk literature has centered on the nature of the distribution of price changes (which, we should note immediately, is an important issue for the efficient markets hypothesis since the nature of the distribution affects both the types of statistical tools relevant for testing the hypothesis and the interpretation of any results obtained). A model implying normally distributed price changes was first proposed by Bachelier [3], who assumed that price changes from transaction to transaction are independent, identically distributed random variables with finite variances. If transactions are fairly uniformly spread across time, and if the number of transactions per day, week, or month is very large, then the Central Limit Theorem leads us to expect that these price changes will have normal or Gaussian distributions.

Osborne [33], Moore [31], and Kendall [21] all thought their empirical evidence supported the normality hypothesis, but all observed high tails (i.e., higher proportions of large observations) in their data distributions vis-à-vis what would be expected if the distributions were normal. Drawing on these findings and some empirical work of his own, Mandelbrot [28] then suggested that these departures from normality could be explained by a more general form of the Bachelier model. In particular, if one does not assume that distributions of price changes from transaction to transaction necessarily have finite variances, then the limiting distributions for price changes over longer differencing intervals could be any member of the stable class, which includes the normal as a special case. Non-normal stable distributions have higher tails than the normal, and so can account for this empirically observed feature of distributions of price changes. After extensive testing (involving the data from the stocks in Table 1), Fama [10] concludes that non-normal stable distributions are a better description of distributions of daily returns on common stocks than the normal. This conclusion is also supported by the empirical work of Blume [7] on common stocks, and it has been extended to U.S. Government Treasury Bills by Roll [37].

Economists have, however, been reluctant to accept these results,[23] primarily because of the wealth of statistical techniques available for dealing with normal variables and the relative paucity of such techniques for non-normal stable variables. But perhaps the biggest contribution of Mandelbrot's work has been to stimulate research on stable distributions and estimation procedures to

---

[23]Some have suggested that the long-tailed empirical distributions might result from processes that are mixtures of normal distributions with different variances. Press [35], for example, suggests a Poisson mixture of normals in which the resulting distributions of price changes have long tails but finite variances. On the other hand, Mandelbrot and Taylor [29] show that other mixtures of normals can still lead to non-normal stable distributions of price changes for finite differencing intervals.

If, as Press' model would imply, distributions of price changes are long-tailed but have finite variances, then distributions of price changes over longer and longer differencing intervals should be progressively closer to the normal. No such convergence to normality

be applied to stable variables. (See, for example, Wise [46], Fama and Roll [15], and Blattberg and Sargent [6], among others.) The advance of statistical sophistication (and the importance of examining distributional assumptions in testing the efficient markets model) is well illustrated in Roll [37], as compared, for example, with the early empirical work of Mandelbrot [28] and Fama [10].

5. "Fair Game" Models in the Treasury Bill Market.

Roll's work is novel in other respects as well. Coming after the efficient markets models of Mandelbrot [27] and Samuelson [38], it is the first weak form empirical work that is consciously in the "fair game" rather than the random walk tradition.

More important, as we saw earlier, the "fair game" properties of the general expected return models apply to

$$z_{jt} = r_{jt} - E(\tilde{r}_{jt}|\Phi_{t-1})$$ (10)

For data on common stocks, tests of "fair game" (and random walk) properties seem to go well when the conditional expected return is estimated as the average return for the sample of data at hand. Apparently the variation in common stock returns about their expected values is so large relative to any changes in the expected values that the latter can safely be ignored. But, as Roll demonstrates, this result does not hold for Treasury Bills. Thus, to test the "fair game" model on Treasury Bills requires explicit economic theory for the evolution of expected returns through time.

Roll uses three existing theories of the term structure (the pure expectations hypothesis of Lutz [26] and two market segmentation hypotheses, one of which is the familiar "liquidity preference" hypothesis of Hicks [18] and Kessel [22]) for this purpose.[24] In his models r_{jt} is the rate observed from the term structure at period t for one week loans to commence at $t + j - 1$, and can be thought of as a "futures" rate. Thus $r_{j+1, t-1}$ is likewise the rate on one week loans to commence at $t + j - 1$, but observed in this case at $t - 1$. Similarly, L_{jt} is the so-called "liquidity premium" in r_{jt}; that is

$$r_{jt} = E(\tilde{r}_{o, t+j-1}|\Phi_t) + L_{jt}$$

In words, the one-week "futures" rate for period $t + j - 1$ observed from the

---

was observed in [10] (though admittedly the techniques used were somewhat rough). Rather, except for origin and scale, the distributions for longer differencing intervals seem to have the same "high-tailed" characteristics as distributions for shorter differencing intervals, which is as would be expected if the distributions are non-normal stable.

[24] As noted early in our discussions, all available tests of market efficiency are implicitly also tests of expected return models of market equilibrium. But Roll formulates explicitly the economic models underlying his estimates of expected returns, and emphasizes that he is simultaneously testing economic models of the term structure as well as market efficiency.

term structure at t is the expectation at t of the "spot" rate for $t + j - 1$ plus a "liquidity premium" (which could, however, be positive or negative.)

In all three theories of the term structure considered by Roll, the conditional expectation required in (10) is of the form

$$E(\tilde{r}_{j,\,t}|\Phi_{t-1}) = r_{j+1,\,t-1} + E(\tilde{L}_{jt}|\Phi_{t-1}) - L_{j+1,\,t-1}$$

The three theories differ only in the values assigned to the "liquidity premiums." For example, in the "liquidity preference" hypothesis, investors must always be paid a positive premium for bearing interest rate uncertainty, so that the L_{jt} are always positive. By contrast, in the "pure expectations" hypothesis, all liquidity premiums are assumed to be zero, so that

$$E(\tilde{r}_{jt}|\Phi_{t-1}) = r_{j+1,\,t-1}$$

After extensive testing, Roll concludes (i) that the two market segmentation hypotheses fit the data better than the pure expectations hypothesis, with perhaps a slight advantage for the "liquidity preference" hypothesis, and (ii) that as far as his tests are concerned, the market for Treasury Bills is efficient. Indeed, it is interesting that when the best fitting term structure model is used to estimate the conditional expected "futures" rate in (10), the resulting variable z_{jt} seems to be serially independent! It is also interesting that if he simply assumed that his data distributions were normal, Roll's results would not be so strongly in support of the efficient markets model. In this case taking account of the observed high tails of the data distributions substantially affected the interpretation of the results.[25]

6. Tests of a Multiple Security Expected Return Model. Though the weak form tests support the "fair game" efficient markets model, all of the evidence examined so far consists of what we might call "single security tests." That is, the price or return histories of individual securities are examined for evidence of dependence that might be used as the basis of a trading system for *that* security. We have not discussed tests of whether securities are "appropriately priced" vis-à-vis one another.

---

[25]The importance of distributional assumptions is also illustrated in Alexander's work on trading rules. In his initial tests of filter systems [1], Alexander assumed that purchases could always be executed exactly (rather than at least) $y\%$ above lows and sales exactly $y\%$ below highs. Mandelbrot [28] pointed out, however, that though this assumption would do little harm with normally distributed price changes (since price series are then essentially continuous), with non-normal stable distributions it would introduce substantial positive bias into the filter profits (since with such distributions price series will show many discontinuities). In his later tests [2], Alexander does indeed find that taking account of the discontinuities (i.e., the presence of large price changes) in his data substantially lowers the profitability of the filters.

But to judge whether differences between average returns are "appropriate" an economic theory of equilibrium expected returns is required. At the moment, the only fully developed theory is that of Sharpe [40] and Lintner [24, 25] referred to earlier. In this model (which is a direct outgrowth of the mean-standard deviation portfolio models of investor equilibrium of Markowitz [30] and Tobin [43]), the expected return on security j from time t to $t + 1$ is

$$E(\tilde{r}_{j, t+1}|\Phi_t) = r_{f, t+1} + \left[\frac{E(\tilde{r}_{m, t+1}|\Phi_t) - r_{f, t+1}}{\sigma(\tilde{r}_{m, t+1}|\Phi_t)} \right] \frac{\text{cov}(\tilde{r}_{j, t+1}, \tilde{r}_{m, t+1}|\Phi_t)}{\sigma(\tilde{r}_{m, t+1}|\Phi_t)} \quad (11)$$

where $r_{f, t+1}$ is the return from t to $t + 1$ on an asset that is riskless in money terms; $r_{m, t+1}$ is the return on the "market portfolio" m (a portfolio of all investment assets with each weighted in proportion to the total market value of all its outstanding units); $\sigma^2(\tilde{r}_{m, t+1}|\Phi_t)$ is the variance of the return on m; cov $(\tilde{r}_{j, t+1}, \tilde{r}_{m, t+1}|\Phi_t)$ is the covariance between the returns on j and m; and the appearance of Φ_t indicates that the various expected returns, variance and covariance, could in principle depend on Φ_t. Though Sharpe and Lintner derive (11) as a one-period model, the result is given a multiperiod justification and interpretation in [11]. The model has also been extended in (12) to the case where the one-period returns could have stable distributions with infinite variances.

In words, (11) says that the expected one-period return on a security is the one-period riskless rate of interest $r_{f, t+1}$ plus a "risk premium" that is proportional to cov$(\tilde{r}_{j, t+1}, \tilde{r}_{m, t+1}|\Phi_t)/\sigma(\tilde{r}_{m, t+1}|\Phi_t)$. In the Sharpe-Lintner model each investor holds some combination of the riskless asset and the market portfolio, so that, given a mean-standard deviation framework, the risk of an individual asset can be measured by its contribution to the standard deviation of the return on the market portfolio. This combination is in fact cov$(\tilde{r}_{j, t+1}, \tilde{r}_{m, t+1}|\Phi_t)/\sigma(\tilde{r}_{m, t+1}|\Phi_t)$.[26] The factor

$$[E(\tilde{r}_{m, t+1}|\Phi_t) - r_{f, t+1}]/\sigma(\tilde{r}_{m, t+1}|\Phi_t)$$

which is the same for all securities, is then regarded as the market price of risk.

Published empirical tests of the Sharpe-Lintner model are not yet available, though much work is in progress. There is some published work, however, which, though not directed at the Sharpe-Lintner model, is at least consistent with some of its implications. The stated goal of this work has been to determine the extent to which the returns on a given security are related to the returns on

---

[26]That is,

$$\sum_j \text{cov}(\tilde{r}_{j, t+1}, \tilde{r}_{m, t+1}|\Phi_t)/\sigma(\tilde{r}_{m, t+1}|\Phi_t) = \sigma(\tilde{r}_{m, t+1}|\Phi_t)$$

other securities. It started (again) with Kendall's [21] finding that though common stock price changes do not seem to be serially correlated, there is a high degree of cross-correlation between the *simultaneous* returns of different securities. This line of attack was continued by King [23] who (using factor analysis of a sample of monthly returns on sixty N.Y.S.E. stocks for the period 1926–60) found that on average about 50% of the variance of an individual stock's returns could be accounted for by a "market factor" which affects the returns on all stocks, with "industry factors" accounting for at most an additional 10% of the variance.

For our purposes, however, the work of Fama, Fisher, Jensen, and Roll [14] (henceforth FFJR) and the more extensive work of Blume [7] on monthly return data is more relevant. They test the following "market model," originally suggested by Markowitz [30] :

$$\tilde{r}_{j,\,t+1} = \alpha_j + \beta_j\,\tilde{r}_{M,\,t+1} + \tilde{u}_{j,\,t+1} \tag{12}$$

where $r_{j,\,t+1}$ is the rate of return on security j for month t, $r_{M,\,t+1}$ is the corresponding return on a market index M, α_j and β_j are parameters that can vary from security to security, and $u_{j,\,t+1}$ is a random disturbance. The tests of FFJR and subsequently those of Blume indicate that (12) is well specified as a linear regression model in that (i) the estimated parameters $\hat{\tilde{\alpha}}_j$ and $\hat{\tilde{\beta}}_j$ remain fairly constant over long periods of time (e.g., the entire post-World War II period in the case of Blume), (ii) $r_{M,\,t+1}$ and the estimated $\hat{u}_{j,\,t+1}$, are close to serially independent, and (iii) the $\hat{u}_{j,\,t+1}$ seem to be independent of $r_{M,\,t+1}$.

Thus the observed properties of the "market model" are consistent with the expected return efficient markets model, and, in addition, the "market model" tells us something about the process generating expected returns from security to security. In particular,

$$E(\tilde{r}_{j,\,t+1}) = \alpha_j + \beta_j E(\tilde{r}_{M,\,t+1}) \tag{13}$$

The question now is to what extent (13) is consistent with the Sharpe-Lintner expected return model summarized by (11). Rearranging (11) we obtain

$$E(\tilde{r}_{j,\,t+1}|\Phi_t) = \alpha_j(\Phi_t) + \beta_j(\Phi_t)E(\tilde{r}_{m,\,t+1}|\Phi_t) \tag{14}$$

where, noting that the riskless rate $r_{f,\,t+1}$ is itself part of the information set Φ_t, we have

$$\alpha_j(\Phi_t) = r_{f,\,t+1}\,[1 - \beta_j(\Phi_t)] \tag{15}$$

and

$$\beta_j(\Phi_t) = \frac{\mathrm{cov}(\tilde{r}_{j,\,t+1}, \tilde{r}_{m,\,t+1}|\Phi_t)}{\sigma^2(\tilde{r}_{m,\,t+1}|\Phi_t)} \tag{16}$$

With some simplifying assumptions, (14) can be reduced to (13). In particular, if the covariance and variance that determine $\beta_j(\Phi_t)$ in (16) are the same for all t and Φ_t, then $\beta_j(\Phi_t)$ in (16) corresponds to β_j in (12) and (13), and the least squares *estimate* of β_j in (12) is in fact just the ratio of the sample values of the covariance and variance in (16). If we also assume that $r_{f,\,t+1}$ is the same for all t, and that the behavior of the returns on the market portfolio m are closely approximated by the returns on some representative index M, we will have come a long way toward equating (13) and (11). Indeed, the only missing link is whether in the estimated parameters of (12)

$$\hat{\alpha}_j \cong r_f(1 - \hat{\hat{\beta}}_j) \tag{17}$$

Neither FFJR nor Blume attack this question directly, though some of Blume's evidence is at least promising. In particular, the magnitudes of the estimated $\hat{\hat{\alpha}}_j$ are roughly consistent with (17) in the sense that the estimates are always close to zero (as they should be with monthly return data).[27]

In a sense, though, in establishing the apparent empirical validity of the "market model" of (12), both too much and too little have been shown *vis-à-vis* the Sharpe-Lintner expected return model of (11). We know that during the post-World War II period one-month interest rates on riskless assets (e.g., government bills with one month to maturity) have not been constant. Thus, if expected security returns were generated by a version of the "market model" that is fully consistent with the Sharpe-Lintner model, we would, according to (15), expect to observe some non-stationarity in the estimates of α_j. On a monthly basis, however, variation through time in one-period riskless interest rates is probably trivial relative to variation in other factors affecting monthly common stock returns, so that more powerful statistical methods would be necessary to study the effects of changes in the riskless rate.

In any case, since the work of FFJR and Blume on the "market model" was not concerned with relating this model to the Sharpe-Lintner model, we can only say that the results for the former are somewhat consistent with the implications of the latter. But the results for the "market model" are, after all, just a statistical description of the return generating process, and they are

---

[27]With least squares applied to monthly return data, the estimate of α_j in (12) is

$$\hat{\alpha}_j = \bar{r}_{j,\,t} - \hat{\beta}_j \bar{r}_{M,\,t}$$

where the bars indicate sample mean returns. But, in fact, Blume applies the market model to the wealth relatives $R_{jt} = 1 + r_{jt}$ and $R_{Mt} = 1 + r_{Mt}$. This yields precisely the same estimate of β_j as least squares applied to (12), but the intercept is now

$$\hat{\alpha}'_j = \bar{R}_{jt} - \hat{\beta}_j \bar{R}_{Mt} = 1 + \bar{r}_{jt} - \hat{\beta}_j(1 + \bar{r}_{Mt}) = 1 - \hat{\beta}_j + \hat{\alpha}_j$$

Thus what Blume in fact finds is that for almost all securities, $\hat{\alpha}'_j + \hat{\beta}_j \cong 1$, which implies that $\hat{\alpha}_j$ is close to 0.

probably somewhat consistent with other models of equilibrium expected returns. Thus the only way to generate strong empirical conclusions about the Sharpe-Lintner model is to test it directly. On the other hand, any alternative model of equilibrium expected returns must be somewhat consistent with the "market model," given the evidence in its support.

B. *Tests of Martingale Models of the Semi-strong Form*

In general, semi-strong form tests of efficient markets models are concerned with whether current prices "fully reflect" all obviously publicly available information. Each individual test, however, is concerned with the adjustment of security prices to one kind of information generating event (e.g., stock splits, announcements of financial reports by firms, new security issues, etc.). Thus each test only brings supporting evidence for the model, with the idea that by accumulating such evidence the validity of the model will be "established."

In fact, however, though the available evidence is in support of the efficient markets model, it is limited to a few major types of information generating events. The initial major work is apparently the study of stock splits by Fama, Fisher, Jensen, and Roll (FFJR) [14], and all the subsequent studies summarized here are adaptations and extensions of the techniques developed in FFJR. Thus, this paper will first be reviewed in some detail, and then the other studies will be considered.

1. Splits and the Adjustment of Stock Prices to New Information. Since the only apparent result of a stock split is to multiply the number of shares per shareholder without increasing claims to real assets, splits in themselves are not necessarily sources of new information. The presumption of FFJR is that splits may often be associated with the appearance of more fundamentally important information. The idea is to examine security returns around split dates to see first if there is any "unusual" behavior, and, if so, to what extent it can be accounted for by relationships between splits and other more fundamental variables.

The approach of FFJR to the problem relies heavily on the "market model" of (12). In this model if a stock split is associated with abnormal behavior, this would be reflected in the estimated regression residuals for the months surrounding the split. For a given split, define month 0 as the month in which the effective date of a split occurs, month 1 as the month immediately following the split month, month −1 as the month preceding, etc. Now define the average residual over all split securities for month m (where for each security m is measured relative to the split month) as

$$u_m = \sum_{j=1}^{N} \frac{\hat{u}_{jm}}{N}$$

where $\hat{u}_{jm}$ is the sample regression residual for security j in month m and N is the number of splits. Next, define the cumulative average residual U_m as

$$U_m = \sum_{k=-29}^{m} u_k$$

The average residual u_m can be interpreted as the average deviation (in month m relative to split months) of the returns of split stocks from their normal relationships with the market. Similarly, U_m can be interpreted as the cumulative deviation (from month -29 to month m). Finally, define u_m^+, u_m^-, U_m^+, and U_m^- as the average and cumulative average residuals for splits followed by "increased" (+) and "decreased" (-) dividends. An "increase" is a case where the percentage change in dividends on the split share in the year after the split is greater than the percentage change for the N.Y.S.E. as a whole, while a "decrease" is a case of relative dividend decline.

The essence of the results of FFJR are then summarized in Figure 1, which shows the cumulative average residuals U_m U_m^+, and U_m^- for $-29 \leqslant m \leqslant 30$. The sample includes all 940 stock splits on the N.Y.S.E. from 1927–59, where the exchange was at least five new shares for four old, and where the security was listed for at least twelve months before and after the split.

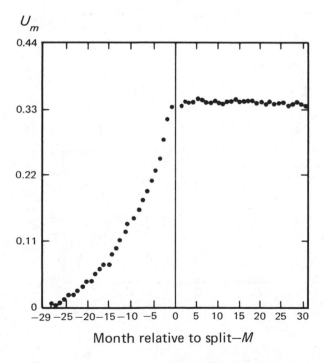

Figure 1a. Cumulative average residuals—all splits.

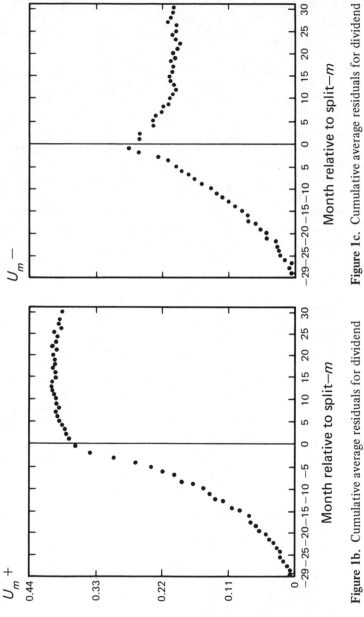

Figure 1c. Cumulative average residuals for dividend "decreases."

Figure 1b. Cumulative average residuals for dividend "increases."

For all three dividend categories the cumulative average residuals rise in the 29 months prior to the split, and in fact the average residuals (not shown here) are uniformly positive. This cannot be attributed to the splitting process, since in only about ten per cent of the cases is the time between the announcement and effective dates of a split greater than four months. Rather, it seems that firms tend to split their shares during "abnormally" good times—that is, during periods when the prices of their shares have increased more than would be implied by their normal relationships with general market prices, which itself probably reflects a sharp improvement, relative to the market, in the earnings prospects of these firms sometime during the years immediately preceding a split.[28]

After the split month there is almost no further movement in U_m, the cumulative average residual for all splits. This is striking, since 71.5 per cent (672 out of 940) of all splits experienced greater percentage dividend increases in the year after the split than the average for all securities on the N.Y.S.E. In light of this, FFJR suggest that when a split is announced the market interprets this (and correctly so) as a signal that the company's directors are probably confident that future earnings will be sufficient to maintain dividend payments at a higher level. Thus the large price increases in the months immediately preceding a split may be due to an alteration in expectations concerning the future earning potential of the firm, rather than to any intrinsic effects of the split itself.

If this hypothesis is correct, return behavior subsequent to splits should be substantially different for the cases where the dividend increase materializes than for the cases where it does not. FFJR argue that in fact the differences are in the directions that would be predicted. The fact that the cumulative average residuals for the "increased" dividends (Figure 1b) drift upward but only slightly in the year *after* the split is consistent with the hypothesis that when the split is *declared*, there is a price adjustment in anticipation of future dividend increases. But the behavior of the residuals for stock splits associated with "decreased" dividends offers even stronger evidence for the split hypothesis. The cumulative average residuals for these stocks (Figure 1c) rise in the few months before the split, but then fall dramatically in the few months after the split when the anticipated dividend increase is not forthcoming. When a year has passed after the split, the cumulative average residual has fallen to about

---

[28]It is important to note, however, that as FFJR indicate, the persistent upward drift of the cumulative average residuals in the months preceding the split is not a phenomenon that could be used to increase expected trading profits. The reason is that the behavior of the average residuals is not representative of the behavior of the residuals for individual securities. In months prior to the split, successive sample residuals for individual securities seem to be independent. But in most cases, there are a few months in which the residuals are abnormally large and positive. The months of large residuals differ from security to security, however, and these differences in timing explain why the signs of the average residuals are uniformly positive for many months preceding the split.

where it was five months prior to the split, which is about the earliest time reliable information about a split is likely to reach the market. Thus by the time it becomes clear that the anticipated dividend increase is not forthcoming, the apparent effects of the split seem to have been wiped away, and the stock's returns have reverted to their normal relationship with market returns.

Finally, and most important, although the behavior of post-split returns will be very different depending on whether or not dividend "increases" occur, and in spite of the fact that a large majority of split securities do experience dividend "increases," when all splits are examined together (Figure 1a), subsequent to the split there is no net movement up or down in the cumulative average residuals. Thus, apparently the market makes unbiased forecasts of the implications of a split for future dividends, and these forecasts are fully reflected in the prices of the security by the end of the split month. After considerably more data analysis than can be summarized here, FFJR conclude that their results lend considerable support to the conclusion that the stock market is efficient, at least with respect to its ability to adjust to the information implicit in a split.

2. Other Studies of Public Announcements. Variants of the method of residual analysis developed in [14] have been used by others to study the effects of different kinds of public announcements, and all of these also support the efficient markets hypothesis.

Thus using data on 261 major firms for the period 1946-66, Ball and Brown [4] apply the method to study the effects of annual earnings announcements. They use the residuals from a time series regression of the annual earnings of a firm on the average earnings of all their firms to classify the firm's earnings for a given year as having "increased" or "decreased" relative to the market. Residuals from regressions of monthly common stock returns on an index of returns (i.e., the market model of (12)) are then used to compute cumulative average return residuals separately for the earnings that "increased," and those that "decreased." The cumulative average return residuals rise throughout the year in advance of the announcement for the earnings "increased" category, and fall for the earnings "decreased" category.[29] Ball and Brown [4, p. 175] conclude that in fact no more than about ten to fifteen percent of the information in the annual earnings announcement has not been anticipated by the month of the announcement.

On the macro level, Waud [45] has used the method of residual analysis to examine the effects of announcements of discount rate changes by Federal Reserve Banks. In this case the residuals are essentially just the deviations of the daily returns on the Standard and Poor's 500 Index from the average daily return. He finds evidence of a statistically significant "announcement effect"

---

[29]But the comment of footnote 28 is again relevant here.

on stock returns for the first trading day following an announcement, but the magnitude of the adjustment is small, never exceeding .5%. More interesting from the viewpoint of the efficient markets hypothesis is his conclusion that, if anything, the market anticipates the announcements (or information is somehow leaked in advance). This conclusion is based on the non-random patterns of the signs of average return residuals on the days immediately preceding the announcement.

Further evidence in support of the efficient markets hypothesis is provided in the work of Scholes [39] on large secondary offerings of common stock (i.e., large underwritten sales of existing common stocks by individuals and institutions) and on new issues of stock. He finds that on average secondary issues are associated with a decline of between one and two per cent in the cumulative average residual returns for the corresponding common stocks. Since the magnitude of the price adjustment is unrelated to the size of the issue, Scholes concludes that the adjustment is not due to "selling pressure" (as is commonly believed), but rather results from negative information implicit in the fact that somebody is trying to sell a large block of a firm's stock. Moreover, he presents evidence that the value of the information in a secondary depends to some extent on the vendor; somewhat as would be expected, by far the largest negative cumulative average residuals occur where the vendor is the corporation itself or one of its officers, with investment companies a distant second. But the identity of the vendor is not generally known at the time of the secondary, and corporate insiders need only report their transactions in their own company's stock to the S.E.C. within six days after a sale. By this time the market on average has fully adjusted to the information in the secondary, as indicated by the fact that the average residuals behave randomly thereafter.

Note, however, that though this is evidence that prices adjust efficiently to public information, it is also evidence that corporate insiders at least sometimes have important information about their firm that is not yet publicly known. Thus Scholes' evidence for secondary distributions provides support for the efficient markets model in the semi-strong form sense, but also some strong-form evidence against the model.

Though his results here are only preliminary, Scholes also reports on an application of the method of residual analysis to a sample of 696 new issues of common stock during the period 1926–66. As in the FFJR study of splits, the cumulative average residuals rise in the months preceding the new security offering (suggesting that new issues tend to come after favorable recent events)[30] but behave randomly in the months following the offering (indicating that whatever information is contained in the new issue is on average fully reflected in the price of the month of the offering).

In short, the available semi-strong form evidence on the effect of various

---

[30]Footnote 28 is again relevant here.

sorts of public announcements on common stock returns is all consistent with the efficient markets model. The strong point of the evidence, however, is its consistency rather than its quantity; in fact, few different types of public information have been examined, though those treated are among the obviously most important. Moreover, as we shall now see, the amount of semi-strong form evidence is voluminous compared to the strong form tests that are available.

C. Strong Form Tests of the Efficient Markets Models

The strong form tests of the efficient markets model are concerned with whether all available information is fully reflected in prices in the sense that no individual has higher expected trading profits than others because he has monopolistic access to some information. We would not, of course, expect this model to be an exact description of reality, and indeed, the preceding discussions have already indicated the existence of contradictory evidence. In particular, Niederhoffer and Osborne [32] have pointed out that specialists on the N.Y.S.E. apparently use their monopolistic access to information concerning unfilled limit orders to generate monopoly profits, and Scholes' evidence [39] indicates that officers of corporations sometimes have monopolistic access to information about their firms.

Since we already have enough evidence to determine that the model is not strictly valid, we can now turn to other interesting questions. Specifically, how far down through the investment community do deviations from the model permeate? Does it pay for the average investor (or the average economist) to expend resources searching out little known information? Are such activities even generally profitable for various groups of market "professionals"? More generally, who are the people in the investment community that have access to "special information"?

Though this is a fascinating problem, only one group has been studied in any depth—the managements of open end mutual funds. Several studies are available (e.g., Sharpe [41, 42] and Treynor [44]), but the most thorough are Jensen's [19, 20], and our comments will be limited to his work. We shall first present the theoretical model underlying his tests, and then go on to his empirical results.

1. Theoretical Framework. In styding the performance of mutual funds the major goals are to determine (a) whether in general fund managers seem to have access to special information which allows them to generate "abnormal" expected returns, and (b) whether some funds are better at uncovering such special information than others. Since the criterion will simply be the ability of funds to produce higher returns than some norm with no attempt to determine what is responsible for the high returns, the "special information" that leads to high performance could be either keener insight into the implications of publicly available information than is implicit in market prices or monopolistic access to specific information. Thus the tests of the performance of the mutual fund industry are not strictly strong form tests of the efficient markets model.

The major theoretical (and practical) problem in using the mututal fund industry to test the efficient markets model is developing a "norm" against which performance can be judged. The norm must represent the results of an investment policy based on the assumption that prices fully reflect all available information. And if one believes that investors are generally risk averse and so on average must be compensated for any risks undertaken, then one has the problem of finding appropriate definitions of risk and evaluating each fund relative to a norm with its chosen level of risk.

Jensen uses the Sharpe [40]-Lintner [24, 25] model of equilibrium expected returns discussed above to derive a norm consistent with these goals. From (14)–(16), in this model the expected return on an asset or portfolio j from t to $t + 1$ is

$$E(\tilde{r}_{j,\,t+1}|\Phi_t) = r_{f,\,t+1}[1 - \beta_j(\Phi_t)] + E(\tilde{r}_{m,\,t+1}|\Phi_t)\beta_j(\Phi_t) \tag{18}$$

where the various symbols are as defined in Section III. A. 6. But (18) is an *ex ante* relationship, and to evaluate performance an *ex post* norm is needed. One way the latter can be obtained is to substitute the realized return on the market portfolio for the expected return in (18) with the result[31]

$$E(\tilde{r}_{j,\,t+1}|\Phi_t, r_{m,\,t+1}) = r_{f,\,t+1}[1 - \beta_j(\Phi_t)] + r_{m,\,t+1}\beta_j(\Phi_t) \tag{19}$$

Geometrically, (19) says that within the context of the Sharpe-Lintner model, the expected return on j (given information Φ_t and the return $r_{m,\,t+1}$ on the market portfolio) is a linear function of its risk

$$\beta_j(\Phi_t) = \mathrm{cov}\,(\tilde{r}_{j,\,t+1}, \tilde{r}_{m,\,t+1}|\Phi_t)/\sigma^2(\tilde{r}_{m,\,t+1}|\Phi_t)$$

as indicated in Figure 2. Assuming that the value of $\beta_j(\Phi_t)$ is somehow known, or can be reliably estimated, if j is a mutual fund, its *ex post* performance from t to $t + 1$ might now be evaluated by plotting its combination of realized return $r_{j,\,t+1}$ and risk in Figure 2. If (as for the point a) the combination falls above

---

[31]The assumption here is that the return $\bar{r}_{j,\,t+1}$ is generated according to

$$\tilde{r}_{j,\,t+1} = r_{f,\,t+1}[1 - \beta_j(\Phi_t)] + r_{m,\,t+1}\beta_j(\Phi_t) + \tilde{u}_{j,\,t+1}$$

and

$$E(\tilde{u}_{j,\,t+1}|r_{m,\,t+1}) = 0 \qquad \text{for all } r_{m,\,t+1}$$

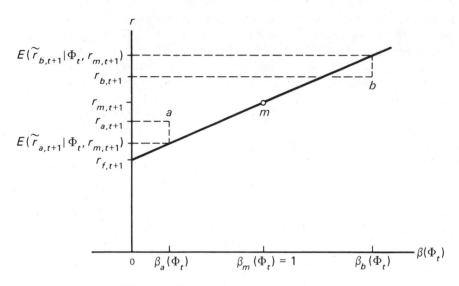

Figure 2. Performance Evaluation Graph.

the expected return line (or, as it is more commonly called, the "market line"), it has done better than would be expected given its level of risk, while if (as for the point b) it falls below the line it has done worse.

Alternatively, the market line shows the combinations of return and risk provided by portfolios that are simple mixtures of the riskless asset and the market portfolio m. The returns and risks for such portfolios (call them c) are

$$r_{c, t+1} = \alpha r_{f, t+1} + (1 - \alpha) r_{m, t+1}$$

$$\beta_c(\Phi_t) = \frac{\text{cov}\,(\tilde{r}_{c, t+1}, \tilde{r}_{m, t+1} | \Phi_t)}{\sigma^2(\tilde{r}_{m, t+1} | \Phi_t)} = \frac{\text{cov}\,((1 - \alpha)\tilde{r}_{m, t+1}, \tilde{r}_{m, t+1} | \Phi_t)}{\sigma^2(\tilde{r}_{m, t+1} | \Phi_t)} = 1 - \alpha$$

where α is the proportion of portfolio funds invested in the riskless asset. Thus, when $1 \geqslant \alpha \geqslant 0$ we obtain the combinations of return and risk along the market line from $r_{f, t+1}$ to m in Figure 2, while when $\alpha < 0$ (and under the assumption that investors can borrow at the same rate that they lend) we obtain the combinations of return and risk along the extension of the line through m. In this interpretation, the market line represents the results of a naive investment strategy, which the investor who thinks prices reflect all available information might follow. The performance of a mutual fund is then measured relative to this naive strategy.

2. Empirical Results. Jensen uses this risk-return framework to evaluate the performance of 115 mutual funds over the ten year period 1955–64. He argues at length for measuring return as the nominal ten year rate with continuous compounding (i.e., the natural log of the ratio of terminal wealth after ten years to initial wealth) and for using historical data on nominal one-year rates with continuous compounding to estimate risk. The Standard and Poor Index of 500 major common stocks is used as the proxy for the market portfolio.

The general question to be answered is whether mutual fund managements have any special insights or information which allows them to earn returns above the norm. But Jensen attacks the question on several levels. First, can the funds in general do well enough to compensate investors for loading charges, management fees, and other costs that might be avoided by simply choosing the combination of the riskless asset f and the market portfolio m with risk level comparable to that of the fund's actual portfolio? The answer seems to be an emphatic no. As far as net returns to investors are concerned, in 89 out of 115 cases, the fund's risk-return combination for the ten year period is below the market line for the period, and the average over all funds of the deviations of ten year returns from the market time is -14.6%. That is, on average the consumer's wealth after ten years of holding mutual funds is about fifteen per cent less than if he held the corresponding portfolios along the market line.

But the loading charge that an investor pays in buying into a fund is usually a pure salesman's commission that the fund itself never gets to invest. Thus one might ask whether, ignoring loading charges (i.e., assuming no such charges were paid by the investor), in general fund managements can earn returns sufficiently above the norm to cover all other expenses that are presumably more directly related to the management of the fund portfolios. Again, the answer seems to be no. Even when loading charges are ignored in computing returns, the risk-return combinations for 72 out of 115 funds are below the market line, and the average deviation of ten year returns from the market line is -8.9%.

Finally, as a somewhat stronger test of the efficient markets model, one would like to know if, ignoring all expenses, fund managements in general showed any ability to pick securities that outperformed the norm. Unfortunately, this question cannot be answered with precision for individual funds since, curiously, data on brokerage commissions are not published regularly. But Jensen suggests the available evidence indicates that the answer to the question is again probably negative. Specifically, adding back all other published expenses of funds to their returns, the risk-return combinations for 58 out of 115 funds were below the market line, and the average deviation of ten year return from the line was -2.5%. But part of this result is due to the absence of a correction for brokerage commissions. Estimating these commissions from average portfolio turnover rates for all funds for the period 1953-58, and adding them back to returns for all funds increases the average deviation from the market line from -2.5% to $.09\%$, which still is not indicative of the existence of special information among mutual fund managers.

But though mutual fund managers in general do not seem to have access to information not already fully reflected in prices, perhaps there are individual funds that consistently do better than the norm, and so provide at least some strong form evidence against the efficient markets model. If there are such funds, however, they escape Jensen's search. For example, for individual funds, returns above the norm in one subperiod do not seem to be associated with performance above the norm in other subperiods. And regardless of how returns are measured (i.e., net or gross of loading charges and other expenses), the number of funds with large positive deviations of returns from the market line of Figure 2 is less than the number that would be expected by chance with 115 funds under the assumption that fund managements have no special talents in predicting returns.[32]

Jensen argues that though his results apply to only one segment of the investment community, they are nevertheless striking evidence in favor of the efficient markets model:

Although these results certainly do not imply that the strong form of the martingale hypothesis holds for all investors and for all time, they provide strong evidence in support of that hypothesis. One must realize that these analysts are extremely well endowed. Moreover, they operate in the securities markets every day and have wide-ranging contacts and associations in both the business and financial communities. Thus, the fact that they are apparently unable to forecast returns accurately enough to recover their research and transactions costs is a striking piece of evidence in favor of the strong form of the martingale hypothesis—at least as far as the extensive subset of information available to these analysts is concerned [20, p. 170].

IV. Summary and Conclusions

The preceding (rather lengthy) analysis can be summarized as follows. In general terms, the theory of efficient markets is concerned with whether prices at any point in time "fully reflect" available information. The theory only has empirical content, however, within the context of a more specific model of market equilibrium, that is, a model that specifies the nature of market equilibrium when prices "fully reflect" available information. We have seen that all of the available empirical literature is implicitly or explicitly based on the assumption that the conditions of market equilibrium can be stated in terms of

---

[32]On the other hand, there is some suggestion in Scholes' [39] work on secondary issues that mutual funds may occassionally have access to "special information." After corporate insiders, the next largest negative price changes occur when the secondary seller is an investment company (including mutual funds), though on average the price changes are much smaller (i.e., closer to 0) than when the seller is a corporate insider.

Moreover, Jensen's evidence itself, though not indicative of the existence of special information among mutual fund managers, is not sufficiently precise to conclude that such information never exists. This stronger conclusion would require exact data on unavoidable expenses (including brokerage commissions) of portfolio management incurred by funds.

expected returns. This assumption is the basis of the expected return or "fair game" efficient markets models.

The empirical work itself can be divided into three categories depending on the nature of the information subset of interest. *Strong-form* tests are concerned with whether individual investors or groups have monopolistic access to any information relevant for price formation. One would not expect such an extreme model to be an exact description of the world, and it is probably best viewed as a benchmark against which the importance of deviations from market efficiency can be judged. In the less restrictive *semi-strong-form* tests the information subset of interest includes all obviously publicly available information, while in the *weak form* tests the information subset is just historical price or return sequences.

Weak form tests of the efficient market model are the most voluminous, and it seems fair to say that the results are strongly in support. Though statistically significant evidence for dependence in successive price changes or returns has been found, some of this is consistent with the "fair game" model and the rest does not appear to be sufficient to declare the market inefficient. Indeed, at least for price changes or returns covering a day or longer, there isn't much evidence against the "fair game" model's more ambitious offspring, the random walk.

Thus, there is consistent evidence of positive dependence in day-to-day price changes and returns on common stocks, and the dependence is of a form that can be used as the basis of marginally profitable trading rules. In Fama's data [10] the dependence shows up as serial correlations that are consistently positive but also consistently close to zero, and as a slight tendency for observed numbers of runs of positive and negative price changes to be less than the numbers that would be expected from a purely random process. More important, the dependence also shows up in the filter tests of Alexander [1, 2] and those of Fama and Blume [13] as a tendency for very small filters to produce profits in excess of buy-and-hold. But any systems (like the filters) that attempt to turn short-term dependence into trading profits of necessity generate so many transactions that their expected profits would be absorbed by even the minimum commissions (security handling fees) that floor traders on major exchanges must pay. Thus, using a less than completely strict interpretation of market efficiency, this positive dependence does not seem of sufficient importance to warrant rejection of the efficient markets model.

Evidence in contradiction of the "fair game" efficient markets model for price changes or returns covering periods longer than a single day is more difficult to find. Cootner [9], and Moore [31] report preponderantly negative (but again small) serial correlations in weekly common stock returns, and this result appears also in the four day returns analyzed by Fama [10]. But it does not appear in runs tests of [10], where, if anything, there is some slight indication of positive dependence, but actually not much evidence of any dependence at all. In any case, there is no indication that whatever dependence exists in weekly returns can be used as the basis of profitable trading rules.

Other existing evidence of dependence in returns provides interesting insights into the process of price formation in the stock market, but it is not relevant for testing the efficient markets model. For example, Fama [10] shows that large daily price changes tend to be followed by large changes, but of unpredictable sign. This suggests that important information cannot be completely evaluated immediately, but that the initial first day's adjustment of prices to the information is unbiased, which is sufficient for the martingale model. More interesting and important, however, is the Niederhoffer-Osborne [32] finding of a tendency toward excessive reversals in common stock price changes from transaction to transaction. They explain this as a logical result of the mechanism whereby orders to buy and sell at market are matched against existing limit orders on the books of the specialist. Given the way this tendency toward excessive reversals arises, however, there seems to be no way it can be used as the basis of a profitable trading rule. As they rightly claim, their results are a strong refutation of the theory of random walks, at least as applied to price changes from transaction to transaction, but they do not constitute refutation of the economically more relevant "fair game" efficient markets model.

Semi-strong form tests, in which prices are assumed to fully reflect all obviously publicly available information, have also supported the efficient markets hypothesis. Thus Fama, Fisher, Jensen, and Roll [14] find that the information in stock splits concerning the firm's future dividend payments is on average fully reflected in the price of a split share at the time of the split. Ball and Brown [4] and Scholes [39] come to similar conclusions with respect to the information contained in (i) annual earning announcements by firms and (ii) new issues and large block secondary issues of common stock. Though only a few different types of information generating events are represented here, they are among the more important, and the results are probably indicative of what can be expected in future studies.

As noted earlier, the strong-form efficient markets model, in which prices are assumed to fully reflect all available information, is probably best viewed as a benchmark against which deviations from market efficiency (interpreted in its strictest sense) can be judged. Two such deviations have in fact been observed. First, Niederhoffer and Osborne [32] point out that specialists on major security exchanges have monopolistic access to information on unexecuted limit orders and they use this information to generate trading profits. This raises the question of whether the "market making" function of the specialist (if indeed this is a meaningful economic function) could not as effectively be carried out by some other mechanism that did not imply monopolistic access to information. Second, Scholes [39] finds that, not unexpectedly, corporate insiders often have monopolistic access to information about their firms.

At the moment, however, corporate insiders and specialists are the only two groups whose monopolistic access to information has been documented. There is no evidence that deviations from the strong form of the efficient markets model permeate down any further through the investment community. For the purposes of most investors the efficient markets model seems a good first (and second) approximation to reality.

In short, the evidence in support of the efficient markets model is extensive, and (somewhat uniquely in economics) contradictory evidence is sparse. Nevertheless, we certainly do not want to leave the impression that all issues are closed. The old saw, "much remains to be done," is relevant here as elsewhere. Indeed, as is often the case in successful scientific research, now that we know we've been in the past, we are able to pose and (hopefully) to answer an even more interesting set of questions for the future. In this case the most pressing field of future endeavor is the development and testing of models of market equilibrium under uncertainty. When the process generating equilibrium expected returns is better understood (and assuming that some expected return model turns out to be relevant), we will have a more substantial framework for more sophisticated intersecurity tests of market efficiency.

References

1. Sidney S. Alexander. "Price Movements in Speculative Markets: Trends or Random Walks." *Industrial Management Review*, 2 (May 1961), 7–26. Also reprinted in [8], 199–218.
2. ——. "Price Movements in Speculative Markets: Trends or Random Walks. No. 2," in [8], 338–72.
3. Louis Bachelier, *Théorie de la Speculation* (Paris: Gauthier-Villars, 1900), and reprinted in English in [8], 17–78.
4. Ray Ball and Phillip Brown. "An Empirical Evaluation of Accounting Income Numbers." *Journal of Accounting Research*, 6 (Autumn, 1968), 159–78.
5. William Beaver. "The Information Content of Annual Earnings Announcements." *Empirical Research in Accounting: Selected Studies, 1968*, supplement to Vol. 7 of the *Journal of Accounting Research*, 67–92.
6. Robert Blattberg and Thomas Sargent. "Regression with Non-Gaussian Disturbances: Some Sampling Results," forthcoming in *Econometrica*.
7. Marshall Blume. "The Assessment of Portfolio Performance." Unpublished Ph.D. thesis, University of Chicago, 1968. A paper summarizing much of this work will appear in the April, 1970, *Journal of Business*.
8. Paul Cootner (ed.). *The Random Character of Stock Market Prices.* Cambridge: M.I.T., 1964.

9. ——. "Stock Prices: Random vs. Systematic Changes." *Industrial Management Review*, 3 (Spring 1962), 24–45. Also reprinted in [8], 231–52.

10. Eugene F. Fama. "The Behavior of Stock Market Prices." *Journal of Business*, 38 (January, 1965), 34–105.

11. ——. "Multiperiod Consumption-Investment Decisions." *American Economic Review*, (March, 1970).

12. ——. "Risk, Return and Equilibrium." Report No. 6831, University of Chicago, Center for Math. Studies in Business and Economics, June, 1968.

13. —— and Marshall Blume. "Filter Rules and Stock Market Trading Profits," *Journal of Business*, 39 (Special Supplement, January, 1966), 226–41.

14. ——, Lawrence Fisher, Michael Jensen and Richard Roll. "The Adjustment of Stock Prices to New Information." *International Economic Review*, X (February, 1969), 1–21.

15. —— and Richard Roll. "Some Properties of Symmetric Stable Distributions." *Journal of the American Statistical Association*, 63 (September, 1968), 817–36.

16. Michael D. Godfrey, C.W.J. Granger and O. Morgenstern. "The Random Walk Hypothesis of Stock Market Behavior." *Kyklos*, 17 (1964), 1–30.

17. C.W.J. Granger and O. Morgenstern. "Spectral Analysis of New York Stock Market Prices," *Kyklos*, 16 (1963), 1–27. Also reprinted in [8], 162–88.

18. John R. Hicks. *Value and Capital.* Oxford: The Clarendon Press, 1946.

19. Michael Jensen. "The Performance of Mutual Funds in the Period 1945–64," *Journal of Finance*, 23 (May, 1968), 389–416.

20. ——. "Risk, the Pricing of Capital Assets, and the Evaluation of Investment Portfolios," *Journal of Business*, 42 (April, 1969), 167–247.

21. Maurice G. Kendall. "The Analysis of Economic Time-Series, Part I: Prices," *Journal of the Royal Statistical Society*, 96 (Part I, 1953), 11–25.

22. Ruben A. Kessel. "The Cyclical Behavior of the Term Structure of Interest Rates," National Bureau of Economic Research Occasional Paper No. 91. New York: Columbia University Press, 1965.

23. Benjamin F. King. "Market and Industry Factors in Stock Price Behavior," *Journal of Business*, 39 (Special Supplement January, 1966), 139–90.

24. John Lintner. "Security Prices, Risk, and Maximal Gains from Diversification," *Journal of Finance*, 20 (December, 1965), 587–615.

25. ——. "The Valuation of Risk Assets and the Selection of Risky Investments in Stock Portfolios and Capital Budgets," *Review of Economics and Statistics*, 47 (February, 1965), 13–37.

26. Fredrich A. Lutz. "The Structure of Interest Rates," *Quarterly Journal of Economics*, 40 (1940–41).

27. Benoit Mandelbrot. "Forecasts of Future Prices, Unbiased Markets, and Martingale Models," *Journal of Business*, 39 (Special Supplement, January, 1966), 242–55.

28. ——. "The Variation of Certain Speculative Prices." *Journal of Business*, 36 (October, 1963), 394–419.

29. —— and Howard M. Taylor. "On the Distribution of Stock Price Differences." *Operations Research*, 15 (November–December, 1967), 1057-62.

30. Harry Markowitz. *Portfolio Selection: Efficient Diversification of Investment*. New York: John Wiley & Sons, 1959.

31. Arnold Moore. "A Statistical Analysis of Common Stock Prices. Unpublished Ph.D. thesis, Graduate School of Business, University of Chicago, 1962.

32. Victor Niederhoffer and M.F.M. Osborne. "Market Making and Reversal on the Stock Exchange." *Journal of the American Statistical Association*, 61 (December, 1966), 897-916.

33. M.F.M. Osborne. "Brownian Motion in the Stock Market," *Operations Research*, 7 (March–April, 1959), 145-73. Also reprinted in [8], 100-28.

34. ——. "Periodic Structure in the Brownian Motion of Stock Prices." *Operations Research*, 10 (May–June, 1962), 345-79. Also reprinted in [8], 262-96.

35. S. James Press. "A compound Events Model for Security Prices." *Journal of Business*, 40 (July, 1968), 317-35.

36. Harry V. Roberts. "Stock Market 'Patterns' and Financial Analysis: Methodological Suggestions." *Journal of Finance*, 14 (March, 1959), 1-10.

37. Richard Roll. "The Efficient Market Model Applied to U.S. Treasury Bill Rates." Unpublished Ph.D. thesis, Graduate School of Business, University of Chicago, 1968.

38. Paul A. Samuelson. "Proof That Properly Anticipated Prices Fluctuate Randomly." *Industrial Management Review*, 6 (Spring, 1965), 41-9.

39. Myron Scholes. "A Test of the Competitive Hypothesis: The Market for New Issues and Secondary Offerings." Unpublished PH.D. thesis, Graduate School of Business, University of Chicago, 1969.

40. William F. Sharpe. "Capital Asset Prices: A Theory of Market Equilibrium under Conditions of Risk." *Journal of Finance*, 19 (September, 1964), 425–42.

41. ——. "Mutual Fund Performance." *Journal of Business*, 39 (Special Supplement, January, 1966), 119-38.

42. ——. "Risk Aversion in the Stock Market." *Journal of Finance*, 20 (September, 1965), 416-22.

43. James Tobin. "Liquidity Preference as Behavior Towards Risk," *Review of Economic Studies*, 25 (February, 1958), 65-85.

44. Jack L. Treynor. "How to Rate Management of Investment Funds." *Harvard Business Review*, 43 (January–February, 1965), 63-75.

45. Roger N. Waud. "Public Interpretation of Discount Rate Changes: Evidence on the 'Announcement Effect.'" forthcoming in *Econometrica*.

46. John Wise. "Linear Estimators for Linear Regression Systems Having Infinite Variances." Unpublished paper presented at the Berkeley-Stanford Mathematical Economics Seminar, October, 1963.
47. Holbrook Working. "A Random Difference Series for Use in the Analysis of Time Series." *Journal of the American Statistical Association*, 29 (March, 1934), 11–24.

2

Proof That Properly Discounted Present Values of Assets Vibrate Randomly

Paul A. Samuelson

1. Review

Consider a random vector sequence: $\ldots, X_t, X_{t+1}, \ldots, X_{t+T}, \ldots$. The dividend of a particular common stock, say General Motors, might be the ith component of that vector: $\ldots, x_{it}, \ldots, x_{i, t+T}, \ldots$; and the jth component might, as in 1965 Samuelson,[1] denote the price of spot wheat at time t. Under some known stochastic process generating the random variables, there will be defined basic conditional probabilities

$$\text{Prob}\left\{ X_{t+T} \leqslant x_{t+T} | X_t = x_t, X_{t-1} = x_{t-1}, \ldots \right\}$$

$$= P_T(x_{t+T}; x_t, x_{t-1}, \ldots; t) \qquad (1)$$

and conditional expected values

$$E\left\{ X_{t+T} | X_t = x_t, X_{t-1} = x_{t-1}, \ldots \right\} = {}_{t+T}Y_t$$

$$= \int_{-\infty}^{\infty} x P_T(dx; x_t, x_{t-1}, \ldots; t)$$

$$= {}_{t+T}F_t(x_t, x_{t-1}, \ldots) \qquad (2)$$

$$E\left\{ {}_{t+T}Y_{t+1} | X_t = x_t, X_{t-1} = x_{t-1}, \ldots \right\}$$

$$= \int_{-\infty}^{\infty} {}_{t+T}F_{t+1}(x_{t+1}, x_t, \ldots) P_1(dx_{t+1}; x_t, x_{t-1}, \ldots; t)$$

$$= E\left\{ {}_{t+T}Y_{t+1} |_{t+T}Y_t \right\} \text{ for short} \qquad (3)$$

The author owes thanks to the National Science Foundation for financial aid, and to Kathryn Kaepplein for valuable assistance.

[1]See [3].

Here a Stieltjes integral is written as $\int_{-\infty}^{\infty} f(x)g(dx)$; and when x is a vector, a *multiple* Stieltjes integral is written as $\int_{-\infty}^{\infty} f(x)g(dx)$.

The two basic 1965 theorems can now be recapitulated.

Theorem 1: For $\tau > t$, the sequence $(_\tau Y_t, _\tau Y_{t+1}, \ldots)$ has the martingale property

$$E\{_\tau Y_{t+k} |_\tau Y_t\} \equiv\ _\tau Y_t \qquad (k = 1, 2, \ldots, \tau - 1) \tag{4}$$

Theorem 2: For the "discounted" sequence,

$$_\tau Z_t \equiv\ _\tau Y_t \prod_{j=1}^{\tau-t} \lambda_{t+j}$$

$$E\{_\tau Z_{t+1} |_\tau Z_t\} = \lambda_{t+1}\ _\tau Z_t \tag{5}$$

$$E\{Z_{t+k} |_\tau Z_t\} = \lambda_{t+1} \lambda_{t+2} \cdots \lambda_{t+k}\ _\tau Z_t$$

2. Expected Present Discounted Values

Suppose that the *i*th component of the vector X_t represents the dividend of a given stock that is to be paid out at time t. Then if $\lambda_{t+1} - 1$ is the interest rate paid at the end of period t on each dollar invested at time t, and if x_{it} were a nonrandom sequence, the classical Fisher present discounted-value rule of capitalization (slightly generalized) defines the value of a stock as

$$V_t = \sum_{T=1}^{\infty} (x_{i\,t+T} \Big/ \prod_{j=1}^{T} \lambda_{t+j}) \tag{6}$$

$$V_{t+1} = \lambda_{t+1} V_t - x_{i\,t+1} \tag{7}$$

If $\lambda_t \equiv 1 + r$, the above denominator takes on the more familiar form $(1 + r)^T$.

But now revert to the supposition that $x_{i,\,t+T}$, and hence V_t, are random variables; and assume that *the market capitalizes the stock at the expected value of V_t*, namely at v_t defined by

$$v_t = E\{V_t | X_t = x_t, X_{t-1} = x_{t-1}, \ldots\} = \sum_{T=1}^{\infty}\ _{t+T} Z_t \tag{8}$$

$$E \, v_{t+1} | v_t \; = \; \sum_{T=2}^{\infty} E\left\{_{t+T} Z_{t+1} |_{t+T} Z_t\right\} \tag{9}$$

Now, by simple use of the principle of superposition, we can derive from (5) our needed generalization or corollary of Theorem 2, namely that stock prices themselves have a martingale or random-walk property.

Theorem 3. If stocks are capitalized at their expected present discounted values defined by (8) and (9), then

$$E\left\{v_{t+1} | v_t\right\} = \lambda_{t+1} v_t - E\left\{x_{i \, t+1} | X_t = x_t, X_{t-1} = x_{t-1}, \ldots\right\} \tag{10}$$

Clearly (10) is the fundamental stochastic generalization of the fundamental nonstochastic relation (7). Note that it holds even for the Pareto-Lévy distributions that lack a finite variance but possess a defined first moment.

Proof of the theorem follows immediately from substituting Theorem 2's relation (5) into each term of (9) and then identifying what remains by use of (8).

3. Example of Brownian Ramble

Suppose that the ratio of dividend to earnings is a constant payout fraction. Let earnings at time t be proportional to a random variable satisfying an independent multiplicative relation. Then we can deduce that dividends will be generated by the stochastic process

$$x_{i, \, t+T} = x_{it} Z_1 \ldots Z_T \tag{11}$$

where the Z's are positive random variables subject to uniform and independent probability distributions

$$\text{Prob}\left\{Z_i \leqslant z\right\} = P(z) \tag{12}$$

$$E\left\{Z_i\right\} = \theta, E\left\{x_{i \, t+T}\right\} = \theta^T x_{it}$$

$$E\left\{\log Z_i\right\} = \mu < \log \theta, \text{Var}\left\{\log Z_i\right\} = \sigma^2$$

Finally, assume a constant interest rate, $\lambda_t \equiv 1 + r > \theta$, which is large enough to keep v_t a finite converging series

$$v_t = x_{it} \left[\frac{\theta}{1+r} + \frac{\theta^2}{(1+r)^2} + \cdots \right] = x_{it}\theta(1 + r - \theta)^{-1} \qquad (13)$$

$$\text{Prob}\{v_{t+1}/v_t \leq z\} = P(z) \qquad (14)$$

$$E\{v_{t+1}|v_t\} = \theta v_t \text{ from (12)}$$

$$= (1 + r)v_t - E\{x_{i\,t+1}\} \text{ from (10)}$$

Actually this model generates the economic or multiplicative Brownian motion of Osborne and Samuelson[2] with the asymptotic log-normal distribution

$$\lim_{T \to \infty} \text{Prob} \left\{ a \leq \frac{\log(v_{t+T}/v_t) - \mu T}{T^{1/2}\sigma} \leq b \right\} = \frac{1}{\sqrt{2\pi}} \int_a^b e^{-1/2\,s^2}\,ds \qquad (15)$$

and its price changes have the white-noise property

$$E\{\log v_{t+1} - \log v_t - \mu\} \equiv 0 \qquad (16)$$

$$\text{covariance}\{\log v_{t+T}, \log v_t\} \equiv 0 \quad T > 0 \qquad (17)$$

Granger[3] has arrived at similar results, including the interesting case where variables are generated as the (possibly infinite) sum of white-noise random variables. Shiller[4] also offers valuable related contributions, particularly in connection with prediction algorithms and also the term structure of interest rates.

4. Probabilities That Obey Economic Law

A second model provides an interesting contrast to the endless wandering of the above model. In it, earnings and dividends continue to have a probability distribution that stays within the same general central range; thus dividends have an ergodic distribution that is determined by economic law, by the fundamentals of the industry's resource scarcities and the capacity of its goods to meet peoples' needs and demands. But, and this is the beauty of the present martingale

---

[2] See [2] and [4], respectively.

[3] In [1].

[4] In [5].

process, the movement of the stock price that capitalizes these determinate dividends is itself a white-noise generalized martingale!

Specifically, let dividends satisfy a damped autoregressive process

$$\log x_{i,\,t+1} = a \log x_{it} + \eta_t \qquad |a| < 1 \tag{18}$$

where η_t is an independently and uniformly distributed random variable, with cov $(\eta_t, \eta_{t \pm k}) = 0$ for $k \neq 0$.

Then, for $|a| < 1$,

$$\lim_{T \to \infty} \text{Prob}\left\{ x_{i\,t+T} \leqslant x | x_{it} = y \right\} = \lim_{T \to \infty} P_T(x,y) = P(x) \tag{19}$$

a limiting ergodic probability distribution that is independent of initial value for x_{it} and which is not log-normal.

Even though dividends and their changes have a nonwhite spectrum, with nonvanishing covariance $x_{it}, x_{i,\,t \pm k}$, the martingale property of Theorem 3's (10) will still be valid. Thus, if the corporation had zero dividend payments over a time interval, and the λ_{t+j} discount factor were at or near unity, the spectrum of $v_{t+k} - v_t$ would be white, in the sense of zero first-order autocorrelation and zero expected values.

The present case of an ergodic probability distribution differs significantly from the log-normal models upon which so much of warrant and option valuations has been based. As applied to calls, which are typically warrants *protected* for dividend payouts, the difference is not so great. Indeed, as my colleague Robert Merton reminds me, even for the present model, once we ask what will be the cumulative value over time of a portfolio that invests back all dividends in this company's common stock, the relevant probability distribution derived from (19) will have properties much like that of (15). In fact, in the following special case, we shall have exactly the same form as (15).

Suppose the corporation selects its optimal algebraic dividend payout so as to leave within the company only that sum of wealth or money which can optimally earn more there than elsewhere. (If the indicated dividend is negative, think of the corporation as selling new shares; for that matter, transaction costs and tax complications aside, a corporation might choose always simply to buy shares *algebraically* in the open market, so that any positive dividend situation would work itself out in each of my shares' becoming more valuable.) Suppose further, for simplicity, that *ex ante* always the same total wealth is to be left in the company: all the random events of the period just past show up in the variable algebraic dividend. Finally, let the relevant interest rates by constant, $\lambda_t \equiv 1 + r$. Then each dollar left invested and reinvested in this company will be subject to the multiplicative probability distribution of (11)'s form; and (15)'s log-normal limit will apply. Even if the amount the company is to reinvest is not completely independent in probability from period to period, the white martingale property assures zero autocorrelation and unbiased means; consequently a slight generalization of the central-limit theorem, to unautocorrelated rather than independent added variates, ought still to enable derivation of a log-normal limit.

5. Qualifications

One person, too small to affect market prices appreciably, could make systematic speculative gains in excess of those shown in (10), if he had more or better information or a better way of evaluating existing information. This would enable him to improve upon the probability distribution of (1). Thus, suppose at time t he could know x_{t+1} exactly, or have a more accurate way of estimating it than from $P_1(x_{t+1}; x_t, x_{t+1}, \ldots; t)$.

An example would be where this investor had private knowledge, or private recognition, of an additional datum m_t, in terms of which he has the probability distribution $Q_1(x_{t+1}; x_t, x_{t-1}, \ldots; m_t; t)$ with the property that $P_1(x_{t+1}; x_t, x_{t-1}, \ldots; t)$ is the "marginal distribution" of $Q_1(\ )$ with m_t integrated out. Suppose

$$P_1(x_{t+1}; x_t, x_{t-1}, \ldots; t) \equiv \int_{-\infty}^{\infty} Q_1(x_{t+1}; x_t, x_{t-1}, \ldots; dm_t; t) \qquad (20)$$

and

$$Q_1(x_{t+1}, x_t, x_{t-1}, \ldots; m_t; t) P_1(x_{t+1}; x_t, x_{t-1}, \ldots; t)^{-1}$$

$$\neq \text{a function of } m_t \text{ alone}$$

Then knowledge of m_t gives extra predictive power of $x_{i\,t+T}$ and of V_{t+k}. Having such knowledge when others do not is highly profitable, since depending upon the level of m_t, the stock becomes an especially good or an especially bad buy. Of course, if this private knowledge becomes widespread, the relevant $P_1(\ )$ will become $Q_1(\ )$ itself, with Theorem 3 and (10) holding in terms of it, and with m_t being just one more element in the relevant x_t. In summary, the present study shows (a) there is no incompatibility in principle between the so-called random-walk model and the fundamentalists' model, and (b) there is no incompatibility in principle between behavior of stocks' prices that behave like random walk at the same time that there exist subsets of investors who can do systematically better than the average investors.

References

1. Granger, C.W.J. "Some Implications of the Fundamentalist's Valuation Model." May 25, 1973 paper for Berlin Workshop on International Capital Markets, September 1973.
2. Osborne, M.F.M. "Brownian Motion in the Stock Market." *Operations Research*, Vol. 7, No. 2 (March–April 1959), pp. 145-173. Also in P.H. Cootner, *The Random Character of Stock Market Prices*, Cambridge, M.I.T. Press, 1967, pp. 100-128.
3. Samuelson, P.A. "Proof That Properly Anticipated Prices Fluctuate Randomly." *Industrial Management Review*, Vol. 6, No. 2, pp. 41–49. This is reproduced as Chapter 198 in Samuelson, *Collected Scientific Papers, Volume III*, Cambridge, M.I.T. Press, 1972.
4. ——. "A Rational Theory of Warrant Pricing." *Industrial Management Review*, Vol. 6, No. 2, pp. 13-39. This is reproduced as Chapter 197 in *Collected Scientific Papers, Volume III*.
5. Shiller, R.J. "Rational Expectations and the Structure of Interest Rates." Unpublished Ph.D. dissertation, M.I.T., 1972.

3 Capital Asset Prices versus Time Series Models as Predictors of Inflation

Patrick J. Hess and James L. Bicksler

The expected real rate of interest and market efficiency

Introduction

In a recent paper Fama has tested the relationship between nominal interest rates on default-free bonds and price level changes.[1] Although this topic has been considered many times in the literature Fama is the first author to test the relationship on an ex ante basis.[2] He concludes that the behavior of nominal yields is consistent with the joint hypothesis that:

1. The expected real returns on 1–6 month Treasury Bills were constant during the period 1/1953–7/1971.
2. the capital markets are efficient in setting the price of the bills since the nominal interest rates summarize all the information about future rates of inflation that is in the time series of past rates.

These results are important for two reasons. First of all, almost all previous studies have concluded that nominal interest rates adjust only after a lag to price level changes, i.e., capital markets are inefficient. Secondly, if the expected real rate of interest is constant for these bills capital market expectations of price level changes may easily be inferred from observable nominal rates.

This paper is a further investigation of the behavior of nominal interest rates under conditions of uncertain inflation. The robustness of nominal interest rates as predictors of inflation are compared to forecasts derived from an

Reprinted with permission of the authors and North-Holland Publishg Company from *Journal of Financial Economics,* Vol. 2, no. 1, December 1975, pp. 341–360.

This paper has benefited greatly from the comments of E. Birch, C. Nelson, M. Rozeff and an anonymous referee. Naturally, any remaining errors or omissions are the responsibility of the authors.

[1] See Fama (1975).

[2] Roll provides a useful documentation of a number of empirical studes. See Roll (1972, pp. 251–277). Pyle has tested the Fisher relationship with polled predictions of the future rate of inflation. See Pyle (1972, pp. 275–280).

integrated auto-regressive-moving-average process (ARIMA). Additionally, the behavior of the expected real rate of interest is investigated in an attempt to distinguish between the constant expected real rate hypothesis and Mundell's framework where the expected real rate is in part determined by the expected rate of inflation.[3] The results of this study are not consistent with Fama's conclusions. Moreover, it appears that the failure to confirm market efficiency is a result of misspecifying the expected real rate. Thus the behavior of interest rates appears to be more complicated than what Fama has suggested.

2. Nominal Yields and the Expected Rate of Inflation

Fama rewrites the Fisher relationship in terms of changes in the purchasing power of money. His equation is

$$E(\widetilde{r}_{j,t}) = I_{j,t} + E(\widetilde{X}_t) + I_{j,t} E(\widetilde{X}_t) \tag{1}$$

where $E(\widetilde{r}_{j,t})$ equals the expected real rate of interest for bill j in period t, $I_{j,t}$ is the nominal interest rate on bill j set at the beginning of period t, and $E(\widetilde{X}_t)$ is the expected relative change in the purchasing power of money or the reciprocal of 1 plus the relative change in the price of consumption at the end of periods $(t-1)$ and (t) less 1.0.[4] If investment horizons are short and $\widetilde{X}_t$ is relatively stable eq. (1) may be approximated by

$$E(\widetilde{r}_{j,t}) = I_{j,t} + E(\widetilde{X}_t) \tag{2}$$

Or, in terms of $\widetilde{X}_t$,

$$E(\widetilde{X}_t) = E(\widetilde{r}_{j,t}) - I_{j,t} \tag{3}$$

Fama estimates the empirical counterpart of eq. (3),

$$\widetilde{X}_t = \alpha_0 + \alpha_1 I_{j,t} + \widetilde{e}_t \tag{4}$$

via OLS. The coefficient α_1 represents changes in the nominal interest rate, $I_{j,t}$, that are due to (a) changes in the equilibrium real rate, $E(\widetilde{r}_{j,t})$, and (b) changes in the expected value of $\widetilde{X}_t$. In the special case where changes in nominal interest rates are due entirely to changes in the expected value of $\widetilde{X}_t$, $\alpha_1 = -1.0$. Furthermore, if $\alpha_1 = -1.0$ the regression coefficient α_0 is an estimate of the expected real rate during the period.

---

[3] Mundell (1963, pp. 280–283).

[4] Fama (1975, p. 3).

Fama estimates eq. (4) for the sample period 1/1953–7/1971. The estimates of α_1 for bills of 1–6 month maturity are always within two standard errors of –1.0. For 1-month bills, the estimates range from –0.33 in the period 3/1959–7/1964 to –1.49 in the sample interval 1/1953–2/1959 and –0.98 during the entire sample period. Thus Fama's evidence is consistant with eq. (3) and the hypothesis that the expected real rate is constant.

3. Derivation of Expectations

The period by period expectations of capital markets are approximated by

$$E(\tilde{Z}_t | B_{t-1}^{cm}) = 1.0/(1.0 + \alpha_0 - I_t) - 1.0 \tag{5}$$

where α_0 is the least square estimate of the equilibrium real rate during the period 1/1953–7/1971 and is equal to 0.00070 [see eq. (4)].[5] $\tilde{Z}_t$ is the relative change in the price of consumption from the end of period $t-1$ to the end of period t. The arbitrarily specified information set consist of the past values of $\tilde{Z}_t; Z_1, Z_2, \ldots, Z_{t-1}$. Expectations for each period t are generated according to the forecasts of the ARIMA model,

$$E(\tilde{Z}_t | B'_{t-1}) = Z_{t-1} + Z_{t-12} - Z_{t-13} - \theta_1 U_{t-1} - \Delta_1 U_{t-12} + \Delta_1 \theta_1 U_{t-13} \tag{6}$$

where θ_1 is a moving average parameter, Δ_1 is a seasonal moving average parameter and U_{t-1}, U_{t-12} and U_{t-13} are errors at lags 1, 12 and 13, respectively.

Eq. (6) is specified such that Z_{t-1} is included in B'_{t-1}. Implicitly we are assuming that Z_{t-1} is in some sense knowable at the end of period $t-1$. This is a tenable assumption since nominal prices are observable, however, it is important to recognize that Z_{t-1} may not be known with certainty at the end of the period. As is noted in the next section we approximate $\tilde{Z}_t$ with the Bureau of Labor Statistics estimate of the rate of inflation which is not published until several weeks after the end of each period. This introduces two complications: (1) the BLS estimate is subject to information that may not have been available at the end of period $t-1$, and (2) the BLS estimate may contain more information than what would be produced by a free market.[6] This means that the BLS estimate may contain less noise than the best estimate available at the end of $t-1$, i.e., the BLS estimate may not have been known at the end of $t-1$. As a result, it is of interest to conduct our tests including and excluding Z_{t-1} from B'_{t-1}.

---

[5] Fama (1975, table 2).

[6] The point here is that the marginal cost of reducing the noise in the estimate at some point exceeds the benefits to the user.

4. The Data

The nominal yields of 30-day treasury bills are used as a proxy for the nominal yields on default-free bonds.[7] The relative changes in the price of consumption are approximated by relative changes in the Consumer Price Index (CPI) published by the Bureau of Labor Statistics. The changes are calculated for monthly intervals. Using the CPI to approximate the price of consumption probably introduces several biases. First of all, the CPI does not include all goods in the consumption set at a point in time. Secondly, the weighting of the goods in the index does not correspond to the proportion of the total value consumed in a period. Thirdly, items in the index are not sampled every month.[8] The effect of the first two limitations are difficult to isolate; however, failure to sample items every month is likely to introduce autocorrelation in the computed series not present in the true variable. The ARIMA model will embed this spurious correlation in the estimated parameters. Efficient capital markets, of course, will ignore it. The result of this is that capital markets may appear to be ignoring 'information'. Unfortunately, better proxies for the price of consumption are unavailable and therefore our tests are limited by these problems.

5. Identification and Estimation of the ARIMA Model

The first step in model identification is to determine the appropriate degree of differencing to achieve stationarity. The estimated autocorrelations for the undifferenced series and first differences are listed in table 1. For the undifferenced series the autocorrelations die off very slowly, e.g., the first 12 are all about 0.30. This is indicative of non-stationarity. In contrast, the estimated autocorrelations of the first difference are large relative to their standard errors only at lags 1, 12 and 36. This behavior is consistent with the seasonal moving average model proposed in section 3. [See eq. (6).]

The parameters are estimated beginning in 1958 with monthly data extending back to 1/1953, e.g., for 1958 the 60-month period 1/1953–12/1957 is used to estimate θ_1 and Δ_1. The estimated model is then used to make forecasts for the subsequent year. The estimation process is an iterative minimization of the sum of squared residuals, however, a number of diagnostic checks are performed to determine the adequacy of the model.[9] As an illustration of the estimation procedure table 2 lists parameter estimates and summary statistics for the sample period 1/1953–12/1970.

---

[7]The nominal rates are from Bildersee (n.d.).

[8]For a description of the consumer price index, see Wallace (1972).

[9]For a more complete description, see Nelson (1973, ch. 5).

Table 1
Autocorrelations

Relative change in the CPI, 1/1953–6/1971

Lags													Est. Std. Error for Row
1–12	0.37	0.36	0.26	0.29	0.28	0.28	0.24	0.33	0.35	0.33	0.26	0.36	0.07
13–24	0.26	0.19	0.30	0.18	0.20	0.18	0.09	0.18	0.20	0.11	0.19	0.18	0.12
25–36	0.12	0.05	0.10	0.07	0.03	0.01	-0.00	0.08	0.16	0.03	0.07	0.17	0.14
37–48	0.03	0.08	0.02	0.03	-0.09	-0.01	-0.05	0.01	0.07	0.04	0.06	0.13	0.14

First differences of relative changes in the CPI, 1/1953–6/1971

Lags													Est. Std. Error for Row
1–12	-0.51	0.10	-0.11	0.05	-0.01	0.01	-0.09	0.05	0.03	0.03	-0.13	0.16	0.07
13–24	-0.03	-0.14	0.17	-0.09	0.04	0.04	-0.15	0.06	0.08	-0.12	0.07	0.03	0.09
25–36	0.03	-0.11	0.06	0.03	-0.02	0.00	-0.10	0.02	0.16	-0.13	-0.07	0.20	0.09
37–48	-0.15	0.09	-0.07	0.13	-0.17	0.11	-0.10	0.00	0.08	-0.05	-0.05	0.14	0.10

Table 2
Parameter Estimates and Summary Statistics, 1/1953–12/1970[a]

Autocorrelation of residuals[b]

Lags													Est. Std. Error
1–12	-0.01	0.15	-0.17	-0.02	0.04	0.06	-0.04	0.08	0.04	0.09	-0.04	-0.06	0.07
13–24	-0.03	-0.07	0.12	-0.02	0.09	-0.01	-0.11	-0.04	-0.01	0.01	0.07	-0.14	0.08
25–36	-0.05	-0.12	-0.06	-0.03	-0.00	-0.07	0.01	0.06	0.07	-0.03	-0.05	-0.00	0.08

Cross correlation of lagged residuals and Z_t

Lags												
1–12	-0.47	0.01	-0.14	0.05	0.07	-0.01	-0.06	0.07	0.08	-0.11	-0.00	-0.49
13–24	0.43	-0.10	0.24	-0.13	0.03	-0.06	-0.01	-0.02	0.03	-0.02	0.09	-0.09
25–36	0.03	-0.03	-0.07	0.07	-0.04	0.02	0.08	0.00	-0.00	-0.06	-0.04	0.11

Cross correlation of current observations of Z_t and future residuals

Lags												
1–12	-0.08	0.24	-0.15	0.03	-0.04	0.00	-0.01	0.04	-0.03	0.12	-0.11	0.06
13–24	-0.02	-0.06	0.11	-0.06	0.03	0.06	-0.01	0.01	-0.08	-0.03	0.13	-0.08
25–36	0.12	-0.15	0.04	-0.14	0.10	-0.08	-0.00	0.01	0.07	-0.00	-0.04	0.02

[a]Estimated parameters: $\theta_1 = 0.867391$, $\Delta_1 = 0.910550$; t-values relative to zero: $t_{\theta 1} = 25.40$, $t_{\Delta 1} = 49.03$; adj. coefficient of determination = 0.709; F-ratio = 248; D.F. = 2 and 201.

[b]Q-statistic: 10 D.F. = 16.5; 22 D.F. = 30.4; 34 D.F. = 38.0.

The estimated parameters θ_1 and Δ_1 are significant at high levels with t-values of 25.40 and 49.03. Also the adjusted coefficient of determination has an F-ratio of 248. Based on these statistics the selected ARIMA model appears to be quite representative of the true model. The residuals, however, appear to exhibit some autocorrelation. In particular, the Q-statistic for 10 degrees of freedom is significant at the 90 percent confidence level and is very close to the critical value of 30.8 for 22 degrees of freedom. This appears to be a result of large values at lags 2 and 3, 0.15 and −0.17, and thus we have some reason to believe that adding moving average parameters at these lags would reduce the residuals to random noise. The autocorrelations at lags 14 and 15 do not support this alternative formulation. Examining the cross correlation of lagged residuals with the current value indicates spikes at the prescribed lags of 1, 12 and 13 and 'smaller' spikes at lags 14 and 15 as the more complicated moving average model would predict. The cross correlation of the current values with the future errors again picks up the autocorrelation at lags 2 and 3. In summary, there is some evidence that the specified model could be improved by adding moving average parameters. This is based on the fact that for the first 12 residuals we can reject the hypothesis that they are white noise. Also there appears to be some cross correlation consistent with excluded parameters at the appropriate lags. At the same time the specified model does not seem to be a bad approximation and probably performs well enough for our purposes.[10]

6. Capital Market Efficiency: Test Statistics

In the most general form capital market efficiency is described as

$$f(X_t | B^{cm}_{t-1}) = f(X_t | B_{t-1}) \tag{7}$$

where $f(X_t | B^{cm}_{t-1})$ equals the density function assessed by capital markets, B^{cm}_{t-1} equals the information set used by capital markets to assess the density function of $\tilde{X}_t$ and $f(X_t | B_{t-1})$ is the true density function given the complete information set available at the beginning of period t, B_{t-1}.[11] In words, eq. (7) specifies a world where capital markets correctly utilize all available information in assessing the likelihood of the possible outcomes of $\tilde{X}_t$.

Two test statistics are utilized in investigating the efficiency of capital markets with regard to the time series of inflation. The first of these is simply a comparison of mean squared forecasting errors. The second is based upon a procedure suggested by Nelson for testing the relationship between two infor-

---

[10]Interestingly enough, for the early periods of estimation there was much less autocorrelation in the residuals.

[11]Fama (1975, p. 4).

mation sets.[12] His procedure utilizes the fact that if one information set (B'_{t-1}) is a subset of another (B^{cm}_{t-1}), the accuracy of forecasts derived from the latter cannot be improved by incorporating the former information set. For the case at hand, this means the forecasting errors of capital markets should be independent of the contemporaneous difference between capital market forecasts and forecasts based upon the arbitrarily specified information set. Thus a composite forecast of the form

$$\tilde{X}_t = \beta[E(\tilde{X}_t|B'_{t-1})] + (1 - \beta)[E(\tilde{X}_t|B^{cm}_{t-1})] + \tilde{e}_t \tag{8}$$

will minimize $\Sigma\tilde{e}_t^2$ for $\beta = 0$.[13] The least squares estimate of β is

$$b = \frac{\Sigma[E(\tilde{X}_t|B'_{t-1}) - E(\tilde{X}_t|B^{cm}_{t-1})][\tilde{X}_t - E(\tilde{X}_t|B^{cm}_{t-1})]}{\Sigma[E(\tilde{X}_t|B'_{t-1}) - E(\tilde{X}_t|B^{cm}_{t-1})]^2} \tag{9}$$

which may be estimated from

$$\tilde{X}_t - E(\tilde{X}_t|B^{cm}_t) = b[E(\tilde{X}_t|B'_{t-1}) - E(\tilde{X}_t|B^{cm}_{t-1})] + \tilde{e}_t \tag{10}$$

via OLS.[14]

7. Empirical Results

The statistical efficiency of capital market forecasts is investigated by computing the ratio of the mean squared forecasting errors of capital markets to the ARIMA model. Thus if the observed ratio is less than 1.0 the forecasts of capital markets are more efficient than those derived from the ARIMA and vice versa for values greater than 1.0. The observed ratios for Z_{t-1} included in B'_{t-1} are enumerated in table 3.

There is a temptation to assume that above ratios have an F distribution. This, of course, is incorrect because the errors of the ARIMA model and capital markets are not independent.[15] As a result the above evidence is not subject to inferential interpretation. At the same time there does not appear to be important differences in the relative accuracy of the competing predictors.

Test results of B'_{t-1} as a subset of B^{cm}_{t-1} are listed in table 4. Since the

[12]Nelson (1972b, pp. 902–917) and (1973, ch. 8).

[13]See footnote 12.

[14]Since we have stated eq. (10) in terms of conditional expectations it follows that they are unbiased and can be estimated via eq. (10).

[15]The estimated correlation coefficient for the entire sample period is 0.65.

Table 3
Tests of Statistical Efficiency for $Z_{t-1} \in B'_{t-1}$

Time Period	Ratio of Mean Squared Forecasting Errors
1/1958–6/1971	0.9735
1/1958–12/1967	0.9424
1/1958–9/1964	0.9388
10/1964–6/1971	1.0234
1/1958–12/1962	0.8574
1/1963–12/1967	1.0875
1/1968–6/1971	1.1214

results given below are for Z_{t-1} as a member of B'_{t-1} significantly positive estimates of the coefficient, b, are not inconsistent with market efficiency. As was previously discussed there is no guarantee that an estimate as robust as the BLS estimate of Z_{t-1} is available at the end of period $t - 1$.

The estimated coefficients and t-values shown in table 4 permit us to reject the hypothesis that the B'_{t-1} is a subset of B^{cm}_{t-1}. It is of some interest to note that the composite forecasts weights the capital market and ARIMA forecasts about equally which suggests that capital markets utilize more than the past values of Z_t in forming expectations. Additionally, if the coefficients are not significantly different from zero when Z_{t-1} is excluded from B'_{t-1} it may be inferred that Z_{t-1} is an important input in assessing the expected value of $\tilde{Z}_t$.

The ratio of mean squared forecasting errors computed for Z_{t-1} excluded from B'_{t-1} are enumerated in table 5.

The results of table 5 are very similar to those of table 3 when Z_{t-1} is included in B'_{t-1}. Although capital markets do slightly better in all the periods, the difference in performance is far from dramatic.

When Z_{t-1} is excluded from B'_{t-1} capital market efficiency implies that B'_{t-1} is a subset of B^{cm}_{t-1} since $Z_1, Z_2, \ldots, Z_{t-2}$ are clearly knowable at the

Table 4
Tests of B'_{t-1} as a Subset of B^{cm}_{t-1} where $Z_{t-1} \in B'_{t-1}$

Time Period	Estimated Coefficient	t-value from Zero	R-squared
1/1958–6/1971	0.4789	5.59	0.1618
1/1958–12/1967	0.4394	4.41	0.1394
1/1958–9/1964	0.4562	3.98	0.1637
10/1964–6/1971	0.5231	4.02	0.1663
1/1958–12/1962	0.4074	3.07	0.1356
1/1963–12/1967	0.4861	2.67	0.1064
1/1968–6/1971	0.5232	2.79	0.1568

Table 5
Tests of Statistical Efficiency for $Z_{t-1} \notin B'_{t-1}$

Time Period	Ratio of Mean Squared Forecasting Errors
2/1958–6/1971	0.9175
2/1958–12/1967	0.8918
2/1958–9/1964	0.8705
10/1964–6/1971	0.9830
2/1958–12/1962	0.7909
1/1963–12/1967	1.0593
1/1968–6/1971	1.0310

Table 6
Test of B'_{t-1} as a Subset of B^{cm}_{t-1} When $Z_{t-1} \notin B'_{t-1}$

Time Period	Estimated Coefficient	t-Value from Zero	R-squared
2/1958–6/1971	0.4403	5.37	0.1520
2/1958–12/1967	0.4037	4.27	0.1331
2/1958–9/1964	0.4148	3.93	0.1618
10/1964–6/1971	0.4915	3.80	0.1514
2/1958–12/1962	0.3807	3.11	0.1410
1/1963–12/1967	0.4577	2.48	0.0933
1/1968–6/1971	0.4529	2.49	0.1290

end of period $t - 1$. Thus the coefficients estimated for this case should not differ significantly from zero. The estimates, t-values and R-squareds are detailed in table 6.

The estimated coefficients listed in table 6 are all significant at a 5 percent confidence level. Thus we can reject the hypothesis that capital markets are efficient in predicting price level changes since the evidence does not support the implication that B'_{t-1} is a subset of B^{cm}_{t-1}. Stated differently, the above evidence suggests that capital markets ignore information in setting prices. This is a very disturbing result since it is inconsistent with a large body of evidence for common stock and other capital market instruments.[16] As a result, it seems likely that there may be other factors that account for these results. Two possible explanations are limitations in our proxy of the rate of inflation and misspecification of capital market expectations. In fact we have a priori reasons to believe

---

[16]Note Fama's conclusion that 'the evidence in support of the efficient markets model is extensive, and (somewhat uniquely in economics) contradictory evidence is sparse'. See Fama (1970, p. 415).

that both of these have occurred. Data limitations were discussed in section 4 and it was noted that our proxy for the rate of inflation is likely to exhibit autocorrelation not present in the true variable. Also, there is no theoretical rationale for a constant expected real rate. Indeed, Mundell has presented a framework that suggests that the expected real rate is inversely related to the expected rate of inflation.[17] Both of these explanations are subject to empirical testing and are investigated in the next section.

8. Data Limitations and the Behavior of the Equilibrium Real Rate

If the proxy variable of the rate of inflation exhibits autocorrelation that is not present in the true variable, the forecasting errors of an efficient capital market would not be independent of the contemporaneous difference between the ARIMA and capital market forecasts. This is simply a result of the fact that capital markets will ignore the 'false' information embedded in the time series of the proxy variable. Furthermore, if the forecasting errors of capital markets are computed relative to the proxy variable they should exhibit autocorrelation. Therefore, the importance of this limitation can be investigated by estimating the autocorrelation of the forecasting errors made by capital markets. These autocorrelations estimated during the period 1/1958–6/1971 are listed for 12 lags in table 7.

Checking the entire set of estimates for significance via the Q-statistic results in a value of 12.7 which is below the critical value of 16.0 for a 90 percent significance level. Thus the evidence does not allow us to reject the hypothesis that the computed forecasting errors are random. The estimate at lag 12, however, is large relative to its standard error. One explanation of this is sampling of a few items, e.g., college tuition, at annual intervals. In other words, the failure to confirm market efficiency may be due to spurious seasonality.[18] While it is difficult to specify the amount of bias induced by sampling some items annually, the potential importance of this bias may be investigated by

---

[17] See Mundell (1963). Kessel and Alchian (1962, p. 528) who makes the same point state:

'The expectation that the cost of holding monetary assets will increase relative to that of real assets implies that the stock of money and other monetary assets is in excess of the desired stocks. Alternatively, the market value of the monetary assets of a community is in excess of the new present worth of the net income stream that these assets are now expected to generate. For real assets the converse is the case. Therefore, there is a community-wide attempt to shift from monetary to real assets. This attempt to substitute real for monetary assets produces, through a complex chain of substitutions, a rise in real asset prices, a rise in the money rate of interest, a fall in the real rate, and a decrease in bond prices.'

[18] We are indebted to an anonymous referee for suggesting this part of the analysis.

Table 7
Autocorrelation of Capital Market Forecasting Errors, 1/1958–6/1971

Lag	Estimate	Std. Error	Lag	Estimate	Std. Error
1	0.10	0.08	7	−0.10	0.08
2	0.12	0.08	8	−0.01	0.08
3	0.01	0.08	9	0.04	0.08
4	−0.03	0.08	10	0.03	0.08
5	0.05	0.08	11	−0.05	0.08
6	0.08	0.08	12	0.17	0.08

conducting the empirical test with a non-seasonal moving average model of order 1. Or simply

$$E(\tilde{Z}_t | B'_{t-1}) = Z_{t-1} - \theta U_{t-1} \tag{11}$$

Empirical results for eq. (11) are reported in tables 8 through 11.

The above results are not consistent with the conclusion that the failure to confirm market efficiency is due to spurious seasonality. While the R-squareds are lower than those reported in tables 4 and 6 the estimated coefficients are approximately the same, and significant at a 5 percent confidence level, except during the subperiods 1/1963–12/1967 and 1/1968–6/1971.

Mundell has argued that the expected real rate of interest is inversely related to the expected rate of inflation, i.e., the expected real rate falls (rises) with increases (decreases) in the expected rate of inflation. Under these conditions the computed forecasting error of capital markets will equal the true forecasting error plus an amount due to misspecification of the forecast of capital markets (due to misspecifying the expected real rate). Similarly the observed differences between the capital markets and ARIMA forecasts will also include

Table 8
Test of Statistical Efficiency with Non-seasonal ARIMA Model When $Z_{t-1} \in B'_{t-1}$

Time Period	Ratio of Mean Squared Forecasting Errors
1/1958–6/1971	0.9988
1/1958–12/1967	1.0168
1/1958–9/1964	1.0213
10/1964–6/1971	0.9706
1/1958–12/1962	0.9826
1/1963–12/1967	1.0666
1/1968–6/1971	0.9328

Table 9
Test of B'_{t-1} as a Subset of B^{cm}_{t-1} with Non-seasonal ARIMA Model When $Z_{t-1} \in B'_{t-1}$

Time Period	Estimated Coefficient	t-Value from Zero	R-squared
1/1958–6/1971	0.5035	3.39	0.0662
1/1958–12/1967	0.4870	2.81	0.0617
1/1958–9/1964	0.5165	2.57	0.0752
10/1964–6/1971	0.5418	2.42	0.0676
1/1958–12/1962	0.4798	2.00	0.0630
1/1963–12/1967	0.4481	0.89	0.0133
1/1968–6/1971	0.2276	0.71	0.0120

Table 10
Test of Statistical Efficiency with Non-seasonal ARIMA Model When $Z_{t-1} \notin B'_{t-1}$

Time Period	Ratio of Mean Squared Forecasting Errors
2/1958–6/1971	0.9703
2/1958–12/1967	0.9941
2/1958–9/1964	1.0008
10/1964–6/1971	0.9351
2/1958–12/1962	0.9603
1/1963–12/1967	1.0393
1/1968–6/1971	0.8891

Table 11
Test of B'_{t-1} as a Subset of B^{cm}_{t-1} with Non-seasonal ARIMA Model When $Z_{t-1} \notin B'_{t-1}$

Time Period	Estimated Coefficient	t-Value	R-squared
2/1958–6/1971	0.4463	3.11	0.0568
2/1958–12/1967	0.4304	2.57	0.0528
2/1958–9/1964	0.4745	2.45	0.0698
10/1964–6/1971	0.4805	2.23	0.0577
2/1958–12/1962	0.4546	2.00	0.0633
1/1963–12/1967	0.2921	0.59	0.0057
1/1968–6/1971	0.1751	0.59	0.0082

a specification error. If the ARIMA forecasts track market forecasts the specification error will not be independent of the ARIMA forecasts, i.e., the specification error will be positive (negative) when the ARIMA forecasts are high (low). It follows then that the computed forecasting error will be positively related to observed differences and therefore capital markets will appear to be ignoring information present in B'_{t-1}.

This proposition is investigated by segregating the computed forecasting errors according to the predictions of the ARIMA model. The segregation is done by classifying the errors according to ARIMA forecasts above or below the average rate of inflation for the period 1/1953–7/1971. If the expected real rate was constant both distributions of forecasting errors should have a mean value of zero. On the other hand, if Mundell's hypothesis is more robust, when the ARIMA forecast is above the average the computed errors will be positive and negative for forecasts below the average. Summary statistics estimated over the period 1/1958–6/1971 are shown in table 12.

The above results support Mundell's hypothesis vis-à-vis the constant expected real rate since both t-values are significant at a 95 percent confidence level. It appears then that this may be an important explanation of the results reported in the previous section and deserves further consideration.

9. Tests for a Changing Equilibrium Real Rate

The evidence of table 12 supports the contention that market expectations are misspecified by assuming a constant expected real rate for the sample interval. Thus tests of market efficiency should incorporate this factor. The most appealing approach to this problem is to derive estimates of the expected real rate

Table 12
Summary Statistics for the Distribution of Forecasting Errors Given the ARIMA Forecasts

---

(A) ARIMA forecast > Average rate of inflation

$[(\tilde{Z}_t - E(\tilde{Z}_t | B^{cm}_{t-1})] = 0.00033$
Standard deviation = 0.001735
No. of observations = 84
t-value from zero = 1.761

(B) ARIMA forecast < Average rate of inflation

$[(\tilde{Z}_t - E(\tilde{Z}_t | B^{cm}_{t-1})] = -0.00056$
Standard deviation = 0.001712
No. of observations = 78
t-value from zero = −2.895

---

from a functional relationship that is specified a priori. Unfortunately, very little is known about the determinants of the expected real rate and therefore this approach is not operational. An alternative procedure is to estimate the expected real rate for each period from the sequence of realized rates. In short, to set the expected real rate, $E(\tilde{\iota}_t)$, equal to the conditional expectation evaluated over the history of realized values, $i_1, i_2, \ldots, i_{t-1}$.[19] It should be recognized that this will result in naive estimates of $E(\tilde{\iota}_t)$ but may improve upon the approximation of the constant equilibrium real rate assumption. Thus capital market expectations of the rate of inflation are approximated by

$$E(\tilde{Z}_t | B_{t-1}^{cm}) = 1.0/(1.0 + E(\tilde{\iota}_t | B_{t-1}^t) - I_t) - 1.0 \tag{12}$$

where $E(\tilde{\iota}_t | B_{t-1}^t)$ is the expected real rate of interest given the past values of $\tilde{\iota}_t; i_1, i_2, \ldots, i_{t-1}$. It may appear that predictions derived from eq. (12) will necessarily subsume the predictions of the ARIMA model. This is not the case, however, since eq. (12) includes both I_t and $E(\tilde{\iota}_t | B_{t-1}^t)$. If capital markets are inefficient with regard to the history of $\tilde{Z}$, there is no guarantee that eq. (12) will either outperform the ARIMA model or predictions derived from the constant expected real rate assumption. On the other hand, if $E(\tilde{\iota}_t)$ is not a constant and the capital markets are efficient with regard to Z_1 thru Z_{t-1} the predictions of eq. (12) should perform better than those derived from the constant expected real rate assumption.

The ARIMA model used to generate the estimates of the expected real rate for each period is

$$E(\tilde{\iota}_t | B_{t-1}^t) = i_{t-12} - \theta_1 U_{t-1} - \theta_2 U_{t-2} - \theta_3 U_{t-3} - \Delta_1 U_{t-12}$$

$$+ \theta_1 \Delta_1 U_{t-13} + \theta_2 \Delta_1 U_{t-14} + \theta_3 \Delta_1 U_{t-15} \tag{13}$$

The estimated autocorrelations for the raw series and seasonal differenced series are listed in table 13 for the sample period 1/1953–6/1971. Summary statistics for the estimated model are listed in table 14 for the same period. The procedure used to estimate the parameters of the model and generate estimates of the expected real rate is identical to that used for $E(\tilde{Z}_t | B_{t-1}')$.

The empirical tests for the expected real rate equal to the ARIMA forecasts [eq. (13)] are set forth in tables 15, 16, 17 and 18. Tables 15 and 16 are a comparison of the ARIMA forecasts of the rate of inflation and capital market forecasts under the assumption that Z_{t-1} is known at the end of $t - 1$. Tables 17 and 18 are for Z_{t-1} excluded from B_{t-1}' and B_{t-1}^t.

The above results are much more consistent with efficient capital markets

---

[19]Nelson (1972a) uses this approach to test competing theories of the term structure of interest rates.

Table 13
Autocorrelations

Lags													Est. Std. Error for Row
Real rate of interest, 1/1953–6/1971													
1–12	0.11	0.12	−0.01	−0.01	−0.02	−0.03	−0.07	0.06	0.10	0.10	0.03	0.20	0.07
13–24	0.08	−0.01	0.15	−0.01	0.03	−0.01	−0.11	0.04	0.09	−0.02	0.10	0.10	0.07
25–36	0.04	−0.07	−0.01	−0.04	−0.08	−0.10	−0.10	0.02	0.14	−0.03	0.02	0.18	
Seasonal differenced real rate of interest, 1/1953–6/1971													
1–12	0.06	0.12	−0.20	−0.03	0.00	−0.00	−0.02	0.04	0.08	0.05	−0.08	−0.39	0.07
13–24	0.01	−0.06	0.25	0.03	0.12	0.04	−0.04	−0.03	−0.04	−0.04	0.08	−0.13	0.07
25–36	0.00	−0.15	−0.12	−0.07	0.00	−0.05	0.06	0.07	0.07	−0.06	−0.08	0.04	0.09

Table 14
Parameter Estimates and Summary Statistics, 1/1953–6/1971[a]

Lags													Est. Std. Error
Autocorrelation of residuals[b]													
1–12	-0.01	-0.00	0.02	0.03	0.08	0.08	0.08	-0.01	0.05	0.11	-0.02	0.02	0.07
13–24	0.05	-0.02	0.16	0.03	0.11	0.07	0.06	-0.09	0.03	0.02	0.06	-0.12	0.07
25–36	0.03	-0.03	-0.09	0.03	0.04	-0.05	0.08	-0.02	0.08	-0.08	-0.03	-0.02	0.08
Cross correlation of lagged residuals and $\tilde{i}_t$													
1–12	0.10	0.09	-0.12	-0.07	0.06	0.04	0.01	-0.05	-0.01	0.11	0.01	-0.58	
13–24	-0.03	-0.15	0.19	-0.01	0.06	-0.00	-0.02	-0.05	-0.02	-0.06	0.04	-0.10	
25–36	0.00	-0.05	-0.15	-0.03	-0.09	-0.05	0.01	0.02	0.07	-0.07	-0.06	0.04	
Cross correlation of $\tilde{i}_t$ and future residuals													
1–12	-0.07	-0.01	-0.07	0.00	-0.03	0.01	0.04	0.04	-0.00	0.10	-0.06	0.09	
13–24	0.04	0.01	0.18	0.02	0.07	0.09	-0.00	-0.05	-0.02	0.03	0.07	-0.10	
25–36	0.03	-0.11	0.00	-0.02	0.10	-0.02	0.11	0.03	0.04	-0.08	-0.04	-0.01	

[a] Estimated parameters: $\theta_1 = -0.105862$, $\theta_2 = -0.247418$, $\theta_3 = 0.126544$, $\Delta_1 = 0.919650$; t-values relative to zero: $t_{\theta 1} = -1.54$, $t_{\theta 2} = -3.73$, $t_{\theta 3} = 1.86$, $t_{\Delta 1} = 55.69$; Adj. coefficient of determination = 0.493; F-ratio = 52.0; $D.F. = 4$ and 206.

[b] Q-statistics; 8 $D.F. = 7.6$; 20 $D.F. = 24.8$; 32 $D.F. = 32.5$.

Table 15
Tests of Statistical Efficiency for $Z_{t-1} \in B'_{t-1}$ and B^t_{t-1}

Time Period	Ratio of Mean Squared Forecasting Errors
1/1958–6/1971	0.8986
1/1958–12/1967	0.8825
1/1958–9/1964	0.8957
10/1964–6/1971	0.9028
1/1958–12/1962	0.8594
1/1963–12/1967	0.9173
1/1968–6/1971	0.9835

Table 16
Tests of B'_{t-1} as a Subset of B^{cm}_{t-1} When $Z_{t-1} \in B'_{t-1}$ and B^t_{t-1}

Time Period	Estimated Coefficient	t-Value from Zero	R-squared
1/1958–6/1971	0.3103	2.210	0.0293
1/1958–12/1967	0.2066	1.200	0.0118
1/1958–9/1964	0.2783	1.45	0.0255
10/1964–6/1971	0.2970	1.43	0.0247
1/1958–12/1962	0.2606	1.19	0.0230
1/1963–12/1967	−0.0678	−0.18	0.0005
1/1968–6/1971	0.3102	1.10	0.0280

Table 17
Tests of Statistical Efficiency for $Z_{t-1} \notin B'_{t-1}$ and $Z_{t-1} \notin B^t_{t-1}$

Time Period	Ratio of Mean Squared Forecasting Errors
2/1958–6/1971	0.8440
2/1958–12/1967	0.8235
2/1958–9/1964	0.8256
10/1964–6/1971	0.8695
2/1958–12/1962	0.7749
1/1963–12/1967	0.9040
1/1968–6/1971	0.9345

Table 18

Test of B'_{t-1} as a Subset of B^{cm}_{t-1} When $Z_{t-1} \notin B'_{t-1}$ and $Z_{t-1} \notin B^t_{t-1}$

Time Period	Estimated Coefficient	t-Value from Zero	R-squared
2/1958–6/1971	0.2356	1.82	0.0201
2/1958–12/1967	0.1042	0.66	0.0036
2/1958–9/1964	0.1731	1.00	0.0123
10/1964–6/1971	0.2580	1.34	0.0216
2/1958–12/1962	0.1560	0.79	0.0103
1/1963–12/1967	−0.1390	−0.38	0.0024
1/1968–6/1971	0.2202	0.84	0.0163

than those enumerated in tables 3, 4, 5 and 6. In particular, only one of the estimated coefficients is significantly different from zero at a 95 percent confidence interval, for the case of Z_{t-1} included in B'_{t-1} and B'_{t-1} during the period 1/1958–6/1971, and this is not inconsistent with market efficiency. However, the evidence on balance favors the conclusion that B'_{t-1} is not a subset of the constructed information set B^{cm}_{t-1}.[20] The importance of the above results is they demonstrate that improving the approximation of the expected real rate, leads to empirical results much more consistent with the efficient markets model than the assumption that the expected real rate is constant. In summary, a constant expected real rate does not seem to be a very robust approximation of real world capital market behavior.

10. Conclusions

The major conclusion of this study is that the behavior of nominal interest rates on 1-month Treasury Bills is not consistent with the joint hypothesis that (1) the expected real rate was constant during the period 1/1958–6/1971, and (2) that capital markets are efficient with regard to predicting price level changes. Two explanations of the results were discussed and investigated; spurious autocorrelation in the variable used as a proxy for the rate of inflation and changes in the expected real rate of interest. Some evidence of spurious autocorrelation was found in the proxy variable, but the level was not important enough to be statistically significant. In contrast, we were able to reject the hypothesis that the computed forecasting errors of capital markets were independent of the expected rate of inflation. Moreover, the distribution of forecasting errors

---

[20] B^{cm}_{t-1} is constructed in the sense that we have forced the expected real rate to equal the conditional expectation given the past series of realized values.

conformed to Mundell's hypothesis that the excepted real rate is inversely related to the rate of inflation. When this result is embedded in our empirical tests, by setting the expected real rate equal to the forecasts of an ARIMA model, the results are much closer to the implications of the efficient markets model. In more positive terms, the failure to confirm market efficiency appears to be the result of naive estimates of the expected real rate. In summary, our results conflict with Fama's conclusion that the expected real rate is constant. Perhaps this is attributable to the fact that a methodology incorporating the ARIMA models is inherently more robust than simple linear regression. More rigorous tests of market efficiency and price level changes are dependent upon a more complete understanding of the determinants of the expected real rate.

References

Bildersee, J., n.d. Some new bond indexes extended and expanded results (Rodney L. White Center for Financial Research, University of Pennsylvania, Philadelphia).

Fama, E., 1970, Efficient capital markets: A review of theory and empirical work, *Journal of Finance*, May.

Fama, E., 1975, Short-term interest rates as predictors of inflation, *American Economic Review*, June.

Kessel, R. and A. Alchian, 1962, Effects of inflation, *Journal of Political Economy*, Dec.

Mundell, R., 1963, Inflation and real interest, *Journal of Political Economy*, June.

Nelson, C., 1972a, The term structure of interest rates (Basic Books, New York).

Nelson, C., 1972b, The prediction performance of the FRB-MIT-PENN model of the U.S. economy, *American Economic Review*, Dec.

Nelson, C., 1973, Applied time series analysis for managerial forecasting (Holden-Day, San Francisco).

Pyle, D., 1972, Observed price expectations and interest rates, *Review of Economics and Statistics*, Aug.

Roll, R., 1972, Interest rates on monetary assets and commodity price index changes, *Journal of Finance*, May.

Wallace, W., 1972, Measuring price changes: A study of the price indexes (Federal Reserve Bank of Richmond).

4

Capital Markets: Theory and Evidence

Michael C. Jensen

1. Introduction

This paper reviews the development of modern capital market theory[1] and the empirical evidence bearing on this theory. There are two main approaches to this problem: the mean-variance models following in the Markowitz tradition, and the state preference models due originally to Arrow and Debreu.[2] Both approaches are generalizations to a world of uncertainty of the work of Irving Fisher on the theory of interest. While the state preference approach is perhaps more general than the mean-variance approach and provides an elegant framework for investigating theoretical issues, it is unfortunately difficult to give it empirical content. I restrict attention here to the mean-variance models.[3]

Section 2 provides a brief review of the historical foundations of capital market theory and a statement of the assumptions and implications of the Sharpe-Lintner mean-variance model of asset pricing. A formal derivation of the model and some of its mathematical properties are outlined in the Appendix for the interested reader. Section 3 provides a review of current empirical knowledge about the process determining the structure of asset prices and returns. Section 4 reviews recent theoretical developments in this area and integrates to some extent those developments with our empirical knowledge. Section 5 contains a brief summary and the conclusions.

---

[1]That is, general equilibrium models of the determination of the prices of capital assets under conditions of uncertainty.

[2]See Markowitz [48, 49], Arrow [1], and Debreu [15].

[3]For an excellent exposition of the state-preference approach see Hirshleifer [31, 32, 33]. The "long run growth" model of Markowitz [49], Chap. 6, Latane [40], Breiman [10, 11], and Hakansson [29] is another approach to the problem of investment choice under uncertainty. See Samuelson [65] for a critique of this approach. Since empirical tests of this model are only just beginning to become available and are as yet somewhat incomplete (cf. Roll [63]), I shall not consider it here. For criticism of the mean-variance approach see Feldstein [25], Borch [9], the rejoinder by Tobin [71], and Samuelson [66], who provides a justification for the mean-variance approach as an approximation to the exact solution when distributions are "compact."

2. The Markowitz Model and the Mean-Variance Asset Pricing Model

The work of Markowitz[4] on portfolio selection resulted in a revolution in the theory of finance and laid the foundation for modern capital market theory. His treatment of investor portfolio selection as a problem of utility maximization under conditions of uncertainty is a pathbreaking contribution. Markowitz deals mainly with the special case in which investor preferences are assumed to be defined over the mean and variance of the probability distribution of single-period portfolio returns, but it is clear that he is aware of the very special nature of these assumptions. In fact, there are very few problems which have received major attention in the literature of this field in the years since the publication of his book that are not at least mentioned there.

Markowitz's treatment of the portfolio problem was almost entirely normative, but other economists began almost immediately to extract positive implications from his approach. The two major directions of these early efforts were (1) Tobin's work[5] utilizing the foundations of portfolio theory to draw implications regarding the demand for cash balances, and (2) the general equilibrium models of asset prices derived by Treynor, Sharpe, Lintner, Mossin, and Fama.[6] Each of these models is an investigation of the implications of the normative Markowitz model for the equilibrium structure of asset prices. They all involve either explicitly or implicitly the following assumptions:

1.   All investors are single-period expected utility of terminal wealth maximizers who choose among alternative portfolios on the basis of mean and variance (or standard deviation) of return.[7]
2.   All investors can borrow or lend an unlimited amount at an exogenously given risk-free rate of interest R_F, and there are no restrictions on short sales of any asset.[8]
3.   All investors have identical subjective estimates of the means, variances, and covariances of return among all assets.
4.   All assets are perfectly divisible and perfectly liquid, i.e., all assets are marketable and there are no transactions costs.
5.   There are no taxes.

---

[4]In [48, 49].

[5][72].

[6][74], [67], [42, 43], [56], and [21, 22], respectively.

[7]Note that representing preferences in terms of mean and standard deviation yields identical results to those obtained with a mean-variance representation.

[8]Sharpe [67] is an exception, since he deals with the case where no short sales are allowed.

6. All investors are price takers.
7. The quantities of all assets are given.

Given these assumptions, the previously mentioned authors demonstrate that the equilibrium expected return, $E(\tilde{R}_j)$, on any asset j will be given by

$$E(\tilde{R}_j) = R_F + \lambda \, \frac{\text{cov}(\tilde{R}_j, \tilde{R}_M)}{\sigma(\tilde{R}_M)} \qquad (1)$$

where R_F is the riskless rate of interest, $\lambda = [E(\tilde{R}_M) - R_F]/\sigma(\tilde{R}_M)$ is the market risk premium per unit of risk, $E(\tilde{R}_M)$ is the expected return on the market portfolio (which consists of an investment in every asset outstanding in proportion to its total value), $\sigma(\tilde{R}_M)$ is the standard deviation of return on the market portfolio, and $\text{cov}(\tilde{R}_j, \tilde{R}_M)$ is the covariance between the return on asset j and the return on the market portfolio. The tildes denote random variables. We now provide a fairly simple derivation of these results and the economic rationale behind them.[9]

A Simple Derivation of the Model

Figure 1 gives a geometric presentation of the Markowitz mean-variance model. Letting $\sigma(\tilde{R})$ be the standard deviation of future return, the shaded area in Figure 1 represents all possible combinations of risk and return available from investments in risk-bearing securities. The portfolios lying on the boundary *ABMD* represent the set of mean standard deviation (or mean-variance) efficient portfolios (since they all represent possible investments yielding maximum expected return for given standard deviation and minimum standard deviation for given expected return).

As Tobin has shown,[10] the normality of security returns and the existence of risk aversion on the part of the investor are sufficient to yield a family of positively-sloping convex indifference curves (represented by I_1, I_2, I_3) in the mean standard deviation plane of Figure 1. The shaded area in Figure 1 represents the opportunity set available to the investor in the absence of a riskless asset, and the upper boundary of this set *ABMD* represents the set of efficient portfolios.[11] An investor limited only to investments in *risky assets* whose

---

[9]An alternative and more formal derivation of the results and some additional discussion of the properties of the model are provided in the Appendix.

[10]In [72].

[11]See Merton [52] for an analytic discussion of the properties of the efficient set.

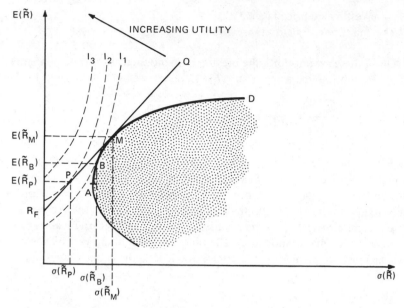

Figure 1. The Maximization of Investor Utility Given the Existence of a Risk-
Free Asset

preferences are summarized by the indifference map shown in Figure 1 maximizes his expected utility by investing in portfolio B, which has expected
return, $E(\tilde{R}_B)$, standard deviation of return, $\sigma(\tilde{R}_B)$, and yields the investor a
level of expected utility denoted by I_1.

Portfolio B portrayed in Figure 1 represents an optimal solution to the
portfolio problem only in the case where investment is restricted to risky assets.
Let us now assume the existence of a *risk-free asset F*, yielding a certain future
return R_F portrayed in Figure 1.[12] An investor faced with the possibility of an
investment in such a risk-free asset, as well as in a risky asset (or risky portfolio),
can construct a combined portfolio of the two assets which allows him to reach
any combination of risk and return lying along a straight line connecting the
two assets in the mean standard deviation plane.[13] Clearly, all portfolios lying

---

[12]Such an instrument might be cash (yielding no positive monetary return), an insured
savings account, or a non-coupon-bearing government bond having a maturity date coincident
with the investor's horizon date. In the latter case, of course, the investor can be assured of
realizing the yield to maturity with certainty if he holds the bond to maturity. Since we
have assumed the investor will not change his portfolio in the interim period, any intermediate fluctuations in price do not present him with risk. We are ignoring the problems
associated with changes in the general price level and shall continue to do so in the remainder
of the paper.

[13]Cf. Tobin [72].

below point M along $ABMD$ are inefficient, since any point on the line $R_F M$ given by

$$E(\tilde{R}) = R_F + \frac{E(\tilde{R}_M) - R_F}{\sigma(\tilde{R}_M)} \sigma(\tilde{R}) \qquad \sigma(\tilde{R}) < \sigma(\tilde{R}_M)$$

represents a feasible solution. Thus the investor may distribute his funds between portfolio M and security F such that his combined portfolio, call it P, yields him $E(\tilde{R}_P)$, $\sigma(\tilde{R}_P)$, and maximum utility of $I_2 > I_1$. In addition, if the investor can borrow as well as lend at the riskless rate R_F, the set of feasible portfolios represented by the line $R_F M$ extends beyond point M.

Under the assumptions outlined above we can see that *all* investors would hold portfolios lying on the line $R_F MQ$ in Figure 1 and thus would attempt to purchase *only* those assets in portfolio M and the riskless security F.[14] The market for capital assets will therefore be out of equilibrium unless M is the "market portfolio," that is, a portfolio which contains every asset exactly in proportion to that asset's fraction of the total value of all assets. In equilibrium, all investors who select *ex ante* efficient portfolios will have mean standard deviation combinations which lie along the line $R_F MQ$, their individual location determined by their degree of risk aversion.

Most important, however, is the result that in equilibrium the expected return on any *efficient portfolio P* will be linearly related to the expected return on the market portfolio in the following manner:

$$E(\tilde{R}_P) = R_F + \lambda \sigma(\tilde{R}_P) \qquad (1a)$$

where from the geometry of Figure 1 we see that $\lambda = [E(\tilde{R}_M) - R_F]/\sigma(\tilde{R}_M)$. Our problem now is to derive the equation for the equilibrium expected returns on an *individual* asset j.[15] If we let h_j be the fraction of the investor's portfolio invested in the jth asset and $1 - \Sigma h_j$ the fraction invested in the riskless asset, the return on his portfolio P can be expressed as

$$\tilde{R}_P = \Sigma h_j \tilde{R}_j + (1 - \Sigma h_j) R_F$$

Further, as long as P is an efficient portfolio lying along the line $R_F MQ$ we can express $\tilde{R}_P$ as

$$\tilde{R}_P = \alpha \tilde{R}_M + (1 - \alpha) R_F$$

---

[14] This is Tobin's well-known separation theorem. *Ibid.*

[15] I am indebted to John Long for this derivation.

where $\tilde{R}_M = \Sigma X_j \tilde{R}_j$ is the return on the market portfolio, $X_j = h_j/\Sigma h_i$ is the fraction of the market portfolio invested in asset j, and $\alpha = \Sigma h_j$. Letting h_j^* represent the optimal investment in the jth asset we can express the expected return and standard deviation of return for any investor's optimal portfolio P (which of course is efficient) as

$$E(\tilde{R}_P) = \Sigma_j h_j^* E(\tilde{R}_j) + (1 - \Sigma_j h_j^*)R_F = \alpha E(\tilde{R}_M) + (1 - \alpha)R_F$$

$$\sigma(\tilde{R}_P) = [\Sigma_j \Sigma_k h_j^* h_k^* \text{cov}(\tilde{R}_j, \tilde{R}_k)]^{1/2} = \alpha\sigma(\tilde{R}_M)$$

where the last equality follows simply from the fact noted above that $\tilde{R}_P$ can be expressed as a linear combination of $\tilde{R}_M$ and R_F.

Now, consider the rate of change of expected return (in equilibrium) in the investor's *optimal* portfolio P as he increases the amount invested in any individual asset h_j by decreasing the amount invested in the riskless asset. To do this we take the derivative of the investor's preference function $U[E(\tilde{R}_P), \sigma(\tilde{R}_P)]$ with respect to h_j and recognize that at the optimum the rate of change of utility must be zero, so at $h_j = h_j^*$ for all j we have

$$\frac{\partial U}{\partial E(\tilde{R}_P)} \cdot \frac{\partial E(\tilde{R}_P)}{\partial h_j} + \frac{\partial U}{\partial \sigma(\tilde{R}_P)} \cdot \frac{\partial \sigma(\tilde{R}_P)}{\partial h_j} = 0$$

Rearranging this and recognizing from Figure 1 and the arguments presented above that at the optimum the slope of the investor's indifference curve $-[\partial U/\partial\sigma(\tilde{R}_P)]/[\partial U/\partial E(\tilde{R}_P)]$ must equal λ, the slope of the capital market line, we have

$$\frac{\partial E(\tilde{R}_P)}{\partial h_j} = \lambda \frac{\partial \sigma(\tilde{R}_P)}{\partial h_j}$$

Substituting for the derivatives obtained from the definitions of $E(\tilde{R}_P)$ and $\sigma(\tilde{R}_P)$ into this expression we obtain

$$E(\tilde{R}_j) - R_F = \lambda \frac{\text{cov}(\tilde{R}_j, \tilde{R}_M)}{\sigma(\tilde{R}_M)} \tag{1b}$$

where at the optimum,

$$\partial\sigma(\tilde{R}_P)/\partial h_j = \Sigma_k h_k^* \text{cov}(\tilde{R}_j, \tilde{R}_k)/\sigma(\tilde{R}_P) = \text{cov}(\tilde{R}_j, \Sigma_k h_k^* \tilde{R}_k)/\sigma(\tilde{R}_P)$$

$$= \alpha \, \text{cov}(\tilde{R}_j, \tilde{R}_M)/\alpha\sigma(\tilde{R}_M)$$

since $\Sigma_k h_k^* \tilde{R}_k = \alpha\tilde{R}_M$. Solving (1b) for $E(\tilde{R}_j)$ then provides the desired result (1).

Thus the equilibrium expected return on any asset[16] is equal to the riskless rate of interest plus a risk premium given by the product of the market risk premium λ and the risk of the jth asset as measured by $\text{cov}(\tilde{R}_j, \tilde{R}_M/\sigma(\tilde{R}_M))$. Although investors take the variance (or equivalently the standard deviation) of their *portfolio* returns as an appropriate measure of risk, these results imply that the appropriate measure of the risk of any *individual* asset is its covariance with the market portfolio, $\text{cov}(\tilde{R}_j, \tilde{R}_M)$, and not its own variance, $\sigma^2(\tilde{R}_j)$. Diversification can eliminate most of the effects of an asset's own variance on the variance (or standard deviation) of a portfolio[17] but cannot eliminate the effects of an asset's covariances with all other assets in the portfolio. In addition, note that $\text{cov}(\tilde{R}_j, \tilde{R}_M)$ is proportional to the marginal impact of the jth asset on the standard deviation of the market portfolio, i.e., $\partial\sigma(\tilde{R}_M)/\partial X_j = \text{cov}(\tilde{R}_j, \tilde{R}_M)/\sigma(\tilde{R}_M)$, where X_j is the weight that asset j receives in the market portfolio.[18] Thus rewriting (1) in terms of $\partial\sigma(\tilde{R}_M)/\partial X_j = \text{cov}(\tilde{R}_j, \tilde{R}_M)/\sigma(\tilde{R}_M)$ and defining λ as $[E(\tilde{R}_M) - R_F]/\sigma(\tilde{R}_M)$ we see that in equilibrium the expected return on an asset is linearly related to its marginal contribution to the total risk to be borne by society, $\sigma(\tilde{R}_M)$.

The main result of the original papers in this area is the demonstration that one can derive the individual's demand function for assets, aggregate these demands to obtain the equilibrium prices (or expected returns) of all assets, and then eliminate all the individual utility information to obtain market equilibrium prices (or expected returns) solely as a function of potentially measurable market parameters.[19] Thus the model becomes testable. In addition, the model may be used to address many important practical issues in a number of areas, including valuation theory, the determination of the "cost of capital," corporate

---

[16]Alternatively (as demonstrated in the Appendix) one can express the equilibrium conditions in terms of the price of each asset, V_j, at time 0 as

$$V_j = \left(\frac{1}{1 + R_F}\right)[E(\tilde{D}_j) - \theta\,\text{cov}(\tilde{D}_j, \tilde{D}_M)] \qquad (2)$$

where $E(\tilde{D}_j)$ is the total dollar payoff on asset j at time 1, $\tilde{D}_M = \displaystyle\sum_{i=1}^{N} \tilde{D}_j$ is the total dollar payoff on all assets at time 1, $\text{cov}(\tilde{D}_j, \tilde{D}_M)$ is the covariance between the total dollar returns on asset j and the total dollar returns on all assets, and $\theta = [E(\tilde{D}_M) - (1 + R_F)V_M]/\sigma^2(\tilde{D}_M)$ is the market "price" per unit of risk. Thus the current equilibrium price of any asset is the certainty equivalent of the expected total dollar outcome at time 1 (the term in brackets) discounted back to the present at the riskless rate of interest.

[17]Note that the variance $\sigma^2(\tilde{R}_j)$ does affect $\text{cov}(\tilde{R}_j, \tilde{R}_M)$ to some extent since $\text{cov}(\tilde{R}_j, \tilde{R}_M) = \Sigma\, X_i\,\text{cov}(\tilde{R}_j, \tilde{R}_i)$ and one of these N terms is $X_j\sigma^2(\tilde{R}_j)$. Hence the effect is on the order of $1/N$, and given positive dependence among most asset returns the effect of an asset's own variance on its risk will be small relative to the effects of the other $N - 1$ covariances. This is the essence of what are commonly called "portfolio effects."

[18]Cf. Fama [20, 21].

[19]Cf. Appendix.

investment decisions, governmental cost benefit analysis, and the term structure of interest rates.[20]

3. Empirical Tests of the Asset Pricing Model

Evidence from Mutual Fund Returns

The Sharpe-Lintner asset pricing model has received widespread attention in the literature in the past five years. Most of the early empirical evidence bearing on the model did not represent direct tests, but rather emanated primarily from attempts to use the asset pricing model to derive portfolio performance evaluation models. Treynor, Sharpe, and Jensen all derived such portfolio evaluation models and applied them to the historical evidence on mutual funds.[21] The evidence presented by Sharpe and Jensen[22] indicated that the returns on open-end mutual funds were positively related to the covariance between the fund returns and the returns on a market index used as a proxy for the market portfolio. As such they provided some indications that the model as given by (1) showed potential promise as a description of the process generating the returns on assets (if one was willing to accept the hypothesis that mutual fund managers were unable to systematically select undervalued securities and did not generate excessively large expenses).

Cross-sectional Tests of the Model

Most direct tests of the asset pricing model have been of the cross-sectional form. The average returns on a cross-sectional sample of securities over some time period are regressed against each security's covariance with a market index. Or, more commonly, equation (1) is rewritten as

$$E(\tilde{R}_j) = R_F + [E(\tilde{R}_M) - R_F]\beta_j \qquad (3)$$

where $\beta_j = \mathrm{cov}(\tilde{R}_j, \tilde{R}_M)/\sigma^2(\tilde{R}_M)$ is what we shall term the *covariance* (or "systematic") risk of the jth asset. Thus the risk of any security is measured

---

[20]See the following for applications of the model to these issues: Bailey and Jensen [3], Black and Scholes [7], Fama [20, 21], Hamada [28], Jensen and Long [39], Long [44, 47], Merton [53, 54], Mossin [57], and Roll [64].

[21]See [73], [68], and [36, 37], respectively.

[22]In [68] and [36, 37].

relative to the total riskiness of the market portfolio.[23] The procedure is then to estimate the cross-sectional regression

$$\bar{R}_j = \gamma_0 + \gamma_1 \hat{\beta}_j + \tilde{e}_j \tag{4}$$

where $\hat{\beta}_j$ is obtained from the regression of a time series of individual security returns on an index used as a proxy for the market portfolio. The estimated coefficients $\hat{\gamma}_0$ and $\hat{\gamma}_1$ obtained from the second-stage regression given by (4) are then compared to R_F and $\bar{R}_M - R_F$, respectively, for the time period under consideration. R_F is usually taken to be the yield to maturity of a government bond, with maturity identical to the length of the time period under examination, and $\bar{R}_M$ is the average return on the market index over the period.[24]

The first published direct test of the asset pricing model was that of Douglas[25] who regressed the returns on a large cross-sectional sample of common stocks on their own variance and on their covariance with an index constructed from the sample. For seven separate five-year periods from 1926 to 1960, the average realized return was significantly positively related to the variance of the security's returns over time but not to their covariance with the index of returns.[26] These results appear to be inconsistent with the relation given by (1), since the variance term should have a coefficient of zero.

Douglas also summarizes some unpublished results of Lintner's that also appear to be inconsistent with equation (1). Lintner estimates equation (4) for a cross section of securities over the period 1954–1963. However, he also adds another variable, $\sigma^2(\tilde{u}_j)$ [the variance of the residuals from the time-series regression given by (5)] to the cross-sectional regression. This variance should

---

[23]Note that if the returns on individual securities are linearly related to the market returns, as in

$$\tilde{R}_{jt} = a_j + b_j \tilde{R}_{Mt} + \tilde{u}_{jt} \tag{5}$$

which is the familiar market (or diagonal model), and if the usual regression assumptions on (5) are satisfied (in particular that $\text{cov}(u_{jt}, u_{it}) = 0, i \neq j$), then $\beta_j = b_j$. Also if (3) is a correct description of the expected returns, then A_j will equal $(1 - \beta_j)R_F$. Cf. Fama [22], Jensen [37], and Black, Jensen and Scholes [8] for discussions of these issues. While the sample estimates of β_j and b_j are always identically equal, this does not imply that the true parameters β_j and b_j are equal. They are equal only if the usual regression assumptions on (5) are satisfied, and the equilibrium asset pricing model implies nothing about this issue. Thus the "market" model and the asset pricing model, while often used jointly, are different models and the asset pricing model implies nothing about the validity of the market model.

[24]Arithmetic averages of annual, quarterly, or monthly returns have generally been used for both $\tilde{R}_j$ and $\tilde{R}_M$, but a number of authors have also used average continuously compounded rates as well.

[25][16].

[26]*Ibid.*, p. 22.

add nothing to the covariance measure of risk incorporated in β_j and therefore should have a zero coefficient in the regressions. In Lintner's tests it did not. The coefficient on the residual variance was positive and as significant as the β_j term (both having t values greater than six). In addition $\hat{\gamma}_0$ was much greater than R_F and $\hat{\gamma}_1$ much less than $\bar{R}_M - \bar{R}_F$.

Miller and Scholes[27] review the theory and the Douglas-Lintner evidence and replicate the Lintner results on a different body of data. They confirm his results and then provide a detailed analysis of the possible econometric difficulties involved in estimating these relationships. For example, the biases introduced by various possible misspecifications of the estimating equation include (1) failure to account adequately for the riskless rate of interest, (2) possible nonlinearity in the risk-return relation, and (3) distortions due to heteroscedasticity. However, after explicit examination of these potential biases they conclude that none of them can explain the Douglas-Lintner results, which seem to indicate that an asset's own variance is as important as (or perhaps even more important than) the asset's covariance or portfolio risk in determining its equilibrium price and expected return.

Miller and Scholes also consider the biases which could be introduced by the variables used to approximate returns and risk in the analysis. They examine both theoretically and empirically the possible bias introduced by (1) measurement errors in the risk variable, $\hat{\beta}_j$; (2) the apparent correlation between the residual risk, $\sigma^2(\tilde{u}_j)$, and the covariance risk, β_j; and (3) the utilization of an improper index as a proxy for the returns on the market portfolio. They conclude that measurement errors in $\hat{\beta}_j$ and the observed correlation between $\sigma^2(\tilde{u}_j)$ and $\hat{\beta}_j$ seem to contribute substantially to the Douglas-Lintner results—the former because of the attenuation bias caused by the measurement errors in $\hat{\beta}_j$ and the latter because of the proxying effects of $\sigma^2(\tilde{u}_j)$ for $\hat{\beta}$. However, they conclude that the improper measurement of the market portfolio returns does not seem to be causing substantial problems, and that the other two sources of difficulty are not sufficient to account for all the observed deviations from the models.

Miller and Scholes also investigate the possible difficulties which could be introduced into the empirical analysis by the presence of skewness in the return distributions and the resulting interdependence of sample moments. They show that these skewness effects could cause serious difficulties, and then demonstrate through Monte Carlo techniques that the combined effects of the measurement errors in $\hat{\beta}_j$ and the skewness difficulties could in principle cause the Douglas-Lintner effects, even if the asset pricing model and market model were a completely accurate description of the process generating security returns. While their analysis does not allow us to conclude that the observed empirical

---

[27]In [55].

results are entirely spurious, they have vividly illustrated many of the econometric difficulties involved in testing the model. As they conclude:[28]

The check tests we have used are adequate to detect the presence of bias, but
too indirect to provide reliable estimates of the "true" relations between risk and
return, and certainly not to settle the issue of whether returns really are approximately proportional to nondiversifiable, covariance risk as certain interesting
special-case versions of the mean-variance model would suggest. Hopefully,
however, more rapid progress in devising test procedures capable of answering
these questions can be made, now that attention has been called to some of the
hidden minefields along the way.

Time-series Tests of the Model

Black, Jensen, and Scholes (B-J-S)[29] present some additional tests of the
Sharpe-Lintner asset pricing model. Most previous studies used cross-sectional
tests of a form similar to (4). B-J-S derive a time-series test using procedures
similar to those employed by Jensen[30] in the evaluation of mutual fund
performance. They argue that if the market model and the asset pricing model
are both valid the *ex post* returns on securities will be generated by[31]

$$\tilde{R}_{jt} = R_{Ft}(1 - \beta_j) + \beta_j \tilde{R}_{Mt} + \tilde{e}_{jt} \tag{6}$$

If we subtract R_{Ft} from both sides of equation (6) and use primes to denote
differences between the return on any asset and the riskless rate we obtain

$$\tilde{R}'_{jt} = \beta_j \tilde{R}'_{Mt} + \tilde{e}_{jt} \tag{7}$$

which asserts that the realized risk premium on any asset for any time period is
proportional to the realized premium on the market portfolio for that time
period plus a random error term with zero expectation. The model can be tested

---

[28]*Ibid.*

[29]In [8].

[30]In [36].

[31]Note that the jump from (3), which is stated in terms of expectations to (6), which is
stated in terms of realized observations, is a non-trivial step. The conditions under which
this *ex post* formulation of the model are valid are discussed in detail in Fama [22],
Jensen [37], and B-J-S [8]. As we shall see below some such *ex post* formulation appears
to be valid.

by running the time-series regression given by (7) but allowing a constant term α_j to enter:

$$\tilde{R}'_{jt} = \alpha_j + \beta_j \tilde{R}'_{Mt} + \tilde{e}_{jt} \tag{8}$$

If the asset pricing model is valid, the intercept α_j in (8) will be zero. Thus a direct test of the model can be obtained by estimating (9) for a security over some time period and testing to see if α_j is significantly different from zero.[32] While this test is simple, it is inefficient to the extent that it makes use of information on only a single security. In order to solve this problem B-J-S perform their tests on portfolio returns over the period 1931–1965, where the portfolios are constructed so as to maximize the dispersion of their systematic risk.[33] They apply their tests to ten portfolios which contain all securities on the New York Stock Exchange in the period 1931–1965. The results indicate that the α's are non-zero and are directly related to the risk level, β. Low risk (i.e., low β) securities earn significantly more, on the average, than that predicted by the model ($\alpha > 0$) and high risk securities earn significantly less, on the average, than that predicted by the model ($\alpha < 0$).[34] These results are consistent with those found by Douglas-Lintner and Miller-Scholes regarding the slope and intercept of the cross sectional relationship between average returns and β, but there is little indication that the residual variance $\sigma^2(\tilde{e})$ contributes much to an explanation of the mean portfolio returns.[35] While the evidence

---

[32] Measurement error in the estimate of β_j causes severe difficulties with bias in the cross-sectional tests of the model. If $\tilde{\beta}_j$ in (4) contains an unbiased measurement error $\tilde{e}$, the large sample regression estimate of γ_1 in (4) is

$$\text{plim } \hat{\gamma}_1 = \frac{\gamma_1}{1 + \dfrac{\sigma^2(\tilde{e})}{S^2(\beta_j)}}$$

where $\sigma^2(\tilde{e})$ is the measurement error variance and $S^2(\beta_j)$ is the cross-sectional sample variance of the true risk parameters, β_j. Thus even for large samples, as long as $\sigma^2(\tilde{e})$ is positive, the estimated coefficient $\hat{\gamma}_1$, will be biased toward zero and $\hat{\gamma}_0$ will be biased away from its true value, R_F. However, this measurement error in β_j introduces no bias whatsoever in the time-series test obtained from (8).

[33] As B-J-S point out, it is important to construct the portfolios in a manner which avoids the introduction of selection bias. This can be accomplished by simply avoiding the use of any data for constructing the portfolios which enters into the calculation of the portfolio returns used in the test regressions.

[34] It should be emphasized that these statements apply to the averages and not to the results for every subperiod. Indeed, as we shall see, for some subperiods the exact opposite results hold.

[35] The cross-sectional squared correlation between $\bar{R}_j$ and β_j for the period 1931–1965 for the ten portfolios (see Figure 2) was 0.9914. This increased to 0.9916 when the residual variance, $\sigma^2(e_j)$, from (8) was also included in the regression. The estimated regression was

indicates that the risk parameters, β_j, are fairly stationary through time there is substantial indication that the intercepts (the α's) are not; a point to which we shall return below. All in all this evidence seems to indicate that the Sharpe-Lintner model *in its most elementary form* does not provide an adequate description of the structure of security returns.

A Two-factor Random Coefficient Model

B-J-S go on to demonstrate that the process generating the returns on individual securities seems to be well represented by a two-factor model of the form

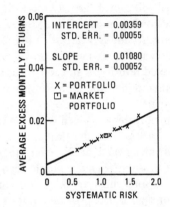

Figure 2. Average Excess Monthly Returns vs. Systematic Risk for Ten Portfolios and the Market Portfolio, 1931–1965

$$\bar{R}_j = \underset{(0.0004)}{0.0039} + \underset{(0.0004)}{0.0102}\,\beta_j + \underset{(0.3577)}{0.9706}\,\sigma^2(e_j) \qquad \bar{\beta} = 1.007,\, s(\beta) = 0.3380$$
$$\bar{\sigma}^2(e) = 0.0004,\, s(\sigma^2(e)) = 0.0004$$

While the coefficient on $\sigma^2(e_j)$ has a t value of 2.71 it explains very little of the mean returns, since the mean of $\sigma^2(\bar{e}_j)$ is only 0.0004 and its variance is only $(0.0004)^2$. Thus while the variable may be statistically significant, its *economic* significance is virtually nil since $\bar{R}_j$ is on the average equal to 0.0142, or roughly 35 times larger than the average contribution of $\sigma^2(e_j)$ to the portfolio returns. However, from one point of view this may not be the relevant test of the significance of the non-covariance risk in explaining security returns. Unless the market model holds exactly, there is no simple direct relationship between the residual variances of the individual securities and the residual variance of the portfolio in which the securities are contained. Thus one could argue that if there were a significant relationship between the residual variance and return on individual securities this relationship might well become masked by the portfolio grouping procedures and the use of $\sigma^2(e)$ for the portfolio in the cross-sectional regression summarized above. The fact that this might occur only serves to highlight how theoretically implausible are the effects of non-covariance risk since portfolios (in the form of open- and closed-end mutual funds and even diversified companies themselves) are possible investment vehicles, and a system in which these assets are valued differently from single asset claims seems extremely unnatural. We shall see, however, that Fama and MacBeth [23] provide an alternative test of the Douglas-Lintner hypothesis using the individual security residual variances and obtain similar results.

$$\tilde{R}_{jt} = (1 - \beta_j)\tilde{R}_{Zt} + \beta_j\tilde{R}_{Mt} + \tilde{e}_{jt} \tag{9}$$

where $\tilde{R}_{Zt}$ represents the return on what they have called the "beta factor," and other variables are as defined earlier. We consider some alternative (and as yet untested) theoretical justifications for this formulation in Section 4 and concern ourselves here only with the empirical results. Rearrnaging (9) into the cross-sectional regression form given by (4) we see that the coefficients γ_0 and γ_1 in (4) now become random and are given by $\tilde{\gamma}_{0t} = \tilde{R}_{Zt}$ and $\tilde{\gamma}_{1t} = \tilde{R}_{Mt} - \tilde{R}_{Zt}$, where the $\tilde{R}_{Zt}$ and $\tilde{R}_{Mt}$ are the values of the returns on the beta and the market factors over the holding period of interest.

B-J-S show that if (9) is the process generating asset returns, the cross-sectional tests of the model will provide grossly misleading significance levels of the departures of the data from the model. The reason for this is quite simple. If (9) held where the returns, $\tilde{R}_j$ and $\tilde{R}_M$, are stated in terms of the risk premiums, and if $E(\tilde{R}_Z) = 0$, then (3) or (7) would provide an accurate description of the unconditional expected returns on an asset. Thus a slightly modified version of the Sharpe-Lintner model would be consistent with (9) if $E(\tilde{R}'_Z)$ were zero. However, for a particular cross section $\tilde{R}_{Zt}$ will be a constant. Thus if one runs the cross-sectional regression given by (4) in risk premium form, the interecept γ_0 will be equal to $\tilde{R}'_{Zt}$ (or if the time interval is over more than one period $\bar{R}'_Z$, where $\bar{R}'_Z$ is the mean value of $\tilde{R}'_{Zt}$ over the period). The crucial issue is whether or not the mean, $E(\tilde{R}'_Z)$, is equal to zero, and the regression test of the significance of γ_0 for a single cross section cannot address this question. The usual tests of significance provide a test of whether $\tilde{\gamma}_{0t}$ for a particular cross section is equal to zero and not whether $E(\tilde{\gamma}_0)$ or equivalently $E(\tilde{R}_Z)$ is equal to zero. The usual cross-sectional tests will not incorporate the variability of $\tilde{R}_{Zt}$ through time. The time series tests of B-J-S described above avoid these difficulties and correctly incorporate the variability of the $\tilde{R}_{Zt}$ over time in the significance tests. As we shall see below Fama and MacBeth[36] provide an alternative way of testing the significance of the difference between the average value of γ_{0t} and zero, which is the crucial comparison to be made.

B-J-S also show how grouping procedures can eliminate most of the difficulties associated with the biases introduced by measurement errors in the β_j in the cross-sectional tests. Figure 2 summarizes the cross-sectional relationship between the average excess returns. $\tilde{R}'_j$, and β's for their ten portfolios (denoted by X's) over the 35-year period 1931–1965. The symbol $\square$ denotes the mean excess return, $\tilde{R}'_M$, and risk (1.0) for the market portfolio estimated by the average excess returns on all securities on the New York Stock Exchange. If the asset pricing model were valid the relationship should be linear and have an intercept of zero, as equation (7) implies. As can be seen from Figure 2 the

---

[36]*Ibid.*

relationship is amazingly linear but the intercept is positive and the slope is less than predicted.[37] From the examination of these cross-sectional relationships between risk and return for 17 subperiods of length 24 months and 4 subperiods of length 105 months it appears that on the average the relationship is highly linear, but the intercepts (and slopes) fluctuate randomly from period to period and are often negative. However, as B-J-S argue, these "nonstationarities" are consistent with the return generating process described by the two-factor model[38] of equation (9), which implies that the intercept and slope in the cross-sectional regression given by (4) will be $\bar{R}_Z$ and $[\bar{R}_M - \bar{R}_Z]$, where the bars denote sample means over the time period covered by the cross section. Since $\bar{R}_Z$ will also be a random variable, equation (9) is consistent with the observed empirical results. Because of the existence of sampling error the intercept in the cross-sectional regression given by (4) would not always be identically equal to the riskless rate even if the Sharpe-Lintner model were correct. However, B-J-S argue that the fluctuations in the estimated intercepts $\hat{\gamma}_0$ and slopes $\hat{\gamma}_1$ from cross section to cross section are far greater than that which could be expected from the sampling error associated with the stochastic error term $\tilde{e}_j$ in (4) alone. The standard deviation of this sampling error is far too small to explain the large fluctuations in the coefficients. Thus B-J-S hypothesize that the process generating the data is a two-factor model of the form given by (9).

B-J-S also provide a tentative procedure for estimating the time series of returns on the beta factor and demonstrate the non-stationarity of its mean $E(\tilde{R}_Z)$ over the period 1931–1965. These findings are consistent with the observed nonstationarity of the intercepts α_j in the time series tests, since for any particular time period α_j in the time series regression, (8) will be equal to $\bar{R}_Z(1 - \beta_j)$.

Jacob[39] in work which is similar in several respects to that of B-J-S also documents the nonstationarity of the risk-return relationship and the inadequacy of the simple form of the Sharpe-Lintner model. Her data include 593 securities listed on the NYSE and covers the period 1946–1965. The results reported by Friend and Blume[40] on the behavior of measures of portfolio performance also appear to be consistent with the B-J-S results and the two-factor model.

---

[37] It should be equal to $\bar{R}'_M = 0.0142$, but it is 0.0108. The standard errors are given in the upper left-hand corner of Figure 2, but the reader should beware of using them to make significance tests for the reasons outlined above.

[38] As we shall see below, relaxation of certain of the assumptions of the simple model lends some theoretical support to the two-factor model given by equation (9).

[39] [34].

[40] In [27].

A Four-factor Random Coefficient Model

Fama and MacBeth (F-M),[41] in a paper extending the B-J-S work, have found that a four-factor random coefficient model of the form

$$\tilde{R}_{jt} = \tilde{\gamma}_{0t} + \tilde{\gamma}_{1t}\beta_j + \tilde{\gamma}_{2t}\bar{\beta}_j^2 + \tilde{\gamma}_{3t}\overline{\sigma_j(u)} + \tilde{\epsilon}_{jt} \tag{10}$$

seems to fit the data better than the simple two-factor linear model postulated in the B-J-S study. β_j is as defined before, $\tilde{\gamma}_{0t}$ plays the role of $\tilde{R}_{Zt}$ in the B-J-S notation, $\bar{\beta}_j^2$ is the average of the β^2 for all individual securities in portfolio j and $\overline{\sigma_j(u)}$ is the average of the residual standard deviations from (5) for all securities in portfolio j. The F-M tests were carried out on 20 portfolios constructed from all securities on the NYSE in the period January 1935–June 1968. Like those of B-J-S, the portfolio construction rules used by F-M were designed to minimize the measurement error bias problems in cross-sectional estimates of the coefficients $\tilde{\gamma}_{0t}$, $\tilde{\gamma}_{1t}$, $\tilde{\gamma}_{2t}$, and $\tilde{\gamma}_{3t}$ in (10). The F-M test procedures are based on an examination of the time series of the coefficients in (10), estimated from cross-sectional regressions for each month in the time interval January 1935–June 1968. They focus on three major implications of the equilibrium properties of the Markowitz mean-variance portfolio model (or in F-M's terms the two-parameter portfolio model):

(H1) The risk-return relationship should be linear.
(H2) No measure of risk in addition to β should be systematically related to expected returns.
(H3) The expected return-risk tradeoff should be positive.

(H1), (H2), and (H3) imply respectively that $E(\tilde{\gamma}_{2t}) = 0$, $E(\tilde{\gamma}_{3t}) = 0$, and $E(\tilde{\gamma}_{1t}) > 0$. F-M also test the implications of the traditional Sharpe-Lintner model which says

(H4) $E(\tilde{\gamma}_{0t}) = R_{Ft}$.

In addition they provide tests of the proposition that each of the period-by-period coefficients are equal to zero $\tilde{\gamma}_{0t} = \tilde{\gamma}_{1t} = \tilde{\gamma}_{2t} = \tilde{\gamma}_{3t} = 0$, and the implication of capital market efficiency that each of the coefficients must behave as a martingale or fair game through time. The latter requirement derives from the fact that, if they did not behave as a fair game, there would exist trading rules based on the past values of the $\tilde{\gamma}$'s which would yield above normal profits—a violation of the efficient markets hypothesis.[42]

---

[41] [23].

[42] Cf. [17].

From an examination of the average values and t statistics for the estimated coefficients $\hat{\gamma}$ from (10) for the entire period and for various five year sub-periods, F-M conclude that the data are consistent with the three major implications of the mean-variance portfolio model (H1)–(H3). The t statistics are defined as

$$t(\overline{\hat{\gamma}}) = \frac{\overline{\hat{\gamma}}}{s(\hat{\gamma})/\sqrt{n}} \qquad (11)$$

where $\overline{\hat{\gamma}}$ and $s(\hat{\gamma})$ are the average and standard deviation of the time series of monthly coefficients and n is the number of months in the period used to calculate $\overline{\hat{\gamma}}$ and $s(\hat{\gamma})$. The average values of $\hat{\gamma}_2$ and $\hat{\gamma}_3$ are generally small and insignificantly different from zero. F-M also confirm the B-J-S results that $E(\widetilde{\gamma}_{0t})$ does not equal R_{Ft} (or in the B-J-S terminology $E(\widetilde{R}_{Zt}) \neq R_{Ft}$), and therefore (H4), the simple Sharpe-Lintner hypothesis, is inconsistent with the data.

The F-M tests of the period-by-period values of the $\widetilde{\gamma}_{jt}$ indicate, however, that while we cannot reject the hypothesis that $E(\widetilde{\gamma}_{2t})$ and $E(\widetilde{\gamma}_{3t})$ equal zero, we can reject the hypothesis that $\widetilde{\gamma}_{2t}$ and $\widetilde{\gamma}_{3t}$ equal zero in each month. Therefore while there are no "systematic" nonlinearities in the risk-return relationship and no "systematic" effects of nonportfolio risk on security returns, such effects do materialize in a random fashion from period to period. That is, the data indicate that $\overline{\beta_j^2}$ and $\overline{\sigma_j(u)}$ do help in explaining the period-by-period returns on securities, although their explanatory power, while significantly different from zero, is small in an absolute sense. The average adjusted coefficient of determination in the 402 monthly cross-sectional regressions from 1/35 to 6/68 increases from .29 to .34 with the addition of these last two factors. Furthermore, knowledge of these effects if of no help to the investor since the coefficients themselves behave as a fair game through time. Thus, the investor can apparently do no better than to act as if the two-factor model suggested by B-J-S is valid.

Unfortunately, while we now have a better idea of the nature of the stochastic process generating asset returns, we as yet have no real theoretical understanding of these effects. We shall argue below that there are a number of possible theoretical justifications for these random elements, but as yet few of them are thoroughly tested. As Fama and MacBeth themselves conclude:

What we have found . . . is that there are variables in addition to $[\beta_j]$ that systematically affect period-by-period returns. Some of these omitted variables are apparently related to $[\beta_j^2]$ and $[\sigma_j(u)]$. But the latter are almost surely proxies since there is no economic rationale for their presence in a stochastic risk-return model. . . . In sum, our results support the important testable implications of the two-parameter portfolio model. We cannot reject the hypothesis that the pricing of common stocks reflects the attempts of risk-averse investors to hold efficient portfolios. On average there seems to be a positive tradeoff between return and risk, with risk measured from the portfolio viewpoint. In addition, although there are "stochastic nonlinearities" from period-to-period, on average their effects are zero and unpredictably different from zero from one period to the next. Thus we cannot reject the hypothesis that in making a portfolio decision, an investor should assume that the relationship between an asset's portfolio risk and its expected return is linear, as implied by the two-parameter model. We also cannot reject the hypothesis of portfolio theory that no measure of risk, in addition to portfolio risk, systematically affects average returns. Finally, the observed "fair game" properties of the coefficients and residuals of our risk-return regressions are consistent with an efficient capital market—that is, a market where prices of securities fully reflect available information.[43]

4. Extensions of the Mean-Variance Asset Pricing Model

The evidence seems to indicate fiarly strongly that the simple version of the asset pricing model as described in Section 2 and the Appendix does not provide an adequate description of the process determining common stock returns. The existence of the second, third, and fourth factors documented by B-J-S and F-M indicate that the nature of the process determining security returns through time is quite complex and not at all well understood at the current time. The mere documentation of the existence of a second factor and stochastic non-linearities in the absence of any real theoretical understanding of the phenomena leaves us in an unsatisfactory state of affairs. In light of this we turn to a closer examination of the theory in search of results which may provide some additional insight into the nature of these phenomena.

Virtually every one of the seven major assumptions (listed in Section 2) upon which the asset pricing model is constructed violates to some degree the conditions observed in the world around us. In attempts to enrich the theory a number of authors have worked on expanding the model by relaxing the seven major assumptions in various ways. The results have indicated that from a theoretical point of view the theory is fairly robust with respect to violations of these assumptions, since many of them are not crucial for the development of the important results of the model. It also appears that some of the extensions of the theory may have in them the seeds of a more complete understanding of the full complexities of the capital markets.

The Single-period Utility of Terminal Wealth Assumption

The assumption that all investors are single-period expected utility of terminal wealth maximizers is clearly erroneous. However, Fama and Long[44] have shown

---

[43] [23].

[44] In [19, 21] and [45], respectively.

that one can, with little additional difficulty, include the current consumption decisions of investors in the model. That is, the investor's decision is characterized by the simultaneous choice of consumption level and portfolio composition. In addition, Fama[45] provides an analysis of the multi-period consumption-investment problem and a justification for the single-period utility of consumption and terminal wealth model.

Fama argues that the investor's problem is more accurately stated as the maximization of his expected lifetime utility of consumption, $U_{\tau+1}$, i.e.:

$$E[U_{\tau+1}(c_{1-k}, \ldots, c_1, \ldots, c_{\tau+1}|\beta_{\tau+1})]$$

where $C_t = (c_{1-k}, \ldots, c_1, \ldots, c_t)$ is the dollar value of consumption from the beginning of his life, period $1 - k$, through period t. The consumer dies[46] at the beginning of period $\tau + 1$, $c_{\tau+1}$ is his bequest, and $\beta_{\tau+1}$ is the "state of the world" at $\tau + 1$ which signifies the set of all events that constitute history up to and including time $\tau + 1$. The consumer's problem is to make an optimal consumption-investment decision for period 1 taking into account that decisions must also be made at the beginning of each future period (which, of course, will depend on future events). Using the backward optimization of dynamic programming, Fama obtains the recursive relation for all possible states of the world β_t and wealth levels, w_t, as

$$U_t(C_{t-1}, w_t|\beta_t) = \max_{c_t H} \int_{\beta_{t+1}} U_{t+1}(C_t, w_{t+1}|\beta_{t+1})dF_{\beta_t}(\beta_{t+1}) \qquad (12)$$

subject to the constraints

$$0 \leqslant c_t \leqslant w_t$$

$$\sum_i h_i = w_t - c_t$$

$$H \geqslant 0$$

where $w_{t+1} = \sum_i h_i \cdot R_i(\beta_{t+1})$ is the investor's wealth at time $t + 1$, $R_i(\beta_{t+1})$ is the one-period per dollar return on asset i in state β_{t+1}, $H = \{h_1, h_2, \ldots, h_n\}$ is the nonnegative vector of dollar amounts invested in each asset at the beginning of period $t + 1$, 0 is the null vector, and $F_{\beta_t}(\beta_{t+1})$ is the distribution function of β_{t+1} given β_t. Fama assumes that consumption goods and portfolio

---

[45] In [19].

[46] As Fama demonstrates, the assumption of known time of death is not crucial to the results. In an earlier version Fama [18] demonstrates that the model can be expanded to allow for the existence of random labor income and for the individual's choice between labor and leisure in each period.

assets are perfectly divisible, there are no transactions costs, and all consumers are price-takers. The function $U_t(C_{t-1}, w_t|\beta_t)$ is the maximum expected utility of lifetime consumption obtainable if the consumer is in state β_t at time t, his wealth is w_t, his past consumption was C_{t-1}, and he makes optimal consumption-investment decisions at time t and in all future periods.

Fama proves that if the utility of lifetime consumption function $U_{\tau+1}(C_{\tau+1}|\beta_{\tau+1})$ displays risk aversion, i.e., is monotone increasing and strictly concave in $C_{\tau+1}$ for all $\beta_{\tau+1}$, then for all t the derived utility functions given by (12) will have these properties. When the consumer makes a decision at time t, the past consumption pattern, $\hat{C}_{t-1}$, is known. Thus the decision at t can be based upon the function

$$V_{t+1}(c_t, \tilde{w}_{t+1}|\beta_{t+1}) = U_{t+1}(\hat{C}_{t-1}, c_t, w_{t+1}|\beta_{t+1}) \tag{13}$$

and since V_{t+1} is monotone increasing and strictly concave in (c_t, w_{t+1}) the function $V_{t+1}(c_t, w_{t+1}|\beta_{t+1})$ has the properties of a risk averter's single-period utility of consumption and terminal wealth function for any given state of the world, β_{t+1}.

Note, however, that V_{t+1} given by (13) does not quite provide a complete justification for the simple asset pricing model, since it allows the investor's utility to be state dependent. Fama argues that such state-dependent utilities can arise from three possible situations: (1) tastes for particular bundles of consumption goods can be state dependent; (2) utilities for given dollars of consumption depend on the particular consumption goods available at each point in time and their prices, either or both of which may be state dependent; and (3) the investment opportunities available in any future period may depend on past events and this will induce state-dependent utilities. To justify the simple asset pricing model in the context of the multi-period problem it is thus sufficient to assume that consumers behave as if the future consumption and investment opportunities are given and that tastes are not state dependent. We can then eliminate β_{t+1} from (13) and characterize the investor's decision as the maximization of the expected value of $V_{t+1}(C_t, w_{t+1})$. Thus even though the consumer must solve a multi-period problem to arrive at his optimal current decisions, Fama's results indicate that if he is risk averse, the consumer's observed market behavior will be "indistinguishable from that of a risk-averse expected utility maximizer who has a one-period horizon."[47] Note that V_{t+1}

---

[47] [19], p. 164. Some confusion has arisen on occasion over the generality of Fama's results, since he does not impose the separability conditions necessary for decomposition which Nemhauser [58], p. 34ff, requires for utilization of the dynamic programming solution technique. Long [44] derives the general class of utility functions satisfying these conditions, but, as he points out, they are not necessary in Fama's approach. In fact, while decomposition vastly simplifies the calculations necessary to obtain a solution, it is not necessary to insure the optimality of Fama's dynamic programming approach. See

is a complicated function which depends on tastes for future consumption and on the consumption-investment opportunities that will be available in future periods. Hence, while Fama's results do not provide an immediately useful normative rule for making consumption-investment decisions, they do provide a positive justification for the characterization of investor decisions *as if* they were made on the basis of a risk-averse single-period utility of consumption and terminal wealth function.

In addition, Fama demonstrates that if V_{t+1} is concave in c_t and w_{t+1} and the probability distributions are normal, investors can choose among alternative portfolios solely on the basis of mean and variance of returns.[48] He also demonstrates that this result extends to a situation where all probability distributions are symmetric stable with finite mean. In this case, of course, the objects of choice are mean and a dispersion parameter, not mean and variance, since the variance is undefined for all stable distributions except the normal. Fama also shows that one can derive equilibrium conditions equivalent to those of the mean-variance form of the asset pricing model in the context of symmetric stable distributions with finite mean.

Merton[49] derives the equilibrium conditions in a continuous-time version of the model, in which all investors are expected utility of lifetime consumption maximizers and returns are functions of Weiner processes. We return to his results and discuss their implications in somewhat more detail below.

Finally, in a recent paper[50] Long provides what is perhaps one of the most general treatments of the nature of equilibrium in a nonstate preference discrete time multi-period consumption-investment model to date. He assumes risk aversion on the part of consumers and makes no restrictions on the forms of the probability distributions of returns other than that the second moment must be finite. Not surprisingly, it turns out to be impossible to get a directly testable equation like that of (1) without making some additional assumptions. Long does, however, provide a theoretical analysis of the nature of the equilibrium solution under various conditions and examines the comparative statics properties of the model in detail, including its implications for the term structure of interest rates. Of particular interest is his use of the model to demonstrate that risk aversion on the part of consumers does not imply the existence of positive liquidity premiums in the equilibrium term structure. Indeed, he illustrates an

---

Bellman [4], pp. 83–86, where Fama's approach is discussed, and White [76], p. 23ff. Essentially the issue boils down to one involving the definition of dynamic programming and need not concern us here. Also, it has recently come to my attention that Stigum [70] appears to derive results similar to Fama's for corporate decisions under uncertainty.

[48] Tobin [72] provided the first proof of this proposition, but he ignored the consumption decision, c_t, in his analysis.

[49] In [53, 54].

[50] [44].

economy made up entirely of risk-averse consumers in which the equilibrium
liquidity premiums are negative. The "risk" which determines the size and sign
of the liquidity premiums is closely related to our usual notion of portfolio risk
and in this case is the covariance between the single-period spot rates and the
marginal utility of consumption for the corresponding future periods.

The Existence of Riskless Borrowing and Lending Opportunities

Sharpe and Lintner[51] originally assumed that the investor had available unlimited borrowing or lending opportunities at some exogenously fixed interest
rate. Mossin[52] assumed the existence of a given quantity of a riskless asset (one
whose future value was known with certainty) whose current price was also
exogenously given. Long and Fama[53] have shown that the introduction of the
consumption decision into the model along with the existence of a fixed
quantity of a riskless asset (with short selling possible) allows the riskless interest
rate to be determined endogenously. One plus the riskless rate will be equal in
equilibrium to the marginal rate of substitution of future for present consumption. Thus the determination of the riskless rate can be brought into the model
without changing any of the other results.

The Model with No Riskless Borrowing and Lending. In a world where there
are no contracts denominated in real magnitudes, the presence of uncertainty
regarding the general level of prices in the future precludes the existence of a
riskless asset. Hence it is important to know to what extent the results of the
asset pricing model are dependent on the assumption of the existence of such
an asset. Fama[54] demonstrates that given homogenous expectations, no riskless
asset, and the ability to sell short all assets, the equilibrium return on any asset
will be linearly related to its systematic (or covariance) risk, β. Of course, in the
absence of the existence of a riskless rate of interest we can no longer interpret
the intercept (or constant) in the equation so easily as in (1) or (3). These
results are consistent with the linearity of the empirical relationship between return
and β documented by B-J-S, but they do not give us any way to determine the
appropriate values of the slope or intercept γ_1 and γ_0 in the cross-sectional
relationship given by (4).

---

[51]In [67] and [42, 43], respectively.

[52]In [56].

[53]In [45] and [19, 21], respectively.

[54]In [21].

Black[55] has demonstrated that one can obtain an equilibrium relationship between risk and return for all assets in a market in which no riskless asset or borrowing or lending opportunities exist (but there are no restrictions on short selling). He proves that in equilibrium the portfolios of all investors consist of a linear combination of two basic portfolios.[56] While this point was recognized earlier,[57] Black lends empirical content to the proposition by demonstrating that the equilibrium conditions imply that one of these two portfolios can be taken to be the market portfolio, M, and the other a portfolio whose returns have zero covariance with the market portfolio.[58] This separation property derives from the fact that given no constraints on short selling, the entire efficient set of portfolios can be generated by a linear combination of these two portfolios,[59] as is demonstrated in Figure 3.[60] The points Z and M represent respectively the standard deviation and expected returns on the zero beta and market portfolios, and since they are uncorrelated, all points on the convex set

---

[55] In [5].

[56] This separation property also holds for the mean-variance portfolio model, as was first pointed out by Tobin [72]. In this case, however, one of the two portfolios was the riskless asset. Cass and Stiglitz [14] proved that the separation property also holds for two risky portfolios for certain classes of utility functions and general return distributions in the absence of a riskless asset. Lintner [41] also investigates the nature of equilibrium in the absence of riskless borrowing or lending for the special case where all investors have preferences which exhibit constant absolute risk aversion and probability distributions are normal.

[57] See Sharpe [69], Chapter 4.

[58] In addition, as Long [46] has pointed out, this portfolio is, of all possible zero covariance portfolios, the one with minimum variance. Black [5] has also shown that the Z portfolio has a covariance with every asset, j, which is proportional to $(1 - \beta_j)$.

[59] Merton [52] also examines this point. In fact the entire frontier of the opportunity set can be generated by linear combinations of any two distinct frontier portfolios.

[60] As pointed out to me by W.F. Sharpe and as shown in Figure 3 the point $E(\bar{R}_Z)$ must be the intercept of a line tangent to the frontier at point M. To see this, note that the mean and standard deviation, $E(R_P)$ and $\sigma(R_P)$, of a combined investment in Z and M are given by:

$$E(\bar{R}_P) = \alpha E(\bar{R}_M) + (1 - \alpha)E(\bar{R}_Z)$$

$$\sigma(\bar{R}_P) = [\alpha^2 \sigma^2(\bar{R}_M) + (1 - \alpha)^2 \sigma^2(\bar{R}_Z)]^{1/2}$$

where α is the fraction invested in the market portfolio M. The slope of the tangent line at point M ($\alpha = 1$) is given by

$$\frac{dE(\bar{R}_P)}{d\sigma(\bar{R}_P)} = \frac{\partial E(\bar{R}_P)/\partial \alpha}{\partial \sigma(\bar{R}_P)/\partial \alpha}\bigg|_{x=1} = \frac{E(\bar{R}_M) - E(\bar{R}_Z)}{\sigma(\bar{R}_M)}$$

and since the line must pass through the point $[E(\bar{R}_M), \sigma(\bar{R}_M)]$ the intercept of the tangent line must be $E(\bar{R}_Z)$.

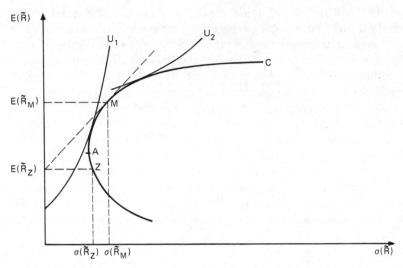

Figure 3. Equilibrium Portfolio Choice (in the Absence of Riskless Borrowing) for Two Investors with Indifference Curves U_1 and U_2.

Note: The market and minimum variance zero beta portfolios are denoted by M and Z, respectively. The efficient set consists of the locus of points on the segment AMC.

given by $ZAMC$ can be obtained by various linear combinations of portfolios Z and M. If all funds are invested in portfolio Z, we obtain the risk-return combination given by Z, and as we reduce the fraction invested in Z and invest the remainder in M, we can obtain all points on the curve ZAM. At point M we have nothing invested in Z and hold only M. In order to move beyond M toward C we sell Z short and invest the proceeds in M. Note that all portfolios in the range AMC are efficient in the Markowitz sense. Each investor maximizes his utility by purchasing that combination of Z and M at which his indifference curve between expected return and standard deviation is just tangent to the efficient set (as is true for indifference curves U_1 and U_2 for hypothetical investors 1 and 2). The equilibrium conditions imply that $E(\tilde{R}_Z)$ must be less than $E(\tilde{R}_M)$[61] and that the holdings of Z must net out to zero for all investors as a whole. Black demonstrates that in equilibrium the expected returns on any asset will be given by

$$E(\tilde{R}_j) = (1 - \beta_j)E(\tilde{R}_Z) + \beta_j E(\tilde{R}_M) \qquad (14)$$

where $E(\tilde{R}_Z)$ is the expected return on the zero beta portfolio. Note that the expected returns on all assets are still a linear function of their systematic or covariance risk and that (14) is almost identical to (3) except that $E(\tilde{R}_Z)$ plays

---

[61]A point originally proven by Long [46] and also proved by Vasicek [75].

the role of R_F, the riskless rate. In addition Mayers[62] demonstrates that if one includes consumption in the model, the expected per dollar returns on the zero beta portfolio will equal a weighted average of the marginal rates of substitution of expected future consumption for present consumption for all individuals; a result which is directly analogous to that obtained for the determination of the riskless rate by Long.[63]

It is also interesting to note that (14) bears a close relationship to the two-factor model suggested by B-J-S. In fact the model given by (9) bears the same relationship to (14) as the market model (5) does to (3), where in (5) A_j is interpreted as equal to $(1 - \beta_j)R_F$. Thus (9) can be interpreted as a two-factor market model, where the expected values of the factors are defined by the equilibrium conditions of the asset pricing model in the context of no riskless borrowing or lending opportunities.

The Model with Riskless Lending but No Borrowing. While the above results are in many ways attractive, one might argue that assumptions have been taken too far. While the nonexistence of perfectly certain real contracts is probably an accurate description of the world, one can argue that the uncertainty introduced by price level changes (at least over relatively short horizons) is infinitesimal. The existence of government bonds which are virtually default-free gives investors the opportunity to lend, if not to borrow, at a rate which is for all practical purposes certain. This suggests investigation of equilibrium in a system with riskless lending opportunities but no riskless borrowing opportunities. Vasicek[64] and Black have demonstrated that the equilibrium risk-return relationships for individual risky securities correspond exactly to that given by equation (14). Their results also imply a piecewise linear relationship between expected return and β for *efficient* portfolios.

Given the existence of riskless lending but no riskless borrowing opportunities, the possible set of standard deviation and expected return combinations available to an investor is portrayed in Figure 4. The efficient set excluding lending opportunities is given by the line segment $ATMC$. The efficient set including optimal utilization of the lending opportunities is given by $R_F TMC$. Vasicek and Black prove that $R_F \leqslant E(\tilde{R}_Z) < E(\tilde{R}_M)$ and that in equilibrium all investors will either hold combinations of portfolio T and the riskless asset (if they are on the segment $R_F T$) or combinations of portfolios Z and M (if they are on the segment TMC). Portfolios M and Z are defined exactly as before, i.e., the market portfolio and the zero beta portfolio respectively, and T is a linear combination of these two portfolios. The expected return on every *individual*

---

[62] In [51].

[63] In [45].

[64] In [75].

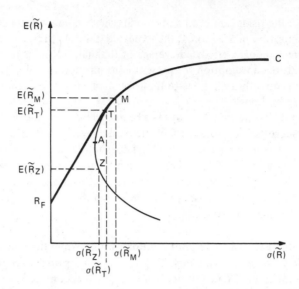

Figure 4. The Locus of Efficient Portfolios, $R_F\,TMC$, When Investors Can Engage in Riskless Lending but No Riskless Borrowing.

Note: The market portfolio, zero beta portfolio, and tangent portfolio are denoted by M, Z, and T respectively.

risky asset or portfolio of risky assets is still given by (14) and lies along the line $E(\widetilde{R}_Z)TMC$ in Figure 5. However, unlike the situation for the other models, equation (14) *does not now hold for all efficient portfolios*. In fact the expected return-β relationship for efficient portfolios is now given by the two straight-line segments making up $R_F TMC$ in Figure 5. All efficient portfolios which consist solely of risky assets lie along the portion *TMC* as in the previous models, *but all efficient portfolios made up of combinations of the riskless asset and portfolio T now lie along the segment* $R_F T$.[65] This result becomes intuitively clear once one notes that if a fraction α is invested in portfolio T and $(1 - \alpha)$ in the riskless asset, the β of the portfolio must equal $\alpha\beta_T$. In addition, the expected returns on the portfolio will equal $\alpha E(\widetilde{R}_T) + (1 - \alpha)R_F$, the weighted average of the returns on portfolio T and the riskless asset. Hence for all values of α in the range zero to one the portfolio must lie on the line $R_F T$ in Figure 5. However, all individual risky assets or imperfectly diversified portfolios must lie somewhere on the line $E(\widetilde{R}_Z)TMC$, and hence those assets and inefficient

---

[65]These results are entirely consistent with the fact pointed out by Fama [21] that the risk of an asset must be measured in terms of its marginal contribution to the riskiness of some relevant efficient portfolio. If we have two efficient portfolios which are relevant to investor choices, it is not surprising that these results occur. However, the fact that the equilibrium expected returns on all risky assets can still be represented by a simple linear function of β like that given by (14) is interesting.

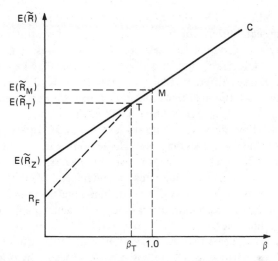

Figure 5. The Relationship between Expected REturn and Systematic Risk, β, where Investors Can Engage in Riskless Lending but No Riskless Borrowing.

Note: All efficient portfolios lie on the two linear segments given by R_F TMC and all individual assets and inefficient portfolios lie on the straight line given by $E(\tilde{R}_Z)$ TMC.

portfolios with $\beta_j < \beta_T$ will appear to dominate the efficient portfolios lying on the segment $R_F T$ in the mean-beta plane in Figure 5. But of course they do not dominate these efficient portfolios in the mean-standard deviation plane, as illustrated in Figure 4.

Since $E(\tilde{R}_Z)$ must be greater than or equal to R_F, the slope of the line $E(\tilde{R}_Z)TMC$ must be less than or equal to the slope of a hypothetical line drawn from R_F through M, which is the slope given by the simple asset pricing model [cf. equation (3)]. Recall the B-J-S empirical results discussed earlier which were based on an examination of portfolios consisting *entirely of risky assets*. This model predicts that the empirical slope of the cross-sectional return-β relationship found in such a study should be less than that implied by equation (3). If we can assume that for sufficiently long periods of time the sample averages $\bar{R}_M$ and $\bar{R}_Z$ are fairly good proxy measures of the *ex ante* expectations, the B-J-S results are consistent with the predictions of this riskless lending but no riskless borrowing model. Over the period 1931–1965 the empirical slope was less than that predicted by equation (3) [cf. Figure 1], and this also was true for three of the four 105-month subperiods examined.[66]

---

[66] Interestingly enough, in the last subperiod, April 1957–December 1965, the empirical slope was slightly negative, which is inconsistent with this model. However, this might be explained by the hypothesis that the observed $\bar{R}_M$ and $\bar{R}_Z$ did not adequately represent the *ex ante* expectations, $E(\tilde{R}_M)$ and $E(\tilde{R}_Z)$. Recall also the qualifications noted in Section 2 regarding the interpretation of significance tests in these cross-sectional relationships.

The Model with Differential Riskless Borrowing and Lending Rates. Brennan[67] derives the market equilibrium conditions assuming that investors can borrow and lend but only at differential rates. He considers two cases: (1) all investors can borrow at a riskless rate r_B and lend at a riskless rate r_L and $r_B > r_L$, and (2) each investor, i, faces different riskless borrowing and lending rates and $r_{Bi} > r_{Li}$. In both cases, Brennan finds that the relationship between an asset's expected return and risk (as measured by β_j) will be linear and identical to (14), the relation obtained by Black for the no riskless borrowing and lending case and by Vasicek for the riskless lending case. He demonstrates that the expected returns on the portfolio Z will be equal to a weighted average of (1) the borrowing rates of borrowers, (2) the lending rates of lenders, and (3) the equivalent riskless rates (marginal rates of substitution) of individuals who neither borrow nor lend. Thus the Black-Vasicek results extend to the general case of differential borrowing and lending rates.

In conclusion, it appears that the relaxation of the assumptions regarding the nature of riskless borrowing and lending opportunities in the original model yields implications which appear to be consistent with some of the observed discrepancies between the empirical results and the simple model documented by B-J-S but do not explain the third and fourth factors involving the nonlinearities and the residual risk components documented by F-M.

The Existence of Nonmarketable Assets

The original asset pricing results are based on the assumption that all assets are perfectly liquid. That is, all assets are marketable and there are no transactions costs. Casual observation indicates that this assumption is violated in reality. For example, most investors hold some claims on probability distributions of future income that are nonmarketable; i.e., they cannot sell these claims in current markets. Claims on labor income ("human capital") represent one of the more important of such assets, but there are undoubtedly many more. Nonmarketable claims on the proceeds of assets held in trust and on the proceeds of governmental transfer payment programs such as social security payments are other examples. In addition, there are many physical assets, such as real estate, for which transactions costs are relatively large. Hence it is important to know whether the relaxation of this assumption of perfect liquidity is crucial to any of the results of the model. It is usually quite difficult to analyze such problems in the context of transactions costs (where buying and selling prices differ), because of the discontinuities introduced into the analysis and the dependence of the solution on the initial distribution of resources. However, Mayers[68]

---

[67] In [12].

[68] In [50].

demonstrates that for the special case where two kinds of assets exist [perfectly liquid (marketable) and perfectly nonliquid (nonmarketable)] the problem is tractable.

Mayers considers a single-period world in which all investors can have claims on the two types of assets, and derives the individual's demand function for marketable assets (which is a function of the covariance of the returns on the individual's nonmarketable assets with all other assets). He aggregates these demand functions to obtain equilibrium conditions and shows that it is still possible to eliminate information about the individual's utilities and to obtain the equilibrium relationship between the expected return of any asset and its covariance risk in terms of market parameters. His result is

$$E(\tilde{R}_j) = R_F + \lambda \, \mathrm{cov}(\tilde{R}_j, \tilde{R}_M^* + \tilde{R}_H^*) \tag{15}$$

where

$$\lambda = \frac{E(\tilde{R}_M) - R_F}{\mathrm{cov}(\tilde{R}_M, \tilde{R}_M^* + \tilde{R}_H^*)}$$

$$= \frac{E(\tilde{R}_M) - R_F}{V_M \sigma^2(\tilde{R}_M) + \mathrm{cov}(\tilde{R}_M, \tilde{R}_H^*)}$$

is the "market price" per unit of risk, $\tilde{R}_M^*$ is the *total* dollar return on all non-marketable assets, V_M is the current total market value of all marketable assets, and all the other variables are as defined earlier except that the asterisks denote total dollar returns. Equation (15) is interesting in several respects, not the least of which is the fact that such a simple equilibrium relationship can be obtained even though investors face widely different efficient sets for their total portfolio opportunities (considering the total probability distribution of returns on marketable and nonmarketable assets). Mayers demonstrates that even with homogeneous expectations, investors will hold widely different portfolios of marketable assets if the nature of the probability distributions on their non-marketable assets differs. One of the unappealing implications of the simple asset pricing model is that the portfolios of risky assets held by all investors are identical in composition to one another and the market portfolio. This implication, which is clearly inconsistent with the actual portfolio holdings of investors, is not implied by this extended version of the model.

In addition, note that (15) seems to be a fairly straightforward generalization of (1), where the risk of an individual asset is now measured as the co-variance of its per dollar returns with the sum of the returns on the market portfolio and all nonmarketable assets (to allow for the proper weighting of the marketable and nonmarketable assets the returns on each are expressed as total dollar returns instead of per dollar returns). Note that λ can still be interpreted as the market price per unit of risk as measured by the risk premium per unit of risk on the market portfolio. However, the risk of the market portfolio now involves not only its total variance but also its covariance with the returns on nonmarketable assets.

Mayers shows that (15) is equivalent to the equilibrium risk-return relationship that can be derived under the assumption that all assets are marketable when the value and returns of only a subset of these assets (say, those securities listed on the New York Stock Exchange) are measured (or measurable). Under these conditions, equation (15) gives the risk-return relationship for all observed assets in terms of the risk premium on the *observed* market portfolio; i.e., we can interpret M in (15) as the observed market portfolio which is only a subset of the true market portfolio and H as the set of nonobserved, but marketable, assets. Thus the structure of asset returns given the existence of nonmarketable assets is identical to that which would be found if all assets were actually marketable but we could obtain only an incomplete measurement of the assets in the true market portfolio. In addition, Mayers[69] shows that the essential nature of these results remains unchanged if there are no riskless borrowing or lending opportunities, except that $E(\tilde{R}_Z)$ plays the role of R_F in the solutions where $\tilde{R}_Z$ is defined as the return on a portfolio which has zero covariance with the *sum* of the total dollar returns on the market portfolio and the total dollar returns on all nonmarketable assets.

Mayers' results indicate that the basic implications of the theory are not weakened in any major respect by the existence of nonmarketable assets and in fact are strengthened, since the expanded model then does not imply that all investors hold identical proportions of all assets in existence. In addition, his results for the case in which some assets transactions costs are infinite provide some indication that the essential results of the model may hold in the context of finite transactions costs; but of course this conjecture remains to be documented. Mayers' results also imply that the problems introduced by the existence of nonmarketable assets are a generalization of those introduced by the incomplete measurement of $\tilde{R}_M$, and hence his work provides some additional insight into the nature of an ideal index of $\tilde{R}_M$ and the appropriate utilization of imperfect indexes in empirical work. It may be that the effects of nonmarketable and omitted assets will explain the third and fourth factors documented by Fama and MacBeth, but empirical evidence on this issue is at present incomplete.

Differential Tax Rates on Dividends and Capital Gains

The assumption that there are no taxes is obviously false as a description of reality. Brennan[70] demonstrates under the assumptions of the simple model

---

[69] In [51].

[70] In [13].

that the equilibrium price of an asset still can be expressed as a linear function of its systematic risk β_j even when investors face differential tax rates on dividends and capital gains if dividend yields are perfectly certain. He assumes that interest and dividend receipts are taxed at the personal income tax rate and that interest payments are tax deductible. His result is somewhat more complex than equation (3):

$$E(\tilde{R}_j) = T_2 R_F + [E(\tilde{R}_M) - T_1 \delta_M - T_2 R_F]\beta_j + T_1 \delta_j \qquad (16)$$

The major variables are defined exactly as before, and $\delta_j = D_j/V_j$, $\delta_M = D_M/V_M$ are respectively the dividend yields on the jth asset and the market portfolio. The other values are

$$T_1 = \frac{T_d - T_g}{1 - T_g} \qquad (17)$$

$$T_2 = \frac{1 - T_d}{1 - T_g} = 1 - T_1 \qquad (18)$$

where T_d and T_g are complicated averages of the marginal tax rates[71] on dividends and capital gains respectively for all investors. If taxes on dividends are greater than the taxes on capital gains, T_1 and T_2 will both be positive. Thus the introduction of differential taxes on capital gains and dividends changes the intercept and slope of the equilibrium risk-return relationship and introduces a new variable, the dividend yield, into the determination of expected returns. However, neither the relevant measure of a security's risk nor the linearity of the risk return trade-off (holding dividend yield constant) for individual assets is altered. Note also that the slope implied by (16) is less than that implied by the simple asset pricing model. In addition, the intercept is now $T_2 R_F$, which will be less than R_F if the capital gains tax rate is less than the dividend rate. Furthermore, (16) implies that the higher is an asset's dividend yield, the higher is its equilibrium before tax expected returns. This seems reasonable since, all other things constant, the after tax expected return would otherwise be *lower* the higher the dividend yield.

Brennan examines the relationship between dividend yield and risk (as measured by β) for 100 portfolios constructed from all securities on the NYSE so as to maximize the dispersion of the dividend yields. He finds that yield and risk are strongly negatively correlated (the squared correlation coefficient was 0.59 over the 20-year period 1946–1965). Brennan also estimates the cross-sectional regression

$$\bar{R}_j = \gamma_0 + \gamma_1 \beta_j + \gamma_2 \delta_j + e_j \qquad (19)$$

---

[71]The result holds even when the tax rates are progressive.

for the period 1946–1965 using a sample of 11 portfolios constructed from all the securities on the NYSE by procedures also designed to maximize the spread in the δ_j among the portfolios. The coefficients and t values are:

$$\hat{\gamma}_0 = 0.051$$
$$(1.89)$$

$$\hat{\gamma}_1 = 0.068$$
$$(3.58)$$

$$\hat{\gamma}_2 = 0.634$$
$$(3.69)$$

and the squared correlation coefficient is 0.65. Since the returns in (19) are defined as the excess returns above the riskless rate (estimated from 90-day Bankers Acceptances), $\hat{\gamma}_0$ should be zero and $\hat{\gamma}_1$ should be equal to T_1 [cf. equation (16)]. Using this result and the fact that $T_2 = 1 - T_1$ [from (18)] Brennan calculates the theoretical value of $\gamma_1 = [E(\tilde{R}_M) - T_1\delta_M - T_2 R_F]$ to be 0.106, which appears to be insignificantly different from $\hat{\gamma}_1$.[72]

Note that γ_2, which is a complex weighted average of the marginal capital gains and dividend tax rates for all investors, falls between zero and one as it should. Brennan also uses instrumental variables procedures in an attempt to eliminate any biases in these results due to specification error and the proxying effects of δ_j for β_j (which are, as indicated earlier, strongly correlated). The results of these tests are virtually the same. Given his estimate of $T_1 = \hat{\gamma}_2$ = 0.610 from the instrumental variables procedures and Bailey's estimate[73] that the average effective tax rate on capital gains is less than 5 percent. Brennan argues that to a rough approximation the results imply that the weighted average dividend tax rate was 63 percent over this period. He notes that this does not differ greatly from the direct estimates obtained by others for various times during his period, which range from 36 percent to 63 percent.[74] On the basis of his regression estimates, Brennan concludes that tax effects on asset yields are important and that his model fits the observed data better than does the simple model.

Black and Scholes[75] also consider the effects of dividend yields on the returns to common stocks. They argue that there is no *a priori* reason to expect

---

[72]However, as noted in Section 2, one must be careful about making literal interpretations of the significance levels obtained from such cross-sectional regressions.

[73]In [2].

[74]Cf. [13], p. 175.

[75]In [7].

the existence of differential taxes on dividends and capital gains to affect the expected returns of any asset. They argue that firms will find it in their best interest to adjust dividend payments so that there is nothing to be gained at the margin from either a reduction or an increase in the total supply of dividends. That is, if some assets sold at either a premium or at a discount (for equivalent risk levels) simply because they had a high dividend yield, other firms would act to eliminate the premium by increasing their dividends or the affected firms themselves could act to eliminate the discount by decreasing or eliminating their dividends. As long as firms are concerned only with the value of their shares and not with the dividend level per se there can be, in equilibrium, no differential values for equivalently risk assets based solely on a differential dividend yield; adjustment on the supply side will eliminate it. Of course, given that dividends are taxed at a higher rate than capital gains, one must assume that some investors prefer dividends to capital gains in order to explain the payment of dividends by any corporation (ignoring constraints imposed by the Internal Revenue Service on the retention of earnings). Brennan does not confront this issue; instead he assumes the supply of dividends is fixed and thus prices need not be equated across differential yield categories by adjustments on the supply side.

Black and Scholes test for the effects of dividends on security prices by using portfolios constructed by ranking securities on dividend yield and then, within a given yield class, ranking all securities on the basis of β_j. They define the yield classes such that 20 percent of all securities on the NYSE in the period 1947–1966 are contained in each class and then divide each of these equivalent yield groups into five portfolios such that the spread on the β's is maximized. When the Brennan cross-sectional regression (19) is run for these 25 portfolios, the coefficients and t values are

$$\hat{\gamma}_0 = 0.0075$$
$$(7.0)$$

$$\hat{\gamma}_1 = 0.0028$$
$$(4.2)$$

$$\hat{\gamma}_2 = 0.0149$$
$$(1.3)$$

and the squared correlation coefficient is 0.46. Thus the intercept and the coefficient on β are "significant" while the coefficient on the dividend yield, δ_j, is much smaller than that obtained by Brennan and "insignificant." To avoid the problems with the interpretation of the significance levels of these cross-sectional tests, Black and Scholes construct a time-series test by combining all the securities into two portfolios by procedures designed to maximize the difference in the dividend yields on the portfolios while constraining the β of each to equal unity. The high yield portfolio has a yield of 6.2 percent and the low yield portfolio, a yield of 4.9 percent. They then run the time-series regression used by B-J-S [equation (8)] to test the asset pricing model. Recall that the intercept α_j in that model should be zero and that B-J-S found that α_j was in fact equal to zero for portfolios with a β of unity but not equal to zero for portfolios with a β different from unity. However, if the dividend yield has an important influence on the total returns of securities, the α on a portfolio which does not have a yield equal to the average value for all securities will not be zero. Thus if dividend yields have an important influence on the returns of assets, as the Brennan model predicts, the intercept α in the time series regression given by (8) should be significantly positive for the high yield portfolio and significantly negative for the low yield portfolio. The coefficients and t values for the period 1947–1966 for the high yield portfolio are:[76]

$$\tilde{R}'_{jt} = 0.00024 + 1.000\ \tilde{R}'_{Mt} \qquad \rho^2 = 0.984$$
$$(0.72)\quad (118.3)$$

and for the low yield portfolio are:

$$\tilde{R}'_{jt} = -0.00024 + 1.000\ \tilde{R}'_{Mt} \qquad \rho^2 = 0.984$$
$$(0.72)\quad (118.3)$$

where ρ is the correlation coefficient. While the signs of the intercepts are consistent with the existence of tax effects, each is insignificantly different from zero, and they are insignificantly different from each other (since the standard deviation of the difference between them is equal to 1.44, because the residuals from the two regressions are perfectly negatively correlated by construction).

Black and Scholes also measure the impact of dividend yields on security returns over several subperiods and over the period 1931–1946 with similar results. On the basis of this evidence they state:[77]

The main conclusion of our analysis is that a dollar of dividends has the same value as a dollar of capital gains in the market. There are virtually no differential returns earned by investors who buy high dividend yielding securities or low dividend yielding securities once we control for the crucial risk variable. The demand for dividends is met by corporations who supply dividends and the end result is a market equilibrium in which the dividend factor is insignificant in magnitude.

---

[76]Note that since Black and Scholes used the average excess monthly return on all their securities for the index $\tilde{R}'_M$ the symmetry of the coefficients is a necessary result of the construction of the test and has no economic connotation.

[77]Black and Scholes [7].

Thus it appears that the Black-Scholes results are inconsistent with the Brennan evidence for reasons that are not readily apparent. Future tests will undoubtedly be required to settle the issue.

The Model in Continuous Time

Black and Scholes and Merton,[78] using a continuous time version of the simple form of the asset pricing model, demonstrate that the simple model given by equation (3) holds where the returns are defined over infinitesimally small time intervals. Their results imply that the equilibrium continuously compounded expected rate of return,[79] $E(\tilde{r}_j)$, over any *discrete* interval for any asset j is given by

$$E(\tilde{r}_j) = \alpha_j + r_F + \beta_j [E(\tilde{r}_M) - r_F] \tag{20}$$

where, except for continuous compounding, all the returns and β_j are defined as before.[80] Note, however, that in addition to the continuous compounding (20) differs from (3) by the addition of the constant α_j, which is given by

$$\alpha_j = [\beta_j \sigma^2(\tilde{r}_M) - \sigma^2(\tilde{r}_j)] / 2 \tag{21}$$

where $\sigma^2(\tilde{r}_M)$ and $\sigma^2(\tilde{r}_j)$ are respectively the variances of the continuously compounded returns on the market portfolio and the jth asset over the time interval of observation.[81] Therefore, this model implies that returns should be defined and measured as continuously compounded rates[82] and that the intercept is not necessarily equal to the riskless return. However, given the assumptions of the market model,

$$\sigma^2(\tilde{r}_j) = \beta_j^2 \sigma^2(\tilde{r}_M) + \sigma^2(\tilde{u}_j)$$

we see that

$$\alpha_j = [(\beta_j - \beta_j^2)\sigma^2(\tilde{r}_M) - \sigma^2(\tilde{u}_j)] / 2 \tag{22}$$

---

[78] In [6] and [53, 54], respectively.

[79] That is, r_j is the natural logarithm of the wealth relative $(P_{jt} + D_{jt})/P_{jt+1}$. Merton [53] also derives a version of the model with no riskless asset in continuous time; his results for instantaneous rates are equivalent to Black's in [5] for discrete time.

[80] Cf. Merton [53].

[81] That is, if the returns refer to monthly continuously compounded rates then the $\sigma^2(\tilde{r}_M)$ and $\sigma^2(\tilde{r}_j)$ are variances of the monthly rates.

[82] See also Jensen [37].

where u_j can be interpreted as the error term in the continuous time version of the market model given by (5). Substituting this result into (20), we see that the model implies the existence of a much more complicated equilibrium relationship than implied by any of the other models:

$$E(\tilde{r}_j) = r_F + \beta_j [E(\tilde{r}_M) - r_F + (1/2)\sigma^2(\tilde{r}_M)]$$

$$- \frac{\sigma^2(\tilde{r}_M)}{2} \beta_j^2 - (1/2)\sigma^2(\tilde{u}_j) \tag{23}$$

Moreover, the relation between risk and return is now nonlinear and involves the residual or nonportfolio risk, and is therefore consistent with the third and fourth factors documented by Fama and MacBeth. Note that (23) implies that $\sigma^2(\tilde{u}_j)$ should be negatively related to the level of expected returns; an implication which is inconsistent with the slightly *positive* relationships described earlier[83] and those reported by Lintner and Douglas, Miller and Scholes, and Fama and MacBeth.[84]

To provide a quick and direct test of this model the following cross-sectional regression was run using the data on the ten portfolios utilized in the B-J-S paper discussed in Section 2:

$$\bar{r}'_j = \gamma_0 + \gamma_1 \beta_j + \gamma_2 \beta_j^2 + \gamma_3 \sigma^2(u_j) + e_j \tag{24}$$

where $\bar{r}'_j = \bar{r}_j - r_F$ is the average continuously compounded excess return on the jth portfolio. For these tests all returns were measured as continuously compounded monthly rates and the β's were calculated using these rates. The results for the 35-year period 1931–1965 and for four 105-month subperiods in this interval are presented in Table 1.[85] As can be seen, the coefficients $\hat{\gamma}_1$ for the entire period and the first two subperiods are close to their theoretical values. The values in the last two subperiods are much farther apart. While the t values are also presented in Table 1, their interpretation must be considered in light of the multicollinearity which exists. The variables β_j and β_j^2 are highly correlated (ρ^2 greater than 0.98 in all cases). While this tends to cause the standard errors of estimate of the coefficients to be unreliable, it does not cause bias in the estimates of the coefficients themselves. Also of interest in Table 1 is the fact that $\hat{\gamma}_2$, the coefficient of β_j^2, is about equal to its theoretical value in the first subperiod and roughly one-half its theoretical value for both the whole period

---

[83] See note 35 above.

[84] See [16], [55], and [23], respectively.

[85] Some of the numbers in Table 1 are somewhat different from those published in Jensen [38] due to a computer error which caused some of the earlier results to be incorrect.

Table 1
Regression Tests of the Continuous Time Model*

Period	Value	γ_0	γ_1	γ_2	γ_3	ρ^{2}**	$\bar{r}_M$	$\sigma^2(\tilde{r}_M)$	$t(\gamma_0)$	$t(\hat{\gamma}_1 - \gamma_1)$	$t(\hat{\gamma}_2 - \gamma_2)$	$t(\hat{\gamma}_3 + \frac{1}{2})$
1/31–12/65	Estimated	0.00055	0.0161	−0.0066	2.129	0.954	0.0105	0.0070	0.225	0.412	1.107	2.750
	Theoretical	0	0.0140	−0.0035	−0.500							
1/31–9/39	Estimated	−0.00884	0.0262	−0.0091	3.483	0.904	0.0108	0.0213	−0.894	0.240	0.143	1.95
	Theoretical	0	0.0214	−0.0106	−0.500							
10/39–6/48	Estimated	0.00249	0.0143	−0.0041	0.804	0.899	0.0128	0.0041	0.378	−0.035	0.280	0.713
	Theoretical	0	0.0148	−0.0020	−0.500							
7/48–3/57	Estimated	0.00286	0.0149	−0.0055	−3.924	0.734	0.0103	0.0013	0.539	0.339	0.467	0.281
	Theoretical	0	0.0110	−0.0006	−0.500							
4/57–12/65	Estimated	0.00092	0.0177	−0.0117	11.198	0.795	0.0082	0.0015	0.106	0.502	1.102	0.938
	Theoretical	0	0.0090	−0.0007	−0.500							

*Cross-sectional regression estimates for equation (24) obtained from ten portfolios containing all securities on the NYSE in the period 1/31–12/65. All returns measured as continuously compounded monthly rates. See equation (23) for the definition of the theoretical values of the coefficients.

**ρ^{2} = squared correlation coefficient.

Table 2
Constrained Regression Test of the Continuous Time Model*

Period	Value	γ_0	γ_1	ρ^2**	$t(\hat{\gamma}_0)$	$t(\hat{\gamma}_1 - \gamma_1)$
1/31–12/65	Estimated	0.00299	0.0112	0.975	4.48	−4.68
	Theoretical	0	0.0140			
1/31–9/39	Estimated	−0.00888	0.0308	0.950	−3.42	7.82
	Theoretical	0	0.0214			
10/39–6/48	Estimated	0.00353	0.0115	0.956	3.86	3.75
	Theoretical	0	0.0148			
7/48–3/57	Estimated	0.00743	0.0036	0.617	7.05	7.50
	Theoretical	0	0.0111			
4/57–12/65	Estimated	0.01645	−0.0016	0.416	16.46	17.0
	Theoretical	0	0.0087			

*Regression estimates for Equation (26) obtained from ten portfolios containing all securities on the NYSE in the period 1/31–12/65. See Equation (27) for the definition of the theoretical values of the coefficients. $\bar{r}_M$ and $\sigma^2(\bar{r}_M)$ are given in Table 1.
**ρ^2 = squared correlation coefficient.

and the second subperiod. In the last two subperiods it is considerably different from its theoretical value. Note also that γ_3, the coefficient of the residual variance, $\sigma^2(u_j)$, bears no relationship at all to its hypothesized value. It is positive in 3 out of 4 subperiods but should be equal to −0.5. Multicollinearity problems can be avoided by substituting from (21) into (20), subtracting r_F, and adding $(1/2)\sigma^2(\tilde{r}_j)$ to both sides:

$$E(\tilde{r}_j') + (1/2)\sigma^2(\tilde{r}_j) = \beta_j[E(\tilde{r}_M') + (1/2)\sigma^2(\tilde{r}_M)] \tag{25}$$

Thus if we run the regression

$$\bar{r}_j + (1/2)\sigma^2(\tilde{r}_j) = \gamma_0 + \gamma_1\beta_j + \tilde{e}_j \tag{26}$$

the coefficients should be given by

$$\gamma_0 = 0 \tag{27a}$$

$$\gamma_1 = [\bar{r}_M' + (1/2)\sigma^2(\tilde{r}_M)] \tag{27b}$$

The regression estimates of (26) are given in Table 2; it is evident that the model does not fit the data. Every coefficient is significantly different from its theoretical value.[86]

While the simple continuous time version of the model is attractive in many ways, these simple tests are not very favorable. However, much more can be done along this line and such work may well prove fruitful.

---

[86]The 5 percent t value for 8 degrees of freedom is 2.31.

A Three-factor Model

Merton[87] in the context of the continuous time intertemporal asset pricing model derives what we might call a three-factor model. The main point of the Merton paper is to show that any violation of the three conditions used by Fama[88] to justify the single-period utility of terminal wealth model[89] will almost certainly negate the simple form of the model. In particular he concentrates on shifting investment opportunity sets and derives an equilibrium model under the assumption that all such shifts can be characterized by changes in a single variable—the riskless interest rate. Merton demonstrates that under these conditions all investors will hold investments in three portfolios, not two.[90] The three portfolios are: (1) the riskless asset, (2) the market portfolio M, and (3) a portfolio (or asset) N which is perfectly negatively correlated with changes in the riskless interest rate. Investors will demand shares of portfolio N in order to hedge against the effects of future unforeseen changes in the riskless interest rate. Merton also demonstrates that as long as investor consumption decisions are not independent of the level of r_F, the *instantaneous* expected return on the jth asset, $E(\tilde{r}_j)$, will be given by

$$E(\tilde{r}_j) = r_F + \lambda_1 [E(\tilde{r}_M) - r_F] + \lambda_2 [E(\tilde{r}_N) - r_F] \qquad (28)$$

where the "risk" measures are now

$$\lambda_1 = \frac{\beta_{jM} - \beta_{jN}\beta_{NM}}{1 - \rho_{NM}^2},$$

$$\lambda_2 = \frac{\beta_{jN} - \beta_{jM}\beta_{NM}}{1 - \rho_{NM}^2},$$

$$\beta_{jk} = \frac{\text{cov}(\tilde{r}_j, \tilde{r}_k)}{\sigma^2(\tilde{r}_k)},$$

and ρ_{NM} is the correlation between the returns on the market portfolio M and the riskless rate N. Thus even if β_{jM}, the usual definition of systematic risk,

---

[87][54].

[88]In [19].

[89]That is, consumption preferences, consumption opportunities (for given wealth), and investment opportunities must be independent of the state of the world.

[90]It is also interesting to note that in this model investors will not in general hold mean-variance efficient portfolios. This isn't surprising, since the Fama [19] theorem regarding the reduction of the multi-period model to a single-period mean-variance model discussed above fails here precisely because one of its conditions is violated. Allowing the interest rate to change over time causes the investment opportunity set to be state-dependent.

were 0, the expected returns on the asset would not be equal to the riskless rate, because the asset returns may be systematically related to changes in the interest rate ($\beta_{jN} > 0$).

There is some evidence that the bond market may not behave in quite the same manner as the equity market and the Merton model may provide some indication of the reasons for this.[91]

Merton argues that in general the sign of λ_2 in (28) will be negative for high beta assets and positive for low beta assets. Furthermore, it can be shown that the sign of $E(\tilde{r}_N) - r_F$ is identical to the sign of $-\partial C/\partial r_F$, where C is the aggregate consumption function. While micro theory tells us nothing about this sign, macro theory usually presumes that aggregate saving is positively related to the interest rate and thus that $E(\tilde{r}_N) - r_F$ should be positive. Merton concludes that this model appears to be consistent with the results found by B-J-S and others that indicate that high beta assets earn less and low beta assets earn more than predicted by the traditional asset pricing model. But until detailed investigation of the empirical implications of the model has been carried out, conclusions on these issues are tentative at best.[92]

The Existence of Heterogeneous Expectations

The model as originally derived (and all of the extensions discussed here) are based on the assumption that all investors view the probability distributions on all assets in exactly the same way: an assumption clearly violated in the world. Some have criticized the reality and even the usefulness of the model on these grounds although it is not exceptional in this respect; most of price theory involves essentially the same approach. Indeed, the assumption of perfect certainty, though much stronger than that of homogeneous expectations, has led to many important insights into the nature of markets and resource allocations. The assumption of identical tastes or a "representative consumer" often used in traditional price theory is quite analogous to that of homogeneous expectations, and while such an assumption is clearly erroneous as a description of reality, it has often been found to yield extremely useful insights into complex problems.

A number of authors[93] have examined the relaxation of the assumption of

---

[91]Roll [62] provides tests of the Sharpe-Lintner model based on taking explicit account of the potential errors involved in using proxy measures of the riskless rate and the market portfolio returns. He applies these tests to a sample of 793 weekly observations on U.S. Treasury bills beginning in 1949. The results seem to indicate that the asset pricing model does not adequately describe the structure of returns in the Treasury bill market.

[92]Recall that (28) is stated in terms of instantaneous rates, and a more complicated expression applies to discrete time returns as in (20).

[93]Primarily Lintner [41, 42]. See also Sharpe [69], Appendix D, and Fama [21].

homogeneous expectations and, as one might expect, it in no way plays a critical role regarding the existence of a market equilibrium solution in the two-period model.[94] In addition, Lintner[95] has demonstrated that the relaxation of the assumption eliminates the somewhat unattractive implication that all investors hold identical portfolios of risky assets, but so does the relaxation of some of the other assumptions, as we have seen. Market equilibrium prices can be written in the same form as that of equation (2) but with $E(\widetilde{D}_j)$, θ, and $\text{cov}(\widetilde{D}_j, \widetilde{D}_M)$ interpreted as very complex weighted averages (involving investor utility information) of all investors' expectations.

Unfortunately, these solutions seem to have little empirical content. It appears to be impossible to eliminate the individual utility information from these solutions to obtain equilibrium relationships stated solely in terms of potentially observable market parameters. It is also difficult to obtain closed form expressions for the equilibrium prices in such models, since they require complete knowledge of the marginal rates of substitution of expected return for variance at all points in the mean-variance plane for all investors. By closed form is meant an expression for the equilibrium prices which involves only exogenously given parameters such as probability assessments, quantities of assets, and investor preferences. However, the marginal rates of substitution of expected return for variance depend in general on the equilibrium position of each investor in the mean-variance plane and therefore are themselves functions of the prices of all assets. Since, given heterogeneous expectations, it is difficult if not impossible in most cases to eliminate the utility information from the equilibrium relationships, we cannot obtain prices solely as a function of exogenous parameters.

However, as Lintner has demonstrated,[96] a closed form solution can be obtained in the special case in which all investors' preferences functions, $U^i[E(\widetilde{R}), \sigma^2(\widetilde{R})]$, can be represented as

$$U^i = E(\widetilde{R}) - \alpha_i \sigma^2(\widetilde{R})$$

that is, the case of constant absolute risk aversion in the Pratt-Arrow sense. Since the marginal rate of substitution, $dE(R)/d\sigma^2(R) = -[\partial U/\partial \sigma^2]/[\partial U/\partial E]$, is a constant, α_i, it is obviously independent of market prices. In this case Lintner shows that equation (2) holds and that the market risk premium θ is proportional to the harmonic mean of the α_i values of all investors. In addition, the expected cash flows, $E(\widetilde{D}_j)$, and covariances, $\text{cov}(\widetilde{D}_j, \widetilde{D}_M)$, in (2) can then be interpreted as very complicated averages involving the probability assess-

---

[94] Although as Radner [59, 60] and Long [44] have pointed out, the situation may not be quite this simple in the context of the multi-period problem.

[95] In [41].

[96] *Ibid.*

ments and preferences of all investors for all assets. While such solutions can be obtained, their usefulness is not clear, other than that they provide an illustration of the fact that the structure of equilibrium prices is in many ways similar to that of the simple model.[97]

5. Conclusions

The mean-variance asset pricing model has thus far provided a major source of empirically testable propositions regarding the nature of risk and its relation to the equilibrium structure of asset prices. The currently available empirical evidence seems to indicate that the simple version of the asset pricing model[98] does not provide an adequate description of the structure of expected security returns.

The recent evidence presented by Black, Jensen, and Scholes and Fama and MacBeth[99] seems to indicate that the two-factor equation for equilibrium expected returns involving the market factor and the beta factor suggested by B-J-S and later derived theoretically by Black, Vasicek, and Brennan[100] may be an adequate representation of the *unconditional* expected return on assets, even though it is far from a complete specification of the stochastic structure of asset returns. Fama and MacBeth also present evidence which indicates the presence of two additional factors involving β_j^2 and the residual risk $\sigma(u_j)$, both of which have random coefficients whose means are zero. We do not as yet have completely satisfactory explanations for the existence of the beta factor, the stochastic nonlinearities, or the stochastic residual risk effects. However, the evidence seems to be entirely consistent with the three major equilibrium implications of the two parameter portfolio model: (1) The *ex ante* relationship between risk and return is linear, (2) no nonportfolio risk measure is systematically related to *ex ante* expected returns, and (3) market risk premiums are positive. In addition the data also seem to be consistent with market efficiency, since the stochastic coefficients in the monthly cross-sectional regression models of Fama and MacBeth and of Black, Jensen, and Scholes all seem to

---

[97]Lintner [41] also examines the equilibrium solution for the special case of constant absolute risk aversion with heterogeneous expectations where (1) 100 percent margin is required on all short sales, (2) no riskless asset exists, (3) no short sales are allowed, and (4) some investors "have no judgements whatsoever" with respect to some stocks in the market. These solutions are similar in many respects to those outlined above for the simple case of heterogeneous expectations, but they are much more complex.

[98]Cf. Sharpe [67], Lintner [42, 43], Mossin [56], and Fama [22].

[99]In [8] and [23], respectively.

[100]In [5], [75], and [12], respectively.

behave as fair game variables, and therefore do not provide any profitable trading opportunities.

The reality of the model has also been criticized by many. Virtually all of its assumptions have been criticized as inappropriate and suggested as the source of the apparent empirical inadequacies documented earlier by a number of authors.[101] However, as we have seen, most of the assumptions of the model have been shown to be capable of relaxation without destroying the essential nature of the results, and (except for heterogeneous expectations) these models are potentially empirically testable. Thus the mean-variance approach to asset valuation under uncertainty shows promise of a remarkable robustness. Perhaps one of the most promising lines of investigation at this time derives from the two-factor model resulting from the assumption of no riskless borrowing or differential interest rates[102] and the three-factor continuous time model derived by Merton.[103]

We now have substantial empirical documentation of the process generating the returns on assets and at least several potential theoretical explanations of these empirical results. Although empirical tests of the alternative theoretical explanations are currently in a rather preliminary state, there is little doubt that explicit empirical tests of alternative theories are forthcoming. While we do not yet have a complete solution to the asset pricing problem, in the recent past we have obtained a much better understanding of the nature of the process generating the returns on assets, and it seems likely that the rate of increase in our knowledge in this area will continue at least into the near future.

------

[101] Douglas [16], Friend and Blume [27], B-J-S [8], and Miller and Scholes [55].

[102] Cf. Black [5], Vasicek [75], and Brennan [12].

[103] In [53, 54].

Appendix

The Mean-Variance Valuation Model

Consider a world in which all investors (denoted by i) are risk-averse single-period expected utility maximizers whose consumption decisions are made independently of their portfolio decisions. Assume also that all investors' orderings of portfolios can be represented by a utility index of the form $G_i(e_i, v_i)$, where e_i is the expected total cash flow to be generated one period hence by the ith investor's portfolio and v_i is the variance of this cash flow. We also assume that $\partial G_i/\partial e_i > 0$, $\partial G_i/\partial v_i < 0$, all assets are infinitely divisible, and transactions costs and taxes are zero. Define

$$e_i = \sum_j X_{ij}\bar{D}_j - rd_i \tag{A1}$$

$$v_i = \sum_j \sum_k X_{ij}X_{ik}\sigma_{jk} \tag{A2}$$

X_{ij} = fraction of the total amount of firm j held by individual i

$\tilde{D}_j$ = the random total dollar cash flow paid to owners of firm j at time i

$\bar{D}_j = E(\tilde{D}_j)$

$$\sigma_{jk} = \begin{cases} \text{var}(\tilde{D}_j), j = k \\ \text{cov}(\tilde{D}_j, \tilde{D}_k), j \neq k \end{cases}$$

$r = (1 + R_F)$, where R_F is the one-period riskless rate of interest at which every consumer can borrow or lend,[104] and

d_i = net debt of individual i ($d_i > 0$ implies borrowing, $d_i < 0$ implies lending)

The individual investor's portfolio problem is

$$\operatorname*{Max}_{X_{ij}, d_i} G_i(e_i, v_i) \tag{A3}$$

---

[104] The model as formulated here can also be interpreted as an infinite time horizon model where all probability distributions of single-period cash flows are assumed stationary and r is the single-period riskless rate of interest (assumed identical for all periods).

subject to the budget constraint

$$\sum_j X_{ij} V_j - d_i = W_i \tag{A4}$$

where V_j = total market value of firm j at time 0, and W_i = total wealth of the ith individual at time 0. Under the assumption that all investors can borrow or lend at the rate R_F and that all investors have homogeneous expectations regarding the $\bar{D}_j$ and o_{jk}, we find the solution to the individual's portfolio problem by forming the Lagrangian

$$L = G_i(e_i, v_i) + \lambda_i [W_i - \sum_j X_{ij} V_j + d_i] \tag{A5}$$

Differentiating with respect to X_{ij} and d_i and eliminating λ_i provides the optimum conditions for each individual i:

$$\frac{\partial G_i}{\partial e_i} (\bar{D}_j - rV_j) + 2 \left(\frac{\partial G_i}{\partial v_i}\right) \sum_k X_{ik} o_{jk} = 0 \quad \text{for all } j \text{ and } i \tag{A6}$$

or equivalently for all pairs (j, t) we have by rearranging (A6) and dividing the equation for asset j by the equation for asset t:

$$\frac{\bar{D}_j - rV_j}{\bar{D}_t - rV_t} = \frac{\sum_k X_{ik} o_{jk}}{\sum_k X_{ik} o_{tk}} \quad \text{for all } i \tag{A7}$$

Market equilibrium requires that all assets be held, and this provides the condition

$$\sum_i X_{ij} = 1 \quad \text{for all } j \tag{A8}$$

Multiplying both sides of (A7) by $\sum_k X_{ik} o_{tk}$, summing over all i, using (A8), and rearranging, we obtain for all pairs (j, t):

$$\frac{\bar{D}_j - rV_j}{\sum_k o_{jk}} = \frac{\bar{D}_t - rV_t}{\sum_k o_{tk}} \tag{A9}$$

Denoting this common ratio by θ we obtain[105]

$$\theta = \frac{\bar{D}_t - rV_t}{\sum_k \sigma_{tk}} \qquad \text{for all } t$$

$$= \frac{\sum_t (\bar{D}_t - rV_t)}{\sum_t \sum_k \sigma_{tk}} = \frac{\bar{D}_M - rV_M}{\sigma_M^2} \qquad (A10)$$

where $\bar{D}_M$ = expected total cash flow paid by all firms in the market, V_M = total value of all firms in the market at time 0, and $\sigma_M^2 = \text{var}(\tilde{D}_M)$ = variance of total cash flow paid by all firms.

Substitution from (A10) into (A9) provides an expression for the equilibrium value of the jth firm:

$$V_j = \frac{1}{r}[\bar{D}_j - \theta \, \text{cov}(\tilde{D}_j, \tilde{D}_M)] \qquad \text{for all } j \qquad (A11)$$

where $\text{cov}(\tilde{D}_j, \tilde{D}_M) = \sum_k \sigma_{jk}$. Thus in equilibrium the value of the jth firm is the present value (discounted at the risk-free rate) of the certainty equivalent of the random payment $\tilde{Y}_j$. The certainty equivalent is simply the expected payment $\bar{D}_j$ minus a risk discount given by the product of θ, the price per unit of risk, and the "systematic" risk of the firm given by the covariance of its cash flow with the total cash flows from all other firms (the sum of its own variance and its covariances with all other firms). In addition, defining the expected return on asset j to be $E(\tilde{R}_j) = (\bar{D}_j/V_j) - 1$ and solving (A11) for $E(\tilde{R}_j)$ provides the expression for the equilibrium structure of expected returns on all assets:

$$E(\tilde{R}_j) = R_F + \lambda \, \text{cov}(\tilde{R}_j, \tilde{R}_M) \qquad (A12)$$

where $\lambda = [E(\tilde{R}_M) - R_F]/\sigma^2(\tilde{R}_M)$ is the market risk premium, $E(\tilde{R}_M) = \sum_i z_i E(\tilde{R}_i)$ is the expected return on the market portfolio, $z_i = V_i/V_M$, $\sigma^2(\tilde{R}_M)$ is the variance of return on the market portfolio, and $\text{cov}(\tilde{R}_j, \tilde{R}_M)$ is the covariance between the return on asset j and the return on the market portfolio.

Investor Preferences and the Market Risk Premium

An alternative interpretation of θ, the market price per unit of risk can be provided. While equation (A10) defines θ in terms of market parameters this

---

[105] Since, if $a_1/b_1 = a_2/b_2 = \ldots a_n/b_n = Z$, then $\sum_{k=1}^{n} a_i \Big/ \sum_{k=1}^{n} b_i = Z.$

"price" can also be interpreted solely in terms of the weighted average marginal rate of substitution of risk and return for each investor in the economy in equilibrium. To state the value equation in terms of investor preferences, we can use a typical equation from (A6). Rewrite the equation for firm j for the ith investor as:

$$\bar{D}_j - rV_j = 2 \left(\frac{\partial e_i}{\partial v_i}\right) \sum_k X_{ik} \sigma_{jk} \qquad \text{for all } i \text{ and } j \qquad (A13)$$

where $(\partial e_i/\partial v_i) = -(\partial G_i/\partial v_i)/(\partial G_i/\partial e_i) > 0$ is the marginal rate of substitution of expected dollar return for variance for individual i. It can be shown[106] that at equilibrium each investor's portfolio contains an identical fraction of the total value of every firm. That is, $X_{ik} = X_{ij} = X_i$ for all k, j, and i. Thus we can rewrite (A13) as

$$\bar{D}_j - rV_j = 2 X_i \left(\frac{\partial e_i}{\partial v_i}\right) \sum_k \sigma_{jk} \qquad \text{for all } i \text{ and } j \qquad (A17)$$

---

[106]Cf. Mossin [56]. In terms of our analysis this is easily seen by representing the system of equations for the ith investor given by (A6) in matrix notation as

$$\left(\frac{\partial G_i}{\partial e_i}\right)(\bar{D} - rV) + 2\left(\frac{\partial G_i}{\partial v_i}\right)\Sigma X_i = 0 \qquad (A6a)$$

where $\bar{D}$ and V are column vectors of expected total cash flows and values respectively, Σ is the covariance matrix for the random cash flows, and X_i is the column vector of the proportions of each company held by the ith individual. Assuming that Σ is non-singular and solving for X_i we have

$$X_i = (1/2)\left(\frac{\partial v_i}{\partial e_i}\right)\Sigma^{-1}(\bar{D} - rV) \qquad (A14)$$

Since the scalar $(\partial v_i/\partial e_i)$ is the only item on the right-hand side of (A14) which is subscripted by i, the composition of every investor's portfolio is identical up to a scale factor. In addition, each of the elements of the vector X_i is identical; that is, the individual i holds the same fraction of the total value of every firm in existence. To see this note that the first conclusion obtained from (A14) indicates

$$X_{ij}/X_{ik} = X_{sj}/X_{sk} \qquad (A15)$$

for any two investors i and s and any two securities j and k. Multiplying both sides of (A15) by X_{sk}, summing over all s, and using the equilibrium condition (A8) we have

$$\frac{X_{ij}}{X_{ik}} = 1 \qquad (A16)$$

and therefore for all individuals i, $X_{ij} = X_{ik} = X_i$ for all assets j and k.

Summing both sides of (A17) over all j, rearranging, and noting that $\sum_j \sum_k \sigma_{jk} = \sigma_M^2$:

$$\frac{\bar{D}_M - rV_M}{\sigma_M^2} = 2 X_i \left(\frac{\partial e_i}{\partial v_i}\right) \quad \text{for all } j \tag{A18}$$

Summing (A18) over all i and using (A8) and (A10) we see that

$$\theta = \frac{2}{L} \left(\frac{\overline{\partial e}}{\partial v}\right) \tag{A19}$$

where L is the total number of investors and

$$\left(\frac{\overline{\partial e}}{\partial v}\right) = \sum_{i=1}^{L} X_i \left(\frac{\partial e_i}{\partial v_i}\right)$$

is the weighted average marginal rate of substitution of return for risk for all investors.[107] (Note that the weight X_i is simply the fractional claim of individual i on the total market cash flow $\tilde{D}_M$.) Thus θ is proportional to the weighted average marginal rate of substitution of expected return for variance for all investors in the economy.

References

1. Arrow, K.J. "Le Rôle des Valeurs Boursieres pour la Repartition la Meilleur des Risques." *International Colloquium on Econometrics*, 1952. Centre

---

[107]Note that $(\overline{\delta e}/\partial v)$ is an equilibrium equal to the harmonic mean of the $(\partial e_i/\partial v_i)$ for all investors. To see this note that

$$2x_i \left(\frac{\partial e_i}{\partial v_i}\right) = \theta \quad \text{for all } i \tag{A20}$$

Solving this expression for X_i, summing both sides over all i, using (A8), and solving the result for θ we have

$$\theta = \frac{2}{\sum\limits_i \frac{1}{\gamma_i}} = \left(\frac{2}{L}\right)\gamma^* \tag{A21}$$

where $\gamma_i = (\partial e_i/\partial v_i)$, and $\gamma^* = L/\Sigma(1/\gamma_i)$ is the harmonic mean of the γ_i's. Note also that substituting from (A21) into (A20) for θ and solving for X_i yields $X_i = \gamma^*/\gamma_i L$.

National de la Recherche Scientifique, Paris, 1953, also in English as "The Role of Securities in the Optimal Allocation of Risk-Bearing," *Review of Economic Studies*, Vol. 31, No. 2 (April 1964), pp. 91–96.

2. Bailey, M. "Capital Gains and Income Taxation," in A.C. Harberger and M.J. Bailey, eds., *The Taxation of Income from Capital*, Washington, D.C.: The Brookings Institution, 1969.

3. —— and Jensen, M.C. "Risk and the Discount Rate for Public Investment," in M.C. Jensen, ed., *Studies in the Theory of Capital Markets* [36].

4. Bellman, R. *Dynamic Programming*, Princeton: Princeton Univ. Press, 1957.

5. Black, F. "Capital Market Equilibrium with Restricted Borrowing." *Journal of Business*, Vol. 45, No. 3 (July 1972), pp. 444–54.

6. —— and Scholes, M. "Capital Market Equilibrium and the Pricing of Corporate Liabilities." Financial Note No. 16c. Mimeographed. Massachusetts Institute of Technology, September 1970, revised January 1971.

7. ——, "Dividend Yields and Common Stock Returns: A New Methodology." Working Paper No. 488–70, Sloan School of Management, Massachusetts Institute of Technology, September 1970.

8. Black, F., Jensen, M.C., and Scholes, M. "The Capital Asset Pricing Model: Some Empirical Tests," in M.C. Jensen, ed., *Studies in the Theory of Capital Markets* [36].

9. Borch, K. "A Note on Uncertainty and Indifference Curves." *Review of Economic Studies*, Vol. 36, No. 1 (January 1969), pp. 1–4.

10. Breiman, L. "Investment Policies for Expanding Business Optimal in a Long Run Sense." *Naval Research Logistics Quarterly* (December 1960).

11. ——. "Optimal Gambling Systems for Favorable Games," in *Fourth Berkeley Symposium on Mathematical Statistics and Probability*, Berkeley, Calif.: Univ. of California Press, 1961.

12. Brennan, M.J. "Capital Market Equilibrium with Divergent Borrowing and Lending Rates." *Journal of Financial and Quantitative Analysis*, Vol. 6, No. 4 (December 1971), pp. 1197–1205.

13. ——. "Investor Taxes, Market Equilibrium and Corporate Finance." Unpublished Ph.D. dissertation, Massachusetts Institute Technology, June 1970.

14. Cass, D. and Stiglitz, J.E. "The Structure of Investor Preference and Asset Returns, and Separability in Portfolio Allocation: A Contribution to the Pure Theory of Mutual Funds." *Journal of Economic Theory*, Vol. 2, No. 2 (June 1970), pp. 122–60.

15. Debreu, G. *Theory of Value*. New York: John Wiley & Sons, Inc., 1959, Chap. 7.

16. Douglas, G.W. "Risk in the Equity Markets: An Empirical Appraisal of Market Efficiency." *Yale Economic Essays*, Vol. 9 (Spring 1969), pp. 3–45.

17. Fama, E.F. "Efficient Capital Markets: A Review of Theory and Empirical Work." *Journal of Finance*, Vol. 25, No. 2 (May 1970), pp. 383–417.

18. ——. "Multiperiod Consumption-Investment Decisions." Report No. 6830, Center for Mathematical Studies in Business and Economics, University of Chicago, revised May 1969.

19. ——. "Multiperiod Consumption-Investment Decisions." *The American Economic Review*, Vol. 60, No. 1 (March 1970), pp. 163–74.

20. ——. "Perfect Competition and Optimal Production Decisions under Uncertainty." *The Bell Journal of Economics and Management Science*, Vol. 3, No. 2 (Autumn 1972), pp. 509–30.

21. ——. "Risk, Return and Equilibrium." *Journal of Political Economy*, Vol. 79, No. 1 (January/February 1971), pp. 30–55.

22. ——. "Risk, Return and Equilibrium: Some Clarifying Comments." *Journal of Finance*, Vol. 23, No. 1 (March 1968), pp. 29–40.

23. —— and MacBeth, J. "Risk, Return and Equilibrium: Empirical Tests." Unpublished manuscript, University of Chicago, July 1972.

24. —— and Miller, M.H. *The Theory of Finance*. New York: Holt, Rinehart & Winston, 1972.

25. Feldstein, M.S. "Mean-Variance Analysis in the Theory of Liquidity Preference and Portfolio Selection." *Review of Economic Studies*, Vol. 36, No. 1 (January 1969), pp. 5–12.

26. Fisher, I. *The Theory of Interest.* Rev. ed. New York: Augustus M. Kelley, 1965.

27. Friend, I. and Blume, M. "Measurement of Portfolio Performance under Uncertainty." *The American Economic Review*, Vol. 60, No. 4 (September 1970), pp. 561–75.

28. Hamada, R.S. "Portfolio Analysis, Market Equilibrium and Corporation Finance." *Journal of Finance*, Vol. 24, No. 1 (March 1969), pp. 13–32.

29. Hakansson, N. "Capital Growth and the Mean-Variance Approach to Portfolio Selection." *Journal of Financial and Quantitative Analysis*, Vol. 6, No. 5 (January 1971), pp. 517–558.

30. Hirshleifer, J. "Efficient Allocation of Capital in an Uncertain World." *The American Economic Review*, Vol. 54, No. 2 (May 1964), pp. 77–85.

31. ——. "Investment Decisions under Uncertainty: Applications of the State-Preference Approach." *Quarterly Journal of Economics*, Vol. 80, No. 319 (May 1966), pp. 252–77.

32. ——. "Investment Decision under Uncertainty: Choice-Theoretic Approaches." *Quarterly Journal of Economics*, Vol. 79, No. 317 (November 1965), pp. 509–36.

33. ——. *Investment, Interest and Capital.* Englewood Cliffs, N.J.: Prentice-Hall, Inc., 1970.

34. Jacob, N. "The Measurement of Systematic Risk for Securities and Port-

folios: Some Empirical Results." *Journal of Financial and Quantitative Analysis*, Vol. 6, No. 1 (March 1971), pp. 815–34.

35. Jensen, M.C. "The Foundations and Current State of Capital Market Theory," in M.C. Jensen, ed., *Studies in the Theory of Capital Markets* [36].

36. ——. "The Performance of Mutual Funds in the Period 1945–1964." *Journal of Finance*, Vol. 23, No. 2 (May 1968), pp. 389–416.

37. ——. "Risk, the Pricing of Capital Assets, and the Evaluation of Investment Portfolios." *Journal of Business*, Vol. 42, No. 2 (April 1969), pp. 167–247.

38. ——, ed. *Studies in the Theory of Capital Markets*. New York: Praeger Publishers, forthcoming.

39. ——, and Long, J.B., Jr. "Corporate Investment under Uncertainty and Pareto Optimality in the Capital Markets." *The Bell Journal of Economics and Management Science*, Vol. 3, No. 1 (Spring 1972), pp. 151–74.

40. Latane, H. "Criteria for Choice Among Risky Ventures." *Journal of Political Economy*, Vol. 67, No. 2 (April 1959), pp. 144–55.

41. Lintner, J. "The Aggregation of Investors' Diverse Judgment and Preferences in Purely Competitive Securities Markets." *Journal of Financial and Quantitative Analysis*, Vol. 4, No. 4 (December 1969), pp. 347–400.

42. ——. "Security Prices, Risk, and Maximal Gains from Diversification." *Journal of Finance*, Vol. 20, No. 5 (December 1965), pp. 587–616.

43. ——. "The Valuation of Risk Assets and the Selection of Risky Investments in Stock Portfolios and Capital Budgets." *The Review of Economics and Statistics*, Vol. 47, No. 1 (February 1965), pp. 13–37.

44. Long, J.B., Jr. "Consumption-Investment Decisions and Equilibrium in the Securities Market," in M.C. Jensen, ed., *Studies in the Theory of Capital Markets* [36].

45. ——. "Corporate Investment under Uncertainty and Pareto Optimality in the Capital Markets." Unpublished manuscript, Graduate School of Management, University of Rochester, August 1970.

46. ——. "Notes on the Black Valuation Model for Risky Securities." Mimeographed. Graduate School of Management, University of Rochester, May 1971.

47. ——. "Wealth, Welfare and the Price of Risk." *Journal of Finance*, Vol. 27, No. 2 (May 1972), pp. 419–33.

48. Markowitz, H.M. "Portfolio Selection." *Journal of Finance*, Vol. 7, No. 1 (March 1952), pp. 77–91.

49. ——. *Portfolio Selection: Efficient Diversification of Investments*. New York: John Wiley & Sons, Inc., 1959.

50. Mayers, D. "Non-Marketable Assets and Capital Market Equilibrium under Uncertainty," in M.C. Jensen, ed., *Studies in the Theory of Capital Markets* [36].

51. ——. "Non-Marketable Assets and the Determination of Capital Asset

Prices in the Absence of a Riskless Asset." Working Paper No. 7114, Graduate School of Management, University of Rochester, November 1971, forthcoming in the *Journal of Business*.

52. Merton, R.C. "An Analytic Derivation of the Efficient Portfolio Frontier." Working Paper No. 493-70, Sloan School of Management, Massachusetts Institute of Technology, October 1970.

53. ———. "A Dynamic General Equilibrium Model of the Asset Market and Its Application to the Pricing of the Capital Structure of the Firm." Working Paper No. 497-70, Sloan School of Management, Massachusetts Institute of Technology, December 1970.

54. ———. "An Intertemporal Capital Asset Pricing Model." Working Paper No. 588-72, Sloan School of Management, Massachusetts Institute of Technology, February 1972, forthcoming in *Econometrica*.

55. Miller, M.H. and Scholes, M. "Rates of Return in Relation to Risk: A Reexamination of Some Recent Findings," in M.C. Jensen, ed., *Studies in the Theory of Capital Markets* [36].

56. Mossin, J. "Equilibrium in a Capital Asset Market." *Econometrica*, Vol. 34, No. 4 (October 1966), pp. 768-83.

57. ———. "Security Pricing and Investment Criteria in Competitive Markets." *The American Economic Review*, Vol. 59, No. 5 (December 1969), pp. 749-56.

58. Nemhauser, G. *Introduction to Dynamic Programming*, New York: John Wiley and Sons, Inc., 1966.

59. Radner, R. "Existence of Equilibrium Plans, Prices, and Price Expectations in a Sequence of Markets." Technical Report No. 5, Center for Research in Management Science, University of California, Berkeley, June 1970.

60. ———. "Problems in the Theory of Markets under Uncertainty." *The American Economic Review*, Vol. 60, No. 2 (May 1970), pp. 454-60.

61. Roll, R. "Assets, Money and Commodity Price Inflation under Uncertainty: Demand Theory." Working Paper No. 48-71-2, Graduate School of Industrial Administration, Carnegie-Mellon University, December 1971.

62. ———. "Bias in Fitting the Sharpe Model to Time Series Data." *Journal of Financial and Quantitative Analysis*, Vol. 4, No. 3 (September 1969), pp. 271-89.

63. ———. "Evidence on the 'Growth Optimum' Model." Working Paper No. 3-71-2, Graduate School of Industrial Administration, Carnegie-Mellon University, July 1971, revised April 1972.

64. ———. "Investment Diversification and Bond Maturity." *Journal of Finance*, Vol. 26, No. 1 (March 1971), pp. 51-66.

65. Samuelson, P.A. "The 'Fallacy' of Maximizing the Geometric Mean in Long Sequences of Investing or Gambling." *Proceedings of the National Academy of Sciences*, Vol. 68 (October 1971).

66. ———. "The Fundamental Approximation Theorem of Portfolio Analysis in

Terms of Means, Variances and Higher Moments." *Review of Economic Studies*, Vol. 38, No. 4 (October 1971), pp. 537–42.

67. Sharpe, W.F. "Capital Asset Prices: A Theory of Market Equilibrium Under Conditions of Risk." *Journal of Finance*, Vol. 19, No. 4 (September 1964), pp. 425–42.

68. ———. "Mutual Fund Performance." *Journal of Business*, Vol. 39, No. 1, Part 2 (January 1966), pp. 119–38.

69. ———. *Portfolio Theory and Capital Markets.* New York: McGraw-Hill Book Co., 1970.

70. Stigum, B. "Entrepreneurial Choice over Time under Conditions of Uncertainty." *International Economic Review*, Vol. 10, No. 3 (October 1969), pp. 426–42.

71. Tobin, J. "Comment on Borch and Feldstein." *Review of Economic Studies*, Vol. 36, No. 1 (January 1969), pp. 13–14.

72. ———. "Liquidity Preference as Behavior towards Risk." *Review of Economic Studies*, Vol. 25 (February 1958), pp. 65–85.

73. Treynor, J.L. "How to Rate Management of Investment Funds." *Harvard Business Review*, Vol. 43, No. 1 (January/February 1965), pp. 63–75.

74. ———. "Toward a Theory of Market Value of Risky Assets." Unpublished manuscript, 1961.

75. Vasicek, O.A. "Capital Asset Pricing Model with No Riskless Borrowing." Unpublished manuscript, Wells Fargo Bank, March 1971.

76. White, D.J. *Dynamic Programming.* San Francisco: Holden-Day, 1969.

**Part II
Implications for
Accounting**

5

Capital Markets Equilibrium,
Information Production, and
Selecting Accounting Techniques:
Theoretical Framework and
Review of Empirical Work

Nicholas J. Gonedes and
Nicholas Dopuch

Section I. Introduction

1.1 Preliminaries

Establishing methods for assessing the desirability and/or effects of alternative
accounting procedures is one of the pressing problems facing accounting policy-
making bodies. This paper deals primarily with one approach towards providing
those assessments—namely, the use of prices of (or rates of returns on) firms'
ownership shares. We provide both a theoretical framework for this approach
and, conditional on the implications of this framework, a review of available
empirical work. Our theoretical analysis and the review of empirical work indicate issues that cannot be, or have not been, resolved by analyses of ownership
share prices. Thus, we were induced to examine some proposed alternative
methods for assessing the desirability and/or effects of alternative accounting
techniques.

This paper deals only with external accounting and, in particular, with
accounting numbers transmitted to capital market agents.

A discussion of the desirability of alternative accounting techniques from
society's perspective requires a concept of social preference. The concept used in
this paper is Pareto optimality, which is a unanimity rule. From a given individual's perspective, desirability is determined by that individual's preference
ordering (see section 4).

The "effects" of changes in accounting techniques refer to the changes, if
any, in agents' assessed distribution functions of returns on ownership shares
induced by the changes in techniques (see section 3 or 8).

The preceding remarks indicate the general topic of interest here. A more
detailed description of our objectives and the structure of this paper is best
motivated by providing some historical perspective on methods used for assessing
the desirability and/or effects of alternative accounting techniques.

Reprinted with permission of the authors and from *Studies on Financial Accounting Objectives,* Supplement to *Journal of Accounting Research,* Vol. 12, 1974, pp. 48–129.

The authors gratefully acknowledge the many detailed comments provided by Joel Demski,
Eugene F. Fama, Ronald W. Masulis, Shyam Sunder and, in particular, John Dickhaut on
earlier drafts of this paper.

1.2 Some Historical Perspective

Equilibrium prices of firms' securities are dependent upon capital market agents' assessed distribution functions of returns to holders of those securities. Such distribution functions are dependent upon the available information about firms' production-investment decisions. The nature of this available information is determined by the results of private and public decisions on investing in information production. The latter decisions are simply additional types of production-investment decisions (see sections 3 and 4). An example of such a decision is one which generates accounting numbers via a particular set of accounting procedures. The selected procedures are parts of the prevailing technology used in the production of these numbers. In different words, the selected accounting procedures define, in part, an experiment. The resulting accounting numbers comprise the sample evidence produced by that experiment. A change in the accounting procedures is equivalent to a change in the underlying experiment. Just as the scheme used to produce, say, automobiles, results from a production-investment decision, the experiment used to produce accounting numbers results from a production-investment decision.

What criteria should be used for optimally selecting accounting techniques by those who produce or regulate the production of accounting numbers? This is one of the vexing questions in the economics of producing accounting numbers. Prior to the mid-1960's, most attempts to deal with this question essentially used "a priori" models whose theoretical underpinnings and rigor were not always apparent. For a review of these models see Nelson [1973]. These models purported to establish criteria for identifying the "best" or "optimal" accounting procedures, conditional on stated (and unstated) assumptions about those who use and produce accounting numbers. Some well-known works that were based upon this approach include Paton and Littleton [1940], Chambers [1966], and Edwards and Bell [1965].

In recent years this approach has come under heavy criticism because of: (1) the theoretical deficiencies of works that advocated or used it; and (2) the fact that it has seemed possible, using this approach, to declare the superiority of just about any set of accounting procedures, depending upon the particular a priori model adopted. Such criticism led to an increased emphasis on the use of empirical analyses in attempting to assess the effects and desirability of alternative procedures. And in 1966 the accounting profession witnessed the first of a series of conferences devoted exclusively to empirical research in accounting.[1]

As we will indicate (see especially section 8.2), many of the available empirical studies dealing with accounting procedures were equally incapable of resolving the indicated assessment problems. This can be ascribed, in part, to the

---

[1]Conference on Emprical Research in Accounting, held by the Institute of Professional Accounting, University of Chicago.

fact that the theoretical underpinnings needed for empirical work appeared to be underdeveloped (see Hakansson [1973]). Since serious empirical work in accounting is a recent phenomenon, this situation is not entirely surprising.

Developments in the theory of, and evidence on, capital market efficiency appear to have provided substantial impetus to the refinement of empirical work in accounting.[2] Recall that an efficient capital market is one in which (1) market prices "fully reflect" available information and, by implication, (2) market prices react instantaneously and unbiasedly to new information. Capital market efficiency played an important role in available assessments of: announcements of accounting numbers (Ball and Brown [1968] and Gonedes [1974]); dividend announcements (Watts [1973]); announcements of changes in accounting techniques (Kaplan and Roll [1972], Ball [1972a and 1972b]), and Sunder [1973a]); and stock-split announcements (Fama, Fisher, Jensen, and Roll [1969]), among other things.

Capital market efficiency also played a critical role in the available attempts to assess the desirability of alternative accounting procedures and regulations pertaining to selections of accounting procedures. This can be seen in the work of Beaver [1972, p. 409], Beaver and Dukes [1972 and 1973], Benston [1973], Friend [1972], Stigler [1964], and others.

There are two critical underpinnings of the arguments advanced in the papers that rely upon capital market efficiency in dealing with alternative accounting procedures:

A.1. Capital market efficiency, taken by itself, provides sufficient justification for using prices of (or rates of return on) firms' ownership shares in assessing the *desirability* of alternative accounting procedures or regulations.

A.2. Capital market efficiency, taken by itself, provides sufficient justification for using prices of (or rates of return on) firms' ownership shares in assessing the *effects* of alternative accounting procedures or regulations.

Not all of the studies that deal with alternative accounting procedures invoke both of these arguments. And in some cases (e.g., Beaver and Dukes [1972]), the position expressed in A.1 is qualified on grounds of incomplete information about the available opportunities for, and the cost of, information production. This qualification is not included in A.1 because, as will be indicated in sections 6 and 8, it is not a central factor in our determining the logical validity of A.1. That is, our analysis of A.1 applies even if one has complete information on the available opportunities for and costs of information production.

If assertion A.1 is accepted then one can proceed as if the prices of (or

---

[2]A review of the theory and evidence pertaining to capital market efficiency is provided in Fama [1970b]. Some implications of capital market efficiency for external reporting are discussed in Gonedes [1972a].

rates of return on) firms' ownership shares provide signals regarding capital market agents' preferences for the results of alternative information-production decisions involving accounting procedures. This seems to point the way around a fundamental deficiency of the other approaches described above; namely, their inability to provide unambiguous means of ranking procedures in terms of capital market agents' preferences, rather than, for example, some researcher's preferences.

Given our objectives (see section 1.1), the logical validity of assertions A.1 and A.2 is of direct concern. The manner in which we deal with this issue is spelled out in the next subsection.

1.3 Details on Objectives and Structure of Paper

The general objectives of this paper were indicated in section 1.1. At a more detailed level, the objectives are as follows:

(0.1)   To determine the extent to which the prices of firms' ownership shares can, in theory, be used to assess the desirability and/or the effects of alternative accounting procedures, conditional on capital market efficiency.

(0.2)   To evaluate available empirical works that used market prices of firms' ownership shares in assessing the effects and/or desirability of alternative procedures.

(0.3)   To consider alternative institutional arrangements for prescribing and regulating the use of accounting procedures.

(0.4)   To review and evaluate "nonprice" methods of assessing the desirability and/or effects of alternative accounting procedures.

The issues associated with (0.1) pertain to the kinds of signals for resource allocation provided by the capital market, conditional on the existing institutional structure. In order to deal with this objective, we need some standards against which aspects of the contemporary institutional setting can be compared. Some of the needed benchmarks are provided by assuming a competitive pricing mechanism for information. This assumption is consistent with the explicit and implicit assumptions of works that rely on either assertion A.1 or A.2, given in section 1.2. It also provides some useful insights on alternative market and non-market settings for information production. Finally—and most importantly—it allows us to highlight the importance of some contemporary factors (e.g., disclosure laws and joint production of information and other commodities) vis-à-vis the logical validity of assertions A.1 and A.2.

Sections 2–5 provide details on a framework for analyzing information-production issues. Section 2 identifies aspects of the market setting underlying this framework. Section 3 provides details on the nature, role, and value of information from the perspective of an individual capital market agent. In section 4 we provide details on the production of information from the perspective of an individual producer. The set of characterizations provided in sections 2–4 is not a set of necessary conditions for the theoretical conclusions given in later sections, but it is a set of sufficient conditions. These characterizations identify a variety of issues on the kinds of individual behavior leading to the equilibrium results of interest to us. Those who are not interested in these details of individual behavior need not read sections 3–4. And if one is not interested in the formal assumptions of the market setting within which individual behavior is assumed to take place then section 2 may be omitted.

Section 5 extends the framework of sections 2–4 to the aggregate level. It is indicated that even though information has the attributes of a public good, it is still meaningful to talk about a competitive price for information—under appropriate market conditions. If one is willing to accept this conclusion on faith then section 5 may be omitted.

Our major theoretical conclusions are provided in section 6. There we investigate the details of some alternative sets of market conditons, all of which are wholly or partially consistent with our competitive-pricing approach. The last set of conditions examined (fifth scenario) captures the essential features of the contemporary institutional setting. This set of conditions allows us to examine the logical validity of assertions A.1 and A.2.

We conclude that as it stands assertion A.1 is logically false.[3] Assertion A.2 is found to have logical validity. The key points leading to these conclusions involve: (1) the rule of excluding nonpurchasers; (2) the relationship between production-investment decisions (e.g., information-production decisions), the market-value rule, and the prices of firms' ownership shares; and (3) the implications of capital market efficiency. Our concluding that assertion A.1 is, as it stands, logically invalid does not imply that one could not construct special cases wherein assertion A.1 would be logically valid. Such special cases might be obtained by, for example, making special assumptions about information production or agents' preference orderings. Some examples of special cases are given in section 10. We believe that developing the details of such special cases is an important area for future work.

Sections 2–6 provide, therefore, a logically complete framework for analyzing information production within the context of competitive markets. The analysis begins with individual consumer-investor and producer behavior; it moves on to consider the existence and nature of market equilibrium; and it examines the implications of equilibrium information-production decisions.

Section 7 provides a summary of the key results of sections 2–6 and moti-

---

[3]It is well to note that some recent criticisms of work based upon capital market efficiency confuse the logical validity of A.1 with that of A.2 by treating remarks on assessing effects as if they were remarks on assessing desirability; see, e.g., May and Sundem [1973] and Abdel-Khalik [1972].

vating remarks for sections 8 and 9, which provide reviews of empirical work. Those who are interested only in these reviews should go directly to section 7.

The logical validity of assertion A.2 justifies an approach for assessing the effects of alternative accounting procedures and regulations (such as SEC disclosure regulations). This approach was used, in one way or another, in a variety of available studies. What have we learned from these studies? What kinds of empirical problems are associated with the approach used in these studies? How can one represent the effects of alternative accounting procedures and regulations? These are among the questions asked in section 8 which is divided into two major subsections. Section 8.1 deals with assessments of effects based upon the two-parameter asset pricing model. Section 8.2 deals with assessments based upon the dividend (earnings) capitalization model.

We conclude (in section 6) that assertion A.1 is logically invalid. In section 8 we observe that available price-oriented studies of effects leave a variety of questions unanswered. This motivated an examination of some "nonprice" approaches for assessing desirability and/or effects. That examination appears in section 9. Our review of each nonprice approach attempts to answer the following questions: (1) If the framework of the approach is accepted as being appropriate can one conclude that the studies using the approach provide reliable evidence on the effects and/or desirability of alternative accounting techniques or regulations? and (2) Is there any theoretical connection between the framework of the approach and capital market agents' resource allocation decisions?

Section 10 briefly summarizes our major conclusions. These conclusions have implications for the institutional arrangements used for selecting and regulating the use of accounting techniques. Some of these implications are identified and discussed in section 10. That section also provides some illustrative special cases wherein the prices of firms' ownership shares can provide some information on the desirability of alternative accounting procedures and regulations.

Section 2. Market Setting

A detailed discussion of the market setting assumed for the production and dissemination of information is given in section 5. Suffice it to note here that the markets for the inputs (e.g., capital and labor) used by firms that produce information are assumed to be perfect markets.

We invoke standard assumptions regarding markets for all other goods and services. Specifically, for these other products, we assume that all firms transact in perfectly competitive markets. It is also assumed that the capital market is perfect (i.e., there are zero transaction costs, any information that is currently publicly available is costlessly available to everybody, etc.). In short, all firms and individuals are assumed to behave as price-takers in frictionless markets.

A characterization of those who produce information will be provided later. Regarding other producers (i.e., other firms), the following characterization is used: Firms purchase and pay for the services of their inputs at the beginning of each period t. They use these services to produce goods and services that will be sold at the beginnings of future periods. At the beginning of period t, firms sell shares in their period $t + 1$ market value (which is a random variable at the beginning of t) in order to finance their outlays at the beginning of period t. The shares sold by firms are the investment assets that consumers hold. Maximization of the current market value of the shares held by its current shareholders is the firm's goal. This is the so-called "market value rule."[4] It is assumed that the technology of the firm is known. This is a restrictive assumption. But relaxing it does not alter the major conclusions of our discussion (those presented in section 6).

Since the technology of each firm is assumed known for all t, there is: (1) no uncertainty about the alternative production-investment decisions that a firm can make at the beginning of each period t and (2) no uncertainty about the inputs required for implementation of each alternative production-investment decision. As of the beginning of period t, the uncertain item is the market value of the firm at the beginning of period $t + 1$, conditional on each of the alternative production-investment decisions.

Consumer-investors are assumed to maximize the expected utility of lifetime consumption, $\underline{c}_T = (c_0, c_1, \ldots, c_t, \ldots, c_T)$, where c_i, $i = 0, 1, \ldots,$ T denotes consumption at the beginning of period i, measured by some numeraire. For simplicity, we assume that the consumer-investor dies, with probability 1, at the beginning of period T; thus c_T is his bequest. The consumer-investor's preferences for lifetime consumption are taken to be representable by a function $V_T(\underline{c}_T)$ that is nondecreasing and strictly concave in each component of $\underline{c}_T$. Some additional notation is defined below. For bervity the phrases "at period t" or "at time t" will often be used instead of the phrase "at the beginning of period t."

$\tilde{\Gamma}_\tau$ = the state of the world prevailing at time τ. (Throughout, tilde denotes a random variable.)

$R_j(\Gamma_\tau)$ = the rate of return on security j over the period $\tau - 1$ to τ when the state at time τ is Γ_τ.

$x_{j\tau}$ = the proportion of the consumer-investor's portfolio invested in security j at time τ; $\sum_j x_{j\tau} = 1$, for each τ.

---

[4]Under appropriate conditions this rule is consistent with shareholders' assumed objective of expected utility maximization. A detailed discussion of sufficient conditions is given by Fama and Miller [1972, pp. 176–81 and 299–301]. The extent to which Pareto optimality is attained when production-investment decisions are made according to the market value rule, the capital market is perfect, and the so-called two-parameter asset pricing model applies is discussed in Fama [1972], Jensen and Long [1972], and Stiglitz [1972]. Note that all of our remarks on the properties of equilibrium in the *market for information* are conditional on the properties of equilibrium in all other markets.

$F(\Gamma_{\tau+1}|\Gamma_\tau)$ = the distribution function of $\tilde{\Gamma}_{\tau+1}$ conditional on $\tilde{\Gamma}_\tau = \Gamma_\tau$.

$\quad w_\tau$ = the consumer-investor's wealth at time τ.

$\quad \underline{c}_\tau = (c_0, c_1, \ldots, c_t, \ldots, c_\tau)$.

$\quad M_\tau$ = the number of securities available in the capital market at time τ.

Suppose that the beginning of period $t > 0$ is the present. The consumer-investor's wealth at time $t + 1$ is given by

$$\tilde{w}_{t+1} = \sum_{j=1}^{M_t} x_{jt}(w_t - c_t)(1 + R_j(\tilde{\Gamma}_{t+1}))$$

Using the backward-optimization approach of dynamic programming (see Bellman [1957, pp. 81–86]), the consumer-investor's problem at time t may be expressed as:

$$V_t(\underline{c}_{t-1}, w_t|\Gamma_t) = \max_{c_t, \underline{x}_t} \int_{\Gamma_{t+1}} V_{t+1}(\underline{c}_t, w_{t+1}|\Gamma_{t+1})dF(\Gamma_{t+1}|\Gamma_t)$$

subject to

$$w_t \geqslant c_t \geqslant 0 \quad \text{and} \quad \sum_j x_{jt} = 1$$

for $t \leqslant T - 1$, where $\underline{x}_t = (x_{1t}, x_{2t}, \ldots, x_{M_t t})$. $V_t(\underline{c}_{t-1}, w_t|\Gamma_t)$, for $t \leqslant T$, is the consumer-investor's maximum expected utility of lifetime consumption conditional on the state, Γ_t, the consumer-investor's wealth, w_t, both at time t, and past consumption expenditures $\underline{c}_{t-1}$. Note that $V_t(\underline{c}_{t-1}, w_t|\Gamma_t)$, for $t < T$, is derived from $V_T(\underline{c}_T)$, the consumer-investor's utility function defined on lifetime consumption. At time t, $\underline{c}_{t-1}$ is known. Thus, for the given $\underline{c}_{t-1}$, we may write

$$U_t(c_t, w_{t+1}|\Gamma_{t+1}) = V_{t+1}(\underline{c}_{t-1}, c_t, w_{t+1}|\Gamma_{t+1})$$

Consequently, the consumer-investor's problem at time t may be reexpressed as

$$\max E\left\{ U_t(c_t, \tilde{w}_{t+1}|\tilde{\Gamma}_{t+1}) \right\}$$

subject to

$$w_t \geqslant c_t \geqslant 0, \qquad \sum_j x_{jt} = 1$$

where the maximization is with respect to $(c_t, \underset{\sim}{x}_t)$. In short, even though we are dealing with a multiperiod problem, the consumer-investor's preferences at the beginning of any period, say, period t, may be represented by the induced "one-period" utility function $U_t(c_t, w_{t+1} | \Gamma_{t+1})$. It can be shown that, given the properties of $V_T(.)$, $U_t(.)$ is nondecreasing and strictly concave in c_t and w_{t+1}; see Fama [1970a]. In the remainder of this paper, the consumer-investor's problem at the beginning of period t will be represented by the induced utility function $U_t(c_t, w_{t+1} | \Gamma_{t+1})$. Also, for added simplicity, we assume that preferences are not "state dependent." Thus, we consider the simplified induced utility function $U_t(c_t, w_{t+1})$. Remarks on state-dependent utility functions are provided by Fama [1970a].

It is important for what follows to note that $E\left\{U_t(c_t, \widetilde{w}_{t+1})\right\}$ is conditional upon assessed distribution functions for returns in each period τ such that $T \geqslant \tau \geqslant t$. That is, as of t and for every firm j, the consumer-investor must assess a distribution function for the *vector* random variable $\underset{\sim}{R}_j = (\widetilde{R}_{jt}, \widetilde{R}_{jt+1}, \ldots, \widetilde{R}_{jT})$.

It is assumed that the activities of firm j, for all j, can be classified into types (e.g., risk classes) and that each investor's assessed multivariate distribution function of rates of return for each type satisfies the following condition: the investor's assessed distribution functions conditional upon different levels of investment (in any period) by the firm in that type of activity are deterministically related to each other. This assumption enables us to avoid some dynamical issues that need not be considered for the major points made here. Its important effect is that, for each firm, each consumer-investor needs only to assess one multivariate distribution function for each type of activity permitted by the known technology of the firm, given the deterministic function connecting the distribution functions for different levels of investment. This assumption functions for different levels of investment. This assumption is satisfied, for example, when each investor's assessed distribution function for each type of activity of a given firm is independent of the firm's levels of investment in that activity over the consumer-investor's lifetime.

The behavior of consumers may now be summarized as follows: Consumers come to the market (at the beginning of each period t) with portfolios of assets (acquired in previous periods) and resources (e.g., labor or services) that may be sold to firms. The consumer needs to select a level of current consumption and a portfolio of assets whose value at the beginning of period $t + 1$ is the value of $\widetilde{w}_{t+1}$. Consumers are assumed to behave in accordance with the rule of maximizing expected utility.

As indicated earlier, this paper deals with information produced for capital

market agents' use on personal account (i.e., "external accounting"). The
mechanism through which the allocation of real resources is affected by this
kind of information can be loosely described as follows. Consumer-investors
must assess the distribution functions of returns on firms' shares in order to
make optimal portfolio decisions. In our framework (see section 3) the exact
distribution functions from which returns will be drawn are random. Without
new information investors must use the marginal distribution functions of
returns. New information permits the use of distributions conditional upon
completely reliable signals on the exact distributions. Thus, produced information affects the distributions used by investors in making optimal portfolio
decisions and, consequently, it affects the equilibrium prices of firms' ownership shares. So, given firms' adherence to the market value rule, this information affects firms' production-investment decisions, or the allocation of real
resources. In short, information produced for investors' use on personal account
affects firms' production-investment decisions via the information's effects on
the prices of firms' ownership shares. Additional details on this issue are provided
by Gonedes [1973a, section 6].

　　We shall want to emphasize equilibrium both in the capital market and
in the "market" for information, as of the beginning of time t. Thus, equilibrium
in all other markets will be taken as given. Equilibrium in the capital market
at the beginning of time t is assumed to be established by a process of tâtonnement with recontracting. That is, no decisions (by firms or consumer-investors)
are final until equilibrium is attained. Prior to that, all prices announced in this
market are tentative and, of course, all decisions made at these prices are
tentative. A clear discussion of this type of process is provided by Patinkin
[1965, pp. 531–40]. The end result of this process is a set of market clearing
prices for investment assets and the corresponding set of firms' optimal production-investment decisions, conditional upon all the information that is publicly
available at period t.

　　Finally, and again for analytical purposes, all the events of period t leading
to capital market equilibrium and equilibrium information-production decisions are assumed to take place "at the beginning of period t."

Section 3. Representations of Information and
Information-Production Opportunities

The major objective of this section is to present a precise analytical framework
for representing both the notion of information and the production of information, conditional on parts of the market setting described in section 2.

　　Consider the consumer-investor's problem at time t. In order to select an
optimal portfolio of investment assets at time t and an optimal level of period t
consumption, c_t, the consumer-investor needs to assess the distribution function

of $\tilde{\underline{R}}_j = (\tilde{R}_{jt}, \tilde{R}_{jt+1}, \ldots, \tilde{R}_{jT})$ for each firm j whose ownership shares are traded in the capital market at time t. Of course, each consumer-investor wants his assessed distribution functions to be identical to the underlying or true distributions of returns, since realized returns will be drawings from the latter distributions.[5] But we will not assume that this identity holds. Instead, we permit differences between assessed and true distributions of returns and use these differences in characterizing the information-production process.[6] Unless otherwise indicated, the following discussion applies to any one capital market agent. This will enable us to avoid excessive use of subscripting to distinguish among capital market agents. The same approach will be used in section 4.

The production of new information will be envisaged as an interaction with Nature. Produced information will be treated as a completely reliable signal from Nature pertaining to the true or underlying distribution functions of returns on assets traded in the capital market. That is, for any given firm, produced information is about the distribution function of returns to holders of that firm's securities, conditional upon the known technology of the firm.

As with the production of other goods and services, the production of information to be used at time $\tau + 1$, for any τ, must be initiated at time τ. For our purposes, it will be sufficient to consider the production of information to be used at the beginning of one period, $t + 1$. So the production of information to be used at any period $\tau > t + 1$ will not be permitted.

At time $t + 1$, capital market equilibrium will be conditional upon two sets of information: (1) newly produced signals associated with information-production decisions made at time t; and (2) all information that is available to capital market agents when they come to the market at $t + 1$ but which is

---

[5]In other words, this identity never leads to lower maximum expected utility if attaining the identity is costless. Consider the following example. Suppose that only one kind of asset is traded in the capital market and that we are dealing with a one-period model. Further suppose that some investor is convinced that the distribution function to be used by Nature will be either F_1, F_2, or F_3. From this investor's perspective, Nature will first pick a distribution function and then draw a rate of return from this distribution function. If the investor must make his consumption-investment decision before the distribution function selected by Nature is revealed then his consumption-investment decision is constrained to be identical for F_1, F_2, and F_3. If, however, he can arrange (at no cost) to receive the realization of a completely reliable signal, say, $\tilde{\theta}$, such that: (a) $\tilde{\theta} = 1$ if Nature chooses either F_1 or F_2 and $\tilde{\theta} = 0$ if Nature chooses F_3 and (b) the realization of $\tilde{\theta}$ will be available before he must make his consumption-investment decision, then his consumption-investment problem will be less constrained. This is because his decision in the latter situation is constrained to be the same for F_1 and F_2, but not for F_3. Consequently, maximum expected utility in the second situation is no less than that in the first (no-information) situation. In short, so long as the cost of doing so is zero, the investor will be motivated to develop schemes for determining Nature's (i.e., the true) distribution function of returns.

[6]The notion of a true distribution is, of course, an analytical device. It is simply a label for the distribution that will ultimately be used by Nature in determining the realized rates of return on assets. Capital market agents need not agree on these distributions.

not associated with agents' period t information-production decisions. We often refer to the second type as the initially available information. This kind of information may be associated, for example, with information-production decisions made prior to time t. Moreover, it includes the details of the assumed known technology of each firm.

The essence of the signal received from Nature can be explained as follows. We represent attributes of the economic environment by scalar random variables. The information-production process will involve selecting (1) an attribute and (2) the system which determines what aspects of that attribute will be made known to an agent by Nature. That which is made known to the agent constitutes the *signal* from Nature. Different signals will pertain to different attributes of the economic environment. Signals pertaining to combinations of attributes will also be considered.

Suppose, for example, that the scalar random variable $\tilde{\theta}$ denotes some attribute of the economic environment. A tilde appears above θ because, before the information-production process is completed, the attribute's value which will be selected by Nature is a random variable. Let $\Omega_i, i = 1, 2, \ldots, N$ be a partitioning of the possible values of $\tilde{\theta}$ into N mutually exclusive and exhaustive sets. Suppose that the signal from Nature is $\tilde{\theta} \in \Omega_i$, for some i. In this case, it is assumed that for any firm $j, j = 1, 2, \ldots, f$, the implied distribution function for the vector of rates of return, $\underline{\tilde{R}}_j$, on the jth firm's shares is $F_j(\underline{R}_j|\Omega_i)$. (The implied distributions for different firms' shares are not assumed to be identical.) The initially available information is that $\tilde{\theta} \in \Omega_0 = \cup_{i=1}^{N} \Omega_i$. Thus, if the signal from Nature is $\tilde{\theta} \in \Omega_0$ then this information is not new, in the sense that it does not have implications differing from those implied by the information available when agents first come to the market.

Suppose (for simplicity) that $\tilde{\theta}$ is a discrete random variable. Then the distribution function of $\underline{\tilde{R}}_j$ would be the marginal distribution function $F_j(\underline{R}_j|\Omega_0) = \Sigma_{i=1}^{N} F_j(\underline{R}_j|\Omega_i) \Pr (\tilde{\theta} \in \Omega_i)$ if no signal from Nature were received. Note that $F_j(\underline{R}_j|\Omega_i) = \Sigma_{\theta \in \Omega_i} F_j(\underline{R}_j|\theta) \Pr (\tilde{\theta} = \theta|\tilde{\theta} \in \Omega_i)$, for $i = 0, 1, 2, \ldots, N$. Thus, if the completely reliable signal from Nature were the scalar-valued realization, say, $\tilde{\theta} = \theta$, then one would know the exact distribution from which the realization of $\underline{\tilde{R}}_j$ will be drawn. When the signal from Nature is the set-realization, say, $\tilde{\theta} \in \Omega_i$ then (in general) one knows only that the value of $\underline{\tilde{R}}_j$ will be drawn from one member of the set of distributions, $F_j(\underline{R}_j|\theta)$ for $\theta \in \Omega_i$.

Signals pertaining to combinations of attributes are easily handled by considering vectors $\underline{\tilde{\theta}} = (\tilde{\theta}_1, \tilde{\theta}_2, \ldots, \tilde{\theta}_\varrho)$ where $\tilde{\theta}_i$ denotes the ith attribute. Let $\underline{\Omega}^k = (\Omega_1^k, \Omega_2^k, \ldots, \Omega_{\overline{N}}^k)$ be the partition for the kth attribute; for each $k, \Omega_i^k, i = 1, 2, \ldots, \overline{N}$, are mutually exclusive and $\Pr (\tilde{\theta}_k \in \cup_i \Omega_i^k) = 1$. For simplicity, we assume that the same value of $\overline{N}$ applies to all attributes. The sample space for all ϱ attributes is $X_{k=1}^{\varrho} \underline{\Omega}^k$, where X denotes Cartesian product. The initially available information on the kth attribute is that $\tilde{\theta}_k \in \Omega_0^k = \cup_{i=1}^{\overline{N}} \Omega_i^k$. We assume that there exist producers of signals pertaining to any

combination of the ℓ economic attributes. Thus, consumer-investors may contemplate purchasing observations pertaining to any of 2^ℓ, where $\tilde{\theta}_j$, $j = 1$,
$2, \ldots, 2^\ell$, where $\tilde{\theta}_j$ now denotes the jth combination of attributes. We assume
that the possible realizations of $\tilde{\theta}_j$, for each j, may be partitioned into N
exhaustive and mutually exclusive subsets, $\underline{S}_1^j, \underline{S}_2^j, \ldots, \underline{S}_N^j$. If the signal received
is $\tilde{\theta}_j \in S_i^j$, for some i, then the implied distribution of returns on the mth firm's
shares is $F_m(\underline{R}_m | \underline{S}_i^j)$. For each i, the dimensionality of $\underline{S}_i^j$ equals j, for all
$j = 1, 2, \ldots, 2^\ell$. The initially available information on the jth combination of
attributes is that $\tilde{\theta}_j \in \underline{S}_0^j = \cup_{i=1}^N \underline{S}_i^j$.

The information conveyed by the realization $\tilde{\theta}_j \in \underline{S}_i^j$, for some j and $i \neq 0$,
is said to have an effect if, for some firm s, $F_s(\underline{R}_s | \underline{S}_i^j) \neq F_s(\underline{R}_s | \underline{S}_0^j)$. That is,
new information has an effect if it induces a change in an agent's assessed
distribution functions.

Note that we made no assumptions on the agreement among agents'
assessments. In particular, we did not (and will not) assume that agents agree
on the distributions of returns implied by a realization of any signal. The results
described in section 5 are based upon some assumptions on the agreement
among agents' assessments. These assumptions will be introduced as needed.
Finally, note that an opportunity to invest in a signal on a specific combination
of attributes using a specified partition defines one opportunity to produce
information.

The production function of each producer of information (viewed from the
perspective of an individual consumer-investor) still needs to be characterized.
We assume that the (known) production function of one who produces information is such that different levels of production costs induce different sample-
space partitions defining the signal produced. In effect, each partition represents
a different experiment; the signal from Nature is the outcome of the experiment.
Moreover, we assume that (given optimal production decisions on the part of
information producers) the refinement of these partitions varies directly with
costs; here, the following definition is used:

Definition. Let $\left\{ \underline{S}_i^j; i = 1, 2, \ldots, N \right\}$ and $\left\{ \hat{\underline{S}}_i^j; i = 1, 2, \ldots, \hat{N} \right\}$ be two different
partitions for the jth signal, $j = 1, 2, \ldots, 2^\ell$. $\left\{ \hat{\underline{S}}_i^j \right\}$ is said to be more refined
than $\left\{ \underline{S}_i^j \right\}$ if for every $\hat{\underline{S}}_i^j \in \left\{ \hat{\underline{S}}_i^j \right\}$ there is a $\underline{S}_i^j \in \left\{ \underline{S}_i^j \right\}$ such that $\hat{\underline{S}}_i^j \subseteq \underline{S}_i^j$.

The stated assumption about the relationship between the total costs
of information production and refinement is analogous to the standard assumption that the total cost of producing any good or service varies directly with the
quantity produced.

We assume that each producer of a signal pertaining to a given combina-
tion of attributes $\tilde{\theta}_j$, $j = 1, 2, \ldots, 2^\ell$ can produce any of a finite number of
partitions, $\left\{ \underline{S}_{ik}^j; i = 1, 2, \ldots, N_k \right\}$, $k = 1, 2, \ldots, n_j$, for the jth attribute, where
n_j is the total number of alternative partitions that can be produced for attribute
j.

Finally, it is assumed that for each j, the subscripting on the partitions is such that partition k is less refined than partition $k + 1$, for $k = 1, 2, \ldots,$ $n_j - 1$.

Section 4. Gains from Information Production

The major objective of this section is to provide details on the way in which opportunities to purchase information affect maximum expected utility of lifetime consumption. The framework given here leads to a precise analytical representation for the gains to be had from purchasing information. The characterizations provided in this section are conditional on the setting described in section 2 and the representations given in section 3.

Recall from the derivation of $U_t(c_t, w_{t+1})$, the consumer's induced one-period utility function, that $U_t(c_t, w_{t+1}) \equiv V_{t+1}(\underline{c}_{t-1}, c_t, w_{t+1})$. Thus,

$$U_t(c_t, w_{t+1}) = \max_{c_{t+1}, \underline{x}_{t+1}} \int_{\Gamma_{t+2}} V_{t+2}(\underline{c}_{t+1}, w_{t+2}) dF(\Gamma_{t+2} | \Gamma_{t+1}) \quad (4.1)$$

where $\tilde{w}_{t+2} = \Sigma_j x_{jt+1}(w_{t+1} - c_{t+1})(1 + R_j(\tilde{\Gamma}_{t+2}))$. Thus, $U_t(c_t, w_{t+1})$ is the value of maximum expected utility at the beginning of $t + 1$, conditional on c_t and the realization $\tilde{w}_{t+1} = w_{t+1}$. As indicated earlier, the decisions made by any consumer-investor at the beginning of any period are also conditional upon the initially available information at the beginning of that period. Let $\underline{S}^I$ denote the information that is publicly available at the beginning of period $t + 1$. Note that $\underline{S}^I = \{\underline{S}_{0k}^j; k = 1, 2, \ldots, n_j; j = 1, 2, \ldots, 2^\ell\}$. That is, if for any attribute j and partition k one observes $\theta_j \in \underline{S}_{0k}^j$ then this realization provides no new information at time $t + 1$.

The dependence of $U_t(c_t, w_{t+1})$ on $\underline{S}^I$, $\underline{x}_{t+1}$, and w_{t+1} will be recognized by writing

$$U_t(c_t, w_{t+1}) = E[U_{t+1}(c_{t+1}^0, \tilde{w}_{t+2}) | \underline{x}_{t+1}^0, \underline{S}^I, w_{t+1}]$$

where $(c_{t+1}^0, \underline{x}_{t+1}^0)$ is the optimal value of $(c_{t+1}, \underline{x}_{t+1})$ at the beginning of period $t + 1$.

Suppose that the consumer-investor receives, at time $t + 1$, a costless drawing based on the kth partition, $\{\underline{S}_{ik}^j; i = 1, 2, \ldots, N_k\}$, for some j. If the realization is $\underline{\theta}_j \in \underline{S}_{ik}^j$, for specified i, then the maximum expected utility that can be had by using this information is:

$$E\left\{U_{t+1}(c_{it+1}^{jk}, \tilde{w}_{t+2}) | w_{t+1}, \underline{x}_{it+1}^{jk}, \underline{S}_{ik}^j, \underline{S}^I\right\}$$

where $(c_{it+1}^{jk}, \underline{x}_{it+1}^{jk})$ is the optimal consumption-investment decision conditional on the signal $\tilde{\theta}_j \in S^j_{ik}$. Since (by assumption) this signal is a completely reliable message "from Nature" about the actual distribution functions of $\tilde{R}_h$, for all h,

$$E\{U_{t+1}(c^{jk}_{it+1}, \tilde{w}_{t+2})|w_{t+1}, x^{jk}_{it+1}, S^j_{ik}, S^I\} \geq E\{U_{t+1}(c^0_{t+1}, \tilde{w}_{t+2})|\underline{x}^0_{t+1}, w_{t+1}, \underline{S}^I\}$$

Next, consider the case where information is not costless. Suppose that the consumer must pay an amount at $t + 1$ equal to K for a signal on $\tilde{\theta}_j$ using partition k. Let

$$\phi_{t+1}(K, S^j_{ik}) = \max_{\{c_{t+1}, \underline{x}_{t+1}\}} E\{U_{t+1}(c_{t+1}, \tilde{w}_{t+2})|w_{t+1} - K, \underline{x}_{t+1}, S^j_{ik}, \underline{S}^I\} \quad (4.2)$$

and

$$W_{t+1}(S^j_{ik}, \underline{S}^I) = E\{U_{t+1}(c^0_{t+1}, \tilde{w}_{t+2})|w_{t+1}, x^0_{t+1}, S^j_{ik}, \underline{S}^I\} \quad (4.3)$$

Consider $E\{\tilde{W}_{t+1}(S^j_{ik}, \underline{S}^I)\}$, where the expectation is taken with respect to the distribution function of the signal on $\tilde{\theta}_j$ using partition k. From the definition of (c^0_{t+1}, x^0_{t+1}), $E\{\tilde{W}(S^j_{ik}, \underline{S}^I)\} = E\{U_{t+1}(c^0_{t+1}, \tilde{w}_{t+2})|w_{t+1}, x^0_{t+1}, \underline{S}^I\}$, the maximum expected utility when no signal on any attribute is purchased before the consumer must make his optimal consumption-investment decision at the beginning of period $t + 1$. Thus, $\phi_{t+1}(0, \underline{S}^I) = E\{\tilde{W}(S^j_{ik}, \underline{S}^I)\}$.

Before the signal about $\tilde{\theta}_j$ is observed, the consumer-investor simply owns a gamble on the signal. The outcome of this gamble will be available at $t + 1$ before the process of attaining capital market equilibrium at $t + 1$ ends. Letting $\pi^j_{ik} = \Pr(\tilde{\theta}_j \in S^j_{ik})$, for $i = 1, 2, \ldots, N_k$, for given k and j, the maximum expected utility of this gamble at $t + 1$ for $K = 0$ is

$$E\{\tilde{\phi}_{t+1}(0, S^j_{ik})\} = \sum_i [\max_{c_{t+1}, \underline{x}_{t+1}} E\{U_{t+1}(c_{t+1}, \tilde{w}_{t+2})|w_{t+1}, \underline{x}_{t+1}, S^j_{ik}, \underline{S}^I\}] \pi^j_{ik}$$
$$(4.4)$$

If no signal, and thus no gamble, is purchased then the maximum expected utility outcome is $\phi_{t+1}(0, \underline{S}^I)$.

It can be shown that $\phi_{t+1}(K, S^j_{ik})$ is a nonincreasing concave function of K.[7] This implies that $E\{\tilde{\phi}_{t+1}(K, S^j_{ik})\}$ is a nonincreasing concave function of K. Thus, there exists a value $K'' \geq 0$ such that $E\{\tilde{\phi}_{t+1}(K'', S^j_{ik})\} = \phi_{t+1}(0, \underline{S}^I)$ and $E\tilde{\phi}_{t+1}(K, S^j_{ik}) \geq \phi_{t+1}(0, \underline{S}^I)$ for $K \leq K''$. All of this says that the consumer-investor gains nothing in terms of maximum expected utility if the cost of the gamble on the signal about $\tilde{\theta}_j$ is K''; he gains (loses) if this cost is less

---

[7] See Luenberger [1969, p. 261]. This result may be more visible if the consumer-investor's maximization problem is formulated in terms of the amounts invested in different securities, rather than the proportions of his portfolio invested in each security.

(greater) than K''. This suggests that one may measure the consumer-investor's gain (or net payoff), at time $t + 1$, from purchasing information by the difference between K'' and the amount that he must actually pay for the gamble on the signal about $\tilde{\underline{\theta}}_j$, for any j.

An information-production opportunity is said to be more desirable than another if the gain from the first opportunity exceeds that from the second. "Indifference" and "less desirable" can be expressed in terms of these gains in obvious ways.

For a given attribute, $\tilde{\underline{\theta}}_j$, the consumer-investor has the option of purchasing a drawing from any partition k, $k = 1, 2, \ldots, n_j$. By construction partition k is less refined than partition $k + 1$, for all $k \leqslant n_j - 1$; see section 3. Consequently, $E\{\tilde{\phi}_{t+1}(0, \underline{S}^j_{ik})\}$, $k = 1, 2, \ldots, n_j$ is a nondecreasing sequence and, by implication, the maximum amount that the consumer-investor would pay for a signal on $\tilde{\underline{\theta}}_j$ using partition k, $k = 1, 2, \ldots, n_j$ is a nondecreasing sequence in k.[8] The logic behind this result is given in Marschak [1967, pp. 9.1-9.2]. Note that this result does not say that the expected net value of a signal on $\tilde{\underline{\theta}}_j$ using partition k is a nondecreasing sequence in k, because $E\ \tilde{\phi}_{t+1}(0, \underline{S}^j_{ik})$ is not adjusted for the cost of such a drawing.

In the above, we assumed that the realized value of the purchased signal is available and is used at the beginning of period $t + 1$ and that payment for the opportunity to receive and use a realization of any signal is made at the beginning of $t + 1$. It is a small matter, however, to consider the same setting but with the payment (for the signal) being made at the beginning of period t.

If payment for the signal (the realization of which is still available for use at $t + 1$) is made at time t then the induced one-period utility function

---

[8]This result strengthens the analogy (given in section 3) between the refinement of the partition defining the signals on a given attribute and the quantity of a good, given the nonsatiation assumption of conventional economic analyses. In general, the nonsatiation assumption allows one to say that: (1) there is some ordering of the quantity of a given commodity (holding the quantities of all other commodities constant) such that every consumer's utility is nondecreasing in the ordered quantities and (2) the appropriate ordering is in terms of increasing quantity. Our result for refinement allows similar statements, namely: (a) there is some ordering of the partitions defining the signals on a given attribute (holding the partitions for other attributes unchanged) such that every consumer's maximum expected utility is nondecreasing in the ordered partitions and (b) the appropriate ordering is in terms of increasing refinement. Note, however, that our result for refinement induces only a partial ordering because two partitions for signals on the same attribute may be such that neither one is more refined than the other. The latter situation does not arise in our discussion because of the production function assumed to characterize any information-producer's operations. Moreover, even if this situation did arise it would not affect any of the main points made in section 6. Finally, just as the nonsatiation axiom (taken by itself) cannot be used to order (in terms of preferences) the quantities of, say, two different commodities, our result on refinement (taken by itself) does not induce an ordering of information-production opportunities pertaining to two different attributes. In order to get such an ordering (for different commodities or different information-production opportunities) one would have to make additional assumptions about, or actually get all the details of, an agent's utility function.

applicable at the beginning of period t is $U_t(c_t, w_{t+1}) = E\{\tilde{\phi}_{t+1}(0, \underline{S}^j_{ik})\}$, for the purchase of a signal on attribute j using partition k. Suppose that an amount equal to L must be paid at time t for this drawing. Then, at time t, the consumer-investor's problem is

$$\max_{\{c_t, \underline{x}_t\}} E\{U_t(c_t, \tilde{w}_{t+1})\} \tag{4.5}$$

subject to

$$(w_t - L) \geqslant c_t \geqslant 0$$

$$\sum_j x_{jt} = 1$$

where $\tilde{w}_{t+1} = \sum_j x_{jt}(w_t - L - c_t)(1 + \tilde{R}_{jt})$. Just as $E\{\tilde{\phi}_{t+1}(K, \underline{S}^j_{ik})\}$ is a nonincreasing concave function of K,

$$\max_{\{c_t, \underline{x}_t\}} E\{U_t(c_t, \tilde{w}_{t+1})\}$$

is a nonincreasing concave function of L. In addition, when $L = 0$

$$\max_{\{c_t, \underline{x}_t\}} E\{U_t(c_t, \tilde{w}_{t+1})\}$$

is a nondecreasing function of refinement. The first result follows from the fact that the payment of $L > 0$ at time t reduces every possible realization of $\tilde{w}_{t+1}$. The payment of $K > 0$ at time $t + 1$ also reduces the value of whatever realization of $\tilde{w}_{t+1}$ happened to be observed at time $t + 1$. Since both payments have the same effect on the ultimate realization of $\tilde{w}_{t+1}$, they affect maximum expected utility at time $t + 1$ in the same way. And since $E\{U_t(c_t, \tilde{w}_{t+1})\}$ is a positive linear combination of maximum expected utility at time $t + 1$, it is affected in the same way by K and L. The behavior of $E\{U_t(c_t, \tilde{w}_{t+1})\}$ as a function of refinement also results from the fact that $E\{U_t(c_t, \tilde{w}_{t+1})\}$ is a positive linear combination of maximum expected utility at time $t + 1$.

It will be helpful for what follows to have an alternative way of characterizing the effects of purchasing information (i.e., drawings on signals). The alternative provided here is expressed in terms of simple and compound lotteries. (Such lotteries or "gambles" are discussed in, e.g., Luce and Raiffa [1957, p. 26] and LaValle [1970, pp. 401–03].)

Suppose that the consumer-investor is now at the beginning of period t and that he decides not to purchase drawings on any signals. When the consumer-investor solves his multiperiod consumption-investment problem, he ends up with an optimal decision rule that defines the optimal consumption-invest-

ment decision for each period conditional upon the realization of wealth in
the predecessor period and the predecessor period's consumption decision. At
the beginning of period t, the investor can derive his conditional distribution
function of wealth for any period $\tau > t$. The conditioning arguments of this
distribution function are the optimal decision rule, c_{t-1}, w_t, and the investor's
assessed distribution functions of rates of return on firms' ownership shares.
Consider the derived conditional distribution function of $\widetilde{w}_{t+2}$, denoted by
$G(w_{t+2})$; for simplicity the aforementioned conditioning arguments will be
left as implicit arguments of $G(\cdot)$.

Now suppose that the investor purchases the right to receive a signal on
attribute j from partition k. This drawing will be available for use at the beginning of period $t + 1$ (as in our earlier analysis). Also suppose that the investor
must pay an amount equal to L for this drawing and the payment must be made
at the beginning of period t. As indicated earlier, when the consumer-investor
purchases such a right his optimal decision at time $t + 1$ is conditional on the
realization of the signal and L, as well as on past realizations of wealth and
past consumption. That is, the investor's decision rule for $t + 1$ now has two
additional arguments: the value of the payment L and the realization of the
signal. Note that the value of L affects the realized value of $\widetilde{w}_{t+1}$, which is an
argument of the optimal decision rule in the no-information case. Once again,
for each realization of the signal about $\widetilde{\theta}_j$ and for the stated value of L, the
investor can derive at time t the distribution function of $\widetilde{w}_{t+2}$ conditional on
c_{t-1}, w_t, L, the realization of the signal about $\widetilde{\theta}_j$, and his associated optimal
decision rule. Consider the case of $\widetilde{\theta}_j \in \underline{S}^j_{ik}$, for some value of i. Denote the
corresponding conditional distribution function of $\widetilde{w}_{t+2}$, constructed at time t,
by $F(w_{t+2} | \underline{S}^j_{ik}, L)$. As of time t, however, this is not the distribution of $\widetilde{w}_{t+2}$
that the investor faces. Since there is one such conditional distribution for each
value of i, the distribution that the investor will ultimately face at $t + 1$ will
be determined by a random selection device. Thus, at time t, the conditional
distribution of $\widetilde{w}_{t+2}$ faced by the investor if $F^*(w_{t+2} | L) = E[\widetilde{F}(w_{t+2} | \underline{S}^j_{ik}, L)]$
$= \Sigma_i F(w_{t+2} | \underline{S}^j_{ik}, L) \Pr(\widetilde{\theta}_j \in \underline{S}^j_{ik})$. In short, relative to the no-purchase-of-informa-
tion case, the consumer-investor is now dealing with a compound gamble. The
first part of the gamble involves a signal about $\widetilde{\theta}_j$ from partition k. The second
part of the gamble involves a drawing on $\widetilde{w}_{t+2}$, with distribution function
$F(w_{t+2} | \underline{S}^j_{ik}, L)$ if $\widetilde{\theta}_j \in \underline{S}^j_{ik}$. The ultimate outcome of this compound gamble can
be described, as of the beginning of period t, by the distribution function
$F^*(w_{t+2} | L)$. Thus, the consumer-investor will decide to purchase, at t, the
signal about j from partition k (where the observed signal becomes available
at $t + 1$) if, at time t, the distribution function $F^*(w_{t+2} | L)$ induces higher
expected utility than the distribution function $G(w_{t+2})$. In the special case
where, for a given value of L, $F^*(w_{t+2} | L)$ and $G(w_{t+2})$ are identical distribution
functions, the consumer-investor would be indifferent towards purchasing or
not purchasing a signal about $\widetilde{\theta}_j$ from partition k.

In the remainder of this paper, the value of L, for a given consumer-investor, will be referred to as the price paid by that consumer-investor for the results of information production.

Section 5. Market Settings for Information Production

We are ultimately interested in determining whether the market prices of firms' ownership shares can be used to assess the effects and/or desirability of information-production decisions made by a firm on behalf of its current owners. As indicated earlier, a given selection of accounting techniques is one type of information-production decision. We cannot pursue our ultimate interest, however, until we say more about the market setting for information production. Thus far, we have indicated (in section 2) only that markets for inputs (e.g., labor and capital) used by information producers are "perfect markets." The output market remains to be considered. In doing so, we shall indicate conditions under which it is meaningful to talk about a *competitive* market for the results of information production.

One of the basic problems in considering the market for the results of information production is that, unlike "private" goods, one person's use of produced information does not reduce the amount of produced information that is available for other users. In short, produced information is a public good. But this does not mean that the market mechanism cannot be used for information production. It does suggest that special care is needed in specifying the kind of market setting that can be used. We shall consider two plausible specifications. One uses the tools of market game theory (see, e.g., Shapley and Shubik [1969]); the other involves a setting appropriate for the private production of public goods under more or less conventional assumptions. Under both of these specifications it is quite appropriate to talk about a competitive pricing mechanism for the results of information production.

5.1 Equilibrium in the Market for Information

Under the *market game theory* scheme, it is assumed that there is costless and unrestricted bargaining among participants in the process of producing and disseminating information. No participant is forced to produce or purchase information. Any number of participants may enter into a contract for information at mutually acceptable terms. Produced information resulting from any such contract is made available only to those who enter into the contract. In short, under this scheme, the production and dissemination of information are handled via the contracting and recontracting of groups or "coalitions." The major tool used to characterize this process is the *core* of a market game. An outcome is said to be in the core if that outcome is consistent with individual rationality, group rationality, and Pareto optimality. An outcome is consistent with group rationality if no subgroup can improve its payoffs, relative to those dictated by the outcome, by not cooperating with others and entering into a contract involving only the members of that subgroup. When information production is the issue at hand, the outcomes or payoffs are the *net gains* from information production; see section 4. Outcomes in the core are such that no agent can do better by using the resources under his control.

Using the assumptions and characterizations provided in sections 2–4, Gonedes [1973a] shows that applying the game-theoretic approach to the problem of information production leads to the following conclusions (among others). (1) A *core* for the problem of information production does exist. Since this result assumes unrestricted competition amongst coalitions and since outcomes in the core are equilibria, the implication is that a competitive equilibrium exists for information production. (2) the net gains of consumer-investors and information-producers converge to a competitive allocation in the classical sense. (3) Each competitive equilibrium is a Pareto optimal state. The derivation of these results uses two assumptions not stated in section 3. First, it is assumed that all consumer-investors agree on the alternative partitions applicable to each attribute. Second, it is assumed that there is agreement among consumer-investors' rankings of information-production opportunities (see section 3), where each consumer-investor's ranking is in terms of the maximum amount that he is willing to pay for each information-production opportunity.

The limiting result given in (2) is obtained when the number of agents of all types becomes arbitrarily large. (See Gonedes [1973a, pp. V.11–V.12].) This result states that, in the limit, the net gain of any agent converges to his marginal contribution to the results of information production. This, in turn, implies the existence of competitive prices (in the limit) for each equilibrium outcome of the information-production process. And these prices fulfill the same roles as competitive prices in more conventional analyses of resource allocation in a competitive situation.

Gonedes' formal results pertain to the implications of information for optimal allocations of real resources via firms' production-investment decisions. The implications of information for trading profits resulting from private access to new information were not given much attention. But his framework does have implications for the latter kind of information, which was recently examined by Fama and Laffer [1971] and Hirshleifer [1971]. When Gonedes' framework is applied to information used for trading purposes, as discussed in the Fama/Laffer and the Hirshleifer papers, no information for trading is produced if doing so requires the use of real resources; see Gonedes [1973a, section II and footnote 4]. We rely upon this result in the following sections which, as was indicated earlier, deal only with external accounting (i.e., the production of information for use by capital market agents). Thus, our remarks pertain directly to information having implications for the allocation of real resources.

Another approach to the information-production problem requires viewing it (from the outset) as one involving the private production of public goods under fully competitive conditions in the usual sense (i.e., zero transaction costs, large numbers of consumer-investors and information-producers, price-taking behavior, etc.). This approach is developed in detail by Demsetz [1970] under the important condition that nonpurchasers of the results of information production can be excluded from using these results. The assumptions and characterizations given in sections 2–4 are consistent with Demsetz's analysis. His analysis uses demand functions. For the problem at hand, the argument of such a function for any *given* attribute would be a measure of the refinement used to define signals, which (as indicated earlier) is analogous to the quantity dimension of a good or service. For Demsetz's analysis we would have to make the standard assumption that each individual's demand function, for a given attribute, is downward sloping. (A necessary condition for this assumption's violation is that the signal on the given attribute be an *inferior* good; see, e.g., Quirk and Saposnik [1968, p. 56] .) The two assumptions (see above) that must be added to those of section 3 in order to obtain Gonedes' results are also required for Demsetz's results.

The analysis provided by Demsetz indicates that the private production of public goods leads to results that satisfy the conditions for competitive equilibrium: markets are cleared; there are no incentives for producers or consumers to alter their allocations of resources; prices are treated as exogenous parameters by every agent, etc. Two important conclusions of this analysis are: (1) given the ability to exclude nonpurchasers, private producers can produce public goods (information, for the problem at hand) efficiently; and (2) the payment of different prices for the same good (or service) is consistent with a competitive equilibrium if the good is a public good. This last result is consistent with the convergence result of the game-theoretic approach; see Gonedes [1973a] .

The results of Demsetz's analysis are consistent with the convergence results of the game-theoretic analysis provided by Gonedes. This is not unexpected, since the assumptions used at the outset of Demsetz's analysis correspond to the limiting conditions in Gonedes' analysis. Since the aspect of capital market behavior considered here is well described by the "large numbers of agents" condition, that limiting result appears applicable (under the stated assumptions).

The major point of the preceding discussion is that conditions similar, or identical, to those familiar to economic analyses can be used in specifying a setting for information production that leads to a competitive pricing mechanism for the results of information production. And the equilibrium induced by this mechanism will consist of a Pareto optimal set of information-production decisions. Much of the discussion in the next section is expressed in terms of such a competitive pricing mechanism. That discussion will indicate the kinds of conditions that must be satisfied in order to justify using the prices of firms' ownership shares in assessing the desirability of alternative information-production schemes. Some implications of disclosure laws and *jointly* selling ownership shares and rights to receive and use information are also considered in that discussion. For brevity, we shall not distinguish between the market-game theory approach and the private-production-of-public-goods approach when information production proceeds under fully competitive conditions.

5.2 Remarks on the Framework

The framework developed in sections 3–4 provides one explicit scheme for representing information, information production, and gains from information production. In some respects, this framework may appear to be overly restrictive. For example, we assumed that the available technology for information production is *known*. Our assumptions rule out various kinds of "learning," among other things.

It is important to recognize, however, that the framework given here does not represent a set of necessary conditions for that which is ultimately desired: a scheme that is consistent with the existence and Pareto optimality of a competitive equilibrium in the market for information. Our framework is sufficient for this result, using either the approach of Gonedes [1973a] or Demsetz [1970].

In short, no matter what characterizations are used for information, information production, and gains from information production, the analytical results to be given in section 6 still will hold so long as the characterizations used are consistent with the existence and Pareto optimality of a competitive equilibrium in the market for information.

Section 6. Determining Optimal Information-Production Decisions: Five Scenarios

This section examines the extent to which prices of firms' ownership shares can be used in assessing the desirability of alternative information-production decisions. Three types of firms will be considered. They are "information-producers," "noninformation-producers," and combined "information-noninformation-producers." Our examination takes the following form: A series of scenarios will be specified and the extent to which desirability can be assessed (using the ownership-share prices of firms of some type) in each

scenario will be considered. The market settings of the scenarios become progressively more realistic. This approach serves to identify the critical aspects
of the contemporary institutional setting which affect the extent to which the
prices of (some type) of firms' ownership shares can be used in assessing the
desirability of alternative information-production decisions (e.g., selections of
accounting procedures). Throughout, the results from a competitive pricing
mechanism will be used as standards for comparison. The applicability of such
a mechanism to information production was discussed in section 5.

The representations of information and information-production opportunities given in section 3 underlie the discussion in this section. Also, the
sequence of events given in sections 3 and 4 is used in this section. The present
is the beginning of period t. The production of information to be used at the
beginning of $t + 1$ must be initiated at the beginning of period t. As indicated
earlier, we do not consider the production of information at the beginning of
any period $\tau > t$ for use in period $\tau + 1$. This restriction does not affect the
conclusions given here; it does simplify the analysis. The manner in which any
consumer-investor assesses the desirability of purchasing results of information
production was described in section 4.

6.1 First Scenario. For this scenario, we specify the following.

S.1: The kind of information produced is information pertaining to individual
firms.
S.2: Information about individual firms is produced by information-producers
that are entities *separated* from the firms to which the information is
related.
S.3: Information production takes place under fully competitive conditions.
S.4: Nonpurchasers of the services provided by information-producers can
be excluded from the use of produced information.

Under this scenario we have two types of firms: (1) those which produce
goods and services other than information about themselves and (2) those
which produce information about other firms.[9] It should be clear that the
only "different" attribute of the second type of firm is its product—information. Except for that feature, a firm of type (2) is the same as any firm of the
first type insofar as economic analysis is concerned. We shall refer to the type
(1) firms as "noninformation-producers" and those of type (2) as "information-producers."

The noninformation-producers sell rights to the goods and services they

---

[9]Just as any economic agent can simultaneously be a producer and a consumer, any
firm can simultaneously be a type (1) and type (2) firm. But in this case, the produced
information is still about some other firm.

produce. Similarly, the information-producers sell rights to receive and use the information which they produce. Recall from section 3 that produced information is a signal about a specific attribute using some partition. And note that the product of an information-producer is a public good in the sense that one person's use of it does not affect the quantity of produced information available for another's use. Thus, the purchase price paid for information is not a price paid for private control over some produced information; instead, it is an entry fee which, once paid, entitles the payer to enter the group of persons allowed to use the produced information.

Both types of firms are assumed to finance their production-investment activities by selling ownership shares. These are shares in the firms' market values at the beginning of period $t + 1$. Also, both types of firms make optimal production-investment decisions according to the market value rule, via the tâtonnement process described in section 2.

Given the specifications of this scenario, it is evident that the determination of optimal information-production decisions is governed by the market mechanism in the usual way. For each firm of either type the optimal production investment decisions are those which maximize the value of the current owners' shares. That is, in this scenario, the prices of information-producers' ownership shares do reflect individuals' assessments of the desirability of alternative information-production decisions. Since part of the technology characterizing information production consists of accounting procedures, the same market mechanism determines optimal accounting procedures.

The existence of competitive prices for the situation at hand was discussed in section 5. For additional insight, we now consider some characteristics of equilibrium prices.

Let P_ℓ be the equilibrium price of one ownership share issued by firm ℓ. Since ownership shares are traded in a perfect market and since these shares provide rights to *private* property, all agents transact at the same equilibrium price, P_ℓ. Let d_j^i be the equilibrium price paid at time t by agent i (to some information-producer) for the right to receive and use (at time $t + 1$) a signal on attribute j. (See sections 3 and 4). Since produced information is a public good, different agents can, in general, pay different equilibrium prices for the same right. (See section 5.)

As indicated in section 4, simultaneous transactions in ownership shares and rights to use produced information are equivalent to the construction of compound gambles. Since neither investors' original assessed distribution functions of returns nor their assessments of the implications of new information are required to be identical, the compound gambles need not be the same for all investors, even if their transactions are identical. Thus, one can only state that (in general) the equilibrium price of any compound gamble must be equal to the price of every other gamble (simple or compound) that is perceived (by a given agent) to be a perfect substitute for the compound gamble.

And in a perfect capital market such a perfect substitute must exist. If, for example, the simultaneous transactions of agent i involve purchasing one ownership share in firm ℓ and a right to receive and use (at time t +1) a signal on attribute j then the price of the compound gamble is $P_\ell + d_j^i$. This is the price that must be equal to the price of another gamble that is deemed, by agent i, to be a perfect substitute for the compound gamble.[10]

For each j an information-producer must select the optimal level of refinement. Since, for each attribute j, a signal is a public good, the quantity to which the marginal cost of refinement must be equated in determining an optimal information-production decision is $\Sigma_{i=1}^Q d_j^i$, where Q is the total number of agents.[11] (See Paul Samuelson [1954 and 1955].) The important feature of this scenario is that there are such guides for the determination of optimal information-production decisions. And, given such guides, the general issue of assessing the optimality of alternative information-production decisions can be solved in a straightforward manner. Indeed, under this scenario, such an assessment is no different from assessing the optimality of production-investment decisions pertaining to private goods.

Note that, in equilibrium, there will be only one information-producer of a signal on attribute j, for each j. Since (1) the costs of producing signals about a given economic attribute are invariant to the number of buyers of rights to receive and use produced information, at each level of refinement, and (2) the revenues of each information-producer vary directly with the number of buyers, at each level of refinement, we have a situation in which there is perfect competition for an entire market rather than within a market. The concept of competition for a market is discussed in detail by Demsetz [1968]. For each type of signal produced, the information-producer that will survive in equilibrium is the one that can produce the signal at the minimum cost. This result also applies to the next three scenarios.

6.2 Second Scenario. For this scenario, we retain specifications S.1, S.3, and S.4 from the first scenario. Specification S.2 is replaced by

S.2.1: Information about a firm may be produced by an information-producer—an entity separated from the firm to which the information is related—or it may be produced by the firm itself. In the latter case, the firm's current shareholders do not automatically get to use produced

---

[10] A *sufficient* condition for two gambles to be perfect substitutes is that the random variables associated with the gambles be *equivalent*. Two random variables, say $\bar{x}$ and $\bar{y}$, are said to be equivalent if Pr $(\bar{x} \neq \bar{y}) = 0$; i.e., $\bar{x}$ and $\bar{y}$ are equivalent if they are equal with probability one.

[11] As indicated in section 4, the level of refinement, for a given j, is somewhat analogous to the quantity of production considered in conventional analyses.

information. They must purchase rights to receive and use produced information, as do the current nonowners of the firm's shares.

This scenario is more realistic than the first to the extent that it allows for firms that produce: (1) goods and services other than information about themselves and (2) information about themselves. Does this difference alter any of the results obtained for the first scenario?

Upon comparing specifications S.2 and S.2.1, one sees that we are now allowing for firms that are combinations of the two types of firms examined under the first scenario. But since specifications S.3 and S.4 still apply, there is really no change in any of the basic results. It is still the case that, in equilibrium, the price paid by an agent for a compound gamble is equal to the price of any other gamble (simple or compound) that is perceived (by that agent) to be a perfect substitute for the compound gamble. Moreover, all of the opportunities (gambles) available to consumer-investors under the first scenario are also available under the second scenario. Indeed, since there is still perfect competition in the production of information of every type, there is no special advantage or disadvantage (for any consumer-investor) to purchasing information from the combined firms rather than from the separate information-producers, at the equilibrium prices.

Under the second scenario, we simply have a situation in which the combined firms are engaged in multiple production activities: the production of information about themselves and the production of other goods and services. Aside from the fact that one of any combined firms' production activities involves a public good, there is nothing unusual about this situation. Indeed, the only difference between the two types of production activities is that payment is received at time t for rights to receive and use information produced by the firm, whereas the payments for the firms' other goods and services are received at time $t + 1$. Thus, the latter payments can only be described, in general, by a probability distribution at time t. Since the payments for rights to produced information are made at time t, each single or multiple activity information-producer can compare its known marginal costs of information production with known marginal revenues in making optimal information-production decisions (and thus optimal selections of accounting techniques). More generally, under the postulated market setting, the single and multiple activity firms can determine optimal production-investment decisions by adhering to the market value rule. As with the first scenario, the important feature of the second scenario is that there is such an unambiguous "price guide" for determining optimal information-production decisions, and thus an optimal selection of accounting procedures.[12]

---

[12]It is probably well to recall that when the combined firms are determining optimal information-production decisions, they are doing so in competition with the separate information-producers. Thus, nothing is gained by attempts to withhold "unfavorable" information.

6.3 Third Scenario. For this scenario, we retain specifications S.1, S.3, and S.4 from the first scenario. We replace S.2 by

S.2.2: Information about a firm may be produced by an information-producer—an entity separated from the firm to which the information is
related—or it may be produced by the firm itself. In the latter case, if
the firm decides to produce information then the firm's ownership
shares and rights to information are *not* separately sold. Rather, a
"tie-in" sale approach is used, whereby the firm's ownership shares
and rights to produced information are jointly sold.

Two aspects of this scenario should be noted: (1) it is still true that information can be purchased from separate information-producers and (2)
noninformation-producers are *not* required to produce information.

Since all markets are perfectly competitive, there is unrestricted entry into
(and exit from) any production activity. Thus, nothing precludes the entry
of noninformation-producers into areas where there are combined noninforma-
tion-/information-producers (the multiple activity firms introduced in the
second scenario). Secondly, any existing combined noninformation-/informa-
tion-producer can decide to invest nothing in information production. Thirdly,
given competing separate information-producers, compound gambles still
can be created by consumer-investors on personal account by, e.g., simultaneously purchasing the ownership shares of a noninformation-producer and the
rights offered for sale by an information-producer. In short, there are always
perfect substitutes for any combined firm's jointly sold ownership shares and
rights to produced information. Indeed, since all options available to consumer-
investors under the first and second scenarios are also available under this third
scenario, we really changed nothing by allowing (but not requiring) the tie-in
sales described in specification S.2.2. Thus, all the implications for optimal
information-production decisions from the first and second scenarios also
apply here.

This scenario partially describes our contemporary institutional framework, since firms whose ownership shares are publicly traded automatically
provide some produced information to the holders of their ownership shares.
But at least two critical aspects of the contemporary setting have not been
considered. They are introduced in the next two scenarios.

6.4 Fourth Scenario. In this scenario we allow for "disclosure laws" requiring
that firms produce some information about themselves. (The accounting
numbers that firms are currently required to report are examples of this kind
of information.) These laws do not simply say that information must be produced. They also stipulate the kinds of information to be produced and the
ways in which these kinds of information should be produced. Stipulating that

certain accounting procedures must, or cannot, be used for information production is one means of constraining the way in which information is produced.

In this scenario, disclosure laws are assumed to have the following attributes: (1) these laws are applied in a nondiscriminatory fashion to all firms; (2) there is no preclusion to producing information in addition to the kinds of information required by disclosure laws or to producing the same kinds of information according to the disclosure laws' specifications as well as to alternative production schemes; and (3) firms are permitted to, and do, disseminate the information produced in accordance with the disclosure laws by selling rights to receive and use the produced information.

In summary, this scenario retains specifications S.1, S.3, and S.4. Specification S.2 is replaced by

S.2.3:   Information about firms may be produced by information-producers or by the firms themselves. The firms must produce information in accordance with disclosure laws (described above). These firms' ownership shares and rights to produced information (including that required by the disclosure laws) are *not* separately sold; instead, they are jointly sold. That is, firms sell only compound gambles.

Nothing in this scenario prevents the current owners of a firm's shares from reselling their information rights to current nonowners of the firm's shares. Thus, even though firms' ownership shares and information rights are jointly sold, current owners still can transform their compound gambles into simple gambles. And current nonowners can transform their simple gambles into compound gambles by purchasing information rights from separate information-producers or current owners. This scenario is, therefore, similar to the third scenario, where there were also joint sales of ownership shares and information rights. When investors are bidding for the compound gambles offered by firms they will take into account the prices at which their rights to receive and use produced information can be resold. The latter prices will, of course, be affected by the competitive behavior of the separate information-producers.

The single most important difference between this and the third scenario is that all firms' information-production decisions are partially constrained by disclosure laws. If disclosure laws are such that, in equilibrium, the rights to information required by disclosure laws are worthless then any firm's use of resources in producing such information will be an inefficient allocation of resources. But once a firm does what is required by disclosure laws it can proceed to make optimal information-production decisions via the market rule. Here, these decisions are optimal conditional on the resource requirements of satisfying the disclosure laws. In making its decisions, each firm will be competing with the separate information-producers. In short, the resources consumed by satisfaction of the disclosure laws constitute a lump-sum loss. Once that loss is incurred, the firms behave just as do the firms in the third scenario insofar as the method of determining optimal information-production decisions is concerned. It should be clear that, in general, there is a lump-sum loss whenever the disclosure laws require an information-production decision by a firm for which the associated information rights have an aggregate market value less than the total cost of that information-production decision.[13] Thus, in general, the disclosure laws (in this scenario) induce an inefficient allocation of resources unless, by coincidence or design, the information-production decisions satisfying the disclosure laws are, in fact, information-production decisions that would have been optimal in the absence of such laws.

As before, the important aspects of this scenario is that there are unambiguous market criteria for firms' determinations of optimal information-production decisions, conditional on any lump-sum loss induced by the disclosure laws. Thus, the existence of the disclosure laws per se is not the source of any problem regarding the existence of market price criteria for determining optimal information-production decisions.

6.5 Fifth Scenario. For this scenario, we retain specifications S.1, S.3, and S.2.1.[14] (The latter specification was used in the second scenario.) However, specification S.4 is no longer retained; i.e., we no longer assume that nonpurchasers of information rights can be excluded from using produced information.

Suppose, as in the first three scenarios, that the separate information-producers or the producers of other goods and services announce (during the tâtonnement process) information-production decisions and offer to sell (at time t) rights to receive and use (at time $t + 1$) produced information. Since no capital market agent will be excluded from using produced information, whether or not he buys rights, no agent will be willing to pay a positive price for any right. And since no vendor of rights is offering to pay any agent to take the rights (i.e., since there are no negative "ask prices"), the equilibrium price of every right, conditional upon every information-production decision, is identically zero. This, in turn, implies that if there are no subsidies for the separate information-producers, and if these producers do not engage in some other profitable activity, then no separate information-producers will exist in equilibrium because they cannot cover any positive amount of production costs.[15]

---

[13]The computation of this market value for the case of a public good was discussed under the first scenario.

[14]S.2.2. can also be used for the fifth scenario; the results to be presented would not be altered in any way, as will be indicated.

[15]It is important to emphasize that the above discussion applies only to the production of information for use by capital market agents on personal account. That is, the analysis deals only with external accounting. It is not intended to deal with information that is produced for use by the firm for internal purposes, such as monitoring the activities of subordinates' behavior. Thus, our analysis does not imply that no information of any kind will be produced in equilibrium.

Upon comparing this situation to that of the second scenario, one sees that the prices of the firms' ownership shares (i.e., the market value rule) can no longer be used in determining optimal information-production decisions. Insofar as the multiple activity firms are concerned, one of their activities (selling rights to receive and use produced information) never contributes a positive amount to the value of the firm, regardless of whether or not the information that can be produced is desired by capital market agents. This result is due to the fact that the rights to receive and use information have equilibrium prices equal to zero, whereas the costs of information production are (by assumption) nonnegative. The same result applies to the production activities of the separate information-producers.

With respect to the multiple activity firms, nothing is achieved by replacing specification S.2.1 by S.2.2. Under the latter specification, joint sales of ownership shares and information rights were used by the producers of goods and services other than information. But under the present scenario, one merely finds that the price of information rights that is implicit in the price of jointly purchased ownership shares and information rights is identically zero. Once again, this is attributable to the nonexclusion of nonpurchasers of information rights from using produced information.

The preceding analysis does not imply that producers of goods and services other than information will find that the prices of their ownership shares are unaffected by any announced information-production decisions. Suppose that such a firm announces an information-production decision. Since all investors can count on getting produced information, the firm's ownership shares (the simple gambles) become compound gambles for all capital market agents. Thus, the price of the firm's ownership shares will reflect the ex ante *effects* of information (i.e., signals) that will be produced in accordance with the firm's announced information-production decision.[16] Clearly, this result also applies to the prices of these firms' ownership shares under scenarios 1–4. In the notation of section 4, these ex ante effects are summarized by the change from the distribution function $G(w_{t+2})$ to $F^*(w_{t+2}|L)$, with $L = 0$ because nonpurchasers of information are not excluded from using information.

In this scenario, as in all others, we assumed that each firm behaves according to the market value rule; see section 2. And we just indicated that the ex ante effects of information-production decisions are reflected in the prices of firms' ownership shares. One might, therefore, be tempted to argue that—even when "exclusion of nonpurchasers" is not enforced—an information-production decision that increases the value of the current owners' shareholdings is better than an equally costly information-production decision that results in a decrease

---

[16] Additional remarks on the effects of new accounting information, and the effects of changes in the techniques used for the production of this information, on the prices of firms' ownership shares (when traded in an efficient capital market) are provided by Gonedes [1972a].

(or smaller increase) in the value of the current owners' shareholdings. For the problem at hand this argument is fallacious. To see this, note that the market value rule is used as a criterion for firms' production-investment decisions because under appropriate market conditions it is consistent with current shareholders' assumed objective of expected utility maximization. (For the details of this argument, see Fama and Miller [1972, pp. 176–81 and 299–301].) But, using the characterizations in sections 3 and 4, it should be evident that producing information (of any type) about a firm may be consistent with maximization of each current owner's expected utility and still induce a decrease in the equilibrium price of that firm's owernship shares. This kind of result will obtain when, for example, the produced information has negative or unfavorable implications about the assessed distributions of returns to holders of those shares.

If one ignores costs then one can assert that information production never decreases expected utility; see section 4. Thus, ignoring costs, it is never disadvantageous to engage in information production, notwithstanding the effects on the equilibrium prices of a firm's ownership shares. Allowing for costs of information production merely requires tradeoffs that are consistent with expected utility maximization. And the decisions implied by these tradeoffs need not maximize the value of a firm's ownership shares. In short, the market value rule cannot (in this situation) be used in determining optimal information-production decisions because the needed correspondence between the value of the firm and expected utility does not, in general, exist. The needed correspondence does exist in scenarios 2–4 where the rule of excluding nonpurchasers is enforced under conditions of perfect competition.

The major implication of the preceding analysis is that, when "exclusion of nonpurchasers" (i.e., specification S.4) is absent, we do not have unambiguous market criteria for determining optimal information-production decisions. Thus, the market value rule cannot be applied to these decisions. In different words, the market prices of firms' ownership shares cannot be used (in this scenario) to assess the desirability of alternative information-production decisions, even though they reflect the ex ante effects of these decisions.

Introducing disclosure laws into the fifth scenario does not alter the major implication of our analysis. Such laws impose information-production decisions on firms, but they do not provide market criteria for assessing the desirability of these decisions! To the extent that disclosure laws impose information-production decisions upon firms, they themselves may be viewed as information-production decisions. The analysis of this scenario implies, therefore, that the prices of firms' ownership shares cannot be used to assess the desirability of disclosure laws, although they can be used in assessing the effects of such laws.

The arguments and conclusions presented above do not imply that there should be no information production because the equilibrium price of every right to produced information is always zero. They merely imply that the competitive pricing mechanism cannot be used in determining optimal information-production decisions when, for whatever reason, the "exclusion of nonpurchasers" rule is not enforced. This is one instance of a classical problem in the economics of public goods; see, e.g., Musgrave [1959, pp. 9 and 73 ff]. Observe, in addition, that our analysis does not imply that the rule of excluding nonpurchasers cannot be used (wholly or partially) for the problem of information production. We simply considered a case in which it is not used. And this case captures the essence of firms' information-production decisions, conditional on the contemporary institutional setting.

Section 7. Partial Summary (Sections 2–6)

The preceding sections examined the extent to which the prices of firms' ownership shares can be used in assessing the effects and desirability of alternative information-production decisions. Selecting accounting procedures and imposing regulations (e.g., disclosure law regulations) on the selection of accounting procedures are examples of information-production decisions.

Attention was given to optional joint (tie-in) sales of ownership shares and rights to produced information, to required "tie-in" sales, and to disclosure laws. Each of these factors is, to some extent, reflected in the contemporary institutional arrangements for the information-production decisions pertinent to accounting. But none of them have any bearing on the extent to which the prices of firms' ownership shares could be used in assessing the effects or desirability of these decisions. The critical factor is the extent to which nonpurchasers of rights to use information are excluded from using it. When the rule of excluding nonpurchasers is not enforced then the prices of firms' ownership shares cannot be used to assess the desirability of the information-production decisions made by (or imposed upon) these firms. Such prices can, however, be used to assess the effects of these information-production decisions.

Under the contemporary institutional setting, "exclusion of nonpurchasers" is not enforced vis-à-vis information produced via the external accounting mechanism (perhaps because of the costs of enforcement). Thus, our conclusions have a direct bearing on the assertions made in works based upon the implications of capital market efficiency (see section 1.2). Recall that the critical assertions made in thes works are:

A.1. Capital market efficiency, taken by itself, provides sufficient justification for using prices of (or rates of return on) firms' ownership shares in assessing the *desirability* of alternative accounting procedures or regulations.

A.2. Capital market efficiency, taken by itself, provides sufficient justification for using prices of (or rates of return on) firms' ownership shares in assessing the *effects* of alternative accounting procedures or regulations.

Assertion A.1 played a critical role in the work of Beaver [1972, p. 409],
Beaver and Dukes [1972 and 1973], Benston [1973], Friend [1972], and
Stigler [1964], among others. Assertion A.2 played a critical role in Kaplan
and Roll [1972], Ball [1972a and 1972b], and Sunder [1973a], among others.
These kinds of studies will be discussed in detail in section 8. Suffice it to note
here that our theoretical analysis implies that assertion A.1 is logically invalid.
Accordingly, the works that relied upon the validity of A.1 cannot be given
the theoretical justification and interpretations that their authors have pro-
pounded.

Our analysis does not imply, however, that there are no conditions (assumptions) which, when added to the assumption of capital market efficiency,
will yield a special case wherein desirability issues can be (wholly or partially)
resolved by empirical analyses of firms' ownership share prices. Some illustrative
special cases will be provided in section 10.

Our conclusion about the logical validity of A.1 is based primarily on one
kind of so-called "market failure," namely, the free-rider problem associated
with not excluding nonpurchasers. There are, of course, a variety of other
things that can, under appropriate assumptions, lead to market failure in an
analysis dealing with information. Some frequently mentioned things pertain
to issues of "adverse selection" in the market for information (Akerloff [1970])
and "signalling" behavior (Spence [1973]). These kinds of issues have not been
considered here because it is not clear that they are consistent with our market
setting (see section 2). The adverse selection issue involves problems induced by
discriminatory terms of trade in the production of information, due to differential costs or opportunities. And the available theory on signalling is applicable
to markets in which agents are infrequent participants, among other things,
which does not seem characteristic of the capital market. More importantly,
introducing these issues would require important departures from the conventional assumptions of the theoretical and empirical works of interest to us
here. And that, we believe, would represent an unfair use of "winter rules."
In short, we have attempted to provide an analysis built upon assumptions
fully consistent with those used in the works that invoke assertions A.1 and/or
A.2, as well as in the bulk of the theoretical literature on asset pricing under
uncertainty in perfect markets.

Since we concluded that assertion A.2 is logically valid, we obviously have
a justifiable approach for assessing the effects of alternative accounting procedures and regulations. And, as indicated, this approach was used in a variety
of studies. What have we learned from these studies? What kinds of empirical
problems are associated with the approach used in these studies? Can their
results be ascribed unambiguous interpretations? Were the "effects," if they
exist, of alternative accounting techniques and regulations appropriately defined,
given available theoretical results? These are among the questions asked in
section 8, which is a review of empirical work based, in one way or another,
on assertion A.2.

In section 8 we shall observe that the available price-oriented studies of effects still leave a variety of questions unanswered. This, plus our conclusion that assertion A.1 is logically invalid, motivated us to examine some "nonprice" approaches for assessing desirability and/or effects. That examination appears in section 9.

Given that firms, accounting bodies (e.g., the FASB), and governmental bodies (e.g., the SEC) face the task of selecting accounting techniques and regulations, the importance of assessing desirability of alternatives, using some concept of social preference, seems obvious. Why are assessments of effects important? Perhaps the easiest way to appreciate such assessments is to recognize that recommendations and prescriptions regarding accounting procedures are often justified (rationalized?) in terms of the effects of the recommended or prescribed procedures and the available alternatives. Such assertions can be found in a variety of APB Opinions and SEC Accounting Releases but they are rarely supported by references to available theory or empirical results.

Since assertions about effects are important parts of the justifications offered for recommendations and prescriptions, we can assess the strength of these justifications by evaluating the theoretical or empirical support for the assertions about effects. And one expects the perceived strength of the justifications to vary directly with the perceived support for the underlying assertions. In short, assessments of the effects of alternative accounting procedures and regulations can be useful to accounting policy-making bodies in making their decisions and to their constituencies in evaluating those decisions.

Section 8. A Review of Empirical Studies on Alternative Accounting Techniques

In this and the next section we provide a critical review of the methods used in empirically assessing the effects or desirability of using alternative accounting techniques. As a starting point, we scanned the "Index of Empirical Research in Accounting," compiled by Ball [1971]. Ball's index contains references to approximately 260 empirical studies published from 1932 through 1970. Approximately 65 of these studies were classified as having dealt with alternative accounting techniques. This group was then enlarged to include similar studies published between 1970 and 1973. Our concern will be with the specific criteria used in these studies and some of the important problems encountered. For the most part, we play the role of "devil's advocates."

We shall not comment on every study dealing with alternative accounting techniques, primarily because many studies employ the same criteria and encounter the same problems. In order to keep our review within manageable proportions, we shall discuss studies that typify the use of different approaches or that attempt to deal explicitly with some important problems associated with a given approach. In general, our review concentrates on recent studies from the accounting literature. We worked back in time only to the extent needed to fulfill our objectives.

The studies selected for review were classified into two groups: those that used security prices (section 8) and those that did not (section 9). The former group is subdivided into studies that used a variant of the two-parameter asset pricing model and studies that essentially used a variant of the dividend (earnings) capitalization model.

It will be evident that our review of empirical work is selective in terms of the issues explicitly identified and discussed. In particular, we chose not to use "all-purpose" criticisms that apply to every kind of empirical work, such as general issues of internal and external validity. We assume that the reader is aware of these ever-present problems and we concentrate on more specific issues. The same general approach is used in section 9.

8.1 Assessments Using the Two-Parameter Model

As indicated earlier, equilibrium prices of firms' securities are dependent upon capital market agents' assessed distribution functions of returns to holders of those securities. Such distributions are, in turn, dependent upon the available information about firms' production-investment decisions. Given a description of capital market equilibrium, one can estimate the effect(s) of new information. One such description is provided by the so-called two-parameter asset pricing model.[17] The descriptive validity of this model has been investigated elsewhere (see footnote 1). Since there is general agreement that the two-parameter asset pricing model has high descriptive validity, relative to the available alternatives, we take descriptive validity as given and concentrate on the problems encountered in applying it to accounting issues.

The two-parameter asset pricing model implies that the equilibrium expected one-period rate of return on the ith asset, for period t, is given by:

$$E(\widetilde{R}_{it}) = [E(\widetilde{R}_{mt}) - S_{mt}\sigma(\widetilde{R}_{mt})] + S_{mt}\sigma(\widetilde{R}_{mt})\beta_{it} \qquad (8.1)$$

where $E(\widetilde{R}_{it})$ and $E(\widetilde{R}_{mt})$ are the expected rates of return on asset i and the market portfolio, m, respectively; S_{mt} is a composite marginal rate of substitution of expected return for risk; $\sigma(\widetilde{R}_{mt})$ is the standard deviation (and measure

---

[17]This model is based upon the work of Tobin [1958], Markowitz [1959], Sharpe [1964], Lintner [1965a and 1965b], Mossin [1966], and Fama [1968]. Derivations of it can be had from several alternative sources, such as Black [1972], Fama and MacBeth [1973], Jensen [1969], and Fama and Miller [1972].

of risk) of the rate of return on the market portfolio; and $\beta_{it} = \text{cov}(\tilde{R}_{it}, \tilde{R}_{mt})/$
$\sigma^2(\tilde{R}_{mt})$ is the relative risk of asset i.

Five sufficient conditions for expression (8.1) are:

(C.1) The capital market is perfect. In particular, all agents behave as price-
takers in a frictionless market.

(C.2) All agents are risk-averse.

(C.3) There is unrestricted short selling of every asset.

(C.4) At each time t, agents behave as if the vector of rates of return on all
assets has a multivariate normal distribution.

(C.5) Investors agree on the multivariate distribution of returns at each t.

If asset z is such that $\beta_{zt} = 0$ then (from (8.1)) $E(\tilde{R}_{zt}) = [E(\tilde{R}_{mt})$
$- S_{mt}\sigma(\tilde{R}_{mt})]$ and, consequently, $S_{mt} = [E(\tilde{R}_{mt}) - E(\tilde{R}_{zt})]/\sigma(\tilde{R}_{mt})$. Substituting for S_{mt} in (8.1), and rearranging, yields:

$$E(\tilde{R}_{it}) = E(\tilde{R}_{zt}) + [E(\tilde{R}_{mt}) - E(\tilde{R}_{zt})]\beta_{it}$$

$$= E(\tilde{R}_{it}|E(\tilde{R}_{zt}), E(\tilde{R}_{mt}), \beta_{it}) \qquad (8.2)$$

Conditional upon a value of the triple $(E(\tilde{R}_{zt}), E(\tilde{R}_{mt}), \beta_{it})$, the effect of
new information on asset i, for period t, is

$$\tilde{\epsilon}_{it} = \tilde{R}_{it} - E(\tilde{R}_{it}|E(\tilde{R}_{zt}), E(\tilde{R}_{mt}), \beta_{it}) \qquad (8.3)$$

Given capital market efficiency, $\tilde{\epsilon}_{it}$ must be a fair game random variable. That
is, $E(\tilde{\epsilon}_{it}) = 0$, and for all $s > 0$, $E(\tilde{\epsilon}_{it+s}|\tilde{\epsilon}_{it+s-1}, \tilde{\epsilon}_{it+s-2}, \ldots, \tilde{\epsilon}_{i0}) = 0$; see
Feller [1971, pp. 209–15]. Moreover, given the assumptions underlying (8.1),
the marginal distribution function, $F(\epsilon_{it})$, is a normal distribution.

Note that $\tilde{\epsilon}_{it}$, as defined in (8.3), has two components that are common to
all firms, namely, $(\tilde{R}_{zt} - E(\tilde{R}_{zt}))$ and $(\tilde{R}_{mt} - E(\tilde{R}_{mt}))$. All of the studies reviewed here assume (implicitly, explicitly, or unknowingly) that there are no
commonalities in the estimated effects of new information.[18] The above two
(but not all) commonalities can be removed by estimating effects conditional
on the contemporaneous values of $\tilde{R}_{zt}$ and $\tilde{R}_{mt}$.

If all returns are distributed according to a multivariate normal distribution
then, for each i,

$$E(\tilde{R}_{it}|R_{zt}, R_{mt}) = \gamma_{it} + \delta_{it}R_{st} + \beta_{it}R_{mt} \qquad (8.4)$$

---

[18]This is the case whenever the statistical estimation procedures and tests used in a study
are applied to cross-sectional observations on the effects of new information using the
assumption of random sampling.

where $\beta_{it} = \text{cov}\,(\tilde{R}_{it}, \tilde{R}_{mt})/\text{var}\,(\tilde{R}_{mt})$.[19] Model (8.1) implies that $\gamma_{it} = 0$ and $\delta_{it} = 1 - \beta_{it}$. Model (8.4), or some variant thereof, is usually referred to as the market model. Conditional on R_{zt} and R_{mt}, the effect of new information is given by:

$$\tilde{e}_{it} = \tilde{R}_{it} - E(\tilde{R}_{it}|R_{zt}, R_{mt}) \qquad (8.5)$$

It is important to note that (8.4), and thus (8.5), is implied by the distributional assumption underlying (8.1). The quantity defined by (8.5), or some variant thereof, is usually used to assess the effect(s) of information on capital market agents' behavior.[20]

The two-parameter model was used by Fama, Fisher, Jensen, and Roll [1969] to assess the effects of stock-split announcements. It was also used by Ball and Brown [1968], Beaver [1968], Benston [1967], May [1971], and Gonedes [1974], among others, to assess the information content of accounting numbers; by Archibald [1972], Ball [1972a and 1972b], Kaplan and Roll [1972], Patz and Boatsman [1972], and Sunder [1973a] to assess the effects of changes in accounting techniques; and by Beaver and Dukes [1972 and 1973] and Benston [1973] to assess the desirability of alternative accounting procedures and disclosure laws.

In general, each of these studies was concerned with an aspect of the distribution of $\tilde{e}_{it}$ conditional on the announcement of interest (e.g., an announced change in accounting techniques). As will be indicated below, Benston also examined the association between disclosure law announcements and relative risk, β_{it}.

The motivation for examining some aspect of the distribution of $\tilde{e}_{it}$ is as follows. Let $\tilde{\theta}_{it}$ be a random variable conveying new information pertinent to valuing firm i in period t. Suppose that the realization of $\tilde{\theta}_{it}$ becomes available after equilibrium expected returns are established. Then, the conditional distribution function $F(e_{it}|\theta_{it}) \neq F(e_{it})$. At the beginning of period t, however, $E[F(e_{it}|\tilde{\theta}_{it})] = F(e_{it})$ and, thus, $E[E(\tilde{e}_{it}|\tilde{\theta}_{it})] = E(\tilde{e}_{it}) = 0$, in an efficient capital market. Any random variable such as $\tilde{\theta}_{it}$ for which $F(e_{it}|\theta_{it}) \neq F(e_{it})$, for some realization, θ_{it}, of $\tilde{\theta}_{it}$, can be said to have information content, in the sense that realizations of that random variable induce equilibrating price adjustments.

The preceding remarks provide a theoretically well-defined framework for empirically assessing the information content of accounting numbers. If any accounting number has information content then that number of one random

---

[19]The critical mathematical results underlying this statement are provided in Cramér [1946, chs. 21–24] and Wilks [1962, sec. 7.4]. See also MacBeth [1973].

[20]The most popular variant of (8.5) assumes that $\text{Var}(\tilde{R}_{zt}) = 0$; i.e., that $\tilde{R}_{zt}$ is a fixed "riskless" rate of return.

variable that can play the role of $\tilde{\theta}_{it}$ in the above. And if the postulated informa-
tion content exists one should observe that $F(e_{it}|\theta_{it}) \neq F(e_{it})$ for some value,
θ_{it}, of $\tilde{\theta}_{it}$.

Note, using (8.3), that β_{it} is one of the conditioning arguments in the
distribution function of $\tilde{\epsilon}_{it}$, and thus $\tilde{e}_{it}$. Thus, some insight into the effect
of new information can be gained by determining whether that information
induces a change in β_{it}. This approach was used in several of the studies reviewed
here.

We shall not comment on those studies that only attempted to assess the
information content of newly announced accounting numbers. We note, however, that these studies do suggest that accounting income numbers reflect
events pertinent to valuing a firm.

Recall that the analysis in section 4 characterized the effects of information
in terms of differences between compound gambles based upon conditional
distribution functions and simple gambles based upon marginal distribution
functions. The framework provided above is one application of the basic approach used in section 4. Here, however, we are dealing with more detailed
conditions, (C.1)–(C.5), on the market setting, individual behavior, and the
distribution functions of returns on firms' ownership shares. Also, in line with
the specifications used in the fifth scenario of section 6, we assume that it is not
necessary to purchase rights to use the information of interest here.

A change in the accounting techniques used for external reporting purposes
can have an effect on capital market equilibrium because (1) the change leads
to the provision of accounting numbers that convey information pertinent to
valuing a firm; (2) the change per se (or, more precisely, the act of making the
change) has a substantive economic impact independent of the accounting
numbers affected by the change in reporting techniques; or (3) the change per
se signals other events that have economic importance. In order to deal with
these kinds of possibilities we need to consider various types of accounting
changes. We shall use the following classification scheme.

(T.1)   A change in the techniques used for external reporting (one result of a
        firm's information-production decisions) that does not affect the
        information-production costs incurred by the firm or the information-
        production decisions and/or costs of agents external to the firm.

(T.2)   A change having the properties of (T.1) except that it does affect a
        firm's information-production costs.

(T.3)   A change having the properties of (T.1) except that it does affect the
        information-production decisions and/or costs of agents external to
        the firm.

(T.4)   A change in the techniques used for external reporting that is, for
        whatever reason, associated with a change in some other aspect of a
        firm's production-investment activities.

(T.5)   A change in the accounting techniques used for tax reporting.

The above types are neither exhaustive nor mutually exclusive; e.g., a change of type (T.1) may also be of type (T.4). But this list of types will suffice for our purposes.

If a change is only of type (T.1) then the change per se will have no effect on equilibrium prices. But the accounting numbers produced by the new technique may affect those prices. They will (not) do so if the information conveyed by those numbers is (not) pertinent to valuing firms, insofar as capital market agents are concerned. If this information is also being provided by a different source then the effect of the accounting change cannot be ascribed to information uniquely associated with the numbers produced by the new reporting technique. But one can still assert that these numbers have information content, in the sense that they convey information pertinent to valuing a firm.

A change of type (T.2) also conveys information pertinent to valuing a firm. In this case, however, part or all of the change's information content is due to its implications about the resources required for implementation of the firm's information-production decisions, a subset of the firm's production-investment decisions.

A type (T.5) change is similar to a type (T.2) change in the sense that it conveys information on a firm's real resources and, thus, information pertinent to valuing the firm. In the case of a type (T.5) change, however, the information content of the change is attributable to its implications for tax purposes, rather than information-production costs or the accounting numbers produced by the new reporting technique. Of course, some changes can simultaneously be of, for example, type (T.1) and (T.5) or (T.2) and (T.5).

A change of type (T.3) can affect capital-market equilibrium because it affects the opportunities available to external agents for information production on personal account or because it induces those agents to alter their information-production activities. We consider the second possibility first.

Suppose that a change in accounting techniques provides numbers that do convey information pertinent to valuing a firm and suppose that these numbers were previously being produced by agents on personal account. If the firm's provision of these numbers induces agents to cease producing them on personal account then the accounting change will have induced a change in the incidence of information-production costs and thus the distribution of wealth. And the redistribution of wealth can alter the details of capital market equilibrium, and perhaps equilibria in other markets.

Similar consequences can characterize the first possibility. Suppose that some types of accounting numbers are inputs to capital market agents' decision models. Further suppose that: (a) the currently used accounting techniques are such that accounting numbers can be converted to numbers based on any set of alternative techniques at a trivial cost; (b) each of the conversions noted in (a) is required by at least one capital market agent's decision model; and (c) the costs of converting to numbers conditional on current techniques from numbers conditional on any alternative set of techniques are quite sizable. Next, suppose that all firms switch their accounting techniques. In this case, and assuming (for simplicity) no changes in decision models, the firms' decisions affect the costs borne by and, thus, the wealths of some capital market agents. This is, of course, an extreme example, but it illustrates another change of type (T.3). Finally, note that our type (T.3) category does not preclude an effect by one firm on available opportunities. This situation is consistent with capital market efficiency. To be sure, if one firm's actions do affect the opportunities available in a given market then that market is not perfect. But we are now talking about the market for information, not the capital market. The latter market can be fully perfect even though the former is not.

Note that the effects of the above two possibilities are not the kinds of effects that model (8.5) is designed to estimate, because they are effects unrelated to the information content of the accounting changes. Those effects are, instead, related to issues of cost incidence and interdependencies amongst agents' information-production opportunities. Consequently, it appears that effects of type (T.3) changes (which are not also of another type) cannot be assessed using the asset pricing model described above.

If the change is of type (T.4) it can have an effect even though (1) the numbers produced by the change convey no information pertinent to valuing a firm and (2) the costs and decisions mentioned in (T.1) are unaffected. This can occur when the change provides signals about other events that are not devoid of economic substance. The "effect" of this type of accounting change is analogous to the "effect" of dividend policy changes in a perfect capital market. Within such a market dividend policy changes per se have no effect on the equilibrium value of a firm. But if dividend policy changes are used by management as a device for disseminating information about the firms' prospects then such changes can affect the equilibrium value of the firm because of the new information indirectly provided via the changes, and not because of the changes themselves. With respect to accounting changes, this kind of situation can arise when, e.g., different accounting techniques are highly associated with different industries. In this case, a change in accounting technique can serve as an indication of a change in a firm's industry membership and the risk of that firm's ownership shares.

Conditional on capital market efficiency, the effects, if any, of changes in accounting techniques can be assessed by using data on the prices of firms' ownership shares. But the interpretations of the empirical results and the appropriateness of alternative statistical tools are critically dependent upon the type of change that is being investigated. For example, if an accounting change is of type (T.4) then the events associated with that change may also be associated with changes in the relative risks of firms (the β_{it}-coefficients in (8.4)). If so then one cannot assume (for estimation purposes) that, for each i, $\beta_{it} = \beta_i^*$ for all t. But then one is obliged, for estimation purposes, to postulate something about the manner in which firms' relative risks change, which introduces nontrivial theoretical and statistical problems. Similar issues arise if the accounting change is both a type (T.2) and (T.3) change and the changes in costs or opportunities experienced by investors, in the aggregate, alter the details of capital market equilibrium—e.g., the value weights that define the market portfolio and, therefore, the β_{it}-coefficients in (8.4). Additionally, if a change in techniques has market-wide effects because of, for example, the kind of information conveyed directly or indirectly by the change then model (8.5) may not be an appropriate vehicle for estimating the overall effects of the change. This is because model (8.5) is based upon a relative pricing model—it specifies a relationship between the expected returns on an asset and on the market portfolio. Market-wide effects will alter the distribution of returns on the market portfolio. But the source of this effect may not induce any changes in the relative prices of a given asset and the market portfolio. In short, use of model (8.5) can, in principle, lead to biased estimates of the overall effects of some types of accounting changes. This issue is currently being investigated by Ray Ball (University of Queensland, Australia).

It appears that change of type (T.3) are the most difficult one to handle in terms of the kinds of problems discussed above. For the most part, the studies reviewed here seem to invoke, as a maintained hypothesis, the condition that a type (T.3) change is not being examined. Moreover, and with one exception (Sunder [1973a]), the null hypothesis in each study is that the change(s) examined has (have) no effect on firms' equilibrium values. Thus, another maintained hypothesis of these studies is that changes of types (T.2) and (T.5) are not being investigated. Finally, these studies assume that any information conveyed by accounting changes does not induce only market-wide consequences.

Before proceeding, it is well to note that if a particular change in accounting techniques is assumed to have no direct or indirect effect of any kind then there is obviously no need to test for the effects of the change. In this case, one can test the hypothesis of capital market efficiency. Testing for the effects of a change is appropriate when the maintained hypothesis is capital market efficiency. This seems like a trivial observation, but a clear distinction between maintained hypotheses and tested hypotheses is required in the review provided below.

Kaplan and Roll [1972] investigated the effect of a switch to the flow-through method of reporting the investment credit, subsequent to the issuance of APB No. 4, and switchbacks from the use of accelerated to straight-line depreciation in external reports. The firms that made the change in depreciation procedure or external reports continued to use accelerated depreciation for tax purposes. Evidently, this led Kaplan and Roll to assume that the depreciation switchback was solely a change of type (T.1). Since the switch to the flow-through method of accounting for the investment credit did not affect tax reports either, the same assumption was made about that change.

In order to assess the effect(s) of their selected changes in accounting technique, they emphasized the expected value of a cumulation of $\tilde{e}_{it}$, as defined in (8.5). Under the null hypothesis of no effect, this expected value is zero, because the expected value of each summand is zero under the null hypothesis. They estimated location and dispersion parameters using cross-sectional data.

Relying strictly on averages, they inferred that the effects of the changes investigated were positive but temporary. The effect associated with the invest-ment-credit change appeared to be statistically significant; the effect associated with the depreciation method change did not. But one of the major differences between their sample of investment-credit switches and depreciation switches is that almost all of the investment credit switches occurred in one year, 1964. This suggests that their analyses may have been heavily influenced by cross-sectional correlation amongst the estimated errors, as defined in (8.5). Such cross-sectional correlation has no effect on the means that they estimated, but it does affect the measures of dispersion that they computed. If, as is usually the case, the estimated errors are positively cross-sectionally correlated then their estimates of dispersion are understated, and the significance of their results is overstated. And, if so, then their results are even more consistent with the null hypothesis that the changes investigated did not alter the changing firms' equilibrium values.

Sunder [1973a] examined a different type of accounting change. He studied the effects of firms' decisions to extend or reduce their usage of the LIFO inventory method. The following cases were examined:

Case 1.—Adopting or extending the use of LIFO for reporting purposes only.

Case 2.—Adopting or extending the use of LIFO for both tax and reporting purposes.

Case 3.—Wholly or partially abandoning LIFO which had been used for reporting purposes only.

Case 4.—Wholly or partially abandoning LIFO for both tax and reporting purposes.

Sunder hypothesized that a change in inventory method for external reporting purposes has no substantive economic effect. A change for tax purposes, type (T.5), was recognized as one that has substantive economic implications because such a change affects cash flows. Thus, Sunder hypothe-sized that the effect of the inventory method change, as measured by the conditional expected value of $\tilde{e}_{it}$, would be positive for case 2, negative for case 4, and zero for cases 1 and 3. He could not, however, discriminate between cases 1 and 2 or 3 and 4 on the basis of available evidence. So he stated his hypothesis in terms of only two cases: (A) firms described either by cases 1 or 2 and (B) firms described either by cases 3 or 4. For firms in group A(B) the effect of the inventory change, measured by the conditional expected value of $\tilde{e}_{it}$, was hypothesized to be nonnegative (nonpositive).

Sunder's results were, in general, consistent with his hypothesis. But these results are not free of statistical problems. His results seem to be heavily influenced by particular industries (especially steel) and years (especially 1946–51). Moreover, since the changes examined by Sunder could also have been of types (T.3) or (T.4), the problem of changes in the parameters of model (8.1) appears. Sunder did observe and attempt to overcome the effects of such changes. But the manner in which this was done was, as in other studies, ad hoc. In particular, it was not based upon any hypothesized relationship between the parameters' behavior and the events affecting firms' operations. This is not surprising because asserting that parameters are nonstationary tells one something about a condition not satisfied by the parameters; it does not, taken by itself, indicate the conditions that the parameters do satisfy.

Ball [1972a and 1972b] faced a somewhat different problem. He attempted to assess the effect(s) of changes in a variety of accounting techniques, some of which could have been of any of the types given earlier. This was explicitly recognized by Ball. But his maintained hypothesis was that the accounting changes had no information content. This is not explicitly stated in the published version of his report (Ball [1972b]); it is explicitly stated in the report from which the published version was taken (Ball [1972a, footnote 5]). So, it appears that he treated his changes as if they were all type (T.1) changes. Of course, changes of type (T.1) may also be of type (T.4), as was indicated earlier. Ball attempted to test the hypothesis of capital market efficiency. In doing so, he observed that the relative risks of the firms in his sample appeared to be non-stationary; and he speculated on some possible reasons for this nonstationarity (such as an association between industry grouping and accounting procedures). The inferred nonstationarity suggests that, on balance, the changes examined by Ball may not have been only type (T.1) changes. He attempted to adjust for the nonstationarities. But, as in Sunder's study, the adjustment procedure was ad hoc. His inferences about information content were based upon estimated means of $\tilde{e}_{it}$. In general, his findings were consistent with capital market efficiency, after abstracting from changes in firms' risks.

Of course, it is also possible to approach Ball's results with the maintained hypothesis of capital market efficiency. If this is done then his results can be viewed as evidence consistent with the "no-information content" hypothesis. We choose to view Ball's study using this perspective.

At this point, it is appropriate to note some additional fundamental problems with all of the above studies. As indicated earlier, if some value, θ_{it}, of the random variable, θ_{it} has information content, then the conditional distribution, $F(e_{it}|\theta_{it})$, of $\tilde{e}_{it}$, as defined in (8.5), should differ from the unconditional distribution function $F(e_{it})$. The usual procedure for assessing the effects of some potentially new information is to consider the mean of the conditional distribution function $F(e_{it}|\theta_{it})$, which pertains to the expected effect of the potentially new information. But this mean is only one attribute of the conditional distribution of interest. Moreover, since the two-parameter asset pricing model does not imply the attributes of the distribution of $\widetilde{e}_{it}$ conditional on a source of new information, one cannot assert (using that model) that a difference between $F(e_{it}|\theta_{it})$ and $F(e_{it})$ implies a difference between $E(\widetilde{e}_{it}|\theta_{it})$ and $E(\widetilde{e}_{it})$. Also, the two-parameter model does not imply that the distribution of $\widetilde{e}_{it}$ conditional on different sources of new information will be the same. Thus, for example, the distribution of $\widetilde{e}_{it}$ conditional upon a newly announced income number with no extraordinary items may differ from that conditional upon a newly announced income number affected by extraordinary items. To date, these kinds of problems have not received much attention.

The fact that some accounting changes appear to be associated with changes in relative risks points to an additional problem: the veil of mystery regarding the kinds of events that are, for whatever reason, associated with changes in accounting techniques. One can, we suppose, argue that some accounting changes are in fact useful signals pertaining to events that induce changes in relative risk. (The analogy with changes in dividend policy given earlier immediately comes to mind.) If there is such a relationship then one must consider issues of information economics in order to assess the effect(s) of such changes. Some of the available techniques for dealing with relative risk changes are discussed in Sunder [1973b].

Another study dealing with the effects of changes in accounting techniques was provided by Archibald [1972], who considered the decision of 65 firms to switch from accelerated to straight-line depreciation for external reporting purposes during the period January 1, 1955 to December 31, 1966. (The same type of change was considered by Kaplan and Roll [1972]; see above.) Archibald essentially assumed that the change investigated was a reporting change of type (T.1). This assumption implies that the expected value of $\widetilde{e}_{it}$, conditional on the change, should be zero conditional on his null hypothesis of no information content.

Unlike the previous authors, Archibald seems to offer no conclusions about the consistency of his results with his hypothesis, probably because his results were quite ambiguous. Specifically, he found that the estimated mean errors for the 23 months prior to the change date and the 24 months subsequent to the change exhibited no really strong pattern.[21] There was, however, a slight tendency for the estimated conditional mean of $\widetilde{e}_{it}$ to fluctuate below (above) its unconditional expected value of zero for the months prior (subsequent) to the change date. There are several statistical problems that may have affected these results.

First, as was the case with the Kaplan and Roll results for the investment

---

[21]The observations from the two-year period on both sides of the announcement date were excluded from the data used in estimating the parameters of the two-parameter model. This conventional procedure was used in order to avoid biasing the estimated expected effects of the accounting changes.

credit switch, Archibald's results may have been affected by cross-sectional correlation, due to the substantial bunching of changes in particular years. Although Archibald did not report the years in which his firms made their changes, we were able to determine these years for 55 of his 65 firms using another of his studies (Archibald [1967]). We found that 29 percent (16) of the 55 firms made their change in 1965. There is some "bunching" of changes in other years, but 1965 is the most affected year. Secondly, as noted by Sunder and others, analyses of estimated mean errors can be particularly treacherous when one's sample size is small. As a result of this, Sunder was led to compare all of his important results to results for randomly selected groups of firms; these groups served as control groups. This exercise led Sunder to ignore the results for the approximately 25 firms in cases 3 and 4 (see above) because the results for that group were erratic and about the same as results for control groups of comparable size. Thirdly, the results presented by Ball and Sunder suggest that firms which change accounting techniques also experience changes in their relative risks, measured by estimates of β_{it}. Archibald's results may have been affected by his assumption that firms' relative risks do not change.

The Patz and Boatsman [1972] study focused on the effects of a newly announced APB Draft Opinion. According to their interpretation, their results are consistent with the statement that capital market agents can distinguish between changes having economic implications and mere accounting acrobatics. Since the deficiencies of their work are more or less the same as those of Archibald's, we shall omit a detailed discussion of their study.

Summing up, the results of the above studies are consistent with the statement that the capital market does distinguish between changes that appear to be reporting changes of no economic importance and those that appear to have substantive economic implications. This inference must, however, be qualified because not all aspects of the conditional distribution, $F(e_{it}|\theta_{it})$, have been examined. In addition, the studies suggest that some types of accounting changes (e.g., those examined by Sunder and Ball) are associated with events affecting firms' relative risks. The nature of this association has not been thoroughly investigated.

The studies discussed thus far limited their analyses to an assessment of the effects of changes in accounting techniques. No attempt was made to infer whether the changes actually made were or were not desirable. As noted earlier, however, Benston [1973], Beaver [1972], and Beaver and Dukes [1972 and 1973] have asserted that essentially the same kinds of empirical analyses can be used to assess the desirability of alternative accounting procedures and constraints (e.g., disclosure laws) in the selection and application of such procedures.

In section 7 we suggested that the Benston, Beaver, and Beaver/Dukes proposals have no theoretical justification (see sections 2-6). This may be more evident if we review the underpinnings of their proposals. (The crux of the arguments given by Beaver is identical to that of the Beaver/Dukes papers. Our references will be to the latter.) At the heart of the Beaver/Dukes proposal is the assertion that:

The association [between the earnings numbers from alternative procedures] and the behavior of security prices will indicate which method the market perceives to be the most related to the information used in setting equilibrium prices. (Beaver and Dukes [1972, p. 321])

They suggest that the "association criterion"

. . . provides a simplified method for preference ordering of alternative measurement methods. A complete analysis would require specification of alternative sources of information and the cost of those alternatives relative to the cost of providing the information in the financial statements. (Beaver and Dukes [1972, p. 321, footnote 5])

This approach was used by Beaver and Dukes in their study on interperiod tax allocation. After inferring that deferral earnings are more highly associated with security price behavior, they concluded that:

If one accepts market efficiency, the results suggest that the APB made the "correct" *policy decision* in requiring interperiod tax allocation. It is a correct decision, in the sense that it requires a method which is most consistent with the information impounded in an efficient determination of security prices. Since the market will incur nonzero costs in adjusting from any other method to the *preferred* one, failing to report the method *preferred* forces the market to incur excessive costs of data processing. Conversely, reporting the method most consistent with the underlying information set reduces the expected cost of data processing by the market. [1972, p. 331; emphasis added]

On our interpretation, this line of argument, which also appears in Beaver [1972], assumes that the prices of firms' ownership shares can be used in assessing the desirability of alternative information-production decisions, including changes in accounting procedures and changes in regulations pertaining to the selection and application of accounting procedures. It also appears to assume that this situation is a direct consequence of capital market efficiency. The same interpretation of the Beaver/Dukes argument was made by May and Sundem [1973, pp. 90 ff.], who also adopted the Beaver/Dukes line of argument. As is indicated in the second quoted passage, this line of argument is qualified only to the extent that one cannot completely specify the available opportunities for information production and/or the costs of those opportunities.

If, however, we accept the arguments of section 6 then we must conclude that this argument is fallacious. In short, our analysis indicates that, under the contemporary institutional setting, capital market efficiency—taken by itself— does not imply that the prices of firms' ownership shares can be used in assessing the desirability of alternative information-production decisions. And note that, contrary to the Beaver/Dukes suggestion, this conclusion is not due to incomplete data on the alternative information-production opportunities, the costs of those alternatives, or the incidence of the latter costs. It is due to the fact that, under the contemporary institutional setting, the prices of firms' ownership shares do not, in general, provide signals regarding preferences for the results of alternative information-production decisions.

The Beaver/Dukes paper is also characterized by some important statistical problems.[22] But, in view of the preceding remarks, we shall not discuss them. The theoretical problems seem to be more fundamental and, in our view, insurmountable.

We should note that there are special cases wherein price analyses can provide some information on desirability. And one of these cases involves the alternative methods used for tax deferral accounting. This is one of the issues to which Beaver and Dukes applied their approach (see Beaver and Dukes [1972]). In section 10 we shall indicate some of the conditions under which a price analysis of this issue may be a valid approach in assessing the desirability of the alternative methods. But the kind of price analysis required involves data based upon firms' actual selections of tax deferral methods. That type of data was not used by Beaver and Dukes [1972].

Benston [1973] attempted to assess the desirability of the SEC disclosure laws via empirical analyses of the prices of firms' ownership shares. These laws *impose* information-production decisions upon firms, but they are still information-production decisions.

The line of thought used by Benston is essentially the same as that used by Beaver and Dukes. This can be seen from his following assertion:

Since numerous studies show that the market adjusts rapidly to new information, the effect, if any, of previously unexpected data in the financial reports of a corporation (j) should be reflected in changes in its stock prices (ΔP_{jt}) in period t when these unexpected financial data (F_{it}^*) become publicly available. [1973, p. 137]

The crux of this statement is, of course, that the capital market is efficient. And this is the only justification provided by Benston for his use of securities' prices in assessing the desirability of the SEC disclosure laws. Our theoretical

---

[22]Some examples pertaining to Beaver and Dukes [1972] are as follows. (1) For each accounting procedure, the authors should have conditioned their tests on the optimal time series model for each firm's accounting numbers. When this is not done one does not know whether the differences apparently induced by the different accounting procedures are more appropriately ascribed to the misspecification of the time series model applied to the accounting numbers generated by one of the procedures examined. (2) Given the design of their study, the authors should have used a multivariate test, rather than a sequence of univariate tests. When this is not done one is more likely to reject their null hypothesis when, in fact, it should not be rejected. (3) The "analysis of differences" provided in their Table 2 does not recognize the cross-sectional correlation amongst the observations used in that analysis. Not recognizing that correlation (if it is important) can induce an overstatement of the significance of one's results.

analysis implies that his justification is not sufficient. So Benston can hardly claim to have used an approach capable of giving desirability assessments.

The Benston paper, can, however, be viewed as an (ambitious) attempt to assess the *effects* of the SEC disclosure laws. This is the perspective adopted below. Since Benston's work pertains to important issues that are not easily handled by empirical research tools, and since serious empirical work on these issues is hard to come by, we shall discuss his work in some detail.

Of particular interest here are the hypotheses used by Benston in structuring his study. These hypotheses pertain to the effects that the passage of the SEC Acts of 1933 and 1934 "should" (in Benston's mind) have had on the behavior of security prices. These hypotheses were expressed in terms of firms' relative risks, β_{it}, in model (8.2), and the effect of new information, $\tilde{e}_{it}$ in model (8.5). Benston's tests involved comparisons (pre- and post-SEC Act of 1934) between firms disclosing sales numbers and those not disclosing sales numbers. He considered the required disclosure of sales numbers to be one of the principal reporting requirements imposed by the 1934 Act. All firms in his primary sample were listed on the New York Stock Exchange at the time of the 1934 Act. He also conducted some tests on firms listed on the NYSE as of 1929 but perhaps delisted some time after 1929 (see Benston [1973, pp. 149 ff.]).

One way to assess the effect(s) of the Acts is to determine whether the expected value of $\tilde{e}_{it}$, conditional on passage of the Acts, is nonzero or whether there were shifts in firms' relative risks around the time that the Acts were passed. Presumably, an analysis of this kind would have to be applied to the previously disclosing and nondisclosing firms separately in order to assess any effects specific to each group of firms. The null hypotheses for this approach would be: (1) the conditional expected value of $\tilde{e}_{it}$ is not different from zero and (2) the value of β_{it} after passage of the Acts did not differ from the value of β_{it} before passage. This approach is similar to that used by, for example, Sunder [1973a] in his examination of changes in inventory costing techniques. But the latter hypotheses do not, taken by themselves, have much interpretive content. Testing them can only lead to inferences about the existence or nonexistence of effects, rather than inferences about specific substantive phenomena that can induce effects. Evidently this led Benston to formulate more detailed hypotheses pertaining to, for example, managements' behavior, the costs imposed upon firms by the SEC Acts, and the benefits realized by shareholders as a result of these Acts. This involves a much more ambitious effort than simply testing for the existence of effects that are not attributed to specific phenomena. But the specific hypotheses ultimately formulated by Benston do not seem testable. So, ambition aside, his results cannot be given any clear-cut interpretations within the framework of his hypotheses. We shall attempt to justify this conclusion by examining each of Benston's five hypotheses.

Benston's first two hypotheses pertain to the behavior of the firms that did not disclose sales numbers prior to the 1934 Act. His first hypothesis states that: "Managers avoided disclosure to hide their poor performance" (p. 144). If so, Benston argued, the effect of the 1934 Act would appear as a negative value of $E(\tilde{e}_{it})$ for the previously nondisclosing firms, conditional on the 1934 Act. He also argued that the relative risks, β_{it}, of the previously nondisclosing firms would increase if the managers of these firms also tried to induce underestimates of their relative risks.

The problem with this hypothesis is that it is not testable. The fact that managers tried to hide poor performance or induce underestimates of risk does not imply that they were successful. And if they were successful there appears little reason to ascribe their success to nondisclosure of accounting numbers. Consequently, even if Benston's first hypothesis were, in fact, true, one could not (using this hypothesis) predict the value or sign of $E(\tilde{e}_{it})$ or the behavior of β_{it} conditional on the 1934 Act. Thus, for example, if $E(\tilde{e}_{it}) < 0$, conditional on the Act, one might infer that such managers did hide poor performance and that disclosure of sales revealed that poor performance. On the other hand, one might also argue that if $E(\tilde{e}_{it}) > 0$, conditional on the Act, the hypothesis is still true and that the newly disclosed numbers simply provided another tool for hiding poor performance and suggesting nonexistent good performance. Finally, if $E(\tilde{e}_{it}) = 0$, conditional on the Act, the hypothesis may still be true, but there may have been information available prior to the Act indicating that poor performance was being hidden. In this regard, it is important to recognize that there was a considerable amount of disclosure of accounting numbers by NYSE firms prior to the 1934 Act. For example, just about all NYSE firms reported annual income numbers prior to the 1934 Act (see Benston [1969, Table I]). In short, the hypothesis really does not imply any unique behavior of $\tilde{e}_{it}$, conditional on the 1934 Act. Similar remarks apply to the hypothesis about β_{it}. It does not do so because it deals only with managers' "attempts" and, secondly, it does not take into account alternative kinds of information available prior to the 1934 Act on the nondisclosing firms.

Benston's second hypothesis states: "Managers did not disclose because they did not realize the value of the information to investors" (p. 144). In this case, he recognized that the hypothesis, if true, cannot be used to predict the behavior of β_{it} or the distribution of $\tilde{e}_{it}$, conditional on the 1934 Act.

His third hypothesis states: "Required disclosure imposes a cost on corporations without compensating benefits to stockholders" (p. 144). In effect, this hypothesis asserts that required disclosure induces an outright waste of resources. Thus, one expects $E(\tilde{e}_{it}) < 0$, conditional on the 1934 Act, for the previously nondisclosing firms. And one might assert the same thing for the disclosing firms if the 1934 Act altered their disclosure activities. The interesting feature of this hypothesis is that its predictions, conditional upon Benston's arguments, are indistinguishable from his first hypothesis, according to which

$E(\widetilde{e}_{it}) < 0$, conditional on the 1934 Act, would represent a beneficial outcome of the Act rather than an undesirable one.[23] This feature was recognized by Benston.

Benston's fourth hypothesis states: "Required disclosure results in benefits to the market as a whole because investors would prefer stocks on registered exchanges to alternative investments. . . . However, some costs are imposed on those firms that would not otherwise have disclosed" (p. 144). He asserted that this situation implies that $E(\widetilde{e}_{it}) < 0$ for the nondisclosure group and $E(\widetilde{e}_{it}) \geqslant 0$ for the disclosure group, conditional on announcement of the 1934 Act. As indicated earlier, however, one cannot expect the "benefits" of information production to be signalled by security price behavior. One can, however, expect the effects of new information to be reflected in price behavior. But Benston's hypothesis specifies only one source of an effect, namely, the marginal costs induced by the 1934 Act. Since nothing else is specified, the hypothesis can hardly be used to predict the distribution of $\widetilde{e}_{it}$, conditional on the 1934 Act.

Finally, Benston hypothesized that: "Required disclosure did not impose sufficient costs or benefits to be measured" (p. 144). This is, of course, as much a statement about the model used as it is about the effects of the 1934 Act. Benston inferred that this is the only hypothesis with which his data are consistent. He interpreted this to mean that ". . . the disclosure provisions of the '34 Act were of no apparent value to investors" (p. 148). We have already indicated that this issue cannot be handled via empirical analysis of price data. But, in any event, it should be clear that Benston's interpretation does not follow from the hypothesis. The hypothesis deals only with the extent to which "costs or benefits" can be measured by the tools he used. An inability to measure costs and benefits via a particular set of procedures does not imply their absence (or presence).

The point of all this is that Benston's results, when viewed as an assessment of the effects of the 1933 and 1934 Acts, are too ambiguous to conclude anything about the Acts. And the main source of ambiguity, it appears, is the set of hypotheses he used in the design of his study. Another problem is that a great many seemingly important events occurred during the time period of interest (January 1926 to November 1941). If, e.g., these events induced serious nonstationarities in the parameters of the models used by Benston and/or serious cross-sectional correlation in the random variables $\widetilde{e}_{it}$, for all i, then it seems unlikely that Benston's procedures are appropriate, given his objectives.[24] Also, since the amount of variability in securities' returns was particularly high during the period of his study (see Officer [1973]), it may be extremely difficult

---

[23]Lest we be accused of being too harsh, we hasten to add that such conflicts are not unusual in empirical work.

[24]Note that the model and theory used by Benston in estimating $\bar{e}_{it}$ do not imply that $\bar{e}_{it}$ is independent of e_{jt}, for $i \neq j$. If not then his cross-sectional tests on estimates of $\bar{e}_{it}$ are not, strictly speaking, justified.

to assess the effects of any single event such as the 1934 Act. That is, such effects (if any) may have been swamped by the high degree of variability induced by contemporaneous events, in the aggregate.

8.2 Assessments Using the Dividend (Earnings) Capitalization Model

Several studies attempted to assess the effects of accounting procedures by using some variant of the dividend (earnings) capitalization model as a basis for their empirical work. Such a model, it may be recalled, played an important role in the work of Modigliani and Miller [1958] and Gordon [1962], among others.

In a world of certainty and perfect capital markets, this model states that the equilibrium price of an ownership share equals the discounted value of all future dividends to be received by the holder of that security, with the discount rate for any one period equal to the equilibrium one-period spot rate of interest. Under conditions of uncertainty, this approach is much more complicated (see, e.g., Long [1972, section 6]). For the most part, applications of this model begin (explicitly or implicitly) with the certainty case and then introduce adjustments (e.g., adjustments for risk) that are supposed to deal with some aspects of uncertainty. But these adjustments are not introduced because of their being implied by some explicit theory of valuation under uncertainty. They are essentially ad hoc. Since they are ad hoc, the interpretations to be ascribed to the model are not entirely clear-cut. And, not unexpectedly, each author used a somewhat different collection of ad hoc adjustments, as will be evident from our review.[25]

The first study to be reviewed is the one by Mlynarczyk [1969], who attempted to assess the effects of using either the flow-through or deferral (normalization) method of accounting for taxes in external reports.[26] Recall that these methods affect only tax expenses appearing in external reports. They have no effect on the actual payments made to the Internal Revenue Service.

Mlynarczyk assumed that the (natural) logarithm of the price of an ownership share in a given period is a linear function of: (1) the log of the latest 12 months' earnings; (2) the log of an index of expected growth of earnings; (3) the log of the preceding period's revenues; (4) the log of the proportion of common equity in the firm's "long-term capital structure," as of the preceding

---

[25] Those familiar with the work by Staubus [1968] may, at some point, wonder why his work on alternative inventory procedures is not reviewed in this section. It is not because it does not provide results based upon actual prices of, or rates of return on, ownership shares. His study uses accounting numbers and "discounted values" of ownership shares, where the latter values were Staubus' own inventions rather than the results of capital market agents' behavior. Similar remarks apply to R. Samuelson [1972].

[26] Some additional useful remarks on Mlynarczyk's study can be had from Neter's review of it; see Neter [1969].

period; (5) a dummy (dichotomous) variable for the exchange (e.g., New York Stock Exchange) on which the firm's ownership shares are traded; and (6) a dummy variable pertaining to the accounting method used by the firm. The latter dummy variable was set equal to unity (zero) if the deferral (flow-through) method was used. The coefficient of the sixth variable was interpreted as a premium (if positive) or discount (if negative) associated with using the deferral rather than the flow-through method, all other things equal. The third and fourth variables are supposed to account for a firm's risk. The first and second variables supposedly pertain to profitability.

Mlynarczyk estimated his regression model for each of the years 1958–62, using cross-sectional data for each year. The estimated coefficient of the accounting procedure dummy variable was positive and declared to be "significantly" different from zero for each of the years 1959–61. According to Mlynarczyk's assertions, these results are inconsistent with the hypothesis that investors do not distinguish between earnings computed according to the different accounting procedures examined. Note he assumed that the selection of either the flow-through or deferral method involved the same kinds of issues as changes that are solely of type (T.1).

That capital market agents do not accept accounting numbers at face value and that they do recognize the effects of bookkeeping mechanics are, it seems to us, plausible propositions. But the extent to which Mlynarczyk's results provide reliable support for these propositions is another matter.

Perhaps the most fundamental problem with his study is that it involves ad hoc procedures in some seemingly important places, such as the measurement of risk and investors' expectations. (See pp. 72–73 of Mlynarczyk's paper for a description of his procedures.) Indeed, his use of the discounting model in a world of uncertainty in a manner analogous to the way it is used in a world of certainty is itself ad hoc because his extension is not justified by any explicit theory of valuation under uncertainty.

Even if one accepts the model stipulated by Mlynarczyk, the interpretations to be ascribed to his results still are not obvious. First, upon examining the independent variables in his model, one is led to expect nontrivial multi-collinearity. For example, since, by definition, the deferral method leads to lower reported earnings (other things equal) one expects the accounting dummy variable and the earnings variable, variable (1), to be inversely dependent (though not necessarily linearly correlated). If multicollinearity is a serious problem then the manner in which any individual estimated regression coefficient should be interpreted is not apparent. Mlynarczyk did attempt to assess the correlation between the accounting dummy variable and the other independent variables via estimated first-order correlation coefficients. Since, however, the accounting variable is a dichotomous variable, such coefficients are, strictly speaking, inappropriate measures of association; see Neter and Maynes [1970]. So we really cannot infer the effect of multicollinearity on his results.

Secondly, the significance tests used by Mlynarczyk for his coefficient estimates assume that the disturbance (error) of his regression model for logs of prices exhibits no cross-sectional correlation. Given the available evidence on common stock prices, this condition probably is not satisfied. Moreover, since all the firms in his sample are from one industry—the electric utility industry— one expects the cross-sectional correlation of the disturbance to be nontrivial. If this cross-sectional correlation is positive then the statistical significance of his results is overstated.

Since Mlynarczyk used cross-sectional analyses, the relevance of serially correlated variables may not be apparent. Note, however, that if log-price is serially correlated, then one should not view his results for each of the years 1958–62 as consisting of five independent sets of results. And assuming that logs of prices (not changes in logs of prices) are serially independent is most certainly inconsistent with the available evidence on prices of ownership shares.

As indicated earlier, Mlynarczyk assumed that the deferral vs. flow-through issue is similar to the issues of type (T.1) changes. For reasons given in his paper (p. 70), he selected all firms in his sample from the electric utility industry. This may, however, be one industry where the deferral vs. flow-through issue does have some direct substantive economic implications of the kind characterizing changes of types (T.2), (T.4), and (T.5). Brigham [1968, section 3] suggested that some lags and inconsistencies in the behavior of regulatory commissions are such that tax accounting methods (flow-through and deferral) can affect, perhaps only temporarily, a utility's cash flows. Under these conditions, a utility's selection of either the deferral or flow-through method may affect its cash flows just as any firm's selection of LIFO or FIFO for tax purposes affects its cash flows. The implications of this phenomenon for Mlynarczyk's study depend upon the behavior of the commissions regulating the firms in his sample. In any event, he seems not to have considered this issue.

The study by Gonedes [1969] also attempted to assess the effects of accounting procedures via a variant of the dividend capitalization model. As in Mlynarczyk's study the dividend capitalization model was used as a basis for formulating regression models. Two regression models were used. They differed only with respect to their dependent variables. One model had observed annual rates of return as its dependent variable; the other had a proxy for the cost of equity capital as its dependent variable. The independent variables consisted of proxies for risk and dummy variables for the use of the following procedures in annual reports: (1) amortization of the investment credit, (2) interperiod tax allocation, and (3) presentation of a funds-flow statement. Both regression models were estimated with cross-sectional data for each of the years 1964–67. The sample of firms consisted of firms from seven industries. Taken at face value, the estimation results for the models did not have unambiguous implications for the effects of the examined procedures. For reasons given in the paper, Gonedes was, however, inclined to interpret his results as suggesting that the procedures did have an effect. (Such are the errors of youth!)

Except for issues unique to the electric utility industry, the deficiencies of the Gonedes study are much the same as those of the Mlynarczyk study. Thus, the results presented by Gonedes are equally suspect when viewed as assessments of the effects of accounting procedures. Similar kinds of ad hockery were needed in order to use the dividend capitalization model in his empirical analyses. And, as before, the theoretical drawbacks of the dividend capitalization model in a world of uncertainty seem not to have been fully appreciated. Perhaps the major differences between Mlynarczyk's and Gonedes' studies are that Gonedes used a sample that contained firms from seven industries and his results were, taken at face value, ambiguous; whereas Mlynarczyk used firms from the electric utility industry and some of his results were, when taken at face value, unambiguous. The different industry characteristics of the samples used may have induced the differences in the results. Since, however, there are also differences regarding the models ultimately estimated, the time periods considered, and the sample sizes, we really cannot ascribe all differences in the results to the industry characteristics of the samples.

We now consider studies that used the price-earnings (P/E) ratio model. This model can be viewed as a special case of the earnings capitalization model. If the price of an ownership share is viewed as the discounted value of a perpetual stream of constant earnings, where the discounting is effected by a constant rate, then the discount rate equals the reciprocal of the P/E ratio. This variant of the capitalization model is, to say the least, crude. And in view of the additional restrictions required by it, as well as the theoretical drawbacks of the general capitalization model in a world of uncertainty, we wonder whether any reliable results can be had by using it. But, like it or not, this model was used in the studies of O'Donnell [1965 and 1968] and Comiskey [1971].

Both studies by O'Donnell dealt with samples of firms from the electric utility industry. A key year in both studies was 1954, the year in which firms were permitted to use accelerated depreciation for tax purposes.[27] In his 1965 (1968) study, the firms in his sample that took advantage of this new provision did so no later than 1956 (1961). O'Donnell was interested in three sub-groups of his firms: (1) firms that used straight-line depreciation for both tax and reporting purposes before and after 1954; (2) firms that used straight-line depreciation for external reports, accelerated depreciation for tax purposes as of some period after 1954, and the flow-through method of tax accounting in external reports as of some period after 1954; and (3) firms using the same procedures as those in (2) except that the deferral method of tax accounting was used for external reports as of some period after 1954. The time period considered in his 1965 study was 1949–61. It was 1961–66 in his 1968 study. He examined averages of P/E ratios for each group for the periods prior and subsequent to 1954 in his first study. For the pre-1954 period, he found that

---

[27]Prior to 1954, a limited form of declining balance depreciation could have been used, subject to the Internal Revenue Service's approval.

the average P/E ratio of the 7 firms in his group (2) was about 108 percent of the average P/E ratio of the 18 firms in his group (3). For the post-1954 period, the average P/E ratio of the 7 firms in group (2) was about 94 percent of the average P/E ratio of the 18 firms in group (3). In his 1968 study, which dealt only with post-1954 years, he found that the average P/E ratio of the 24 firms in his new sample of group (2) firms was about 95 percent of the average P/E ratio of the 32 firms in his new set of group (3) firms. (We do not know whether the larger sample used in his 1968 study included firms from the sample used in his 1965 study.)

O'Donnell [1968] interpreted his results as indicating that: (1) flow-through firms "sold at a discount" relative to the deferral-method firms (p. 550) and, by implication, (2) that earnings computed under the flow-through method were viewed as being of "lower quality" than earnings computed under the deferral method (p. 551). It is not clear, however, that his first assertion is necessarily implied by his results. Since he examined the behavior of P/E ratios, his results cannot be used to make inferences about the numerator of the ratio, even when all other things are assumed to be equal. Since his second statement is not independent of the first, it is not on any stronger ground.[28]

The implications of cross-sectional and serial correlation were noted when we discussed Mlynarczyk's study. Similar problems characterize the variable examined by O'Donnell, namely, P/E ratios. His tests and interpretations do not, however, reflect recognition of these problems.

A fundamental problem with O'Donnell's study is the absence of any analysis of regulatory commissions' behavior. As indicated earlier, the electric utility industry may be one in which the flow-through versus deferral issue does have substantive economic implications of the kind characterizing changes of types (T.2), (T.4), and (T.5), contrary to the implicit assumption of O'Donnell's analyses. There are, for example, various ways that a utility commission can adjust permitted rates of return in response to a firm's selection of either the flow-through or deferral method. And some of these ways can affect the firm's cash flows. For example, a utility using the deferral method may be allowed to treat the additional reported tax expense as an allowable charge for rate-making purposes, even though this additional expense does not correspond to an additional cash outflow. Also, if the regulatory commission includes the "deferred taxes" account in the so-called rate-base then the deferral method will further increase the firm's cash inflows. Under these conditions, and assuming all other things equal, the firm using the deferral method should have a higher equilibrium market value (because its cash inflows are higher) and thus a higher P/E ratio.

---

[28]According to O'Donnell's logic, his conclusions actually apply to flow-through firms relative to deferral firms and flow-through firms relative to firms using straight-line depreciation for both tax and external reporting purposes. He concentrates on the flow-through/deferral comparison, perhaps because the flow-through/straight-line comparison induces results that are not easily interpreted.

Yet, it should be clear that this higher P/E ratio would have nothing whatsoever to do with the quality of earnings or any misstatement of reported earnings, unless the economic issues mentioned above motivated O'Donnell's use of these characterizations.

The study by Comiskey [1971] dealt with the decisions of 11 steel firms to switch from the accelerated to the straight-line depreciation method for external reporting purposes in the year 1968. This switch made the 1968 earnings of each firm higher than they otherwise would have been. The question asked by Comiskey was: Were the increases in 1968 earnings (relative to what they would have been) viewed by capital market agents as being merely the results of accounting acrobatics or did the increases actually affect the values of the firms that switched procedures? He used the P/E ratio model in dealing with this question. The P/E ratios of the switching firms might have been affected by events other than the changes in accounting technique. So in an attempt to control for such other events Comiskey compared the changes in the P/E ratios of the switching firms to the changes in the P/E ratios of 14 steel firms that did not change their depreciation procedure. The changes in the P/E ratios were computed using data for 1967 and 1968. He reasoned that the P/E ratio changes for the switching firms should have been less than those for the nonswitching firms if the increases in the switching firms' earnings were viewed as being accounting artifacts. He interpreted his results as being consistent with the latter statement.

The appropriate interpretation of Comiskey's results is, it seems to us, not as clear-cut as he suggests. As indicated in section 8.1, two published studies (Ball [1972b] and Sunder [1973a]) of changes in accounting techniques suggest that, for some reason, firms which made changes in their accounting techniques seem to have undergone changes in their relative risks (as defined in the two-parameter asset pricing model). The same phenomenon may have characterized the switching firms in Comiskey's sample. If so, then the P/E ratio differences observed by Comiskey may have had little to do with changes in depreciation methods per se; they may have been associated with risk changes.[29] Finally, note that Comiskey neither adjusted for nor mentioned the effects of cross-sectional correlation among the changes in P/E ratios used in his analysis. If this cross-sectional correlation is important and (as is likely) positive then the statistical significance of his results is overstated.

In general, the implications of the results presented in the P/E ratio studies are not apparent to us. Admittedly, we view such results as being suspect because there is so little theory available for interpreting results based upon the P/E ratio model or even designing a study conditional upon that model. For example, we know of no theory indicating the behavior of P/E ratios that should

---

[29]One framework for examining the behavior or relative risk in a study using P/E ratios is described in Beaver and Dukes [1973, pp. 557–58].

be observed across firms or time. Moreover, an appropriate scheme for computing P/E ratios is not even apparent. For the numerator of this ratio, some have
used the closing price of the period to which the P/E ratio pertains. Others have
used averages of high and low prices for that period. Another scheme (used by
Comiskey) involves the use of moving averages. But these alternative computational schemes were always selected in an arbitrary way and the sensitivity of
empirical results to the alternative schemes is not known. Also, little (if anything) is known about the distribution function of P/E ratios. Thus, one cannot
even assess the extent to which conventional (parametric) statistical tests are
appropriate.

Section 9. Alternative Methods of Assessing the Effects or Desirability of Alternative Accounting Techniques

Recall that the emphasis of this paper is on the theoretical support for using
analyses of the prices of firms' ownership shares in assessing the effects and
desirability of alternative accounting techniques. This approach has considerable
appeal because those prices are determined by the actual decisions of capital
market agents, in the aggregate. Therefore, they can be ascribed useful economic
interpretations. It should be obvious, however, that the evidence available from
studies based upon analyses of these prices does not answer all of our questions
about the effects of alternative accounting techniques (see section 8), nor can
they answer any questions about the desirability of alternative techniques (see
section 6).

The limitations of the results from price studies provide some motivation
for asking whether studies not using the prices of firms' ownership shares
provide additional reliable evidence on the effects and/or desirability of alternative techniques. At the outset, we claim that the extent to which they do so is
minimal, at best. The main reason for this is that they are not based upon a
strong theoretical foundation that provides the necessary linkage between the
accounting techniques examined and the resource allocation decisions of capital
market agents. Of course, the "nonprice" methods reviewed below may be
capable of yielding reliable evidence on issues other than those examined in this
paper. But given our objectives, that possibility need not be considered here.

Additional motivation for our review of nonprice methods is provided by
the fact that the nonprice methods reviewed here are often proposed as methods
which can provide evidence on the external accounting issues examined in this
paper, namely the desirability and effects of alternative accounting techniques.
Moreover, those who use these methods in empirical work often present and
discuss their results as if they had implications for those external accounting
issues. And the latter results are often interpreted by subsequent writers as
having such implications.

For convenience, we have classified the nonprice studies into four broad categories: Laboratory and Field Studies; Questionnaire Results on Alternative Accounting Techniques; Studies of Time Series Properties; and Studies of the Consistency of Different Accounting Techniques within the Historical Cost Framework. A listing of studies in each category is provided in Exhibit 1.

For the most part, our review of the studies in each category will be confined to some basic technical and theoretical issues. This will enable us to cover these studies in much less detail than that provided in section 8. Our review of the studies in each category will attempt to respond to the following questions: (1) If the framework of the studies is accepted as being appropriate can one conclude that the studies provide evidence on the effects and/or desirability of accounting techniques? and (2) Is there any theoretical connection between the framework used by the studies and capital market agents' resource allocation decisions?

9.1 Laboratory and Field Studies

Each study listed in this category (see Exhibit 1) focused on either an "investment" or "operating" decision of subjects as functions of accounting techniques. In general, the subjects were students, businessmen, financial analysts, or industry specialists. With one exception (Dickhaut [1973]), the same approach was used in each study. The characteristics of the decision situation were held constant over all subjects except that some received a (supposedly) pertinent accounting report based on one technique (e.g., the FIFO inventory costing technique) and the others received the same type of report based upon a different accounting technique (e.g., the LIFO inventory costing technique). In some studies, a third subset of the subjects received a report containing enough information for conversion from either of the examined techniques to the other. The studies attempted to determine whether the decisions of those receiving a report conditional upon one of the techniques differed from the decisions of those receiving a report conditional upon the other technique. The remarks provided below pertain only to the studies dealing with "investment" decisions, since this is the decision setting of interest in this paper. Studies dealing with operating or managerial decisions were omitted from the Exhibit.

With one known exception (Dopuch and Ronen [1973]), the studies listed abstracted from tax considerations and emphasized the effects of accounting techniques only on external reporting. For the most part, these studies attempted to test the following simple null hypothesis: subjects' decisions are not altered by changes in accounting techniques. Evidence consistent with this hypothesis was interpreted as indicating that subjects "saw through" the purely reporting differences induced by the different accounting techniques and, consequently, that the techniques per se had no effect on decisions. The motivation for testing this hypothesis was provided by the belief that subjects would have difficulty in distinguishing between: (1) purely reporting differences induced by the different accounting techniques and (2) substantive economic differences (if any). This hypothesis became formalized as the functional fixation hypothesis (see Ijiri, Jaedicke, and Knight [1966]), which states that users of accounting reports will treat all purely reporting differences as if they reflected substantive economic differences, unless they are informed about and understand the changes in accounting procedures.

The results of these studies are mixed. In some, the results appear to be consistent with the crux of the functional fixation hypothesis (see, e.g., Dyckman [1964] and Jensen [1966]); in some, the results appear to be inconsistent with this hypothesis (see, e.g., Barrett [1971] and McIntyre [1973]); and in another, the observed results were dependent upon the way in which the accounting numbers were manipulated (see Dopuch and Ronen [1973]).

It appears that the results of these studies were influenced by: (1) the kinds of subjects used (see, e.g., McIntyre [1973], Elias [1972], and Dickhaut [1973]); (2) the type of accounting technique examined; and (3) the decision model that the experimenter (knowingly or unknowingly) used to describe and interpret his subjects' behavior.

If these kinds of factors really do have systematic effects on the observed results then they should have been identified as important factors by some body of theory. In the absence of such a theory, we do not know what variables must be controlled in the invented decision settings of the lab/field studies. And it appears that such theoretical considerations were not given serious attention in most of the available studies.

The above remarks are all more or less related to aspects of individual behavior. As such, they point to a fundamental deficiency of the lab/field studies: they were not based upon a sufficiently rich theoretical framework pertinent to an individual's allocation of resources under uncertainty. Such a framework should characterize decision-making behavior and link this behavior to formation production, in general, and the production of accounting numbers, in particular. Some effects of this deficiency can be seen by considering the frequently made assumption that subjects' resource allocation decisions are primarily determined by properties of accounting income numbers. Conditional on this assumption, the relevant effects of alternative accounting techniques should appear via the techniques' effects on accounting income numbers. Typically, the importance ascribed to accounting income numbers is never deduced from theoretical considerations; it is simply asserted. But this approach can have an important (and seemingly undesirable) effect on interpretations of observed results. For example, Dopuch and Ronen [1973] found that when a firm's financial statements were converted from FIFO to LIFO, the firm's income number decreased, but its rate of return on common equity increased (i.e., the cumulative effect of the switch had a greater proportional effect on common equity than did the switch's effect on current income). Subjects who stated that their decisions were based upon income numbers showed a preference for the FIFO firm, whereas those whose decisions were based upon rates of return on common equity preferred the same firm when it used LIFO. The point here is that inferences and interpretations may differ depending upon whether income numbers or rates of return are assumed to be the major determinants of subjects' decisions. And without resorting to theoretical considerations, it is certainly not obvious that all importance should be ascribed to income numbers.

Even if these studies were based upon an explicit theory of resource allocation by individuals, it still is not apparent that their results would be pertinent to issues of reporting to capital market agents. To see this, consider the implications of capital market efficiency and competition in the market for information.[30]

Recall that the kind of efficient market considered here is simply a competitive market, a market within which each individual is a price-taker. Given this type of market, any generalizations made about the aggregate behavior of capital market agents on the basis of results from lab/field studies are extremely tenuous.[31] Specifically, given an efficient capital market, studies of the behavior of particular types of investors (e.g., "average" investors or "financial analysts") are not likely to lead to reliable generalizations about the relationship between the production of accounting information and capital market equilibrium. To see this, recall that, within a competitive market, market behavior is a function of the interactions among rivalrous price-takers. The attainment of equilibrium in such a market is induced by the workings of the system as a whole, or *aggregate* market behavior, and not by the actions of particular individuals. Since the lab/field studies concentrated on individual behavior rather than competitive market phenomena, their relevance to the issues at hand seems nonexistent.[32]

Note also that available lab/field studies fail to simulate competition among sources of information. Indeed, the information available to subjects is usually deliberately limited to accounting information. This limitation makes the settings of these studies even further removed from the setting within which the equilibrium prices of firms' ownership shares appear to be established; see Gonedes [1972a].

To be sure, the indicated deficiencies of lab/field studies can, in principle,

---

[30]The following remarks on capital market efficiency and competition in the market for information are based upon the discussion in Gonedes [1972a and 1973c].

[31]The results of at least one behavioral experiment were, however, clearly described as pertaining only to individual behavior; see Dickhaut [1973].

[32]This statement does not imply that lab/field approaches are irrelevant to all accounting issues. Indeed, these approaches may be particularly helpful in resolving some issues of managerial accounting.

be overcome. But to our knowledge, few (if any) attempts to do so have been completed or are even underway.

9.2 Questionnaire Results on Alternative Accounting Techniques

The questionnaire studies listed in Exhibit 1 can be viewed as minimally controlled types of lab/field studies. Some aspects of questionnaire studies are, of course, not exhibited by lab/field studies. But at a fundamental level, the deficiencies of the available questionnaire studies are much the same as the lab/field studies. Thus, we omit direct discussion of the questionnaire studies.

9.3 Studies of Time Series Properties

Under this heading, we listed all studies that compare some attribute of the process generating an accounting number under one accounting technique with the same attribute of the process induced by an alternative technique. This collection of studies includes all of the so-called "materiality studies," studies that focused on aspects of underlying stochastic processes, and the so-called "smoothing studies."

Materiality Studies. In general, these studies sought to determine whether the process generating an accounting number according to one accounting technique is significantly different from the process generating the same number according to a different technique. "Significance" is often determined by comparing observed values of the number conditional upon one technique with contemporaneous values of the number conditional upon the other technique. Usually, a percentage rule is used. If the contemporaneous values of the number (where each value is conditional upon a different technique) differ by more than x percent then the techniques are asserted to have a material effect. The conventional value of x is 10. This approach is most often applied to accounting income numbers. There is, however, no reason why the approach cannot be applied to other accounting numbers.

Evidently, the implicit assumption of the materiality criterion is that users' decisions will be affected if a change in accounting technique induces changes in accounting numbers that violate the percentage rule. And the frequently asserted corollary to this is that users' decisions will not be affected if the percentage rule is not violated. This approach is, therefore, analogous to the control chart schemes used in managerial accounting contexts.

The materiality criterion is a widely used rule of thumb. And it is certainly easy to apply. But it should be clear that the policy implications of results based

upon using this criterion are somewhat mysterious. This is, we believe, attributable to its not having any explicit theoretical underpinnings. Evidently, the
only way to ascribe concrete interpretations to results based upon applying this
criterion is to invoke appeals to authority (e.g., APB Opinions), as was done by
Rosenfield [1969].

It is also well to note that the materiality rule, as described above, attempts
to determine when two stochastic processes are different without ever attempting
to infer the major characteristics of the underlying processes. This is not a trivial
matter because different accounting techniques may induce different stochastic
processes even though given samples of observations from these processes are
consistent with the percentage rule.

Studies Dealing with Aspects of Underlying Stochastic Processes. Exhibit 1
shows five studies in this category. In four of the studies, properties of stochastic
processes that were alleged to provide surrogates for preference rankings were
used to assess the desirability of alternative techniques. In contrast, the Dopuch
and Watts [1972] study only attempted to detect some effects of different
techniques. Since some aspects of the Dopuch/Watts study provide insights into
the underpinnings of the other studies, we begin our review with it.

Dopuch and Watts proposed that the significance (materiality) of switching
from one accounting technique to another be determined by assessing the effect
of the change on the parameters of the process generating any accounting
number of interest. According to their argument, a change in an accounting
technique has a potential impact on users' decisions if it alters the process
generating the accounting number examined. The essence of their procedure
involves inferring whether the parameters of the best-fitting time series model
prior to the change are identical to the parameters of that model after the
change. This is equivalent to asking whether the underlying generating process
was affected by the change of technique.

Dopuch and Watts offered the following rationale for their approach.
Suppose that some accounting number is used as an input for capital market
agents' decision models. Further suppose, in line with the "theory of rational
expectations" (see Muth [1961]), that agents attempt to recognize and exploit
the systematic behavior of this number by inquiring into its underlying generating process. The identified underlying process provides some information for
prediction. If a change in accounting techniques forces agents to reidentify
the underlying process then—according to the Dopuch/Watts argument—that
change is declared to be significant. Of course, the processes identified by capital
market agents may not be identical to the ones identified by the Dopuch/Watts
procedures. Moreover, the accounting numbers investigated by Dopuch and
Watts may not be inputs to capital market agents' decision models. Thus, their
approach is not free from deficiencies.

It should be clear that the Dopuch/Watts proposal merely involves a different scheme for assessing materiality. As with the percentage-rule approach, its theoretical underpinnings are somewhat scanty. The important part of the proposal is, however, that it attempts to incorporate more aspects of the process generating accounting numbers. That this is important can be seen from the following.

Consider the Dopuch and Drake [1966] study. They attempted to assess the variability of an accounting income number process computed under each of two techniques: (1) the use of historical costs to measure the income from long-term investments and (2) the use of changes in the market values of these investments to measure income. Using estimated variances, they inferred that the historical cost techniques induced income number processes with less dispersion. Frank [1969] compared the predictive ability of income computed under historical cost and current cost schemes; the adjustments for the different schemes were made to inventory and fixed-asset accounts. Predictive ability was assessed in terms of average percentage differences between observed income and income predicted under each of the alternative techniques using a restrictive set of prediction models.

The statistical tools used in the studies by Dopuch and Drake and by Frank are appropriate for certain kinds of stochastic processes. But none of these studies examined the nature of the processes with which they dealt. Thus, we do not know whether the results of these studies yield substantive implications about the effects of accounting techniques or whether they merely reflect the effects of inappropriate estimation procedures. This is the kind of issue which can be examined with the Dopuch/Watts procedures.

These studies are, however, not deficient on only technical grounds. There remains the question about whether variability or predictive ability is a sufficient basis for selecting from among alternative accounting techniques. Presumably, accounting numbers are supposed to convey information on events pertinent to evaluating firms. Given this argument, there is little reason to select an accounting technique solely because it induces an accounting number process with "low" variability. In short, this approach is just as theoretically deficient as others relying upon rules of thumb.

Similar conceptual deficiencies characterize the simulation studies of Simmons and Gray [1969] and Greenball [1968 and 1969]. In addition, they also suffer from the fact that the numbers examined are not actual accounting numbers. So one does not know whether the results of these studies have any descriptive validity.

Smoothing Studies. Many of the above remarks apply with equal force to the numerous studies that attempted to determine whether managers select accounting techniques so as to "smooth" the processes generating accounting numbers.

Exhibit 1
Empirical Studies Which Use Other than Price Data to Evaluate Accounting Alternatives

Laboratory and Field Studies	Materiality of Differences	Time Series Properties of Different Methods			Questionnaires
		Time Series Analyses	Smoothing Studies	Consistency Studies	
	1947 R.W. King				
	1949 R.C. Jones				
	1953 A.L. Bell				
	M.J. Gordon				
	J.F. Weston				
	1954 D. Corbin				
	J. Dean				
	T.J. McNichols and F.V. Boyd				
	G. Warner				1955 C. Horngren
	1955 D.A. Corbin				
	P. Mason				
	1956 H.J. Bierman, Jr.				
	1959 W.T. Baxter				
	1962 H.R. Jaenicke		1962 H.R. Jaenicke	1962 S.R. Sapienza	
				1963 S.R. Sapienza	
1964 T. Dyckman	1964 G.C. Holdren				
	1965 C.H. Spencer and T.S. Barnhisel				
1966 T. Dyckman R. Jensen	1966 S. Davidson and J.M. Kohlmeier N. Dopuch and D.F. Drake	1966 N. Dopuch and D.F. Drake	1966 M.J. Gordon, B. Horwitz, and P. Meyers		
			1967 T.R. Archibald J-M. Gagnon J. Meyers	1967 O. Johnson J.L. Livingstone	
		1968 M. Greenball	1968 R.M. Copeland and R.D. LiCastro	1968 W. Voss D. McDonald	1968 R. Estes

1969 T. Dyckman

1969 R. Abel
G. Foster
P. Rosenfield

1969 M. Greenball
W. Frank
J.K. Simmons and
J. Gray

1969 —— and J.F.
Wojdak
R.H. Simpson
B. Cushing

1969 J.L. Livingstone
R. Sterling and
R. Radosevich

1970 V. Brenner

1970 P.O. Dietz and
G.P. Williams,
Jr.

1970 P.E. Dasher and
R.E. Malcolm
G.E. White

1970 Y. Peles

1971 G. Fogelberg

1971 M. Barrett

1971 R. Barefield and
E. Comiskey
J-M. Gagnon

1971 L. Chasteen
J.C. McKeown

1972 N. Elias

1972 N. Dopuch and
R. Watts

1972 R. Barefield and
E. Comiskey
G.E. White

1973 E.V. McIntyre
N. Dopuch and
J. Ronen
J. Dickhaut

1973 R.J. Peterson

The alleged motivation for this behavior is a desire to reduce the extent to which "bad times" and—at the other extreme—"good times" are revealed by reported accounting numbers. It is suggested by some that a smoothed series of accounting numbers, particularly income numbers, will enhance the value of a firm. A typical statement of this argument was provided by Hepworth [1953, p. 34] : "Certainly the owners and creditors of an enterprise will feel more confident toward a corporate management which is able to report stable earnings than if considerable fluctuation of reported earnings exists."[33]

This group of studies is, however, not based upon a well-developed theoretical base. One characteristic of the available studies of the income-smoothing hypothesis is a lack of rigorously derived explicit statements about what one should expect if, in fact, income smoothing is practiced. Such statement are particularly important for empirical tests of the smoothing hypothesis, since it is difficult to test for the existence of something that cannot even by identified, if that something exists at all. Indeed, with one exception, the available studies do not even consider whether income smoothing is optimal, given the stochastic process applicable to the accounting numbers of interest and the alleged objectives of income-smoothing actions; the one exception is a study by Ball and Watts [1972].[34] The available studies also pay little (if any) attention to the multiperiod consequences of income-smoothing actions; the importance of this factor is discussed in detail in Gonedes [1972b, section III]. Finally, note that the crux of the smoothing hypothesis is in direct conflict with the evidence on capital market efficiency, evidence suggesting that the kinds of manipulations needed for smoothing will not "fool" capital market agents.

We might also add that, like the materiality studies, most smoothing studies do not inquire into the appropriateness of the statistical methods used in the studies. Thus, we cannot determine whether the results reflect substantive phenomena or model misspecifications.

9.4 Consistency Studies

The studies in this group sought to determine whether firms select accounting techniques in a manner consistent with prescriptions of "policy-making" or "authoritative" bodies. (The AICPA's Accounting Research and Terminology Bulletins and the APB's Opinions are two sources of such prescriptions.) As is indicated by Exhibit 1, the number of studies in this group is seemingly small.

---

[33]This argument involves some strong (implicit) assumptions about the information on risk conveyed by accounting numbers. Empirical results bearing on this issue are provided in: Ball and Brown [1969]; Beaver, Kettler, and Scholes [1970]; Pettit and Westerfield [1972]; Beaver and Manegold [1973]; and Gonedes [1973b and 1973d].

[34]Their conclusions about the "optimality" of smoothing actions are not, however, as general as one might infer from their discussion; see Gonedes [1972b, p. 583].

Perhaps one of the reasons for this is that the data needed to directly test the consistency of accounting techniques are seldom available. We illustrate this by beginning our review with the deferred-tax/flow-through controversy.

Should firms use the deferred tax method to account for the differences between "book" and tax income induced by using accelerated depreciation for tax purposes and straight-line depreciation for external reporting purposes? Originally, this question was answered by determining whether a firm's deferred tax account could really be viewed as a liability (induced by the differences between book and tax income numbers). Davidson [1958] argued that firms which increase or maintain their investment in fixed assets will never be forced to "pay off" the aggregate amount of deferred taxes. According to his argument, this suggests that the flow-through method is more appropriate for these firms. The empirical results subsequently provided by Livingstone [1967 and 1969] and Voss [1968] suggest that in fact, deferred tax accounts are rarely reduced. At the very least, this evidence suggests that neither method is best for every firm, where "best" is determined by recourse to the so-called liability criterion.

There are two important ingredients in this situation: A clear statement of the criterion to be used (assuming that one is willing to invoke appeals to authority) and data on the object of analysis. (In the above case, the data are observations on the process generating the deferred tax number.) Upon reflection it seems clear that either or both of these ingredients are absent when one extends the consistency approach to other controversies over accounting techniques. Consider, for example, the debates over depreciation techniques. The conventional argument (see, e.g., Grady [1965, p. 126]) is that the costs of using the services provided by fixed assets should be charged to the periods during which these services are consumed. But there is (as yet) no well-defined *general* scheme for measuring the periodic consumption of these services. In short, even within the conventional historical cost framework, there is no unambiguous means of empirically testing the consistency of a firm's chosen depreciation techniques with the prescriptions of Generally Accepted Account-Principles (GAAP).

A similar absence of unambiguous criteria exists with respect to inventory costing techniques. Consider, for example, the LIFO vs. FIFO controversy. The contemporary tax laws prohibit the use of LIFO unless that technique is also used for external reports. The primary consideration in selecting either LIFO or FIFO is probably the effect of the techniques on a firm's tax payments. Thus, it seems unlikely that any empirical study of the consistency of firms' inventory costing techniques with GAAP will provide much other than negative results. This, we believe, is what Chasteen [1971] observed.

Chasteen attempted to infer the consistency of the inventory costing techniques used by firms for external reporting with criteria set forth by the 1938 AI(CP)A Committee on Federal Taxation. He inferred that there was little

consistency. This appears, however, to be a misleading inference.[35] The 1938
Committee actually dealt with conditions under which LIFO and FIFO would
lead to significantly different values of accounting numbers and, in particular,
significantly different tax payments. The Committee did not argue that the
conditions it set forth identified the inventory costing technique that is superior
from the view of GAAP. At best, Chasteen's study probably provides evidence
on the importance of LIFO's tax consequences, rather than its superiority for
firms with certain kinds of operating characteristics. But this brings us back to
the main problem with attempts to use consistency arguments: the absence
of unambiguous (and general) criteria for assessing the consistency of alternative
techniques.

The severity of this problem is also apparent in attempts to assess the
consistency of techniques applied to "intangibles," such as advertising (see
Peles [1970]) and research and development (see Johnson [1967]). Here the
problem is to determine whether expenditures for intangibles should be capitalized or expensed and, if they are capitalized, to determine which depreciation
technique is appropriate. The major difficulty here is identical to that associated
with other depreciation problems, namely, determining the extent to which the
benefits from the expenditures can be associated with particular periods. But, in
general, determining that is rarely (if ever) possible. Peles and Johnson attempted
to deal with some aspects of this problem. Yet, ignoring statistical problems, the
acceptability of their results is wholly dependent on the extent to which their
modeling of "future benefits" is accepted. There is, however, no evidence on
the adequacy of these models.[36]

Thus far, we have considered applications of the consistency criterion to
some individual types of accounts. The framework used in the papers by
McDonald [1968], McKeown [1971], and Sterling and Radosevich [1969] uses
the consistency approach in a more general way. This framework involves
evaluating accounting techniques (pertaining to any type of account) in terms
of their consistency with the "objectivity principle." Each uses the "consensus"
interpretation of objectivity advanced by Ijiri and Jaedicke [1966]. According
to this view, objectivity varies directly with the extent to which two or more
accountants quantifying the effects of the same event arrive at identical results.
In line with this interpretation, Ijiri and Jaedicke suggested that the estimated
variance of the accountants' measurements be used as a measure of objectivity.

Ijiri and Jaedicke also discussed the reliability of alternative accounting
techniques, where reliability is measured by the expected squared deviation of
the measurement from the "true value" of an event's effect. The latter quantity

---

[35]For one misinterpretation of Chasteen's results, see Sterling [1973].

[36]We should note that the models and tests used by Peles have more intuitive appeal than
those used by Johnson because Peles's models and tests tried to exploit more aspects of
economic theory.

is equal to the variance of the measurement *plus* the squared bias term, where bias is equal to the mean of the measurement *minus* the true value of the event's effect. Since, however, the true value of an event's effect is usually never known (and often undefined), studies that use the Ijiri/Jaedicke framework ignore the bias component of reliability, and thus focus on the objectivity component.

Suppose, however, that the true value of some event's effect is known and that the estimated mean conditional on accounting technique A(B) is equal (not equal) to this value. Also suppose that the estimated variance of measurement conditional on A exceeds that of B. Even if the estimated reliability (i.e., estimated variance plus squared bias) of the two methods is identical, it is not obvious that a user of accounting reports would be indifferent between the two methods. That is, there is a potential for trading off variance against bias and, without additional information, we do not see how the tradeoffs should be made.

Similar questions arise when only objectivity is considered. One technique may induce a measurement with both a higher mean and a higher variance relative to a competing technique.[37] Should a choice of one method or the other be made on the basis of variances only? Or should coefficients of variation (i.e., square roots of variances divided by means) be used?

The point of all this is that the objectivity criterion is not so well developed that it can actually be used in assessing alternative techniques. Moreover, even if an unambiguous indicator of objectivity were available, its pertinence to capital market agents' behavior would have to be established before it could be of much use in assessing alternative techniques.

9.5 Summary

The available studies that did not use the prices of firms' ownership shares in examining the effects of alternative techniques do not, in our judgment, provide much reliable evidence on the effects of alternative accounting techniques. Their failure to do so can be attributed to deficiencies at two basic levels of analysis.

First, suppose that the framework of each nonprice study is accepted as being appropriate. Even if this is done, these studies are characterized by some major theoretical and technical problems. In some cases these problems are statistical ones. In other cases, the problems arise because the framework (e.g., the theory of individual behavior in the lab/field studies and the specification

---

[37]This problem was actually encountered by McDonald who dealt with it by scaling his estimated variances. His reasons for doing so, however, were not made explicit in his paper. Moreover, neither McDonald nor others who assessed objectivity considered the problems that arise when the probability distributions of measurements are not normal.

of materiality in the materiality approach) is not so well developed that it can yield reliable results. These problems may not be insurmountable; perhaps some of them can be alleviated by using improved statistical tools and by devoting more effort to the specification of the frameworks used.

The second level of analysis involves the connection between whatever framework is used in a nonprice study and capital market agents' behavior. In each of the above subsections, we observed that the relationship between the specific framework adopted and capital market agents' resource allocation decisions was never apparent. Thus, the relevance of each framework to the issues at hand is most certainly not obvious. And this would be the case even if each framework were completely well specified and even if all data needed for its application were available.

The above remarks should not be interpreted to mean that a study is deficient simply because it is a nonprice study. Rather, we are suggesting that the *available* nonprice studies were not successful in overcoming some seemingly major technical and theoretical problems.

Section 10. Summary and Remarks on Institutional Arrangements

Establishing methods for assessing the desirability and/or effects of alternative accounting procedures is one of the main problems facing accounting policy-making bodies. Much of this paper has dealt with one approach for making these assessments, namely, the use of prices of (or rates of return on) firms' ownership shares. The considerable appeal of this approach seems to have been induced by developments in the theory of, and evidence on, capital market efficiency, upon which the approach relies. This reliance upon capital market efficiency is based upon two critical assertions:

A.1 Capital market efficiency, taken by itself, provides sufficient justification for using prices of firms' ownership shares in assessing the *desirability* of alternative accounting techniques or regulations.

A.2 Capital market efficiency, taken by itself, provides sufficient justification for using prices of firms' ownership shares in assessing the *effects* of alternative accounting procedures or regulations.

Pareto optimality is the concept of social preference used in discussing the desirability of alternative techniques and regulations from a social perspective. From a given individual's perspective, desirability is determined by reference to that individual's preference ordering.

The "effects" of changes in techniques or regulations refer to the changes (if any) in agents' assessed distribution functions of returns on ownership shares induced by the changes in techniques or regulations.

The theoretical framework developed in Sections 2–6 was used to assess the logical validity of assertions A.1 and A.2. Our analysis indicated that assertion A.1 is logically invalid and that assertion A.2 is logically valid. These conclusions are conditional upon the contemporary institutional setting. Our analysis also indicated some alternative market settings wherein assertion A.1 would be logically valid.

The logical validity of A.2 justifies an approach for empirically assessing the effects of alternative accounting procedures and regulations, such as SEC disclosure regulations. In section 8 we reviewed studies that used that approach. Not unexpectedly, the results of these studies were observed to have several limitations. And, as indicated above, the approach used in these studies could not provide desirability assessments. Thus, we were motivated to review some nonprice approaches for assessing desirability and/or effects. That review was provided in section 9.

As is evident from our review, we are inclined to ascribe more descriptive validity to studies based upon an explicit and descriptively valid theory of asset valuation under uncertainty. Given the available evidence, we therefore ascribe relatively more descriptive validity to those studies (reviewed here) that are based upon the two-parameter asset pricing model. In general, the results from these studies are consistent with the statement that capital market agents (in the aggregate) behave as if they do distinguish between changes in accounting techniques that have substantive economic implications and those that do not. Some necessary qualifications of this inference are given in section 8.

It is somewhat fashionable to criticize accounting policy-making bodies (such as the Accounting Principles Board or the Securities and Exchange Commission) for ignoring empirical evidence pertaining to alternative accounting techniques. Our theoretical analysis and the review of empirical work suggest, however, that available evidence cannot be used to fully resolve the main issues with which these bodies deal (i.e., conditions under which different accounting techniques should be used). Thus, we should neither expect nor want such bodies to rely exclusively on the kinds of evidence reviewed in this paper.[38]

On the other hand, evidence on the price effects of alternative procedures (see section 8.1) can provide some information for making optimal information-production decisions. Suppose, using the classification scheme of section 8.1, the available evidence indicates that a choice from a set of procedures involves a change in the external reporting process of type (T.1), and, perhaps, type (T.3), but not any other type. In this special case there may be little reason to even deliberate over what procedure should be used when accounting numbers produced under one procedure can be almost costlessly transformed (by a user)

---

[38]Another reason for this is that some of the studies reviewed here (see, e.g., sec. 9) are so theoretically and/or technically deficient that their results should be viewed as being more or less useless.

to numbers conditional on any of the alternative procedures. If such transforma-
tions are less costly when a particular procedure is used for reporting purposes
then a seemingly reasonable approach is to select the method producing results
that can be converted to results conditional on alternative methods at the
lowest conversion cost. In the latter situation, we would be dealing with a
change of type (T.1) and (T.3). The choice of the deferred-tax method for
industrial firms provides a good example of how this approach could be used.
A change involving this procedure and the flow-through method would seem
to be of type (T.1) and (T.3). By using the deferred-tax method, the firm
provides sufficient information for anyone to convert the firm's accounting
numbers to the flow-through basis. Moreover, use of the deferred-tax method
provides sufficient information for computing the after-tax effects of using
accelerated rather than straight-line depreciation (for the same class of firms).
The question as to whether anyone would want to make these computations
is irrelevant here. The point is that the option to do so is made available.[39]

The above example also motivates another special case. Consider the
same type of procedures discussed in the preceding paragraph. This time,
however, suppose that the additional cost to a firm of producing numbers
conditional on one of the procedures is truly trivial if numbers conditional on
one of the other procedures are already being produced. In this case, it seems
reasonable to produce information conditional on both procedures, rather than
wasting resources by deliberating over which method should be used. This
approach can, it appears, also be used when the choice of technique affects the
information-production costs incurred by agents external to the firm. But in the
latter case, one has to consider social costs and benefits rather than only private
costs and benefits. Thus, the additional social costs of any one technique would
have to be trivial before we could advocate a change in the information-
production mechanism.

The point to emphasize is that decisions such as those described above
should not be based upon the prevalent belief (among accountants) that capital
market agents may be confused by accounting numbers based upon several
techniques and that this "confusion" will affect capital market equilibrium.
Such beliefs appear to have no supporting empirical evidence.

In general, when the selection of an accounting technique affects the
available opportunities for information production or the costs of these opportunities then the appropriate route for optimally selecting techniques is not
clearly identified. A general resolution of this problem involves profound issues
of social choice (see section 6). If we rule out dictatorial schemes or the
(somewhat mysterious) "rule by convention" schemes then we are essentially
left with the market mechanism or some type of political (voting) scheme; see
Arrow [1963]. In general, the market mechanism cannot be used by firms to

---

[39]For the special case considered here, our conclusions are the same as Beaver's [1973, p.
52]. However, Beaver also applies these conclusions to items that do not appear to satisfy
the conditions of this special case.

optimally select accounting techniques, given the current institutional setting; see section 6. If the current institutional framework is taken as given then the remaining alternative involves using an organization that is akin to a governmental body in a democracy in order to make the public choices under examination.

One example of such a political organization is the recently founded Financial Accounting Standards Board (FASB). To be sure, the decisions of this institution are partially influenced by (somebody's) accounting theory. But, in the end, it is a political institution (nominally under private-sector control). Consequently, the actions of this (and any similar) organization should be viewed as political outcomes, rather than as outcomes of a process that is supposed to operationalize and implement an accounting theory in a pure and pristine manner.

The political perspective can, we believe, facilitate understanding of the actions taken by a policy-making body such as the FASB or the now defunct APB. Consider, for example, the APB's responsiveness to criticisms of its "exposure drafts." The APB's tendency to alter its position in response to such criticism was often considered to be something of a deficiency. Yet, in line with our argument, this tendency should have been expected and welcomed. If this had not occurred the APB might have become overly dictatorial. Indeed, assuming that the latter result was not desired, we wonder why the APB did not use other schemes for eliciting criticisms of and votes on its proposed Opinions from those directly affected by them.

Observe that our theoretical framework merely identifies a political organization as one vehicle for making the social choices under examination. It does not identify the details of the organization's operating rules or its composition. Thus, it most certainly does not identify the FASB as the organization that is needed.[40] Many alternative institutional forms should be viewed as competitors vis-à-vis the FASB.

One possibility is to have a political body whose members are directly elected by the agents that this body is supposed to represent, namely, the users of accounting information. Those elected could then select accounting procedures in much the same way that the U.S. Congress passes laws. This approach has the same benefits and limitations as other legislative bodies in a democracy.[41]

Another possibility is to allow a government body staffed by appointments

---

[40]Nor does it give details on the FASB's objectives. It was, however, recently argued that one of the major roles of the FASB is to "prevent superior returns accruing from inside information" (Beaver [1973, p. 56]). This is not implied by our analysis. Moreover, one can argue via the theory of competitive markets that the use of inside information is consistent with a well-functioning capital market and a well-functioning market for information; see, e.g., Manne [1966]. Thus, one cannot flatly assert that the aforementioned role of the FASB is implied by the theory of competitive markets, or any other part of economic theory.

[41]See, e.g., Arrow [1963], Downs [1957], Buchanan and Tullock [1962], Tullock [1970 and 1971], and Stigler [1970].

(e.g., the SEC) to act as the representative of those who use information produced via the accounting mechanism. An obvious potential problem here is that this body may be secondarily responsive to those users and primarily responsive to those who control its appointments (and budget).[42]

These are simply some of the more obvious alternatives to the type of organization represented by the FASB. We shall not debate the relative merits of each here. The important point is not which type is "best"; it is that there are alternative kinds of political schemes. Unfortunately, there is little evidence in the accounting literature indicating that such alternatives have been seriously considered. Typically, all that is available is a somewhat emotional objection to governmental influence on accounting. And if the alternatives to the FASB have not even been seriously considered then it is somewhat difficult to assess desirability.

In general, the political approach is not the only one available. We can also consider alterations in the contemporary institutional setting that will allow use of the market mechanism. Consider the following example. Currently, there are private firms that locate, for a fee, requested information that is on file at the SEC.[43] Why can we not have similar firms producing and selling, for a fee, information on firms' operations?[44] If these firms serve as agents for stockholders then they could exercise the stockholders' rights to examine corporate records. More generally, there would have to be laws establishing the rights of such agents to gain access to corporate records. Under this approach, the users of information initiate requests for and bid on the services of information producers. This is in contrast to contemporary procedures whereby a firm initiates requests for and bids on the services of information producers (often to satisfy disclosure laws).

To be sure, our last suggestion involves some seemingly radical departures from the contemporary institutional setting. And a complete analysis (not undertaken here) would involve some heady issues regarding property rights, social costs, and social benefits, among other things.[45] Our purpose here, however, is not to suggest that either the market or the political approach is preferable. Rather, we want to emphasize (again) that there is a wide range of

---

[42]Cf. Tullock [1971].

[43]This was pointed out to the authors by James Mikes, then a student at the University of Chicago's Law School.

[44]These sales can be effected via the selling of rights to receive and use produced information; see section 6.

[45]See the references given in fn. 4, Coase [1960], Roberts [1973], Demetz [1964 and 1969], and Sen [1970] for discussions of pertinent issues. Also note that the problems associated with use of the market mechanism are no more complex than those associated with designing an appropriate political mechanism.

alternative schemes for making the kinds of information-production decisions considered in this paper.[46]

References

Abdel-Khalik, A. Rashad. "The Efficient Marketing Hypothesis and Accounting Data: A Point of View," *The Accounting Review* (October 1972): 791-93.

Abel, R. "A Comparative Simulation of German and U.S. Accounting Principles," *Journal of Accounting Research* 7 (Spring 1969): 1-11.

Akerloff, G.A. "The Market for 'Lemons': Quality Uncertainty and the Market Mechanism," *Quarterly Journal of Economics* (August 1970): 488-500.

Archibald, T. Ross. "The Return to Straight-Line Depreciation: An Analysis of a Change in Accounting Method," *Empirical Research in Accounting: Selected Studies, 1967*. Supplement to *Journal of Accounting Research* 5: 164-80.

——. "Stock Market Reaction to the Depreciation Switch-Back," *The Accounting Review* 47 (January 1972): 22-30.

Arrow, Kenneth J. *Social Choice and Individual Values*. 2d ed. New Haven, Conn.: Yale University Press, 1963.

Ball, Raymond J. "Index of Empirical Research in Accounting," *Journal of Accounting Research* 9 (Spring 1971).

——. "Changes in Accounting Techniques and Stock Prices." Draft of Ph.D. dissertation, University of Chicago, June 1972a.

——. "Changes in Accounting Techniques and Stock Prices," *Empirical Research in Accounting: Selected Studies, 1972*. Supplement to *Journal of Accounting Research* 10 (1972b).

——, and Brown, P. "An Empirical Evaluation of Accounting Income Numbers," *Journal of Accounting Research* 6 (Autumn 1968): 159-77.

——, and ——. "Portfolio Theory and Accounting," *Journal of Accounting Research* 7 (Autumn 1969): 300-323.

——, and Watts, Ross. "Some Time Series Properties of Accounting Income," *Journal of Finance* (June 1972): 663-82.

Barefield, Russell M., and Comiskey, Eugene E. "Depreciation Policy and the

---

[46]Also note that the implications of the political approach described here are quite different from arguments recently advanced by Horngren [1973]. Horngren virtually asserts that we should want a more dictatorial scheme. Indeed, he states that the FASB should strive to convince others (e.g., the SEC) that is the "premier group of experts on accounting standards" (p. 65). He also states that the FASB should "stress that, to benefit society at large, it is generally desirable to allow the experts to make the decisions without harassment" (p. 65). Our own argument points to a very different scheme—one with no (intended) dictatorial features.

Behavior of Corporate Profits," *Journal of Accounting Research* 9 (Autumn 1971): 351–58.

——, and ——. "The Smoothing Hypothesis: An Alternative Test," *The Accounting Review* 47 (April 1972): 291–98.

Barrett, M. Edgar. "Accounting for Intercorporate Investments: A Behavior Field Study," *Empirical Research in Accounting: Selected Studies, 1971.* Supplement to *Journal of Accounting Research* 9: 50–65.

Baxter, W.T. "Inflation and the Accounts of Steel Companies," *Journal of Accountancy* (May and June 1959 [2 parts]): 250–75; 308–14.

Beaver, William H. "The Information Content of Annual Earnings Announcements," *Empirical Research in Accounting: Selected Studies, 1968.* Supplement to *Journal of Accounting Research* 6: 67–92.

——. "The Behavior of Security Prices and Its Implications for Accounting Research (Methods)," Supplement to *The Accounting Review* (1972): 407–36.

——. "What Should Be the FASB's Objectives?" *Journal of Accountancy* (August 1973): 49–56.

——, and Dukes, R.E. "Interperiod Tax Allocation, Earnings Expectations, and the Behavior of Security Prices," *The Accounting Review* (April 1972): 320–32.

——, and ——. "Interperiod Tax Allocation and δ-Depreciation Methods: Some Empirical Results," *The Accounting Review* (July 1973): 549–59.

Beaver, William H.; Kettler, P.; and Scholes, M. "The Association Between Market Determined and Accounting Determined Risk Measures," *The Accounting Review* (October 1970): 654–82.

——, and Manegold, James. "The Association Between Market-Determined and Accounting-Determined Measures of Systematic Risk: Some Further Evidence." Manuscript, Stanford University, 1973.

Bell, Albert L. "Fixed Assets and Current Costs," *The Accounting Review* 28 (January 1953): 44–53.

Bellman, R.E. *Dynamic Programming.* Princeton, N.J.: Princeton University Press, 1957.

Benston, George J. "Published Corporate Accounting Data and Stock Prices," *Empirical Research in Accounting: Selected Studies, 1967.* Supplement to *Journal of Accounting Research* 5: 1–14 and 22–54.

——. "The Effectiveness and Effects of the SEC's Accounting Disclosure Requirements," in Manne (1969): 23–80.

——. "The Value of the SEC's Accounting Disclosure Requirements," *The Accounting Review* (July 1969): 515–32.

——. "Required Disclosure and the Stock Market: An Evaluation of the Securities Exchange Act of 1934," *American Economic Review* (March 1973): 132–55.

Bierman, Harold, Jr. "The Effect of Inflation on the Computation of Income of Public Utilities," *The Accounting Review* 30 (April 1956): 258–62.

Black, F. "Capital Market Equilibrium with Restricted Borrowing," *Journal of Business* (July 1972): 444–55.

Brenner, Vincent C. "Financial Statement Users' Views of the Desirability of Reporting Current Cost Information," *Journal of Accounting Research* 8 (Autumn 1970): 159–66.

Brigham, E.F. "The Effects of Alternative Depreciation Policies on Reported Profits," *The Accounting Review* (January 1968): 46–61.

Buchanan, James M., and Tullock, G. *The Calculus of Consent.* Ann Arbor: University of Michigan Press, 1962.

Chambers, R.J. *Accounting, Evaluation, and Economic Behavior.* Englewood Cliffs, N.J.: Prentice-Hall, 1966.

Chasteen, Lanny G. "An Empirical Study of Differences in Economic Circumstances as a Justification for Alternative Inventory Methods," *The Accounting Review* 46 (July 1971): 504–8.

Coase, R.H. "The Problem of Social Cost," *Journal of Law and Economics* (October 1960): 1–44.

Comiskey, Eugene E. "Market Response to Changes in Depreciation Accounting," *The Accounting Review* 46 (April 1971): 279–85.

Copeland, Ronald M. "Income Smoothing," *Empirical Research in Accounting: Selected Studies, 1968.* Supplement to *Journal of Accounting Research* 6: 101–16.

——, and Li Castro, Ralph D. "A Note on Income Smoothing," *The Accounting Review* 43 (July 1968): 540–45.

——, and Wojdak, Joseph F. "Income Manipulation and the Purchase-Pooling Choice," *Journal of Accounting Research* 7 (Autumn 1969).

Corbin, D. "The Impact of Changing Prices on a Department Store," *The Journal of Accountancy* 97 (April 1954): 430–40.

——. "A Case Study of Price-Level Adjustments," *The Accounting Review* 30 (April 1955): 268–81.

Cramér, H. *Mathematical Methods of Statistics.* Princeton, N.J.: Princeton University Press, 1946.

Cushing, Barry E. "An Empirical Study of Changes in Accounting Policy," *Journal of Accounting Research* 7 (Autumn 1969): 196–203.

Dasher, Paul E., and Malcolm, Robert E. "A Note on Income Smoothing in the Chemical Industry," *Journal of Accounting Research* 8 (Autumn 1970): 253–59.

Davidson, Sidney. "Accelerated Depreciation and the Allocation of Income Taxes," *The Accounting Review* 33 (April 1958): 173–80.

——, and Kohlmeier, John M. "A Measure of the Impact of Some Foreign Accounting Principles," *Journal of Accounting Research* 4 (Autumn 1966): 183–212.

Dean, Joel. "Measurement of Real Economic Earnings of a Machinery Manufacturer," *The Accounting Review* 29 (April 1954): 255–66.

Demsetz, Harold. "The Exchange and Enforcement of Property Rights," *Journal of Law and Economics* 7 (1964): 11–26.

——. "Why Regulate Utilities?" *Journal of Law and Economics* 11 (1968): 55–65.

——. "Perfect Competition, Regulation, and the Stock Market," in Manne (1969): 1–22.

——. "The Private Production of Public Goods," *Journal of Law and Economics* 13 (1970): 293–306.

Dickhaut, John W. "Alternative Information Structures and Probability Revisions," *The Accounting Review* 48 (January 1973): 61–79.

Dietz, Peter O., and Williams, George P., Jr. "Influence of Pension Fund Asset Valuations on Rate of Return," *Financial Executive* (May 1970): 32–35.

Dopuch, Nicholas, and Drake, David F. "The Effect of Alternative Accounting Rules for Nonsubsidiary Investments," *Empirical Research in Accounting: Selected Studies, 1966.* Supplement to *Journal of Accounting Research* 4: 192–219.

——, and Ronen, J. "The Effects of Alternative Inventory Valuation Methods— An Experimental Study," *Journal of Accounting Research* 11 (1973), in press.

——, and Watts, Ross. "Using Time Series Models to Assess the Significance of Accounting Changes," *Journal of Accounting Research* 10 (Spring 1972): 180–94.

Downs, Anthony. *An Economic Theory of Democracy.* New York: Harper and Brothers, 1957.

Dyckman, Thomas R. "On the Investment Decision," *The Accounting Review* 39 (April 1964): 285–95.

——. "On the Effects of Earnings-trend, Size and Inventory Valuation Procedures in Evaluating a Business Firm," in Jaedicke *et al.*, eds., *Research in Accounting Measurement.* New York: American Accounting Association, 1966.

——. *Investment Analysis and General Price-Level Adjustments.* New York: American Accounting Association, 1969.

Edwards, Edgar O., and Bell, Philip W. *The Theory and Measurement of Business Income.* Berkeley: University of California Press, 1965.

Elias, Nabil. "The Effects of Human Asset Statements on the Investment Decision: An Experiment," *Empirical Research in Accounting: Selected Studies, 1972.* Supplement to *Journal of Accounting Research* 10 (1972).

Estes, Ralph W. "An Assessment of the Usefulness of Current Cost and Price-Level Information by Financial Statement Users," *Journal of Accounting Research* 6 (Autumn 1968): 200–207.

Fama, Eugene F. "Risk, Return and Equilibrium: Some Clarifying Comments," *Journal of Finance* (March 1968): 29–40.

——. "Multiperiod Consumption-Investment Decisions," *American Economic Review* (March 1970a): 163–74.

——. "Efficient Capital Markets: A Review of Theory and Empirical Work," *Journal of Finance* (May 1970b): 383–417.

——. "Perfect Competition and Optimal Production Decisions Under Uncertainty," *Bell Journal of Economics and Management Science* (Autumn 1972): 509–30.

——; Fisher, L.; Jensen, M.; and Roll, R. "The Adjustment of Stock Prices to New Information," *International Economic Review* (February 1969): 1–21.

——, and Laffer, A.B. "Information and Capital Markets," *Journal of Business* (July 1971): 289–98.

——, and Macbeth, J. "Risk, Return and Equilibrium: Empirical Tests," *Journal of Political Economy* (May/June 1973): 607–36.

——, and Miller, M.H. *The Theory of Finance.* New York: Holt, Rinehart and Winston, 1972.

Feller, W. *An Introduction to Probability Theory and Its Applications.* vol. 2, 2d ed. New York: John Wiley & Sons, 1971.

Fogelberg, Graeme. "Interim Income Determination: An Examination of the Effects of Alternative Measurement Techniques," *Journal of Accounting Research* 9 (Autumn 1971): 215–35.

Foster, George J. "Mining Inventories in a Current Price Accounting System," *Abacus* 5 (December 1969); 99–118.

Frank, Werner. "A Study of the Predictive Significance of Two Income Measures," *Journal of Accounting Research* 7 (Spring 1969): 123–36.

Friend, Irwin. "The SEC and the Economic Performance of Securities Markets," in Manne (1969): 185–216.

——. "The Economic Consequences of the Stock Market," *American Economic Review* (May 1972): 212–19.

——, and Herman, E.S. "The SEC Through a Glass Darkly," *Journal of Business* (October 1964): 382–405.

Gagnon, Jean-Marie. "Purchase versus Pooling of Interests: The Search for a Predictor," *Empirical Research in Accounting: Selected Studies, 1967.* Supplement to *Journal of Accounting Research* 5: 187–204.

——. "The Purchase-Pooling Choice: Some Empirical Evidence," *Journal of Accounting Research* 9 (Spring 1971): 52–69.

Gonedes, Nicholas J. "The Significance of Selected Accounting Procedures: A Statistical Test," *Empirical Research in Accounting: Selected Studies, 1969.* Supplement to *Journal of Accounting Research* 7: 90–113.

——. "Efficient Capital Markets and External Accounting," *The Accounting Review* (January 1972a): 11–21.

——. "Income Smoothing Under Selected Stochastic Processes," *Journal of Business* (October 1972b): 570–84.

——. "Properties of Accounting Numbers: Models and Tests." Report No. 7202, Center for Mathematical Studies in Business and Economics, University of Chicago, 1972c. *Journal of Accounting Research* 11 (1973), in press.

——. "Information-Production and Capital Market Equilibrium." Report No.

7256, Center for Mathematical Studies in Business and Economics, University of Chicago, November 1972d. Revised, October 1973a. *Journal of Finance*, in press.

——. "Evidence on the Information Content of Accounting Numbers: Accounting-Based and Market-Based Estimates of Systematic Risk," *Journal of Financial and Quantitative Analysis* (June 1973b): 407–44.

——. "Remarks on 'Empirical Research in Accounting 1960–70: An Appraisal,' " *Accounting Research 1960–70: A Critical Evaluation.* Edited by Nicholas Dopuch and Lawrence Revsine. Urbana: Center for International Education and Research in Accounting, University of Illinois, 1973c: 179–91.

——. "A Note on Accounting-Based and Market-Based Estimates of Systematic Risk." Manuscript, University of Chicago, 1973d. *Journal of Financial and Quantitative Analysis*, in press.

——. "Capital Market Equilibrium and Annual Accounting Numbers: Empirical Evidence." Revised manuscript, University of Chicago, 1974. *Journal of Accounting Research* 12 (1974), in press.

Gordon, Myron J. "The Valuation of Accounts at Current Cost," *The Accounting Review* 28 (July 1953): 373–84.

——. *The Investment, Financing, and Valuation of the Corporation.* Homewood, Ill.: Richard D. Irwin, 1962.

——; Horwitz, B.; and Meyers, P. "Accounting Measurements and Normal Growth of the Firm," in Jaedicke *et al.*, eds., *Research in Accounting Measurement.* New York: American Accounting Association, 1966.

Grady, Paul. "Inventory of Generally Accepted Accounting Principles for Business Enterprises," *Accounting Research Study No. 7.* New York: American Institute of Certified Public Accountants, 1965.

Greenball, M. "The Accuracy of Different Methods of Accounting for Earnings—A Simulation Approach," *Journal of Accounting Research* 6 (Spring 1968): 114–29.

——. "Appraising Alternative Methods of Accounting for Accelerated Tax Depreciation: A Relative Accuracy Approach," *Journal of Accounting Research* 7 (Autumn 1969): 262–89.

Hakansson, Nils. "Empirical Research in Accounting, 1960–70: An Appraisal," *Accounting Research, 1960–70: A Critical Evaluation.* Edited by Nicholas Dopuch and L. Revsine. Urbana: Center for International Education and Research in Accounting, University of Illinois, 1973: 137–73.

Hepworth, Samuel. "Smoothing Periodic Income," *The Accounting Review* 28 (January 1953): 32–39.

Hirshleifer, Jack. "The Private and Social Value of Information and the Reward to Inventive Activity," *American Economic Review* (September 1971): 561–74.

Holdren, George C. "Lifo and Ratio Analysis," *The Accounting Review* 39 (January 1964): 70–85.

Horngren, Charles T. "Security Analysts and the Price Level," *The Accounting Review* 30 (October 1955): 575-81.

——. "The Marketing of Accounting Standards," *Journal of Accountancy* (October 1973): 61-66.

Ijiri, Yuji, and Jaedicke, R. "Reliability and Objectivity of Accounting Measurements," *The Accounting Review* 41 (July 1966): 474-83.

Ijiri, Yuji; Jaedicke, R.; and Knight, Kenneth E. "The Effects of Accounting Alternatives on Management Decisions," in Jaedicke *et al.*, eds., *Research in Accounting Measurement.* New York: American Accounting Association, 1966: 186-99.

Jaedicke, Robert K.; Ijiri, Yuji; and Nielson, Oswald, eds. *Research in Accounting Measurement.* New York: American Accounting Association, 1966.

Jaenicke, Henry R. "Management's Choice to Purchase or Pool," *The Accounting Review* 37 (October 1962): 758-65.

Jensen, Michael. "Risk, the Pricing of Capital Assets, and the Evaluation of Investment Portfolios," *Journal of Business* (April 1969): 167-247.

——, and Long, J.B., Jr. "Corporate Investment Under Uncertainty and Pareto Optimality in the Capital Markets," *Bell Journal of Economics and Management Science* (Spring 1972): 151-74.

Jensen, Robert E. "An Experimental Design for Study of Effects of Accounting Variations in Decision Making," *Journal of Accounting Research* 4 (Autumn 1966): 224-38.

Johnson, Orace. "A Consequential Approach to Accounting for R&D," *Journal of Accounting Research* 5 (Autumn 1967): 164-72.

Jones, Ralph Coughenor. "Effect of Inflation on Capital and Profits: The Record of Nine Steel Companies," *The Journal of Accountancy* (January 1949): 9-27.

Kaplan, R.S., and Roll, R. "Investor Evaluation of Accounting Information: Some Empirical Evidence," *Journal of Business* (April 1972): 225-57.

King, Robert W. "Effect of Inventory Valuation Methods on Profits," *The Accounting Review* 22 (January 1947): 45-53.

La Valle, Irving H. *An Introduction to Probability, Decision, and Inference.* New York: Holt, Rinehart and Winston, 1970.

Lintner, J. "The Valuation of Risk Assets and the Selection of Risky Investments in Stock Portfolios and Capital Budgets," *Review of Economics and Statistics* (February 1965a): 13-37.

——. "Security Prices, and Maximal Gains from Diversification," *Journal of Finance* (December 1965b): 587-615.

Livingstone, John Leslie. "Accelerated Depreciation and Deferred Taxes: An Empirical Study of Fluctuating Asset Expenditures," *Empirical Research in Accounting: Selected Studies, 1967.* Supplement to *Journal of Accounting Research* 5: 93-117.

——. "Accelerated Depreciation, Tax Allocation, and Cyclical Asset Expenditures of Large Manufacturing Companies," *Journal of Accounting Research* 7 (Autumn 1969): 245–56.

Long, John B., Jr. "Consumption-Investment Decisions and Equilibrium in the Securities Market," *Studies in the Theory of Capital Markets.* Edited by M. Jensen. New York: Praeger, 1972: 146–222.

Luce, R. Duncan, and Raiffa, H. *Games and Decisions.* New York: John Wiley & Sons, 1957.

Luenberger, D.G. *Optimization by Vector Space Methods.* New York: John Wiley & Sons, 1969.

Macbeth, J.D. "Tests of the Two-Parameter Model of Capital Market Equilibrium," Ph.D. dissertation proposal, University of Chicago, 1973.

Manne, Henry G. *Insider Trading and the Stock Market.* New York: The Free Press, 1966.

———, ed. *Economic Policy and the Regulation of Corporate Securities.* Washington, D.C.: American Enterprise Institute, 1969.

Markowitz, H. *Portfolio Selection: Efficient Diversification of Investments.* New York: John Wiley & Sons, 1959.

Marschak, Jacob. "Economic Theory of Information." Working paper No. 118, Western Management Science Institute, University of California, Los Angeles, 1967.

Mason, Perry. "The Price-Level Study of the American Accounting Association," *The Accounting Review* 30 (January 1955): 37–44.

May, Robert G. "The Influence of Quarterly Earnings Announcements on Investor Decisions as Reflected in Common Stock Price Changes," *Empirical Research in Accounting: Selected Studies, 1971.* Supplement to *Journal of Accounting Research* 9: 119–63.

———, and Sundem, Gary L. "Cost of Information and Security Prices: Market Association Tests for Accounting Policy Decisions," *The Accounting Review* (January 1973): 80–94.

Mc Donald, Daniel, L. "A Test Application of the Feasibility of Market Based Measures in Accounting," *Journal of Accounting Research* 6 (Spring 1968): 38–49.

Mc Intyre, Edward V. "Current-Cost Statements and Investment Decisions," *The Accounting Review* 48 (July 1973): 575–85.

Mc Keown, James C. "An Empirical Test of a Model Proposed by Chambers," *The Accounting Review* 46 (January 1971): 12–29.

Mc Nichols, Thomas J., and Boyd, F. Virgil. "Adjustment of Fixed Assets to Reflect Price Level Changes," *The Accounting Review* 29 (January 1954): 106–13.

Meltzer, Allan H. "On Efficiency and Regulation of the Securities Industry," in Manne (1969): 217–42.

Mlynarczyk, Francis A., Jr. "An Empirical Study of Accounting Methods and Stock Prices," *Empirical Research in Accounting: Selected Studies, 1969.* Supplement to *Journal of Accounting Research* 7: 63–81.

Modigliani, Franco, and Miller, Merton H. "The Cost of Capital, Corporation Finance, and the Theory of Investment," *American Economic Review* (June 1958): 261-97.

Mossin, Jan. "Equilibrium in a Capital Asset Market," *Econometrica* (October 1966): 768-83.

Musgrave, R.A. *The Theory of Public Finance.* New York: McGraw-Hill, 1959.

Muth, J.F. "Rational Expectations and the Theory of Price Movements," *Econometrica* (July 1961): 315-35.

Myers, John H. "Depreciation Manipulation for Fun and Profits," *Financial Analysts Journal* (November-December 1967): 117-23.

Nelson, Carl L. "A Priori Research in Accounting," *Accounting Research 1960-70: A Critical Evaluation.* Edited by Nicholas Dopuch and Lawrence Revsine. Urbana: Center for International Education and Research in Accounting, University of Illinois, 1973.

Neter, John. "Discussion of 'An Empirical Study of Accounting Methods and Stock Prices,'" *Empirical Research in Accounting: Selected Studies, 1969.* Supplement to *Journal of Accounting Research* 7: 85-89.

——, and Maynes, E.S. "Correlation Coefficient with 0, 1 Dependent Variable," *Journal of the American Statistical Association* (June 1970): 501-9.

O'Donnell, John L. "Relationships Between Reported Earnings and Stock Prices in the Electric Utility Industry," *The Accounting Review* 40 (January 1965): 135-43.

O'Donnell, John L. "Further Observations on Reported Earnings and Stock Prices," *The Accounting Review* 43 (July 1968): 549-53.

Officer, R.R. "The Variability of the Market Factor of the New York Stock Exchange," *Journal of Business* (July 1973): 434-53.

Patinkin, Don. *Money Interest and Prices.* 2d ed. New York: Harper & Row, 1965.

Paton, W.A., and Littleton, A.C. *An Introduction to Corporate Accounting Standards.* New York: American Accounting Association, 1940.

Patz, Dennis H., and Boatsman, James R. "Accounting Principle Formulation in an Efficient Markets Environment," *Journal of Accounting Research* 10 (Autumn 1972): 392-403.

Peles, Yoram. "Amortization of Advertising Expenditures in the Financial Statements," *Journal of Accounting Research* 8 (Spring 1970): 128-37.

Peterson, Russell J. "General Price-Level Impact on Financial Information," *The Accounting Review* 48 (January 1973): 34-43.

Pettit, R.R., and Westerfield, R. "A Model of Capital Asset Risk," *Journal of Financial and Quantitative Analysis* (March 1972): 1649-68.

Quirk, James, and Saposnik, R. *Introduction to General Equilibrium Theory and Welfare Economics.* New York: McGraw-Hill, 1968.

Roberts, Blaine. "An Extension of Optimality Criteria: An Axiomatic Approach to Institutional Choice," *Journal of Political Economy* (March/April 1973): 386-400.

Rosenfield, Paul. "Accounting for Inflation—A Field Test," *Journal of Accountancy* (June 1969): 45–50.

Samuelson, Paul A. "The Pure Theory of Public Expenditure," *Review of Economics and Statistics* (November 1954): 387–89.

——. "Diagrammatic Exposition of a Theory of Public Expenditure," *Review of Economics and Statistics* (November 1955): 350–56.

Samuelson, Richard A. "Prediction and Price-Level Adjustment," *Journal of Accounting Research* 10 (Autumn 1972): 322–44.

Sapienza, Samuel R. "Pooling Theory and Practice in Business Combinations," *The Accounting Review* 37 (April 1962): 263–78.

——. "Business Combinations: A Case Study," *The Accounting Review* 38 (January 1963): 91–101.

Sen, Amartya K. *Collective Choice and Social Welfare.* San Francisco: Holden-Day, 1970.

Shapley, Lloyd S., and Shubik, M. "On Market Games," *Journal of Economic Theory* 1 (1969): 9–25.

Sharpe, W.F. "Capital Asset Prices: A Theory of Market Equilibrium Under Conditions of Risk," *Journal of Finance* (September 1964): 425–42.

Simmons, J.K., and Gray, Jack. "An Investigation of the Effect of Differing Accounting Frameworks on the Prediction of Net Income," *The Accounting Review* 44 (October 1969): 757–76.

Simpson, Richard H. "An Empirical Study of Possible Income Manipulation," *The Accounting Review* 44 (October 1969): 806–17.

Spence, M. "Job Market Signalling," *Quarterly Journal of Economics* (August 1973): 356–74.

Spencer, Charles H., and Barnhisel, Thomas S. "A Decade of Price-Level Changes —The Effect on the Financial Statements of Cummings Engine Company," *The Accounting Review* 40 (January 1965): 144–53.

Staubus, George J. "The Association of Financial Accounting Variables with Common Stock Values," *The Accounting Review* 40 (January 1965): 119–34.

——. "Testing Inventory Accounting," *The Accounting Review* 43 (July 1968): 413–24.

Sterling, Robert R. "A Test of the Uniformity Hypothesis," *Abacus* 5 (September 1969): 37–47.

——. "Accounting Power," *Journal of Accountancy* (January 1973): 61–67.

——, and Radosevich, R. "A Valuation Experiment," *Journal of Accounting Research* (Spring 1969): 90–95.

Stigler, George J. "Public Regulation of the Securities Markets," *Journal of Business* (April 1964): 117–42.

——. "The Optimum Enforcement of Laws," *Journal of Political Economy* (May/June 1970): 526–36.

Stiglitz, J. "On the Optimality of the Stock Market Allocation of Investment,"

Quarterly Journal of Economics (February 1972): 25–60.

Sunder, Shyam. "Relationships Between Accounting Changes and Stock Prices: Problems of Measurement and Some Empirical Evidence," *Empirical Research in Accounting: Selected Studies, 1973.* Supplement to the *Journal of Accounting Research* 11 (1973a), in press.

——. "An Empirical Study of Stock Price and Risk as They Relate to Accounting Changes in Inventory Methods." Ph.D. dissertation, Carnegie-Mellon University, 1973b.

Tobin, J. "Liquidity Preference as Behavior Towards Risk," *Review of Economic Studies* (February 1958): 65–86.

Tullock, G. *Private Wants, Public Means.* New York: Basic Books, 1970.

——. "Public Decisions as Public Goods," *Journal of Political Economy* (July/August 1971): 913–18.

Voss, William M. "Accelerated Depreciation and Deferred Tax Allocation," *Journal of Accounting Research* 6 (Autumn 1968): 262–69.

Warner, George H. "Depreciation on a Current Cost Basis," *The Accounting Review* 29 (October 1954): 628–33.

Watts, Ross. "The Information Content of Dividends," *Journal of Business* (April 1973): 191–211.

Weston, J. Fred. "Revaluations of Fixed Assets," *The Accounting Review* 28 (October 1953): 482–90.

White, Gary E. "Discretionary Accounting Decisions and Income Normalization," *Journal of Accounting Research* 8 (Autumn 1970): 260–73.

——. "Effects of Discretionary Accounting Policy on Variable and Declining Performance Trends," *Journal of Accounting Research* 10 (Autumn 1972): 351–58.

Wilks, S.S. *Mathematical Statistics.* New York: John Wiley & Sons, 1962.

The Association between Market Determined and Accounting Determined Risk Measures

William Beaver,
Paul Kettler, and
Myron Scholes

Although the accounting profession has accepted the premise that the purpose of accounting is to facilitate decision making, the implementation of this approach within the area of financial statement preparation has been impeded by an inability to specify the decision processes of external users of accounting data. Recent research in portfolio theory provides some *a priori* and empirical knowledge of the decision processes of one external user, the investor in the firm's securities. This study extends that research in terms of its implications for accounting.

The accounting system generates information on several relationships that are considered by many to be measures of risk. Previous research would suggest that financial statement ratios can be used as measures of default risk, but little is known of their association with the concept of risk as defined in portfolio theory. The problem is compounded by the fact that portfolio theory specifies its risk measures solely in terms of market determined interactions (i.e., security price variables). An issue of paramount concern to the accounting profession is—what is the relationship between the accounting determined and market determined measures of risk? An answer to this question is central to a meaningful evaluation of accounting data in at least three respects.

1. Our knowledge of risk determination is incomplete as long as we do not know what exogenous variables (i.e., nonprice data) are impounded in assessments of security prices and price changes. Observed prices (and price changes) are the net result of the decision processes of the entire investing community. They are also the ultimate decision variables that determine both what return and what risk an investor incurs during his holding of a security. We cannot hope to construct an accounting system or evaluate the current system in terms of a decision-making criterion without a knowledge of the interaction between the accounting data and the market price variables.

In particular, this study will examine the contemporaneous association between the accounting determined and market determined measures of risk. By

Reprinted with permission of the authors and American Accounting Association from *Accounting Review*, October 1970, pp. 654–682.

doing this, we intend to determine what accounting data are impounded in the market price data, such as to give rise to a given level of risk. If an association is observed, the evidence supports the joint hypothesis that accounting data reflect the underlying events that determine securities' riskiness and that such events are also reflected in the market prices of securities.

2.   We also will determine the extent to which accounting risk measures can be used to assess the risk parameters for a *future* decision period. The tradi-tional role of accounting data in security valuation has been within the context of "intrinsic value" analysis, where accounting data were used to assess the intrinsic value of securities for the purpose of detecting "overvalued" or "under-valued" securities (e.g., Graham, Dodd, and Cottle [17]). The recent studies by Fama and others [see references 2, 5, 11, 14] suggest that the securities market is efficient in the following sense: (a) Security prices behave as if, at any point in time, they are unbiased estimates of the intrinsic value. (b) The market reacts virtually instantaneously and, on the average, in an unbiased manner to the new information as it is announced. The implications of this research for intrinsic value analysis is that, unless the investor has "inside information," searching for overvalued and undervalued securities is not an optimal decision strategy.

If the notion of an efficient market is accepted, what role have accounting data to play in the decisions of investors? One answer is that accounting data can be useful to the investor in assessing (i.e., forecasting) the riskiness of securi-ties, such that he can select the portfolio which maximizes his utility. If account-ing data can be used to form superior risk forecasts, it will be a tangible demonstration of one area where the use of accounting data can lead to an improvement in decision making, at the level of the *individual* decision maker.

3.   One of the most promising aspects of the study is its implications for the evaluation of specific accounting measurement controversies. The study can provide a basis for dealing with such issues as: (a) Where several measurement rules are being reported, which measurement alternative produces accounting risk measures with the highest degree of association with the market determined risk measure? (b) Does the market determined risk measure appear to adjust for differences in reporting methods across firms and for changes in reporting methods over time? (c) Are there measurement controversies where a *nonre-ported* measurement alternative (e.g., the capitalization of leases) produces accounting risk measures with a higher degree of association with the market determined risk measure than does the *reported* accounting method?

Our attempt to explore the relationship between accounting and market risk measures will be described in the following sections: I. Summary of Litera-ture Concerning Market Determined Risk Measures; II. Definition of Accounting Determined Measures of Risk; III. Sample Design; IV. Analysis of Contemporane-ous Association; V. Forecasting Ability of Accounting Risk Measures; VI. Evaluation of Alternative Accounting Measurements; VII. Concluding Remarks.

I. Summary of Literature on Market Determined Risk Measures

In recent years, Sharpe and others [Sharpe (37), Lintner (25, 26), and Mossin (33)] have extended the earlier work of Markowitz [(29), (30)] to a simplified portfolio model (hereafter referred to as the diagonal model) and to a capital asset pricing model, which determines the equilibrium prices for all securities.[1] Markowitz defined the riskiness of a portfolio of assets in terms of the variance of the portfolio's return [$\sigma^2(R_p)$].[2] Under certain conditions the variance is the appropriate measure of risk. The conditions are:

1. That the utility function of the investor have the following properties:
   a. The first derivative be positive and
   b. The second derivative be negative (i.e., a risk averse utility function for wealth); and
2. That the return distributions of the individual securities are stable with a finite variance (i.e., a normal distribution).

The use of the variance is not as restrictive as it might first appear. Empirical evidence [Fama (11)] has shown that return distributions are adequately characterized as symmetric and that at the portfolio level the variance is highly correlated with other popular dispersion measures, such as the mean absolute deviation, the semi-standard deviation, the range, the interquartile range, and higher central moments of the distribution.

The variance of a portfolio's return is the sum of two terms. For convenience and without loss of generality, assume that an equal dollar amount is invested in each security. It can be shown that

$$\sigma^2(R_p) = (1/N)\overline{\sigma^2(R_i)} \tag{1}$$

$$+ \quad \frac{N-1}{N} \quad \overline{\sigma(R_i, R_j)}$$

$$= \frac{1}{N} \text{ average variance}$$

$$+ \quad \frac{N-1}{N} \quad \text{average covariance}$$

---

[1] An excellent review of the literature on portfolio theory, capital asset pricing, and the behavior of security prices appears in Jensen [20].

[2] Throughout the paper, the term *return* will refer to rate of return.

where

$\sigma^2(R_p)$ = variance of portfolio's return

$\sigma^2(R_i)$ = mean of the variances of the individual securities in the portfolio,

$$\frac{\displaystyle\sum_{i=1}^{N} \sigma^2(R_i)}{N}$$

$\overline{\sigma(R_i, R_j)}$ = mean of the covariance of each individual security with every other security

$$\frac{\displaystyle\sum_{i=1}^{N} \sum_{j=1, j \neq 1}^{N} \sigma(R_i, R_j)}{N(N-1)}$$

N = number of securities in portfolio.

As N increases the first term, $[(1/N \cdot \sigma^2(R_i)]$, converges to zero, and the second term, $[(N - 1/N) \cdot \overline{\sigma(R_i, R_j)}]$, converges to the average covariance among the securities that comprise the portfolio [i.e., $\lim_{N \to \infty} \sigma^2(R_p) = \overline{\sigma(R_i, R_j)}$]. For a diversified portfolio (i.e., where N is large), a security's contribution to the risk of the portfolio is measured by its average *covariance* with all other securities in the portfolio, *not its variance.*[3]

Because the concept of covariance is so crucial to an understanding of risk, it will be described in intuitive terms. Essentially, the covariance reflects the extent to which security returns move together. Two security returns are said to have positive covariance if, when one security's *ex post* return is larger than its expected value, the other security's *ex post* return is also larger than expected. Two securities are said to possess negative covariance with one another if, when one security's return is above its expected value, the other return is below its expected value.

A security's return may have a high variance, but, if it has low covariance (ideally, negative covariance) with other securities, it is not really a risky security to hold, because its addition to the portfolio will tend to reduce the variance of the portfolio's return. Empirically, there may be positive association

---

[3] The covariance is defined as $E([(\tilde{R}_i - E(\tilde{R}_i)] \, [\tilde{R}_j - E(\tilde{R}_j)])$.

between a security's variance and its average covariance with other securities. However, *a priori* there is no obvious reason why such association would have to exist.

One limitation of the Markowitz model is the enormous amount of parameter estimation required in order to assess the variance of return for a portfolio. For an N security portfolio, the factor is $[N \cdot (N + 1)/2]$, which for $N = 1,000$ is 500,500. In order to reduce the number of parameters to estimate, Sharpe [36] has offered the diagonal model, which specifies the following relationships:

$$\tilde{R}_i = \alpha_i + \beta_i \tilde{R}_M + \tilde{\epsilon}_i \tag{2}$$

where

$$E(\tilde{\epsilon}) = 0$$
$$\sigma(\tilde{R}_M, \epsilon_i) = 0$$
$$\sigma(\tilde{\epsilon}_i, \tilde{\epsilon}_j) = 0$$

$\tilde{R}_i$ = return on security i,

$\tilde{R}_M$ = return on all other capital assets in the market (hereafter referred to as the "market return").

$\tilde{\epsilon}_i$ = an individualistic factor reflecting that portion of security i's return which is not a linear function of R_M.

α_i, β_i = intercept and slope associated with the linear relationship.

The model asserts that a security's return can be decomposed into two elements, a systematic component $(\beta_i R_{Mt})$ which reflects common movement of a single security's return with the average return of all other securities in the market, and an individualistic component $(\alpha_i + \epsilon_{it})$, which reflects that residual portion of a security's return that moves independently of the market-wide return. Intuitively, a motivation for the model can be provided by viewing events as being classified into one of two categories: (1) those events that have economy-wide impacts which are reflected in the returns of all securities; and (2) those events which have an impact only upon one particular security. Dichotomizing events in this fashion is obviously highly abstractive. In fact, a third class of events immediately would come to mind—industry-wide events. However, previous empirical studies [Fama, *et al.*, (14), Ball and Brown (2, 8)] suggest that the omission of an explicit industry factor in the equation is not a serious misspecification of the model.

Within the context of the diagonal model, the variance of portfolio return is defined as,

$$\sigma^2(R_p) = \frac{1}{N} \ \overline{\sigma^2(\epsilon_i)} + (\overline{\beta})^2 \sigma^2(R_M) \tag{3}$$

where

$\overline{\sigma^2(\epsilon_i)}$ = mean of the variances of the individualistic factors.

$$\overline{\beta} = \text{mean of } \beta_i\text{'s} = \sum_{i=1}^{N} \beta_i$$

$\sigma^2(R_M)$ = variance of the market return, R_M.

For $N = 1$ (i.e., for an individual security),

$$\sigma^2(R_i) = \sigma^2(\epsilon_i) + \beta_i^2 \sigma^2(R_M) \tag{3a}$$

Note that, analogous to the Markowitz model, the variance is composed of two elements. As N increases, the first term goes to zero and the portfolio variance becomes equal to the second term, $\overline{\beta}^2 \sigma^2(R_M)$. $\sigma^2(R_p)$ will differ among portfolios solely according to the magnitude of $\overline{\beta}$, the average of the β_i's of the securities comprising the portfolio. Hence, an individual security's contribution to the riskiness of the portfolio is measured by its β_i, not $\sigma^2(\epsilon)$.

As equation (3a) shows, the variance of a security's return can differ from that of other securities because of one of two factors, either $\sigma^2(\epsilon)$ or β_i. The first factor is referred to as the individualistic or avoidable risk of a security, because that risk can be driven to zero through diversification (i.e., by increasing N). The risk averse investor (i.e., one who prefers less risk to more risk, for a given expected return), will select a portfolio where the individual riskiness is essentially zero. Such a portfolio is known as an efficient portfolio. The β_i is the systematic or unavoidable risk of the security and measures the security's sensitivity to market-wide events. It is called the systematic or unavoidable risk because it is that portion of the variance of the security's return that cannot be diversified away by increasing the number of securities in the portfolio.

As would be expected, β_i bears a direct relationship to the concept of covariance. In particular, it can be shown that, if security returns are normally distributed,

$$\beta_i \cong \frac{\sigma(R_i, R_M)}{\sigma^2(\widetilde{R}_M)} \tag{4}$$

where

$\sigma(R_i, R_M)$ = covariance of security i's returns with the market returns

$\sigma^2(R_M)$ = variance of the market return.

Hence our previous statements that the security's riskiness be measured in terms of its covariance is entirely compatible with using β as a measure of security riskiness. The following statements can be made concerning the magnitude of β: (1) the larger the value, the greater the riskiness of the security; and (2) a β of one implies an "average" riskiness.

Remember that the original motivation for the diagonal model was to reduce the number of parameters to estimate. The variance of a portfolio, using the diagonal model, requires an estimation of $2N + 1$, which for $N = 1000$ is 2001 (as compared with 500,500 for the Markowitz model).

Another advantage of the diagonal model is that it can be extended to the more general cases where security return distributions are characterized by the Stable family of distributions, of which the normal distribution is a special case. This is an important property because there is considerable evidence [Fama (11), Mandelbrot (28), and Roll (34)] that the distributions of security returns most closely conform to those members of the Stable family, which have finite expected values but infinite variances and covariances. Fama [12] has shown that the β can still be interpreted as a measure of risk even in cases where the covariance and variance, strictly speaking, are undefined.

Sharpe and others [Sharpe (37), Lintner (25, 26), and Mossin (33)] have extended the earlier work on portfolio models to capital asset pricing models, which determine the equilibrium prices for all securities in the market. Essentially the models start from the assumption that investors are generally risk averse and show that, in equilibrium, capital assets will be priced such that

$$E(\tilde{R}_i) = R_F(1 - \beta_i) + \beta_i E(\tilde{R}_M) \qquad (5)$$

where

$E(\tilde{R}_i)$ = expected return of asset i.

R_F = rate of return on a riskless asset.

$E(\tilde{R}_M)$ = expected return on "market" portfolio.

$$\beta_i \cong \frac{\sigma(\tilde{R}_i, \tilde{R}_M)}{\sigma^2(\tilde{R}_M)}$$

The capital asset model states that the only variable which determines differential expected returns among securities is the systematic risk coefficient, β_i. The model further asserts there is a linear relationship bewteen β_i and expected return, such that the greater the risk the higher the expected return.

Note that the variability of the individualistic component of return does not enter into the pricing of capital assets, since that component can be eliminated through diversification. Although the models were originally developed under the assumption of finite variance and covariance, Fama (13) has shown that the results extend to the broader class Stable distributions with finite expected values but infinite variances and covariances.

Empirical assessments of α_i and β_i can be obtained from a time series, least-squares regression of the following form:

$$R_{it} = a_i + b_i R_{Mt} + e_{it} \qquad t = 1, T \tag{6}$$

where R_{it} and R_{Mt} are *ex post* returns for security i and the market, respectively, and where e_{it} is the disturbance term in the equation. King's study of monthly security returns [23] found that, on the average, approximately 52 percent of the variation in an individual security's return could be explained by its comovement with a marketwide index of return. The percentage has been secularly declining since 1926, and, for the final 101 months of the study (ending with December, 1960), the proportion explained was 30 percent.

The assessment of β_i from a time series regression assumes that β_i was stationary during that period. Evidence by Blume [6] and by Jensen [20] suggests that stationarity does exist, especially at the portfolio level. The empirical evidence [Fama et al., (14)] also indicates that the resulting equation conforms well to other assumptions of the linear regression model (i.e., linearity, serial independence of the disturbance terms and homoscedasticity), with one exception. The distribution of the estimated residuals is leptokurtic (i.e., has fatter tails than would be expected under normality). This departure from normality is consistent with Fama's [11] findings that security returns are members of the Stable family of distributions with finite means but infinite variances. However, Wise [42] has shown that for Stable distributions with finite expected values, least-square estimates of β_i are unbiased and consistent, although not efficient.

In sum, portfolio theory provides a measure of security riskiness that has both *a priori* and empirical support. Our knowledge of risk determination is incomplete in one important respect, as long as we do not know what exogenous data (i.e., nonprice data) are impounded in the assessments of prices and price changes such as to give rise to a given value of β. This study will attempt to shed some light on that issue by examining some accounting-based risk measures by the financial statement analysis literature.

II. Accounting Measures of Risk

Although none of the traditional accounting risk measures are explicitly defined in terms of covariance of returns, they do attempt to highlight several aspects of the *uncertainty* associated with the earnings (or return) stream of the firm. In particular, the accounting risk measures can be viewed as surrogates for the *total* variability of return of a firm's common equity securities. Thus, the accounting measures reflect both the systematic and individualistic risk components (see equation 3a for the decomposition of the variance in this fashion). If the systematic and individualistic components are positively correlated (at the extreme, perfectly correlated), then it is reasonable to view the accounting measures as surrogates for systematic risk as well. The evidence indicates that positive correlation does exist (e.g., securities with a larger than average β tend to have a larger than average variance of the individualistic component). The appropriateness of using these measures as surrogates for systematic risk will be taken up again at the end of this section.

It is not our contention that the following list of accounting risk measures is exhaustive, but it is believed that the list captures most of the important relationships suggested in the literature. The list includes: (1) dividend payout, (2) growth, (3) leverage, (4) liquidity, (5) asset size, (6) variability of earnings, and (7) covariability of earnings.

1. *Dividend Payout.* It is often asserted that *ceteris paribus* firms with low payout ratios (i.e., cash dividends/earnings available for common stockholders) are more risky. The assertion not only appears in the security valuation literature, but Sorter *et al.* [41] found that management of large corporations also perceive a significant association between low payout policies and risk taking behavior.

The belief can be rationalized in the following manner: If firms follow a policy of dividend stabilization (i.e., firms are reluctant to cut back, once a dividend level has been established), and are adverse to paying out more than 100 percent (or x percent) of earnings in any single fiscal period, then firms with greater volatility in earnings will pay out a lower percentage of expected earnings. Thus, the payout ratio can be viewed as a surrogate for management's perception of the uncertainty associated with the firm's earnings.

The payout ratio has two disturbing properties. If earnings in any period is zero or close to zero, the ratio becomes extremely large. Computing an average of the payout ratios over several years does not adequately deal with this problem, because one extreme year will still dominate the average. Thus, the average payout ratio is defined here as the sum of cash dividends paid out over the period for which the average is being computed divided by the sum of earnings over that same time period. The result is equal to a weighted average of the yearly payout ratios, where each year's weights are equal to the proportion of each year's earnings to the total earnings over the averaging period. This procedure will prevent years with near-zero income from dominating the average. In fact, it may create a bias in the opposite direction, but it is felt that the effect of such a bias would be relatively small when compared with the alternative of simply averaging the yearly payout ratios. Another computation difficulty also arises. It is possible for the average payout to be negative, if the sum of earnings over the averaging period is negative. In such instances, the payout ratio was arbitrarily defined to be 100 percent. Since a negative ratio occurs only three times out of a possible 614 occurrences, the empirical results are not sensitive to the particular procedure used to remove this anomoly. These difficulties arise because the payout ratio must be computed on observed (*ex post*) earnings rather than expected (or permanent) earnings. This problem is not unique to the payout ratio and is present to varying degrees in all of the risk measures.

2. *Growth.* An above normal growth rate is a function of at least three factors: (a) "excessive" earnings opportunities for the firm (i.e., where the expected earnings rate on new asset acquisitions is greater than the cost of capital); (b) the *ex post* rate of return exceeds the expected return for several consecutive periods (i.e., a run of positive transitory earnings components); and (c) a payout policy that results in a retention of a higher than average proportion of earnings. To what extent are each of these factors related to risk?

For factor (a) initially it is not obvious that new investments must on balance be more or less risky than the assets already held by the firm. It is intuitively appealing to think of areas of asset expansion where the earnings stream is more uncertain (e.g., research and development, moving into new product areas, etc.). However, counter-examples could be just as easily cited, so argument at this level is not very persuasive. The more convincing line of reasoning, at least to us, is to argue that in a competitive economy the excessive earnings opportunities of any firm will erode as other firms enter. The question is—how long will such excessive opportunities continue to exist? While the answer will depend upon many factors (such as ease of entry, patents, special skills, etc.), it is argued that these excessive earnings streams are more uncertain (i.e., volatile) than the "normal" earnings stream of the firm. Thus, factor (a) would result in a positive association between growth rates and risk.

In the case of factor (b), it could be argued that risky (large β) securities are more likely to have a series of large positive transitory terms in earnings, but it is also true that they are more likely to have a string of large negative terms as well. Thus it is difficult to see that growth due to this factor has any monotonic relationship to risk, as in the case of factor (a).

Factor (c) has really already been discussed. Firms with lower payout ratios, *ceteris paribus,* will have higher growth rates. Yet it was argued above that low payout implies greater riskiness. If so, then growth rate would be positively associated with risk—the same relationship that was posited with respect to factor (a).

It is interesting to speculate on the relative stationarity of these two factors over time. In a competitive economy it would be expected that abnormal growth rates due to factor (a) would not persist for long periods. At the same time, factor (c) would be relatively permanent if payout policies among firms are stationary. Empirical evidence [Little (24), Craig and Malkiel (9), and Lintner and Glauber (27)] suggests that growth rates are near random over time, which could imply that factor (a) tends to dominate.

Thus far we have not been explicit in defining *growth*, because the arguments would have been essentially the same regardless of how the term was defined. The most popular definition is growth in earnings. It has its origins in instrinsic value analysis, which requires estimates of earnings growth in order to determine the multiplier to apply to current earnings. However, growth is defined in this study as growth in total assets. In particular, the growth variable was defined as the natural logarithm of the ratio of the terminal asset size divided by the initial asset size. The log of the asset relatives was then divided by the number of years between the initial and terminal dates. The resulting number is the "average" annualized rate of change in assets over the time period for which the average is computed.

There may be some potential measurement error in the growth variable induced by the effect of mergers. It could be argued that mergers are merely the combining of two or mroe firms and do not imply any excessive earnings opportunities. We do not pretend to have a solution to the perplexing problem of why firms merge. However, we can only recognize that a potential measurement error does exist and say that it is still not obvious why mergers cannot be viewed in the same context as any other asset acquisition.

3. *Leverage.* It can be easily shown that as debt is introduced, the earnings stream of the common stockholders becomes more volatile [Modigliani and Miller (32)]. Hence the leverage ratios can be used as a measure of the risk induced by the capital structure. The leverage ratio was defined as total senior securities (including current liabilities) divided by total assets. The numerator includes all fixed claim holders with prior claim to earnings to the common stockholders. This particular definition was used because previous research [Beaver (4)] has shown this form of the leverage relationship exhibits the highest association with default risk. In a pilot study, several leverage ratios were analyzed but the results were consistent with the previous study of default risk, in that the definition described above was superior to all others tested.

4. *Liquidity.* It can be argued that liquid assets or current assets have a less volatile return than noncurrent assets. At the extreme cash can be viewed as a "risk free" asset (ignoring purchasing power risk) with zero (explicit) return and zero volatility associated with that return. However, it is an argument which we prefer not to pursue too far, because it is our belief that the differential riskiness among firms is more explained by the differential riskiness in

their noncurrent assets than it is by the fraction of noncurrent assets they hold. Our priors are that liquidity relationships will not have high association with the market determined risk measure. The liquidity measure selected was the current ratio, largely because of its popularity. In a pilot study, other liquidity relationships were also examined, but all performed about the same as the current ratio.

5. *Asset size.* It is widely believed that larger firms are less risky than smaller firms. In terms of default risk, the evidence indicates that the belief is a correct one. The aggregate statistics published by Dun and Bradstreet [10] reveal the frequency of failure per 1,000 firms is lower for the large size classes. Horrigan [19] has shown that the most single important financial statement variable in predicting the bond rating of a firm was total assets. Hickman [18] finds that, at least in aggregate, the bond ratings are associated with relative frequency of default.

Furthermore, it can be shown that, if individual asset returns are less than perfectly correlated, larger firms will have a lower variance of rate of return than smaller firms. In fact, if the asset returns are independent, the variance will decrease in direct proportion to the difference in asset size (i.e., as firm size doubles, the variance of the rate of return will be cut in half). Empirical work by Alexander [1] has found that the cross section dispersion of the net income to net worth ratios does in fact decrease as average firm size increases.

In terms of portfolio theory, the previous analysis merely suggests that larger firms become more efficient by increasing the number of assets in the portfolio (i.e., firm). However, they may not be less risky. As long as the investor can diversify out of the individualistic risk (either directly or through an investment company), he is indifferent to whether an individual firm is an efficient portfolio in and of itself. In a portfolio theory context, larger firms are less risky than smaller firms only if the average β of the assets in which they invest is lower than that of the smaller firms. There is no *a priori* reason or empirical evidence why this need be so.

The size variable used in this study is the natural logarithm of total assets. The log transformation was used because its distribution more nearly conforms to the properties of symmetry and normality. Also the cross section coefficient of variation is greatly reduced with the log transform.

6. *Variability in earnings.* All of the previous variables discussed can be viewed as measures that attempt to reflect some aspect of the total variability of the earnings stream. It would seem reasonable to explicitly introduce a variability measure.

The measurement selected was the standard deviation of an earnings-price ratio (i.e., income available for common stockholders to market value of common stock outstanding). In a pilot study, the standard deviation of net income available for common to book value and the standard deviation of total net income to total assets were also included in the analysis. These ratios performed about the same as, but consistently slightly poorer than, the variable described above.

7. *Covariability in earnings.* If β is being used as the market determined concept of risk, then the most direct approach would be to compute a β value on accounting earnings data. The earnings variable chosen was net income available for common deflated by the market value of common stock outstanding (i.e., the earnings-price ratio). The accounting β can be derived in a similar manner to the market β (see equation 6)—that is, from a time series regression with the firm's earnings-prices ratio as the dependent variable (i.e., R_i) and some economy-wide average of earnings-price as the independent variable (i.e., R_M). The precise procedure by which this is done will be described in the next section.

At this point it is appropriate to ask—why not restrict the study solely to the accounting β? What is to be gained by also examining the other accounting risk measures? There are at least two reasons for expanding the scope of the study to include the other measures:

1. The accounting β for each security will be estimated on a few number of observations, which implies that estimates will be subject to a large amount of sampling error. To isolate the systematic risk component (i.e., covariability of earnings) from total variability involves the loss of an additional degree of freedom, which is a substantial reduction considering the small number of observations per firm (only 9 observations per period, see section III for details). Because of the potential inability to separate the systematic and individualistic risk components, measures of total variability might perform as well or better than an accounting β. As a result, other accounting measures are also being studied.

2. The other accounting measures are commonly offered by the literature on financial statement analysis and security analysis as measures of risk. Moreover, it is likely that such measures are, in fact, used by investors as surrogates for risk. For these reasons, it is important to know to what extent a strategy of selecting portfolios according to the traditional accounting risk measures is equivalent to a strategy that uses the market-determined risk measures.

III. Sample Design and Preliminary Analysis of Data

The study is based upon an analysis of the 307 firms whose financial statement data were available on the Compustat Industrial Tape for the years 1947 through 1965, inclusive, and whose dividend and security price data were available on the Center for Research in Security Prices (CRSP) Tape for that same period. The CRSP Tape contains monthly security price information for all New York

Stock Exchange (NYSE) common stocks from January, 1926, through June, 1966. The advantage of studying Compustat NYSE firms is the accessibility of their data with a commensurate reduction in the data collection chore. It is difficult to specify what bias may be introduced by the use of these selection criteria, except that they lead to the selection of the larger, older, and more successful firms in the economy. However, there is no compelling reason to believe that the associations of interest to the study would be consistently higher or lower for these firms as opposed to nonmembers of this population. Most importantly, we contend that the firms selected are of interest in their own right, even if subsequent research were to discover that their findings cannot be extended to nonmembers of the population. The market value of their common stock represents approximately 67 percent of the total market value of all common stocks listed on the NYSE.

The years 1947 through 1965 were selected because they represent the full extent of overlap between the Compustat and CRSP tapes. The nineteen year period was further divided into two subperiods of ten years (1947-1965) and nine years (1957-1965), respectively. The partitioning of the total time period will permit an analysis of the stationarity of the relationships over time and an examination of the ability of accounting data to forecast into a future period.

Market Determined Risk Measure

The market determined risk measure, β_i, can be assessed *ex post* for a given time period by means of a (time series) least-squares regression of the following form:

$$R_{it} = a_i + b_i R_{Mt} + e_{it} \qquad t = ML, NL \qquad (6a)$$

where

$$R_{it} = n \left[\frac{D_{it} + P_{it}}{P'_{it-1}} \right]$$

$$R_{Mt} = n \frac{(L)_t}{(L)_{t-1}}$$

ML = January, 1947 (period one) or January, 1957 (period two),

NL = December, 1956 (period one) or December, 1965 (period two),

D_{it} = cash dividend payable on common stock i in month t

P_{it} = closing price for common stock i at end of month t,

P'_{it-1} = closing price at end of month $t - 1$, adjusted for capital changes (e.g., stock splits and stock dividends),

L_t = Fisher's link relative, a market price index of all firms on the NYSE at the end of month t, adjusted for dividends and all capital changes.

R_{it} is the *ex post* rate of return for security i during period t, assuming instantaneous or continuous compounding, although R_{it} could have been defined in terms of discrete compounding.[4]

R_{Mt} is an index of the *ex post* return for all NYSE firms during month t (i.e., the market rate of return). The measure is based upon Fisher's index, which is the only one available for 1947 through 1965 that is both comprehensive (all NYSE firms) and properly treats cash dividends. A more complete discussion of construction and merits of the index versus alternative indices appears in Fisher [15]. Previous studies (Fisher [15], Fama, *et al.* [14]) indicate that: (a) the Standard & Poor's and Dow-Jones indices are highly correlated with the Fisher index; and (b) their findings were essentially the same regardless of which market index was used.

The slope of the regression equation, b_i, is the empirical estimate of systematic risk, β_i. Note that a separate regression must be computed for each security and for each subperiod. Thus, for the 307 firms in our sample, 307 regressions were computed for each of the two subperiods, resulting in a total of 614. As indicated earlier, b_i can also be viewed as an estimate of the covariance between security i's return and the market return, divided by the variance of the market return (i.e., $\sigma(R_i, R_M)/\sigma^2(R_M)$). An examination of the properties of the regression equations revealed that they conform to the assumptions of the linear regression model to the same extent and in the same respects as was noted by the previous research employing this model. The mean, standard deviation, and range of b_i are reported in Table 1.

It is interesting to note that the mean b_i is .991 and .987, respectively for each of the two subperiods. Since a value of one represents "average" riskiness, the finding implies that the average riskiness of the sample is essentially the same as that of all NYSE firms (i.e., the firms that comprise the market index). Hence, there appears to be no bias arising from the sample selection criteria, at least in this one respect. The range of b_i's (see Table 1) indicates the sample is drawn from a wide segment of the risk continuum. Comparing the range with that of previous studies suggests that essentially the entire risk continuum is represented here, and hence the scope of inference is essentially unrestricted. In other words, there is no evidence that the sample

---

[4]Evidence indicates that the estimated b_i is essentially the same whether continuous or discrete compounding is used. A more complete discussion appears in King [23] and Fisher [15].

Table 1

Summary Statistics for Distributions of Estimates of Systematic Risk (b)

	Mean	Standard Deviation	Range
Period one (1947–1956)	.991	.336	.17 to 2.15
Period two (1957–1965)	.987	.342	-.05[a] to 2.19

[a]Only negative value of b_i in distribution.

selection criteria drew firms from only a small, restricted segment of the risk spectrum. The standard deviation also is essentially the same as that obtained in previous research.

Estimating β in the manner described above assumes that the β is constant (stationary) throughout the time period for which the regression is being computed. The stationarity of the β_i's was examined by computing the cross-sectional correlation between the b_i in period one (1947-1956) and b_i in period two (1957-1965). The Spearman rank correlation coefficient (r_s) was .626, while the product-moment correlation was .594. There is a significant positive association between the b_i's in successive time periods (i.e., for $N = 307$, $r_s^* = .14$ at the .01 level of significance). Although the association is by no means perfect, it does suggest that the assumption of stationarity is not seriously violated by the data. The stationarity was also examined at the portfolio level. The firms were arrayed according to the b_i's in period one and were divided into portfolios. Each portfolio's b_p was computed as the average of the b_i's of the securities that comprise that portfolio. A cross-sectional correlation was computed between the b_p's in period one versus period two. The analysis was conducted for portfolios of five securities each (leading to a total of 61 portfolios and for twenty securities each (leading to 15 portfolios). The results are reported in Table 2.

As would be expected, the association is higher than at the individual security level. In fact, at the level of portfolios with 20 securities each, the association is virtually perfect. The correlation coefficients have been adjusted

Table 2

Association between Market Determined Risk Measure in Period One (1947–56) versus Period Two (1957–65)

No. of Sec. in Portfolio	Rank Correlation	Product-Moment Correlation
1	.626	.594
5	.876	.875
20	.989	.965

for the loss of degrees of freedom through aggregation. The rank and product-moment correlations are about the same. This will also hold for the other associations examined in the remainder of the study. The stationarity has also been observed by Blume [6], Jensen [20], and Sharpe [39]. A more complete discussion of the implications of and motivation for aggregation into portfolios will be discussed shortly.

Accounting Determined Risk Measures

Since the market determined risk measure is estimated over a given time period accounting risk measures must be computed in a similar manner. Each of the seven risk measures was defined in the following manner for each firm, for each of the two subperiods (all of the definitions below should carry a subscript i to denote security i):

$$\text{average payout} = \frac{\sum_{t=1}^{T} \text{cash dividends paid to common stockholders}_{,t}}{\sum_{t=1}^{T} \text{income available for common stockholders}_{,t}}$$

$$\text{average asset growth} = n \left[\frac{\text{total assets}_T}{\text{total assets}_0} \right] T$$

$$\text{average leverage} = \sum_{t=1}^{T} \frac{\text{total senior securities}_t}{\text{total assets}_t} \, T$$

$$\text{average asset size} = \sum_{t=1}^{T} n(\text{total assets}_t)/T$$

$$\text{average liquidity} = \sum_{t=1}^{T} \frac{\text{current assets}_t}{\text{current liabilities}_t} \, T$$

$$\text{earnings variability} = \left(\sum_{t=1}^{T} (E_t/P_{t-1} - [\bar{E}/P])^2 /T \right)^{1/2}$$

where

$$E_t/P_{t-1} = \frac{\text{income available for common stockholders}_t}{\text{market value of common stock}_{t-1} \text{ (valued at fiscal year-end)}}$$

$$[\bar{E}/P] = \left(\sum_{t=1}^{T} E_t/P_{t-1} \right) T,$$

$$\text{accounting } \beta \text{ (covariability of earnings)} = \frac{\sum_{t=1}^{T} (E_t/P_{t-1} - [\bar{E}/P])(M_t - \bar{M})}{\sum_{t=1}^{T} (M_t - \bar{M})(M_t - \bar{M})}$$

$$\cong \frac{\text{covar}(E_t/P_{t-1}, M_t)}{\text{var}(M_t)}$$

where

$$M_t = (\Sigma_{i=1}^{N} E_{it}/P_{it-1})/N,$$
$$\bar{M} = (\Sigma_{t=1}^{T} M_t)/T,$$

T = number of years in subperiod (10 in period one and 9 in period two),

N = number of NYSE, Compustat firms for which earnings and price data were available for year t.

Appendix A indicates what elements in the Compustat data array were used in defining the components of the variables defined above.

The reasons for selecting these variables and for defining them precisely in this fashion were discussed in the previous section and will not be repeated here. However, there are a few additional comments that are in order at this point. In the case of the two earnings variables, a lagged market price term appears in the denominator of the ratio. The resulting earnings-price ratio (E_t/P_{t-1}) can be viewed as a measure of rate of return, where income is defined in accounting terms (in contrast to dividend plus capital gains). The use of a lagged market price term will make the ratio consistent with the market rate of return, which also has the lagged price term in the denominator. The lagged term is used because it represents the investment base of the security at the beginning of the period.

The first earnings variable listed above is the standard deviation of the earnings-price ratio, while the second variable is an estimate of the "accounting β" (denoted by B_i, as opposed to b_i) measuring the covariance of security i's earnings (or rate of return) with that of an overall market average of earnings, M_t. This method of estimating the accounting β is equivalent to estimating B from a linear regression of the form of equation (6), where R_{it} is defined as E_t/P_{t-1} and R_{Mt} is defined as M_t. As indicated above, M_t was defined as the arithmetic mean of individual earnings-price ratios in year t. An alternative definition, which weighs each security's ratio by its market value, was also used but not reported here. The results were insensitive to which definition was used, but the first definition had the convenient property that it would produce an average accounting β approximately equal to one. Another measure of an accounting β was also computed for most of the results but again was not reported here. The definition involved the first differences of the earnings-price ratio, rather than the ratio itself. Previous research (Ball and Brown [2]) indicates there is some reason to believe that the first differences form of the variable might be a better specification of the process generating the earnings variable. However, in this study the first differences transformation performed consistently poorer than the measure reported here. The cross-sectional means and standard deviations of each of the seven variables for both time periods are reported in Table 3.

For the most part, there are no dramatic shifts in the mean values. The major exception is earnings variability, where the mean in period two is one-half of the value in period one. The reduction in earnings variability is consistent with the findings of King [23] and others, which indicate that the magnitude of the variability due to economy-wide movements has experienced a secular decline throughout the last forty years. A casual inspection of the magnitude

Table 3
Summary Statistics for Accounting Risk Measures

Variable	Mean		Standard Deviation	
	(1947–56)	(1957–65)	(1947–56)	(1957–65)
Payout	.482	.532	.182	.241
Growth	.085	.064	.046	.038
Leverage	.401	.384	.142	.142
Liquidity	3.214	3.587	2.061	5.914
Size	4.575	5.237	1.251	1.282
Earnings Variability	.062	.033	.052	.035
Accounting Beta (B)	.979	.908	1.164	1.280

of changes in GNP or market price indices would also suggest that the entire economy has become less volatile in recent years.

The accounting β_i has mean values close to one but slightly below one, similar to those of the market-determined b_i. Note, however, that the standard deviation of the accounting measure is almost four times as large as that of the market b_i (see Table 1). In fact, 9 percent and 12 percent of the accounting B_i's were negative, in each of the subperiods, respectively.

One reason is the relatively small number of observations upon which the accounting β is being computed. The number of observations for the market determined b is 120 and 108, in each subperiod, while the number is only 9 for each subperiod in the case of the accounting measure (N.B., period one loses one observation because of the lagged market value term). The sampling error for such a small number of observations is very large. When the accounting B_i's are computed over the entire 19-year period, the standard deviation reduces to .791. Another approach to reducing the error (see Kennelly [22]) is to estimate the accounting b_i from quarterly data to see if more efficient estimates can be obtained.

Another area for concern is the behavior of M_t, used as the economy-wide measure of earnings-price ratio. It exhibits a strong downward trend over the 19 years studied, and the first order autocorrelation in the series is extremely high. Its counterpart, the market-determined R_{Mt}, exhibits no trend nor any serial correlation. It is possible that economy-wide changes in accounting methods (e.g., the switch to accelerated forms of depreciation) in part account for such behavior in M_t. A more thorough examination of the behavior of M_t is planned for future extensions of the study.

Both factors just discussed may result in a reduction of the association between the accounting and market determined b's, especially at the individual security level. This concern increases when the stationarity of the accounting risk measures are examined (see Table 4).

Table 4 reports the cross-sectional correlation coefficients between a given

Table 4
Association between Accounting Risk Measures in Period One versus Period Two

Variable	Rank Correlation[a]	Product-Moment Correlation[a]
Payout	.463	.429
Growth	.199	.205
Leverage	.731	.768
Liquidity	.774	.883
Size	.959	.963
Earnings Variability	.443	.410
Accounting Beta (B)	.034	−.060

[a]The table refers to the correlations at the individual security level.

risk measure in period one and that same risk measure in period two. Remember that a similar analysis for the market-determined risk measure yielded correlations of .626 (rank) and .594 (product-moment). The correlation of the accounting B is the lowest of the seven variables studied. In fact, there appears to be virtual independence between the accounting B in each of the two periods.

The evidence suggests that the accounting B may be subject to a large amount of error and that other accounting measures of risk will have to be introduced in searching for correlates with the market risk measure. In this respect, it is interesting that the other risk measures do exhibit stationarity over time. In fact, asset size, leverage, and liquidity exhibit a much higher degree of stationarity than the market-determined b does (see Table 2). This finding suggests that perhaps these measures are "too stationary" (i.e., too insensitive to changes in systematic risk).

Earlier we argued that the number of observations might be too few to adequately isolate the systematic risk and individualistic risk from the accounting earnings stream. The evidence cited above is consistent with that contention. We also contended that, under such circumstances, a measure ot *total* variability, such as the standard deviation of the earnings-price ratio, might perform as well as or better than the accounting B. In this respect, note that the earnings variability measure has approximately the same degree of stationarity as the market b does (see Tables 1 and 4).

IV. Contemporaneous Association between Accounting and Market Risk Measures

The major purpose of this analysis is to discover the extent to which accounting risk measures are impounded in the market risk measure. Empirically this issue will be addressed by examining the contemporaneous association between the accounting risk measures and the market b. In particular, for each subperiod cross sectional correlations at the individual security level were computed between b and each of the seven accounting variables. The results are reported in Table 5.

In every instance except one, the sign of the coefficient is in the predicted direction. The exception is the rank correlation of the liquidity measure in period two, and in this case the correlation is near-zero. Any rank correlation whose absolute value is larger than .10 (.14) is "significant" at the .05 (.01) level [see Siegel, (40)].[5] Four variables possess coefficients larger than .14 in both periods: payout, leverage, and both earnings variables. The degree of

---

[5]Similar statistics will not be given for the product-moment correlations, because tests for normality have not been conducted on the accounting variables and even a casual examination of the normal probability plots of the distributions suggests that normality is seriously violated in some cases.

Table 5

Contemporaneous Association between Market Determined Measure of Risk and Seven Accounting Risk Measures[a]

Variable	Period One (1947–56)		Period Two (1957–65)	
	Individual Level	Portfolio[b] Level	Individual Level	Portfolio[b] Level
Payout	−.49	−.79	−.29	−.50
	(−.50)	(−.77)	(−.24)	(−.45)
Growth	.27	.56	.01	.02
	(.23)	(.51)	(.03)	(.07)
Leverage	.23	.41	.22	.48
	(.23)	(.45)	(.25)	(.56)
Liquidity	−.13	−.35	.05	.04
	(−.13)	(−.44)	(−.01)	(−.01)
Size	−.06	−.09	−.16	−.30
	(−.07)	(−.13)	(−.16)	(−.30)
Earnings Variability	.66	.90	.45	.82
	(.58)	(.77)	(.36)	(.62)
Accounting Beta (B_i)	.44	.68	.23	.46
	(.39)	(.67)	(.23)	(.46)

[a]Rank correlation coefficients appear in top row, and product-moment correlations appear in parentheses in bottom row.

[b]The portfolio correlations are based upon 61 portfolios of 5 securities each.

association is strongest for earnings variability, the payout variable is next, the accounting B is third, and the liquidity variable exhibits the least amount of association.

Correlations were also conducted at the portfolio level. In order to form the portfolios for a given correlation, the securities were arrayed according to the magnitude of the *accounting variable* involved in the correlation. The data were then grouped into portfolios of five securities each, with the first portfolio consisting of those five securities with the largest values of the accounting variable (and similarly for the remaining portfolios). The risk measure b_p of each portfolio was defined as the arithmetic mean of the b_i's of the five securities. The result is 61 portfolios ranked according to a given accounting risk measure. An intuitive explanation of the procedure follows: Suppose an investor chose the strategy of selecting portfolios on the basis of the payout ratio (or any accounting variable) where the payout variable is being used as a surrogate for risk. When a strategy is applied, 61 portfolios are formed and then ranked according to risk, as measured by the payout variable. The portfolio correlations will reveal the similarity between this ranking and that obtained by ranking the same portfolios according to b_p.

The primary justification for the analysis of portfolios is that the portfolio, rather than the individual security, is the relevant decision-prediction entity for investors, just as the variance of return of the portfolio, not the variance of an individual security's return, is the relevant concept of risk. Thus, it is the degree of association at the *portfolio* level that is of concern to the study.

Before discussing the portfolio correlations, it is important to specify the precise relationship between the individual security and portfolio correlations. Assume the following relationship bewteen two variables, $\tilde{X}$ and $\tilde{Y}$:

$$\tilde{Y}_i = \alpha + \beta \tilde{X} + \tilde{\epsilon}_i \qquad i = 1, N$$

where

$$E(\tilde{\epsilon}_i) = 0 \qquad \sigma(\tilde{\epsilon}_i, \tilde{\epsilon}_j) = 0 \qquad \sigma^2(\tilde{\epsilon}_i) = \sigma^2$$

Assume each M observations are pooled into a single observation. The result is the following relationship:

$$\tilde{\tilde{Y}}_k = \alpha + \beta \tilde{\tilde{X}}_k + \tilde{\tilde{\epsilon}}_k \qquad k = 1, N/M$$

where

$$\tilde{\tilde{Y}}_k = \sum_{i=IX}^{IZ} \tilde{Y}_i \quad M,$$

$$\tilde{\tilde{X}}_k = \sum_{i=IX}^{IZ} \tilde{X}_i \quad M,$$

$$\tilde{\tilde{\epsilon}}_k = \sum_{i=IX}^{IZ} \tilde{\epsilon}_i \quad M$$

$$IX = (k-1)M + 1$$

$$IZ = (k-1)M + M = k \cdot M$$

Of special concern is the behavior of $\sigma^2(\tilde{\tilde{\epsilon}})$. If the data have been aggregated such that $\sigma(\tilde{\epsilon}_i, \tilde{\epsilon}_j)$ is zero within the pooled observation, then

$$\sigma^2(\tilde{\tilde{\epsilon}}) = \sigma^2(\tilde{\epsilon})/M$$

In other words, the variance of the disturbance terms, will decrease in direct proportion to M. If independence of disturbance terms is not preserved, then the reduction will be less. At the extreme of perfect correlation, there would be no reduction at all in $\sigma^2(\tilde{\bar{\epsilon}})$.

The primary implication of the model is that the correlations are expected to improve as a result of the aggregation, because of the reduction in the unexplained variance (i.e., the variance of the disturbance terms).[6] The reason for aggregating into portfolios is *not* the fact that such aggregated data will exhibit higher correlations. As stated earlier, the reason for aggregation is dictated by portfolio theory, which tells us that the portfolio level is the relevant level to decision-makers in terms of the prediction and measurement of risk.

Implications can also be drawn in terms of the nature of measurement and specification errors that are of concern from a decision-making viewpoint. Errors, random or independent in nature, can effectively be diversified away and are not of major concern. Only systematic errors, which still persist at the portfolio level, are deterimental to optimal predictions and decisions. Thus portfolio theory provides us with a decision context within which to evaluate measurement errors in accounting data.

The sources of measurement error are many-fold, including the following factors: (1) the inability to disentangle the *ex ante* from the *ex post* in measurements of earnings and other variables; (2) the existence of different accounting measurement alternatives being used at the same time by different firms (e.g., inventory and depreciation methods); and (3) the existence of "uniform" methods that produce nonuniform errors across firms (e.g., historical cost).

The portfolio correlations are reported in Table 5. The degree of association is strongest in earnings variability, where the rank correlations are .90 and .82, respectively in each period. The payout variable is next, with correlations of −.79 and −.50, and the accounting B is third (.71 and .46). The evidence indicates that accounting risk variables can be used to select and to rank portfolios such that the ranking has a high degree of correlation with ranking the same portfolios according to the market risk measure. The evidence is consistent with the contention that the accounting risk measures are impounded in the market risk measure.

It is worth noting that aggregation into portfolios did not materially reduce the range of the market risk measure. For example, ranking by the earning variability measure yielded portfolios whose b_p range was 1.11 (.42 to 1.53). Also, a second analysis was conducted where the portfolios were ranked according to b_i, and essentially the same levels of correlations were obtained. The results reported in Table 5 do not appear to be sensitive to the variable on which the data are arrayed before they are aggregated into portfolios.

---

[6] Aggregation may also result in a reduction in the variance of the dependent variable. This reduction would reduce or possibly even eliminate the increase in correlation due to the above factors.

V. The Forecasting Ability of the Accounting Risk Measures

The purpose of the analysis described in this section is to discover the extent to which accounting risk measures can forecast future market determined risk measures relative to the forecasting ability of a naive forecast model. The major distinction between this analysis and the one presented in the previous section is it is dealing with the decision processes at the *micro,* rather than the *macro,* level. The previous analysis was concerned with what accounting data were impounded in market prices, where the market prices reflect the net effect of the decision processes of the entire investing community. At that level it is dealing with the issue of what data does the accounting system, in aggregate, provide to decision makers, in aggregate, and, as such, it is an examination of the usefulness of accounting data at a macro level.

This section will examine the question of the ability of individual decision makers to use accounting data to provide assessments of the risk parameters of their decision models for the next decision period. As such, the analysis will concern itself with the usefulness of accounting data at the micro level. The distinction is important because, as the discussion will indicate shortly, an affirmative answer to the macro question does not dictate a similar answer at the micro level.

Specifically, the analysis in this section will concern itself with the ability of accounting risk measure in period one (1947-56) to forecast the market-determined risk measure, b_i, in period two (1957-65). An evaluation of forecasting ability must involve some standard against which that forecasting ability can be compared. Fortunately, such a standard is readily available, in the form of the estimated market risk measure b_i in period one. Thus, a naive forecasting model states that the b_i in period two will be equal to the b_i in period one.

Previous analysis (Table 1) indicated that the two measures are correlated (.626 at the individual security level and .876 at the portfolio level). Thus the empirical evidence would suggest that the naive model is not easy to beat. However, this holds only if the observed b_i is measuring the "true," underlying β_i with little or no error. The existence of error can provide accounting risk measures with the opportunity to possess superior forecasting ability.

Specifically, we will examine the ability of accounting data to serve as instrumental variables in forming estimates of β in period one that will reduce or eliminate the errors in the observed b's. The instrumental variables approach has been used by Miller and Modigliani [31] and by Brown [7] in removing measurement errors in observed earnings data, for the purpose of generating better earnings estimates to be used in empirical tests of valuation theories of the firm.

The use of instrumental variables is one of several solutions to the errors-in-the-variables problem. Within the context of this study, the problem can be stated as follows: (All variables should carry a subscript i to denote security i.)

We wish to examine the relationship between β_i (β in period one) and β_2 (β in period two). In particular, we are assuming that

$$\beta_2 = \delta_{10} + \delta_{11}\beta_1 \quad \text{where} \quad \delta_{10} = 0$$

$$\delta_{11} = 1$$

However, we cannot observe either β_i or β_2 directly, but must examine b_1 and b_2 (the observed estimates of β_1, β_2), where both are subject to error.

$$b_1 = \beta_1 + u$$
where u and v are error terms
$$b_2 = \beta_2 + v$$

One source of the error may be due to misspecifications in equation (6), such as the use of *ex post* rather than *ex ante* variables. The instrumental variables approach states that, although β_1 may be directly unobservable, it is linearly related to n observable variables, z_1 through z_n, (called instrumental variables):

$$\beta_1 = \phi_0 + \phi_1 z_1 + \ldots + \phi_n z_n$$

β_1 can then be estimated from the following cross section linear regression equation:

$$b_1 = c_0 + c_1 z_1 + \ldots + c_n z_n + w$$

where

$$\hat{b}_1 = b_1 - w$$

z_i = accounting risk measure i

w = error term, reflecting error in b_1

b_1 = measure of β_1 obtained from diagonal model [equation (6)].

The $\hat{b}_1$ is the estimate of β_1 obtained by removing the error (w) from b_1. There are several features of the instrumental variables approach worth noting. (1) The adequacy of the approach is a function of how well the instruments were selected. Suboptimal selection of instruments will lead to some of the error still being impounded in b_1. (2) The instruments are assumed to be independent of the error terms u and v. If this assumption does not hold, there will be a reduction in the efficacy of the instrumental equation. At the extreme, if the accounting variables (i.e., the instruments) contain the same measurement errors as b_1, this approach will be futile. It is often difficult empirically to determine whether the independence holds, since u and v are both unobservable. The instrumental variables approach and the errors-in-the-variables problem are discussed in greater detail in Johnston [21], Goldberger [16], Miller and Modigliani [31], and Brown [7].

Since there is no well specified procedure for the selection of the instrumental variables, initially all seven accounting risk measures were included in the regression equation. An examination of the regression statistics indicated that the inclusion of all seven variables was unnecessary and potentially harmful. There was multicollinearity between the two earnings variables (the product-moment correlation was .61), and the partial correlation coefficients for the leverage, liquidity and size variables were near zero. In fact the standard error of the estimate began to increase as the latter variables were added. As a result, the final instrumental equation contained only three accounting measures—payout, growth, and earnings variability. The multicollinearity between these three variables was low. An examination of the correlations in period two between growth and b_2 (see Table 5) would suggest that even the growth term is unnecessary. However, it was included because a decision maker would only have period one data available to him when constructing the instrumental equation, and we wish to approximate the decision context as much as possible. The summary statistics for the instrumental equation are reported in Table 6. The data are also summarized in four plates (Figures 1 through 4).

Table 6
Summary Statistics for Instrumental Variable Equation, Period One
(Dependent Variable, b_1)

Variable	Statistic
Standard deviation of b_1	.337
Constant	1.016
(T-value)	(14.040)
Regression coefficient	
Payout	−.584
(T-value)	(−5.969)
Growth	.835
(T-value)	(2.533)
Earnings variability	3.027
(T-value)	(10.213)
Standard error of estimate	.251
Correlation coefficient (R)	.668
R^2	.447

Normal Probability Plot

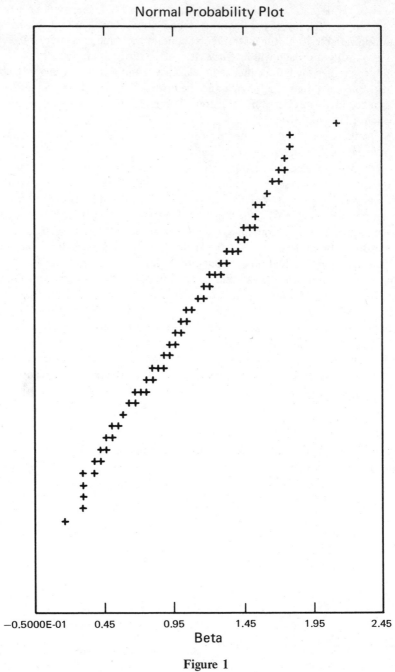

Figure 1

Normal Probability Plot

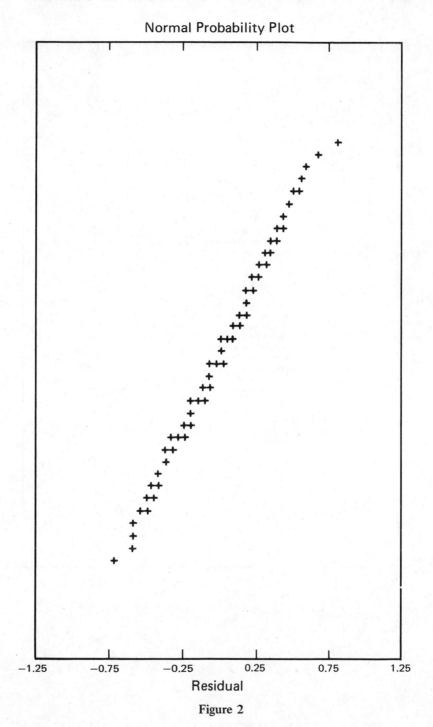

Residual

Figure 2

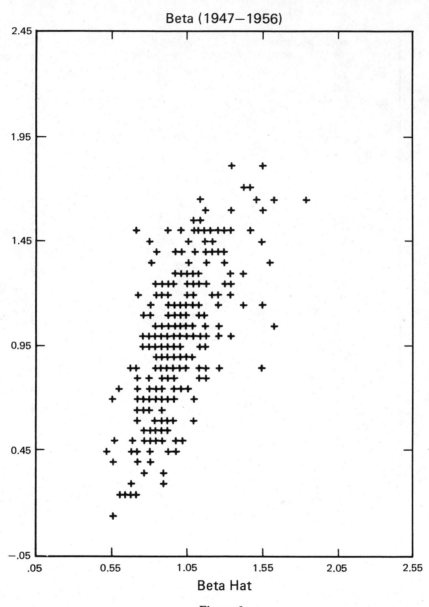

Figure 3

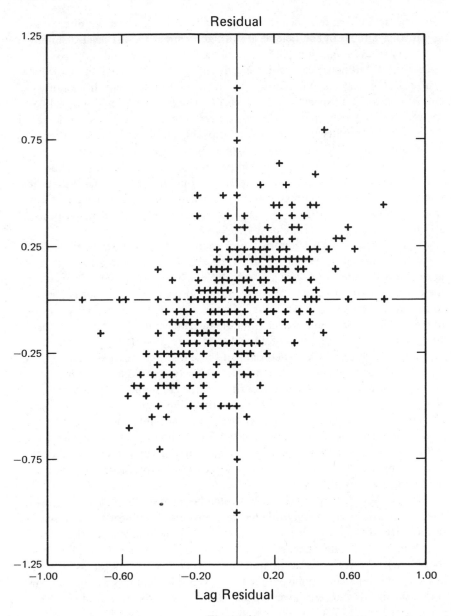

Figure 4

The signs of the regression coefficients are all in the predicted direction, and the magnitudes of coefficients are all significant at the .01 level, assuming normality (that assumption will be examined shortly). The constant also has a large T-value, but no special significance is placed upon this finding, since there is no reason to test the null hypothesis that the constant is zero. In fact, it is almost impossible to specify what value of b_1 should be expected when all the values of the independent variables are zero, because the payout variable and earnings variability bear opposite relationships to b_1 and to each other. The multiple correlation coefficient is .668, implying an R^2 of .447.

It is also difficult to indicate whether the observed level of correlation is a desirable one. Extremely low correlation would probably indicate that the wrong instruments were chosen. On the other hand, extremely high correlation would result in a $\hat{b}_1$ essentially equal to b_1, which would defeat the purpose of attempting to remove measurement errors in b_1.

The plot in Figure 1 is a normal probability plot of the dependent variable in the instrumental equation (b_1). The vertical axis is transformed such that a normal distribution would plot as a straight line. There is a slight tendency for the tail areas to depart from normality, although the departure does not appear to be a very "serious" one. The plot in Figure 2 is a normal probability plot of the residuals or disturbance terms from the instrumental equation. Again the conformity to the assumption of normality is quite good. It would require much more extensive tests to determine if these distributions are in fact normal or really a member of the stable family that closely approximates normality. Previous research, indicating that security returns are stable but nonnormal, would imply that perhaps a similar distribution is appropriate for b_1. However, for our purposes, the distinction is relatively unimportant, since the T-values are so large that even if they were adjusted for the nonnormality they would still be significant at "respectable" levels. More importantly, the real test of the instrumental equation will be measured in terms of its forecasting ability, not the significance of its regression coefficients.

Figure 3 is a plot of b_1 versus $\hat{b}_1$ (called beta hat in the plot). The data appear to conform reasonably well to the assumptions of linearity and homoscedasticity. Although it may not be readily apparent from viewing the plot, the assumption of independence of the disturbance terms is not met. Figure 4 should make the autocorrelation more obvious. Positive correlation is reflected in the preponderance of points in the first and third quadrants. In forming this graph, the disturbance terms were ranked according to the magnitude of the dependent variable (b_1). The positive correlation is induced by the fact that, for the lowest value of b_1, the residual is almost always negative (actual below estimate) and conversely for the largest values of b_1. If β_1 is being measured with error, the lowest b_1 values are more likely to contain a negative error term and the largest values a positive one. If the instrumental equation is fulfilling its purpose, positive correlation in error terms should be expected. Estimates of the regression coefficients are still unbiased, but are not efficient.

Table 7 reports summary statistics of the analysis of the forecasting errors observed when b_1 and $\hat{b}_1(b_1 - w)$ were used as forecasts of b_2. Results are reported for forecasts at the individual security level, and at the portfolio level (61 portfolios of 5 securities each). The portfolio analysis involved two forecasts of b_{2p}, one where portfolios were formed by ranking securities according to $\hat{b}_1$ and the other where securities were ranked according to b_1.

The mean error was very small in all cases, because the mean of b_1 was .991, b_2 was .987, and the $\hat{b}_1$ mean was the same as the b_1 mean by necessity (i.e., the mechanics of linear regression require this). The mean of the squared errors and the mean of the absolute value of the errors is consistently larger for the naive model (b_1). The difference is larger at the portfolio level, and the implication is the difference in forecasting ability cannot be diversified away but, in fact, grows proportionately larger. This can be more readily seen by deflating the mean square error by the variance of b_2, and mean absolute error by M.A.D. (mean of the absolute value of the deviations from the mean) of b_2. At the individual security level the percentage of variance explained is 21 for b_1 versus 24 for $\hat{b}_1$, while at the portfolio level 42 (37) percent of the variance is explained by b_1 and 69 (63) percent explained by $\hat{b}_1$. The superiority of $\hat{b}_1$ can also be seen by comparing the percentage of M.A.D. explained.

An analysis of the percentage of times that one model had a lower error than the other model also reveals the consistently superior performance of the instrumental variables (I.V.) approach. At the individual security level, the split is 54–46 in favor of the I.V. model, and at the portfolio level the split increases to 57–43 and 66–34, respectively, for each of the portfolio rankings. Although the overall performance of $\hat{b}_1$ is consistently superior to that of the naive model and the margin of superiority increases at the portfolio level, the analysis of overall performance tends to understate the usefulness of the I.V. model.

Earlier it was noted that we expected the measurement error in b_1 to be greater in the tails of the distribution, because the lowest values of b_1 were expected to have negative error and conversely for the largest values. An analysis of the forecast errors confirms that belief. Hence we would suspect that the power of the I.V. is greatest in the tail areas of the distribution, which incidentally are probably the areas where accurate forecasts are most needed. Table 7 reports the percentage of times that the I.V. model had a lower error than the naive model in the "tail" areas (operationally defined to be the upper and lower deciles at the individual level and the upper and lower quartiles at the portfolio level). At the individual security level the split in favor of the I.V. approach is 78–22 and at the portfolio level 88–12 and 76–24, respectively. A comparison of the other error measures would reveal the same margin of superiority in favor of $\hat{b}_i$.

Two extensions of this basic analysis were conducted but will not be reported in detail here. (1) The errors were expressed in percentage terms and the analysis repeated. The thrust of the findings was essentially the same as

Table 7
Analysis of Forecast Errors

	Forecasting Model					
	Naive (b_1)			Instrumental Variable ($\hat{b}_1$)		
	Individual Securities	Portfolios		Individual Securities	Portfolios	
Item		$(A)^a$	$(B)^b$		$(A)^b$	$(B)^b$
Mean error	−.004	−.006	−.006	−.004	−.003	−.004
Mean square error	.093	.030	.027	.089	.016	.016
Mean absolute error	.239	.139	.130	.230	.104	.100
Percentage of times lower error	.46	.43	.34	.54	.57	.66
Percentage of times lower in tail areas	.22	.12	.24	.78	.88	.76
Mean of b_2	.987	.990	.990	.987	.990	.990
Variance of b_2	.117	.052	.043	.117	.052	.043
Mean of absolute deviations from mean (b_2)	.269	.196	.160	.269	.196	.160
Percentage explained variance	.21	.42	.37	.24	.69	.63
M.A.D.	.11	.29	.19	.14	.47	.38

[a]Portfolios of 5 securities each ranked according to b_1.
[b]Portfolios of 5 securities each ranked according to $\hat{b}_1$.

that reported here. (2) Another model was examined, where $\hat{b}_1$ was defined as the mean b_1 of all firms in the same industry (defined at the two-digit level). The performance of this model was poorer than that of the naive model at the individual security level, was about the same in the first portfolio analysis (with portfolios selected on basis of $\hat{b}_1$) and was only slightly better in the second portfolio analysis (portfolios selected according to b_1). But in all cases the industry model performed worse than the I.V. model. Both extensions reinforce the contention that accounting risk variables provide superior forecasts of risk for future decision periods.

VI. Evaluation of Alternative Measurements in Accounting

One of the most promising extensions of the models developed here is their potential application to the evaluation of specific accounting measurement controversies. Currently one extension is underway concerning interperiod tax allocation. Some opponents of comprehensive allocation argue that the probability of a reversal in the deferred tax account is so small that the expected value of the amount of reversal (made even smaller when present value considerations are included) is closer to zero than it is to the number currently being placed on the income statement.

For a subset of 92 firms, the earnings variability measure was computed under the assumption of allocation and then under the assumption of non-allocation. The preliminary results indicate that nonallocation form of the variable exhibits a consistently higher association with the market determined risk measure, b, than does the allocation form. This is particularly impressive because the allocated numbers that are currently being reported to investors in annual reports, and there is potentially a bias in favor of reported methods showing higher association, since they are more visable to investors. Although the results are clearly tentative in nature, they offer encouraging prospects for further research. Efforts are also currently underway to apply this methodology to the financial lease controversy, depreciation rules, and direct versus absorption costing.

VII. Concluding Remarks

(1) The evidence supports the contention that accounting measures of risk are impounded in the market-price based risk measure. There is a high degree of contemporaneous association between the accounting and market risk measures. More precisely, a strategy of selecting and ranking portfolios according to the accounting risk measures is essentially equivalent to a strategy of ranking those same portfolios according to the market-determined risk measure. This finding

is consistent with the joint hypothesis that accounting data do reflect the underlying events that determine differential riskiness among securities and that such events are also reflected in the market prices of securities.

The finding is also consistent with other hypotheses, which are highlighted by raising the following two issues:

(a) Does the evidence imply that investors *actually* use accounting risk measures in making portfolio decisions?
(b) To what extent can market-price based dependent variables, such as the β value, be used as a "standard" against which to evaluate accounting data?

With respect to issue (a), the evidence is open to two interpretations. The first is that investors actually do use accounting risk measures in their decisions. The second interpretation is that the market risk measure and accounting data are jointly reflecting the same underlying events and that investors are reacting to those events, rather than to the accounting data themselves. Additional research is needed to determine which interpretation is the "correct" one. One area for further study would be the specification of other variables to which investors might react and the determination of their association with the accounting measures and the market risk measure. Another area for study is an examination of the announcement effects of accounting data, such as annual earnings announcements. Initial research in this area [Beaver (5)] suggests that investors do react directly to the accounting data. However, it is worthwhile noting that under either interpretation it can be said that accounting data impound the underlying events that affect a security's risk. In this sense, the study's findings provide important insight into the utility of accounting data, regardless of the outcome of the issue discussed above.

With respect to issue (b), the evidence is open to the further interpretation that neither the accounting data nor the market-price based risk measure reflect the "true" underlying risk, but that investors falsely perceiving accounting data to have utility, make decisions such that the accounting data are impounded in the market prices.

There is some evidence of an indirect nature that suggests that such an interpretation is not a correct one. The empirical research in the behavior of security prices indicates the securities market is "efficient," in the sense that information appears to be impounded in security prices rather quickly and, on the average, in an unbiased manner. However, further research of a more direct sort is needed to resolve the issue. In particular, the research must deal with such questions as: (i) Is there a bias in favor of the reported method showing an association with market price variables, because it is more visible than non-reported methods? (ii) Are investors "fooled" by the reported numbers and fail to make proper adjustments for measurement errors in the accounting data?

(iii) Do investors fail to compensate for differences in reporting methods across firms and for changes in reporting methods for a given firm over time?

Until questions of this sort are answered, the observed associations are open to both interpretations, and it is difficult to ascertain to what extent market-price based dependent variables can be used as "standards" against which to evaluate accounting measurements. However, the existence of such an unresolved issue in no way detracts from the usefulness of the study's findings. In fact, if one admits the importance of resolving such issues, the study takes on special significance, since its findings and research method provide a foundation for dealing with such questions, as the pilot study on interperiod tax allocation illustrates. In fact, it was our concern about the importance of such issues that motivated us to conduct the study.

(2) Accounting data provided superior forecasts of the market determined risk measure for the time periods studied. This test provides tangible demonstration of at least one area where accounting data can lead to an improvement in prediction, at the level of the individual decision maker. There are also other areas of improvement in decision making which have not been made explicit. The findings of the study also suggest that accounting risk measures can be applied to decision-settings where market determined risk measures are not available. Two such situations immediately come to mind: privately-held firms "going public" for the first time, and multi-division firms with divisions operating on different parts of the risk spectrum. (3) The methodology can be applied to the evaluation of specific measurement controversies in accounting, as suggested by the preliminary results of an application to the issue of interperiod tax allocation.

In summary, we hope this study will provide some additional insight into the interaction between accounting data and market price variables and will help to provide a foundation for structuring the accounting system in a way that will facilitate decisions by investors.

References

[1] S. Alexander, "The Effect of Size of Manufacturing Corporation on the Distribution of the Rate of Return," *Review of Economics and Statistics* (August 1949), pp. 229–235.

[2] Ray Ball and Philip Brown, "An Empirical Evaluation of Accounting Income Numbers," *Journal of Accounting Research* (Autumn 1968), pp. 159–178.

[3] Ray Ball, and Ross Watts, "Predictions of Earnings" (Unpublished manuscript, The University of Chicago, 1968).

[4]   William Beaver, "Financial Ratios as Predictors of Failure," *Journal of Accounting Research* (supplement to Autumn 1966 issue), pp. 71-111.

[5]   —— "The Information Content of Annual Earnings Announcements," *Empirical Research in Accounting: Selected Studies, 1968,* supplement to the *Journal of Accounting Research* (Autumn 1968).

[6]   Marshall Blume, "The Assessment of Portfolio Performance" (Unpublished Ph.D. dissertation, University of Chicago, 1968).

[7]   Philip Brown, "Some Aspects of Valuation in the Railroad Industry" (Unpublished Ph.D. dissertation, University of Chicago, 1968).

[8]   —— and Ray Ball, "Some Preliminary Findings on the Association between the Earnings of a Firm, Its Industry, and the Economy," *Journal of Accounting Research* (supplement to Autumn 1967, pp. 55-77).

[9]   J. G. Craig, and B. G. Malkiel, "The Consensus and Accuracy of Some Predictions of the Growth of Corporate Earnings," *Journal of Finance,* XXIII (March 1968), pp. 67-84.

[10] Dun and Bradstreet, *Dun's Review,* published monthly.

[11] Eugene Fama, "The Behavior of Stock-Market Prices," *Journal of Business,* XXXVII (January 1965), pp. 34-105.

[12] ——, "Portfolio Analysis in a Stable Paretian Market," *Management Science* (January 1965), pp. 404-419.

[13] ——, "Risk, REturn, and Equilibrium," Report No. 6831 (Center for Mathematical Studies in Business and Economics (University of Chicago, June 1968).

[14] ——, Lawrence Fisher, Michael Jensen, and Richard Roll, "The Adjustment of Stock Prices to New Information," Report No. 6715, Center for Mathematical Studies in Business and Economics, (University of Chicago, January 1967).

[15] Lawrence Fisher, "Some New Stock Market Indexes," *Journal of Business,* XXXIX (January 1966), pp. 191-225.

[16] Arthur S. Goldberger, *Econometric Theory* (John Wiley and Sons, Inc., 1964).

[17] Benjamin Graham, David L. Dodd, and Sidney Cottle, *Security Analyses* (McGraw-Hill Book Co., Inc., 1962).

[18] W.B. Hickman, *Corporate Bond Quality and Investor Experience* (Princeton University Press, for the National Bureau of Economic Research, 1958).

[19] James Horrigan, "The Determination of Long-Term Credit Standing with Financial Ratios," Supplement to *Journal of Accounting Research,* (Autumn 1966), pp. 44-62.

[20] Michael C. Jensen, "Risk, the Pricing of Capital Assets, and the Evaluation of Investment Portfolios," *Journal of Business,* XLII (April 1969), pp. 167-247.

[21] J. Johnson, *Econometric Methods,* (McGraw-Hill, 1963).

[22] John W. Kennelly, "The Utility of Interim Reporting," (Unpublished manuscript, 1969).

[23] Benjamin King, "Market and Industry Factors in Stock Price Behavior," *Journal of Business,* XXXIX, Part II (January 1966), pp. 139-190.

[24] I.M.D. Little, "Higgledy Piggledy Growth," (Institute of Statistics, November 1962).

[25] John Lintner, "The Valuation of Risk Assets and the Selection of Risky Investments in Stock Portfolios and Capital Budgets," *Review of Economics and Statistics,* XLVII (February 1965), pp. 13-37.

[26] ——, "Security Prices, Risk and Maximal Gains from Diversification," *Journal of Finance,* XX (December 1965), pp. 587-616.

[27] —— and Robert Glauber, "Higgledy Piggledy Growth in America?" *Proceedings of the Seminar on the Analysis of Security Prices* (May 1967).

[28] Benoit Mandelbrot, "The Variation of Certain Speculative Prices," *Journal of Business,* XXXVI (October 1963), pp. 394-419.

[29] Harry Markowitz, "Portfolio Selection," *Journal of Finance,* VII (March 1952), pp. 77-91.

[30] ——, *Portfolio Selection: Efficient Diversification of Investments* (Wiley, 1959).

[31] Merton H. Miller, and Franco Modigliani, "Some Estimates of the Cost of Capital to the Electric Utility Industry, 1954-1957," *American Economic Review* (June 1966), pp. 333-391.

[32] Franco Modigliani and Merton H. Miller, "The Cost of Capital, Corporation Finance, and the Theory of Investment," *American Economic Review,* XLVII (June 1958), pp. 261-297.

[33] Jan Mossin, "Equilibrium in a Capital Asset Market," *Econometrica,* XXXIV (October 1966), pp. 768-783.

[34] Richard Roll, "The Efficient Market Model Applied to U.S. Treasury Bill Rates," (Unpublished Ph.D. dissertation, Chicago, 1968).

[35] Myron Scholes, "A Test of the Competitive Market Hypothesis: An Examination of the Market for New Issues and Secondary Offerings" (Unpublished Ph.D. Dissertation, University of Chicago, 1969).

[36] William F. Sharpe, "A Simplified Model for Portfolio Analysis," *Management Science* (January 1963), pp. 277-293.

[37] ——, "Capital Asset Prices: A Theory of Market Equilibrium Under Conditions of Risk," *Journal of Finance,* XIX (September 1964), pp. 425-442.

[38] ——, "Risk Aversion in the Stock Market," *Journal of Finance,* XX (September 1965), pp. 416-422.

[39] ——, "Mutual Fund Performance," *Journal of Business,* XXXIX, Part 2, (January 1966), pp. 119-138.

[40] Sidney Siegel, *Nonparametric Statistics* (McGraw-Hill, 1956).

[41]   George H. Sorter, Selwyn W. Becker, T. Ross Archibald, and William H. Beaver, "Accounting and Financial Measures as Indicators of Corporate Personality—Some Empirical Findings," *Research in Accounting Measurement* (American Accounting Association, 1966).

[42]   John Wise, "Linear Estimation for Linear Regressions Systems Having Infinite Variances" (Unpublished paper presented at Berkeley-Stanford Mathematical Economics Seminar, October 1963).

Appendix A

Compustat Industrial Format (Annual) Binary Type Tape

J	Data (J.K.)	Units
1	Cash and Equivalent	MM$
2	Receivables	MM$
3	Inventories	MM$
4	Current Assets	MM$
5	Current Liabilities	MM$
6	Total Assets/Liabilities	MM$
7	Gross Plant	MM$
8	Net Plant	MM$
9	Long Term Debt	MM$
10	Preferred Stock	MM$
11	Common Equity	MM$
12	Net Sales	MM$
13	Operating Income	MM$
14	Depreciation and Amortization	MM$
15	Fixed Charges	MM$
16	Income Taxes	MM$
17	Non-Recurring Income/Expense (Not Net of Tax)	MM$
18	Net Income (Before Netted Non-Recurring)	MM$
19	Preferred Dividends	MM$
20	Available for Common	MM$
21	Common Dividends	MM$
22	Stock Price—High	$ and 8ths
23	Stock Price—Low	$ and 8ths
24	Stock Price—Close	$ and 8ths
25	Number of Shares Outstanding	Thous.
26	Dividends per Share	$ and ¢
27	Adjustment Factor	Ratio
28	Number of Shares Traded	Thous.
29	Number of Employees	Thous.
30	Capital Expenditures	MM$
31	Investment and Advances to Subsidiaries	MM$
32	Investment and Advances—Other	MM$
33	Intangibles	MM$
34	Debt in Current Liabilities	MM$
35	Deferred Taxes and Investment Cr. (B.S.)	MM$
36	Number of Common Shares Purchased/Sold (Net)	Thous.
37	Total Invested Capital	MM$
38	Minority Interest and Sub. Pfd. Stock (B.S.)	MM$
39	Amount of Conv. Debt and Pfd. Stock	MM$
40	Number of Shares Reserved for Conversion	Thous.
41	Cost of Goods Sold	MM$
42	Labor and Related Expense	MM$
43	Pension and Retirement Expense	MM$
44	Incentive Compensation Expense	MM$
45	Selling and Advertising Expense	MM$
46	Research and Development Expense	MM$
47	Rental Expense	MM$
48	Non-Recurring Income/Expense (Net of Taxes)	MM$
49	Minority Interest (I.A.)	MM$

Compustat Industrial Format (Annual) Binary Type Tape (*continued*)

J	Data (J.K.)	Units
50	Deferred Taxes (I.A.)	MM$
51	Investment Credit (I.A.)	MM$
52	Carry Forward Tax—Loss	MM$
53	Unconsolidated Subsidiaries—Excess Equity	MM$
54	Unconsolidated Subsidiaries—Unremitted Earnings	MM$
55	Unconsolidated Subsidiaries—Remitted Earnings	MM$
56	Preferred Stock at Redemption Value	MM$
57	Potentially Diluted Earnings Per Share	$ and ¢
58	Earnings per Share as Reported	$ and ¢
59	Inventory Valuation	Code
60	Inventory Cost	Code

(Note: MM = millions)

Name of Variable Component	Definition in Terms—DATA(J)
Total Assets	DATA(6)
Income Available for Common	DATA(20)
Market Value of Common Stock	DATA(24) * DATA(25) * 1000
Total Senior Securities	DATA(5)+DATA(9)+DATA(10)
Current Assets	DATA(4)
Current Liabilities	DATA(5)
Cash Dividends	DATA(21)

7

Investor Evaluation of Accounting Information: Some Empirical Evidence

Robert S. Kaplan and
Richard Roll

I. Introduction

Accounting statements are a principal means for disseminating information about the economic events of corporations. Because accounting reports are utilized for a variety of purposes, a well-defined set of rules has been established to govern methods of reporting. These rules frequently limit the value of accounting reports to some users, but accountants hope that consistent and objective measurement will enable all users to properly interpret and act upon the events being reported.

In recognition, though, of the complexity and diversity of business transactions, generally accepted accounting procedures still permit a firm to have considerable control over the numbers that appear in its published financial statements. The methods of reporting depreciation, inventory valuation, or income and expense recognition are determined by the firm's officers but subject to the approval by its auditors. If a firm can reduce its tax liability by choosing a different method of reporting (e.g., by using accelerated depreciation), a real economic impact can be obtained. But frequently, the method selected will be used only for financial reporting to stockholders and will therefore not affect tax payments. In such a situation, the firm is essentially choosing among different forms of communicating the same information.

The firm and its auditors are responsible for disclosing the accounting conventions used in preparing financial statements. Any change in method that occurs (e.g., a switch in reporting depreciation) should be specifically mentioned at the time that an earnings or financial-position report is issued or, at the very latest, in the annual report for the year in which the accounting change occurred. Sophisticated investors should be able to understand detailed financial statements and properly interpret the accounting conventions used by a company to describe its operations. Thus, the existence of sophisticated traders who are able to correctly "price" a stock should preclude a company being able to influence its stock price through the manipulation of accounting conventions.

However, this view of efficient capital markets, where stock prices correctly reflect all information, is not universally held. Almost every week a column in

Reprinted with permission of the authors and University of Chicago Press from *The Journal of Business,* Vol. 46, 1972, pp. 225–245. © 1972 by University of Chicago Press.

Barrons, "Up and Down Wall Street," contains a detailed exposé of the accounting manipulations performed by a company ostensibly attempting to influence
is stock price. Since the information used in these exposés is generally obtained
by meticulous reading and analysis of footnotes to financial statements, the
assumption must be that the investing public is unable to perform these calculations. A number of other articles in *Barrons*[1] have gone to great lengths to
explain the accounting manipulations that are possible while still keeping
auditors' approval of "generally accepted accounting principles."

Similar articles may be found in professional publications for financial
analysts. Two articles in the *Financial Analysts Journal* entitled "Depreciation
Manipulation for Fun and Profits"[2] have described in detail how companies
have increased their reported profits by switching back from accelerated
depreciation to straight-line depreciation. Articles have appeared in accounting
journals describing and analyzing companies that have increased reported
earnings through changing depreciation methods,[3] using the flow-through
method for reporting the investment credit,[4] and accounting for mergers by
pooling of interests.[5] A recent dissertation[6] provides an extensive survey of
companies that have made accounting changes. The evidence there indicates
that companies are most likely to use accounting changes in an attempt to
smooth their reported income streams. There are occasional instances of
"housecleaning"—implementing accounting changes with an adverse effect on
earnings at a time when earnings are already depressed.[7]

Company executives must believe such practices affect securities prices or

---

[1] E.g., J.S. Seidman, "Pooling Must Go," *Barron's,* July 1, 1968; and Abraham Briloff,
"Much-abused Goodwill," *Barron's,* April 28, 1969.

[2] John Myers, "Depreciation Manipulation for Fun and Profit," *Financial Analysts Journal*
23 (November–December 1967): 117–23; and 25 (September–October 1969): 47–56.

[3] T. Ross Archibald, "The Return to Straight-Line Depreciation: An Analysis of a Change in
Accounting Method," *Journal of Accounting Research* 5, suppl. (1967): 164–80; and Francis
Bird, "A Note on 'The Return to Stright-Line Depreciation,' " *Journal of Accounting Re-
search* 7 (Autumn 1969): 328–31.

[4] Archibald; and M. Gordon, B. Horowitz, and P. Myers, "Accounting Measurements and
Normal Growth of the Firm," in Jaedicke, Ijiri, and Nelson, *Research in Accounting
Measurement,* ed. R. Jaedicke, Y. Ijiri, and O. Nelson (Iowa City, Iowa: American Ac-
counting Association, 1966).

[5] Jean-Marie Gagnon, "Purchase versus Pooling of Interests: The Search for a Predictor,"
Journal of Accounting Research 5, suppl. (1967): 187–204.

[6] Barry Cushing, "The Effects of Accounting Policy Desisions on Trends in Reported
Corporate Earnings Per Share" (Ph.D. diss., Michigan State University, 1969).

[7] For development of the income-smoothing hypothesis, see S. Hepworth. "Smoothing
Periodic Income," *Accounting Review* 28 (January 1953): 32–39; Myron Gordon, "Postu-
lates, Principles and Research in Accounting," *Accounting Review* 39 (April 1964): 251–63;
Gordon et al.; and Ronald Copeland and Ralph Licastro, "A Note on Income Smoothing,"
Accounting Review 43 (July 1968): 540.

they would not take the trouble to change accounting procedures, hinder inter-period and intercompany comparisons, and incur a qualification or supplementary statement in the auditors' report. So far, however, no published evidence is available to support executives' beliefs, and indeed, few systematic studies have been made. Those that are available examine the impact on price-earnings ratios of companies, within a single industry, that implemented accounting methods affecting reported income but not taxable income.[8] They suggest that investors do compensate for accounting changes and do not blindly compute earnings per share without examining the methods used to generate earnings. However, these studies either failed to control for important factors that affect stock prices (e.g., general market movements) or else introduced errors in the measurement of some of the variables (e.g., growth rate, risk).

In this paper, we employ a recently developed technique (see Sec. III) to measure the effect that two widely adopted accounting changes had on stock prices of firms in many different industries. Both changes affected only the financial statements prepared for stockholders and had no effect on taxes, cash, or any other real economic asset or liability of the firm.

The first was the switch, in 1964, to the flow-through method or reporting the investment credit. When the investment credit was first introduced in 1962, the recommended method was to take the tax saving into income over the life-time of the asset. An alternative method also allowed a company to take 48 percent of the investment credit into income immediately with 52 percent deferred to subsequent accounting periods. In 1964, the accounting treatment was modified to give a company the option of reporting the entire amount of the credit in the year that the asset was purchased. Many companies were quick to adopt this new accounting procedure, and some obtained an even larger earnings jolt in the first year by taking deferred reserves, which had been built up in the first few years of the investment credit, into income too. Of course, many companies continued to use the recommended and more conservative convention of amortizing the credit over the productive life of the asset. The 48–52 method faded from use in 1964 because virtually all the companies that had used it switched to the flow-through method. One might suspect that those companies which were able to increase their reported earnings by adopting the flow-through method should have had relatively higher increases in stock prices than those companies which continued to report their earnings conserva-

---

[8]See J.L. O'Donnell, "Relationships between Reported Earnings and Stock Prices in the Electric Utility Industry," *Accounting Review* 40 (January 1965): 135–43; and "Further Observation on Reported Earnings and Stock Prices," ibid. 43 (July 1968): 549–53; and F.A. Mlynarczyk, "An Empirical Study of Accounting Methods and Stock Prices," *Journal of Accounting Research* 7, suppl. (1969): 63–81, for studies of the effect of flow-through versus normalization accounting in the electric utility industry. E.E. Comiskey, "Market Response to Changes in Depreciation Accounting," *Accounting Review* 46 (April 1971): 279–85, examines the impact on price-earnings ratios of companies in the steel industry that switched from accelerated to straight-line depreciation for financial reporting.

tively. If the market was dominated by sophisticated investors, however, that portion of a company's earnings which was obtained through the flow-through of the investment credit should have been apparent and discounted properly, thus resulting in no price change.

The second change studied was the switch back from reporting accelerated depreciation to reporting straight-line depreciation. This switch-back has been performed by many companies recently, and there is even an industry effect; for example, paper companies switched back in 1965, steel companies in 1968. Again, since these companies continued to use accelerated depreciation for tax purposes, the change to reporting straight-line depreciation had no effect on the economic position of the firm.

Section II describes the sources and types of accounting data collected for companies that implemented either change in accounting practice since 1962. Section III presents the financial model used to test the impact of changes in accounting practice. Discussion of procedures for statistical inference when the underlying distribution is from the class of symmetric stable distributions also appears in Section III. The findings from estimating and testing the financial model are reported in Section IV. Briefly, they indicate that any price effect from a change in accounting procedure of the type investigated in this paper is temporary. Additional tests and findings are reported in Section V. Summary and conclusions are presented in Section VI.

II. Accounting Data

The names of companies that switched to the flow-through method of reporting the investment credit were obtained from the 1965 edition of *Accounting Trends and Techniques*. This publication surveys the annual reports of 600 companies and summarizes the form and terminology used in the financial statements of the companies. It also presents the various treatments of transactions and items that affect the financial statements. The 600 companies are intended to be a cross-section of U.S. industrial firms, and, while most of the largest companies are in the sample, many small companies whose securities are not traded on the New York or American Exchange are also included. No utility companies are in the sample. We are unaware of any bias in selecting companies for inclusion in this publication which would make the results reported in this paper unrepresentative for industrial corporations in general.

The 1965 edition of *Accounting Trends and Techniques* had a detailed section on the investment credit because of the issuance of Opinion No. 4 of the Accounting Principles Board (APB) in March 1964. This opinion granted that "the alternative method of treating the credit as a reduction of Federal income taxes of the year in which the credit arises is also acceptable." There were 302 companies which indicated that they switched to the flow-through method permitted by Opinion No. 4. In contrast to these, sixty-eight companies continued to use the method recommended in APB Opinion No. 2, December 1962, of reflecting the investment credit "in net income over the productive life of the acquired property and not in the year in which it is placed in service." Two companies continued to use the 48–52 method.

The remaining 228 companies either did not make specific reference to the use of the investment credit or else used other accounting variations which were not identified. The identity of the 372 companies which were using either the productive-life or flow-through method was disclosed so that we had both a group of companies that switched their method and a control group of companies that did not switch their accounting treatment of the investment credit. Because of data limitations described in the following section, only companies whose stock was listed on the New York or American Exchange could be analyzed. In addition, tape errors or an insufficient number of stock price observations for some companies limited the sample somewhat further. At this point we had 263 companies which switched to the flow-through method and sixty-nine which retained the productive-life or 48–52 method in 1964. More recent editions of *Accounting Trends and Techniques* were scanned to identify companies that switched methods in later years. This yielded twelve more companies, so that our final sample had 275 companies which switched and fifty-seven companies which retained the productive-life method.

For each of the 332 companies that were in the final sample, the date was obtained when the earnings were announced for the fiscal year in which the investment-credit method switch could have or actually occurred. This was accomplished by finding the first record of a fiscal-year earnings report as published in the *Wall Street Journal*. Such information was readily available by utilizing the *Wall Street Journal Index* in the appropriate year. There was, in general, no specific mention in the *Index* as to whether the investment credit treatment had been disclosed prior to or at the same time as the earnings report. We assumed that this information was generally known at the time of the earnings announcement or shortly thereafter when the annual report appeared. This assumption was tested in another context when we considered companies that switched depreciation methods.

We used the earnings announcement data as the base date for measuring the effect of accounting changes, since previous studies[9] have indicated that this is a time when new information about the company is disseminated. Significant price adjustments are likely to occur at this point as investors revise their expectations about a company's future prospects. If a company is able to

---

[9]Ray Ball and Philip Brown, "An Empirical Evaluation of Accounting Index Numbers," *Journal of Accounting Research* 6 (Autumn 1968): 159–78; and William Beaver, "The Information Content of Annual Earnings Announcements," *Journal of Accounting Research* 6, suppl. (1968): 67–92.

influence its stock price by an accounting change, the principal impact should occur when the announcement is made of the first full year of earnings in which the accounting change was implemented. Certainly, in the first few years after the switch, companies using the flow-through method, and not significantly decreasing their level of investment, will consistently report higher earnings than if they used the productive-life or 48–52 method. However, since the largest change in year-to-year earnings will occur in the first year in which the switch was implemented, this date was used in our analysis.[10]

A similar procedure was used to identify companies that switched from using an accelerated method of depreciation to the straight-line method for financial reporting. As with the investment credit, this switch had the immediate effect of increasing the reported earnings in the first year the change was implemented over what would have been reported had the accounting change not been made. *Accounting Trends and Techniques* again provided a good source of companies that had implemented this change in reporting depreciation, and it was cross-checked against a list compiled by Cushing.[11] The names of additional companies were obtained from studies reported by Myers, Archibald, and Bird.[12] The final sample included seventy-one companies.

For each company, the date of first earnings announcement was recorded from the *Wall Street Journal* for the fiscal year when the change in depreciation method was implemented. In addition to this information, we attempted to identify when the change in depreciation method was first announced. Every mention of a company as indicated in the *Wall Street Journal Index* during the year in which the depreciation change occurred (and shortly thereafter) was checked in the *Journal* itself to see whether it included mention of the accounting change. There is no guarantee that the earliest date so obtained was when the investment community was first informed by the change, but it certainly provided an upper bound and we were not able to obtain a better estimate. For many companies, this date turned out to be the same as for the year-end earnings announcement. However, a number of companies did announce the accounting change prior to this report, and in one instance, a company announced its intentions to change its depreciation method in the annual report for the prior year. Thus, we were able to test whether there was an effect due solely to the announcement, in advance, that earnings were going to be increased by an accounting change.

In contrast to the investment-credit switch which was first implemented in

---

[10]We observed stock returns for thirty weeks on either side of the announcement date so that an earlier price adjustment, say after a six- or nine-month earnings report which included the effect of the accounting change, would have been detected. In face, as reported later, the major impact did occur at the year-end announcement date.

[11]See n. 6 above.

[12]See Myers (n. 2 above) and Archibald and Bird (n. 3 above).

Table 1
Corporations Switching from Accelerated to Straight-Line Depreciation for Financial Reporting

Year	Number of Firms
1962	9
1963	6
1964	3
1965	17
1966	12
1967	3
1968	21
Total	71

most companies in the same year, 1964, the depreciation change occurred throughout the 1960s. Table 1 presents for each year the number of companies in our sample which switched back to reporting straight-line depreciation for that year.

III. Financial Data and Methodology

In attempting to judge the real impact of accounting changes, we are faced with the unfortunate circumstance that many other causes are simultaneously affecting market prices. Whether these are general market movements or changes in dividends, labor contracts, interest rates, or technology, they are all nuisances and must be eliminated in order to clearly perceive the effects of the events under study.

To accomplish this, we employed two techniques: First, by constructing models based on the capital asset pricing theory of Sharpe and Lintner,[13] we intended to eliminate two variables that are broadly related to all securities. These variables were interest rates and general economic conditions, the latter as measured by an index of stock prices. Second, we hoped to purge the effects of many other influences on stock prices by cross-sectional averaging over a large sample of heterogeneous firms. Of course, this technique only eliminated the impact of events that were independent among firms.

The Sharpe-Lintner theory of capital asset pricing is based on the normative risk-avoidance prescription of Markowitz.[14] A diversified portfolio of im-

---

[13]William F. Sharpe, "Capital Asset Prices: A Theory of Market Equilibrium under Conditions of Risk," *Journal of Finance* 19 (September 1964): 425–42; and John Lintner, "The Valuation of Risk Assets and the Selection of Risky Investments in Stock Portfolios and Capital Budgets," *Review of Economics and Statistics* 47 (February 1965): 13–37.

[14]Harry M. Markowitz, *Portfolio Selection: Efficient Diversification of Investments* (New York: John Wiley & Sons, 1959).

perfectly correlated securities has a lower expected variance of return than a value-weighted average of the individual security returns. Sharpe was the first to show how capital market equilibrium prices (and expected returns) are formed under pure competition when investors behave as portfolio diversifiers. Although his analysis required several rather unrealistic assumptions,[15] his model has been successfully applied to a variety of capital assets[16] and seems to fit common stocks particularly well.

Sharpe-Lintner equilibrium is characterized by the following expression:

$$\bar{R}_{j,t} = R_{F,t} + \beta_j(\bar{R}_{m,t} - R_{F,t}) \tag{1}$$

where $\bar{R}_{j,t}$ is the expected return on stock j in time t; $R_{F,t}$ is a riskless return; $\bar{R}_{m,t}$ is the average return expected on all risky assets; and β_j is a risk coefficient. In this paper, we followed the common practice of converting $(1)^{17}$ to a regression model:

$$R_{j,t} = \gamma_j R_{F,t} + \beta_j R_{m,t} + \epsilon_{j,t} \tag{2}$$

where $\epsilon_{j,t}$ is a disturbance term whose mean is assumed to be zero. Variables in equation (2) were measured weekly by the quantities given in table 2. For each security, the record of weekly prices begins, at the earliest, on July 5, 1962 and ends, at the latest, on September 25, 1969. To have been included in the sample, at least twelve observations (weeks) must have been available on each side of the accounting change date.

Most securities included here provide a complete record of observations from mid-1962 to the end of 1968, a total of 338 weeks. Some, however, were listed on the New York or American Exchange for less than the full period.[18]

---

[15]That is, all investors have the same expectations, only two periods are considered, and a riskless asset exists.

[16]Eugene Fama, Lawrence Fisher, Michael C. Jensen, and Richard Roll, "The Adjustment of Stock Prices to New Information," *International Economic Review* 10 (February 1969): 1–21; Michael C. Jensen, "Risk, the Pricing of Capital Assets, and the Evaluation of Investment Portfolios," *Journal of Business* 42 (April 1969): 167–247; Marshall E. Blume, "Portfolio Theory: A Step toward Its Practical Application," *Journal of Business* 43 (April 1970): 152–73; Ray Ball and Philip Brown (n. 9 above); and Richard Roll, "Bias in Fitting the Sharpe Model to Time Series Data," *Journal of Financial and Quantitative Analysis* 4 (September 1969): 271–89.

[17]This conversion is valid only under specific assumptions about the joint probability distribution of R_j and R_m (see Roll, especially p. 272).

[18]Only securities listed on the two major U.S. exchanges are included on the source ISL tapes. Some securities in the sample were listed from the over-the-counter market, were delisted, or merged during the sample period. If a company in the sample merged with a larger company, the record was stopped at the merger time. If the company merged with a smaller concern, the record was continued and calculations were based on the entire period.

Table 2
Empirical Definitions of Financial Variables

Variable	Definition	Source
$R_{j,t}$	Weekly return,* $\log_c[(P_{j,t} + D_{j,t})/ P_{j,t-1}]$	
$P_{j,t}$	Market price of security j at end of week t adjusted for splits and stock dividends	ISL daily historical stock price tapes, Standard
$D_{j,t}$	Cash dividend paid to stockholders of record of firm j during week t (also adjusted for splits, etc.)	Statistics Corporation
$R_{F,t}$	Average rate on short-term government debt obligations at beginning of week t	
$R_{m,t}$	Market return, $\log_e(I_t/I_{t-1})$	Standard and Poor's trade
I_t	Value of Standard and Poor's composite stock price average at end of week t	statistics

*Ordinarily, the time subscript was in increments of one week. In some cases, however, most frequently when a trading day was a holiday, the span was six or eight days. Every return was adjusted to an equivalent per annum return before any calculations were performed. Ordinarily, this was done by simply multiplying the weekly return by 52. If the return was for six or eight days, however, it was multiplied by 364/6 or 364/8, respectively. Naturally, if the security return spanned six or eight days, all explanatory variables spanned the same interval.

Table 3 provides a frequency distribution of weekly observations available for the 364 stocks in the sample.

The market model (2) is of intrinsic interest and has been examined in detail by many others,[19] but we only employed it to remove the influence of extraneous variables (R_F and R_m). We were not searching for either efficient coefficient estimates or optimal functional forms. In searching for maximum explanatory power, however, we checked several alternative specifications. First, regression calculations were performed with and without suppressing the constant term. When a constant term is allowed, the coefficient of R_F becomes much more uncertain. This seems to be due to the extremely low variance of R_F relative to R_m and R_j. The constant term has been suppressed in all reported results.

Second, we checked for temporal nonstationarity by comparing regression coefficients calculated during subperiods. This did not provide any additional explanatory ability. (We could have taken advantage of a systematic nonstationarity in the coefficients.)

In the few cases of merger encountered, there was no ambiguity about which firm was larger. For companies that changed depreciation methods in 1968, additional records of prices through September 1969 were collected from the *Wall Street Journal*.

[19] In particular, see George W. Douglas, "Risk in the Equity Market: An Empirical Appraisal of Market Efficiency," *Yale Economic Essays* 9 (Spring 1969): 3–45; Jensen (n. 16 above); and Blume (n. 16 above).

Table 3
Distribution of Numbers of Observations (Weeks)

Observations (N)	Securities (N)	Proportion of Securities
⩾ 300	265	0.728
200–299	78	0.214
100–199	20	0.055
⩽ 100	1	0.003

Third, we checked for excessive serial dependence in regression residuals using the Durbin-Watson test and again found no significant effect.

Regression equation (2) was fitted to the data sample available for each security; but observations thirty weeks before and after the earnings announcement date associated with an accounting change were excluded[20] to avoid another econometric problem: If accounting changes affect stock prices, the disturbance term $\epsilon_{j,\,t}$ will not have a mean of zero when t is near the earnings announcement date.[21] A summary of regression results from model (2) is presented in table 4.

Using coefficients $\hat{\gamma}_j$ and $\hat{\beta}_j$ estimated from (2) and concurrent values of $R_{j,\,t}, R_{F,\,t}$, and $R_{m,\,t}$, we calculated predicted disturbance terms for thirty weeks on each side of the earnings announcement date for each security:

$$u_{j,\,t} = R_{j,\,t} - \hat{\gamma}_j R_{F,\,t} - \hat{\beta}_j R_{m,\,t} \qquad t = 1, \ldots, 60 \qquad (3)$$

Next, these "abnormal returns," $u_{j,\,t}$, were averaged cross-sectionally to obtain

$$\bar{u}_t = \frac{1}{N} \sum_{j=1}^{N} u_{j,\,t} \qquad (4)$$

Emphasis must again be placed on t, a measure of time relative to the earnings announcement date which is generally not the same chronological date for different firms. Thus, for example, $\bar{u}_{31}$ estimates an average historical return, abstracting from market and interest rate effects, that occurred during a week when earnings that had been affected by an accounting change were announced. Generally speaking, $\bar{u}_{31-k}$ measures the average abnormal return in a week ending k weeks before earnings were announced.

Finally, an estimate of the total abnormal return that would have been

---

[20]The thirty-week period was chosen a priori as likely to be long enough to contain any discernible price movement caused by the accounting change.

[21]This procedure was also followed, for the same reason, in Fama et al. (n. 16 above).

Table 4

Summary of Regression Results (Applying Eq. [2] to Weekly Observations)

	$\bar{R}_j$	$\hat{\gamma}$ ~	$t_{\hat{\gamma}}$	$\hat{\beta}$	$t_{\hat{\beta}}$	R^2
Investment-credit changes ($N = 332$):						
Mean	16.2	1.52	0.555	1.00	6.44	0.148
Median	15.7	1.43	0.514	0.995	6.40	0.141
Interquartile range	11.7	2.76	1.10	0.442	3.20	0.108
Depreciation changes ($N = 71$):						
Mean	15.0	1.17	0.425	1.07	6.75	0.151
Median	14.5	0.785	0.304	1.05	6.54	0.149
Interquartile range	14.2	2.59	1.05	0.443	2.31	0.083

earned by a holder of shares during the weeks surrounding a change can be more distinctively seen by accumulating $\bar{u}_t$ over time. The next section, therefore, will report

$$U_T = \sum_{t=1}^{T} \bar{u}_t, \quad T = 1, \ldots, 60 \tag{5}$$

For example, U_{31} is the total abnormal return which would have accrued on the average to stockholders over the thirty weeks preceding, plus the one week containing, an earnings announcement.

The underlying returns, R_j, R_F, and R_m, are, of course, random variables, and true quantities which correspond to estimates $\hat{\gamma}_j$, $\hat{\beta}_j$, $\bar{u}_t$, and U_T are exposed to uncertainty. Since these estimates are all linear functions of the individual abnormal returns, $u_{j,t}$, the sampling distribution of $u_{j,t}$ must be used to derive probability inferences from $\bar{u}_t$ and U_T. This sampling distribution is unknown to begin with, and we were impelled to ease the search problem by restricting the class of contenders. Consequently, we assumed that $u_{j,t}$ had achieved, by virtue of the generalized central limit theorem, a sampling distribution that is a symmetric member of the stable class.

Stable distributions occur as the only possible limiting distributions for sums of independent, identically distributed random variables.[22] The Gaussian (or normal) is a member of this class and undoubtedly owes its wide employment[23] to the normal central limit theorem. But the Gaussian is only a special

---

[22]William Feller, *An Introduction to Probability Theory and Its Applications* (New York: John Wiley & Sons, 1966), vol. 2.

[23]In empirical work, probability statements are rarely made without the aid of a standard Gaussian probability table.

case that has no prior justification. A more general assumption is both costless and less likely to yield misleading results.

All symmetric stable distributions are described by three parameters: δ, for location (the mode and median and in some cases the mean); s, for scale (in the Gaussian case, s^2 is one-half the variance); and α, the characteristic exponent, which portrays the type.[24] (For the Gaussian, $\alpha = 2$, while for the Cauchy, $\alpha = 1$.) A different probability table is required for each value of α.

All three parameters can be estimated from the order statistics of a sample.[25] The estimators are for δ, a truncated mean; for s, an interfractile range; and for α, a function of the ratio of two interfractile ranges. Details are given in Appendix A. We shall denote these estimates by $\hat{\delta}(x)$, $\hat{s}(x)$, and $\hat{\alpha}(x)$, where x is the random variable. For example, $\hat{\alpha}(u_{j,\,t})$ is the estimated characteristic exponent of the cross-sectional distribution of abnormal returns from (3) for week t.

To verify that economic quantities such as $u_{j,\,t}$ actually *are* sums of random variables and are thus potentially modeled by stable distributions, one only need recall that they represent market quantities and are thus aggregates of many individual transactions. We can offer no additional justification for restricting our analysis to stable distributions, but we can fashion a refuge by comparing it to the much more stringent normality assumption that has been traditionally employed (although usually unstated) in economic data analysis. The data remain as final arbiters of the procedure's validity.

IV. Empirical Results

Description of Figures and Tables

Stock price changes associated with accounting changes are illustrated in figure 1, Panels *A–C*. Each panel plots these data as functions of time relative to the earnings announcement week, $t = 31$. The numbers used in plotting figure 1 are tabulated in Appendix B.

On each panel, the top chart gives the 80 percent acceptance interval for the mean abnormal return, $\bar{u}_t$, in percentage per week. This interval provides a probability measure of $\bar{u}_t$ and can be interpreted in either of two ways: the probability is .8 that the given interval contains the true value of $\bar{u}_t$; or, given a diffuse prior, the posterior probability is .8 that $\bar{u}_t$ falls within

---

[24] Asymmetric members of the stable class have a fourth parameter.

[25] Eugene Fama and Richard Roll, "Some Properties of Symmetric Stable Distributions," *Journal of the American Statistical Association* 63 (September 1968): 817–36; and "Parameter Estimates for Symmetric Stable Distributions," ibid. 66 (June 1971): 331–38.

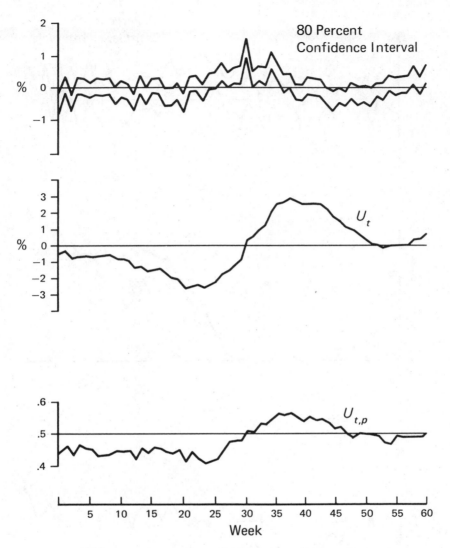

Figure 1. Panel *A*.–Investment-credit Changes.

the given interval.[26] Using figure 1, Panel A, as an example, the return from holding a security in a week when a company announces earnings that are

---

[26]Each acceptance interval was derived from probability tables of symmetric stable distributions with characteristic exponent $\alpha = 1.6$. This value of α was chosen because the mean values of $\alpha(_{j, t})$ computed for securities in panels A, B, and C over sixty weeks were α_A = 1.58, α_B = 1.63, and α_C = 1.57. The α's estimated for each week are given in Appendix B, table B1. For details of the derivation of $\alpha(u_{j, t})$, see Appendix A. The 80 percent interval was chosen because it has a lower sensitivity to the choice of α than the 90 or 95 percent intervals.

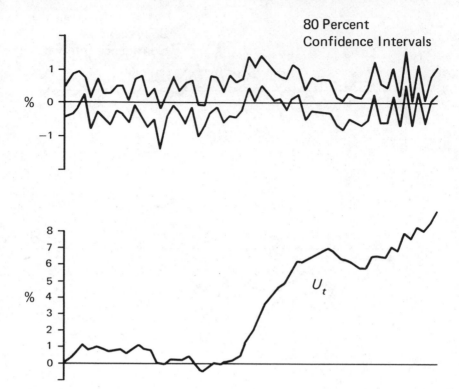

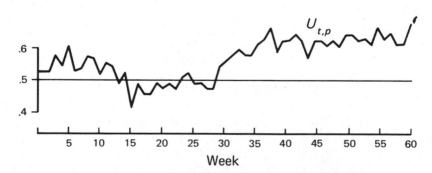

Figure 1. Panel B.—Investment-credit control group

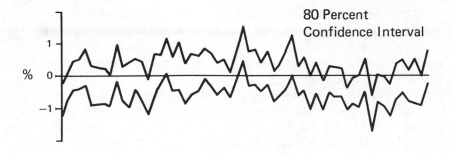

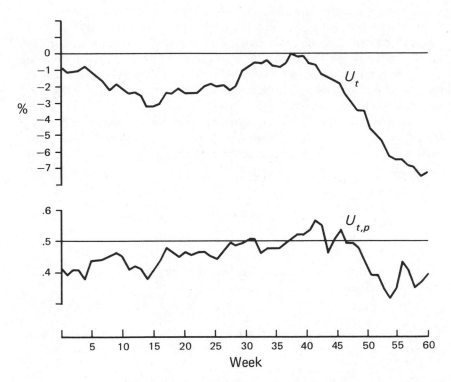

Figure 1. Panel *C*.—Depreciation changes

increased by a change in investment-credit accounting (week 31) falls in the interval 0.889 to 1.476 percent per week[27] with probability .8; and, of course, this return abstracts from the security's normal responses to movements of interest rates and other stock prices during the same week.

---

[27]From 46.2 to 76.8 percent per annum!

Mean cumulative abnormal returns, U_T, are plotted just below the 80 percent confidence intervals in each panel. Since cumulative returns are sums beginning in week 1, their units are percentage per T weeks. For $T = 52$, the units are percentage per annum; for example, $U_{52} = -0.058$ percent per annum for investment-credit changes.

Confidence bands for the cumulative abnormal average return are not reported for every week. As an example, however, table 5 reports the 80 percent confidence interval for U_T for week 52 assuming $\bar{u}_t$ is temporally independent. The table provides intervals for two widely separated values of α (1.3 and 2.0) and also the interval for $\hat{\alpha}$, the arithmetic mean of $\hat{\alpha}$ taken over the sixty weeks around each earnings announcement date.[28]

These results show how sensitive probability statements are to the normality assumption. When normality is assumed, securities in Panels B and C of figure 1 have highly significant cumulative abnormal returns in week 52 (positive for B, negative for C); but when more reasonable distributional assumptions are made, the confidence intervals become wider and the results for week 52 agree more with those obtained from the nonparametric measure of cumulative return, $U_{t,p}$, discussed below.

A nonparametric measure of cumulative abnormal return is given by $U_{T,p}$ (charted by ticked curve below U_t). The term $U_{T,p}$ is the proportion of individual securities with positive cumulative abnormal returns in week T; that is, define

$$U_{T,j} \equiv \sum_{t=1}^{T} u_{j,t}$$

where $u_{j,t}$ is the individual abnormal return of stock j in week t given by equation (3). Then

$$U_{T,p} \equiv \frac{1}{N_T} \sum_{j=1}^{N_T} \max(0, \text{sign } U_{T,j})$$

where N_T is the number of stocks available in week T.

If the u_j's are mutually independent, $N_T U_{T,p}$ has a binomial distribution and the quantity

$$(U_{T,p} - \pi)/\sqrt{\pi(1-\pi)/N_T}$$

---

[28]See n. 26.

Table 5
80 Percent Confidence Intervals for Cumulative Abnormal Average Return in Week 52 (Percentage per Annum)

Assumed Type of Distribution	Panel A: Investment-Credit Changes	Panel B: Investment-Credit "Control Group"	Panel C: Depreciation Changes
$\alpha = 2.0$	−0.935 to −0.819	4.44 to 8.40	−7.19 to −2.93
$\alpha = 1.3$	−12.9 to 11.7	−11.5 to 24.3	−25.1 to 14.4
$\alpha = \hat{\alpha}$	−3.74 to 2.58	1.52 to 11.3	−11.9 to 1.75

is asymptotically normal with mean zero and variance 1 under the null hypothesis: $E(U_{T,p}) = \pi$. We are, of course, interested in the hypothesis $E(U_{T,p}) = \frac{1}{2}$. For example, in figure 1, Panel A, week 31, $N_{31} = 275$ and the 95 percent acceptance interval on $E(U_{31,p}) = \frac{1}{2}$ is approximately $\frac{1}{2} \pm 0.059$. Since $U_{31,p}$ was calculated as 0.509, we cannot reject, at the .05 level of significance, the hypothesis that cumulative abnormal returns are zero $[E(U_{31,p}) = \frac{1}{2}]$ in week 31.

One should note that $U_{T,p}$ is not independent across T.

Interpretation of Investment-Credit Changes

Securities of firms that increased reported earnings by adopting the flow-through method of accounting for the investment credit experienced abnormally good times in the ten weeks surrounding their earnings announcement. This is indicated in figure 1, Panel A, by the uniformly positive average abnormal returns, $\bar{u}_t$, from weeks 25 to 36. These positive returns are responsible for the rapid rise in U_T, the cumulative abnormal return, during the same weeks. The proportion of securities with individually positive cumulative returns rises more than 14 percent from 0.416 in week 25 to 0.562 in week 36.[29] This is a significant movement in security prices, and its coincidence with increased accounting earnings is highly suggestive of a positive relation.

Unfortunately for stockholders, market prices did not remain high. In weeks 39–53, these securities experienced abnormally *bad* times on the average. The proportion of securities with positive cumulative abnormal returns declined to 0.471 in week 53.

It seems prudent to emphasize now that patterns in figure 1 are averages and need bear no resemblance to the patterns of individual prices. Indeed,

---

[29] As indicated by positive returns in weeks 26–30, the favorable earnings report seems to have been anticipated by stock prices. However, the largest abnormal average return did not occur until week 31, when the higher earnings were announced. In week 31, the *lower* end of the 80 percent confidence interval was 0.889 percent per week.

movements in averages, both up and down, reflect nonsynchronous movements of individual components. For example, in figure 1, Panel A, the movement down in weeks 39–53 must be due to a trickling of information about the true reason for previously reported high earnings. Investors could have learned that earnings had been manipulated by reading the annual report. Its publication occurs sometime after the earnings announcement in the financial press, and part of the downtrend after week 39 could be attributed to its receipt and accompanying investor actions. We have no firm estimate of the normal lag in the report's publication, but it seems unlikely to be delayed until week 53, twenty-one weeks after earnings are announced. This fact, plus the sharp downward movement in prices beginning in week 44, suggests another possibility: a reaction to subsequent quarterly reports that began to appear about thirteen weeks after the original earnings announcement date. These later quarterly reports may have indicated that the increased rate of earnings growth anticipated because of the previous investment-credit switch could not be sustained. (No additional earnings manipulations were available.)

Panel B of figure 1 portrays the "control group" of firms that were specifically mentioned in the 1965 *Accounting Trends and Techniques* as continuing to reflect the investment credit over their assets' productive lines. These firms voluntarily reported earnings below the potential permitted by accepted accounting practice. Stockholders must not have been too upset, however, because their shares not only increased in value around the earnings announcement date but, in contrast to the companies that switched accounting methods, remained at the higher level. On the average, holders of these shares from weeks 1 to 52 earned 6.42 percent per annum in addition to the normal return associated with interest rates and stock market averages.

You can now appreciate why we enclose "control group" in quotes. The performance reported in figure 1, Panel B, strongly suggests the presence of preselection bias in this group of companies, since a random selection should show no abnormal return over an extended time period. A possible explanation is this: Managers of these firms knew that their earnings were going to be higher than anticipated even without the help of an accounting change—so why bother? The change to flow-through of the investment credit could be postponed until a later date when earnings might not be so favorable. (This is consistent with an income-smoothing model for predicting the timing of a firm's account changes.)

Interpretation of Depreciation Changes

Firms that switched from accelerated to straight-line depreciation between 1962 and 1968 were, on average, dismal performers. Shareholders from week 1 to week 52 lost 5 percent more than they would have anticipated given interest rate and general stock price movement. In week 60, less than 40 percent of these firms had positive cumulative abnormal returns. These results are only suggestive, however, because none of the performance measures significantly rejects, in the statistical sense, the hypothesis that $E(\bar{u}_t) = 0$, that is, that these firms were unaffected by accounting changes and earnings announcements. Even the low proportion of firms with positive cumulative abnormal returns, $U_{t,p}$, is not significant at the 5 percent level.

But if we rely on the average patterns, the data suggest two conclusions about firms that increase earnings by switching to straight-line depreciation. First, there is a temporary positive effect around the earnings announcement date. This may be due to unexpectedly higher reported earnings which investors accept as valid, not suspecting they resulted from an accounting change. Second, the patterns suggest that firms that increase earnings by changing depreciation reporting are likely to be performing poorly. This is indicated by the general downtrend in cumulative abnormal average return which is only ameliorated in the weeks adjacent to the earnings announcement. This is consistent with the income-smoothing hypothesis of when accounting methods are likely to be changed. We conclude, however, that such practices are unsuccessful in permanently affecting stock prices.

V. Additional Tests and Findings

Truncating the Sample

When analyzing data from symmetric stable distributions, one can obtain better measures of central tendency by using a truncated sample to estimate the mean.[30] For our purposes, truncation would provide an added benefit by verifying that observed patterns were due to co-movements by many stocks rather than by relatively few.

Plots of the cumulative abnormal return, U_t (see the middle plots in fig. 1, Panels A–C), were made with both the extreme 5 percent and 25 percent of the residuals deleted in each week. The general shape of U_t remained the same for the truncated and the untruncated samples. This verified that we had been seeing a general movement of prices. However, the level of these returns decreased with the degree of truncation. Subsequent analysis revealed that this downward shift was due to positive skewness in the residuals. The effect of skewness on our probability measures is discussed in Appendix B, where we argue that conclusions in Section IV remain valid, and perhaps are even strength-

---

[30] See n. 25 above.

ened. We also believe that skewness makes untruncated sample statistics more reliable measures of accounting change effects.

Advancing the Analysis Forward in Time

In an experiment to verify that observed patterns were significantly related to accounting changes and not due to some artifact, we advanced the analysis forward by thirty weeks for investment-credit changes. The sixty-week period now started at the earnings announcement date for the year that the change occurred and ended slightly more than a year later, so that the announcement date for the following year should have been within the period studied. The shape of the U_t plot for the entire sample of stocks showed a strong positive increase over this period, but this was due to a few extreme observations and was, consequently, not a significant pattern. When the sample was truncated by deleting 5 percent of the extreme observations of either sign in each week, the pattern of U_t reverted, essentially, to random fluctuations. This is important to note, since truncating the sample in the original sixty-week period affected the level of the plot but left the basic shape unchanged.

Treatment of Investment-Credit Reserves

Companies that switched to the flow-through method for the investment credit varied in their treatment of reserves that had been built up in previous years. About half took the previous years' deferred credits directly into current income, thereby inflating earnings for the most recent year even more. A number of companies made no reference to the treatment of this reserve. The remainder continued to amortize the reserve over a period of years, took the reserve into retained earnings,[31] or transferred it to the federal income tax liability account. These remaining firms thus did not try to increase the current year's earnings by the use of credits developed in previous years.

We subdivided investment-credit switchers into three groups according to their treatment of the previous years' reserves, and we made a plot of the mean cumulative abnormal return, U_t, for each group. The mean cumulative returns of the firms that took the reserve directly into current income or did not report their treatment replicated the pattern reported in figure 1, Panel A. Firms that took a more conservative treatment of the reserve performed more like the control group in figure 1, Panel B. Therefore, the downward trend that is apparent in figure 1, Panel A, is due solely to companies that attempted to obtain the maximum impact from earnings manipulation. Firms that were really performing better were less likely to have made an accounting change.

---

[31]Such as by restating a prior year's income.

Effect of Prior Announcement of Accounting Change

The sample of companies which switched from accelerated to straight-line depreciation was subdivided according to whether the change was announced prior to or simultaneously with the fiscal-year earnings report. We were trying to determine whether investors respond differently to the fiscal-year earnings report when they had prior knowledge of the accounting change. Because there were only a small number of companies in each group, the results are only suggestive.

Those companies that announced the accounting change prior to the fiscal-year earnings report (in week 31) had an increasing mean cumulative abnormal return, U_t, prior to week 31. As with the investment-credit switchers, a steady decline in U_t started in week 43 and reached zero by week 60.

Companies which postponed announcement of the accounting change until the year-end report had a declining mean cumulative abnormal return prior to week 30, a greater positive movement in weeks 30–39, but a steady decline thereafter that became significantly negative by week 60. Thus, the companies that were more honest in announcing their intentions in advance fared somewhat better. This could again be due to a selection effect, with firms whose fortunes were on the wane postponing the announcement until the last possible moment in an attempt to get a bigger impact from the increased earnings arranged by a depreciation change.

A final subdivision of the depreciation-switching companies was created by placing all companies that switched in 1968 in one group and all those that switched in prior years in another group. We were trying to determine whether investors had become more perceptive over time, so that smaller transient effects would be observed for companies that switched methods in 1968. In fact, just the opposite result was suggested. The plot of U_t for those companies that switched prior to 1968 was virtually identical to that obtained for the entire sample. (This is not totally surprising, of course, since these companies comprised five-sevenths of the total sample.) The companies that switched in 1968 exhibited a strong positive price movement in advance of the year-end announcement date, and this level was maintained for about twelve weeks. But again, a decline started around week 43 which returned the mean cumulative abnormal return back to its level prior to week 20. This movement, however, could have been a random fluctuation (the sample size was only twenty-one).

Abstracting from Industry Effects

As mentioned before, there were some industries in which several firms switched back from accelerated to straight-line depreciation in the same year. Professor Ray Ball pointed out that such coincidental action might have confounded the results. Since the sample size of the depreciation group is relatively small (seventy-one) and since a small but significant proportion of a security's price variation can be explained by an industry factor,[32] he argued correctly that the ability of cross-sectional averaging to eliminate factors other than the accounting change from the "abnormal return" may have been hampered. To make a rough measure of the possible bias introduced, we recomputed the abnormal returns for the depreciation group after taking out the industry effect for the four most heavily represented industries[33] in the sample. This was accomplished by adding a third explanatory variable, the return on an industry index,[34] to regression model (2). Then the abnormal return was calculated net of this industry index return (and net of the total market return and the interest rate, too). The results can scarcely be distinguished from those reported in figure 1, Panel C, and in table B1, Panel C, for depreciation changes where the effect of heavily represented industries was not eliminated.[35]

VI. Summary

Earnings manipulation may be fun, but its profitability is doubtful. We have had difficulty discerning any statistically significant effect that it has had on security prices. Relying strictly on averages, however, one can conclude that

---

[32] The first and definitive study of the industry factor was by Benjamin F. King, "Market and Industry Factors in Stock Price Behavior," *Journal of Business* 39, suppl. (January 1966): 139–90

[33] These industries were steels, nine firms; papers, eight firms; cement, four firms; and glass and metal containers, three firms; these comprised a total of twenty-four of the seventy-one firms in the sample. No other industry was represented by more than two firms.

[34] The industry index return was defined by

$$R_{i,t} = \log_e [\text{IND}_{i,t}/\text{IND}_{i,t-1}],$$

where $\text{IND}_{j,t}$ is the Standard and Poor index for industry i at time t. It might have been better to construct an industry index that is orthogonal to the market index (see King, n. 32 above). However, the uniformly significant industry and total market coefficients in all twenty-four cases where the industry factor was included led us to believe that multi-collinearity was not a serious problem. In the twenty-four regressions, the lowest t-ratio associated with the industry effect was 1.8 and only three were below 3.0. Among the t-ratios associated with the total market return, nineteen of twenty-four were above 3.0.

[35] The patterns are almost identical. The only difference is a small downward shift in the abnormal returns from weeks 10 through 60. For example, the cumulative abnormal returns (U_t's) were previously –5.058 percent in week 52 and –0.31 percent in week 38 (U_t reached a relative peak in week 38). After we abstracted from the four industries, these cumulative abnormal returns were $U_{52} = -6.00$ and $U_{38} = -1.59$ percent. If anything, this strengthens our conclusion that switching back to straight-line depreciation has little permanent effect. In addition, the temporary effect is lowered. Previously, the cumulative abnormal return increased 2.24 percent from week 28 to week 38. After we netted out the industry return; this temporary increase was only 1.85 percent.

security prices increase around the date when a firm announces earnings inflated by an accounting change. The effect appears to be temporary, and, certainly by the subsequent quarterly report, the price has resumed a level appropriate to the true economic status of the firm. In the present sample, firms that manipulated earnings seem to have been performing poorly. If this is generally true, one would predict that earnings manipulation, once discovered, is likely to have a depressing effect on market price because it conveys an unfavorable management view of a firm's economic condition.

8

Portfolio Analysis, Stock Valuation and Capital Budgeting Decision Rules for Risky Projects

Richard C. Stapleton

I. Introduction

This paper derives decision rules for corporate capital budgeting when cash flows resulting from the acceptance of projects are risky. The decision rules are in terms of a project's discounted value and rate of return, the two familiar measures of investment profitability under certainty.[1] The analysis of capital projects assumes throughout that stock values are determined in perfect capital markets and also ignores complications which arise due to taxation of corporations and individuals. The results are therefore of theoretical rather than direct practical relevance.

A capital project may be defined as profitable, and should be accepted by a shareholder's wealth maximizing corporation if, and only if, acceptance of it adds to the stock value of the corporation more than it costs the shareholders. The prerequisite for developing capital budgeting decision rules is, therefore, a theory of stock valuation. The questions answered in this paper include the following. What is the stock value of the corporation in terms of its future, risky cash flow, earnings, and dividends? What determines the cost of capital to a corporation? How can the relevant or significant risk of a capital project be measured? Given measures of the relevant risk of a project's cash flows, how can the project be evaluated?

Sharpe [14] and Lintner [5, 6] have shown convincingly that the stock value of a corporation cannot be determined from information regarding the size and risk of the corporation's dividend stream alone. Some risk attaching to

Reprinted with permission of the author and publisher from *The Journal of Finance*, Vol. 26, no. 1, March 1971, pp. 95–117. I would like to thank the referee for helpful comments and suggestions.

[1]Lintner [5] has developed rules for corporate capital budgeting under uncertainty. The simpler rules developed here stem from one approximation introduced in section II which has the same effect as an assumption used by Sharpe [14] in his portfolio model. The decision rules differ considerably from those suggested in recent texts on corporation finance (see for example Van Horne [19], chs. 4 and 5), in that they result from valuation models developed in a portfolio framework. Similar attempts to develop capital budgeting rules from the Sharpe-Lintner portfolio models have been made by Tuttle and Litzenberger [18] and Litzenberger [8]. Another recent contribution which includes corporate leverage in a portfolio valuation model is that of Hamada [3].

returns on a corporation's stock can be avoided by shareholders holding a portfolio of many stocks. Risk that cannot be avoided by holding a well diversified portfolio of stocks is 'significant' risk and is relevant to valuation. The implication of portfolio analysis is clear. Stock values of individual corporations can only be determined when stocks are viewed as part of a portfolio. Conventional analyses of stock value in terms of the size and risk of corporate earnings or dividends such as found in Solomon [16] are inadequate. Section II of this paper develops a theory of stock valuation using a multi-period portfolio model. In this section a new definition and measure of the relevant risk of a dividend is derived. Section III proves a well known theorem that dividend policy is irrelevant to stock valuation given the investment policy of the corporation.[2] This result allows the stock value of a corporation to be expressed in terms either of its net cash flow, its earnings or its dividend stream. The earnings model is then used to find the determinants of the 'cost of equity capital' to the corporation.

Section IV employs the stock value theory of section III to derive optimal decision rules for the evaluation of individual capital projects. Three different approaches to project evaluation are considered. The first approach uses the probability distributions of the net discounted value (NDV), or the rate of return (R R) of a project to derive either the certainty equivalent NDV or the certainty equivalent RR. It is shown that if the certainty equivalent NDV of a project is positive it should be accepted by a shareholder wealth maximising corporation. Similarly if the certainty equivalent RR exceeds the rate of interest the project should be accepted. The second approach derives these same certainty equivalent measures of investment value by computing the certainty equivalent cash flows of the project. The third and most complicated approach uses the expected value of the cash flows of the project. These cash flows may be discounted at a risk-adjusted discount rate to compute the certainty equivalent NDV of the project. Alternatively, the expected RR of the project may be computed from the expected cash flows and compared with a risk adjusted discount rate or required rate of return which is dependent on the risk of the project. As Lintner [5] has pointed out, this risk adjusted discount rate is hard to determine.[3] In section IV it is shown that it is possible to simplify analysis using risk-adjusted discount rates by modifying the definition of the rate of return. It is proved that all three approaches, each of which allows of a net present value and rate of return variant, lead to identical accept-reject capital budgeting decisions.

---

[2]Miller and Modigliani [11] prove the irrelevance of dividend policy, given investment policy, in the absence of transaction costs and personal taxes.

[3]Robichek and Myers [13], Ch. 5, have pointed out some of the dangers and anomalies of using an average risk-adjusted discount rate to evaluate project cash flows.

II. Portfolio Analysis and the Stock Value of a Corporation

General Approaches to Stock Valuation

It has been shown, if (1) capital markets are perfect, and (2) the future is known with certainty, that the stock value of the corporation is the present value of its future dividends, discounted at the market rate of interest.[4] If dividend payments $d_1, d_2, ---, d_n$ are to be made at future points in time, $1, 2, ---, n$, and if the market rate of interest is i per period, the stock value of the corporation at time 0, after the payment of time 0 dividend, is

$$P_0 = \sum_{t=1}^{n} d_t (1 + i)^{-t} \tag{1}$$

The contribution to the stock value of the corporation of a particular dividend d_t is

$$d_t (1 + i)^{-t}$$

and depends upon the dividend's size and timing.

If each future dividend $d_1, d_2 ---, d_n$ is a random variable possessing a known normal probability distribution, the size of a particular dividend d_t may be measured by its expected value, $E(d_t)$, and its standard deviation, σ_{dt}, is a measure of its risk. The contribution of such a dividend to the stock value of the corporation will be dependent upon its size, risk and timing. There are two possible ways of stating the contribution of d_t to stock value. The contribution is

$$C(d_t)(1 + i)^{-t}$$

---

[4]See for example Miller and Modigliani [11]. One important qualification of the above statement should be noted. Since the stock value of the corporation at a point in time t is the total value of the stock in issue at time t, the future dividends will be paid to holders of the stock in issue at time t only if no new issues of stock are made at future points in time. If new issues are to be made in the future, some proportion of the corporation's dividends in periods subsequent to the new issues will not accrue to the holders of the stock to be valued at time t. There are two ways of overcoming this problem. Dividends entering valuation equations may be defined net of the dividends receivable on stock to be issued in the future. Alternatively, dividends may be defined as the net cash flows between the corporation and its shareholders, that is net of any new issue contributions made by the shareholders. This second definition of the dividend stream is adopted in this paper as there is a simple relationship between dividends so defined and the net cash flows received by the corporation.

where $C(d_t)$ is the certainty equivalent of the dividend, d_t, derived in some way from its probability distribution, and where i is the riskless rate of interest.[5] Alternatively the contribution is

$$E(d_t)(1 + \bar{r}_t)^{-t}$$

where $\bar{r}_t$ is a risk-adjusted discount rate determined by the riskless rate i, and the risk of the dividend d_t. The stock value of a corporation may therefore be given by

$$P_0 = \sum_{t=1}^{n} C(d_t)(1 + i)^{-t} \tag{2}$$

or by[6]

$$P_0 = \sum_{t=1}^{n} E(d_t)(1 + \bar{r}_t)^{-t} \tag{3}$$

A third and very convenient formulation of stock value is

$$P_0 = C(DVd) \tag{4}$$

where DVd is the discounted value of dividends computed by discounting future dividends at the riskless rate of interest, i. The stock value equation (4) follows from a special case of (2) and the meaning of discounted value. Consider the special case where a corporation is to pay only one dividend, d_0, payable immediately, and assume that d_0 is a random variable. From (2), the value of the corporation's stock is

$$P_0 = C(d_0) \tag{2a}$$

---

[5] Note that $C(d_t)$ should be read as "the certainty equivalent of d_t" and not as "d_t multiplied by C." C is used as an operator similar to E in $E(d_t)$ which is to be read as the "expected value of d_t."

[6] There must also be some average discount rate $\bar{r}$ which satisfies the equation

$$P_0 = \sum_{t=1}^{n} E(d_t)(1 + \bar{r})^{-t} \tag{3a}$$

However, this formulation of stock value leads to many problems since only under very special circumstances will $\bar{r} = \bar{r}_1 = \bar{r}_2 = \cdots = \bar{r}_n$, and only in this case is (3a) a useful generalization of (3). See Robichek and Myers [13], ch. 5, pp. 79–86.

where $C(d_0)$, the certainty equivalent of the immediate dividend, is derived from its probability distribution. Now by the definition of discounted value a stream of future dividends with discounted value DVd is of identical value to a single immediate dividend of $d_0 = DVd$. If the future dividends of a corporation when discounted form a probability distribution of DVd

$$
\begin{array}{cc}
p_1 & DVd_1 \\
p_2 & DVd_2 \\
\cdot & \cdot \\
\cdot & \cdot \\
\cdot & \cdot \\
p_h & DVd_h
\end{array}
$$

this probability distribution can be treated as equivalent to a probability distribution of immediate dividends:

$$
\begin{array}{cc}
p_1 & d_{10} \\
p_2 & d_{20} \\
\cdot & \cdot \\
\cdot & \cdot \\
\cdot & \cdot \\
p_h & d_{h0}
\end{array}
$$

Since from (2a) the stock value of a corporation which is to pay an immediate dividend, d_0, is the certainty equivalent of that dividend, the stock value of a corporation paying a stream of future dividends must be as shown by (4).[7]

The equations (2), (3), and (4) represent three approaches to stock valuation theory when future dividends are subject to risk. The theoretical problems remain in determining, either in equation (2), the certainty equivalents, $C(d_t)$, for each future dividend from the probability distributions of the d_t, or in equation (3), the risk adjusted discount rates which discount the expected dividends, $E(d_t)$, to their market value, or in equation (4), the certainty equivalent discounted value of the dividend stream, $C(DVd)$, from the probability distribution of that discounted value.

The second approach to valuation appears to be the most popular in the literature in spite of the fact that its theoretical basis is the most complex.[8] Note that the first and third approaches, which determine the $C(d_t)$ and $C(DVd)$

---

[7] Forming a probability distribution of discounted value to analyze the risk of cash flows from an investment project is suggested by Lutz and Lutz [9], pp. 179–192. The approach is also used by Lintner [5].

[8] For example both Sharpe [14] and Lintner [5] derive the one period expected rate of return from holding stocks.

from probability distributions of d_t and DVd respectively, separate the theoretical effect of risk on valuation from the effect of timing. Thus, determining the $C(d_t)$ from probability distributions of the d_t considers the effect of risk first. The certainty equivalent dividends may then be substituted in (2) to yield stock value. By forming a probability distribution of the discounted value of dividends, DVd, the third approach considers the effect of dividend timing before determining the effect of risk on value. The second approach attempts to solve for stock value by finding risk-adjusted discount rates which simultaneously account for the risk and timing of dividends. It is the most complex approach for this reason. In this paper the third approach is adopted since, compared with the first, it avoids the multiperiod problem of determining the effect of risk on each future dividend. By forming the probability distribution of the discounted value of dividends, the risk-valuation problem becomes equivalent to finding the certainty equivalent of a single immediate dividend from its probability distribution.

Certainty Equivalent Values from Portfolio Theory

Sharpe [14] and Lintner [5, 6] have derived the relationship between the expected rate of return on a stock and the rate of interest. Their major results may be used in deriving the parallel relationship between the expected discounted value of dividends from holding a stock and the market value of the stock. If there are k corporations' stocks on the market and if the probability distributions of the discounted value of dividends are known for each of the k corporations, the problem is to derive the stock value for any corporation j from the probability distribution of DVd_j. The solution follows from an analysis of investors' portfolio selections.

An investor with an amount of funds F at time 0 has to decide what proportions α_k of F to invest in the stocks of the k corporations whose stocks are on the market. Given the market prices of a share of each of the k corporations' stocks, the investor knows how many shares of each corporation's stock he could obtain if he invested all of his funds F in a particular stock. Given also the probability distributions of the discounted value of dividends to be paid in total by each corporation he can compute the probability distribution of V_k, the discounted value of the dividends he would receive from investing all his funds F in the stocks of corporation k. For convenience, V_k will be termed the return from investing funds F in the stock of corporation k. By investing funds F in the stock of a particular corporation j the investor receives a return with expected value, $E(V_j)$, and standard deviation, σ_{Vj}. However, by investing proportions α_k in the k corporations' stocks, he may diversify and obtain a portfolio return on his funds F with expected value $E(V)$ and standard deviation σ_V. An efficient portfolio for the risk averse investor may be defined as one which maximises the expected return $E(V)$ on funds F for a given level of risk σ_V.[9] The portfolio returns on the line DMH in Figure 1 are returns on efficient portfolios if the investor is required to invest all his funds in the k corporations' stocks. However, by investing only a proportion of F in the portfolio yielding the return M in Figure 1, and the remainder of F in bonds yielding a certain rate of interest, i, he may obtain any return on the line MF.[10] All portfolios yielding returns on DM are therefore sub-optimal. Similarly, if the investor may borrow additional funds at the market rate of interest he may obtain any return on MG, and all portfolios yielding returns on MH are also sub-optimal.[11]

To attain his desired risk, expected return position the investor will first choose the optimal portfolio, M, and then either invest a proportion of his

---

[9]The assumption that the probability distribution of all dividends are known means that investors' expectations are homogeneous. Each investor is faced with the same set of efficient portfolios shown in Fig. 1. It is also assumed that investors are risk averse (i.e., their indifference curves are concave to the $E(V)$ axis in Figure 1). This assumption does not imply that all investors have identical risk-return preferences. For a discussion of these points see Markovitz [10], Sharpe [4], or Lintner [5, 6].

[10]Investment of an amount F in bonds yields a series of interest payments whose discounted value is by definition equal to F. Investment of a proportion $(1 - \alpha)$ of F in the portfolio yielding return M and a proportion α of F in bonds yields the investor a return with expected value

$$E(V) = (1 - \alpha)E(V_M) + \alpha F \tag{5}$$

and standard deviation

$$\sigma_V = (1 - \alpha)\sigma_{VM} \tag{6}$$

Substituting from (6) in (5) yields the relationship

$$E(V) = F + \frac{[E(V_M) - F]\sigma_V}{\sigma_{VM}} \tag{7}$$

which is linear. Investment of a proportion of F in the portfolio yielding return M and the remainder in bonds yields a return on the line MF in Fig. 1.

[11]If the investor borrows an amount αF at the interest rate, i, the discounted value of his future interest payments is αF. Investing his increased funds $(1 + \alpha F)$ in the portfolio yielding return M gives him a net return with expected value

$$E(V) = (1 + \alpha)E(V_M) - \alpha F \tag{5a}$$

and standard deviation

$$\sigma_V = (1 + \alpha)\sigma_{VM} \tag{6a}$$

Substitution of (6a) in (5a) yields equation (7) of the previous footnote. The return from "levering up" the portfolio with return M lies on the same straight line FMG in Fig. 1, this time to the right of point M.

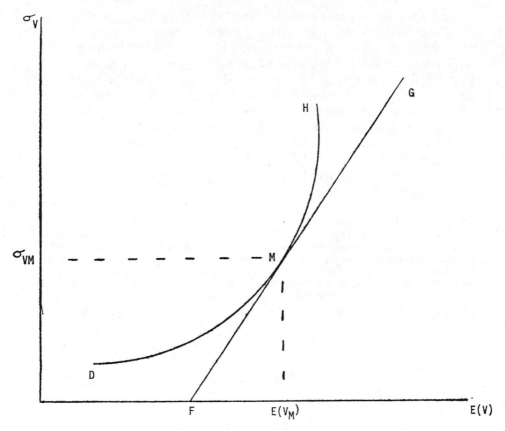

Figure 1. Portfolio Solution.

funds in the portfolio and a proportion in bonds, or lever himself up to invest more than his initial funds, F, in the portfolio.[12]

The slope of the line *FMG* is important in the subsequent analysis. It is given by S' in

$$\sigma_V = S'[E(V) - F] \tag{8}$$

The value of S' may be derived by noting that the return on the optimal portfolio M is given by a point on the line. Thus

---

[12]Since all investors will invest in the same portfolio M, satisfying their individual risk preferences by borrowing or lending to invest more or less than their original funds, the proportions α_k of the individual stocks making up the portfolio M must equal the ratios of the market values of the stocks to the total market value of all stocks, if the market is to be in equilibrium. The portfolio M may there be termed *the market portfolio* (see Fama [2]).

$$\sigma_{VM} = S'[E(V_M) - F] \tag{8a}$$

and

$$S' = \frac{\sigma_{VM}}{[E(V_M) - F]} \tag{9}$$

The reciprocal of S'

$$S = 1/S' = \frac{E(V_M) - F}{\sigma_{VM}} \tag{10}$$

may be termed the *market risk aversion factor,* since by rearranging (10),

$$F = E(V_M) - S\sigma_{VM} \tag{11}$$

states that the certainty equivalent or market value of the return V_M equals its expected value less an amount S times its standard deviation. F is the market value of V_M since V_M can be purchased by investing F in the portfolio M.

Both Sharpe [14] and Lintner [6] derive the risk premium for an individual corporation's stock.[13] They each show that

$$E(V_j) - F = \left[\frac{E(V_M) - F}{\sigma_{VM}^2} \right] \text{Cov}(V_j, V_M) \tag{12}$$

The excess of the expected return on a particular stock j over its purchase price is linearly dependent on the covariance of the return on the stock j with the return on the optimal portfolio M. The result in (12) may be restated in terms of the market risk aversion factor S and the relevant risk of return on stock j by noting that the correlation between the return on stock j and the return on the optimal portfolio is defined as

$$R_{jM} = \frac{\text{Cov}(V_j, V_M)}{\sigma_{Vj}\sigma_{VM}} \tag{13}$$

---

[13]Sharpe's and Lintner's models yield an expression for the excess of the expected rate of return on a stock over the rate of interest. Exactly the same argument may be used to derive the excess $E(V_j) - F$ in the equation (12) by substituting the discounted value of dividends V_j for the rate of return on stock, and the invested amount F for the rate of interest, i. Fama [2] proves that the Sharpe and Lintner models are identical with respect to their conclusions regarding the risk premium. Specifically Fama shows that the expression for the risk premium derived by Sharpe [14, footnote 22] is identical to Lintner's [6, equation 11]. Thus equation (12) derives from either model.

Equation (12) can therefore be written as

$$E(V_j) - F = \left[\frac{E(V_M) - F}{\sigma_{VM}}\right] R_{jM} \sigma_{Vj} \qquad (12a)$$

or, substituting from (10),

$$E(V_j) - F = S R_{jM} \sigma_{Vj} \qquad (12b)$$

Rearranging (12b) yields

$$F = E(V_j) - S R_{jM} \sigma_{Vj} \qquad (14)$$

Equation (14) states that F, which is the market value of the return V_j, equals its expected value less an amount equal to the market risk aversion factor multiplied by its *relevant* risk. The relevant risk of the return on stock j is not its standard deviation but its standard deviation multiplied by the correlation between the return on the stock and the return on the optimal portfolio.

Equation (14) expresses the market value of a proportion of corporation j's stock. A proportion $E(V_j)/E(DVd_j)$ of j's stock can be purchased for the amount F, where $E(DVd_j)$ is the expected value of the discounted value of the dividends on the total stock of j. The value of j's outstanding stock is therefore

$$P_{0j} = F\frac{E(DVd_j)}{E(V_j)} = E(DVd_j) - S R_{jM} \sigma_{DVdj} \qquad (15)$$

where σ_{DVdj} is the standard deviation of discounted value of j's dividends.[14]

The equation (15) is the fundamental result of portfolio theory which will be used in this paper. Before using the result to analyze investment decisions a useful approximation to (15) is introduced and explained.

A Simplified Measure of Relevant Risk

The analysis of stock value and the corporation's capital budgeting decision that follows rests on one assumption which, if accepted as a reasonable approximation, allows a straightforward and simple solution to an otherwise

---

[14]Equation (15) follows from the fact that V_j is a proportion of the total return DVd_j and thus

$$\frac{\sigma Vj}{E(Vj)} = \frac{\sigma DVdj}{E(DVdj)}$$

complex problem. The immediate consequence of the assumption is that the relevant risk of a dividend, or of the discounted value of a stream of dividends, can be measured without forming inevitably complex probability distributions and without estimating correlations with an optimal portfolio return. The assumption is that

$$R_{jM} \triangleq R_{jm} \text{ (for all corporations } j) \tag{16}$$

where m is some index which is almost perfectly correlated with the return on the optimal portfolio M. The choice of the appropriate index m depends upon the determinants of the optimal portfolio return.

The optimal portfolio M is superior to other portfolios because it is diversified. The risks attaching to the returns of the individual stocks in the portfolio are in part avoided by holding the stocks in a portfolio. The risk which cannot be avoided in a portfolio of stocks is risk which affects all stocks held. Taking first an extreme example to illustrate the optimal portfolio, assume that the correlation between any two stocks on the market is zero. By forming a portfolio of all stocks it would be possible to avoid almost all the risk to which individual stocks were subject (given independence of returns, holding such a portfolio is akin to playing a game of chance a large number of times). However, only in the limit, when an infinite number of stocks make up the portfolio, is the risk of the portfolio zero. Also, with any finite number of stocks in the portfolio, the portfolio will be dependent to some extent on the return outcome of an individual stock, j. Thus $R_{jM} > 0$, although very small. For practical purposes it would be justifiable to use an approximation $R_{jM} = 0$.

Now assume that correlations between most stocks are positive, but less than unity, due to common dependence on future general economic conditions. Each stock's return is subject to risk because its dividends will be determined in part by the future state of the economy and to risk due to factors peculiar to the individual corporation. By combining these stocks in a portfolio it is the second type of risk that may be avoided. In the limit, the portfolio return will be perfectly correlated with an index of the future state of the economy, and the approximation (16) would be an equality.[15] The relationship in (16) is an approximation therefore to the extent that portfolios are not perfectly diversified. Since there are in practice a very large number of stocks on the market it is hard to see (16) not being a good approximation.[16]

---

[15]If m is the index and the optimal portfolio return is perfectly correlated with m, R_{Mm} = 1, and R_{jM} must equal R_{jm}.

[16]Lintner's analysis [5] is excessively complex because he does not assume perfect diversification of portfolios. Sharpe [14] makes a slight error in his analysis which has exactly the same effect as the approximation introduced in the text. Fama [2] argues that the differences between Lintner and Sharpe are in practice trivial.

Assuming that the return, V_M, on the optimal portfolio is solely determined by the future state of the economy, the most sensible index, m, is the growth rate of GNP. The return V_M is the discounted value of a future stream of dividends, and since individual dividends in the stream will be dependent upon the state of the economy at particular points in time, the discounted value of the stream will depend upon some weighted average of the states of the economy at future points in time. A seemingly appropriate weighted average is the growth rate of GNP.[17]

As R_{jm} is the linear correlation of the return on stock j and the index m, consider the linear regression of DVd_j on the index m. This is given by

$$DVD_j = a + bm + \epsilon \tag{18}$$

where a and b are constants and ϵ a random error term with expected value, $E(\epsilon) = 0$. By definition of the least squares estimate b,[18]

$$b\sigma_m = R_{jm}\sigma_{DVdj} \tag{19}$$

and $b > 0$ when $R_{jm} > 0$ and $b < 0$ when $R_{jm} < 0$.

If a new variable DVd'_j is defined by the equation

$$DVd'_j = a + bm \tag{20}$$

DVd'_j is the expected discounted value of dividends given a particular level of

---

[17]The choice of the appropriate index cannot strictly be determined *a priori.* The index chosen must satisfy the condition that it is almost perfectly linearly correlated with the optimal portfolio return. Although the growth rate of GNP does give weight to the state of economic activity in all future periods of time, it is not obvious that the optimal portfolio return will be linearly correlated with this index. The appropriate index may be the logarithm or some more complex function of the GNP growth rate. Choice of the index m must therefore await empirical conclusion as to the determination of returns on diversified portfolios.

[18]The correlation R_{jm} is defined as

$$R_{jm} = \frac{\text{COV}(DVdj, m)}{\sigma_m \sigma_{DVdj}}$$

and b is given by

$$b = \frac{\text{COV}(DVdj, m)}{\sigma_m^2}$$

Equation (19) follows directly from these two definitions.

the index m. The correlation between this new variable and the index m is either perfect positive or perfect negative. It follows from (20) that[19]

$$\sigma_{DVd'j} = b\sigma_m \qquad b > 0, R_{jm} > 0$$

$$\sigma_{DVd'j} = -b\sigma_m \qquad b < 0, R_{jm} < 0 \tag{21}$$

and since from (19), $b\sigma_m = R_{jm}\sigma_{DVdj}$,

$$\sigma_{DVd'j} = R_{jm}\sigma_{DVdj} \qquad b > 0, R_{jm} > 0$$

$$\sigma_{DVd'j} = -R_{jm}\sigma_{DVdj} \qquad b < 0, R_{jm} < 0 \tag{22}$$

The stock valuation equation (17) may therefore be rewritten as

$$P_{0j} = E(DVd_j) - S\,\sigma_{DVd'j} \qquad R_{jm} > 0$$

$$= E(DVd_j) + S\,\sigma_{DVd'j} \qquad R_{jm} < 0 \tag{23}$$

(The subsequent discussion will use (23) assuming $R_{jm} > 0$ which is the general case. It should be borne in mind that all following conclusions are reversed for the case of "defensive" stocks or investments where returns are negatively correlated with the index m.)

The advantage of the measure of relevant risk in (23) is that the probability distribution of DVd'_j is very easy to form. The probability distribution of DVd'_j gives the expected discounted value of dividends for each level of the index m, and the probability of each value of m. For a given level of m, DVd'_j is found by discounting the stream of expected dividends, given this level of m at the rate of interest. Since from (18) and (20) $E(DVd'_j) = E(DVd_j)$, the probability distribution of DVd'_j provides all the information required to solve for the stock value of corporation j (apart of course from the market risk aversion factor S). Table 1 illustrates the information required to compute the expected value and standard deviation of DVd' (the subscript referring to the particular corporation is dropped for notational convenience). Expected divi-

---

[19]When DVd'_j and m are perfectly and positively correlated:

$$COV(DVd'j, m) = \sigma_m \sigma_{DVd'j}$$

and

$$b = \frac{\sigma DVd'j}{\sigma_m}$$

Table 1
Information for Computation of Relevant Risk

State of Index, m	Probability of Index State	Expected Dividends Given Index State		
		Time 1	2	...n
1	p_1	d'_{11}	$d'_{12} \ldots d'_{1n}$	
2	p_2	d'_{21}	$d'_{22} \ldots d'_{2n}$	
.	.	.	. ... .	
.	.	.	. ... .	
.	.	.	. ... .	
h	p_h	d'_{h1}	$d'_{h2} \ldots d'_{hn}$	

dends form a matrix of order $h \times n$ if there are h possible states of the index m, and n future points in time at which dividends could be paid. Note that, since the rows of the matrix contain elements which have identical probabilities, the expected dividends $d'_1, d'_2 \text{ ---}, d'_n$ to be paid at future points in time are perfectly correlated.[20] This property implies that there are two equivalent methods of computing $E(DVd)$ and $\sigma_{DVd'}$. First, the probability distribution of DVd' may be formed as in Table 2. Alternatively these quantities may be computed from the probability distributions of the d'_t since

$$E(DVd) = \sum_{t=1}^{n} E(d'_t)(1 + i)^{-t} \tag{24}$$

and, due to the perfect correlation of the d'_t,[21]

$$\sigma_{DVd'} = \sum_{t=1}^{n} \sigma_{d'_t}(1 + i)^{-t} \tag{25}$$

---

[20]It is important to note that no restrictive assumptions have been made regarding the probability distributions of individual dividends in the stream of future dividends. Whatever the degree of dependence or independence of the dividends d_t in the stream, the d'_t which are expected dividends given the state of the index m must be perfectly correlated with each other by definition. The crucial advantage of the equation (23) formulation of stock value is that only risk due to the index state m need be considered. Although the actual probability distributions of the d_t may take on any form, all that is required for stock value determination are the streams of *expected* dividends for different states of the index, m, and the probability distribution of m.

[21]See Hillier [4], pp. 447–449.

Table 2
Probability Distribution of Dividend Discounted Value

State of Index m	Probability of Index State	Present Value of Dividends
1	p_1	$DVd'_1 = \displaystyle\sum_{t=1}^{n} d'_{1t}(1+i)^{-t}$
2	p_2	$DVd'_2 = \displaystyle\sum_{t=1}^{n} d'_{2t}(1+i)^{-t}$
. . .	. . .	. . .
h	p_h	$DVd'_h = \displaystyle\sum_{t=1}^{n} d'_{ht}(1+i)^{-t}$

Using the relationships in (24) and (25) it is now possible to redefine the stock value in terms of certainty equivalent dividends, i.e., to solve for the values $C(d_t)$ in equation (2). Substitution of (24) and (25) in (23) yields

$$P_0 = \sum_{t=1}^{n} E(d'_t)(1+i)^{-t} - S\left[\sum_{t=1}^{n} \sigma_{d't}(1+i)^{-t}\right]$$

$$= \sum_{t=1}^{n} [E(d'_t) - S\sigma_{d't}](1+i)^{-t} \tag{23a}$$

The certainty equivalent values of the dividends d_t in equation (2) have therefore been shown to be given by

$$C(d_t) = E(d'_t) - S\sigma_{d't}$$

The market risk aversion factor, S, may be used to compute the certainty equivalent of each dividend in the future stream.

III. Earnings and Cash Flow Models of Stock Value and the Cost of Equity Capital

The theory of stock value developed in section II is a dividend theory. The stock value is the value of future dividends (the future cash flow between the corporation and its shareholders). Capital projects, however, subtract from and add to the cash flow of the corporation and only indirectly affect the future dividend stream. This section provides a vital link between the dividend stock value theory of section II and the analysis of projects in terms of their cash flow effect in section IV.

Net Cash Flow and Corporate Earnings

The net cash flow of a corporation $X_1, X_2, ---, X_n$ states the future net cash returns or net outlays receivable or payable by a corporation and available for distribution to shareholders. The net cash flow depends upon the assets owned by the corporation and its future investment policy. Net cash flow therefore includes returns from assets currently owned and the costs and returns from all future investments. Corporate earnings may be defined as the maximum perpetuity dividend that a corporation could pay given this net cash flow and the rate of interest i, at which it may borrow and lend.[22] When net cash flow is known with certainty, earnings may be defined as Y in the equation

$$\frac{Y}{i} = \sum_{t=1}^{n} X_t (1 + i)^{-t} \qquad (27)$$

By borrowing and lending appropriate quantities of cash at the interest rate, i, the corporation can change the net cash flow $X_1, X_2, ---, X_n$ into a perpetuity Y which has the same discounted value as the net cash flow.[23]

---

[22]This definition is essentially that used by Lintner [7], p. 55. The maximum perpetual dividend may be termed earnings because a dividend equal to this amount may be paid out by a corporation without diminishing its subsequent earnings and (given a constant interest rate) its capital value. Note that as the cash returns of all future investments are included in net cash flow, earnings as defined do take account of future investment opportunities. Earnings should not be interpreted as earnings solely from the currently owned assets of the corporation. The earnings definition given in the text thus differs from that used by Miller and Modigliani [11].

[23]The definition of earnings in equations (27) and (28) holds when the interest rate i is assumed constant through time. If the rate of interest changes over time the computation of earnings would be more complex. Earnings defined as the maximum perpetual dividend

Earnings are therefore:

$$Y = i \sum_{t=1}^{n} X_t (1 + i)^{-t} \tag{28}$$

When each element in the net cash flow stream is subject to risk, earnings will be subject to risk and, given the section II conclusions as to relevant risk, the probability distribution of earnings may be formed.[24] If, for any given state h of the index m, the expected net cash flow is $X'_{h1}, X'_{h2}, ---, X'_{hn}$, expected earnings given this index state are

$$Y'_h = i \sum_{t=1}^{n} X'_{ht} (1 + i)^{-t} \tag{29}$$

$$= iDVX'_h \tag{29a}$$

where DVX'_h is the discounted value of expected cash flows given the index state h.

The expected earnings $E(Y)$ and a measure of the relevant risk of earnings, $\sigma_{Y'}$ may be then computed from the probability distribution of Y'.

Stock Value When Net Cash Flow or Earnings
Paid as Dividends

The first dividend policy to be considered is that of paying out net cash flow as dividends. If net cash flow is paid out as dividends then $d_t = X_t$ for all points in time t, and the X_t may be substituted in either (23) or (23a) to yield stock value. Substitution in (23) yields

$$P_0 = E(DVX) - S \sigma_{DVX'} \tag{30}$$

$$= C(DVX)$$

---

that could be paid would be computed by discounting cash flows period by period at the appropriate rates and then solving for that perpetuity Y which, given the period rates of interest, had the same discounted value.

[24]It will again be assumed that the interest rate is constant over time. Further it is assumed throughout that the interest rate is not itself subject to risk. If the interest rate is itself influenced by the level of the index, m, the expected interest rate given the state of m would have to be used to compute expected earnings for that state.

The stock value is the certainty equivalent of the discounted net cash flow. Substitution in (23a) yields

$$P_0 = \sum_{t=1}^{n} [E(X'_t) - S\sigma_{X'_t}](1 + i)^{-t} \tag{30a}$$

The stock value is the discounted value of the certainty equivalent cash flows in the net cash flow stream.

A second dividend policy is the payment of earnings as dividends. Payments of earnings as dividends means that

$$d_1 = d_2 = \cdots = d_\infty = Y \tag{31}$$

and each dividend has an expected value, $E(Y)$, and relevant risk, $\sigma_{Y'}$. Substitution of (31) in the stock value equation (23) yields

$$P_0 = E(DVY) - S\sigma_{DVY'} \tag{32}$$

Similarly substitution in (23a) yields

$$P_0 = \sum_{t=1}^{n} [E(Y') - S\sigma_{Y'}](1 + i)^{-t} \tag{32a}$$

which with $n \to \infty$ reduces to

$$P_0 = \frac{E(Y') - S\sigma_{Y'}}{i} = \frac{C(Y)}{i} \tag{32b}$$

Stock value is the present value of certainty equivalent earnings.

It can now be easily verified that (30) and (32) yield identical values and that under the assumptions of this analysis it does not matter which of the two dividend policies is adopted by the corporation.[25] From the definition of earnings for a given state h of the index m in (29a), the discounted value of earnings for that level is given by

---

[25] The relevant assumptions are that the investment policy of the company and thus net cash flow is unaffected by dividend policy, that the company can borrow and lend at the rate of interest and that there are no investor taxes. The dividend policy irrelevance proposition has been proved by Miller and Modigliani [11]. The conclusion is affected by the presence of transactions costs and differential taxes on dividends and capital gains.

$$DVY'_h = DVX'_h \tag{33}$$

Thus (30) and (32) are identical. It could similarly be shown that given the net cash flow of a corporation any dividend policy will produce a stock value in (23) or (23a) identical to the stock values in (30) or (30a) and (32) and (32a). Dividend policy is irrelevant to stock valuation and either the dividend, cash flow, or earnings model of stock value may be used.

The Cost of Equity Capital

The expected rate of return to share holders who buy the stock of a corporation is often referred to as the cost of equity capital to the corporation. The expected rate of return from purchasing the stock of a corporation j and holding the stock indefinitely is defined by r_j in[26]

$$P_{0j} = \sum_{t=1}^{n} E(d_{tj})(1 + r_j)^{-t} \tag{34}$$

where r_j is an average risk adjusted discount rate which discounts expected dividends into equality with stock value. If earnings are paid out as dividends, (34) simplifies to

$$P_{0j} = \frac{E(Y_j)}{r_j} \tag{35}$$

showing that r_j is the expected earnings yield on the stock. The value of r_j may be determined by equating (35) with stock value equation (32b). This substitution yields

$$r_j = \frac{i}{1 - So_{Y'_j}/E(Y_j)} \tag{36}$$

The expected rate of return on the stock depends upon the rate of interest, i, the relevant risk of earnings as measured by the ratio $\sigma_{Y'_j}/E(Y_j)$, and the market risk aversion factor S. The value of r_j in (36) is often referred to as the "cost of

---

[26]If any of the future dividends are negative, i.e., new issue contributions by shareholders (see footnote 4), the rate of return may have to be redefined. The same problems arise as those encountered in project evaluation when sign changes occur in the cash flow stream. For a full discussion of this sign change problem see Duguid and Laski [1], or Teichroew, Robichek, Montalbano [17].

equity capital" to the corporation because under certain (restrictive) circumstances it is the minimum expected rate of return that a corporation may earn
on the investment of additional shareholders funds. The investment decision is
the subject of section IV.

IV. Capital Budgeting Decision Rules for Risky Projects

For the purposes of this paper a capital project will be defined as an opportunity to invest a certain amount of cash, X_0, at time 0, which has the effect of
changing the future cash flows to the corporation. It will be assumed that the
project is to be financed by equity capital raised from a new issue of shares,
and that the decision to be taken is whether to accept or reject the project.[27]
A wealth maximising corporation will accept such a project if the difference in
its stock value, due to accepting rather than rejecting the project, exceeds the
cost, X_0, which is to be raised from shareholders. If P_{0j} is the stock value of
company j if it rejects the investment and $P*_{0j}$ its stock value if it accepts the
project, then the condition for project acceptance is

$$P^*_{0j} - P_{0j} > X_0 \tag{37}$$

Let the net cash flow of the corporation without the project be $X_{1j}, X_{2j},$
$\ldots, X_{nj}$, and with the project, $X*_{1j}, X*_{2j}, \ldots, X*_{nj}$. From equation (30) the
stock value without the project must be

$$P_{0j} = E(DVX_j) - S\sigma_{DVX'j}$$

Stock value with the project is

$$P^*_{0j} = E(DVX^*_j) - S\sigma_{DVX*'j}$$

Substituting these two values in (37) yields the condition

$$E(DVX^*_j) - E(DVX_j) - S(\sigma_{DVX*'j} - \sigma_{DVX'j}) > X_0 \tag{37a}$$

The quantities in the condition for project acceptance (37a) may be determined
with reference only to the incremental cash flows produced by the project.
The incremental cash flows of the project are $X_1, X_2, \text{---}, X_n$, where X_t

---

[27]In the absence of taxes, exactly the same decision rules would apply if projects were
financed with debt capital. The Modigliani-Miller theorem assures this (see Modigliani and
Miller [12]). Complications arise because of the tax deductibility of interest payments but
these will not be explored in this paper. In this context see Hamada [3].

$= X^*_{tj} - X_{tj}$. The difference between the expected discounted values with and without the project must be the expected present value of the incremental cash flows resulting from acceptance of the project; thus,

$$E(DVX^*_j) - E(DVX_j) = E(DVX) \tag{38}$$

where $E(DVX)$ is the expected value of the discounted cash flows from the project. Second, it must be the case that

$$\sigma_{DVX'} = \sigma_{DVX*'j} - \sigma_{DVX'j} \tag{39}$$

where $\sigma_{DVX'}$ is computed from the probability distribution of DVX' which in turn is the expected value of the discounted cash flows of the project resulting from different states of the index, m. Equation (39) holds because the variables DVX'_j and DVX' are perfectly correlated.[28] They are determined by the outcome of the same event, the state of the index m. The advantage of the definition of relevant risk introduced in section II should now be clear. In effect it allows projects to be analyzed individually in terms of the relevant risk of the cash flow produced by the project. The relevant risk of the project's cash flow and that of the company's cash flow without the project are additive. The important conclusion of the portfolio theory that only relevant risk, which cannot be diversified by shareholders in stock portfolios, affects stock value means that the diversification effect of investments within the company can be ignored. The company cannot benefit its shareholders by diversifying investments within the company.[29]

Substitution of equations (38) and (39) in (37a) yields the condition for project acceptance,

$$E(DVX) - S\sigma_{DVX'} > X_0 \tag{37b}$$

---

[28] The standard deviation of the addition of two variables A and B is given by

$$\sigma_{AB} = \sqrt{\sigma_A^2 + \sigma_B^2 + 2R_{AB}\sigma_A\sigma_B}$$

when the two variables are perfectly correlated, $R_{AB} = 1$, and

$$\sigma_{AB} = \sigma_A + \sigma_B.$$

[29] This is not to say that there is no diversification effect when a new project is accepted. No restrictive assumption has been made regarding the correlation of the project cash flow and the cash flow without the project. If σ_{DVXj} measures the total risk of the discounted flows without the project (computed from the probability distribution of $DVXj$), and σ_{DVX} is a similar measure for the project, then if the cash flow discounted values are less than perfectly correlated σ_{DVX*j}, the total risk including the project will be less than the sum of σ_{DVXj} and σ_{DVX}. This is the diversification effect of the project. However, it is not total risk which determines value but relevant or nondiversifiable risk and the effect of the project on this risk must always be additive as shown in equation (39).

which is solely in terms of the project's cash flows. All the decision rules which follow derive from (37b).

Analysis of Projects Using Certainty Equivalent NDV and RR

The two most commonly advocated measures of investment worth are the Net Discounted Value (*NDV*) of a project, and the Rate of Return (RR) of the project. When projects yield risky cash flows, they can be evaluated by considering the probability distributions of NDV and RR. The decision rule in terms of *NDV* derives directly from the condition (37b).

As the initial cash outlay on the project, X_0, is assumed certain, the expected *NDV* of the project must be

$$E(NDV) = E(DVX) - X_0 \qquad (40)$$

Also, due to the assumption that X_0 is certain, the relevant risk of the net discounted value of the project must be the relevant risk of the discounted value of future cash flows

$$\sigma_{NDV'} = \sigma_{DVX'} \qquad (41)$$

Substituting in (37b) the condition for project acceptance becomes

$$E(NDV) - S\sigma_{NDV'} > 0 \qquad (42)$$

and if

$$C(NDV) = E(NDV) - S\sigma_{NDV'} \qquad (43)$$

is defined as the certainty equivalent net discounted value of the project, the project should be accepted if

$$C(NDV) > 0 \qquad (42a)$$

The first derived decision rule is therefore that a project should be accepted if its certainty equivalent *NDV* is positive. The certainty equivalent *NDV* may be found from the probability distribution of *NDV'*, if the market risk aversion factor S is known. To form the probability distribution of *NDV'*, the expected *NDV* is computed for each level of the index, m.

The rate of return of a project costing X_0 and yielding cash flows $X_1, X_2,$ - - -, X_n is normally defined as r in the equation

$$-X_0 + \sum_{t=1}^{n} X_t(1 + r)^{-t} = 0 \tag{44}$$

However, it has been shown that r in (44) may be an unreliable measure of project profitability if any of the cash flows $X_2, X_3, - - - X_n$ are negative.[30] An alternative and more general definition of the rate of return of a project will be used here, the perpetuity equivalent rate of return. This measure of profitability if defined as r_p in the equation

$$-X_0 + \frac{i \sum_{t=1}^{n} X_t(1 + i)^{-t}}{r_p} = 0 \tag{45}$$

The numerator of the second term in (45) is the perpetuity which has the same present value as the X_t, or the contribution of the X_t to the earnings of the corporation. Re-arranging (45) gives:

$$r_p = \frac{i \sum_{t=1}^{n} X_t(1 + i)^{-t}}{X_0} = \frac{i[NDV + X_0]}{X_0} \tag{46}$$

The certainty equivalent perpetuity rate of return can be calculated in a similar manner to the certainty equivalent NDV. If a probability distribution of r'_p is formed, and its expected value and standard deviation computed, the certainty equivalent rate of return is

$$C(r_p) = E(r'_p) - S\sigma_{r'p} \tag{47}$$

If this certainty equivalent rate of return is greater than the rate of interest, the project should be accepted.[31]

---

[30]More than one sign change is a necessary but not sufficient condition for r in equation (44) to fail as a measure of project profitability. For a thorough analysis of the sign change problem, see Duguid and Laski [1] or Teichroew, Robichek, Montalbano [17].

[31]In order to prove this, note that

$$E(r'_p) = \frac{E[i(NDV' + X_0)]}{X_0} = \frac{iE(NDV) + X_0}{X_0} \tag{48}$$

Only when the certainty equivalent NDV of the project exceeds zero will the certainty equivalent rate of return exceed the rate of interest.[32] Analysis of a project using the certainty equivalent rate of return is consistent with the previously derived NDV certainty equivalent analysis and hence provides an alternative decision rule.

Analysis of Projects Using Certainty Equivalent Cash Flows

Equation (30a) expressed stock value in terms of the certainty equivalent cash flows of the corporation. The individual investment project may similarly be analyzed in terms of its certainty equivalent cash flows. If certainty equivalent cash flows can be derived, the certainty equivalent NDV or RR of the project may be used to judge its profitability.

In terms of the individual cash flows of the project, the expected NDV in (42) is

$$E(NDV) = -X_0 + \sum_{t=1}^{n} E(X_t)(1 + i)^{-t} \tag{50}$$

and the standard deviation relevant to valuation is[33]

$$\sigma_{NDV'} = \sigma_{DVX'} = \sum_{t=1}^{n} \sigma_{X't}(1 + i)^{-t} \tag{51}$$

and

$$\sigma_{r'p} = \sqrt{E\left\{\frac{i[NDV' + X_0]}{X_0} - \frac{i[E(NDV) + X_0]}{X_0}\right\}}$$

$$= \frac{i}{X_0} \sqrt{E[NDV' - E(NDV)]^2} = \frac{i}{X_0} \sigma_{NDV'} \tag{49}$$

Substitution in (47) yields

$$C(r_p) = \frac{i}{X_0} [E(NDV) - S\sigma_{NDV'}] + i$$

$$C(r_p) = \frac{i}{X_0} C(NDV) + i \tag{47a}$$

[32]See previous footnotes (31), equation (47a).

[33]This follows from the fact that the X'_t are by definition perfectly correlated through time. They are all dependent solely upon the state of the index, m.

Substitution in (42) yields a condition for project acceptance:

$$-X_0 + \sum_{t=1}^{n} [E(X_t) - S\sigma_{X't}](1 + i)^{-t} > 0 \qquad (52)$$

or

$$-X_0 + \sum_{t=1}^{n} C(X_t)(1 + i)^{-t} > 0 \qquad (52a)$$

where $C(X_t)$ is the certainty equivalent of the cash flow, X_t.

A project's certainty equivalent NDV may therefore be computed from the certainty equivalent cash flows. If this value, the left hand side of (52a), is greater than zero, the project should be accepted.

The certainty equivalent perpetuity RR of the project can similarly be computed from the certainty equivalent cash flows. This rate of return is given by $C(r_p)$ in

$$-X_0 + \frac{i \sum_{t=1}^{n} C(X_t)(1 + i)^{-t}}{C(r_p)} = 0 \qquad (53)$$

If the rate of return $C(r_p)$ in (53), computed from the certainty equivalent cash flows, is greater than the rate of interest, i, the project should be accepted.[34]

Analysis Using Risk Adjusted Discount Rates

The third approach to capital budgeting under risk is to use a discount rate adjusted for the risk of the project either as a rate at which to discount expected

---

[34]This is easily proved by noting that the certainty equivalent NDV is

$$C(NDV) = \sum_{t=1}^{n} C(X_t)(1 + i)^{-t} - X_0 \qquad (54)$$

Substituting in (53) and rearranging yields

$$C(r_p) = \frac{i}{X_0} C(NDV) + i \qquad (47a)$$

cash flows to their present value, or as a hurdle rate which the expected rate of return must exceed for the project to be acceptable. Lintner [5] has shown that, given his stock value model, the appropriate risk-adjusted discount rate is extremely difficult to determine, being a complex function of the rate of interest and the risk of each cash flow generated by the project. Also Robichek and Myers [13] have shown the danger of using an average risk-adjusted discount rate to discount all expected cash flows of the project. As the risk-adjusted discount rate approach is perhaps the most commonly used method of project appraisal, it is desirable to formulate rules for project analysis in these terms. Contrary to Lintner's conclusions it is found that, although the appropriate discount rate is unique to the particular project under analysis, it is fairly easily derived if a project's cash flows are first reduced to an equivalent perpetuity.

The equivalent perpetuity cash flow of a project is the increase in the earnings of the corporation due to the project, where earnings are defined as in section III of this paper. The appropriate risk-adjusted discount rate to use in evaluating a project is determined by the risk of these increased earnings and may be derived from the earnings model of stock value. Let the cash flows of the corporation without the project again be $X_{1j}, X_{2j}, ---, X_{nj}$, and earnings Y_j. Stock value from equation (32b) is

$$P_{0j} = \frac{E(Y_j) - S_{Y'j}}{i} \qquad (32b)$$

or from (35)

$$P_{0j} = \frac{E(Y_j)}{r_j} \qquad (35)$$

where r_j is the 'cost of equity capital' of corporation j. If the project costing X_0 yields cash flows $X_1, X_2, ---, X_n$, the corporation's cash flows after accepting the project are $X^*_{1j}, X^*_{2j}, ---, X^*_{nj}$, and earnings rise to Y^*_j, where $X^*_{tj} = X_{tj} + X_t$, and $Y^*_j = Y_j + Y$, and where Y is the increase in earnings contributed by the project. If the project is accepted stock value rises to

$$P^*_{0j} = \frac{E(Y^*_j) - S\sigma_{Y^{*'}j}}{i} \qquad (32c)$$

The condition for project acceptance is

$$P^*_{0j} - P_{0j} > X_0 \qquad (37)$$

or[35]

$$\frac{E(Y) - S\sigma_{Y'}}{i} - X_0 > 0 \tag{55}$$

This appropriate risk-adjusted discount rate which can be used to discount the expected earnings of the project to their market value must be $\bar{r}$ in the equation

$$\frac{E(Y)}{\bar{r}} = \frac{E(Y) - S\sigma_{Y'}}{i} \tag{56}$$

since it is known from (55) that if

$$\frac{E(Y)}{\bar{r}} - X_0 > 0 \tag{57}$$

the project should be accepted. The risk adjusted discount rate from (56) is therefore

$$\bar{r} = \frac{i}{1 - S\sigma_{Y'/E(Y)}} \tag{58}$$

As would be expected the appropriate rate is a function of the rate of interest, the risk of the project as measured by the ratio $\sigma_{Y'/E(Y)}$, and the market risk aversion factor. It will equal r_j, the so-called "equity cost of capital" of corporation j, if, and only if, the risk ratio of the increased earnings of the project is the same as the risk ratio of the earnings of the corporation without the project.

When the risk-adjusted discount rate has been determined, analysis of the project may proceed using either a net discounted value or a rate of return approach. The *NDV* approach simply tests whether the left hand side of (57) is positive or not. If positive the *NDV* of the project is positive and it should be accepted. The rate of return approach requires the computation of the expected rate of return of the project which may then be compared with the risk-adjusted discount rate to judge the project. If the increase in expected

---

[35]Substituting (32b) and (32c) in (37) yields (55) because again Y^*_j and Y'_j are perfectly correlated and thus $\sigma_{Y^*_j} = \sigma_{Y'_j} + \sigma_{Y'}$.

earnings due to acceptance of the project is $E(Y)$, the expected perpetuity rate of return of the project must be

$$E(r_p) = \frac{E(Y)}{X_0} \tag{59}$$

This is the expected rate of return of the project, and if it exceeds the risk-adjusted discount rate in (58) which is the minimum acceptable rate of return given the risk of the project, the project should be accepted. Comparison of equations (57) and (59) reveals that if the rate of return $E(r_p)$ in (59) exceeds $\bar{r}$ in (57), then (57) is necessarily positive. The risk-adjusted discount rate $\bar{r}$ is thus the hurdle rate that the expected rate of return $E(r_p)$ must exceed for the project to be acceptable.

Conclusions and Qualifications

This paper has derived capital budgeting decision rules based on stock value models derived within a portfolio framework. The most important conclusion to be drawn from portfolio analysis is that only risk that cannot be avoided by shareholders holding portfolios is relevant to valuation. The shareholder wealth-maximizing corporation may ignore all diversifiable risk when considering capital projects. The diversification effect of investments within the corporation can be ignored and individual capital projects may be appraised separately. The decision rules developed require the corporation to predict cash flows from projects for each possible state of an index, m, where this index is chosen so that it is perfectly correlated with the return on the optimal portfolio. Any of the decision rules in section IV may then be applied, given knowledge of the market risk aversion factor.[36]

A number of limitations of the analysis should be noted. It has been assumed throughout that the probability distributions of future cash flows are known and that they are normal. Thus the whole analysis has required only two parameters of these probability distributions. Market imperfections have been assumed away. Corporations and investors could borrow and lend at the known and constant rate of interest. Also the paper has only considered project analysis when investments are financed with new issues of equity capital. Although the Modigliani-Miller theorem could be applied, adjustments would have to be incorporated for the effect of corporate taxes on valuation. Another problem not dealt with is that of the choice between mutually exclusive investment

---

[36]It is significant to note that Sharpe [15] has attempted to measure the empirical value of the risk aversion factor, S, by comparing mutual fund rates of return over time. He concludes that S is approximately 0.5.

projects and the selection of investment programs. However, the basic analysis of individual projects could be extended to solve these problems.

The practical application of the decision rules developed is difficult due to these limitations and to the lack of convincing empirical evidence on stock valuation. The definition of relevant risk derived in this paper must be of practical significance, however, due to the observed fact that investors do hold portfolios of stocks. When considering investment project decisions, management should consider only this nondiversifiable risk, which is relevant to valuation in a portfolio framework. Finally, it should prove possible to adapt some of the theoretically sound alternative decision rules derived in section IV to take account of the market imperfections and differential taxes which serve to complicate the investment decision of the corporation.

References

1. A.M. Duguid and J.G. Laski. "The Financial Attractiveness of a Project," *Opeartional Research Quarterly* 14 (December, 1964,) pp. 317-329.
2. E.F. Fama. "Risk, Return and Equilibrium: Some Clarifying Comments," *Journal of Finance* XXIII (March, 1968), pp. 29-40.
3. R.S. Hamada. "Portfolio Analysis, Market Equilibrium and Corporation Finance," *Journal of Finance* XXIV (March, 1969), pp. 13-31.
4. F.S. Hillier. "The Derivation of Probabilistic Information for the Evaluation of Risky Investments," *Management Science* 9 (April, 1963), pp. 443-457.
5. J. Lintner. "The Valuation of Risk Assets and the Selection of Risky Investments in Stock Portfolios and Capital Budgets," *Review of Economics and Statistics* XLVII (February, 1965), pp. 13-37.
6. ——. "Security Prices, Risk and Maximal Gains from Diversification," *Journal of Finance* XX (December, 1965), pp. 587-615.
7. ——. "Optimal Dividends and Corporate Growth Under Uncertainty," *Quarterly Journal of Economics* LXXVIII (February, 1964), pp. 49-95.
8. R. H. Litzenberger. "Equilibrium in the Equity Market Under Uncertainty," *Journal of Finance* XXIV (September, 1969), pp. 663-671.
9. F. Lutz and V. Lutz. *The Theory of the Investment of the Firm.* Princeton University Press, 1951.
10. H. Markovitz. "Portfolio Selection," *Journal of Finance* VII (March, 1952), pp. 77-91.
11. M.H. Miller and F. Modigliani. "Dividend Policy, Growth, and the Valuation of Shares," *Journal of Business* XXXIV (October, 1961), pp. 411-433.
12. F. Modigliani and M.H. Miller. "The Cost of Capital, Corporation Finance, and the Theory of Investment," *American Economic Review* XLVIII (June, 1958), pp. 261-297.
13. A.A. Robichek and S.C. Myers. *Optimal Financing Decisions.* Prentice-Hall, 1965.

14. W.F. Sharpe. "Capital Asset Prices: A Theory of Market Equilibrium Under Conditions of Risk," *Journal of Finance* XIX (September, 1964), pp. 425–442.
15. W.F. Sharpe. "Risk Aversion in the Stock Market: Some Empirical Evidence," *Journal of Finance* XX (September, 1965), pp. 416–422.
16. E. Solomon. *The Theory of Financial Management.* Columbia University Press, 1963.
17. D. Teichroew, A.A. Robichek and M. Montalbano. "An Analysis of Criteria for Investment and Financing Decisions under Certainty," *Management Science* 12 (November, 1965), pp. 151–179.
18. D.L. Tuttle and R.H. Litzenberger. "Leverage, Diversification and Capital Market Effects on a Risk Adjusted Capital Budgeting Framework," *Journal of Finance* XXIII (June, 1968), pp. 427–443.
19. J.C. Van Horne. *Financial Management and Policy.* Prentice-Hall, 1968.

**Part III
Implications for
Finance**

An Approach to the Valuation of
Uncertain Income Streams

M. S. Brennan

I. Introduction

In the last decade substantial advances have been made in the theory of the
valuation of assets under uncertainty, such work being based mainly on what
has come to be known as the Capital Asset Pricing Model,[1] which itself grew
out of the static theory of portfolio selection originally due to Markowitz
[1959].

More recently the theory of portfolio selection has been extended under
certain assumptions to the problem of an individual planning his investment
and consumption under uncertainty over a multi-period horizon.[2] As yet,
however, the theory of the market valuation of individual assets has not
paralleled this development, and remains almost entirely within a one-period
context. Exceptions of this generalization are the work of Black and Scholes
[1971] on warrant valuation, and an unpublished paper by Black [1969],
recently brought to the author's attention, which, drawing on some earlier work
by Treynor, anticipates in a more general context part of the theoretical
development presented here. Other efforts to apply modern capital market
theory to multi-period asset valuation and investment decisions include the
work of Tuttle and Litzenberger [1968] and that of Stapleton [1971], both
of which differ in significant respects from the approach adopted here.

The Tuttle and Litzenberger paper, which derives appropriate criteria for
optimal corporate investment decisions, takes as given the effects on a firm's
market risk[3] of adopting a particular investment project. The paper therefore
leaves open the questions both of the determinants of this risk effect, and of
the way in which the risk of projects is to be assessed. The model presented
here is more complete, in that investment decision criteria are developed

Reprinted with permission of the author and publisher from *The Journal of Finance,*
Vol. 28, no. 3, June 1973, pp. 661–674.

The author is grateful for helpful discussion with Fischer Black and Irwin Tepper, as well as
for the suggestions of a referee.

[1] See Jensen [1971].

[2] See Merton [1969], Samuelson [1969], and others.

[3] By 'market risk' is meant the risk characteristics of a firm's securities as perceived by investors.

assuming only that the decision-maker has information on the conditional distributions of the project's cash flows.

Stapleton, on the other hand, while purporting to develop a theory of stock valuation using a multi-period portfolio model,[4] actually employs a single-period certainty-equivalent approach in which it is assumed that the joint probability distribution of all the future dividend payments on a share can be reduced to a probability distribution on the present values at the end of one period of all the possible future dividend streams. The probability distribution of these deferred present values is then valued using the single-period Capital Asset Pricing Model. This procedure would be legitimate only if, at the end of one period, the investor were to know with certainty the precise pattern of dividend payments over the remainder of the horizon; this of course is highly unrealistic and ignores the fact that information about future dividends becomes available only gradually through time.

As a result of its predominantly one-period framework, the relevance of the theory of valuation under uncertainty is severely restricted, for most assets provide risky income streams over an indefinite future life, and unless these income streams can be valued in a market equilibrium context, there can exist no theory of the valuation of the assets which provide them. The most obvious consequence of this lack of available theory lies in the unsatisfactory state of normative models of the corporate investment decision under uncertainty; such models, when they incorporate the maximization of the current value of the firm as an appropriate objective of policy, either rely on a risk-adjusted discount rate to value the uncertain future income stream of the investment, or make use of certainty-equivalents to adjust the expected cash flows, before discounting them at the risk-free rate of interest.[5] Lacking in both approaches is any theory for the determination of the appropriate discount rate or certainty-equivalent adjustment.

A further consequence of the single-period nature of available valuation models is the lack of any rigorous theory of the determinants of the market risk of firms;[6] this has impeded the integration of corporate finance with modern capital market theory except within the confines of a limited single-period model.[7]

This paper has as its major aim, the development of a theory of the valuation of uncertain future cash flows and hence of the valuation of the assets which provide them. The basic framework is a model of multi-period capital market

---

[4]Stapleton [1971], pp. 95–96.

[5]For an excellent discussion of these two approaches see Robichek and Myers [1965].

[6]Some progress towards developing such a theory has been made by Pettit and Westerfield [1971], drawing on some unpublished work by Daniel Rie.

[7]See for example Mossin [1969].

equilibrium developed from an optimizing model of the individual's lifetime portfolio selection problem due to Merton [1969], to which the reader is referred. To this model of capital market equilibrium is introduced an extremely simple expectations generating mechanism which, it is hoped, will serve to capture the basic dynamic nature of information arrival. It is then shown that the behavior of the value of a cash flow claim must follow a simple differential equation: this differential equation approach to valuation was inspired by the article of Black and Scholes on warrant valuation, referred to above. Solution of this differential equation yields the present value of a claim to a risky future cash flow. By aggregating the market values of claims to risky cash flows in different periods, the net present values of risky income streams and therefore of the assets which provide them may be computed, permitting a relatively straightforward approach to the problem of the corporate investment decision under uncertainty.

In Section II the conditions for equilibrium in a multi-period capital market are derived. Section III introduces the expectations generating mechanism and gives the present value of a risky cash flow claim. Some implications of the model are discussed in Section IV.

II. Multi-Period Capital Market Equilibrium

We shall consider first the conditions for the instantaneous portfolio equilibrium of an individual investor planning his consumption and investment under uncertainty: aggregation of the resulting individual asset demands will then yield a condition for instantaneous capital market equilibrium.

Individual Equilibrium

Assume that the investor is considered with maximizing the expected utility of both consumption over a known lifespan and terminal wealth; that he has no labour income, and that he is free to adjust his investment portfolio instantaneously without incurring transactions costs. The investor may place his wealth in two types of asset: first, a riskless asset whose yield at each future instant in time is a known constant, r; second, in risky assets whose yields are uncertain but are assumed to be serially independent.

The investor may then be represented at time t as maximizing expected utility, given by:

$$E\left[\int_t^H e^{-\rho s}\, U(C_s)\, ds + B(W_H)\right]$$

constrained by his initial wealth $W(t)$, and investment opportunities. $U(C_s)$ is his utility function, defined on his instantaneous rate of consumption, C_s; ρ is his rate of time preference; H is his date of death; and $B[W_H]$ is the utility to be gained from dying with net worth W_H. The investor is assumed to exhibit risk aversion so that U and B are strictly concave. The decision variables in this planning problem are C_s, the instantaneous rate of consumption, and $w_j(s)$, the proportion of instantaneous wealth, W_s, that the investor places in each of the risky assets $(j = 1 .. n)$ at each instant of time, s.

Define the investor's optimal value function (i.e., the maximum expected value of discounted utility at time t), $\phi[W_t, t]$ as:

$$\phi[W_t, t] \equiv \underset{C_s, w_j(s)}{\text{Max}} E\left[\int_t^H e^{-\rho s} U(C_s)\, ds + B(W_H)\right] \tag{1}$$

Note that the optimal value function, which may also be referred to as the investor's derived utility function, depends only on current wealth and time, because of the posited serial independence of asset yields.

Then it may be shown that, providing the risky asset yields possess 'compact' probability distributions,[8] the optimal instantaneous consumption and investment decisions are found by maximizing G w.r.t. $w_j(t)$ and C_t, where

$$G \equiv e^{-\rho t}U(C_t) + \frac{\partial \phi}{\partial W_t}$$

$$\left\{W_t\left[\sum_{j=1}^n w_j(t)\,(\alpha_{jt} - r) + r\right] - C_t\right\} + \frac{1}{2}\frac{\partial^2 \phi}{\partial W2}\,W_t^2 \sum_{j=1}^n \sum_{k=1}^n w_j(t)w_k(t)\sigma_{jkt} \tag{2}$$

and

α_{jt} — the expected instantaneous rate of return on asset j $(j = 1 .. n)$

σ_{jkt} — the instantaneous rate of covariance between the yields on assets j and k.

r — the risk free rate of interest.

---

[8]Merton [1969] obtains this result when asset yields are generated by a Wiener Brownian motion process. The extension to the more general case of compact probability distributions follows from Samuelson [1970].

Differentiating w.r.t. $w_j(t)$ and C_t, we obtain the following first order conditions for the maximum of G:[9]

$$\frac{\partial G}{\partial C_t} = e^{-\rho t} \, U' - \frac{\partial \phi}{\partial W} = 0 \tag{3}$$

$$\frac{\partial G}{\partial w_j(t)} = \frac{\partial \phi}{\partial W_t} W_t(\alpha_{jt} - r) + \frac{\partial^2 \phi}{\partial W_t^2} W_t^2 \sum_{k=1}^{n} w_k(t) \, \sigma_{jkt} = 0 \tag{4}$$

Then the vector of the ith investor's equilibrium *dollar holdings* of the n risky assets, $Z^i(t)$, is given by

$$Z^i(t) = a_t^i \, \Omega_t^{-1} \, (\alpha_t - rj) \tag{5}$$

where

$$a_t^i = - \left(\frac{\partial \phi}{\partial W_t} \Big/ \frac{\partial^2 \phi}{\partial W_t^2} \right) - \text{a measure of the investor's absolute risk aversion.}$$

Ω_t — the instantaneous variance-covariance matrix of risk asset yields.

α_t — the vector of expected instantaneous risk asset yields.

j — an n-dimensional vector of units.

The superscript i has been added to a_t^i and $Z_{(t)}^i$ to show that these symbols refer to the ith investor ($i = 1 \, .. \, n$).

Market Equilibrium

To obtain the conditions for instantaneous capital market equilibrium we set the vector of aggregate dollar amounts demanded of each risky asset equal to the vector of aggregate dollar supplies, S_t, assuming that all investors agree on the joint probability distribution of asset yields,

---

[9]See Merton [1969]. Satisfaction of the second-order conditions is guaranteed by the concavity of U and B.

i.e.,
$$\sum_{i=1}^{m} Z^i_{(t)} = \left(\sum_{i=1}^{m} d^i_t \right) \Omega_t^{-1} (\alpha_t - j) = S_t \qquad (6)$$

Re-arranging equation (6) we obtain:

$$\alpha_t - rj = \left(\sum_{i=1}^{m} d^i_t \right)^{-1} \Omega_t S_t \qquad (7)$$

which may be interpreted as an equation for the vector of expected asset yields α_t conditional on the vector of asset supplies, S_t. Equation (7) states that, in equilibrium, the excess of the expected instantaneous yield of each risky asset over the risk-free rate of interest is proportional to its weighted average instantaneous rate of covariance with the yields on all the risky assets. It is the continuous time analogue of the single period Capital Asset Pricing Model.

This market equilibrium condition may be readily, if somewhat tediously, transformed in the familiar way[10] to yield

$$\alpha_{jt} - r = \beta_{jt} (\mu_t - r) \qquad (j = 1 .. n) \qquad (8)$$

where β_{jt} is the instantaneous slope of the regression of the yield on asset j $(j = 1 .. n)$ against the yield on the market portfolio of all risky assets, and μ_t is the instantaneous expected yield on this same market portfolio.

It will be recalled that when the conditions for the instantaneous portfolio equilibrium of the individual investor were being derived, it was assumed that individual asset yields were serially independent. Conditions for such independence and for the expected yield on the market portfolio to be a constant are discussed in an Appendix. Assuming that such conditions are satisfied, the market equilibrium condition may be written

$$\alpha_{jt} - r = \beta_{jt} (\mu - r) \qquad (8')$$

It is this relationship we shall use in the following section

III. The Valuation of Risky Cash Flow Claims

At every instant in time, t, investors are assumed to trade in claims to uncertain future cash flows which will be realized at instants in time T, where $T > t$.

---

[10]See Fama [1968].

Initially we assume that the total quantity of such claims is given; later we shall allow an individual firm to create additional claims to finance investment projects, but maintain the assumption that the total quantity of such issues is arbitrarily small so that the market equilibrium conditions are not affected. A particular cash flow will be denoted generically by $\tilde{C}_{jT}$, and the problem to be considered is the determination of the value at time t of a claim to such a cash flow, which value we shall denote generically by $V_t(\tilde{C}_{jT})$. First it is necessary to describe the process by which expectations about future cash flows are generated.

The Expectations Generating Mechanism

Investors are assumed to form their expectations about future cash flows conditional on an index of expectations for the economy as a whole,

i.e.,
$$E_t[\tilde{C}_{jT} | \tilde{I}_t] = {}_t a_{jT} + b_{jT} \tilde{I}_t \tag{9}$$

where $\tilde{I}_t$ is the current value of the expectations index; $b_{jT} \tilde{I}_t$ is the index-dependent component of the jth cash flow expected at time T; and ${}_t a_{jT}$ is the index-independent component, as assessed at time t.

It is apparent that changes in the expected value of a particular cash flow can come from two sources: changes in the overall index, $\tilde{I}_t$, and changes in ${}_t a_{jT}$. We make the diagonal assumption about the expectations generating mechanism, that all the covariance between expectations about different cash flows is due to changes in the index, $\tilde{I}_t$; in other words, changes in ${}_t a_{jT}$ are independent across securities. We further assume that claims to index-dependent components and index-independent components of claims to future cash flows may be traded separately.[11]

It is a property of rational expectations that such expectations should follow a martingale sequence, since by definition rational expectations can change only on receipt of new (i.e. unexpected) information. Hence

$$E_t[\tilde{I}_{t+h}] = \tilde{I}_t$$

$$E_t[{}_{t+h} a_{jT}] = {}_t a_{jT}$$

$$h > 0$$

We assume that the variance rate on the expectations index is $I_t^2 \sigma^2$, and that all random variables possess compact probability distributions.

---

[11] This assumption guarantees satisfaction of condition (ii) for the serial independence of asset yields. See Appendix.

At any instant in time, the market value of all claims to future cash flows will consist of two components: the market value of claims to all index-independent cash flows and the market value of all index-dependent cash flows. Given the existence of a large number of such claims the market value of the former will be a function of time only, since by construction it is independent of the other state variable, $\tilde{I}_t$. Investment in the portfolio of all index-independent claims will therefore be essentially riskless, and we may, without loss of generality, define the net value of all index-independent claims to be part of the net supply of riskless securities so that the true risky asset portfolio consists only of claims to index-dependent cash flows.

We denote the current value of this risky asset portfolio by $\tilde{M}_t$, and assume that it has a constant cash flow yield or dividend yield, δ, and a constant expected rate of price appreciation γ.

Since $E_t[\tilde{I}_{t+h}] = \tilde{I}_t$, this implies

$$\tilde{M}_t = K_0 e^{\gamma t} \tilde{I}_t \tag{10}$$

where K_0 is an arbitrary scaling constant, assuring that the rate of return on the risky asset portfolio has a constant variance, σ^2. The reasonableness of these assumptions about the risky market portfolio will be examined in more detail below.

A Differential Equation for the Value of a Claim

The value of a cash flow claim at any instant in time depends upon:

(i)   the current instant of time t
(ii) the current value of the market index, $\tilde{I}_t$
(iii) the current assessment of the index-independent component of the cash flow expectation, $_ta_{jT}$.

Since there is a one-to-one relationship between the current value of the expectations index and the current value of the risky market portfolio, M_t, given by (10), we may write

$$V_t(\tilde{C}_{jT}) = y(\tilde{M}_t, t, {}_ta_{jT}) \tag{11}$$

where $y_1 = \partial y/\partial \tilde{M}_t; y_2 = \partial y/\partial_t; y_3 = \partial y/\partial_t a_{jT}$.

Then, invoking the market equilibrium condition (8') for the expected return on a security, we see that over any short period of time h, the expected return from holding a cash flow claim must be given by

$$\frac{1}{y} E[\Delta y] = \text{r.h.} + \frac{My_1}{y} \sigma^2 (\gamma + \delta - r)h \qquad (12)$$

for $My_1/y \, \sigma^2$ is the instantaneous rate of covariance between the yield on the claim and the yield on the risky market portfolio.

Now
$$\Delta y = y[M + \Delta M, t + h, {}_{t+h}a_{jT}] - y[M, t, {}_t a_{jT}]$$

$$= y_1 \Delta M + y_2 h + y_3 \Delta a + \frac{1}{2} y_{11}(\Delta M)^2 + \frac{1}{2} y_{22} h^2$$

$$+ \frac{1}{2} y_{33}(\Delta a)^2 + \frac{1}{2} y_{12} \Delta M \cdot h + \frac{1}{2} y_{21} \Delta M \cdot h$$

$$+ \frac{1}{2} y_{13}(\Delta M)(\Delta a) + \frac{1}{2} y_{31}(\Delta M)(\Delta a)$$

$$+ \frac{1}{2} y_{23}(\Delta a)h + \frac{1}{2} y_{32}(\Delta a)h$$

where terms of higher order than the second in h have been dropped, and $\Delta a = {}_{t+h}a_{jT} - {}_t a_{jT}$.
Then, taking the expectation and dropping terms in h^2,

$$E[\Delta y] = y_1 M \gamma h + y_2 h + \frac{1}{2} y_{11} M^2 \sigma^2 h + \frac{1}{2} y_{33} \xi^2 h \qquad (13)$$

where $\xi^2 h = E[\Delta a]^2$.
Substitute for $E[\Delta y]$ in (12), divide by h, and let $h \to 0$.

$$My_1 \gamma + y_2 + \frac{1}{2} y_{11} M^2 \sigma^2 + \frac{1}{2} y_{33} \xi^2 - yr - My_1 (\gamma + \delta - r) = 0$$

or

$$y_2 + \frac{1}{2} y_{11} M^2 \sigma^2 + \frac{1}{2} y_{33} \xi^2 - yr + y_1 M(r - \delta) = 0 \qquad (14)$$

(14) is then a differential equation governing the behavior of the value of a claim to a risky cash flow. The equation is formally almost identical to that employed by Black and Scholes [1971] for valuing warrants.

The boundary condition for the differential equation is in terms of the expectations index, $\tilde{I}_T$,

i.e.,
$$V_T(\tilde{C}_{jT}) = y(M_T, T, {}_T a_{jT}) = {}_T a_{jT} + b_{jT} \tilde{I}_T \tag{15}$$

For this reason we write the solution to the differential equation in terms of I_t, as

$$V_t(\tilde{C}_{jT}) = {}_t a_{jT} e^{-r(T-t)} + b_{jT} \tilde{I}_t e^{-(\gamma+\delta)(T-t)} \tag{16}$$

It is apparent from inspection that this equation satisfies the boundary condition (15).

Writing this solution in terms of $\tilde{\tilde{M}}_t$

$$V_t(C_{jT}) = {}_t a_{jT} e^{-r(T-t)} + \frac{b_{jT}}{K_0} M_t e^{\delta t - (\gamma+\delta)T} \tag{17}$$

it is readily verified that this expression also satisfies the differential equation (14) for

$$y_1 = \frac{b_{jT}}{K_0} e^{\delta t - (\gamma+\delta)T}$$

$$y_{11} = 0$$

$$y_{33} = 0$$

$$y_2 = \delta \frac{b_{jT}}{K_0} \tilde{M}_t e^{\delta t - (\gamma+\delta)T} + r\, {}_t a_{jT} e^{-r(T-t)}$$

Characteristics of the Risky Market Portfolio and the Structure of Security Returns

Having derived an expression for the value of an individual cash flow claim we are now in position to examine the implications of our earlier assumptions that the value of the risky market portfolio has a constant expected rate of appreciation γ, and a constant dividend yield δ. For this to hold, it is sufficient that $b_T = \sum_j b_{jT}$, be given by:

$$b_T = b_0 e^{\gamma T} \tag{18}$$

for then
$$K_t = \int_{T>t} b_T e^{-(\gamma+\delta)(T-t)} \, dT$$

$$= \int_{T>t} b_0 e^{(\gamma+\delta)t - \delta T} \, dT$$

$$= \frac{b_0}{\delta} e^{\gamma t} \tag{19}$$

and K_t grows at the constant rate γ, so that the risky market portfolio also has a constant rate of expected appreciation, γ. Moreover, the dividend yield is given by

$$\frac{b_t I_t}{K_t I_t} = \frac{b_0 e^{\gamma t}}{b_0 e^{\gamma t}} \, \delta = \delta \tag{20}$$

and is a constant, independent of time and the current level of the expectations index.

Thus the nature of investors' wealth in this simple capital market is as follows: the supply of securities representing claims to future cash flows is given. One component of net wealth consists of claims to riskless future cash flows, while the other consists of claims to index-dependent cash flows. Investors always expect the sum of these index-dependent cash flows to grow at the same rate γ. However the actual growth rate is stochastic.

In spite of the extremely simplistic nature of this model, it does have one feature which is consistent with the observed nature of security returns. Specifically, it implies that security returns will be generated by a diagonal model, which several authors have found to represent adequately the actual security return generating process.[12] The diagonal return generating process in this model stems of course from the assumption that changes in expected cash flows are linked only through the single common index of expectations, I_t.

IV. Some Implications of the Cash Flow Valuation Equation

Investment Criteria

Under the usual assumptions of a perfectly competitive securities market the individual firm is able to take market prices as given in making its investment decisions. Hence, although the valuation equation (16) was derived on the assumption of fixed security supplies, it may be used to value marginal increases in the supply of securities (cash flow claims) of an individual firm such as accompany on investment decision.

---

[12]See King [1966] and Blume [1970]. However, for evidence of departures from the diagonal model see Black, Jensen and Scholes [1970], and Brennan [1971].

Re-writing the valuation equation (16) as

$$V_t(\widetilde{C}_{jT}) = {}_ta_{jT}e^{-r(T-t)} + b_{jT}\widetilde{I}_te^{-\mu(T-t)} \tag{16'}$$

where $\mu = \gamma + \delta$ permits a fairly straightforward approach to the corporate investment decision under uncertainty. The information requirements include the index-independent and index-dependent components of all the cash flows associated with the project, viz. ${}_ta_{jT}$ and b_{jT} for all $T > t$, where the subscript j refers to the jth project. Given these, and knowledge of the expected return on the market portfolio, μ, the decision-maker may compute the net present value of the project by applying the valuation equation (16') to each individual cash flow. Given the assumption of perfect security markets, the resulting net present value represents the effect on stockholder wealth of adopting the project, and hence provides a simple criterion for project acceptance.

The similarity of this result to that obtained by Mossin [1969] in a single-period framework may be noted. In particular, although both models are founded upon the portfolio equilibrium of the individual investor, they do not require the firm itself to adopt a portfolio selection approach to project selection as has been suggested by several writers;[13] in other words projects are risk-independent.[14] Furthermore, the net present value of a particular project is a given number in this model, and not a random variable the properties of whose distribution must be examined before the decision on project acceptance can be made. Despite the simplifying assumptions made in this model it seems probable that these conclusions hold more generally.

This model also throws further light on the certainty-equivalent and cost-of-capital approaches to the investment decision. The certainty-equivalent of a particular cash flow, C_{jT}, is now an objective, market-determined phenomenon, and not derived from a manager's utility function. It is defined by

$$CE_t(\widetilde{C}_{jT}) = V_t(\widetilde{C}_{jT})e^{r(T-t)}$$

where $CE_t(\widetilde{C}_{jT})$ denotes the certainty-equivalent at time t.

Substituting for $V_t(\widetilde{C}_{jT})$ from (16') and recalling the expression for the expected value of the cash flow (9), the relationship between the expected value and the certainty-equivalent of a cash-flow is:

$$CE_t(\widetilde{C}_{jT}) = E_t(\widetilde{C}_{jT}) - b_{jT}\widetilde{I}_te^{-(\mu-r)(T-t)} \tag{21}$$

Thus the risk premium $(E_t(\widetilde{C}_{jT}) - CE(\widetilde{C}_{jT}))$ is a simple exponential function of the time to realization of the cash flow.

---

[13]For example Van Horne [1969], Cohen and Elton [1967].

[14]The term is Myers' [1968].

While there always exists a number, the 'cost of capital' which, if used to discount the expected cash flows from an investment project, will yield the net present value, it should be clear from (16') that this number is an extremely complex function of $_t a_{jT}$ and b_{jT} ($T = t \ldots$); the very difficulty of computing the cost of capital even for a single project should give pause to those who would apply a single cost of capital standard for all of a company's investments.[15] However, it is outside the scope of this paper to consider the nature of the biases likely to result from such a procedure.

Finally, because of its explicit consideration of risk in a multi-period context, the model should permit examination of such questions as the conditions under which it is optimal to substitute fixed for variable costs, e.g., by accepting a new labour contract, or by installing automated machinery with high fixed and low variable costs.

Security Risk Measures

It is well-known that the relevant measure of the risk of a security in the framework of capital market equilibrium is the covariance between the rate of return on the security and the rate of return on the market portfolio, or more simply its beta coefficient, β_{jt}. For an individual cash flow claim the beta coefficient is given by:

$$\beta_{jt} = \frac{M}{V} \frac{dV}{dM} \tag{22}$$

$$= \frac{b_{jT} \tilde{I}_t e^{-\mu(T-t)}}{_t a_{jT} e^{-r(T-t)} + b_{jT} I_t e^{-\mu(T-t)}} \tag{23}$$

from equations (16) and (17).

Assuming that $b_{jT} > 0$

$$\beta_{jT} \genfrac{}{}{0pt}{}{>}{<} \Big\} 1 \quad \text{as} \quad _t a_{jT} \genfrac{}{}{0pt}{}{<}{>} \Big\} 0$$

Moreover if $_t a_{jT} > 0$ so that $\beta_{jT} < 1$, then with unchanged expectations, β_{jT} will increase as the cash flow realization date approaches; on the other hand,

---

[15] This procedure is usually justified on the assumption that the new investment has risk characteristics similar to those of the firm's existing assets. Since new investments will generally have income streams stretching further ahead than the income stream of the existing assets of the firm, it is unlikely that the same cost of capital will be appropriate for both existing assets and net investment.

if $_{t}a_{jT} < 0$, β_{jT} will decline towards unity from above as the realization date approaches.

The beta coefficient for a firm is of course simply the market value weighted average of the betas of all the firm's expected cash flows. It is difficult to derive a simple expression for this save under highly restrictive assumptions. However, if both components of a firm's expected cash flows grow at a constant rate g, (where $g < r$), so that

$$_{t}a_{fT} = a_f e^{gT}$$

$$b_{fT} = b_f e^{gT}$$

where the subscript f refers to the firm, then the value of the firm at time t, V_{ft}, is given by

$$\tilde{V}_{ft} = e^{gT} \int_{T>t} [a_f e^{(g-r)(T-t)} + b_f I_t e^{(g-\mu)(T-t)}] \, dT = \left[\frac{a_f}{r-g} + \frac{b_f \tilde{I}_t}{\mu - g} \right] e^{gt} \tag{24}$$

The firm's beta coefficient, β_{ft}, is given by

$$\tilde{\beta}_{ft} = \frac{1}{\tilde{V}_{ft}} \int_{T>t} \frac{b_{fT} \tilde{I}_t e^{-\mu(T-t)}}{_{t}a_{fT} e^{-r(T-t)} + b_{fT} I_t e^{-\mu(T-t)}} \, (_{t}a_{fT} e^{-r(T-t)} + b_{fT} \tilde{I}_t e^{-\mu(T-t)} \, dT$$

$$= \frac{(r-g) b_f \tilde{I}_t}{a_f(\mu - g) + (r-g) b_f \tilde{I}^t} \tag{25}$$

Note that equation (25) implies that the beta coefficient of the firm is non-stationary but depends upon the level of the expectations index, $\tilde{I}_t$.[16] Moreover the beta coefficient of the firm is clearly shown to depend upon the conditional distributions of the firm's underlying cash flows.

V. Conclusion

In this paper we have developed, under highly simplified assumptions about the process by which investors' expectations are generated, a model for the valuation of risky future cash flows and income streams. Despite the simplicity of the expectations mechanism, the model has two features which accord well with the observed nature of security returns: it implies that they will be generated by a

---

[16]For the suggestion that empirical beta coefficients are non-stationary, see Fisher [1971].

diagonal model and that the beta coefficients will be non-stationary. Nevertheless, a more sophisticated model of expectations is obviously desirable, and further empirical research is required on the process by which investors form expectations.

However, within the limited scope of this paper, we have been able to show the crucial role of dynamic expectations formation in determining the risk of cash flows, and to demonstrate the possibility of incorporating the investment decision under uncertainty into the mainstream of finance, by employing the same net present value tools employed elsewhere.

Appendix

Inspection of (7) shows that expected risky asset yields at time t are dependent on the vector of dollar values of all risky assets outstanding in the market at time t. The instantaneous market values of these risky assets will depend upon the capital gains and hence the yields realized on these assets in previous instants, thus introducing a dependence between realized asset yields in one instant and expected asset yields in the following instant. This dependence will be compounded by any possible effects on the term

$$\left(\sum_{i=1}^{m} a_i^t \right)^{-1}$$

of unanticipated capital gains and losses in the previous instant.[17] Therefore it is necessary to examine in more detail the conditions under which this serial dependence will be absent, for only under such conditions will the model of capital market equilibrium developed above be internally consistent.

The market equilibrium relationship (7) may be written

$$\alpha - rj = M \left(\sum_{i=1}^{m} \phi^i W^i \right)^{-1} \Omega w \tag{26}$$

where

M — the value of the market portfolio of all risky assets

w — an n-dimensional vector giving the proportion of M accounted for by each risky asset

---

[17] It will be recalled that this term reflects the risk aversion of investors which may well be different at different wealth levels.

$\phi^i = a^i/W^i$—the relative risk aversion of the derived utility function of
  investor $i(i = 1 - m)$

W^i — the wealth of investor i.

The time-subscripts have been removed from the variables to avoid unnecessary complexity. The sufficient conditions for the serial independence of
asset yields are then:

(i) $\lambda = M\left(\displaystyle\sum_{i=1}^{m} \phi^i W^i\right)^{-1}$ is constant, and

(ii) the vector w is known.

(iii) If ϕ^i and W^i are uncorrelated we may write $\lambda = M/WR$, where

$$R = \frac{1}{m} \sum_{i=1}^{m} \phi^i$$

and $W = \displaystyle\sum_{i=1}^{m} W^i$. But $W = M + B$, where B is the net value of riskless assets
held in investor portfolios, so that

$$\lambda = \frac{M}{(M + B)R}$$

Therefore, sufficient conditions for λ to be independent of realized yields
on investment portfolios are that:
    a) the derived utility functions of all investors exhibit constant relative risk
aversion, and ϕ^i is uncorrelated with W^i.
    b) B is small relative to M.
ii) w will be known if the market value of each risky asset bears a known relationship to the value of the market portfolio of all risky assets. It is a property
of the cash flow claims considered in this paper that they either have values
bearing a known relationship to that of the risky market portfolio or have
returns uncorrelated with the returns on the market portfolio, which therefore
have constant expected values equal to the risk-free rate of interest.
    While the above assumptions are somewhat restrictive, they have some
empirical support in that extensive tests indicate that equity security returns
tend to be distributed independently through time.[18]

---

[18]See, for example, the papers contained in Cootner [1964].

Finally, premultiplying equation (26) by w' it is readily seen that the market portfolio will have a constant expected rate of return, $= w'\alpha$, so long as the variance rate $w'\Omega w$ is constant.

References

1. Fischer Black. "Corporate Investment Decisions", Associates in Finance, Financial Note No. 2B, May 1969.
2. Fischer Black, Michael C. Jensen and Myron S. Scholes. "The Capital Asset Pricing Model: Some Empirical Tests", University of Rochester Systems Analysis Program Working Paper No. 57030, November, 1970.
3. Fischer Black and Myron S. Scholes. "Capital Market Equilibrium and the Pricing of Corporate Liabilities", Associates in Finance, Financial Note No. 16C, January 1971.
4. Marshall Blume. "Portfolio Theory: A Step Towards its Practical Application", *Journal of Business*, Vol. 43, (April 1970), pp. 152–174.
5. Michael J. Brennan. "Capital Asset Pricing and the Structure of Security Returns", paper presented at the Wells Fargo Symposium on Modern Capital Theory, San Francisco, 1971.
6. Kalman J. Cohen and Edwin J. Elton. "Inter-Temporal Portfolio Analysis Based Upon Simulation of Joint Returns", *Management Science*, Vol. 14 (September 1967), pp. 5–18.
7. Paul Cootner (ed). *The Random Character of Stock Market Prices*, M.I.T. Press, Cambridge, 1964.
8. Eugene, F. Fama. "Risk, Return and Equilibrium: Some Clarifying Comments", *Journal of Finance*, Vol. 23, (March 1968), pp. 29–40.
9. Lawrence Fisher. "On the Estimation of Systematic Risk", paper presented at the Wells Fargo Symposium on Modern Capital Theory, San Francisco, 1971.
10. Michael C. Jensen. "The Foundations and Current State of Capital Market Theory", forthcoming in *Studies in the Theory of Capital Markets*, M.C. Jensen (ed.), Praeger Publishers, 1971.
11. Benjamin, F. King. "Market and Industry Factors in Stock Price Behavior", *Journal of Business*, Vol. 39, (January 1966), pp. 139–189.
12. Harry Markowitz. *Portfolio Selection*, John Wiley & Sons, New York, 1959.
13. Robert C. Merton. "Lifetime Portfolio Selection Under Uncertainty: The Continuous Time Case", *Review of Economics and Statistics*, Vol. 51, (August 1969), pp. 247–257.
14. Jan Mossin. "Security Pricing and Investment Criteria in Competitive Markets", *American Economic Review*, Vol. 59, (December 1969) pp. 749–756.
15. Stewart Myers Co. "Procedures for Capital Budgetary Under Uncertainty", *Industrial Management Review*, Vol. 9 (Spring, 1968), pp. 1–15.

16. R. Richardson Pettit and Randolph Westerfield. "A Model of Market Risk", paper presented at the annual meetings of the Western Finance Association, Vancouver, 1971.
17. Alexander A. Robichek and Stewart C. Myers. *Optimal Financing Decisions*, Prentice-Hall, Englewood Cliffs, 1965.
18. Paul A. Samuelson. "Lifetime Portfolio Selection by Dynamic Stochastic Programming", *Review of Economics and Statistics*, Vol. 51, (August 1969), pp. 239-246.
19. Paul A. Samuelson. "The Fundamental Approximation Theorem of Portfolio Analysis in Terms of Means, Variances and Higher Moments", *Review of Economic Studies*, Vol. 37, (October 1970), pp. 538-542.
20. Richard C. Stapleton. "Portfolio Analysis, Stock Valuation and Capital Budgeting Rules for Risky Projects", *Journal of Finance*, Vol. 26 (March 1971), pp. 95-118.
21. Donald L. Tuttle and Robert H. Litzenberger. "Leverage, Diversification and Capital Market Effects on a Risk Adjusted Capital Budgeting Framework", *Journal of Finance*, Vol. 23, (June 1968), pp. 427-444.
22. James C. Van Horne. "Capital Budgeting Decisions Involving Combinations of Risky Investments", *Management Science*, Vol. 13 (October 1966), pp. 84-92.

10

The Effect of the Firm's Capital Structure on the Systematic Risk of Common Stocks

Robert S. Hamada

I. Introduction

Only recently has there been an interest in relating the issues historically associated with corporation finance to those historically associated with investment and portfolio analyses. In fact, rigorous theoretical attempts in this direction were made only since the capital asset pricing model of Sharpe [13], Lintner [6], and Mossin [11], itself an extension of the Markowitz [7] portfolio theory. This study is one of the first empirical works consciously attempting to show and test the relationships between the two fields. In addition, differences in the observed systematic or nondiversifiable risk of common stocks, β, have never really been analyzed before by investigating some of the underlying differences in the firms.

In the capital asset pricing model, it was demonstrated that the efficient set of portfolios to any individual investor will always be some combination of lending at the risk-free rate and the "market portfolio," or borrowing at the risk-free rate and the "market portfolio." At the same time, the Modigliani and Miller (MM) propositions [9, 10] on the effect of corporate leverage are well known to the students of corporation finance. In order for their propositions to hold, personal leverage is required to be a perfect substitute for corporate leverage. If this is true, then corporate borrowing could substitute for personal borrowing in the capital asset pricing model as well.

Both in the pricing model and the MM theory, borrowing, from whatever source, while maintaining a fixed amount of equity, increases the risk to the investor. Therefore, in the mean-standard deviation version of the capital asset pricing model, the covariance of the asset's rate of return with the market portfolio's rate of return (which measures the nondiversifiable risk of the asset— the proxy β will be used to measure this) should be greater for the stock of a

Reprinted with permission of the author and publisher from *The Journal of Finance*, Vol. 27, no. 2, May 1972, pp. 435–452.

The research assistance of Christine Thomas and Leon Tsao is gratefully acknowledged. This paper has benefited from the comments made at the Finance Workshop at the University of Chicago, and especially those made by Eugene Fama. Remaining errors are due solely to the author.

firm with a higher debt-equity ratio than for the stock of another firm in the same risk-class with a lower debt-equity ratio.[1]

This study, then , has a number of purposes. First, we shall attempt to link empirically corporation finance issues with portfolio and security analyses through the effect of a firm's leverage on the systematic risk of its common stock. Then, we shall attempt to test the MM theory, or at least provide another piece of evidence on this long-standing controversial issue. This test will not rely on an explicit valuation model, such as the MM study of the electric utility industry [8] and the Brown study of the railroad industry [2] . A procedure using systematic risk measures (βs) has been worked out in this paper for this purpose.

If the MM theory is validated by this procedure, then the final purpose of this study is to demonstrate a method for estimating the cost of capital of individual firms to be used by them for scale-changing or nondiversifying investment projects. The primary component of any firm's cost of capital is the capitalization rate for the firm if the firm had no debt and preferred stock in its capital structure. Since most firms do have fixed commitment obligations, this capitalization rate (we shall call it $E(R_A)$; MM denote it $\rho\tau$) is unobservable. But if the MM theory and the capital asset pricing model are correct, then it is possible to estimate $E(R_A)$ from the systematic risk approach for individual firms, even if these firms are members of a one-firm risk-class.[2]

With this statement of the purposes for this study, we shall, in Section II, discuss the alternative general procedures that are possible for estimating the effect of leverage on systematic risk and select the most feasible ones. The results are presented in Section III. And finally, tests of the MM versus the traditional theories of corporation finance are presented in Section IV.

II. Some Possible Procedures and the Selected Estimating Relationships

There are at least four general procedures that can be used to estimate the effect of the firm's capital structure on the systematic risk of common stocks.

---

[1]This very quick summary of the theoretical relationship between what is known as corporation finance and the modern investment and portfolio analyses centered around the capital asset pricing model is more thoroughly presented in [5], along with the necessary assumptions required for this relationship.

[2]It is, in fact, this last purpose of making applicable and practical some of the implications of the capital asset pricing model for corporation finance issues that provided the initial motivation for this paper. In this context, if one is familiar with the fair rate of return literature for regulated utilities, for example, an industry where debt is so prevalent, adjusting correctly for leverage is not frequently done and can be very critical.

The first is the MM valuation model approach. By estimating ρ^τ with an explicit valuation model as they have for the electric utility industry, it is possible to relate this ρ^τ with the use of the capital asset pricing model to a nonleveraged systematic risk measure, $_A\beta$. Then the difference between the observed common stock's systematic risk (which we shall denote $_B\beta$) and $_A\beta$ would be due solely to leverage. But the difficulties of this approach for all firms are many.

The MM valuation model approach requires the specification, in advance, of risk-classes. All firms in a risk-class are then assumed to have the same ρ^τ— the capitalization rate for an all-common equity firm. Unfortunately, there must be enough firms in a risk-class so that a cross-section analysis will yield statistically significant coefficients. There may not be many more risk-classes (with enough observations) now that the electric utility and railroad industries have been studied. In addition, the MM approach requires estimating expected asset earnings and estimating the capitalized growth potential implicit in stock prices. If it is possible to consider growth and expected earnings without having to specify their exact magnitude at a specific point in time, considerable difficulty and possible measurement errors will be avoided.

The second approach is to run a regression between the observed systematic risk of a stock and a number of accounting and leverage variables in an attempt to explain this observed systematic risk. Unfortunately, without a theory, we do not know which variables to include and which variables to exclude and whether the relationship is linear, multiplicative, exponential, curvilinear, etc. Therefore, this method will also not be used.

A third approach is to measure the systematic risk before and after a new debt issue. The difference can then be attributed to the debt issue directly. An attractive feature of this procedure is that a good estimate of the market value of the incremental debt issue can be obtained. A number of disadvantages, unfortunately, are associated with this direct approach. The difference in the systematic risk may be due not only to the additional debt, but also to the reason the debt was issued. It may be used to finance a new investment project, in which case the project's characteristics will also be reflected in the new systematic risk measure. In addition, the new debt issue may have been anticipated by the market if the firm had some long-run target leverage ratio which this issue will help maintain; conversely, the market may not fully consider the new debt issue if it believes the increase in leverage is only temporary. For these reasons, this seemingly attractive procedure will not be employed.

The last approach, which will be used in this study, is to assume the validity of the MM theory from the outset. Then the observed rate of return of a stock can be adjusted to what *it would have been* over the same time period had the firm no debt and preferred stock in its capital structure. The difference between the observed systematic risk, $_B\beta$, and the systematic risk for this adjusted rate of return time series, $_A\beta$, can be attributed to leverage, if the MM theory is correct. The final step, then, is to test the MM theory.

To discuss this more specifically, consider the following relationship for the dollar return to the common shareholder from period $t - 1$ to t:

$$(X - I)_t(1 - \tau)_t - p_t + \Delta G_t = d_t + cg_t \qquad (1)$$

where X_t represents earnings before taxes, interest, and preferred dividends and is assumed to be unaffected by fixed commitment obligations; I_t represents interest and other fixed charges paid during the period; τ is the corporation income tax rate; p_t is the preferred dividends paid; ΔG_t represents the change in capitalized growth over the period; and d_t and cg_t are common shareholder dividends and capital gains during the period, respectively.

Equation (1) relates the corporation finance types of variables with the market holding period return important to the investors. The first term on the left-hand-side of (1) is profits after taxes and after interest which is the earnings the common and preferred shareholders receive on their investment for the period. Subtracting out p_t leaves us with the earnings the common shareholder would receive from currently-held assets.

To this must be added any change in capitalized growth since we are trying to explain the common shareholder's market holding period dollar return. ΔG_t must be added for growth firms to the current period's profits from existing assets since capitalized growth opportunities of the firm—future earnings from new assets over and above the firm's cost of capital which are already reflected in the stock price at $(t - 1)$—should change over the period and would accrue to the common shareholder. Assuming shareholders at the start of the period estimated these growth opportunities on average correctly, the expected value of ΔG_t would not be zero, but should be positive. For example, consider growth opportunities five years from now which yield more than the going rate of return and are reflected in today's stock price. These growth opportunities will become one year closer to fruition at time t than at time $t - 1$ so that their present value would become larger. ΔG_t then represents this increase in the present value of these future opportunities simply because it is now four years away rather than five.[3]

Since the systematic risk of a common stock is:

$$_B\beta = \frac{\text{cov}(R_{B_t}, R_{M_t})}{\sigma^2(R_{M_t})} \qquad (2)$$

---

[3]Continual awareness of the difficulties of estimating capitalized growth, or changes in growth, especially in conjunction with leverage considerations, for purposes such as valuation or cost of capital is a characteristic common to students of corporation finance. This is the reason for the emphasis on growth in this paper and for presenting a method to neutralize for differences in growth when comparing rates of return.

where R_{B_t} is the common shareholder's rate of return and R_{M_t} is the rate of return on the market portfolio, the substitution of (1) into (2) yields:

$$_B\beta = \frac{\text{cov}\left[\dfrac{(X-I)(1-\tau)_t - P_t + \Delta G_t}{S_{B_{t-1}}}, R_{M_t}\right]}{\sigma^2(R_{M_t})} \tag{2a}$$

where $S_{B_{t-1}}$ denotes the market value of the common stock at the beginning of the period.

The systematic risk for the same firm over the same period *if* there were no debt and preferred stock in its capital structure is:

$$_A\beta = \frac{\text{cov}(R_{A_t}, R_{M_t})}{\sigma^2(R_{M_t})}$$

$$= \frac{\text{cov}\left[\dfrac{X(1-\tau)_t + \Delta G_t}{S_{A_{t-1}}}, R_{M_t}\right]}{\sigma^2(R_{M_t})} \tag{3}$$

where R_{A_t} and $S_{A_{t-1}}$ represent the rate of return and the market value, respectively, to the common shareholder if the firm had no debt and preferred stock. From (3), we can obtain:

$$_A\beta S_{A_{t-1}} = \frac{\text{cov}[X(1-\tau)_t + \Delta G_t, R_{M_t}]}{\sigma^2(R_{M_t})} \tag{3a}$$

Next, by expanding and rearranging (2a), we have:

$$_B\beta S_{B_{t-1}} = \frac{\text{cov}[X(1-\tau)_t + \Delta G_t, R_{M_t}]}{\sigma^2(R_{M_t})} - \frac{\text{cov}[I(1-\tau)_t, R_{M_t}]}{\sigma^2(R_{M_t})} - \frac{\text{cov}(p_t, R_{M_t})}{\sigma^2(R_{M_t})} \tag{2b}$$

If we assume as an empirical approximation that interest and preferred dividends have negligible covariance with the market, at least relative to the (pure equity) common stock's covariance, then substitution of the LHS of (3a) into the RHS of (2b) yields:[4]

---

[4]This general method of arriving at (4) was suggested by the comments of William Sharpe, one of the discussants of this paper at the annual meeting. A much more cumbersome and less general derivation of (4) was in the earlier version.

$$_B\beta S_{B\,t-1} = {}_A\beta S_{A\,t-1} \tag{4}$$

or

$$_A\beta = \left(\frac{S_B}{S_A}\right)_{t-1} {}_B\beta \tag{4a}$$

Because $S_{A\,t-1}$, the market value of common stock *if* the firm had no debt and preferred stock, is not observable since most firms do have debt and/or preferred stock, a theory is required in order to measure what this quantity *would have been* at $t-1$. The MM theory [10] will be employed for this purpose, that is:

$$S_{A\,t-1} = (V - \tau D)_{t-1} \tag{5}$$

Equation (5) indicates that if the Federal government tax subsidy for debt financing, τD, where D is the market value of debt, is subtracted from the observed market value of the firm, V_{t-1} (where V_{t-1} is the sum of S_B, D and the observed market value of preferred), then the market value of an un-leveraged firm is obtained. Underlying (5) is the assumption that the firm is near its target leverage ratio so that no more or no less debt subsidy is capitalized already into the observed stock price. The conditions under which this MM relationship hold are discussed carefully in [4].

It is at this point that problems in obtaining satisfactory estimates of $_A\beta$ develop, since (4) theoretically holds only for the next period. As a practical matter, the accepted, and seemingly acceptable, method of obtaining estimates of a stock's systematic risk, $_B\beta$, is to run a least squares regression between a stock's and market portfolio's *historical* rates of return. Using past data for $_B\beta$, it is not clear which *period's* ratio of market values to apply in (4a) to estimate the firm's systematic risk, $_A\beta$. There would be no problem if the market value ratios of debt to equity and preferred stock to equity remained relatively stable over the past for each firm, but a cursory look at these data reveals that this is not true for the large majority of firms in our sample. Should we use the market value ratio required in (4a) that was observed at the start of our regression period, at the end of our regression period, or some kind of average over the period? In addition, since these different observed ratios will give us different estimates for $_A\beta$, it is not clear, without some criterion, how we should select from among the various estimates.

It is for this purpose—to obtain a standard—that a more cumbersome and more data demanding approach to obtain estimates of $_A\beta$ is suggested. Given the large fluctuations in market leverage ratios, intuitively it would appear that the firm's risk is more stable than the common stock's risk. In that event, a leverage-free rate of return time series for each firm should be derived and the market model applies to this time series directly. In this manner, the beta coefficient wold give us a *direct* estimate of $_A\beta$ which can then be used as a criterion to determine if any of the market value ratios discussed above can be applied to (4a) successfully.

For this purpose, the "would-have-been" rate of return for the common stock if the firm had no debt and preferred is:

$$R_{A_t} = \frac{X_t(1-\tau)_t + \Delta G_t}{S_{A_{t-1}}} \tag{6}$$

The numerator of (6) can be rearranged to be:

$$X_t(1-\tau)_t + \Delta G_t \equiv [(X-I)_t(1-\tau)_t - p_t + \Delta G_t] + p_t + I_t(1-\tau)_t$$

Substituting (1):

$$X_t(1-\tau)_t + \Delta G_t = [d_t + cg_t] + p_t + I_t(1-\tau)_t$$

Therefore, (6) can be written as:

$$R_{A_t} = \frac{d_t + cg_t + p_t + I_t(1-\tau)_t}{S_{A_{t-1}}} \tag{7}$$

Since $S_{A_{t-1}}$ is unobservable for the firms with leverage, the MM theory, equation (5), will be employed; then:

$$R_{A_t} = \frac{d_t + cg_t + p_t + I_t(1-\tau)_t}{(V-\tau D)_{t-1}} \tag{8}$$

The observed rate of return on the common stock is, of course:

$$R_{B_t} = \frac{(X-I)_t(1-\tau)_t - p_t + \Delta G_t}{S_{B_{t-1}}} = \frac{d_t + cg_t}{S_{B_{t-1}}} \tag{9}$$

Equation (8) is the rate of return to the common shareholder of the same firm and over the same period of time as (9). However, in (8) there are the underlying assumptions that the firm never had any debt and preferred stock and that the MM theory is correct; (9) incorporates the exact amount of debt and preferred stock that the firm actually did have over this time period and no leverage assumption is being made. Both (8) and (9) are now in forms where they can be measured with available data. One can note that it is unnecessary to estimate the change in growth, or earnings from current assets since these should be captured in the market holding period return, $d_t + cg$.

Using CRSP data for (9) and both CRSP and Compustat data for the components of (8), a time series of yearly R_{At} and R_{Bt} for $t = 1948\text{--}1967$ were derived for 304 different firms. These 304 firms represent an exhaustive sample of the firms with complete data on both tapes for all the years.

A number of "market model" [1, 12] variants were then applied to these data. For each of the 304 firms, the following regressions were run:

$$R_{Ait} = {}_A\alpha_i + {}_A\beta_i R_{Mt} + {}_A\epsilon_{it} \tag{10a}$$

$$R_{Bit} = {}_B\alpha_i + {}_B\beta_i R_{Mt} + {}_B\epsilon_{it} \tag{10b}$$

$$\ln(1 + R_{Ait}) = {}_{AC}\alpha_i + {}_{AC}\beta_i \ln(1 + R_{Mt}) + {}_{AC}\epsilon_{it} \tag{10c}$$

$$\ln(1 + R_{Bit}) = {}_{BC}\alpha_i + {}_{BC}\beta_i \ln(1 + R_{Mt}) + {}_{BC}\epsilon_{it} \tag{10d}$$

$$i = 1, 2, \ldots, 304$$

$$t = 1948\text{--}1967$$

where R_{Mt} is the observed NYSE arithmetic stock market rate of return with dividends reinvested, α_i and β_i are constants for each firm-regression, and the usual conditions are assumed for the properties of the disturbance terms, ϵ_{it}. Equations (10c) and (10d) are the continuously-compounded rate of return versions of (10a) and (10b), respectively.[5]

III. The Results

An abbreviated table of the regression results for each of the four variants, equations (10a)–(10d), summarized across the 304 firms is shown in Table 1.

---

[5]Because the R_{Mt} used in equations (10) is defined as the observed stock market return, and since adjusting for capital structure is the major purpose of this exercise, it was decided that the same four regressions should be replicated on a leverage-adjusted stock market rate of return. The major reason for this additional adjustment is the belief that the rates of return over time and their relationship with the market are more stable when we can abstract from all changes in leverage and get at the underlying risk of all firms.

For the 221 firms (out of the total 304) whose fiscal years coincide with the calendar year, average values for the components of the RHS of (8) were obtained for each year so that R_{Mt} could be adjusted in the same way as for the individual firms—a yearly time series of stock market rates of return, if all the firms on the NYSE had no debt and no preferred in their capital structure, was derived. The results, when using this adjusted market portfolio rate of return time series, were not very different from the results of equations (10), and so will not be reported here separately.

Table 1
Summary Results over 304 Firms of Equations (10a)–(10d)

	Mean	Mean Absolute Deviation*	Standard Deviation	Mean Standard Error of Estimate
$A\hat{\alpha}$	0.0221	0.0431	0.0537	0.0558
$A\hat{\beta}$	0.7030	0.2660	0.3485	0.2130
$A\hat{R}^2$	0.3799	0.1577	0.1896	
$A\hat{\rho}$	0.0314			
$B\hat{\alpha}$	0.0187	0.0571	0.0714	0.0720
$B\hat{\beta}$	0.9190	0.3550	0.4478	0.2746
$B\hat{R}^2$	0.3864	0.1578	0.1905	
$B\hat{\rho}$	0.0281			
$AC\hat{\alpha}$	0.0058	0.0427	0.0535	0.0461
$AC\hat{\beta}$	0.7263	0.2700	0.3442	0.2081
$AC\hat{R}^2$	0.3933	0.1586	0.1909	
$AC\hat{\rho}$	0.0268			
$BC\hat{\alpha}$	-0.0052	0.0580	0.0729	0.0574
$BC\hat{\beta}$	0.9183	0.3426	0.4216	0.2591
$BC\hat{R}^2$	0.4012	0.1602	0.1922	
$BC\hat{\rho}$	0.0262			

*Defined as: $\displaystyle\sum_{i=1}^{n} |x_i - \bar{x}|/N$, where $N = 304$. ρ = first order serial correlation coefficient.

The first column designated "mean" is the average of the statistic (indicated by the rows) over all 304 firms. Therefore, the mean $_A\hat{\alpha}$ of 0.0221 is the intercept term of equation (10a) averaged over 304 different firm-regressions. The second and third columns give the deviation measures indicated, of the 304 point estimates of, say, $_A\hat{\alpha}$. The mean standard error of estimate in the last column is the average over 304 firms of the individual standard errors of estimate.

The major conclusion drawn from Table 1 is the following mean β comparisons:

$$_B\hat{\beta} > {_A\hat{\beta}} \quad \text{i.e., } 0.9190 > 0.7030$$

$$_{BC}\hat{\beta} > {_{AC}\hat{\beta}} \quad \text{i.e., } 0.9183 > 0.7263$$

The directional results of these betas, assuming the validity of the MM theory, are not imperceptible and clearly are not negligible differences from the investor's point of view. This is obtained in spite of all the measurement and data problems associated with estimating a time series of the RHS of (8) for each firm. One of the reasons for the "traditional" theory position on leverage is precisely this point—that small and reasonable amounts of leverage cannot be discerned by the market. In fact, if the MM theory is correct, leverage has explained as much as, roughly, 21 to 24 per cent of the value of the mean β.

We can also note that if the covariance between the asset and market rates of return, as well as the market variance, was constant over time, then the systematic risk from the market model is related to the expected rate of return by the capital asset pricing model. That is:

$$E(R_{A_t}) = R_{F_t} + {}_A\beta[E(R_{M_t}) - R_{F_t}] \tag{11a}$$

$$E(R_{B_t}) = R_{F_t} + {}_B\beta[E(R_{M_t}) - R_{F_t}] \tag{11b}$$

Equation (11a) indicates the relationship between the expected rate of return for the common stock shareholder of a debt-free and preferred-free firm, to the systematic risk, ${}_A\beta$, as obtained in regressions (10a) or (10c). The LHS of (11a) is the important $\rho\tau$ for the MM cost of capital. The MM theory [9,10] also predicts that shareholder expected yield must be higher (for the same real firm) when the firm has debt than when it does not. Financial risk is greater, therefore, shareholders require more expected return. Thus, $E(R_{B_t})$ must be greater than $E(R_{A_t})$. In order for this MM prediction to be true, from (11a) and (11b) it can be observed that ${}_B\beta$ must be greater than ${}_A\beta$, which is what we obtained.

Using the results underlying Table 1, namely the firm and stock betas, as the criterion for selecting among the possible observed market value ratios that can be used, if any, for (4), the following cross-section regressions were run:

$$({}_B\beta)_i = a_1 + b_1\left(\frac{S_A}{S_B} \;{}_A\beta\right)_i + u_{1i} \quad i = 1, 2, \ldots, 102 \tag{12a}$$

$$({}_{BC}\beta)_i = a_2 + b_2\left(\frac{S_A}{S_B} \;{}_{AC}\beta\right)_i + u_{2i} \quad i = 1, 2, \ldots, 102 \tag{12b}$$

$$({}_A\beta)_i = a_3 + b_3\left(\frac{S_B}{S_A} \;{}_B\beta\right)_i + u_{3i} \quad i = 1, 2, \ldots, 102 \tag{13a}$$

$$({}_{AC}\beta)_i = a_4 + b_4\left(\frac{S_B}{S_A} \;{}_{BC}\beta\right)_i + u_{4i} \quad i = 1, 2, \ldots, 102 \tag{13b}$$

Because the preferred stock market values were not as reliable as debt, only the 102 firms (out of 304) that did not have preferred in any of the years were used. The test for the adequacy of this alternative approach, equation (4), to adjust the systematic risk of common stocks for the underlying firm's capital structure, is whether the intercept term, a, is equal to zero, and the slope coefficient, b, is equal to one in the above regressions (as well as, of course, a high R^2)–these requirements are implied by (4). The results of this test would also indicate whether future "market model" studies that only use common stock rates of return without adjusting, or even noting, for the firm's debt-equity ratio will be adequate. The total firm's systematic risk may be stable (as long as the firm stays in the same risk-class), whereas the common stock's systematic risk may not be stable merely because of unanticipated capital structure changes–the data underlying Table 3 indicate that there were very few firms which did not have major changes in their capital structure over the twenty years studied.

The results of these regressions, when using the average S_A and average S_B over the twenty years for each firm, are shown in the first column panel of Table 2. These regressions were then replicated twice, first using the December 31, 1947 value of S_{Ai} and S_{Bi} instead of the twenty-year average for each firm, and then substituting the December 31, 1966 values of S_{Ai} and S_{Bi} for the 1947 values. These results are in the second and third panels of Table 2.[6]

From the first panel of Table 2, it appears that this alternative approach via (4a) for adjusting the systematic risk for the firm's leverage is quite satisfactory (at least with respect to our sample of firms and years) only if long-run averages of S_A and S_B are used. The second and third panels indicate that the equations (8) and (10) procedure is markedly superior when only one year's market value ratio is used as the adjustment factor. The annual debt-to-equity ratio is much too unstable for this latter procedure.

Thus, when forecasting systematic risk is the primary objective–for example, for portfolio decisions or for estimating the firm's cost of capital to apply to prospective projects–a long-run forecasted leverage adjustment is required. Assuming the firm's risk is more stable than the common stock's risk,[7] and if

---

[6]The point should be made that we are not merely regressing a variable on itself in (12) and (13). (12a) and (12b) can be interpreted as correlating the $_B\beta_i$ obtained from (10b) and (10d)–the LHS variable in (12a) and (12b)–against the $_B\beta_i$ obtained from rearranging (4)–the RHS variable in (12a) and (12b)–to determine whether the use of (4) is as good a means of obtaining $_B\beta_i$ as the direct way via the equations (10). We would be regressing a variable on itself only if the $_A\beta_i$ were calculated using (4a), and then the $_A\beta_i$ thus obtained, inserted into (12a) and (12b).

Instead, we are obtaining $_A\beta_i$ using the MM model in *each* of the twenty years so that a leverage-adjusted 20 year time series of R_{A_i} is derived. Of course, if there were no data nor measurement problems, and if the debt-to-equity ratio were perfectly stable over this twenty year period for each firm, then we should obtain perfect correlation in (12a) and (12b), with a = 0 and b = 1, as (4) would be an identity.

[7]A faint, but possible, empirical indication of this point may be obtained from Table 1. The ratio of the mean point estimate to the mean standard error of estimate is less for the firm β than for the stock β in both the discrete and continuously compounded cases.

Table 2
Results for the Equations (12a), (12b), (13a), and (13b)*

	Using 20-Year Average for $(S_A/S_B)_i$			Using 1947 Value for $(S_A/S_B)_i$			Using 1966 Value for $(S_A/S_B)_i$		
	a	b	R^2	a	b	R^2	a	b	R^2
Eq. (12a)	-0.022	1.062	0.962	0.150	0.842	0.781	0.085	0.905	0.849
	(0.021)	(0.021)		(0.048)	(0.045)		(0.041)	(0.038)	
constant suppressed		1.042	0.962		0.966	0.781		0.976	0.849
		(0.009)			(0.021)			(0.017)	
Eq. (12b)	-0.003	1.016	0.984	0.159	0.816	0.773	0.124	0.843	0.859
	(0.013)	(0.013)		(0.047)	(0.044)		(0.037)	(0.034)	
constant suppressed		1.014	0.984		0.952	0.773		0.947	0.859
		(0.005)			(0.019)			(0.015)	

	Using 20-Year Average for $(S_B/S_A)_i$			Using 1947 Value for $(S_B/S_A)_i$			Using 1966 Value for $(S_B/S_A)_i$		
	a	b	R^2	a	b	R^2	a	b	R^2
Eq. (13a)	0.030	0.931	0.969	0.112	0.843	0.888	0.080	0.898	0.902
	(0.016)	(0.017)		(0.028)	(0.030)		(0.027)	(0.030)	
constant suppressed		0.960	0.969		0.948	0.888		0.976	0.902
		(0.007)			(0.015)			(0.014)	
Eq. (13b)	0.007	0.979	0.988	0.119	0.852	0.902	0.063	0.942	0.911
	(0.010)	(0.011)		(0.026)	(0.028)		(0.026)	(0.029)	
constant suppressed		1.004	0.911		0.967	0.902		1.005	0.911
		(0.012			(0.013)			(0.012)	

*Standard error in parentheses.

there is some reason to believe that a better forecast of the firm's future leverage can be obtained than using simply a past year's (or an average of past years') leverage, it should be possible to improve the usual extrapolation forecast of a stock's systematic risk by forecasting the total firm's systematic risk first, and then using the independent leverage estimate as an adjustment.

IV. Tests of the MM vs. Traditional Theories of Corporation Finance

To determine if the difference, $_B\beta - {_A}\beta$, found in this study is indeed the correct effect of leverage, some confirmation of the MM theory (since it was assumed to be correct up to this point) from the systematic risk approach is needed. Since a direct test by this approach seems impossible, an indirect, inferential test is suggested.

The MM theory [9, 10] predicts that for firms in the same risk-class, the capitalization rate if all the firms were financed with only common equity, $E(R_A)$, would be the same—regardless of the actual amount of debt and preferred each individual firm had. This would imply, from (11a), that if $E(R_A)$ must be the same for all firms in a risk-class, so must $_A\beta$. And if these firms had different ratios of fixed commitment obligations to common equity, this difference in financial risk would cause their observed $_B\beta$s to be different.

The major competing theory of corporation finance is what is now known as the "traditional theory," which has contrary implications. This theory predicts that the capitalization rate for common equity, $E(R_B)$, (sometimes called the required or expected stock yield, or expected earnings-price ratio) is constant, as debt is increased, up to some critical leverage point (this point being a function of gambler's ruin and bankruptcy costs).[8] The clear implication of this constant, horizontal, equity yield (or their initial downward sloping cost of capital curve) is that changes in market or covariability risk are assumed not to be discernible to the shareholders as debt is increased. Then the traditional theory is saying that the $_B\beta$s, a measure of this covariability risk, would be the same for all firms in a given risk-class irregardless of differences in leverage, as long as the critical leverage point is not reached.

Since there will always be unavoidable errors in estimating the β's of individual firms and in specifying a risk-class, we would not expect to find a set of firms with identical systematic risk. But by specifying reasonable a priori risk-classes, if the individual firms had closer or less scattered $_A\beta$s than $_B\beta$s, then this would support the MM theory and contradict the traditional theory.

---

[8]This interpretation of the traditional theory can be found in [9, especially their figure 2, page 275, and their equation (13) and footnote 24 where reference is made to Durand and Graham and Dodd].

If, instead, the $_B\beta$s were not discernibly more diverse than the $_A\beta$s, and the leverage ratio differed considerably among firms, then this would indicate support for the traditional theory.[9]

In order to test this implication, risk-classes must be first specified. The SEC two-digit industry classification was used for this purpose. Requiring enough firms for statistical reasons in any given industry, nine risk-classes were specified that had at least 13 firms; these nine classes are listed in Table 3 with their various leverage ratios.[10] It is clear from this table that our first requirement is met—that there is a considerable range of leverage ratios among firms in a risk-class and also over the twenty-year period.

Three tests will be performed to distinguish between the MM and traditional theories. The first is simply to calculate the standard deviation of the unbiased β estimates in a risk-class. The second is a chi-square test of the distribution of β's in an industry compared to the distribution of the β's in the total sample. Finally, an analysis of variance test on the estimated variance of the β's between industries, as opposed to within industries, is performed. In all tests, only the point estimate of β (which should be unbiased) for each stock and firm is used.[11]

The first test is reported in Table 4. If we compare the standard deviation of $_{AC}\beta$ with the standard deviation of $_{BC}\beta$ by industries (or risk-classes), we can note that $\sigma(_{AC}\beta)$ is less than $\sigma(_{BC}\beta)$ for eight out of the nine classes. The probability of obtaining this is only 0.0195, given a 50% probability that $\sigma(_{AC}\beta)$ can be larger or smaller than $\sigma(_{BC}\beta)$. These results indicate that the systematic risk of the firms in a given risk-class, if they were all financed only with common

---

[9] The traditional theory also implies that $E(R_A)$ is equal to $E(R_B)$ for all firms. Unfortunately, we do not have a functional relationship between these traditional theory capitalization rates and the measured βs of this study. Clearly, since the $_A\beta$s were obtained assuming the validity of the MM theory, they would not be applicable for the traditional theory. In fact, no relationship between the $_A\beta$ and $_B\beta$ for a given firm, or for firms in a given risk-class, can be specified as was done for the capitalization rates.

[10] The tenth largest industry had only eight firms. For our purpose of testing the uniformity of firm βs relative to stock βs within a risk-class, the use of the two-digit industry classification as a proxy does not seem as critical as, for instance, its use for the purpose of performing an MM valuation model study [8] wherein the ρ^τ must be pre-specified to be exactly the same for all firms in the industry.

[11] Since these βs are estimated in the market model regressions with error, precise testing should incorporate the errors in the β estimation. Unfortunately, to do this is extremely difficult and more importantly, requires the normality assumption for the market model disturbance term. Since there is considerable evidence that is contrary to this required assumption [see 3], our tests will ignore the β measurement error entirely. But ignoring this is partially corrected in our first and third tests since means and variances of these point estimate βs must be calculated, and this procedure will "average out" the individual measurement errors by the factor $1/N$.

Table 3
Industry Market Value Ratios of Preferred Stock (P) and Debt (D) to Common Stock (S)

Industry Number	Industry	Number of Firms		P/S	D/S	P+D/S
20	Food and Kindred Products	30	Mean*	0.22	0.81	1.04
			ROM**	0.00 / 0.00	0.00 / 0.00	0.00 / 0.00
			ROCR***	1.18 / 2.52	3.55 / 8.10	4.13 / 10.01
28	Chemicals and Allied Products	30	Mean	0.07	0.25	0.33
			ROM	0.00 / 0.00	0.00 / 0.00	0.00 / 0.00
			ROCR	0.51 / 1.54	0.90 / 2.07	1.20 / 2.92
29	Petroleum and Coal Products	18	Mean	0.06	0.22	0.27
			ROM	0.00 / 0.00	0.00 / 0.00	0.03 / 0.00
			ROCR	0.26 / 0.83	0.55 / 1.54	0.57 / 2.30
33	Primary Metals	21	Mean	0.14	0.54	0.68
			ROM	0.00 / 0.00	0.00 / 0.00	0.00 / 0.00
			ROCR	1.31 / 4.69	1.95 / 6.20	3.04 / 7.49
35	Machinery, except Electrical	28	Mean	0.07	0.33	0.40
			ROM	0.00 / 0.00	0.00 / 0.00	0.00 / 0.00
			ROCR	0.49 / 1.28	1.92 / 6.92	2.32 / 7.62
36	Electrical Machinery & Equipment	13	Mean	0.06	0.35	0.41
			ROM	0.00 / 0.00	0.00 / 0.00	0.01 / 0.00
			ROCR	0.29 / 1.13	1.31 / 2.53	1.33 / 2.53
37	Transportation Equipment	24	Mean	0.08	0.38	0.47
			ROM	0.00 / 0.00	0.00 / 0.00	0.00 / 0.00
			ROCR	0.54 / 2.33	0.93 / 3.76	1.32 / 6.09
49	Utilities	27	Mean	0.25	1.03	1.28
			ROM	0.00 / 0.00	0.49 / 0.12	0.52 / 0.12
			ROCR	0.53 / 3.12	2.64 / 16.40	3.12 / 19.52
53	Dep't Stores, Order Houses & Vending Mach. Operators	17	Mean	0.13	0.49	0.62
			ROM	0.00 / 0.00	0.01 / 0.00	0.01 / 0.00
			ROCR	0.38 / 1.09	1.52 / 3.19	1.87 / 3.66

*"Mean" refers to the average ratio over 20 years and over all firms in the industry.
**"Range of Means" (ROM) refers to the lowest firm's mean (over 20 years) ratio and the highest firm's mean (over 20 years) ratio in the industry.
***"Range of Company Ranges" (ROCR) refers to the lowest and highest ratio in the industry, regardless of the year.

Table 4

Mean and Standard Deviation of Industry β's

Industry Number	Industry	Number of Firms		A^β	B^β	AC^β	BC^β
20	Food & Kindred Products	30	Mean β	0.515	0.815	0.528	0.806
			σ(β)	0.232	0.448	0.227	0.424
28	Chemicals & Allied Products	30	Mean β	0.747	0.928	0.785	0.946
			σ(β)	0.237	0.391	0.216	0.329
29	Petroleum & Coal Products	18	Mean β	0.633	0.747	0.656	0.756
			σ(β)	0.144	0.188	0.148	0.176
33	Primary Metals	21	Mean β	1.036	1.399	1.106	1.436
			σ(β)	0.223	0.272	0.197	0.268
35	Machinery, except Electrical	28	Mean β	0.878	1.037	0.917	1.068
			σ(β)	0.262	0.240	0.271	0.259
36	Electrical Machinery and Equipment	13	Mean β	0.940	1.234	0.951	1.164
			σ(β)	0.320	0.505	0.283	0.363
37	Transportation Equipment	24	Mean β	0.860	1.062	0.875	1.048
			σ(β)	0.225	0.313	0.225	0.289
49	Utilities	27	Mean β	0.160	0.255	0.166	0.254
			σ(β)	0.086	0.133	0.098	0.147
53	Department Stores, etc.	17	Mean β	0.652	0.901	0.692	0.923
			σ(β)	0.187	0.282	0.198	0.279

equity, is much less diverse than their observed stock's systematic risk. This supports the MM theory, at least in contrast to the traditional theory.[12]

Our second test, the chi-square test, requires us to rank our 300 $_A\beta$s into ten equal categories, each with 30 $_A\beta$s (four miscellaneous firms were taken out randomly). By noting the value of the highest and lowest $_A\beta$ for each of the ten categories, a distribution of the number of $_A\beta$s in each category, by risk-class, can be obtained. This was then repeated for the other three betas. To test whether the distribution for each of the four β's and for each of the risk-classes follows the expected uniform distribution, a chi-square test was performed.[13]

---

[12]Of course, there could always be another theory, as yet not formulated, which could be even more strongly supported than the MM theory. If we compare $\sigma(_A\beta)$ to $\sigma(_B\beta)$ by risk-classes in Table 4, precisely the same results are obtained as those reported above for the continuously-compounded betas.

[13]By risk-classes, seven of the nine chi-square values of $_A\beta$ are larger than those of $_B\beta$, as are eight out of nine for the continuously-compounded betas. This would occur by chance with probabilities of 0.0898 and 0.0195, respectively, if there were a 50% chance that either the firm or stock chi-square value could be larger. Nevertheless, if we inspect the individual chi-square values by risk-class, we note that most of them are large so that the

Even with just casual inspection of these distributions of the betas by risk-class, it is clear that two industries, primary metals and utilities, are so highly skewed that they greatly exaggerate our results.[14] Eliminating these two industries, and also two miscellaneous firms so that an even 250 firms are in the sample, new upper and lower values of the β's were obtained for each of the ten class intervals and for each of the four β's.

In Table 5, the chi-square values are presented; for the total of all risk-classes, the probability of obtaining a chi-square value less than 120.63 is over 99.95% (for $_A\beta$), whereas the probability of obtaining a chi-square value less than 99.75 is between 99.5% and 99.9% (for $_B\beta$). More sharply contrasting results are obtained when $_{AC}\beta$ is compared to $_{BC}\beta$. For $_{AC}\beta$, the probability of obtaining less than 128.47 is over 99.95%, whereas for $_{BC}\beta$, the probability of obtaining less than 78.65 is only 90.0%. By abstracting from financial risk, the underlying systematic risk is much less scattered when grouped into risk-classes than when leverage is assumed not to affect the systematic risk. The null hypothesis that the β's in a risk-class come from the same distribution as all β's is rejected for $_{AC}\beta$, but not for $_{BC}\beta$ (at the 90% level). Although this, in itself, does not tell us *how* a risk-class differs from the total market, an inspection of the distributions of the betas by risk-class underlying Table 5 does indicate more clustering of the $_{AC}\beta$s than the $_{BC}\beta$s so that the MM theory is again favored over the traditional theory.

The analysis of variance test is our last comparison of the implications of the two theories. The ratio of the estimated variance between industries to the estimated variance within the industries (the F-statistic) when the seven industries are considered (again, the two obviously skewed industries, primary metals and utilities, were eliminated) is less for $_B\beta$ ($F = 3.90$) than for $_A\beta$ ($F = 9.99$), and less for $_{BC}\beta$ ($F = 4.18$) than for $_{AC}\beta$ ($F = 10.83$). The probability of obtaining these F-statistics for $_A\beta$ and $_{AC}\beta$ is less than 0.001, but for $_B\beta$ and $_{BC}\beta$ greater than or equal to 0.001. These results are consistent with the results obtained from our two previous tests. The MM theory is more compatible with the data than the traditional theory.[15]

---

probabilities of obtaining these values are highly unlikely. For all four βs, the distributions for most of the risk-classes are nonuniform.

[14]Primary metals have extremely large betas; utilities have extremely small betas.

[15]All of our tests, it should be emphasized, although consistent, are only inferential. Aside from assuming that the two-digit SEC industry classification is a good proxy for risk-classes and that the errors in estimating the individual βs can be safely ignored, the tests rely on the two theories exhausting all the reasonable theories on leverage. But there is always the use of another line of reasoning. If the results of the MM electric utility study [8] are correct, and if these results can be generalized to all firms and to all risk-classes, then it can be claimed that the MM theory is universally valid. Then our result in Section III does indicate the correct effect of the firm's capital structure on the systematic risk of common stocks.

Table 5
Chi-Square Results for All β's and All Industries (except Utilities and Primary Metals)

Industry		A^β	B^β	AC^β	BC^β
Food and Kindred	Chi-Square	18.67	11.33	26.00	9.33
	P $x^2 <$ * =	95–97.5%	70–75%	99.5–99.9%	50–60%
Chemicals	Chi-Square	9.33	10.67	12.00	7.33
	P $x^2 <$ =	50–60%	60–70%	75–80%	30–40%
Petroleum	Chi-Square	17.56	25.33	18.67	22.00
	P $x^2 <$ =	95–97.5%	99.5–99.9%	95–97.5%	99–99.5%
Machinery	Chi-Square	19.14	12.00	24.86	9.14
	P $x^2 <$ =	97.5–98%	75–80%	99.5–99.9%	50–60%
Electrical Machinery	Chi-Square	13.92	7.77	12.38	9.31
	P $x^2 <$ =	80–90%	40–50%	80–90%	50–60%
Transportation Equipment	Chi-Square	15.17	16.83	13.50	6.83
	P $x^2 <$ =	90–95%	90–95%	80–90%	30–40%
Dep't Stores	Chi-Square	14.18	3.59	14.18	3.59
	P $x^2 <$ =	80–90%	5–10%	80–90%	5–10%
Miscellaneous	Chi-Square	12.67	12.22	6.89	11.11
	P $x^2 <$ =	80–90%	80–90%	30–40%	70–75%
Total	Chi-Square	120.63	99.75	128.47	78.65
	P $x^2 <$ =	over 99.95%	99.5–99.90%	over 99.95%	90.0%

*Example: $P\left\{ x^2 < 18.67 \right\}$ = 95–97.5% for 9 degrees of freedom.

V. Conclusions

This study attempted to tie together some of the notions associated with the field of corporation finance with those associated with security and portfolio analyses. Specifically, if the MM corporate tax leverage propositions are correct, then approximately 21 to 24% of the observed systematic risk of common stocks (when averaged over 304 firms) can be explained merely by the added financial risk taken on by the underlying firm with its use of debt and preferred stock. Corporate leverage does count considerably.

To determine whether the MM theory is correct, a number of tests on a contrasting implication of the MM and "traditional" theories of corporation finance were performed. The data confirmed MM's position, at least vis-à-vis our interpretation of the traditional theory's position. This should provide another piece of evidence on this controversial topic.

Finally, if the MM theory and the capital asset pricing model are correct, and if the adjustments made in equations (8) or (4a) result in accurate measures of the systematic risk of a leverage-free firm, the possibility is greater, without resorting to a fullblown risk-class study of the type MM did for the electric utility industry [8], of estimating the cost of capital for individual firms.

References

1. M. Blume. "Portfolio Theory: A Step Toward Its Practical Application," *Journal of Business* 43 (April, 1970), 152-173.
2. P. Brown. "Some Aspects of Valuation in the Railroad Industry," Unpublished Ph.D. dissertation, Graduate School of Business, University of Chicago, 1968.
3. E. Fama. "The Behavior of Stock Market Prices," *Journal of Business* 38 (January, 1965), 34-105.
4. E. Fama, and M. Miller. *The Theory of Finance.* Chapter 4, Holt, Rinehart and Winston, 1972.
5. R. Hamada. "Portfolio Analysis, Market Equilibrium and Corporation Finance," *Journal of Finance* (March, 1969), 13-31.
6. J. Lintner. "The Valuation of Risk Assets and the Selection of Risky Investments in Stock Portfolios and Capital Budgets," *Review of Economics and Statistics* (February, 1965), 13-37.
7. H. Markowitz. *Portfolio Selection: Efficient Diversification of Investments.* New York: John Wiley & Sons, Inc., 1959.
8. M. Miller, and F. Modigliani. "Some Estimates of the Cost of Capital to the Electric Utility Industry, 1954-57," *American Economic Review* (June, 1966), 333-91.

9. F. Modigliani, and M. Miller. "The Cost of Capital, Corporation Finance and the Theory of Investment," *American Economic Review* (June, 1958), 261–97.

10. ——. "Corporate Income Taxes and the Cost of Capital: A Correction," *American Economic Review* (June, 1963), 433–43.

11. J. Mossin. "Equilibrium in a Capital Asset Market," *Econometrica* (October, 1966), 768–83.

12. W. Sharpe. "A Simplified Model for Portfolio Analysis," *Management Science* (January, 1963), 277–93.

13. ——. "Capital Asset Prices: A Theory of Market Equilibrium under Conditions of Risk," *Journal of Finance* (September, 1964), 425–42.

11

Risk and Return: The Case of Merging Firms

Gershon Mandelker

1. Introduction

Mergers are a controversial issue in economic literature. At one extreme is the view that in the acquisitions market 'big business' uses its power to exploit imperfections in the capital market to gain monopolistic power in the product market. It is frequently argued that stockholders of acquiring firms earn abnormal returns from mergers.[1] In discussing mergers, many textbooks present famous mergers of successful firms, and conclude that mergers are profitable. Consequently frequent waves of mergers have been regarded as a threat to the free enterprise system for which the heavy hand of the regulator is needed.

At the other extreme is the position that assumes the separation of control from ownership in the modern multi-owner corporation.[2] In this view management pursues size maximization, often at the expense of maximization of owners' wealth. This implies that firms engage in acquisitions even when the marginal cost of acquisition is higher than the marginal increase in the value of the firm. Stockholders are thus expected to earn lower than normal returns. This approach seems to have considerable empirical support. Indeed most of the empirical studies on the profitability of the acquiring firms yield the surprising result that, on the average, mergers are unsuccessful.[3] In a recent survey article which reviews the last fifty years' empirical research on the profitability of mergers, Hogarty concludes that mergers have a *negative* effect on the profit-

Reprinted with permission of the author and North-Holland Publishing Company from the *Journal of Financial Economics,* Vol. 1, issue 4, December 1974, pp. 303–335.
This paper is adapted from my Ph.D. thesis at the University of Chicago. I am deeply grateful to my thesis committee, Eugene F. Fama (Chairman), Fischer Black, and Merton H. Miller for their invaluable advice. I owe a special debt of gratitude to Professor Fama for his penetrating criticisms of numerous drafts of my dissertation. I would also like to thank Jeffrey F. Jaffe for his insightful comments. The editorial and technical aid of Michael C. Jensen and David Mayers are gratefully acknowledged. Needless to say, I retain responsibility for any remaining errors or lack of clarity.

[1] Firm X is referred to as the acquiring firm if it acquires more than 50% of the equity of firm Y (the acquired firm).

[2] This position follows the arguments of Berle and Means (1932), and, more recently, those of Baumol (1959), Williamson (1966), and Mueller (1969). See also Kaysen (1965) and Larner (1966).

[3] See, for example, recent studies by Hogarty (1970), Gort and Hogarty (1970), Reid (1968, 1971), and Gilbert (1971).

ability of the acquiring firms, and a neutral effect on the *sum* of acquired plus acquiring firms. He believes that acquiring firms engage in this unprofitable activity because 'mergers are an attractive form of investment for those firms whose managers are risk takers . . . (since) some mergers produce extraordinary profits . . .' (St. John's Law Review, 1969)—while most produce losses to the acquiring firms. However, previous studies suffer from various shortcomings. Most employ small sample sizes and use rather primitive models, i.e., they neither adjust for risk nor do they take into consideration changes in risk. In this study we attempt to incorporate these factors.

In contrast to the above two views, the basic presumption of this study is that the expected return from an acquisition is the same as from any other investment–production activity with similar risk. That is, we expect the market for acquisitions to operate competitively. Consequently two basic questions will be examined:

(a) Are mergers in fact associated with abnormal positive or negative returns? If so, how are the abnormal returns shared between the shareholders of acquired and acquiring companies?

(b) Is the capital market efficient with respect to mergers? That is, is information on mergers reflected immediately in the stock prices of the merging firms? Statements that contradict the Efficient Capital Markets Hypothesis by assuming a long period for learning are found quite often in the literature on mergers.[4] We hope to bring some evidence to bear on this.

The following section presents some competing hypotheses. In section 3, data sources and research methodology are discussed. In section 4, empirical evidence is presented and analyzed. Section 5 summarizes the results.

2. Hypotheses

2.1. The Perfectly Competitive Acquisitions Market (PCAM) Hypothesis

In a perfectly competitive market, competition will equate the expected rates of return on assets of similar risk. If the acquisitions market offers higher expected returns than equivalent activities of similar risk, more resources will be directed to this activity until expected rates of return are reduced to a competitive level. The reverse holds if the acquisitions market has lower expected returns than equivalent activities of similar risk. The PCAM hypothesis implies that for an acquiring firm there are no monopolistic sources of gains due solely to merging as a way of obtaining productive capacity.

---

[4]For an excellent exposition of the theory of efficient capital markets and the relevant empirical research, see Fama (1970).

We could, however, envisage an acquisitions market in which perfect competition prevails on only one side. For example, the acquiring firms might be in a perfectly competitive acquisitions market, but the firms to be acquired might have some 'unique' resources. In this situation only the acquiring firms' stockholders will earn normal levels of expected returns from an acquisition. If a firm to be acquired has some resources which are not used effectively and which could provide economic gains to other firms by merger, then competition among these firms will cause any abnormal returns from the merger to go to the stockholders of the acquired firm. We can envisage situations in which such unique resources can be released only by the agreement to merge (e.g., the acquired firm has had large losses which it cannot hope to use against future profits to lower taxes).

Some economists argue that firms merge to achieve synergy.[5] However, in a steady-state economy this argument is inconsistent with a perfect market in business organizations. In a perfect market firms are able to achieve synergy equally by internal or external growth. They are not expected to be able to acquire a firm at prices which are lower than the cost of reproducing that firm's assets internally.

2.2. The Efficient Capital Markets Hypothesis

The efficient capital markets hypothesis says that stock prices adjust instantaneously to new information. Thus stock prices provide unbiased signals for efficient resource allocation. If the capital market is efficient with respect to mergers, then any information about a merger should be incorporated instantaneously into the corresponding stock prices. The efficient markets hypothesis does not rule out monopolistic elements in the acquisitions market. Mergers could imply gains for either the acquiring or for the acquired firms. The hypothesis states only that the stock market reacts efficiently to information about a forthcoming merger.

In fact, many of the reasons for mergers proposed in the literature are based on the assumption that the capital market is inefficient. Some of these arguments are presented below.

2.3. Some Traditional Hypotheses

By contrast to the PCAM and efficient market hypotheses, the mergers literature contains hypotheses on the reasons for mergers which tend to fall under one or more of the following headings.

---

[5] See, for example, Weston, in: Alberts and Segall (1966).

2.3.1. The 'Abnormal Gains' Hypothesis. This hypothesis states that information concerning a forthcoming acquisition is generally considered 'good' news for the stockholders of the acquiring firm. Various reasons for economic gains from mergers are usually given. These include economies of scale, attainment of monopoly or economic power that stems from 'bigness',[6] financial advantages,[7] tax considerations,[8] undervalued securities,[9] diversification,[10] improvement of the 'marketability' of stocks,[11] and others.

One of the most comprehensive articles written in support of this hypothesis is Lintner's most recent attempt to develop a theory of mergers (1971). He presents many diverse reasons why mergers are bound to provide abnormal returns to the acquiring firm's stockholders and summarizes thoroughly most of the traditional arguments. Among those he mentions (p. 106): 'gains from favorable tax treatment, gains from greater leverage and/or lower borrowing costs due to size, and possible gains from merging imperfectly correlated income streams to preserve expected returns with reduced risk'.

Lintner also adds an original contribution to the theory of mergers in the framework of the capital-asset-pricing model. He argues that, even in a pure conglomerate merger where no economies of scale are involved, investors will gain in *perfect* capital markets if non-identical subsets of investors are holding the stocks of each of the merging firms (i.e., if there is some market segmentation).[12] Lintner cites a recent empirical Ph.D. dissertation by Lynch as evidence for some of his theoretical conclusions. But Lynch explicitly chose for his sample only ex-post successful conglomerates. In order to be included in his sample a firm had to show 'superior' performance for shareholders [Lynch (1969, p. 3)]. This is hardly evidence that mergers in general produce this result.

2.3.2. The 'Chain Letter' Hypothesis. The second view found in the mergers literature is the 'chain letter' hypothesis.[13] It states that investors rely on very

---

[6]See Edwards (1955, pp. 331–352) for a well-known and much-quoted article on the dangers of big business and its power.

[7]Levy and Sarnat (1970, p. 801), Lewellen (1971), Lintner (1971, p. 107). Some counterarguments are in Weston (1971).

[8]Butters, Lintner and Cary (1951), Lintner (1971, p. 107).

[9]Butters, Lintner and Cary (1951), Lintner (1971), Mead (1969), and Weston and Brigham (1972, p. 690).

[10]See the discussion in Gort (1966), and Levy and Sarnat (1970).

[11]Weston (1953, p. 73) and Lintner (1971, pp. 109–110) discuss this argument favorably.

[12]Rubinstein (1974) raises some important issues concerning Lintner's Model.

[13]The 'chain letter' hypothesis in the mergers literature usually refers to the earnings-per-share argument as will be described below. But in this manuscript the term will be used also for any other accounting manipulation which may mislead investors as to the profitability of a merger.

few sources of information, the main ones being financial and accounting numbers. Lintner mentions that mergers enhance opportunities for accountants to manipulate accounting income numbers in reports to stockholders by means of 'dirty pooling', suppression of asset costs at the time of the merger in order to mislead shareholders. Also, instantaneous increases in earnings per share from P/E ratio differences among the merging firms tend to raise stockholders' assessments of future earnings. Thus he argues, 'the current aggregate value of the merging companies in equilibrium will be raised, ceteris paribus, even in a 'pure' conglomerate case in strictly perfect securities markets . . .' [Lintner (1971, p. 110)].

The 'chain letter' hypothesis implies that shareholders are misled by manipulation of accounting numbers so that the announcement of a forthcoming merger is followed by a rise in stock prices of the acquiring firm. But in this context, the information conveyed by the E.P.S. and other accounting numbers would be misleading. If we assume that equilibrium in the stock prices is eventually reached, then stock prices have to adjust downward finally, to reflect their equilibrium values. In any case, the 'chain letter' hypothesis is based on the assumption that capital markets operate inefficiently.

2.3.3. The 'Growth Maximization' Hypothesis. The third view that has received much support lately in the literature in light of recent empirical results is the 'growth maximization' hypothesis.[14] This hypothesis is presented by Mueller (1969, p. 644) as follows:

'. . . managers maximize, or at least pursue as one of their goals, the growth in physical size of their corporation rather than its profits or stockholder welfare . . . both the pecuniary and nonpecuniary rewards which managers receive are closely tied to the growth rate of their firm. Managerial salaries, bonuses, stock options, and promotions all tend to be more closely related to the size or changes in size of the firm than to its profits. Similarly, the prestige and power which managers derive from their occupations are directly related to the size and growth of the company and not to its profitability.'

Thus, due to the separation of control from ownership in the modern giant corporation, the managers can pursue their own personal goals. The firm's goal, therefore, is not to maximize profits. However, if companies merge not for the sake of increasing profits, but merely for the sake of increasing size, their profits or rates of return on common stock should be abnormally low when this policy becomes known to the market.[15] Reid (1968) in his comprehensive empirical work supports this conclusion. Indeed other empirical studies, some of which

---

[14]See Reid (1968, 1971), Bossons, Cohen and Reid (1966), Mueller (1969), and Williamson (1964).

[15]Mueller (1970, p. 675): '. . . a growth-maximizing management can be expected to push its acquisition program beyond the point that maximizes stockholder welfare.'

were mentioned earlier also suggest that mergers result in low returns to stock-holders of the acquiring firms.

3. Methodology and Data

3.1. Methodology

We have stated that, in equilibrium, expected returns on common stocks of firms of similar risk are equalized. However, the measurement of risk and its relationship to expected return must be stated more precisely.

Within the framework of a two-parameter model, in equilibrium, each asset is priced, and its one-period expected return is determined by the attempts of investors to hold mean-standard deviation efficient portfolios.[16] The capital-asset-pricing model[17] states that the relationship between risk and expected return in such a world is as follows:[18]

$$E(\tilde{R}_i) = E(\tilde{R}_0) + [E(\tilde{R}_m) - E(\tilde{R}_0)]\beta_i \tag{1}$$

where

$E(\tilde{R}_i)$ = expected rate of return on asset i,

$E(\tilde{R}_m)$ = expected rate of return on the market portfolio,

$E(\tilde{R}_0)$ = expected rate of return on any asset that is uncorrelated with the market portfolio,

$\beta_i = \mathrm{cov}(\tilde{R}_i, \tilde{R}_m)/\sigma^2(\tilde{R}_m)$ represents the risk of asset i relative to the total risk of the market portfolio m, and is proportional to the contribution of asset i to the total risk of the market portfolio.

The model implies that the expected return on an asset is equal to $E(\tilde{R}_{0t})$ (the expected return on an asset, at time period t, that is riskless with respect to the market portfolio), plus a risk premium, equal to $\{E(\tilde{R}_{mt}) - E(\tilde{R}_{0t})\}\beta_i$. The market portfolio m includes all the assets in the market, each weighted in proportion to the total market value of outstanding units. The model implies

---

[16] A portfolio is efficient if no other portfolio with the same or higher expected return has lower standard deviation of return.

[17] This model was originally developed by Sharpe (1964), Lintner (1965), Mossin (1966), Fama (1968, 1971), extended recently by Black (1972) and tested by Black, Jensen and Scholes (1972), Miller and Scholes (1972) and Fama and MacBeth (1973).

[18] Tildes ($\sim$) denote random variables.

a linear relationship between the expected return on a stock and its risk in the market portfolio.

The following model is consistent with the capital-asset-pricing model and does fairly well as a model of a stochastic process generating asset returns:[19]

$$\tilde{R}_{jt} = \tilde{\gamma}_{0t} + \tilde{\gamma}_{1t}\beta_{jt} + \tilde{\epsilon}_{jt} \quad j = 1, 2, \ldots, N \tag{2}$$

where

$\tilde{R}_{jt}$ = the percentage rate of return on security j during period t,

$\tilde{\gamma}_{0t}, \tilde{\gamma}_{1t}$ = market determined variables representing the ex-post relation between rates of return and risk at time period t; they can vary stochastically from period to period, but $E(\tilde{\gamma}_0) = E(\tilde{R}_0)$ and $E(\tilde{\gamma}_1) = E(\tilde{R}_m) - E(\tilde{R}_0)$ in (2),

$\tilde{\epsilon}_{jt}$ = a stochastic disturbance term in the return on asset j at month t, assumed to have zero mean, to be independent of β_i and uncorrelated across j,

β_{jt} = represents the relative risk of asset j at time period t.

In this model, the return on an asset is a function of the general market variables $\tilde{\gamma}_{0t}, \tilde{\gamma}_{1t}$ and also the firm-specific variables, β_{jt} and $\tilde{\epsilon}_{jt}$. It is usually assumed that β_j is constant over time.

3.1.1. Estimation of the General Market Variables $\tilde{\gamma}_{0t}$ and $\tilde{\gamma}_{1t}$[20]. We use data on monthly percentage returns (adjusted for dividends, capital gains, splits and stock dividends) available for all common stocks traded on the New York Stock Exchange for the period February 1926 to June 1968.

(a) the first four years, 1926–1929, are used to estimate β_i for each stock. β_i's are estimated by the following formula:

$$\hat{\beta}_i = \widehat{\text{cov}}(\tilde{R}_i \tilde{R}_m)/\hat{\sigma}^2(\tilde{R}_m) \tag{3}$$

where for $\tilde{R}_m$ we use 'Fisher's Arithmetic Index' [Fisher (1966)].

(b) Each stock is allocated to one of twenty portfolios by a ranking procedure. The five percent of stocks with the highest $\hat{\beta}_i$'s are placed in the first portfolio, the five percent of stocks with the next highest $\hat{\beta}_i$'s form the second portfolio, etc.

---

[19]For recent empirical work, see Black, Jensen and Scholes (1972) and Fama and MacBeth (1973).

[20]See Fama and MacBeth (1973) for a more thorough description of the procedure and the theoretical reasoning behind it.

(c) Data for January 1930–December 1934 are used to recompute the $\hat{\beta}_i$, and these estimates are averaged across securities within each portfolio, to obtain twenty portfolio estimates of $\tilde{\beta}_{pt}$. To allow for delisting of securities during each month of the following four years, 1935–1938, the $\hat{\beta}_{pt}$ are recomputed as averages of $\hat{\beta}_i$ of the individual securities which were listed at month t. The $\hat{\beta}_i$ of individual securities are themselves recomputed yearly for 1930 to 1935, 1936 and 1937.

(d) For each portfolio, the month-by-month returns R_{pt} are computed with equal weighting of each security every month during period 1935–1938.

(e) The month-by-month returns of the twenty portfolios, R_{pt}, are regressed on the estimates $\hat{\beta}_{p,t-1}$ derived in (c),

$$R_{pt} = \hat{\gamma}_{0t} + \hat{\gamma}_{1t}\hat{\beta}_{p,t-1} + \hat{U}_{pt} \qquad p = 1, 2, \ldots, 20 \qquad (4)$$

In this equation, $\hat{\beta}_{p,t-1}$ is used as the explanatory variable while $\hat{\gamma}_{0t}$ and $\hat{\gamma}_{1t}$ are least squares estimates of $\tilde{\gamma}_{0t}$ and $\tilde{\gamma}_{1t}$. The steps above are repeated for other periods by using seven years to form portfolios; the next five years to compute the initial $\hat{\beta}_{p,t-1}$ and the next four years are used to compute $\hat{\gamma}_{0t}$ and $\hat{\gamma}_{1t}$.

(f) Using the estimates $\hat{\gamma}_{0t}$ and $\hat{\gamma}_{1t}$, and rearranging (2), we compute

$$\hat{\epsilon}_{jt} = R_{jt} - \hat{\gamma}_{0t} - \hat{\gamma}_{1t}\hat{\beta}_{jt} \qquad (5)$$

where

$\hat{\epsilon}_{jt}$ is the residual or the abnormal performance of stock j at month t,

β_{jt} is re-estimated by ordinary least squares regression for each stock by using the last 60 monthly rates of return up to month t (henceforth $t - 59$ to t).

This estimating procedure was adopted in order to account for possible changes in risk. As will be shown later there are changes in risk of the firms in this sample. The ex-post return R_{jt} contains the market adjustment to any new information generated during period t concerning stock j. That part of the return of a security which is not accounted for by the interrelationships among securities as summarized by the market factor $\tilde{R}_{mt}$ and the common factor $\tilde{\gamma}_{0t}$ will be observed in $\hat{\epsilon}_{jt}$. The residual $\hat{\epsilon}_{jt}$ captures the effect of company-specific events on the returns of a given stock.

The specific event under study is a merger. We want to investigate what information, if any, a merger conveys to the market about the constituent firms, and how such information affects the behavior of their stock prices.

Blume (1968) shows that the constant β assumption is reasonable, at least for large portfolios. However, β's of individual stocks may be influenced by specific company-connected events. An acquisition might influence risk through a change in the mix of products produced by the acquiring firm. It might also indicate changes in its investment and growth policy. Substantiated economic theory implies that expected rates of return on an asset are a positive function of risk. If, after a merger, the risk of acquiring firms tends to be lower than before that event, then this phenomenon should result in lower returns for stockholders after the merger.[21] However, the stock prices do not have to change in any specific direction if these lower returns are subject to an appropriately lower risk level.

3.1.2. Cumulation of Residuals.

In order to see whether stockholders of merging firms gain from mergers we want to look at the residual $\hat{e}_{jt}$, remaining after subtracting out the effects of market-wide effects $\hat{\gamma}_{0t}$, $\tilde{\gamma}_{1t}$ and of $\hat{\beta}_{jt}$.

Define month 0 as the month of the merger. Month –1 represents one month before the month in which a merger took place and month +1 represents one month after the month of the merger. Residuals, $\hat{e}_{jt}$ are averaged for each month τ (where τ is measured relative to the merger month) across firms by

$$\bar{e}_\tau = \frac{1}{N} \sum_{j=1}^{N} \hat{e}_{jt} \tag{6}$$

where

N is the number of firms having a computed residual for month τ,

$\bar{e}_\tau$ is the average residual across firms for month τ.

We want to examine the cumulative effects of abnormal returns in the months surrounding the merger.

Eq. (7) shows the cumulation procedure,

$$\bar{\bar{e}}_T = \sum_{\tau=-K}^{T} \bar{e}_\tau \tag{7}$$

where $\bar{\bar{e}}_T$ is the cumulated average residual, C.A.R., from month $(-)K$ through month T.

---

[21] This hypothesis was proposed in a discussion with E.F. Fama regarding a term paper in the spring of 1969, and its subsequent confirmation led for the first time, by this author's knowledge, to the procedure of adjusting for changes in risk, since conducted in a few other empirical studies. See Mandelker (1972) for findings on changes in risk due to mergers and implications on corresponding changes in rates of return.

3.2. The Data

The main sources of data are the Federal Trade Commission listing of mergers during the period 1948–1967, the CRSP file,[22] Moody's industrials and Standard and Poor's Corporation records. The CRSP file was the source of data on monthly rates of return. For a firm to be included in the sample it is required that its records be available on the CRSP files, i.e., it has been listed on the New York Stock Exchange during the relevant period. The mergers included in this study have been consummated during the period November 1941 to August 1962. About 91% were consummated after January 1951.

For each of the acquired firms, its acquiring firm is listed on the N.Y.S.E. Usually the acquiring firm is the larger of the two firms and its stocks continue to be listed on the New York Stock Exchange after the merger. In the month of the merger about 85 percent of the acquired firms are removed from the N.Y.S.E.

4. Empirical Results

4.1. Moving Beta Series

Table 1 presents the C.A.R. of acquiring firms accumulated according to formula (7) for the period (–40 to +40), i.e., from 40 months before the merger to 40 months after the merger. We require that all firms included in table 1 have data for the whole period studied, i.e., (–100 to +40).[23] This restricts our sample size to 241 acquiring firms. The C.A.R. rises during the 40 months prior to the merger by 5.1 percent and decreases during the next 40 months by 1.7 percent. The average β decreases by approximately eight percent, five percent of which occurs after the merger. The results of table 1 appear to be consistent with the theories that postulate positive results (either temporary or permanent) of mergers on stock prices of acquiring firms:

(a) The 'abnormal gains' hypothesis states that mergers cause either economies of scale, monopoly power, or advantages that Lintner's new arguments suggest. Accordingly, news about a forthcoming merger should result in higher returns for stockholders of the acquiring firm.

---

[22]Center for Research in Security Prices file. For a description of the CRSP file, see Fisher and Lorie (1964).

[23]Therefore these empirical results are for acquiring firms which have been listed on the N.Y.S.E. for a relatively long period of time, both before and after the acquisition. In that respect our results are biased towards firms that have not been acquired and were not subject to bankruptcy, for a long period. This bias towards more successful firms may account for some of the positive returns observed.

Table 1

Average Residuals, Cumulative Average Residuals, Average Beta and Percentage of Negative Residuals for 241 Acquiring Firms during Period (−40 to +40)[a]

Month	Average Residual	C.A.R.	Average Beta	Percentage of Negative Residuals
−40	0.0025	0.002	1.085	0.56
−30	0.0029	−0.008	1.090	0.52
−29	0.0011	−0.007	1.090	0.50
−28	0.0014	−0.006	1.091	0.56
−27	0.0028	−0.003	1.095	0.51
−26	0.0010	−0.002	1.096	0.51
−25	0.0023	0.000	1.093	0.51
−24	−0.0027	−0.002	1.088	0.54
−23	0.0010	−0.001	1.086	0.49
−22	0.0057	0.005	1.091	0.54
−21	0.0066	0.011	1.092	0.47
−20	−0.0001	0.011	1.090	0.51
−19	−0.0012	0.010	1.090	0.51
−18	0.0001	0.010	1.093	0.55
−17	0.0031	0.013	1.092	0.49
−16	0.0004	0.014	1.087	0.49
−15	0.0061	0.020	1.086	0.50
−14	0.0002	0.020	1.077	0.49
−13	0.0024	0.022	1.076	0.51
−12	−0.0038	0.019	1.073	0.57
−11	0.0088	0.027	1.073	0.48
−10	0.0034	0.031	1.076	0.56
−9	0.0003	0.031	1.076	0.52
−8	0.0040	0.035	1.073	0.49
−7	0.0035	0.038	1.073	0.53
−6	0.0094	0.048	1.079	0.47
−5	0.0013	0.049	1.077	0.54
−4	0.0067	0.056	1.075	0.50
−3	−0.0054	0.050	1.070	0.60
−2	−0.0015	0.049	1.072	0.54
−1	0.0001	0.049	1.067	0.54
0	0.0018	0.051	1.066	0.54
1	0.0013	0.052	1.063	0.54
2	0.0034	0.056	1.061	0.48
3	−0.0015	0.054	1.066	0.55
4	−0.0005	0.054	1.066	0.51
5	−0.0070	0.047	1.065	0.61
6	0.0018	0.048	1.066	0.49
7	0.0002	0.049	1.063	0.51
8	0.0001	0.049	1.065	0.54
9	0.0022	0.051	1.064	0.54
10	−0.0017	0.049	1.068	0.54

[a]All of the 241 acquiring firms in this table are analyzed below in tables 9, 10, 11. For some of these tables it was required that data be available for the period (−40 to +70). Since stock prices on the CRSP tape were available up to June 1968, the mergers analyzed here were consummated at least 70 months before this date, i.e., up to August 1962.

Table 1 continued

Month	Average Residual	C.A.R.	Average Beta	Percentage of Negative Residuals
11	0.0023	0.052	1.066	0.50
12	0.0052	0.057	1.064	0.49
13	−0.0010	0.056	1.061	0.54
14	−0.0026	0.053	1.060	0.55
15	0.0001	0.053	1.062	0.52
16	−0.0031	0.050	1.058	0.51
17	−0.0039	0.046	1.054	0.58
18	0.0056	0.052	1.050	0.50
19	0.0019	0.054	1.050	0.50
20	−0.0021	0.052	1.047	0.52
21	−0.0003	0.051	1.045	0.54
22	0.0039	0.055	1.039	0.50
23	−0.0023	0.053	1.040	0.53
24	−0.0009	0.052	1.040	0.49
25	0.0058	0.058	1.040	0.50
26	−0.0048	0.053	1.038	0.55
27	−0.0056	0.047	1.038	0.56
28	0.0010	0.048	1.036	0.52
29	−0.0064	0.042	1.038	0.57
30	0.0003	0.042	1.035	0.51
40	0.0068	0.037	1.017	0.49

(b) The 'chain letter' hypothesis states that mergers cause an increase in stock prices because of their positive effect on the price–earnings ratio or on earnings-per-share, even though the merger may not cause any real economies at all.

These results suggest that the informational impact of a forthcoming merger is spread over approximately thirty months before the event.[24] The subsequent decrease in C.A.R. after the merger might be viewed as consistent with the hypotheses which assume that people are fooled by acquisitions. Accordingly, it has been argued that people believe that a merger implies higher performance of the acquiring firm and therefore revise their expectations upward. However, on the average, they are 'overshooting' and after the merger they revise their expectations downward.[25]

Since leaks of information into the market about a forthcoming merger would include the identity of both the acquiring and the acquired firms, we

---

[24]During (−40:−30) C.A.R. decreases by 1.0 percent and for the next 30 months (−30:0) it increases by about 2.0 percent during each of the 10-months periods (−30:−20), (−20:−10), and (−10:0). Table 7, to be presented later, shows that such results extend in fact over the last 8 years before the merger.

[25]Gort and Hogarty (1970), Reid (1968), and Gilbert (1971) report that acquiring firms' stockholders lose after the merger.

turn now to analyze the performance of the acquired firms. This may help us both to identify the period in which such information becomes available to the market and to evaluate the performance of the stocks involved.

Table 2 shows the C.A.R. of acquired firms for the period (-40 to -1). Since most of the acquired firms cease to be listed on the New York Stock Exchange in the month of the merger, we are able to present results up to one month before the merger.

In contrast to table 1, the C.A.R. in table 2 shows a dramatic rise of about 14 percent (an average of 2 percent per month) during the last seven months before the merger. However, the C.A.R. is slightly negative during period (-35 to -7), and its lowest level is in month (-9). During the 12-month period (-20 to -9) eight of the monthly average residuals are negative. The percentage of negative residuals (column 5) is consistently low during the last seven months before the merger and especially so in the last 4 months. This may indicate that for some mergers, positive information regarding acquisitions, or any other 'good' news correlated with acquisitions, starts leaking out to the market about 7 months before the merger.

It should be noted that the increase in the cumulative average residuals during the period (-7 to -1) does not necessarily imply abnormal returns for those investors who purchase stocks of firms to be acquired after the acquisition has been announced. The residuals of individual stocks typically do not follow the behavior of the average residuals across stocks. Plots of successive residuals of individual stocks indicate that they are independent. Each stock has some high residuals in some months and these differ from stock to stock.[26] The average residuals are high for all seven months because the timing of abnormal residuals differs from stock to stock. In the next section we employ some probability tests in order to examine whether the C.A.R. of tables 1 and 2 are significantly different from zero.

4.2. Some Probability Tests on the Average Portfolio Residuals

It is well known that common security effects such as industry effects can cause residuals across securities in a given month to be correlated. A test-statistic should not assume independence of residuals across securities in a given month since this would overstate the t-values. Therefore it makes sense to build portfolios in order to appropriately incorporate the dependencies in the residuals, $\tilde{\epsilon}_{jt}$, of the different securities [cf. Black, Jensen and Scholes (1972, p. 84)], and thus produce independent drawings. In order to produce identically distributed

---

[26]This can be observed in the percentage of negative errors in table 2. Otherwise, we would have observed a much lower percentage of negative residuals for all 7 months.

Table 2

Average Residuals, Cumulative Average Residuals, Average Beta and Percentage of Negative Residuals for 252 Acquired Firms during Period (–40 to –1)

Month	Average Residual	C.A.R.	Average Beta	Percentage of Negative Residuals
–40	0.0012	0.001	1.093	0.53
–39	0.0087	0.010	1.095	0.51
–38	–0.0046	0.005	1.098	0.59
–37	–0.0013	0.004	1.096	0.56
–36	0.0014	0.005	1.098	0.57
–35	–0.0118	–0.006	1.093	0.60
–34	–0.0011	–0.007	1.096	0.56
–33	–0.0047	–0.012	1.095	0.60
–32	0.0008	–0.011	1.090	0.54
–31	–0.0023	–0.014	1.092	0.58
–30	0.0004	–0.013	1.095	0.52
–29	–0.0022	–0.015	1.092	0.56
–28	–0.0054	–0.021	1.097	0.59
–27	–0.0066	–0.026	1.102	0.58
–26	0.0025	–0.025	1.103	0.54
–25	–0.0010	–0.026	1.106	0.58
–24	0.0012	–0.025	1.112	0.51
–23	0.0049	–0.020	1.111	0.50
–22	0.0008	–0.019	1.111	0.53
–21	–0.0013	–0.020	1.107	0.54
–20	–0.0036	–0.024	1.108	0.58
–19	0.0023	–0.021	1.015	0.52
–18	0.0067	–0.015	1.100	0.50
–17	–0.0028	–0.018	1.096	0.57
–16	0.0072	–0.010	1.096	0.48
–15	–0.0047	–0.015	1.096	0.54
–14	0.0002	–0.015	1.087	0.56
–13	–0.0047	–0.020	1.085	0.56
–12	–0.0006	–0.020	1.091	0.55
–11	–0.0016	–0.022	1.093	0.53
–10	–0.0040	–0.026	1.091	0.59
–9	–0.0040	–0.030	1.093	0.54
–8	0.0067	–0.023	1.090	0.54
–7	0.0118	–0.011	1.084	0.50
–6	0.0121	0.001	1.093	0.51
–5	0.0223	0.023	1.079	0.48
–4	0.0274	0.050	1.073	0.40
–3	0.0303	0.081	1.068	0.37
–2	0.0217	0.102	1.066	0.42
–1	0.0174	0.120	1.064	0.44

drawings as required for a t-test, we standardize their residuals by the estimated residual standard deviation.

The strategy is as follows. An investor is assumed to build a portfolio by adopting a policy of buying securities at a predetermined period relative to a merger and keeping them for one period. This will enable us to test whether

Table 3
Probability Tests on the Cumulative Average Portfolio Residuals of Acquired Firms[a]

Portfolio formation period	K L	-6 -6	-6 -5	-6 -4	-6 -2
	Average residuals	0.0230^b	0.0256	0.0288	0.0269^c
	t-statistic[d]	5.76	9.20	12.37	13.80
	No. of portfolios[e]	139	180	192	197

[a]Since for most of the acquired firms there is no data on the CRSP tape for the merger month (i.e., month 0), residuals for this month were not computed.

[b]This is $e_{K,L}$ [see formula (11b) in the appendix], i.e., the average monthly residual on a portfolio that consists of merging firms where the securities of the merging firms are purchased at the end of the 6th month before the merger and sold at the end of the 5th month before the merger [i.e., month (–5)].

[c]This corresponds to investing in securities that merged during the period $t + 6$ to $t + 2$ and holding them from period (t) to $(t + 1)$.

[d]This is $t_{K,L}$ [see formula (12) in the appendix].

[e]The number of portfolios for the different estimation periods is not constant because each one of the periods requires different amounts of data. The closer the estimation period is to the month of the merger, the smaller is the required number of prior monthly rates of return.

stockholders of merging firms gain from mergers. First we shall employ some probability tests on the average portfolio residuals earned by buying stocks before or after the merger. The tests examine whether the average portfolio residuals are statistically different from zero. The probability tests are explained in the appendix.

4.2.1. Empirical Results. Table 3 presents results for different values of K and L for *acquired* firms.[27] The t-values are very high, i.e., 5.8 to 13.8, and imply that during the last 5 months before the merger the average residual terms are significantly greater than zero, and amount to about 2 to 3 percent per month. This is consistent with the results in table 2 and indicates that there is a very low probability of their occurrence by pure chance.

In table 4 we present some probability tests for the average residuals of the acquiring firms. In part I of this table, probability tests are designed for the period in which the acquired stocks' average residuals have high t-values, i.e., period (–6 to –1). The acquiring stocks do not have such 'significant' results. The t-values are very low, and thus the low level of the average residuals could have been obtained by pure chance. It is difficult to say whether the stockholders of the acquiring firms gain from mergers. For example, the average residuals of portfolios formed for the period (–7 to –4) is 0.24% per month, and

[27]As explained in the appendix, K and L relate to the number of months before the merger that the investor invests in the merging firms.

Table 4
Probability Tests on the Cumulative Average Residuals of the Acquiring Firms[a]

		I. Use of pre-merger beta[b] (−8)		
Portfolio				
formation	K	−7	−7	−7
period	L	−7	−4	−1
	Average residuals	0.0035	0.0024	0.0005
	t-statistic	0.93	0.74	0.04
	No. of portfolios	93	150	158
		II. Use of post-merger beta (+70) for pre-merger period		
Portfolio				
formation	K	−20		−20
period	L	−10		−1
	Average residual	0.0032		0.0023
	t-statistic	1.84		1.73
	No. of portfolios	139		159
		III. Post-merger beta (+70) for post-merger period		
Portfolio				
formation	K	1		1
period	L	10		20
	Average residual	0.0006		0.0003
	t-statistic	0.04		0.33
	No. of portfolios	177		197

[a]Included are only acquiring firms that acquired firms listed on the N.Y.S.E. It is only for these firms that we could estimate the returns for their acquired firms and determine the time when the abnormal returns occurred. However, similar results were obtained for the whole sample of acquiring firms. See footnotes to table 3 for further definitions of items in the table.

[b]Beta used is of month (−8), estimated by ordinary least squares regression by using 60-monthly rates of return up to month −8, i.e., $(m_i - 67)$ to $(m_i - 8)$. β_{-8} is used under the assumption that the impact, if any, of the forthcoming merger is minor during this period.

the *t*-statistic is 0.74, which is far from being significant. However, the true average residual might amount to 0.7% or 1.0% per month and this would mean that the stockholders gain from acquisitions. On the other hand, the true average residual might be zero and this would be consistent with no abnormal gains to stockholders. Anyway our results seem to be inconsistent with abnormal losses to stockholders from acquisitions.

Part II of table 4 uses β's of month (+70), i.e., post-merger β's which, according to table 1, are considerably lower than pre-merger β's. These β's are used to investigate the same question, under the hypothesis that immediately before the merger the true underlying β's are better estimated by post-merger data (i.e., because information about the forthcoming merger will be immediately incorporated in the stock prices). Since post-merger β's in our sample are lower than pre-merger β's, we can expect that the above procedure may lead to higher residuals in the pre-merger period. The t-statistics are indeed, 1.84 for the period (–20 to –10), and, unexpectedly, somewhat lower, 1.73 for the period (–20 to –1). These t-statistics are on the border of what is usually considered 'significant' in statistical sampling theory. But the magnitude of the average residuals is quite low, i.e., 0.0032 and 0.0023 per month. It is, again, difficult to say definitely what these results imply. They certainly do not imply that the acquiring firms' stockholders lose from mergers (as some previous studies concluded). But both because of the specific procedure and the magnitude of the t-values, it is difficult to conclude whether the stockholders earn normal or abnormal positive returns from mergers.

In part III of table 4 we use post merger β's for post-merger data. The t-statistics are very small as are the average residuals. This is consistent with the hypothesis that there are no abnormal (i.e., positive or negative) returns for the stockholders after the merger. The results for the acquiring firms are consistent with the hypothesis that the capital market reacts 'efficiently' to information regarding mergers since we did not detect any specific increase or decrease in C.A.R. after the merger in spite of the changes in β.

4.3. Comparing Results of the Acquiring and the Acquired Firms

The above results are consistent with the hypothesis that the acquired firms earn abnormal returns in the last seven months before the acquisition, and point to the hypothesis that during this period the information on mergers becomes available in the market.[28]

However, the acquiring firms' C.A.R. before the merger does not follow a similar pattern. The C.A.R. is positive in the last 30 months before the merger, but the t-statistics are small. Also, the time pattern behavior of the cumulative average residuals of the acquiring firms (in table 1) is different from that of the acquired firms. During period (–40 to –9) the average residuals of the acquired firms are mostly negative (i.e., 19 out of 32, or about 59 percent) but those of the acquiring firms are not (i.e., only 10 are negative, or about 31 percent). The acquired firms' C.A.R. accumulates during this period –3.0 percent while the acquiring firms' C.A.R. accumulates 3.1 percent. The average percentage of negative residuals in the last 7 months before the merger is 44.5 percent for the acquired firms while this average is 53.1 percent for the acquiring firms.[29]

Table 5 presents results for 167 acquiring firms who acquired firms that

---

[28]Another possible hypothesis is that mergers follow abnormal returns for ths stockholders of the acquired firms (i.e., abnormal returns may be the reason for the take-over).

[29]Derived from column 5 of tables 2 and 1, respectively.

Table 5
Average Residuals, Cumulative Average Residuals, Average Beta and Percentage
of Negative Residuals for 167 Acquiring Firms during Period (–20 to +10)

Month	Average Residual	C.A.R.	Average Beta	Percentage of Negative Residuals
–20	0.0025	0.003	1.073	0.54
–19	0.0008	0.003	1.072	0.49
–18	0.0067	0.010	1.067	0.49
–17	0.0034	0.013	1.064	0.50
–16	0.0059	0.019	1.061	0.47
–15	0.0029	0.022	1.062	0.50
–14	–0.0044	0.018	1.055	0.56
–13	0.0036	0.021	1.051	0.43
–12	–0.0035	0.018	1.051	0.56
–11	0.0113	0.029	1.052	0.47
–10	–0.0001	0.029	1.056	0.56
–9	0.0093	0.039	1.053	0.41
–8	–0.0012	0.037	1.052	0.57
–7	–0.0003	0.037	1.052	0.55
–6	–0.0001	0.037	1.052	0.53
–5	0.0066	0.044	1.050	0.48
–4	0.0019	0.045	1.049	0.52
–3	–0.0022	0.043	1.047	0.55
–2	–0.0047	0.038	1.049	0.58
–1	–0.0101	0.028	1.045	0.64
0	–0.0005	0.028	1.048	0.53
1	0.0079	0.036	1.047	0.50
2	–0.0042	0.032	1.048	0.59
3	0.0030	0.035	1.051	0.53
4	0.0002	0.035	1.049	0.53
5	–0.0025	0.032	1.050	0.53
6	–0.0020	0.030	1.046	0.49
7	–0.0024	0.028	1.043	0.54
8	–0.0014	0.027	1.046	0.54
9	0.0007	0.027	1.050	0.59
10	–0.0050	0.022	1.053	0.57

were listed on the New York Stock Exchange and who had enough data for
estimation during period (–20 to –1).[30] This enables us to compare directly the
performance of acquiring firms with their respective acquired firms. Table 6
presents results for the corresponding acquired firms. The requirement that the
acquired firms be listed on the New York Stock Exchange probably causes
this subsample to include relatively larger acquisitions than the sample of
table 1. In table 5 the C.A.R. of the acquiring firms is 2.8 percent at month (–1).
During the period (–7 to –1) there is no increase in C.A.R. (in fact it decreases

---

[30]This requirement restricts our results to acquisitions where both constituent firms are
listed and traded on the N.Y.S.E.

Table 6
Average Residuals, Cumulative Average Residuals, Average Beta and Percentage of Negative Residuals for 167 Acquired Firms during Period (–20 to –1)

Month	Average Residual	C.A.R.	Average Beta	Percentage of Negative Residuals
–20	–0.0063	–0.006	1.092	0.60
–19	0.0098	0.003	1.089	0.46
–18	0.0034	0.007	1.086	0.52
–17	0.0014	0.008	1.081	0.54
–16	0.0113	0.020	1.081	0.47
–15	–0.0063	0.013	1.080	0.56
–14	0.0034	0.017	1.069	0.56
–13	–0.0040	0.013	1.067	0.56
–12	–0.0020	0.011	1.069	0.56
–11	0.0026	0.013	1.073	0.53
–10	–0.0068	0.006	1.066	0.61
–9	0.0024	0.009	1.066	0.58
–8	0.0095	0.018	1.064	0.51
–7	0.0091	0.028	1.058	0.53
–6	0.0169	0.044	1.053	0.49
–5	0.0132	0.058	1.051	0.47
–4	0.0259	0.084	1.048	0.41
–3	0.0241	0.108	1.039	0.38
–2	0.0247	0.132	1.034	0.39
–1	0.0167	0.149	1.029	0.45

by 0.9 percent). In contrast to these results, the C.A.R. of the acquired firms rises by 13.1 percent during this same 7-month period prior to the merger. These results are consistent with those found in tables 1 and 2, which include larger samples, but relatively smaller mergers. They point to the possibility that for the stockholders of the acquiring firms, 'news' of an acquisition may not be worthwhile news, since no abnormal behavior is in fact observed during the period (–7 to 0).[31] The abnormal returns earned long before the merger may have nothing to do with the acquisition per se.

4.4. Changes in Beta

Table 7 shows results for the period (–100 to 40) for 128 acquiring firms who have not been engaged in other major acquisitions during the period (–80 to

---

[31]We should however qualify this inference. One could envisage a seemingly unlikely case in which the market reaction to the merger for the acquiring firm occurs before the reaction for the acquired firm. In such cases the somewhat positive C.A.R. for the acquiring firms prior to month (–4) might be viewed as due to the merger, and interpreted as positive information for these firms too.

Table 7

Cumulative Average Residuals per Ten-month Periods, and Average Beta for 128 Acquiring Firms[a] during Period (−100 to +40)

Period	C.A.R. per Ten-month Period	C.A.R. at End of Period	β at End of Period
(−100)		−0.003	1.002
(−100: −90)	+0.026	0.023	1.014
(−90: −80)	+0.008	0.031	1.028
(−80: −70)	+0.038	0.069	1.045
(−70: −60)	+0.005	0.074	1.073
(−60: −50)	+0.001	0.075	1.068
(−50: −40)	+0.025	0.100	1.079
(−40: −30)	−0.028	0.072	1.089
(−30: −20)	+0.017	0.089	1.103
(−20: −10)	+0.035	0.124	1.073
(−10:0)	+0.002	0.126	1.057
(0: +10)	−0.007	0.119	1.058
(+10: +20)	−0.003	0.116	1.039
(+20: +30)	−0.002	0.114	1.029
(+30: +40)	−0.015	0.099	1.005

[a]Firms which did not have other major mergers in the period surrounding the date of the merger studied.

80). During the period (−7 to −1) the C.A.R. accumulates only 0.2 percent. During the period (0 to 40) the C.A.R. decreases by 2.7 percent compared to an increase of 2.6 percent during the pre-merger period (−40 to 0). During the period (−100 to 0) C.A.R. accumulates 12.6 percent, 7.5 percent accumulated during period (−100 to −50) and only 5.1 percent during period (−50 to 0). This is especially interesting because information about mergers probably becomes available during this latter period (mostly during the last part of this period).

These results again point to our previous observation that the positive C.A.R. before the merger and the slightly negative C.A.R. after the merger may not be due to the merger per se. One possible explanation for these phenomena is changes in beta and the way it is estimated. In table 7 $\bar{\beta}$ increases during the period (−100 to −20) by approximately 10 percent, and decreases during period (−20 to 0) by approximately 5 percent and by the same percentage during period (0 to 40). So the value of $\bar{\beta}$, after increasing by 10 percent and decreasing subsequently by 10 percent, reaches at month (+40) the same level as at month (−100). For a sample whose $\bar{\beta}$ changes so much, the estimation procedure for beta may be of significant importance in estimating the C.A.R. As described in the methodology section, we are using past data [i.e., monthly rates of return as of period ($t - 59$ to t) to estimate β_t]. For example, if beta

Table 8
Cumulative Average Residuals and Average Beta for 241 Acquiring Firms, Estimated by Using Both Past and Future Data[a] during Period (−40 to +40)

Month	C.A.R.	Average Beta
−40	0.002	1.076
−30	−0.008	1.076
−20	−0.001	1.073
−10	0.019	1.064
0	0.029	1.046
10	0.028	1.028
20	0.026	1.021
30	0.008	1.019
40	0.003	1.008

[a]β_t was estimated while using 60 monthly observations of the periods [$(t − 30$ to $t − 1)$ and $(t + 1$ to $t + 30)$].

is increasing during the period (−100 to −40) then the estimated $\beta_{j,-50}$ may be lower than the one estimated by using both past and future data.[32] This causes the estimate of the market component of return at month (−50) to be lower than one estimated by a procedure which uses both past and future data for estimation. Consequently the residuals will be positive. This, in fact, seems to be occurring in table 7 for the period (−100 to approximately −40). The reverse may be occurring for the period (0 to +40).[33] Table 8 shows results for the sample of acquiring firms of table 1, using the following procedure for estimating β. The β_t for firm i is estimated by least-squares regression using data from period $(t − 30$ to $t + 30)$, excluding month t, i.e., both past and future data has been used. Changes in $\bar{\bar{\beta}}$ in table 1 precede changes in $\bar{\bar{\beta}}$ of table 8. The changes over time in $\bar{\bar{\beta}}$ of this sample causes the C.A.R. in table 8 at the month of the merger to reach only half the level of that in table 1. There is no adequate theoretical reason to justify one procedure over the other. The procedure used in table 1, though, is more consistent with the estimation procedure of $\tilde{\gamma}_{0t}$ and $\tilde{\gamma}_{1t}$, which uses past data.

Table 9 presents data on the distribution of $\bar{\bar{\beta}}$ before and after the merger in the sample of 241 firms of table 1. In month (−40) β is 1.085, seventy months after the merger it decreases to 0.992. However, for 58.5 percent of the acquiring firms $\bar{\bar{\beta}}$ decreases, whereas for 41.5 percent of the firms $\bar{\bar{\beta}}$ increases. In the next section we examine whether these decreases in β are typical of all subperiods.

---

[32]For example, if $\beta_{j,-50}$ is estimated by using both past and future data [e.g., $(t − 30)$ to $(t + 30)$], the resulting beta will be higher than the one we are using in the above tables.

[33]Indeed in that period, C.A.R. is negative.

Table 9
Distribution of $\beta(-40)$, $\beta(+70)$ and β-difference for 241 Firms

Deciles	Beta in Month $(-40)^a$	Beta in Month $(+70)^b$	Distribution of Changes in β $\beta_i(-40) - \beta_i(+70)^c$
1	0.626	0.527	−0.386
2	0.817	0.670	−0.223
3	0.897	0.799	−0.127
4	0.984	0.823	−0.006
5	1.068	0.970	0.084
6	1.157	1.078	0.192
7	1.269	1.190	0.268
8	1.372	1.302	0.431
9	1.565	1.482	0.608
Median	1.067	0.971	0.081
Mean	1.085	0.992	0.093
Standard deviation	0.37	0.38	0.42
No. of positive beta-difference − 140 (58.5 percent)			
No. of negative beta-difference − 101 (41.5 percent)			

[a]Data used to estimate β as of period (−100 to −40).

[b]Data used to estimate β as of period (+10 to +70).

[c]β_i-difference is calculated separately for each firm i. Note that the three columns represent three separate orderings.

4.4.1. Changes in β by Subperiods. The results of table 10 are obtained by breaking down the sample of 241 acquiring firms into subperiods according to the dates of mergers. $\bar{\beta}$ changes differently for the various subperiods.[34] For the subperiod December 1950–February 1955, the average beta rises both before and after the merger. For the period January 1959–August 1962, the average beta decreases sharply during the period (−40 to −10) in which very little, if any, information is known about a forthcoming merger [for example, to estimate β_{-10} we use data for period (−69 to −10)], and it continues to decrease long after the merger. In both subperiods, December 1950–February 1955 and January 1959–August 1962, $\bar{\beta}$'s change during the relative period (−40 to +70) but the merger date does not serve as a turning point for these changes.

A possible implication is that changes in risk indeed occurred during and surrounding merger periods, but subperiod results suggest that the direction of the change is not predictable.

5. Interpretation of Results and Some Alternative Hypotheses

Our results for the acquired firms are consistent with the hypothesis that mergers are a mechanism by which the market system replaces incompetent

---

[34]β's were estimated as for table 1.

Table 10
Levels of $\bar{\beta}$ of 241 Acquiring Firms in Various Months Relative to Month of Merger and in Various Subperiods[a]

| Subperiod | Month Relative to Merger | | | | | | | | | | | | No. of Firms |
	-40	-30	-20	-10	0	10	20	30	40	50	60	70	
Dec. 1950–Feb. 1955	1.04	1.06	1.08	1.06	1.07	1.08	1.07	1.06	1.07	1.11	1.13	1.10	45
Dec. 1950–Dec. 1958	1.07	1.07	1.10	1.10	1.11	1.12	1.11	1.10	1.08	1.07	1.06	1.05	146
Jan. 1959–Aug. 1962	1.11	1.12	1.09	1.05	1.02	1.00	0.99	0.97	0.95	0.96	0.95	0.94	95

[a]β's were calculated as for table 1.

management.[35] If managers of a firm do not operate efficiently, the stock prices of the firm will fall and the firm might become a good buy. Replacement of the incumbent management may then be a source of gains for the acquired entity. This explanation is also consistent with some other empirical studies.[36]

In table 2 the cumulative average residuals of the acquired firms are indeed negative and continue to decrease up to month (–9). In addition, the percentage of negative residuals is high (compare, for example, our results for the acquiring firms in table 1). The C.A.R. is negative up to month (–7). During the 7-month period (–15 to –9) only one average residual is positive. (The C.A.R. accumulates by –2.0 percent.)

If the firm to be acquired has relatively inefficient management, then this information should have been impounded in its stock prices at some point in time in the past. Afterwards its stockholders should earn 'normal' returns. Since for each firm this information is revealed in a different month, we would not expect to detect its effect on the stock prices, in any specific month, for the sample as a whole. The level of the stock prices will reflect both the relative inefficiency of the firm's operations and the probability that this management will be replaced. However, incumbent management can resist an acquisition. As long as the management continues to successfully resist a take-over, the stock prices will probably continue at low levels. Indeed, it is very difficult to acquire a firm if its management resists forcefully.[37]

In a competitive acquisitions market where there are other firms who

---

[35]See, for example, Manne (1965), Samuelson (1970, p. 505), Solow (1967), and Williamson, in: Manne (1969, pp. 281–336) for support of this view.

[36]Hayes and Taussig (1967) report that companies being acquired by cash take-over bids suffered losses, on the average, before those bids were announced. However, the announcement of a bid resulted in an increase in the stock prices. But if the bid was not successful, the stock prices tended to decrease. This is consistent with quite a few alternative hypotheses concerning the competitiveness of the market for acquisitions.

The Bureau of Economics of the F.T.C. measured the rates of return on equity of 165 large corporations acquired during 1951–1963. [See statement of Mueller, Director of Bureau of Economics, F.T.C. before the U.S. Senate Sub-committee on Antitrust and Monopoly (1965, p. 129)]. The average rate of return one year *prior* to the acquisition was 8.2%. At the same period the average rate of return for all manufacturing firms was 10.0%. Based on these findings, the Bureau concludes that the acquired firms perform poorly before the merger.

Hale and Hale (1962) have also found, by a survey questionnaire on merger motivation, that 35% of 136 firms based their decisions to acquire on the belief that improved management of the acquired firm would increase their profits.

However, we certainly realize that these studies suffer, as well, from problems similar to those mentioned earlier.

[37]This is probably the reason for the relatively small percentage of mergers that result from proxy fights or tender offer bids. For a recent fight over a $1 billion tender offer by Northwest Industries for the acquisition of B.F. Goodrich, see O'Hanlon (1969). This case demonstrates that even an offer worth 30 percent more than the market value of the company's common stock can be refused if management so desires.

expect, similarly, to improve the operations of the firm to be acquired, competition among potential acquiring firms will raise the price of the former. Consequently, the acquiring firm should earn a normal rate of return. However, if only one firm can make such an improvement, then the two constituent firms will share equally any abnormal profits.[38] The stockholders of the acquired firms may gain in both cases.

This hypothesis is also consistent with the view that there exists a market for corporate control. As noted by Manne (1965, p. 314), 'under almost all state statutes the board of directors of a corporation must approve a merger before it is submitted to shareholders for a vote . . .'[39] When a firm is confronted with a tender offer a conflict of interest between management and shareholders may result. Although the stockholders of the acquired firm are likely to profit from the merger more than any other party involved, incumbent management may stand to lose the most, for they may forfeit their controlling position with all the accompanying benefits. If the incumbent management objects to a take-over, the bidding firm has the option of making either a proxy fight or a tender offer. However, these latter types of acquisitions are relatively rare.[40] They are usually considered to be too expensive, because incumbent management has, to a certain degree, all the economic resources of the firm at their disposal to resist an undesired merger.[41]

---

[38]This case is consistent with Halpern's (1971) findings.

[39]Samuelson (1969, pp. 89–90) argues, 'Barring blatant incompetence, managment can count on remaining in office . . . (so) long as management possesses the confidence of the board (of directors) . . .'

[40]Hayes and Taussig (1967, p. 140) found in their study that only 29 out of 83 cash tender offers resulted in mergers. They found that 'the median premium offered by bidders was 16% over the market price two days before the offer. Premiums ranged from zero to 44%.' The greater the resistance by management, the higher the premium offered. They also cite a study by D.V. Austin who found that out of 28 proxy fights, only 9 were successful.

[41]In the tender offer cited earlier [O'Hanlon (1969)], the management of B.F. Goodrich responded to the tender offer by Northwest Industries with the following strategy: (a) It took out a loan of $250 million under the stipulation that the loan would be in default in the event of a take-over. Moreover, the company considered using up to $200 million of the loan to prepay such items as income taxes and accounts payable, and to make contributions to retirement funds. It was intended that the acquirer would have to make arrangements to borrow this amount of money elsewhere in advance of the close of his tender offer. (b) Goodrich acquired another company which was in the same line of business as Northwest Industries and in so doing caused an injunction by the antitrust division of the Justice Department. (c) Goodrich searched for other companies willing to acquire it. (d) It made other arrangements to 'defend' itself by putting obstacles in the way of the tender offer. Among these was a whole program to ask various state securities commissions to prohibit the registration of debentures and warrants offered by Northwest Industries. (e) It initiated a review of the investment policy of B.F. Goodrich in order to restore its profitability and efficiency. (f) It contacted a Chicago based law firm whose previous member served as the head of the antitrust division at the Justice Department. The tender offer, consequently, failed.

Some other possible reasons for higher returns to the stockholders of the acquired firms are suggested below:

(1) One hypothesis is that firms are acquired due to new positive information about their business. That is, the acquisition occurs after some new positive information has been impounded into its stockprices. So, there is a rise in the stock prices of the firm to be acquired without any relation to the subsequent acquisition. We have not tested this hypothesis. But it remains at least as one reason why our results could also be consistent with a perfectly competitive market for acquisitions on both sides, i.e., for the acquiring as well as for the acquired firms.

(2) Tax considerations: In many cases the stockholders of the acquired firms have to pay capital–gains taxes.[42] Therefore the price paid for the acquired common stocks should be sufficiently higher to compensate for the costs involved in paying taxes that the owner may otherwise have to pay only at an actual sale of his stocks. This assumes that capital gains do, in fact, exist.

(3) Relative size of acquisition: In mergers where there are expectations for synergism if the two constituent firms share equally any synergy gains, then the stockholders of the smaller firm may gain proportionately more. While we have seen that stockholders of acquired firms enjoy abnormal gains, we see in table 5 that the acquiring firms' stocks do not show any abnormal gains, during the period (–7 to –1).[43] Another way to check this hypothesis is to look at the percentage of positive (or negative) residuals before the merger. A comparison of these measures in tables 6 or 2 with those of tables 5 or 1 at period (–7 to –1) reveals that the percentage of positive residuals of stocks of acquiring firms is about the same as in any other period. On the other hand, stocks of the acquired firms show exceptionally high percentages of positive residuals during that period. Nevertheless, this hypothesis, too, could account for part of the abnormal gains observed, at least for some individual acquiring firms.

(4) Effect of changes in beta of the acquired firms due to the expected acquisition: Information that firm X is going to be acquired by firm Y five months hence, should affect immediately (i.e., equilibrium in capital markets will be reached immediately) the level of risk of both firms. Since the firm to be acquired is usually much smaller, its level of risk will change more drastically. Using past data for estimation of β of the acquired firms, may therefore be highly inappropriate, and may erroneously result in abnormally high residuals if there is a substantial decrease in β. We will now present another estimation

---

[42]If other than voting stock is used for payment (e.g., non-voting stocks, cash, bonds, convertible securities, etc.) the stockholders of the acquired firms have to pay capital–gains taxes, at the year of merger.

[43]In table 5 are included firms which acquired firms that were listed on the NYSE and only these latter firms were included in the analysis of table 6.

Table 11
C.A.R.'s of 192 Acquired Firms When Using Post-merger β's of the Corresponding Acquiring Firms[a]

Month Relative to Merger	Average Residual	C.A.R.
−20	−0.0088	−0.009
−19	−0.0063	−0.015
−18	−0.0041	−0.019
−17	0.0041	−0.015
−16	0.0086	−0.007
−15	−0.0058	−0.011
−14	0.0008	−0.012
−13	0.0011	−0.011
−12	−0.0001	−0.011
−11	−0.0008	−0.012
−10	−0.0003	−0.012
−9	0.0126	0.001
−8	0.0076	0.008
−7	0.0171	0.026
−6	0.0122	0.038
−5	0.0234	0.061
−4	0.0253	0.086
−3	0.0353	0.122
−2	0.0271	0.149
−1	0.0189	0.168

[a] β was estimated from data of acquiring firms from month (−7) to month (+43).

procedure which tries to remedy this problem. This procedure uses data of the merged firm, XY.

Using a sample of 192 acquisitions, we conduct the following experiment.[44] For the acquired firm X, we use β_{xy} estimated by employing rates of return of the corresponding acquiring firm Y from month (−7 to +43). If the appropriate information reaches the market at month (−7), and if the merger is by exchange of shares, then the level of β of the acquiring firm, henceforth, should be the appropriate one for the acquired firm during the period (−7 to −1). Table 11 presents the following results. During period (−7 to −1) the C.A.R. of the acquired firms accumulates 15.9 percent which is about the same magnitude as the 14.3 percent shown in table 2. That is, on average we get similar results with both β_x and β_{xy}. In fact, a comparison of the pre-merger betas of the acquired firms in table 2 with those of the acquiring firms in table 1 (or 5) implies that we can expect such C.A.R.'s. Consequently, the changes in beta between per-merger and post-merger values for the acquired firms' stocks do not seem to explain the high A.R. during the period (−7 to −1).

---

[44] See table 11.

6. Summary and Conclusions

The purpose of this study has been to investigate empirically the market for acquisitions. The profitability for stockholders of the acquiring and the acquired firms was examined. Two basic assumptions were tested: the perfectly competitive acquisitions market hypothesis, and the efficient capital market hypothesis, the latter with respect to information on acquisitions.

6.1. The Perfectly Competitive Acquisitions Market Hypothesis

In much of the literature on mergers where various market imperfections have been assumed, the conclusions have been that acquiring firms and, by implication, their stockholders, gain abnormal returns from acquisitions. However, few empirical results have supported these conclusions. Surprisingly, in most of the empirical studies, it was found that acquisitions entail losses for the acquiring firms and their stockholders after the merger.

The findings of this study are consistent with the hypothesis that the acquiring firms operate in a perfectly competitive market, in that the prices they pay for the acquired firms' stocks enable their stockholders to earn normal returns on the acquisitions, (i.e., they earn a rate of return equal to other investment—production activities of similar risk). However, there is some indication that the stockholders of the acquiring firms may be gaining somewhat from mergers. Even though the t-values in panel I of table 4 are low, the average residuals are generally positive before the merger and the true value of the average residuals may be positive (as is suggested in panel II of table 4). However, there is no evidence to indicate that the acquiring firms overpay and thus lose from mergers, as some studies have previously concluded.

However, the stockholders of the acquired firms earn abnormal gains from mergers. That is, most of the gains from mergers go to the stockholders of the acquired firms. This result may imply that these stockholders are operating in a market in which they have some unique resources whose potential gains are realized at the time of the merger.[45] Our results are consistent with economic gains associated with mergers and with economic rent for the acquired firms.

6.2. The Efficient Capital Markets Hypothesis

As described in section 2, many previous studies and hypotheses concerning mergers have explicitly assumed, or implied, that the stock market operates

---

[45]Some other hypotheses were suggested in section 5.

inefficiently with respect to information on mergers.[46] Our results, however, are consistent with the hypothesis that anticipatory price movements preceding the effective date of a merger exhaust all valuable information in mergers. Thus, the stock prices of the constituent firms at the time of the merger already reflect all economic gains expected from the acquisition. No post-merger adjustment was observed in the stock prices of the merged firm. Significant changes in β were observed. However, rates of return adjusted efficiently to changes in risk.

The results of this study are therefore not consistent with some of the traditional hypotheses described in section 2. The stockholders are apparently not misled by accounting manipulations in mergers or by increases in earnings-per-share due to acquisitions (contrary to the 'chain letter' hypothesis). The 'growth maximization' hypothesis was not confirmed, at least so far as it implies losses to the acquiring stockholders.

The results of this study are consistent with the two-parameter portfolio models and emphasize the importance of appropriate measures of risk in estimating expected returns. It is shown that failure to take into account changes in risk led to erroneous results in some previous research on mergers.

6.3. Implications and Suggestions for Further Research

The results of this study have some implications for public policy. There is a widely held view that mergers are related to imperfections in the market place. It is frequently stated that the acquiring firms gain some monopoly power by acquisitions which then result in high returns. Our findings are consistent with the hypothesis that the acquiring firms earn normal returns from mergers.[47] This raises the question whether there is any real need to regulate merger activity.

The present study also has some implications for the current debate on the theory of the firm. Merger activity is regarded by many economists as an expression of the capital market discipline.[48] Samuelson (1970, p. 505) says that 'take-overs, like bankruptcy, represent one of Nature's methods of eliminating deadwood in the struggle for survival. A more open and more efficiently responsive-corporate society can result'. The results of this study are consistent

---

[46]See for example the discussion in section 2 on the 'chain letter' and the 'growth maximization' hypotheses.

[47]However, one might argue that all monopoly gains are realized by the stockholders of the acquired firms. Also, Goldberg's (1972) results cast some doubt on the monopoly hypothesis.

[48]Hindley (1969, p. 431) views mergers as 'the only external constraint upon managerial exploitation of the owners'.

with this view in as much as the acquired firms' stockholders have lower than normal returns, prior to the merger, and thus represent those firms which have not been doing as well as stockholders have been expecting. Efforts to limit merger activity may result, therefore, in misallocation of resources, and regulation may lead to a less efficient economy.

Future research might investigate the profitability of acquired firms before tender-offers or propositions to merge, and cases in which incumbent management is replaced subsequent to the acquisition. Such a study should distinguish between 'voluntary' and 'involuntary' mergers. It might also prove fruitful to investigate firms that were targets of unsuccessful take-over bids, inquiring whether the threat of a take-over led to subsequent changes in management or policies, and what effect these changes produced in stockholder returns.

Appendix

Probability Tests on the Average Portfolio Residuals
(or Excess Returns)

Following is a method of estimating the likelihood that residuals (or excess returns) of the magnitude shown in some previous tables may have arisen by chance. We construct a trading rule[49] which says in every calendar month t invest \$1.00 equally in each firm which acquires another firm (or alternatively which is acquired by another firm) during period ($t - L$ to $t - K$). In other words, for a merger to be included in portfolio t the following condition must hold,[50]

$$t - L \leqslant m_i \leqslant t - K \tag{8}$$

where

$\qquad m_i$ = calendar month for the merger of firm i,

$\qquad K, L$ = specific integers where $K, L \leqslant 0$ and $K \leqslant L$.

Hold this portfolio for one month. Calculate the excess return from period

---

[49] See Jaffe (1974) for a similar probability test, but for entirely different purposes. In 'Jaffe's method' the parameters K and L are not allowed to vary.

[50] Note that if $K, L > 0$, the investments are made after the merger, while if $K, L < 0$ they are made before the merger.

(t to $t + 1$) for each one of the firms in portfolio t. Calculate the average excess return on this portfolio across firms by

$$\hat{e}_{p,t+1} = \frac{1}{N} \sum_{i=1}^{N} \hat{e}_{i,t+1}$$

where

$\hat{e}_{i,t+1}$ = the residual of stock i during month $(t + 1)$,

N = number of firms in portfolio t,

$\hat{e}_{p,t+1}$ = the average residual of portfolio t, during month $(t + 1)$.

A few examples might clarify the procedure. For example, assume t is June 1962, and $K = -6$, $L = -6$. Portfolio t (i.e., June 1962) will include firms who merged during the month of December 1962 (i.e., $t = m_i - 6$). Calculating the excess returns for month $(t + 1)$ (i.e., July 1962) we will find the excess returns for an investor who invests in firms 6 months before they merge and sells them one month hence.

If $K = -6$ and $L = +4$ then in June 1962 the investor invests in firms which merge during the period February 1962 to December 1962. Portfolio $t =$ June 1962 which is invested for one month from the end of June to end of July 1962 (i.e., $t + 1$) will be an investment during different months relative to the month of merger. For example, a firm whose merger date is December 1962 will be included in portfolio June 1962 and its excess return during July 1962 will be calculated, i.e., 5 months before the merger. Another firm whose merger date is February 1962 will also be included in portfolio $t =$ June 1962; and its excess return 5 months *after* the merger (i.e., July 1962) will be calculated. In this example, firms that merge from February 1962 to December 1962 are included in portfolio June 1962.

This portfolio method produces independent drawings. But we still don't have identically distributed drawings which are required for a t-test. This is why we want to standardize each portfolio residual $\hat{e}_{p,t+1}$ by some measure of variability. We will use the estimated standard deviation of the residual term of portfolio t during the last fifty months ($t - 49$ to t);

$$\hat{Sd}_{t+1} = \sqrt{\left\{ \frac{1}{49} \sum_{j=1}^{50} \left(\hat{e}_{p,t-j+1} - \frac{1}{50} \sum_{i=1}^{50} \hat{e}_{p,t-i+1} \right)^2 \right\}} \qquad (9)$$

By dividing $\hat{e}_{p,t+1}$ by $\hat{Sd}_{t+1}$ we get the standardized residual term for portfolio t, which is, by itself, a t-statistic,

$$\hat{es}_{t+1} = e_{p,t+1}/\hat{Sd}_{t+1} \tag{10}$$

In this way we have one standardized portfolio for each calendar month t. We want to test whether portfolios formed by this procedure have an average standardized residual which is statistically different from zero.

The average standardized residual term is:

$$\overline{es}_{K,L} = \frac{1}{N} \sum_{t=X}^{Y} es_{t+1} \times D_t \tag{11a}$$

where

$D_t = 1$ if a portfolio for calendar month t was formed,

$\quad = 0$ if a portfolio for calendar month t was not formed,

$N =$ number of calendar months for which portfolios were formed, i.e.,

$$N = \sum_{t=X}^{Y} D_t$$

$X, Y =$ are April 1939 and June 1968, respectively, for which data is available on the CRSP file for estimation of the residual,

$\overline{es}_{K,L} =$ the average monthly standardized residual across all N portfolios.

The average residual term mentioned in the text and given in tables 3 and 4 is *unstandardized* and is represented as:

$$\overline{e}_{K,L} = \frac{1}{N} \sum_{t=X}^{Y} \hat{e}_{p,t+1} \times D_t \tag{11b}$$

The t-test is used to test whether the average residual terms are different from zero,

$$t_{K,L} = \overline{es}_{K,L}/(S/\sqrt{N}) \tag{12}$$

where

$t_{K,L}$ = a t-statistic for portfolios formed by a specific pair of K and L
over all t,

S = an estimate of the standard deviation of the residual terms of these
portfolios; since each residual term was already standardized in (10)
by the Sd_{t+1} the value of S is one ($S = 1$).

Since each of the N standardized residuals is t-distributed with forty-nine
degrees of freedom, the t-value of each portfolio in (12) has also forty-nine
degrees of freedom. If the number of portfolios is N then the degrees of freedom
are 49 $\times$ N.[51] Therefore, a normal distribution table will be appropriate.

Each pair of K and L will form a different standardized residual term and
a different t-statistic. The results are presented in tables 3 and 4.

References

Alberts, W.W. and J. Segall, eds., 1966, The corporate merger (University of
Chicago Press, Chicago, Ill.).

Ball, R., 1972, Changes in accounting techniques and stock prices, unpublished
Ph.D. dissertation (University of Chicago, Chicago, Ill.).

Baumol, W.J., 1959, Business behavior, value and growth (MacMillan, New
York).

Berle, A. and G. Means, 1932, The modern corporation and private property
(MacMillan, New York).

Black, F., 1972, Capital market equilibrium with restricted borrowing, Journal
of Business 45, 444–455.

Black, F., M. Jensen and M. Scholes, 1972, The capital asset pricing model:
Some empirical tests, in: M. Jensen, ed., Studies in the theory of capital
markets (Praeger, New York).

Blume, M., 1968, The assessment of portfolio performance, unpublished dissertation (University of Chicago, Chicago, Ill.).

Bossons, J., K.J. Cohen and S.R. Reid, 1966, Mergers for whom—managers or
stockholders, in: Economic concentration—Part 5, Hearings before the
Subcommittee on Antitrust and Monopoly, U.S. Senate, 89th Congress,
2nd Session (U.S. Government Printing Office, Washington, D.C.).

Brownlee, K.D., 1965, Statistical methods in science and engineering (Wiley,
New York).

Butters, J.K., J. Lintner and W.L. Cary, 1951, Effects of taxation on corporate

---

[51] See Brownlee (1965, pp. 297–304).

mergers (Graduate School of Business Administration, Harvard University, Boston, Mass.).

Edwards, C.D., 1955, Conglomerate bigness as a source of power, in: Business concentration and price policy, Conference of the universities N.B.E.R. (Princeton University Press, Princeton, N.J.).

Fama, E.F., 1968, Risk, return and equilibrium: Some clarifying comments, Journal of Finance 23, 29–40.

Fama, E.F., 1971, Risk, return and equilibrium, Journal of Political Economy 79, 30–55.

Fama, E.F., 1970, Efficient capital markets: A review of theory and empirical work, Journal of Finance 25, 383–417.

Fama, E.F. and J.D. MacBeth, 1973, Risk, return and equilibrium: Empirical tests, Journal of Political Economy 71, 607–636.

Federal Trade Commission, 1968, Statistical report.

Fisher, L., 1966, Some new stock market indices, Journal of Business 49, supplement, 191–225.

Fisher, L. and J.H. Lorie, 1964, Rates of return on investments in common stocks, Journal of Business 37, 1–21.

Gilbert, D., 1971, Mergers, diversification and the theories of the firm, unpublished dissertation (Harvard University, Cambridge, Mass.).

Goldberg, L., 1972, The effects of conglomerate mergers on competition, unpublished Ph.D. dissertation (University of Chciago, Chicago, Ill.).

Gort, M., 1966, Diversification, mergers and profit, in: W.W. Alberts and J. Segall, eds., The corporate merger (University of Chicago Press, Chicago, Ill.) 31–44.

Gort, M. and T. Hogarty, 1969, New evidence on mergers, paper presented at the Seminar on Conglomerates (University of Chicago) appeared in: Journal of Law and Economics 13, 53–62.

Hale, R.S. and G.E. Hale, 1962, More on mergers, Journal of Law and Economics 5, 119–130.

Halpern, P., 1971, Empirical estimates of the expected economic gains from mergers and an analysis of their division among companies in the merger, unpublished Ph.D. dissertation (University of Chicago, Chicago, Ill.).

Hayes, S.L. and R.A. Taussig, 1967, Tactics of cash takeover bids, Harvard Business Review 45, 135–148.

Hindley, B., 1969, Capitalism and the corporation, Economica 36, 426–438.

Hogarty, T., 1970, The profitability of corporate mergers, Journal of Business 43, 317–327.

Jaffe, J.F., 1974a, Special information and insider trading, The Journal of Business 47, 410–428.

Jaffe, J.F., 1974b, The effect of regulation changes on insider trading, Bell Journal of Economics and Management Sciences 5, 93–121.

Kaysen, C., 1965, Another view of corporate capitalism, Quarterly Journal of Economics 79, 41–51.

Larner, R.J., 1966, The 200 largest nonfinancial corporations, American Economic Reivew 56, 779–787.

Levy, H. and M. Sarnat, 1970, Diversification, portfolio analysis and the uneasy case for conglomerate mergers, Journal of Finance 25, 795–802.

Lewellen, W.G., 1971, A pure financial rationale for the conglomerate merger, Journal of Finance 26.

Lintner, J., 1965, The valuation of risk assets and the selection of risky investments in stock portfolios and capital budgets, Review of Economics and Statistics 47, 13–37.

Lintner, J., 1971, Expectations, mergers and equilibrium in purely competitive securities markets, American Economic Review 61, 101–111.

Lynch, H., 1969, Acquisitive conglomerate performance, unpublished thesis (Graduate School of Business Administration, Harvard University, Cambridge, Mass.).

Mandelker, G. and C. Sophonpanich, 1969, Some new evidence on the behavior of stock prices involved in mergers, unpublished term paper (Graduate School of Business, University of Chicago, Chicago, Ill.).

Mandelker, G., 1972, Risk and return on stocks of merging firms, presented at the Workshop in Finance (Graduate School of Business, University of Chicago, Chicago, Ill.).

Manne, G.H., 1965, Mergers and the market for corporate control, Journal of Political Economy 73, 110–120.

Manne, G.H., ed., 1969, Economic policy and the regulation of corporate securities, Symposium sponsored by the National Law Center, George Washington University and American Enterprise Institute for Public Policy Research (Washington, D.C.).

Mead, W.J., 1969, Instantaneous merger profit as a conglomerate merger motive, Western Economic Journal 7, 295–306.

Miller, M.H. and M. Scholes, 1972, Rates of return in relation to risk: A reexamination of recent findings, in: M. Jensen, ed., Studies in the theory of capital markets (Praeger, New York).

Mossin, J., 1966, Equilibrium in a capital asset market, Econometrica 24, 768–783.

Mueller, D.C., 1969, A theory of conglomerate mergers, Quarterly Journal of Economics 83, 643–660.

Mueller, D.C., 1970, Reply, Quarterly Journal of Economics 84, 674–679.

O'Hanlon, T., 1969, Goodrich's four-ply defense, Fortune 80, 110–114.

Reid, R.S., 1968, Mergers, managers and the economy (McGraw-Hill, New York).

Reid, R.S., 1971, A reply to the Weston–Manshinghka criticisms dealing with conglomerate mergers, Journal of Finance 26, 937–946.

Rubenstein, M.E., 1973, Corporate financial policy in segmented securities markets, Journal of Financial and Quantitative Analysis 8, 749–761.

Samuelson, P., 1969, Economics, 7th ed. (McGraw-Hill, New York).

Samuelson, P., 1970, Economics, 8th ed. (McGraw-Hill, New York).

Sharpe, W.F., 1964, Capital asset prices: A theory of market equilibrium under conditions of risk, Journal of Finance 19, 425–442.

Solow, R.M., 1967, The new industrial state or son of affluence, The Public Interest 3, 107–113.

Stiglitz, J.E., 1972, Some aspects of the pure theory of corporate finance: Bankruptcies and take-overs, The Bell Journal of Economics and Management Science 3, 458–482.

St. John's Law Review 44, Spring 1970, special ed., Conglomerate mergers and acquisitions: Opinion analysis.

U.S. Senate, 1965, Committee on the Judiciary, Hearings before the Subcommittee on Antitrust and Monopoly, Economic concentration, Part 2, Mergers and other factors affecting industry concentration, Statement of Dr. Willard F. Mueller, Director, Bureau of Economics, Federal Trade Commission, 89th Congress, first session.

Weston, J.F., 1953, The role of mergers in the growth of large firms (University of California Press, Berkeley, Calif.).

Weston, J.F., 1971, Discussion, American Economic Review 61, 125–127.

Weston, J.F. and E.F. Brigham, 1972, Managerial finance (Holt, Rinehart and Winston, New York).

Williamson, J., 1966, ptofit, growth and sales maximization, Economica 33.

Williamson, O.E., 1964, The economics of discretionary behavior: Managerial objectives in a theory of the firm (Prentice Hall, Englewood Cliffs, N.J.).

12 Imperfections in International Financial Markets: Implications for Risk Premia and the Cost of Capital to Firms

Richard A. Cohn and
John S. Pringle

The effects of diversification on portfolio efficiency have been examined extensively over the past decade since the pioneering works of Markowitz [10], and later Sharpe [12] and Lintner [7]. The great majority of the empirical work has been limited to common stocks in the U.S. capital market. Recently papers have begun to appear examining the merits of diversifying across international boundaries ([1], [2], [4], [5], [6], [11]). The purpose of this paper is to examine several theoretical implications of such international diversification, with particular attention to the effects of imperfections in international financial markets on risk premia for capital assets, the cost of capital to firms, and the efficiency with which capital is allocated.

Development of Capital Market Theory

The theory of portfolio selection proposed by Markowitz [10] was essentially normative. Later, assuming that investors did in fact behave according to the dictates of the Markowitz theory, and invoking some additional assumptions,[1] Sharpe [12] and Lintner [7] independently developed a positive theory of capital asset pricing. This theory yielded the important result that, for a shareholder able to combine shares into portfolios in an efficient market, the only relevant risk in the case of a single security is the non-diversifiable component, measured by the correlation of the security's return with those of all other securities in the opportunity set. At equilibrium, the expected return on an individual security was shown to be

$$E(R_i) = R_f + \left[\frac{E(R_m) - R_f}{\sigma_m} \right] \rho_{im} \sigma_i \qquad (1)$$

Reprinted with permission of the authors and publisher from *The Journal of Finance*, Vol. 28, no. 1, March, 1973, pp. 59–66.

[1]The principal assumptions underlying capital market theory are risk aversion, homogeneous expectations, risk-free borrowing and lending at the same constant rate of interest, and perfect capital markets.

where R_i is the return on the ith security, R_f the risk-free rate of interest, R_m the return on the market portfolio, σ_m and σ_i are respectively the standard deviation of the return on the market portfolio and on the ith security, and ρ_{im} the coefficient of correlation of security i's return with that of the market portfolio. The market portfolio consists of all risky securities in the same proportions that their market values bear to the total market value of all risky securities. $E(R_i)$, the rate of return expected by investors in the shares of the ith firm, is, from the point of view of the firm, its cost of equity capital. The quantity in brackets, $[E(R_m) - R_f]/\sigma_m$, represents the slope of the capital market line and is the marginal rate of substitution of risk for return (henceforth $\text{MRS}_{\sigma R}$) for all risky assets and portfolios and for all investors. The quantity $\rho_{im}\sigma_i$ represents non-diversifiable risk of the ith security.

Limitations in a Single Economy

Given perfect markets, $E(R_i)$ will always exceed R_f to the extent that non-diversifiable risk exists among returns of individual securities, i.e., to the extent that returns of securities are positively correlated. Returns on common stocks in the United States are correlated, and *ex ante* returns on securities do exceed the risk-free rate, as the Sharpe/Lintner theory predicts.

Correlation among returns on securities can be traced to the fact that returns on the underlying real assets, to which the securities represent claims, are themselves correlated. Assuming productive uncertainty only and no transactions uncertainty,[2] correlation of returns on real assets can be explained on the basis of the national business cycle and the Hicks-Slutsky income effect. A cyclical change in income tends to cause a change in the quantity demanded for all goods and services, and hence tends to affect returns to capital assets in the same direction. In any single economy, this correlation of returns on capital assets imposes a definite upper limit on the benefits of portfolio diversification.

International Diversification

To the extent that economic activity in different economies is less than perfectly correlated, diversification across international boundaries should improve investors' risk-reward opportunities. While studies of correlation of security returns in different countries are few in number ([1], [2], [5], [6], [11]), there is at least some evidence that correlation is relatively low between foreign securities and the United States market portfolio, as one would expect.

To see the effects of international diversification more clearly, consider

---

[2]See Hirshleifer ([3], pp. 243–244) for a discussion of this distinction.

a case in which a prohibition of international diversification heretofore in effect between separated but otherwise perfect national capital markets suddenly is lifted. From the point of view of an investor in any particular country, additional securities possessing low correlation with the prior market portfolio suddenly are added to the investment opportunity set.[3]

The lifting of the restriction on international diversification affects risk-return relationships and security prices in two ways. First, the non-diversifiable risk of each security, $\rho_{im}\sigma_i$, declines as the market portfolio is broadened to include more securities. Second, as will be demonstrated below for two classes of utility functions, logarithmic and exponential, the slope of the capital market line, $MRS_{\sigma R}$, itself also declines. In terms of Equation (1), these two effects both operate in the direction of reducing the required return $E(R_i)$, and concomitantly raising the price, of individual securities. The two effects are analyzed below in more detail.

Non-Diversifiable Risk

Upon lifting of the restriction on international diversification, returns on all risky securities should adjust. Assuming for the moment that $[E(R_m) - R_f]/\sigma_m$, i.e., $MRS_{\sigma R}$, does not rise,[4] there should be a decline in the premium return provided by individual risky securities over the return yielded by the risk-free asset. This result follows from the fact that in perfect world capital markets, the correlation of the return on any single risky security with the return on the augmented market portfolio is likely to be less than the correlation of the security's return with the return on the old market portfolio, owing to the addition of "low-correlation" securities to the market portfolio. The resulting decline in ρ_{im} in Equation (1) causes $E(R_i)$ to decline. This decline in required returns takes place for individual capital investment projects as well as for securities.

The downward adjustment in *ex ante* risk premia brought on by a sudden change from imperfect to perfect world financial markets would cause a corresponding upward adjustment in prices of risky securities and thus result in windfall gains to holders of risky assets. The higher the positive correlation of a security's return with the old market portfolio, the greater would be the security's proportional rise in price.[5]

---

[3] It is assumed that both real investment and international trade restrictions are held constant.

[4] It will be shown below that $MRS_{\sigma R}$ is likely to fall.

[5] Two possible exceptions to the above result should be noted. In the case of firms whose earnings were more closely related to other national economies than to the domestic economy, exporters for example, ρ_{im} could rise (and share prices fall) with the addition of shares of firms from the other national economies. A second exception would occur in the

The Slope of the Capital Market Line

The second of the two effects of a lifting of restrictions on international diversification concerns the impact on $\text{MRS}_{\sigma R}$, the slope of the capital market line. This effect is explored below for two classes of investor utility functions for wealth.

In the case of logarithmic utility, investors act as if they wish to maximize the asymptotic rate of growth of wealth. Logarithmic utility has the further desirable properties of decreasing absolute risk aversion and constant relative risk aversion in the Pratt-Arrow sense. If all investors display logarithmic utility, then the slope of the capital market line, $\text{MRS}_{\sigma R}$, can be expressed as $\sigma_w/\bar{W}$, where $\bar{W}$ is aggregate expected end-of-period wealth for all investors, and σ_w is the standard deviation of W.[6]

Prior to the lifting of restrictions on international diversification, each country has its own ratio, $\sigma_w/\bar{W}$. When restrictions are lifted, the denominators of these national ratios combine additively to form a new aggregate $\bar{W}$ for all economies, whereas the numerators combine less than additively when, as is likely, national economies are less than perfectly correlated. Hence the new aggregate ratio $\sigma_w/\bar{W}$ is lower than the old individual ratio for most countries,

---

case of securities whose returns had been negatively correlated with the prior market portfolio (if indeed any such securities existed). In this case, ρ_{im} whose rise and prices fall as such securities became less useful for reducing dispersion of portfolio returns.

[6]Whe investors behave as though they have logarithmic utility functions, the market price of the ith firm has been shown by Litzenberger and Budd [9] to be

$$P_i = \frac{1}{1 + R_f}\left[E(Y_i) - \frac{1}{\sum_k \bar{W}_k}\sum_j \text{cov}(Y_i, Y_j)\right]$$

where Y_i is the total end-of-period dollar return (price plus dividend for the period) on each firm and $\bar{W}_k$ is the expected end-of-period wealth for the kth investor. It can be shown that this expression is equivalent to

$$P_i = \frac{1}{1 + R_f}\left[E(Y_i) - \frac{\sigma_w}{\bar{W}}\rho_{iw}\sigma_{Y_i}\right]$$

where $\bar{W}$ is the aggregate expected end-of-period wealth for all investors, σ_w the standard deviation of W, σ_{Y_i} the standard deviation of the dollar return on the ith firm, and ρ_{iw} the coefficient of correlation between Y_i and W. This expression can be rewritten to give:

$$E(R_i) = R_f + \frac{\sigma_w}{\bar{W}}\rho_{iw}\sigma_{R_i}$$

where R_i is rate of return on shares of the ith firm. The ratio $\sigma_w/\bar{W}$ represents the slope of the capital market line, $\text{MRS}_{\sigma R}$.

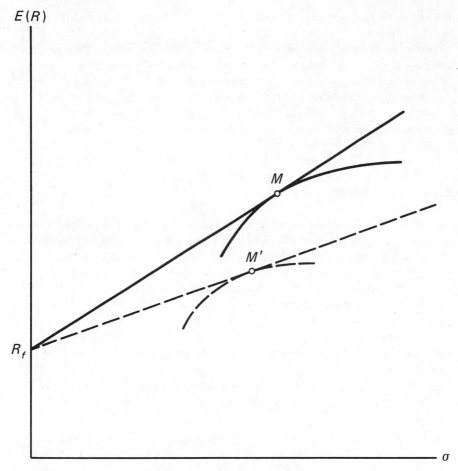

Figure 1

and for the typical country the slope of the capital market line declines as shown in Figure 1 below (dotted line).

Under an alternative assumption that investors have exponential utility functions, the $MRS_{\sigma R}$ can be shown to be

$$\frac{\sigma_w}{\underset{k}{\Sigma}\left(\dfrac{1}{a_k}\right)}$$

where σ_w is the standard deviation of aggregate end-of-period wealth and a_k

is investor k's Pratt-Arrow risk aversion coefficient, $-U''/U'$.[7] If a_k and the standard deviation of end-of-period per capita wealth do not differ greatly across countries, then $\text{MRS}_{\sigma R}$ will fall with the removal of restrictions on international financial flows, for the denominator will increase additively with a widening of the market while the numerator σ_w will increase less than additively.

If investors' utility functions are assumed to be quadratic, the analysis is not so straightforward. Because of certain properties of the quadratic utility function, the effects of unrestricted international diversification on $\text{MRS}_{\sigma R}$ cannot be determined unambiguously.[8]

Effect on Risk Premia

Free international movements of financial capital thus reduce the risk-premium component of the cost of capital to firms through the joint action of two effects. Not only will the non-diversifiable risk of the typical firm, $\rho_{im}\sigma_i$, decline as a result of the elimination of market imperfections, but $\text{MRS}_{\sigma R}$, the slope of the capital market line, is likely to decline as well. The resulting downward shift in the risk-premium component of the cost of capital to firms is an indicator of increased allocational efficiency. Investments that were deemed too risky vis-à-vis their expected returns in a world of separate national capital markets might well be deemed worth undertaking in the presence of a world capital market.

The overall effects of a lifting of restrictions on international diversification are illustrated in Figure 1 below depicting portfolio risk and return in mean-

---

[7]See Lintner [8] for development of the negative exponential utility function. Assuming that investors display exponential utility and returns are normally distributed, Litzenberger and Budd [9] have noted that the price of the ith firm is given by

$$P_i = \frac{1}{1 + R_f}\left[E(Y_i) - \frac{1}{\sum\limits_k \frac{1}{a_k}}\, \sum\limits_j \text{cov}(Y_i, Y_j)\right]$$

with terms defined as above. It can be shown that the slope of the capital market line in this case is given by

$$\frac{\sigma_w}{\sum\limits_k\left(\dfrac{1}{a_k}\right)}$$

[8]The assumption of quadratic utility has been very useful in the development of capital market theory and as an approximation in generating hypotheses for empirical studies. However, as is well known, the quadratic utility function has certain undesirable theoretical properties, namely increasing absolute risk aversion and negative marginal utility of wealth over part of its range. These properties prevent a clear interpretation of the effect on $\text{MRS}_{\sigma R}$ of a lifting of restrictions on international diversification.

standard deviation space. The curved lines represent efficient sets of portfolios in the absence of risk-free lending and borrowing. The lines tangent to the curved lines are "capital market lines" that represent the loci of efficient sets of portfolios when investors are free to lend and borrow at R_f. The slope of the capital market line is $MRS_{\sigma R}$. M and M' represent market portfolios under different sets of conditions discussed below. The graphical analysis in Figure 1 is based on the assumption that the risk-free rate of interest, R_f, did not change when restrictions were lifted. The risk-free rate of interest is discussed further below.

For a typical country, the riskiness, σ_m, of the new (international) market portfolio will be less than the riskiness of its old (national) market portfolio.[9] Since the slope of the capital market line declines (dotted line), it follows that, for most countries, the new (international) market portfolio, M', will lie below and to the left of the old (national) market portfolio, M. Hence, for most countries, $E(R_m)$ declines toward the risk-free rate of interest when restrictions on diversification are lifted.

While international diversification is possible at present, many factors exist which constitute market imperfections and the removal of which should lead to the effects hypothesized above.[10] However, very little empirical work has been done in the way of constructing internationally diversified portfolios and analyzing their returns (see [1], [5], [6]), and there is far too little empirical evidence yet available to permit any definitive conclusions.

The Risk-Free Rate of Interest

The analysis to this point has abstracted from the question of the magnitude and determination of the risk-free rate of interest and has focused only on risk premia. The risk-free rate was assumed to be exogenously determined. Although an analysis of the way in which the risk-free rate is set in the market is beyond the scope of this paper, a few observations can be made.[11]

As noted above, Figure 1 and related analysis assumed that the risk-free rate of interest did not change when restrictions on international financial movements were lifted. In general, however, where risk-free rates differed among countries prior to the removal of financial barriers, the rates would converge to a common equilibrium rate after the removal of barriers.

---

[9]For countries that previously had a market portfolio of low risk, it is theoretically possible that the new (international) σ_m could be higher. For example, investors in a country that previously had only riskless investments available to them now would be faced with a σ_m greater than zero.

[10]Examples of such factors are the interest equalization tax, exchange controls and other restrictions on capital flows, witholding taxes on dividends to foreigners, and the existence of exchange rate risk. Another factor, perhaps even more important in practice, is the availability and cost of information on foreign securities.

The lifting of restrictions on international diversification should lead to a rise in the general level of the risk-free rate, as measured by the new (world-wide) equilibrium rate relative to the previous (national) rates. This rise is a direct result, assuming time-independent utility, of the increased per-capita certainty-equivalent future consumption endowment caused by merging national capital markets.[12] If such a rise occurred, it would operate in the direction of decreasing the slope of the capital market line, thus reinforcing the decline in the marginal rate of substitution of risk for return described earlier.

Some observations also can be made regarding the nature of the risk-free asset itself. Assuming fixed exchange rates,[13] and hence (in effect) a single world currency, in the absence of restrictions on capital mobility the risk-free rate should be the same everywhere. In the presence of any non-zero probability that these "fixed" rates could change, however, such an ideal situation breaks down. Given exchange rate risks, it is difficult to conceive of a single asset that wold be "risk-free" to all investors in all countries. U.S. Treasury bills, the most often employed empirical proxy for the risk-free asset in the U.S. literature, would be risk-free only from the standpoint of U.S. investors. Another nation's government bills, while risk-free from the viewpoint of investors in that country, would enter into the opportunity set of risky securities for U.S. investors. Of course, strictly speaking, government bills are risk-free, even in perfect markets, only if there is no inflation *and* their maturity coincides in time with a need on their holder's part to liquidate the security, for only at maturity is their nominal value certain.

Conclusions

The almost universal practice in the empirical literature of finance has been to treat diversified portfolios of common shares listed on the New York Stock Exchange as a proxy for the market portfolio of investment opportunities in the Sharpe-Lintner model of capital market equilibrium. But this opportunity set itself contains a large component of diversifiable risk if the market portfolio is extended to securities of other nations.

The relatively high *ex post* returns provided by internationally diversified portfolios of securities may well be related to market imperfections. If current restrictions on international capital flows, to say nothing of other market imperfections, were removed, returns on internationally diversified portfolios

---

[11] See Hirshleifer [3] for a discussion of the risk-free rate of interest.

[12] For a discussion of this effect within the context of the state-preference approach to uncertainty, see Hirshleifer ([3], pp. 256–257).

[13] The case of flexible exchange rates is more complex and will not be considered here.

would be expected to decline relative to the risk-free rate of interest. More importantly, the equilibrium rate of exchange of risk and return should decline for most countries, non-diversifiable risk should decline for most projects, and the resulting reduction in the risk-premium component of the cost of capital to firms should improve the efficiency of real capital allocation.

References

1. H.G. Grubel. "Internationally Diversified Portfolios: Welfare Gains and Capital Flows," *American Economic Review*, LVIII (December 1968), pp. 1299-1314.
2. —— and K. Fadner. "The Interdependence of International Equity Markets," *Journal of Finance*, XXVI (March 1971), pp. 89-94.
3. J. Hirshleifer. *Investment, Interest and Capital*. Englewood Cliffs, N.J.: Prentice-Hall, 1970.
4. C.H. Lee. "A Stock-Adjustment Analysis of Capital Movements: The United States-Canadian Case," *Journal of Political Economy*, LXXVII (July/August 1969), pp. 512-523.
5. D.R. Lessard. "Multinational Portfolio Diversification for Developing Countries," unpublished doctoral dissertation, Stanford University, 1970.
6. H. Levy and M. Sarnat. "International Diversification of Investment Portfolios," *American Economic Review*, LX (September 1970), pp. 668-675.
7. J. Lintner. "The Valuation of Risk Assets and the Selection of Risky Investments in Stock Portfolios and Capital Budgets," *Review of Economics and Statistics*, XLVII (February 1965), pp. 13-37.
8. ——. "The Market Price of Risk, Size of Market and Investor's Risk Aversion," *Review of Economics and Statistics*, LII (February 1970), pp. 87-99.
9. R.H. Litzenberger and A.P. Budd. "A Note on Geometric Mean Portfolio Selection and the Market Prices of Equities," *Journal of Financial and Quantitative Analysis*, VI (December 1971), pp. 1277-1282.
10. H. Markowitz. "Portfolio Selection," *Journal of Finance*, VII (March 1952), pp. 77-91.
11. A.A. Robichek, R.A. Cohn, and J.J. Pringle. "Returns on Alternative Investment Media and Implications for Portfolio Construction," *Journal of Business*, XLV (July 1972), pp. 427-443.
12. W.F. Sharpe. "Capital Asset Prices: A Theory of Market Equilibrium Under Conditions of Risk," *Journal of Finance*, XIX (September 1964), pp. 425-442.

13

A Mean–Variance Synthesis of Corporate Financial Theory

Mark E. Rubinstein

In recent years the elaboration of portfolio theory has shattered the conventional partitions within the field of finance. While it has always been desirable, it is now possible to treat security valuation, asset expansion decision rules, and capital structure policies as derivatives of market equilibrium models under uncertainty. Additionally, these models provide benchmarks for measuring the efficiency of markets and investment performance. Portfolio theory, providing as it does, theories of individual choice of securities and the determination of their market prices, therefore comprises the theoretical substructure of finance. The objective of this essay is to demonstrate that an integration of much of the subject matter of finance is possible at a relatively introductory level. No attempt is made to cover all the applications of portfolio theory; I have rather concentrated on the contributions of the popular mean-variance theory[1] to corporate finance, and consequently this essay is divided into three parts treating the three major problems of corporate finance: security valuation, asset expansion, and capital structure, in that order.

Much of the theory, informally treated in the text with formal arguments banished to footnotes, is contained in the existing literature, in particular Sharpe [15] on security valuation, Mossin [11] on asset expansion and Stiglitz [16] on capital structure.[2] However, several results will not be found in the published literature: (1) development of mean-variance capital budgeting criteria for mutually exclusive projects, capital rationing, and mutually interdependent projects; (2) proof that although non-synergistic merging typically reduces the probability of bankruptcy, shareholders will nonetheless be indifferent; (3) proof of the Modigliani-Miller Proposition I with risky corporate debt and

---

Reprinted with permission of the author and publisher from *The Journal of Finance,* Vol. 28, no. 1, March 1973, pp. 167–181. Thanks are due to Professor Fred Weston for many helpful discussions and the opportunity to test and refine the pedagogic approach in this essay in the classroom.

[1] The state-preference theory, developed for example by Myers [12], from which this theory can be derived as a special case, is omitted from this synthesis. However, while empirical tests of the more general theory are lacking, they are available for the mean-variance theory in increasing abundance in recent years. Jensen [4] provides an excellent summary of these results. He concludes that the model in its simplest form fails to explain adequately the structure of security returns; however, slightly generalized forms of the model which do not destroy its basic features appear more promising.

[2] Portions of several other papers are summarized in the text, including those of Hamada [3], Lintner [5], Modigliani and Miller [9], and Mossin [10].

corporate taxation; (4) proof of the Modigliani-Miller Proposition II revised for
risky corporate debt; (5) analysis of the separate effects of operating risk and
financial risk on equity risk premiums; (6) analysis of the components of
operating risk; and (7), in the Appendix, a relatively elegant proof of the mean-
variance security valuation theorem.

I. Security Valuation

Let us start from the familiar mean-variance security valuation theorem that
under certain assumptions[3] it follows that for any security j

$$E(R_j) = R_F + \lambda \text{Cov}(R_j, R_M) \tag{1}$$

---

[3]The most important assumptions are (1) its single-period context, (2) no restrictions on
short-selling and borrowing, and (3) a perfect and competitive securities market. However, Fama [1] has demonstrated that even though an individual has a concave multiperiod
utility function, he will nonetheless behave in the first period as if he possesses some
concave single-period utility function. This theorem is significant since if security returns
are assumed normally distributed and intertemporarily statistically independent, equation
(1) applies even in a multiperiod setting where R_j represents a first period rate of return.
Nonetheless, the model remains incapable of valuing irregular or non-perpetual income
streams over time and hence has not rigorously been applied to the analysis of dividend
policy and capital budgeting projects with multiperiod receipts. Only if firms can in some
way estimate the probability distribution of the market value of a project at the end of the
first period (without knowing future discount rates) and sale of the project at that time
does not result in synergistic losses will the mean-variance model be appropriate. However,
this model should not be criticized too heavily on this account since the present failure of
theorists to produce any multiperiod (i.e., permitting portfolio revision over time) security
valuation model under uncertainty consistent with maximizing expected utility (see
Hakansson [2]) is very likely the most pressing theoretical problem in the field of finance.
    The assumption of a *perfect* securities market precludes personal or corporate taxes,
brokerage fees, underwriting costs, bankruptcy penalties, or other types of transactions
costs as well as indivisibilities of securities. Relaxation of this assumption provides no
analytical complications provided the imperfection is confined to a proportional reduction
(possibly different for different securities) in the rate of return on a security; that is,
stochastic constant returns must prevail. Otherwise, the necessary first order conditions in
the Appendix must be drastically revised. However, if certain imperfections are admitted
(as we will do in the case of proportional corporate income taxes) the capital structure and
merger irrelevancy propositions do not strictly hold. Bankruptcy penalties, though not
proportional corporate income taxes, create an incentive to merge since mergers almost
invariably diminish the probability of bankruptcy. However, proportional personal income
taxes do not affect any of the conclusions in this essay.
    With a *competitive* securities market, the same security investment opportunities are
available to all investors and no investor believes he can influence the rate of return on any
security by his market transactions. No such assumption is made for firms in Sections I
and III. However, in Section II, a firm's capital budgeting decisions are assumed to have
negligible impact on the capitalized opportunities of other firms. The implications of
relaxing the assumption of a competitive securities market have received little attention
in the theoretical literature.
    Rubinstein [13] demonstrates that the assumption of (4) the existence of a risk-free
(i.e. zero variance) security is not substantive provided at least two risky securities exist

where

R_j (random variable) is the rate of return on security j,

R_F is the rate of return on a risk-free security,

R_M (random variable) is the rate of return on the market portfolio of risky securities, and

λ is a positive constant.

See the Appendix for a short proof of this theorem. This market equilibrium relationship between security risk and return may be interpreted in perhaps more familiar language by defining $R_j \equiv \tilde{P}_j/P_j$ where P_j is the present price of security j and P_j (random variable) is the change in price of security j.[4] With this definition it follows immediately that

$$P_j = \frac{E(\tilde{P}_j)}{R_F + \lambda \text{Cov}(R_j, R_M)} = \frac{E(\tilde{P}_j) - \lambda \text{Cov}(\tilde{P}_j, R_M)}{R_F}$$

the first equality representing a risk-adjusted discount rate formula, the second

---

in which case the symbol R_F in this paper may be replaced at every point by $E(R_p)$ where p is a portfolio with Cov $(R_p, R_M) = 0$. The strong short-selling assumption, by circumventing the issue of personal bankruptcy, makes this possible. Restrictions on short-selling leading to Kuhn-Tucker conditions have been examined by Lintner [5,6].

If the assumption of (5) homogeneous subjective probabilities is omitted, as Lintner [6] has shown, a concept similar to λ remains well-defined. However expected rates of return and covariances must be replaced by weighted averages. Furthermore, the convenient separation property of the model (i.e. all individuals regardless of differences in wealth levels of preferences, divide their wealth between the same two mutual funds, one of which is risk-free and the other the market portfolio of risk securities) no longer holds. As Stiglitz [16] proves, this failure of the separation property invalidates the Modigliani-Miller Proposition I in the presence of risky corporate borrowing. However, if corporate debt is risk-free, the proposition still holds. A similar qualification applies to the asset expansion propositions; see Lintner [8] and Myers [12].

The assumption that (6) all individuals evaluate portfolios by only two parameters, expectation and variance of future wealth, of omitted leads to a more complex security valuation equation which nonetheless preserves many of the characteristics of the simpler mean-variance case; see Rubinstein [13]. However, in this case the separation property is more difficult to obtain. Finally, if the assumption of (7) risk aversion is omitted, equation (1) remains necessary but no longer sufficient for market equilibrium.

[4] If R_j is defined as a *rate* of return, $\tilde{P}_j$ must be interpreted as a perpetual flow. Alternatively, R_j can be regarded as *one plus* the rate of return in which case $\tilde{P}_j$ must be interpreted as the future price of security j, a stock variable. With this latter definition of $\tilde{R}_j$ all equations in the text remain unchanged; however, all flow variables must be regarded as stock variables and, in particular, τ_j must be considered as a *wealth* tax rate on equity. To see this, observe that equation (1) holds if and only if

$$E(1 + R_j) = (1 + R_F) + \lambda \text{Cov}(1 + R_j, 1 + R_M)$$

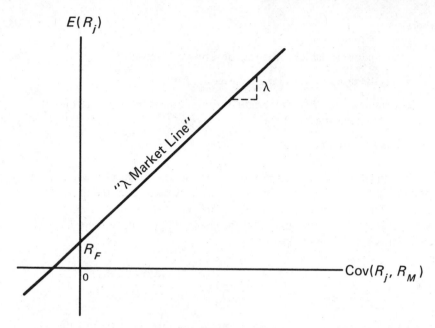

Figure 1

equality a certainty-equivalent formula.[5] Equation (1) is illustrated graphically in Figure 1. Since λ and R_F are market parameters, all securities have risk and return characteristics which fall along the "λ market line" in equilibrium. Define α_j as the proportion of the value of an arbitrary portfolio p assigned to security j. Observing that $R_p = \Sigma_j \alpha_j R_j$, it is easily demonstrated that all possible portfolios of securities fall along this same market line;[6] that is, for any portfolio p,

$$E(R_p) = R_F + \lambda \mathrm{Cov}(R_p, R_M)$$

Further since the market portfolio of risky securities is itself a portfolio, its risk and return characteristics fall along the market line; that is,

$$E(R_M) = R_F + \lambda \mathrm{Cov}(R_M, R_M) = R_F + \lambda \mathrm{Var} R_M$$

---

[5]In the traditional risk-adjusted rate and certainty-equivalent dividend capitalization equations, the relationship between the risk premium or certainty-equivalent factor in each period and the risk characteristics of the dividend stream are unspecified. Unless some relationship is postulated, the equations remain merely *definitions* of the risk premiums or certainty-equivalent factors. In this context, the contribution of the mean-variance security valuation *theorem* is to provide the needed specification of the risk premium and certainty-equivalent factor.

[6]To see this, merely multiply equation (1) by α_j and take the summation over all j.

or alternatively,

$$\lambda = \frac{E(R_M) - R_F}{\text{Var} R_M}$$

Two popular alternative formulations of the equation (1) are

$$E(R_j) = R_F + \lambda^* \rho(R_j, R_M)\sqrt{\text{Var} R_j} \qquad (2)$$

$$E(R_j) = R_F + \lambda^{**} \beta_j \qquad (3)$$

where

$$\lambda^* \equiv \lambda \sqrt{\text{Var} R_M} = [E(R_M) - R_F] \sqrt{\text{Var} R_M},$$

$$\lambda^{**} \equiv \lambda \text{Var} R_M = E(R_M) - R_F,$$

$$\beta_j \equiv \text{Cov}(R_j, R_M)/\text{Var} R_M, \text{ and}$$

$\rho(R_j, R_M)$ is the correlation coefficient between R_j and R_M.

Unlike λ and λ^{**}, λ^* is dimensionless. These equations are derived from the definition of correlation coefficient and the result that the market portfolio of risky securities falls along the market line. These results can be described by similar graphical representations (see Figure 2). Equation (2) permits convenient distinctions between types of risk. Held alone as a portfolio, the risk of security j to an individual can be measured by $\sqrt{\text{Var} R_j}$; in a market or well-diversified portfolio context, the risk is measured by $\rho(R_j, R_M)\sqrt{\text{Var} R_j}$ (see equation (2)). The former may be called the *total risk* and the latter the *nondiversifiable or systematic risk.* Since $-1 \leq \rho(R_j, R_M) \leq 1$, $\rho(R_j, R_M)$ may be interpreted as the percentage of total risk that cannot be eliminated by diversification without sacrificing expected rate of return. The difference between total and non-diversifiable risk, $[1 - \rho(R_j, R_M)] \sqrt{\text{Var} R_j}$, measures the portion of the total risk that can be eliminated by diversification and hence can be called *diversifiable* or *nonsystematic risk.* All these results can, of course, be shown to hold for portfolios as well as securities.

If all diversifiable risk has been eliminated from a portfolio, we define that portfolio to be *efficient.* In this case

$$[1 - \rho(R_e, R_M)] \sqrt{\text{Var} R_e} = 0$$

where subscript e denotes an efficient portfolio. For this equation to hold, $\rho(R_e, R_M) = 1$; or, in other words, all efficient portfolios are perfectly positively correlated with the market portfolio of risky securities (with the exception of the efficient portfolio containing only risk-free securities). It follows that

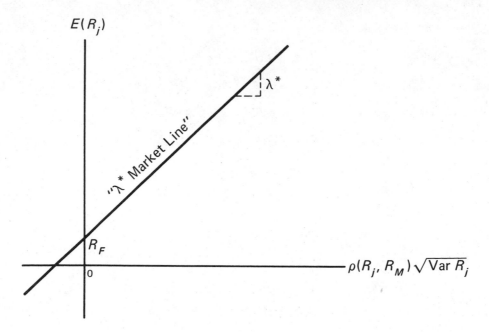

Figure 2

$\rho(R_p, R_M)$ may be interpreted as a dimensionless measure of the degree of diversification of any portfolio p. This analysis provides a method of segregating the efficient portfolios from other portfolios and securities which fall along the "λ^* market line" by noting that an "efficient portfolio market line" is described by setting the correlation coefficient equal to 1 in equation (2), and hence

$$E(R_\epsilon) = R_F + \lambda^*\sqrt{\operatorname{Var} R_\epsilon}$$

This, by the way, is the same line each individual will derive in a Markowitz efficient set analysis with the existence of a risk-free security and homogeneous subjective probabilities.

II. Asset Expansion

The mean-variance security valuation theorem is readily applied to capital budgeting decisions for share price maximizing firms.[7] Consider j now as refer-

---

[7] The following theory does not actually require share price maximizing behavior for firms; it merely indicates the influence of capital budgeting decisions on share prices.

ring to firm j and R_j as representing the rate of return on the equity of firm j. It is easily demonstrated that firm j should accept a project only if

$$E(R_j^0) > R_F + \lambda \mathrm{Cov}(R_j^0, R_M)^8$$

where

X_j^0 (random variable) is the dollar return of the project,

COST_j^0 is the cost of the project,[9] and

$R_j^0 \equiv X_j^0/\mathrm{COST}_j^0$ (random variable) is the rate of return of the project.

This decision rule advises acceptance of a project only if its expected internal rate of return $E(R_j^0)$ exceeds the appropriate risk-adjusted discount rate for the project, $R_F + \lambda \mathrm{Cov}(R_j^0, R_M)$; this discount rate is equal to the expected rate of return on a security with the same risk as the project. Graphically, in Figure 3, the acceptance criterion implies a firm should accept a project only if the *project's* risk-return order pair plots above the market line, such as projects A and B. In this case, when the firm accepts such favorable projects, there must be an upward revision of the firm's share price. To see this, after acceptance of a favorable project but before the price adjustment, the firm can be viewed in temporary disequilibrium with the firm's risk-return ordered pair temporarily plotting above the line. To restore equilibrium, individuals cause $E(R_j)$ to be lowered to the market line by bidding up the share price of firm j.[10]

The constant slope of the market line, λ, may be interpreted as the *risk-*

---

[8]Alternative present value risk-adjusted discount rate and certainty-equivalent forms of this criterion are easily derived. Further, the criterion also has alternative formulations analogous to equations (2) and (3). However, the version given by Mossin [11, p. 755] similar to $[E(R_j^0) - R_F/\mathrm{Cov}(R_j^0, R_M)] > \lambda$ is only correct provided $\mathrm{Cov}(R_j^0, R_M) > 0$.

[9]X_j^0 and COST_j^0 should be understood to represent, respectively, the entire marginal dollar return and cost of the project to the firm. Synergistic benefits could clearly cause the same project to have different marginal dollar returns and costs to different firms. Again, X_j^0 may be interpreted as a perpetual flow of income or as the future market value of the project, with corresponding interpretations for R_j^0; see footnote 4.

[10]The asset expansion criterion is demonstrated formally under the convenient, though unnecessary, assumption of all-equity financed firms and projects. Consider firm j for which

P_j' is the revised present price after acceptance of the new project,

N_j is the number of shares before acceptance of the new project,

N_j^0 is the additional shares issued at price P_j' to finance the project, and

X_j (random variable) is the dollar value of net operating income before acceptance of the new project.

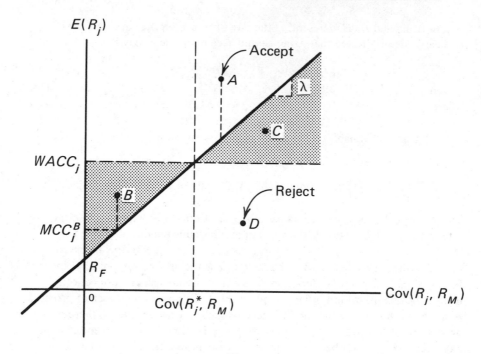

Figure 3

standardized cost of capital appropriate to all firms and all projects since, if $\mathrm{Cov}(R_j^0, R_M) > 0$, then a firm should accept a project only if

$$\frac{E(R_j^0) - R_F}{\mathrm{Cov}(R_j^0, R_M)} > \lambda$$

From equation (1), before acceptance of the project since $R_j = X_j/(N_j P_j)$

$$E(X_j) = R_F N_j P_j + \lambda \mathrm{Cov}(X_j, R_M) \tag{a}$$

After acceptance of the project

$$E(X_j + X_j^0) = R_F(N_j + N_j^0)P_j' + \lambda \mathrm{Cov}(X_j + X_j^0, R_M) \tag{b}$$

Since be definition $X_j^0 = R_j^0 (\mathrm{COST}_j^0)$ and $\mathrm{COST}_j^0 = N_j^0 P_j'$, from equations (a) and (b)

$$R_F N_j (P_j - P_j') = (\mathrm{COST}_j^0)[R_F + \lambda \mathrm{Cov}(R_j^0, R_M) - E(R_j^0)] \tag{c}$$

The asset expansion criterion follows since both $R_F N_j$ and COST_j^0 are positive. This analysis, however, ignores second order effects on R_M, and hence on λ. In U.S. capital markets such effects are likely to be insignificant. See Myers [12, pp. 12,13] for a more probing discussion of this point.

We will call this result the "market price of risk" (MPR) asset expansion criterion. All firms in the economy may use λ as a cutoff value for all projects;[11] this contrasts with the traditional "weighted average cost of capital" (WACC) criterion which must be computed separately for each firm, and as we will shortly show, is generally invalid. Further, since the contribution of the project to the firm's variance of equity rate of return does not affect the accept or reject decision given by the MPR criterion, *diversification* (i.e., reduction of Var R_j) can be ignored in capital budgeting decisions. That is, in the absence of *synergy* (i.e., if $R_j^0 = R^0$, the rate of return if the project were itself a firm), each project is evaluated on its own merits without reference to the firm's existing investments.[12] This conclusion also follows from the observation that individuals, by their own diversification, can costlessly eliminate any diversifiable risk present in a firm's investment portfolio so that the firm need not diversify for individuals.[13]

A common interpretation of the WACC criterion can easily be shown to be generally invalid. This interpretation advises that a project should be accepted only if $E(R_j^0) >$ WACC$_j$, that is, graphically, only if it falls above the horizontal dotted line in Figure 3, such as projects A and C. Therefore, for projects that fall in the shaded areas, such as B and C, the WACC and MPR criteria lead to contradictory decisions. The WACC criterion is obviously invalid because it fails to consider the risk of projects. For example, projects with $E(R_j^0) >$ WACC$_j$ but with very high risk, such as C, will be improperly accepted. In fact, the WACC criterion will only lead to the correct cut-off rate for projects in the same "risk class" as the firm; that is, projects for which Cov(R_j^0, R_M) = Cov(R_j^*, R_M) where R_j^*(random variable) is the rate of return shareholders would earn if the firm kept its existing investments intact but altered its capital structure so that it became debt free. Cov(R_j^*, R_M) therefore reflects only the "business" or "operating risk" of the firm as distinct from its "financial risk." In Section III, we will show that the ordered pair (Cov(R_j^*, R_M), WACC$_j$) falls on the market line. Graphically, a project will be in the same "risk class" as the firm only if it plots on the vertical dotted line in Figure 3, from which it

---

[11]λ, therefore, is an important economy-wide variable. Several studies have attempted to measure the related λ^* from *ex-post* data; and the comparative statics analyses of Lintner [7] and Rubinstein [14] permit a theoretical examination of the determinants of λ^* and its behavior over time.

[12]Since R_M reflects the existing investments of firm j as well as all other firms, this statement is not formally accurate. However, in U.S. capital markets the influence of a single firm's investments on R_M is likely to be insignificant.

[13]The "homemade diversification" theorem should be regarded as one of the major discoveries in corporate financial theory. Despite lack of recognition in several recent papers, the theorem was first formally proven by Mossin [10, pp. 779–781]. Myers [12] has demonstrated a similar proposition with a state-preference model under complete (i.e., Arrow-Debreu) markets for securities and under incomplete (i.e., generalized) markets with the existence of security risk classes.

can be visually verified that only for such projects will the WACC criterion provide the appropriate cut-off rate. A second explanation of the failure of the WACC criterion is that it is not a marginal criterion. The appropriate marginal cost of capital (MCC_j^B) for project B is indicated on the vertical axis in Figure 3. The MCC_j^0 depends on the risk of a project and is equal to the appropriate discount rate for the project, $R_F + \lambda \text{Cov}(R_j^0, R_M)$.

Mutually exclusive projects, capital rationing and mutually interdependent projects are easily treated in this framework. Suppose projects A and B in Figure 3 are mutually exclusive. It can be readily shown that the firm should accept the project with the highest excess expected internal rate of return weighted by its cost,[14] that is, the highest $(\text{COST}_j^0)[E(R_j^0) - R_F - \lambda \text{Cov}(R_j^0, R_M)]$. Note that the excess expected internal rate of return for project A, for example, is measured graphically by the vertical distance between A and the market line in Figure 3. With capital rationing, the proper procedure is again to reject all projects falling below the line. Of the remaining projects consider all possible bundles of projects satisfying the rationing constraint. These bundles are in effect mutually exclusive; therefore the firm should accept the bundle with the highest excess expected internal rate of return weighted by its cost. If n superscripts projects in a feasible bundle, this is equivalent to accepting that bundle for which $\Sigma_n (\text{COST}_j^n)[E(R_j^n - R_F - \lambda \text{Cov}(R_j^n, R_M)]$ is the highest. With mutually interdependent projects, selection is determined by appropriately increasing the number of mutually exclusive projects. Assume, for example, that projects A and C are mutually interdependent; in this case in addition to projects A and C treated separately, the joint acceptance of A and C is considered as a single project.

Decision rules regarding mergers are easily derived. Consider firms j and k which are contemplating merger. Let X_j, X_k, and X_{jk} (random variables) be the net operating income (EBIT) of firms j, k, and the pro-forma post-merger firm, respectively. In the absence of *synergy*, that is, if $X_{jk} = X_j + X_k$, the post-merger firm can be considered equivalent to a portfolio containing all the securities of firms j and k. Since all possible portfolios, as well as securities, fall along the market line, the post-merger firm will fall along the market line and it will be impossible for the shareholders of both j and k to benefit from the merger. Again, the intuitive reason for this result is costless "homemade diversification." Alternatively, since an individual could have held the stock of both j and k in his portfolio before the merger, his portfolio becomes no more diversified if he holds the post-merger firm.[15] Therefore, as in capital budgeting, the diver-

---

[14]This result follows immediately from equation (c) of footnote 10 and is equivalent to accepting the project with the highest net present value.

[15]Before the merger, the shares of firms j and k could have been held in any proportion in an individual's portfolio; however, after the merger, shares in firms j and k can, in effect, be held only in a fixed proportion. It may be argued, therefore, that mergers destroy opportunities for individual portfolio selection and hence even a merger with positive

sification effects of a merger will not affect equity values. However, mergers with synergy will affect equity values and such mergers can be analyzed similarly to capital budgeting projects, since with synergy, *from the point of view of firm j,* the risk-return ordered pair of firm k may not plot on the market line.

It has been argued (see Lintner [8, p. 107]) that with risky corporate borrowing, merging decreases the probability of bankruptcy (provided the separate net operating incomes of the merging firms are not perfectly correlated). As a result, the merged firm can borrow on more favorable terms thereby increasing the value of equity. However, an offsetting consequence of merging is overlooked in this argument. The effects of bankruptcy are double-edged since mergers also have the unfavorable consequence of removing the separated limited liabilities of the merging firms. Consider two firms j and k: prior to merger bankruptcy of k does not affect the returns to shares of j; subsequent to merger, the returns from j's portion of the merged firm would be reduced by the requirement of meeting k's defaulted portion of the merged firm's obligations.[16]

III. Capital Structure

The mean-variance security valuation theorem is also readily applied to the effect of capital structure on the value of a firm. Consider firm j for which

X_j (random variable) is the dollar value of net operating income,

B_j is the present dollar value of debt,

S_j is the present dollar value of equity,

---

synergy could reduce equity values. However, the portfolio separation property of the mean-variance model insures that relevant opportunities will remain intact.

[16]The irrelevancy of mergers is formally demonstrated even where corporate debt is explicitly risky. Define R_{Fj}, R_{Fk}, and R_{Fjk} (random variables) as the borrowing rates for firms j, k, and jk. To reflect the influence of bankruptcy, for example, the probability distribution of R_{Fj} could be defined such that $\bar{R}_{Fj} \equiv R_{Fj}$ if $X_j \geqslant \bar{R}_{Fj}B_j$ and $R_{Fj} \equiv X_j/B_j$ if $X_j \leqslant \bar{R}_{Fj}B_j$ where $\bar{R}_{Fj}$ is the promised or contracted rate of interest (see text for definitions of B_j and V_j). From equation (1) and since $R_j = (X_j - R_{Fj}B_j)/(V_j - B_j)$, $E(X_j) - B_jE(R_{Fj}) = R_F V_j - B_j R_F + \lambda \,\mathrm{Cov}(X_j, R_M) - B_j\lambda \,\mathrm{Cov}\,(R_{Fj}, R_M)$. Since risky debt is also a security, $E(R_{Fj}) = R_F + \lambda \,\mathrm{Cov}\,(R_{Fj}, R_M)$; therefore

$$E(X_j) = R_F V_j + \lambda \,\mathrm{Cov}\,(X_j, R_M) \qquad \text{(a)}$$

Similar arguments may also be made for firms k and jk, so that

$$E(X_k) = R_F V_k + \lambda \,\mathrm{Cov}\,(X_k, R_M) \text{ and (c) } E(X_{jk}) = R_F V_{jk} + \lambda \,\mathrm{Cov}\,(X_{jk}, R_M) \qquad \text{(b)}$$

These equations will hold regardless of the effects of reduced probability of bankruptcy on R_{Fjk}. Since $X_{jk} = X_j + X_k$, adding equations (a) and (b) and comparing the sum to equation (c) yields the result $V_{jk} = V_j + V_k$.

$V_j \equiv B_j + S_j$ is the present total dollar value of the securities of the firm, and

$R_j \equiv (X_j - R_F B_j)/S_j$ (random variable) is the rate of return on equity.

Define these variables for a second firm denoted by a * superscript for which $B_j^* = 0$. Since the risk-return ordered pairs of all securities fall along the market line,

$$\frac{E(R_j) - R_F}{\rho(R_j, R_M)\sqrt{\operatorname{Var} R_j}} = \frac{E(R_j^*) - R_F}{\rho(R_j^*, R_M)\sqrt{\operatorname{Var} R_j^*}} = \lambda^* \tag{4}$$

If $X_j = X_j^*$, it follows that $V_j = V_j^*$ by substituting the definitions of R_j and R_j^* in equation (4).[17] Interpreting this result, as a firm alters its capital structure, but before price adjustment, the firm moves along, not off, the market line achieving the precise risk-return trade-off which leaves the market indifferent and hence its stock price unchanged.[18]

---

[17]This proposition is demonstrated formally in the presence of corporate taxes and risky corporate debt where superscript denotes after tax variables, τ_j is the corporate income tax rate for firm j, and R_{Fj} (random variable) denotes the rate of return on the risky debt of firm j. Since $E(R_j) = R_F + \lambda \operatorname{Cov}(R_j, R_M)$ and $R_j \equiv (X_j - R_{Fj}B_j)(1 - \tau_j)/S_j$, it follows in the levered case that

$$E(X_j)(1 - \tau_j) - E(R_{Fj})B_j(1 - \tau_j) = R_F S_j + \lambda(1 - \tau_j)\operatorname{Cov}(X_j, \hat{R}_M) - \lambda(1 - \tau_j)B_j\operatorname{Cov}(R_{Fj}, \hat{R}_M)$$

$$\text{(a)}$$

By similar reasoning since in the unlevered case $\hat{R}_j^* \equiv X_j(1 - \tau_j)/V_j^*$

$$E(X_j)(1 - \tau_j) = R_F V_j^* + \lambda(1 - \tau_j)\operatorname{Cov}(X_j, \hat{R}_M) \tag{b}$$

Further since risky debt is also a security, $E(R_{Fj}) = R_F + \lambda\operatorname{Cov}(R_{Fj}, R_M)$. Substituting this equation and equation (b) into equation (a) and recalling that by definition $V_j \equiv S_j + B_j$, it follows that $V_j = V_j^* + \tau_j B_j$. This is the familiar result of Modigliani-Miller which holds even in the presence of risky debt.

It should be emphasized, as Stiglitz [16] has shown, for more general models which lack the separation property, the Modigliani-Miller Proposition I, with or without taxes, will not hold in the presence of risky debt. The separation property in the mean-variance model insures that changes in capital structure will not alter relevant opportunities available to individuals.

[18]It is not difficult to demonstrate that if $V_j = V_j^*$, then $P_j = P_j^*$ where P_j and P_j^* refer to share prices. Imagine that a firm is first in an unlevered position so that $V_j^* = S_j^* = N_j^* P_j^*$ where N_j^* is the number of shares. The firm now levers its capital structure without affecting its net operating income by purchase of ΔN shares of equity at price P_j (a priori, possibly different from P_j^*) and financing $(\Delta N)P_j$ with debt so that $(\Delta N)P_j = B_j$. Hence

$$V_j \equiv S_j + B_j = (N_j^* - \Delta N)P_j + (\Delta N)P_j = N_j^* P_j$$

and since $V_j = V_j^*$, then $P_j = P_j^*$.

To show that the ordered pair $(\rho(R_j^*, R_M)\sqrt{\text{Var } R_j^*}, \text{WACC}_j)$ falls on the "λ^* market line" (or, alternatively, that $(\text{Cov}(R_j^*, R_M), \text{WACC}_j)$ falls on the "λ market line") we need only recall that by definition

$$\text{WACC}_j \equiv R_F \left[\frac{B_j}{V_j} \right] + E(R_j) \left[\frac{S_j}{V_j} \right] = \frac{E(X_j)}{V_j}$$

and since $X_j = X_j^*$ and $V_j = V_j^*$,

$$\text{WACC}_j = \frac{E(X_j)}{V_j} = \frac{E(X_j^*)}{V_j^*} = E(R_j^*)$$

Since R_j^* is independent of capital structure, it follows that the weighted average cost of capital is also.

The precise relationship between expected rate of return to equity and capital structure is easily demonstrated since by substitution of $R_j \equiv (X_j - R_F B_j)/S_j$ and $R_j^* = X_j/V_j$:

$$\rho(R_j, R_M) = \rho(R_j^*, R_M) \quad \text{and} \quad \sqrt{\text{Var } R_j} = \sqrt{\text{Var } R_j^*} \left[1 + \frac{B_j}{S_j} \right] \quad (5)$$

Therefore, from equation (2),

$$E(R_j) = R_F + \lambda^* \rho(R_j^*, R_M)\sqrt{\text{Var } R_j^*} \left[1 + \frac{B_j}{S_j} \right] \quad (6)$$

Equation (6) quantifies the effect of financial leverage on the risk of a firm and hence on its expected rate of return to equity. Equation (5) indicates that since the correlation coefficient is invariant to changes in financial leverage, the full impact of financial risk is absorbed by the standard deviation $\sqrt{\text{Var } R_j}$. Further, since both λ^* and $\sqrt{\text{Var } R_j^*}$ are positive, the direction of the influence of changes in financial leverage on $E(R_j)$ depends on the sign of $\rho(R_j^*, R_M)$, so that $E(R_j)$ could conceivably decrease with increased financial leverage. In more familiar terms, equation (6) is a specialization of the Modigliani-Miller Proposition II,

$$E(R_j) = E(R_j^*) + [E(R_j^*) - R_F] \left[\frac{B_j}{S_j} \right] \quad (7)$$

for the attitudes toward risk implied by the mean-variance security valuation theorem.[19] Both equations (6) and (7) permit separate analysis of operating risk and financial risk. Equation (6) can be written

$$E(R_j) = R_F + \lambda^* \rho(R_j^*, R_M)\sqrt{\text{Var } R_j^*} + \lambda^* \rho(R_j^*, R_M)\sqrt{\text{Var } R_j^*} \left[\frac{B_j}{S_j}\right] \quad (8)$$

thereby separating the effects of the risk-free rate of return, operating risk, and financial risk on the expected rate of return to equity.[20]

It is further interesting to develop the components of operating risk. Consider, for firm j, product m for which

Q_m (random variable) is the output in units,

v_m is the variable cost per unit,

---

[19]If corporate debt is risky, equation (7) is generalized by replacing the symbol R_F with $E(R_{Fj})$. To see this, applying the definitions $R_j \equiv (X_j - R_{Fj}B_j)/S_j$, $R_j^* \equiv X_j/V_j^*$ and $V_j = B_j + S_j$, it is easy to demonstrate that the revised equation (7) holds if and only if $V_j = V_j^*$, but this last equality has already been demonstrated in the absence of taxes in footnote 17. Since $E(R_{Fj})$ exceeds R_F for most firms in U.S. capital markets, the consideration of risky debt will cause $E(R_j)$ to be less than it would otherwise be if debt were assumed risk-free. This is intuitively plausible since with risky debt, the total risk of net operating income is shared by both equity and debt holders.

[20]This result can be used to explain the size of observed *ex post* values of β_j in equation (3). Defining $\beta_j^* \equiv \text{Cov}(R_j^*, R_M)/\text{Var } R_M$, it can be shown with adjustment for corporate income taxes that

$$\left[\beta_j = \beta_j^* \left(1 + \frac{B_j(1 - \tau_j)}{S_j} \right) \right]$$

From data in *Moody's Handbook of Common Stocks:* First Quarter, 1971, on General Motors (GM) and Chrysler (C) for 1960–1969, $\beta_{GM}^* = .77$ and $\beta_C^* = 1.69$ with $\beta_{GM} = .86$ and $\beta_C = 2.48$. We might infer that not only was Chrysler's "operating risk" about double General Motors' but the substantially higher financial leverage ratio for Chrysler (B_{GM}/S_{GM} = .2 and B_C/S_C = 1.0) caused Chrysler's nondiversifiable risk (operating plus financial) to be about triple General Motors'.

An alternative approach is to use equation (8) directly. The results for General Motors and Chrysler (adjusted for corporate income taxes) are summarized in the following table:

	$E(R_j)$	Risk-Free Rate R_F	Operating Risk $\lambda^* \rho(R_j^*, R_m)\sqrt{\text{Var } R_j^*}$	Financial Risk	
				$\lambda^* \rho(R_j^*, R_m)\sqrt{\text{Var } R_j^*}$	$\frac{B_j(1 - \tau_j)}{S_j}$
GM	.10	.045	.050	.005	
C	.21	.045	.110	.055	

p_m is the sales price per unit,

F_m is the fixed cost, and

α_m is the proportion of assets (i.e., V_j) devoted to its production.

Therefore, assuming all fixed costs of the firm can be allocated, $X_j = \Sigma_m$ $(Q_m p_m - Q_m v_m - F_m)$. Since $R_j^* = \alpha_m X_j / \alpha_m V_j$, it is not difficult to demonstrate that operating risk

$$p(R_j^*, R_M)\sqrt{\text{Var } R_j^*} = \Sigma_m [\alpha_m (p_m - v_m) p(Q_m, R_M)\sqrt{\text{Var }(Q_m / \alpha_m V_j)}]$$

where α_m measures the relative influence of each product line (assuming all assets of the firm can be allocated to products), $p_m - v_m$ reflects operating leverage, $\rho(Q_m, R_M)$ the pure influence of economy-wide events on output, and $\sqrt{\text{Var }(Q_m / \alpha_m V_j)}$ the uncertainty of output per dollar of assets which could be interpreted as a measure of the uncertainty of "operating efficiency."

Illustration of the effect of corporate income taxes on the relationship between capital structure and firm values is easily analyzed by equation (4) upon substitution of

$$R_j = \frac{(X_j - R_F B_j)(1 - \tau_j)}{V_j - B_j} \quad \text{and} \quad R_j^* = \frac{X_j(1 - \tau_j)}{V_j^*}$$

where τ_j is the corporate income tax rate of firm j.[21] We immediately derive the familiar result $V_j = V_j^* + \tau_j B_j$. This result can be given a similar interpretation to the acceptance of a project with a risk-return ordered pair falling above the market line. After an increase in financial leverage, but before price adjustment, the risk-return ordered pair of the firm's equity moves temporarily above the market line. To restore equilibrium, individuals cause $E(R_j)$ to be lowered to the market line by bidding up the share price of the firm.

In contrast to Modigliani and Miller [9], whose ingenious "risk class" assumption insulated their partial equilibrium approach from a need to provide a theory of the market risk premium, at some sacrifice of generality (see footnote 3), the mean-variance market equilibrium model provides this theory. By straightforward extensions, the most important concepts of corporate finance can be demonstrated by use of virtually a single diagram. Furthermore, quantification of risk premiums supplies the key to practical implementation.

---

[21] The corporate income tax is assumed to be proportional and with full loss offset. See footnote 17 for formal proof for the more general case of risky corporate debt.

In general, with the introduction of taxes, while all securities still fall along the market line, the slope of the line will change; see Rubinstein [14].

Appendix[22]

A short proof of the mean-variance security valuation theorem follows under the special case of quadratic utility.[23] In addition to the variables already used in this paper consider individual i for which

S_{ij} is his present dollar value holdings of risky security j,

B_i is his present dollar value holdings of risk-free securities,

$W_i = \Sigma_j S_{ij} + B_i$ is his present wealth,

$\widetilde{W}_i = \Sigma_j S_{ij} R_j + B_i R_F$ (random variable) is his future wealth (interpreting R as 1 + rate of return), and

$U_i(\widetilde{W}_i)$ is his twice continuously differentiable measurable utility of future wealth function where $U_i' > 0$.

In this context, closure requires $S_j = \Sigma_i S_{ij}$ and $R_M = \Sigma_j S_j R_j / \Sigma_j S_j$. These definitions imply the simple Lagrangian form of optimization

$$\max_{S_{ij}, B_i} E[U_i(\widetilde{W}_i)] + L_i[W_i - \Sigma_j S_{ij} - B_i]$$

with first order conditions[24]

$$E[U_i' R_j] = E[U_i' R_F] = L_i \quad \text{for all } j \quad \text{and} \quad W_i = \Sigma_j S_{ij} + B_i$$

These conditions imply $E[U_i'(R_j - R_F)] = 0$ which in turn implies $E(U_i')E(R_j$

---

[22]This proof as well as other arguments in this essay utilize freely and without comment basic properties of expectation operators. Specifically, if X and Y are any two random variables, a and b are nonrandom parameters, and i is an index, then (1) $E(a + bX) = a + bE(X)$, (2) $E(\Sigma_i X_i) = \Sigma_i E(X_i)$, (3) $\text{Var}(a + bX) = b^2 \text{Var } X$, (4) $\text{Cov}(X,Y) = \text{Cov}(Y,X)$, (5) $\text{Cov}(a + bX,Y) = b \text{ Cov}(X,Y)$, (6) $\text{Cov}(\Sigma_i X_i,Y) = \Sigma_i \text{Cov}(X_i,Y)$, (7) $\text{Cov}(X,Y) = E(XY) - E(X)E(Y)$, and (8) if $b > 0$, $\rho(a + bX,Y) = \rho(X,Y)$. It is, of course, assumed that all random variables have finite variances (and hence finite means).

[23]Mossin [10] provides a more general proof assuming only ordinal utility functions with future value portfolio mean and variance as arguments. In a more recent paper, Mossin [11] offers another proof which sacrifices generality by assuming all individuals have measurable quadratic utility functions for future wealth; however, Mossin's new proof has the virtue of simplicity and provides detailed information about the determinants of λ. Nonetheless, as this appendix demonstrates, his new proof is needlessly lengthy. For the mean-variance security valuation equation to be consistent with measurable utility, one can alternatively assume that all securities have normally distributed rates of return; see Rubinstein [14].

[24]These first order conditions will be necessary and sufficient for a unique global maximum if $U_i''(\widetilde{W}_i) < 0$ and no security rate of return is perfectly correlated with the rate of return of any portfolio excluding it.

$-R_F) + \text{Cov}(U_i', R_j - R_F) = 0$. If $U_i = W_i - a_i W_i^2$ where a_i is a nonrandom parameter, then $U_i' = 1 - 2a_i W_i$ and therefore

$$[E(R_j) - R_F]\, \frac{E(U_i')}{2a_i} = \text{Cov}(R_j, W_i)$$

Since this equation will hold for all individuals in the market,

$$[E(R_j) - R_F]\, \Sigma_i \frac{E(U_i')}{2a_i} = \Sigma_i \text{Cov}(R_j, \tilde{W}_i) = \text{Cov}(R_j, \Sigma_i \tilde{W}_i)$$

Closure requires that $\Sigma_i \tilde{W}_i = \Sigma_j S_j R_j + \Sigma_i B_i R_F = R_M \Sigma_j S_j + R_F \Sigma_i B_i$; however, since $\Sigma_j S_j$ and $R_F \Sigma_i B_i$ are nonrandom, $\text{Cov}(R_j, \Sigma_i W_i) = \text{Cov}(R_j, R_M \Sigma_j S_j) = (\Sigma_j S_j)\,\text{Cov}(R_j, R_M)$. Therefore,

$$E(R_j) = R_F + \left[\frac{\Sigma_j S_j}{\Sigma_i \dfrac{E(U_i')}{2a_i}} \right] \text{Cov}(R_j, R_M)$$

and if the quantity in brackets is identified with λ,[25] then

$$E(R_j) = R_F + \text{Cov}(R_j, R_M)$$

References

1. E.F. Fama. "Multiperiod Consumption-Investment Decisions," *American Economic Review,* March, 1970.
2. N.H. Hakansson. "On the Dividend Capitalization Model under Uncertainty," *Journal of Financial and Quantitative Analysis,* March, 1969.
3. R.S. Hamada. "Portfolio Analysis, Market Equilibrium, and Corporation Finance," *Journal of Finance,* March, 1969.
4. M.C. Jensen. "The Foundations and Current State of Capital Market Theory," ed. M.C. Jensen, *Studies in the Theory of Capital Markets* (forthcoming).
5. J. Lintner. "The Valuation of Risk Assets and the Selection of Risky Investments in Stock Portfolios and Capital Budgets," *Review of Economics and Statistics,* February, 1965.
6. ——. "The Aggregation of Investor's Diverse Judgments and Preferences in

---

[25]If $U_i'' < 0$, then $2a_i > 0$. From this it follows that $\lambda > 0$ since both $\Sigma_j S_j$ and U_i' are assumed positive.

Purely Competitive Markets," *Journal of Financial and Quantitative Analysis,* December, 1969.

7. ——. "The Market Price of Risk, Size of Market, and Investor's Risk Aversion," *Review of Economics and Statistics,* February, 1970.

8. ——. "Expectations, Mergers and Equilibrium in Purely Competitive Securities Markets," *American Economic Review,* May, 1971.

9. F. Modigliani and M.H. Miller. "The Cost of Capital, Corporation Finance, and the Theory of Investment," *American Economic Review*, June, 1958.

10. J. Mossin. "Equilibrium in a Capital Asset Market," *Econometrica,* October, 1966.

11. ——. "Security Pricing and Investment Criteria in Competitive Markets," *American Economic Review,* December, 1969.

12. S.C. Myers. "Procedures for Capital Budgeting under Uncertainty," *Industrial Management Review,* Spring, 1968.

13. M.E. Rubinstein. "The Fundamental Theorem of Parameter-Preference Security Valuation," *Journal of Financial and Quantitative Analysis,* January, 1973.

14. ——. "A Comparative Statics Analysis of Risk Premiums," (forthcoming in *Journal of Business*).

15. W.F. Sharpe. *Portfolio Theory and Capital Markets,* McGraw-Hill, 1970.

16. J.E. Stiglitz. "A Re-Examination of the Modigliani-Miller Theorem," *American Economic Review,* December, 1969.

14

Some Aspects of the Performance of Non-Convertible Preferred Stocks

John S. Bildersee

Non-convertible preferred stocks[1] have been the subject of far less discussion than bonds and common stocks. Some of these discussions suggest that preferred stocks combine some features that are inferior to those of bonds with some features that are inferior to those of common stocks.[2] Such discussions suggest that preferred stocks may represent an inferior class of investments relative to bonds and common stocks. However, portfolio theory suggests that every security, including preferred stocks, is an integral part of the marketplace since the investor is always adequately compensated for any perceived risk by the return he expects from the security. This paper employs the market model from portfolio theory and a multiple regression analysis to investigate the holding period returns to preferred stocks. In particular, we investigate and quantify some traditional thoughts about the performance of preferred stocks as well as integrate and compare the performance of preferred stocks with the performance of common stocks of the same company and with the performance of the alternative assets in the marketplace. Our sample also gives us an opportunity to do some further tests of the empirical strength of the market model.

As we shall see, the results obtained here appear consistent with those expected for the market model. Section II describes the measure of risk, beta, to be used and discusses its usefulness in this context briefly. After describing the sample in Section III, Section IV presents the results obtained from applying the market model. Section V presents a multiple regression analysis of the preferred stocks.

Reprinted with permission of the author and publisher from *The Journal of Finance*, Vol. 28, no. 5, December 1973, pp. 1187–1201. The author is grateful to Merton Miller, Eugene Fama, Nicholas Gonedes, Robert Hamada, Charles Nelson, Harry Roberts and Joshua Ronan for helpful remarks, but is of course responsible for any errors. This paper is based on the author's dissertation.

[1]We consider only non-convertible preferred stocks in this paper.

[2]See Amling (2), p. 155, for a typical statement of this position. Amling, however, does not suggest that this approach is the proper one to take with respect to preferred stocks.

II. Beta as a Measure of Risk

The market model, as proposed by Markowitz (12) and developed by Sharpe (16, 17), Fama (7, 8) and others,[3] states that we can represent the return on a security j in period t, $\widetilde{R}_{jt}$,[4] as

$$\widetilde{R}_{jt} = \alpha_j + \beta_j \widetilde{R}_{mt} + \widetilde{\epsilon}_{jt}$$

where α_j and β_j are parameters indicating the relation between the return on asset j and the return on the market portfolio in period t, $\widetilde{R}_{mt}$. The $\widetilde{\epsilon}_{jt}$ are random variables with mean zero and variance $\sigma^2(\widetilde{\epsilon}_j)$ and represent the independent factors unique to security j.

Beta for any investment j is a measure of the systematic risk investors associate with that particular investment relative to the risk of the market portfolio. Moreover, beta can have any value and measure any level of systematic risk relative to the market.[5] Since beta is a continuous variable we shall be able to compare the relative systematic risk of preferreds directly with that for any other preferreds and with common stocks.

Phrases stating that a preferred stock is "like a bond" or "like a common stock" take an additional meaning in the context of this paper. In this paper these phrases refer to the general performance characteristics of the security. Thus preferred stocks that behave "like bonds" would be those that have betas and average returns like those of bonds, whereas preferred stocks that behave "like common stocks" would be those that have betas and average returns like those of common stocks.[6]

III. The Preferred Stock Sample

Our goal in this paper is to study the risk-return performance of preferred stocks. To achieve this goal we selected a sample of securities that emphasizes the variety of large companies issuing preferred stocks. We assumed that such a sample was most likely to enable us to investigate a wide range of investment preformances during the sample period. Our sample includes month-end wealth relatives, adjusted for dividends and capital changes, for 72 preferred stocks

---

[3] Fama (6) provides a useful review of the model's current status.

[4] The tilde (~) denotes a random variable.

[5] Typical traditional quality ratings (e.g., Moody's and Standard and Poor's) use discrete rating schemes and use rating procedures and scales that are separate and distinct for each class of securities.

[6] This does not mean that a preferred stock that is "like a bond" or "like a random stock" has to have a perfect positive correlation with some bond or common stock.

listed on the New York Stock Exchange continuously from March, 1956 to March, 1966. These securities represented 60 industrial, utility, transportation and financial corporations. For a corporation to qualify for the study its common stock also had to be listed on the N.Y.S.E. for the entire period.[7]

Moreover, at least one preferred security issued by each company in the study had to pass a minimum trading requirement.[8] The minimum trading requirement helps to ensure up-to-date prices or relatively narrow bid-ask spreads for the estimation of market prices.[9] The sample might be atypical if there were any systematic differences among the performances of securities with large numbers of outstanding shares relative to typical preferred securities. However, up to two additional preferred stocks per company were added to the sample. These preferred stocks were listed on the N.Y.S.E. during the full sample period, but did not have to meet the trading requirement.[10] These securities, which tend to compensate for any systematic characteristics of the sample due to the minimum trading requirements, will also give us an opportunity to observe the performance of multiple equivalent securities issued by given companies.[11]

We restricted the number of utility preferred stocks in the sample and included 16 of the qualifying utility preferreds. We assumed that inclusion of additional utility corporations and their preferreds would not have increased the variety of the securities in the sample.[12]

---

[7]This requirement imparts a survivorship bias on the sample. However, tests using a sample of securities on the exchange for portions of this period yielded results virtually identical with those stated in the paper.

The March 1956 to March 1966 period was chosen as it was the most recent 10 year period available on the Chicago tape developed by the Center for Research in Security Prices, University of Chicago. Such data are necessary for some of our tests. These tapes have since been updated. See Bildersee (3) for a full discussion of the preferred stock sample.

[8]We required that securities trade at least 4,000 shares between January 1966 and March 1966. Since the number of shares outstanding fell during the period for the typical preferred stock, this trading requirement suggests that the typical preferred in the sample may have been more active earlier in the period.

[9]If there were no trading price for the security in question, the mean of the bid and ask quotes was used as a substitute for the price.

[10]Eight companies were represented by two preferreds and two companies were represented by three preferreds.

[11]Equivalent securities in this paper are those securities which have equal rights to assets and to dividends as stated by Moody's manuals.

[12]The results obtained in this paper support this assumption. In addition some traditional rating agencies, like Moody's, show less differentiation among rated utility preferreds than they do among other rated preferreds. In addition, we subsequently looked at a sample of 28 additional NYSE preferreds. The observations obtained for this sample are consistent with those reported for the utility preferreds included in this paper.

IV. Preferred Stocks and the Market Model

In this section we shall use a common stock index to represent the 'basic underlying factor' of the market model. Then we shall employ a bond index and a 'market' index in the same model. In each case we shall investigate the betas generated for our sample.

We shall use time series data of ex-post returns in risk premium form to estimate the distributions of expected risk premiums for each security in the sample.[13] That is, we assume the process is of the form

$$(\widetilde{R}_j - R_F) = \beta_j(\widetilde{R}_m - R_F) + \widetilde{e}_j$$

where $(\widetilde{R}_j - R_F)$ is the holding period risk premium for security j, $(\widetilde{R}_m - R_F)$ is the holding period risk premium for the market portfolio and $\widetilde{e}_j$ is a random variable with an expected value zero and a variance σ_j^2.[14] In this paper we use the one month treasury bill rate to represent the riskless rate.

Several tests were performed to check the adequacy of the market model as a return generating mechanism for preferred stocks. For the most part, the results were similar to those obtained by other researchers in the case of common stocks.

Of special interest is the examination of the structural stability of the regression relation between each preferred stock and the common stock index in time. For this test we divided the observations for each security into two equal periods and estimated beta for each period for each security. If the beta estimated from the observations for the second half of the period was over two standard errors away from the beta estimated for the first half of the period, then we said that the betas for each half of the period were drawn from different distributions of risk premiums and that beta was not stationary for the security.

We found that 16 of the 72 preferreds appeared to lack stationarity. However, when we looked at the 10 preferreds which either missed at least one preferred dividend or paid off an existing arrearage at some time during the period, we found that 8 preferreds appeared to lack structural stability. This

---

[13]Roll (15) indicates that, without adjustment for the riskless rate, use of the returns from time series data would bias the results of the analysis as the riskless rate varies from period to period. See Friend and Blume (10), Miller and Scholes (13) and Black, Jensen and Scholes (4) for discussions of additional problems encountered when using the market model and the capital asset pricing model to explain differential returns in the market.

[14]For simplicity of exposition we will use the standard deviation and variance of distributions as measures of dispersion. This replaces measures of dispersion which are associated with the stable Paretian distributions that appear to describe returns on assets. This issue is not critical as we will be concerned primarily with the betas.

Table 1

Distributions of Beta from Regressions on the Common Stock Index

Sample	Observations	Mean	Std. Dev.	Aver. R^2
Preferreds	72	0.198	0.262	0.061
SCCS−(Same Company's Common Stock)	60^{17}	0.999	0.383	0.284

Sample	Ranges of Beta		Range of R^2
	Inter-Quartile	Extremes	Extremes
Preferreds	0.053–0.211	−0.029–+1.538	0.0^34–0.334
SCCS	0.693–1.216	+0.356–+2.025	0.071–0.532

result, which is discussed more fully in Bildersee (3), raises the possibility that much of the lack of structural stability among preferreds was concentrated among those companies that broke their regular dividend policy.

A. *Preferred Stocks and a Common Stock Index*

In this section we shall use Fisher's Link Relative Common Stock Index to represent the market index.[15]

We would expect a beta for a company's preferred stock to be less than the beta for the same company's common stock. Owners of each security suffer the same business risks relative to the market. However, since common stockholders have subordinated ownership relative to preferred stockholders, common stockholders suffer financial risks relative to the market in excess of those suffered by preferred stockholders. As expected and as can be seen from Figure 1, every company's preferred stocks had betas which were less than the beta for the same company's common stock.[16] Furthermore, in every case where multiple preferred stocks of the same company had equal right to assets and to dividends, the betas for these preferred stocks were not significantly different from each other.

Table 1 contains the distributions of beta for the preferred stocks and for the common stocks from regressions using the common stock index. It appears that the preferred stocks in this sample were issued by companies issuing common stocks with a typical set of risks. The mean of the beta distribution for

---

[15]See Fisher (9).

[16]The figure also shows one point far apart from the others. The tests were repeated excluding this point and yielded virtually identical results.

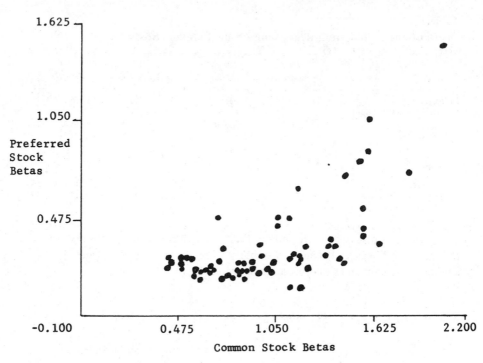

Figure 1. Distribution of Preferred Stock Betas and the Same Company's
Common Stock Betas (SCCS).

the common stocks is not different from 1.0, the expected mean for a random
sample of common stocks.

Note from Table 1 that the distribution of preferred stock betas has less
dispersion than does the distribution of common stock betas. Note also that
the mean beta for preferred stocks is significantly less than the expected mean
for common stocks. This suggests that the preferred stock class may be narrower
than the common stock class and that the typical preferred stock has less risk
than the typical common stock. The mean beta for preferreds is also greater
than zero so preferreds appear positively correlated with the common stock
index. However, the relatively low average R^2 suggests that the relation between the typical preferred stock and the common stock index may be weaker
than the relation between the typical common stock and the common stock
index.

Figure 2 compares the distributions of the preferred stock and SCCS

---

[17]Each firm is represented once in the same company's common stock sample regardless
of the number of preferred stocks representing the company.

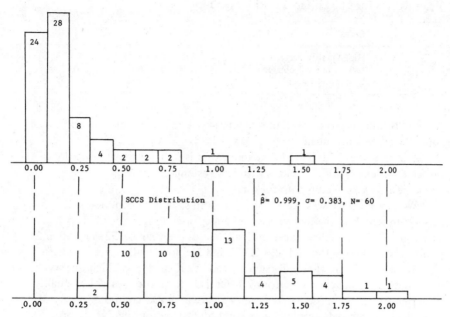

Figure 2. Preferred Stock and SCCS Distributions.

samples. Both distributions appear skewed to the right. Moreover, the distributions overlap each other so that it is possible to speak of a range of beta values
which appear primarily representative of preferred stocks, a range which appears
representative of common stocks and a range which includes securities from
both the preferred and common stock classes. The figure also shows that the
preferred stocks of some companies have more systematic risk than common
stocks of some other company.

The figure suggests a way of grouping preferred stocks which may provide
an immediate, simple test of the value of using a market approach to consider
the risk and performance of preferreds. In particular, we can divide our preferred stock sample into a sample of preferreds with betas within the range
which appears to be representative primarily of preferred stocks and into a
sample of preferreds with betas outside this range. Purchasers of preferred
stocks may want the benefits of a senior security. However, if they invest in
a preferred stock with a beta that is not within the range of betas that appears
to be representative primarily of preferred stocks, then they will not get the
benefits of a preferred stock in the sense that they could also purchase a common stock that would provide the systematic risk associated with the beta
value of this particular preferred security. Since the latter type of preferred

Table 2
Mean Return for Chosen Indexes Risk Premium Form

Index	Mean
High Quality Preferreds	0.041%/mo.
Low Quality Preferreds	0.269
Common Stocks	0.846

stock illustrates as great a level of systematic risk as some junior security, it could be called a low quality preferred stock.[18]

The securities with betas in the range that is representative primarily of preferred stocks provide investors with less systematic risk than common stocks relative to the common stock index.

We can use the lowest beta from a random sample of common stocks (0.152) to represent the low end of the range for common stock betas.[19] There are 46 'high quality' preferreds with betas less than 0.152. The other 26 preferreds have betas that are over 0.152 and are 'low quality' preferreds.[20]

To test the value of this division we can ask if the typical high quality preferred stock, so defined, performs differently from the typical low quality preferred stocks. In particular, we can compare an index composed solely of high quality preferreds with an index composed solely of low quality preferreds.[21]

Note from Table 2 and Table 3 that the risk premium, the variance and the covariance with the common stock index are all lower if one invests solely in high quality preferreds than if he invests solely in low quality preferreds. It appears that low quality preferreds behave more like common stocks than do high quality preferreds. Moreover, Table 4 suggests that the performance of the

---

[18]This use of quality is not identical with the term as it is used by rating agencies. We are talking about an expected performance for a given holding period whereas rating agencies speak primarily of the probability of default before or at some maturity date for bonds or of the dividend yield stability for preferreds.

[19]Other potential criteria include a split based on T-values, a split based on correlations and a split using beta equal to 0.25 as the dividing line. These procedures, which provided results that were very similar to those reported are all correlated with the one we chose. When we used a likelihood ratio and split the preferreds into high and low quality groups depending on whether their observed betas were more likely to be from the preferred or common stock distributions, we obtained similar results.

[20]Subsequent examination of the stationarity problem mentioned above indicated that 13 of the 16 preferreds lacking structural stability (and all of the preferreds that suffered any arrearage problems) were low quality preferreds, i.e., preferreds which suffered systematic risk like that obtainable from purchasing a common stock. See Bildersee (3).

[21]Each preferred stock index contains every security from the appropriate group. Each security carries equal weight in the index.

Table 3

Variance-Covariance Matrix for Chosen Indexes

Index	High Qual. Preferreds	Low Qual. Preferreds	Common Stocks
High Quality Preferreds	1.778	1.209	1.249
Low Quality Preferreds		3.589	5.379
Common Stocks			13.854

Table 4

Correlation Matrix for Chosen Indexes

	High Qual. Preferreds	Low Qual. Preferreds	Common Stocks
High Quality Preferreds	1.0	0.518	0.252
Low Quality Preferreds		1.0	0.763
Common Stocks			1.0

typical low quality preferreds appears more closely correlated to that of the common stocks than to that of the high quality preferreds.

Table 5 indicates that the beta distribution for the high quality preferreds was tighter than that for low quality preferreds. In addition, it suggests that the association between the high quality preferred index and the common stock index was less than that between the low quality preferred index and the common stock index.

B. *Preferred Stocks and a Bond Index*

We also compared the performance of preferred stocks and common stocks to that of a bond index. The index, which is described fully in Bildersee (3), is based on holding period returns of a broad sample of U.S. Government treasury bills, notes and bonds.

The index is composed of several subindexes of U.S. Government bonds. At any time, each subindex includes only those government bonds with approximately the same term to maturity. These terms to maturity are listed in Table 6. In time any subindex has an approximately constant term to maturity and each bond moves from one subindex to the subindex with the next shorter

---

[22]Every utility preferred is in the high quality preferred category. The distributions of utility preferreds had a mean beta of 0.065 and a standard deviation of 0.039. The non-utility high quality preferreds had a distribution with a mean beta of 0.073 and a standard deviation of 0.049.

Table 5

Distributions or Beta from Regressions on the Common Stock Index

Sample	Obser-vations	Mean	Std. Dev.	Aver. R^2
High Quality Preferreds[22]	46	0.070	0.046	0.022
Low Quality Preferreds	26	0.423	0.329	0.130

term to maturity as the bond approaches maturity. Since each subindex remains a constant proportion of the Government bond index in time, the index, which has an average risk premium of 0.034% per month and a variance of 0.282, also has a fairly constant term to maturity in time.

The bond index does not represent the performance of any single bond. Instead, the bond index should indicate the performance of the typical bond-like security with a constant term to maturity and may best indicate the responsiveness of bonds and bond-like securities to events typically thought to affect the bond market.

Preferred stocks are that "like bonds" should show a relatively strong association with this index. In particular, high quality preferreds which were different from common stocks might perform like bonds—the other form of security to which preferreds are usually compared. We would expect that high quality preferreds which perform most like bonds to be riskier than government bonds and hence to have high betas and a high correlation relative to the government bond index. However, lower quality preferreds are less likely to be affected solely by those events affecting government bonds and should have

Table 6

Terms to Maturity for Subindexes Contained in the Government Bond Index

Subindex	Range of Terms to Maturity Included in Subindex*
1	1 month
2	2 months
3	3–6 months
4	7–12 months
5	13–24 months
6	25–36 months
7	37–48 months
8	49–72 months
9	73–108 months
10	109–180 months
11	Over 15 years

*To be included in a given subindex for a given month a security had to have a term to maturity associated with that subindex at the end of the month.

Table 7

Distributions of Betas from Regressions on the Government Bond Index

Sample	Obser-vations	Mean	Standard Deviation	Average R^2
Preferred Stocks	72	0.820	1.118	0.089
SCCS	60	-1.228	1.790	0.022

	Ranges of Beta		Range of R^2
Sample	Interquartile	Extremes	Extremes
Preferred Stocks	0.346-1.676	-3.201 - +2.821	$0.0^3$4-0.360
SCCS	-2.288 - +0.141	-5.384 - +1.825	$0.0^4$1-0.102

a lower correlation relative to the government bond index. They are also likely to have lower betas relative to the bond index.[23]

Table 7 shows that the typical preferred stock was related positively to the bond index. It appears that preferred stocks are more strongly associated with bonds than are the same company's common stocks. However, the average and range for R^2's for the preferreds were about the same as when the preferred stocks were regressed on the common stock index. Thus the average association between preferreds and the bond index appears no stronger than does the association between preferreds and the common stock index. It appears that the preferred stocks in this sample are not, as a group, more closely associated with bonds or common stocks than with the other security.

However, this result may not hold for individual preferred stocks. In particular, the performance of our high quality preferreds relative to the bonds may differ substantially from the performance of our low quality preferreds relative to the bonds index. Note from Table 8 that the bond index is more closely related to the index of high quality preferreds than it is to the index of low quality preferreds. Moreover, the correlation between the high quality preferreds index and the bond index is about as high as that between the high quality preferreds index and the low quality preferreds index. This result, with the result suggesting that low quality preferreds perform more like common stocks than like high quality preferreds, from Table 4, suggests that there may be a dichotomy of performance between the two sets of preferreds.

There were many negative betas when the preferred stocks were regressed

---

[23]Since beta equals the correlation between the risk premium on security j and that on the index multiplied by the standard deviation of security j's risk premiums divided by the standard deviation of the risk premium of the market index, beta will decrease with a decrease in the correlation unless the standard deviation the security risk premiums increase sufficiently to compensate for the decrease. In practice, the standard deviation of the security's risk premium does increase. However, this increase is not enough to offset the decline in the betas due to the decline in the correlation.

Table 8
Correlation Matrix for Chosen Indexes

	Government Bonds	High Quality Preferreds	Low Quality Preferreds
Government Bonds	1.0	0.538	−0.016
High Quality Preferreds		1.0	0.518
Low Quality Preferreds			1.0

on the bond index. Table 9 shows the direction of the association appears related
to the quality of the preferred stock. Individual high quality preferreds appeared
to be related positively with the bond index, but the results were mixed for the
low quality preferreds. Note from Table 10 the difference in the strength of the
association between preferreds of each quality and the bond index. This table
and Table 5 suggest that the typical high quality preferred may be associated
more closely with bonds than with common stocks. However, these tables also
suggest that the typical low quality preferred stock appeared to be associated
more closely with common stocks than with bonds.

C. Preferred Stocks and a "Market" Index

A performance index composed solely of common stocks or of government
bonds may not provide an appropriate measure of the performance of the entire
market. In this section we shall use an index composed of 65% common stocks,
5% preferred stocks and 30% government bonds to represent a market index.[24]
      As Table 11 shows the beta distributions have higher means and greater
dispersion when the market index is used than when the common stock index
was used. Because the variance of returns to the typical common stock is much
greater than for preferreds and for bonds, common stocks dominate the market
index. It turns out that the results obtained from this index differ only in scale.
In particular, they are about 50% greater than those obtained from using
the common stock index. If our market index represents the market well, it
appears that preferred stocks have less systematic risk than the market while
common stocks suffer more risk than the market. Other conclusions reached
from using beta distributions based on this index are not different from using
the beta distributions based on the common stock index.

---

[24]Several alternative mixes of these assets were tested as possible market indices. As long
as common stock represents a medium to a large portion of the market, the performance
of each of the potential indices was correlated with our chosen market index at levels often
in excess of 0.99.

Table 9

Signs of the Preferred Stock Betas from Regressions on the Government Bond Index

| | Sign | | |
Sample	+	−	Total
High Quality Preferreds	45	1	46
Low Quality Preferreds	13	13	26
Total	58	14	72

Table 10

Distributions of Beta from Regressions on the Government Bond Index

Sample	Observations	Mean	Standard Deviation	Average R^2
High Quality Preferreds	46	1.413	0.728	0.131
Low Quality Preferreds	26	−0.229	1.099	0.016

Table 11

Distributions of Beta from Regressions on the Market Index

Sample	Observations	Mean	Standard Deviation	Average R^2
Preferred Stocks	72	0.325	0.391	0.069
SCCS	60	1.516	0.568	0.282

| | Ranges of Beta | | Ranges of R^2 |
Sample	Inter-Quartile	Extremes	Extremes
Preferred Stocks	0.115–0.341	−0.028 – +2.345	0.0^57–0.334
SCCS	1.070–1.848	+0.571 – +3.066	0.069–0.501

V. Preferred Stocks and Multiple Indexes

The market model suggests that one index may be sufficient to estimate the systematic risk of a security. However, there have been many suggestions for the use of multiple indexes to identify distinct sources of risk including identification of industries, particular classes of securities and different nations.[25]

The correlation between the common stock index and the government bond index was −0.149 and the correlation between the market index and the

---

[25] For example, see King (11), Cohen and Pogue (5) and Agmon (1).

Table 12

Distributions of Coefficients When Preferred and Common Stocks are Regressed on the Common Stock Index and the Bond Index in Multiple Regression Form

Sample		Common Stock Index			Bond Index		
	Obs.	Mean	St. Dev.		Mean	Std. Dev.	Aver. R^2
Preferred Stocks	72	0.227	0.252		1.015	1.017	0.161
		(0.198)*	(0.262)*		(0.820)*	(1.118)*	(0.061)*
							(0.089)†
SCCS	60	0.986	0.379		−0.146	1.565	0.298
		(0.999)*	(0.383)*		(−1.228)*	(1.790)*	(0.284)°
							(0.022)†

*The numbers in parentheses are the results obtained from regressing the chosen sample on the chosen index alone. They are taken from Tables 1 and 7 for comparison purposes.

°Average R^2 obtained from using the common stock index alone as the independent variable.

†Average R^2 obtained from using the bond index alone as the independent variable.

government bond index was −0.007. These indexes, with correlations suggestive of zero correlation, will be used in multiple regressions to test if an additional variable would increase the explanatory power of the market model substantially.[26] We should remember that the bond index does not represent any single security. Since the bond index maintains a relatively constant term-to-maturity and since there is no default risk associated with the securities in the index, the index should respond primarily to changes in the interest rate.[27]

Table 12 shows the results when preferred stocks and the same companies' common stocks are regressed on the common stock index and the government bond index in multiple regression form. In the case of the preferreds, both of the coefficients for the multiple regression were greater than the betas generated when the indexes were used alone. The coefficient relative to the common stock index for the SCCS sample was slightly less than the beta based on the common stock index alone. The coefficient for the bond index increased substantially in the multiple regression. However, the bond index adds little to the regression in this case.

The variance explained for the common stock sample isn't improved substantially by addition of the bond index to the common stock index for the multiple regression. However, the improvement obtained with the multiple

---

[26]A zero corrlation may not mean independence. In fact, the market index includes the bond index as a component. The goal of the market index was to approximate the true market index. The low correlation between the market index and the bond index was a coincidental by-product of the aforementioned goal.

[27]See Miller and Scholes (14) for a more complete discussion of this problem. More theoretical work is needed in this area.

Table 13

Significant Estimates Obtained When Using the Common Stock Index and the Bond Index in a Multiple Regression

Sample Obs.			Significant Estimates*			
			Common Stock Index Only**	Bond Index Only**	Both Indexes°	At Least 1 Sig. Obs.
Preferred Stocks	72	$T = 2^*$	26	17	24	67
		$T = 1^*$	15	4	52	71
SCCS	60	$T = 2^*$	44	0	16	60
		$T = 1^*$	29	0	31	60

*A significant estimate is one that is accompanied by a T-Value with an absolute value of at least 2(1).

**When the multiple regression was used, the only significant estimate was for the stated index. If we use the same row T-Value as the appropriate dividing line between significance and nonsignificance for the other index, then the estimate based on the other index was not significant.

°Estimate based on each of the independent variables were significant in the multiple regression.

regression approach for the preferred stock sample suggests that use of these uncorrelated indexes may aid in the analysis of the performance of some classes of assets.

Table 13 also suggests that multiple regressions may improve the analysis of a security's performance. When we used the multiple regression, many common stocks showed significant associations with both indexes. Preferred stocks showed a variety of results. If a T-Value greater than two is taken as indicating that a coefficient is significantly different from zero, then we found that 26 preferreds were associated only with the common stock index in the multiple regression. We also observed 17 preferreds that appeared to have significant associations only with the bond index in the multiple regression. Moreover, 24 preferreds appeared to be associated significantly with both indices simultaneously. If we take a T-Value over one as a measure of significance, then 52 preferreds and 31 common stocks were related to both indexes at once.

Note from Table 14 that if the preferred stocks were divided by quality, there was a distinct difference between the high and low quality preferreds. The low quality preferreds showed a pattern similar to that for common stocks. However, the high quality preferreds appeared to be significantly related to bonds alone or to both the bond and common stock indices more often than to common stocks alone.

Table 15 shows the distributions of the coefficients for each index when the securities were divided by quality. Most of the coefficients were about

Table 14

Significant Estimates Obtained When Using the Common Stock Index and the Bond Index in a Multiple Regression

			Significant Estimates*			
Sample	Obs.		Common Stock Index Only**	Bond Index Only**	Both Indexes°	At Least 1 Sig. Obs.
High Quality	46	$T = 2*$	3	17	21	41
Preferreds		$T = 1*$	1	4	40	45
Low Quality	26	$T = 2*$	23	0	3	26
Preferreds		$T = 1*$	14	0	12	26

*A significant estimate is one that is accompanied by a T-Value with an absolute value of at least 2(1).

**When the multiple regression was used, the only significant estimate was for the stated index. If we use the same row T-Value as the appropriate dividing line between significance and nonsignificance for the other index, then the estimate based on the other index was not significant.

°Estimates based on each of the independent variables were significant in the multiple regression.

equal to the coefficients obtained when each index was used alone as the independent variable. However, the average coefficient for the low quality preferreds relative to the bond index changed from negative to positive. No test presented here has suggested that this particular relationship is definitely positive or negative.

It is possible that some of these results are due simply to a misspecification of the 'true' market index, as we used the common stock index in this analysis. We explored this possibility as we also regressed each preferred and

Table 15

Distributions of Coefficients-Regression on the Common Stock Index and the Bond Index in Multiple Regression Form

		Common Stock Index		Bond Index	
Sample	Obs.	Mean	S.D.	Mean	S.D.
High Quality	46	0.102	0.049	1.434	0.745
Preferreds		(0.072)*	(0.047)*	(1.326)*	(0.732)*
Low Quality	26	0.427	0.317	0.218	0.851
Preferreds		(0.412)*	(0.304)*	(−0.178)*	(1.152)*

*The numbers in the parentheses are the results obtained from regressing the chosen sample on the chosen index alone. They are stated here for comparison only.

common stock of each company on our estimate of the market index and the government bond indices in multiple regression form. The results were virtually identical to those obtained from our use of the common stock and government bond indices together.[28]

Conclusions

Our sample provided us with further tests of the consistency of the market model and of the applicability of that model to an additional class of securities. In particular, the preferred stock sample enabled us to observe the consistency of the relationship between different classes of equity securities issued by the same firm and among equivalent securities issued by the same firm. In addition, it appears that preferreds with low betas relative to the common stock index perform primarily like bonds in the market while preferreds with higher betas perform primarily like common stocks in the market. Our study also suggests that a multiple regression approach to an analysis of risk may be a useful extension of the market model and may aid studies of some classes of securities.

References

1. Tamir Agmon. "Interrelations Among International Equity Markets: An Application of Portfolio Analysis to Share Price Comovements in the United States, United Kingdom, Germany and Japan," Unpublished dissertation proposal, School of Business, University of Chicago, 1971.
2. Frederick Amling. *Investments—An Introduction to Analysis and Management,* 2nd Edition, Prentice-Hall, Inc. 1970.
3. John S. Bildersee. "Risk and Return on Preferred Stocks," Unpublished Ph.D. Dissertation, University of Chicago, 1971.
4. Fischer Black, Michael Jensen and Myron Scholes. "The Capital Asset Pricing Model: Some Empirical Tests," in Michael Jensen, ed., *Studies in the Theory of Capital Markets,* Praeger (forthcoming).
5. K.J. Cohen and J. Pogue. "An Empirical Evaluation of Alternative Portfolio Selection Models," *Journal of Business,* XL (April 1967).
6. E.F. Fama. "Efficient Capital Markets: A Review of Theory and Empirical Work," *Journal of Finance,* XXV (May 1970).
7. ——. "Risk, Return and Equilibrium," *Journal of Political Economy,* LXXIX (January–February 1971).

---

[28]One could argue that the market index is a synthetic variable. However, the results obtained from using the market index and the bond index together as independent variables in multiple regression form are very similar to those expressed in the paper. This suggests that the results are not merely the result of using such a variable.

8. ——. "Risk, Return and Equilibrium: Some Clarifying Comments," *Journal of Finance,* XXIII (March 1968).

9. Lawrence Fisher. "Some New Stock-Market Indexes," *Journal of Business,* XXXIX (January 1966).

10. Irwin Friend and Marshall Blume. "Measurement of Portfolio Performance Under Uncertainty," *American Economic Review,* LX, 4 (September 1970).

11. Benjamin F. King. "Market and Industry Factors in Stock Price Behavior," *Journal of Business,* XXXIX (January 1966).

12. Harry M. Markowitz. *Portfolio Selection,* Cowles Foundation, Monograph 16, John Wiley and Sons, Inc., 1959.

13. Merton H. Miller and Myron Scholes. "Rates of Return in Relation to Risk: A Re-examination of Some Recent Findings," Report No. 7035, Center for Mathematical Studies in Business and Economics, University of Chicago, 1970.

14. Merton H. Miller and Myron Scholes. *Risk and Return: Some Additional Results* (forthcoming).

15. Richard Roll. "Bias in Fitting the Sharpe Model to Time Series Data," *Journal of Finance and Quantitative Analysis,* 4 (September 1969).

16. William F. Sharpe. "A Simplified Model for Portfolio Analysis," *Management Science,* 9 (January 1963).

17. ——. "Capital Asset Prices: A Theory of Market Equilibrium Under Conditions of Risk," *Journal of Finance,* XIX (September 1964).

**Part IV
Implications for Investment
Portfolio Management**

15

Futures Trading and Investor Returns: An Investigation of Commodity Market Risk Premiums

Katherine Dusak

I. Introduction

Considerable controversy exists over the amount and the nature of the returns earned by speculators in commodity futures markets. At one extreme is the position first set forth by J.M. Keynes in his *Treatise on Money* (1930, pp. 135–44) that a futures market is an insurance scheme in which the speculators underwrite the risks of price fluctuation of the spot commodity. The non-speculators or "hedgers" on the other side of the market must expect to pay and, according to Keynes, they do in fact pay, on the average a significant premium to the speculator-insurers for this service. At the other extreme have been those such as C.O. Hardy (1940) who argue that for many speculators a futures market is a gambling casino. Far from demanding and receiving compensation for taking over the risks of price fluctuation from the hedgers, speculators, as a class, are willing to pay for the privilege of gambling in this socially acceptable form (with the losers continually being replaced at the tables by new arrivals). Despite many empirical studies, the conflict between the insurance interpretation and the gambling interpretation of returns to speculators in futures markets remains unresolved.[1]

This paper offers another and quite different interpretation of the returns to speculators in futures markets. It is argued that futures markets are no different in principle from the markets for any other risky portfolio assets. Futures markets are perhaps more colorful than many other sub-segments of the capital market such as the New York Stock Exchange or the bond market, and the terminology of futures markets is perhaps more arcane, but these differences in form should not obscure the fundamental properties that futures market assets share with other investment instruments: in particular, they are all candidates for inclusion in the investor's portfolio.

Reprinted with the permission of the author and University of Chicago Press from *Journal of Political Economy*, Vol. 81, no. 6, November–December 1973, pp. 1387–1406. © 1973 University of Chicago Press. I am indebted to Eugene Fama, Charles Nelson, Harry Roberts, and especially Merton H. Miller for many helpful comments and suggestions.

[1] Among the most influential papers devoted to the Keynes-Hardy controversy have been those of Telser (1958, 1960, 1967) and Cootner (1960*a*, 1960*b*). Other studies of the returns to speculation in futures markets include Houthakker (1957), Gray (1961), Smidt (1965), Rockwell (1967), and Stevenson and Bear (1970).

The portfolio approach, by itself, makes no presumption as to whether returns to speculators are positive, as Keynes hypothesized, or zeroish to negative, as Hardy believed. It says, rather, that returns on any risky capital asset, including futures market assets, are governed by that asset's contribution, positive, negative, or zero, to the risk of a large and well-diversified portfolio of assets (in fact, all assets, in principle). In contrast to this portfolio measure of risk, Keynes and his later followers identify the risk of a futures market asset solely with its price variability.[2] These differences in the proposed measures of risk make it possible to test the portfolio and Keynesian interpretations of futures markets against each other and, in principle, also against the Hardy gambling casino view.

It turns out that for each of the commodity futures studied (wheat, corn, and soybeans) returns and portfolio risk are both close to zero during the sample period even though variability or risk in the Keynesian sense is high. Hence, as far as this set of observations is concerned, the data conform better to the portfolio point of view than to the Keynesian insurance interpretation. The sample did not permit any direct confrontation between the portfolio interpretation and the Hardy view, but some indirect light is thrown on this part of the controversy and some suggestions for further tests are offered.

In the next section the salient points of the equilibrium pricing of portfolio assets are noted, and futures contracts are analyzed within this context. Measures of Keynesian and portfolio asset risk are then developed and interpreted in the light of the returns observed.

II. Capital Asset Pricing: The Determination of an Equilibrium Risk-Return Relation

A model of the equilibrium pricing of portfolio assets was proposed originally by Sharpe (1964) and extended by Lintner (1965), Mossin (1966), and Fama (1971).[3] Sharpe showed that conditions exist under which the equilibrium risk-return relation for any capital asset i can be represented as

---

[2]This is at least the conventional interpretation of the Keynesian position as suggested by the following quotation: "It will be seen that, under the present regime of very widely fluctuating prices for individual commodities, the cost of insurance against price changes —which is additional to any charges for interest or warehousing—is very high" (Keynes 1930, p. 144). A somewhat broader interpretation emphasizes the insurance premium and tries to relate the size and sign of this premium to variations in the stocks of the commodity over the production cycle (see Cootner 1960a, 1960b).

[3]The description of the equilibrium pricing model presented here assumes some familiarity on the part of the reader. For a more complete discussion, see Sharpe (1964) or Lintner (1965). A detailed exposition of the model is also given in Fama and Miller (1972, chap. 7).

$$E(\tilde{R}_i) = R_f + \left[\frac{E(\tilde{R}_w) - R_f}{\sigma(\tilde{R}_w)} \right] \frac{\partial \sigma(\tilde{R}_w)}{\partial x_i} \tag{1}$$

where $\tilde{R}_i$ is the random rate of return on asset i, $E(\tilde{R}_i)$ is its mathematical expectation, and R_f is the pure time return to capital or the so-called riskless rate of interest; $\tilde{R}_w$ is the random rate of return on a representative dollar of total wealth or, equivalently, the return on a portfolio containing all existing assets in the proportions, x_i, in which they are actually outstanding: $E(\tilde{R}_w)$ is the expected rate of return on total wealth, and $\sigma(\tilde{R}_w)$, the standard deviation of the return on total wealth, is a measure of the risk involved in holding a representative dollar of total wealth. The term $[\partial\sigma(\tilde{R}_w)]/\partial x_i$ is the marginal contribution of asset i to the risk of the return on total wealth, $\sigma(\tilde{R}_w)$. Thus expression (1) says that, in equilibrium, the expected rate of return on any asset i will be equal to the riskless rate of interest plus a risk premium proportional to the contribution of the asset to the risk of the return on total wealth.

To see some of the broader implications of this proposition and especially to highlight its fundamental difference from the simple Keynesian approach to risk, note that since

$$\sigma(\tilde{R}_w) = \left[\sum_{i=1}^{N} \sum_{j=1}^{N} x_i x_j \, \text{Cov}\,(\tilde{R}_i, \tilde{R}_j) \right]$$

it follows that

$$\frac{\partial\sigma(\tilde{R}_w)}{\partial x_i} = \frac{1}{\sigma(\tilde{R}_w)} \left[\sum_{j=1}^{N} x_j \, \text{Cov}\,(\tilde{R}_i, \tilde{R}_j) \right]$$

$$= \frac{1}{\sigma(\tilde{R}_w)} \left[x_i \sigma^2(\tilde{R}_i) + \sum_{j \neq i}^{N} x_j \, \text{Cov}\,(\tilde{R}_i, \tilde{R}_j) \right]$$

Thus what governs the riskiness of any asset i is not merely its own variance $\sigma^2(\tilde{R}_i)$ but its weighted covariance with all the other assets making up total wealth. Normally the latter terms can be expected to swamp the former, since there are $N - 1$ terms making up the covariance portion and only one in the variance portion, and that one, moreover, weighted by a very small number, x_i.

Additional insight into the equilibrium risk-return relation is gained by noting that the expression

$$\sum_{j=1}^{N} x_j \, \text{Cov} \, (\tilde{R}_i, \tilde{R}_j)$$

can be rewritten as $\text{Cov} \, (\tilde{R}_i, \tilde{R}_w)$, the covariance of return on asset i with that of total wealth. Hence we can rewrite (1) as

$$E(\tilde{R}_i) = R_f + \left[\frac{E(\tilde{R}_w) - R_f}{\sigma(\tilde{R}_w)} \, \frac{\text{Cov} \, (\tilde{R}_i, \tilde{R}_w)}{\sigma(\tilde{R}_w)} \right] \qquad (2)$$

or equivalently as

$$E(\tilde{R}_i) - R_f = [E(\tilde{R}_w) - R_f] \, \beta_i \qquad (3)$$

where $\beta_i \equiv [\text{Cov} \, (\tilde{R}_i, \tilde{R}_w)] / \sigma^2 (\tilde{R}_w)$. The coefficient β_i can be interpreted as the relative risk of asset i, since it measures the risk of asset i relative to that of total wealth. Equation (3) then says that the risk premium expected on asset i is proportional, in equilibrium, to its systematic risk β_i, the factor of proportionality being the risk premium expected on a representative dollar of total wealth.

Needless to say, the capital asset pricing model rests on a set of fairly strong assumptions. Nevertheless, it has proven to be remarkably robust empirically. Studies by Miller and Scholes (1972), Black, Jensen, and Scholes (1972), and Fama and MacBeth (1972) indicate that while simple expressions such as equations (2) and (3) may not be entirely satisfactory descriptions of the relations between return and relative risk, there is a strong connection between them, whereas there seems to be virtually none between the risk premium and measures of nonportfolio risk.[4]

III. Application of the Capital Asset Pricing Model to Futures Contracts

One difficulty in applying the Sharpe model of capital asset pricing to the risk-return relation on futures contracts is that of defining the appropriate capital asset and its rate of return. Since virtually all futures contracts are bought (and sold short) on margins that typically range from 5 to 10 percent of the face value of the contract, it might seem at first sight that we can treat the margin

---

[4]Recently Black (1972) has generalized the Sharpe model by replacing the riskless asset having return R_f with another asset whose return is a random variable but whose covariance with total wealth is zero. Empirical tests by Black, Jensen, and Scholes (1972) and Fama and Macbeth (1972) seem to indicate that the generalized model fits the data somewhat better than the Sharpe version.

as the capital investment and treat the ratio of the net profit at closeout to the initial margin as the rate of return on investment. In fact, one theoretical study, that of Schrock (1971), takes this point of view and makes it the basis of a standard mean-variance portfolio analysis, à la Markowitz (1959), though restricting attention only to futures market assets.

This appealing procedure for computing futures market returns breaks down, however, as soon as we trace the subsequent history of the payment that is turned over to the broker. Unlike other capital assets such as common stocks where the margin is transferred from buyer to seller, the margin on a futures contract is kept in escrow by the broker. Not only does the seller of the futures contract not receive the capital transfer from the buyers, but he actually has to deposit an equivalent amount of his own funds in the broker's escrow account. At closeout, the broker returns the escrowed margin plus or minus any profits or losses (net of commissions in the case of profits and inclusive of commissions in the event of losses) that occurred over the period.

The margin, despite surface appearances, is thus not a portfolio asset in the sense of the Sharpe general-equilibrium model, but merely a good-faith deposit to guarantee performance by the parties to the contract. If the brokers had other ways of ensuring that traders did not make commitments beyond their resources, then no such performance bonds would be required. For example, forward foreign exchange markets, where firms deal through their own banking connections, typically operate without any explicit margins, whereas participants in public futures currency markets are required to post margins.[5]

Although the rate of return on the margin is not a meaningful number from a general-equilibrium point of view, and need not even exist if other types of guarantees could serve, there is another natural candidate which can always be computed: namely, the percentage change in the futures price. We cannot interpret this percentage change as a rate of return comparable to the $\tilde{R}_i$, in equation (2) above, since the holder invests no current resources in the contract.

---

[5] That entering into a future contract need involve no margin or other specific payment that could be interpreted as an "investment" (and hence that could serve as the basis for computing a "rate of return") does not mean that the mean-variance portfolio model cannot be applied at the microlevel to analyze an investor's decision process. The price changes on the contracts held will affect *terminal* wealth, just as in the case of any other asset; but the contracts do not appear in the *initial* wealth constraint. For a rigorous treatment in the context of forward foreign exchange, see Leland (1971). A study by Johnson (1960) of futures spot commodity holdings also proceeds in this way. That is, the entire analysis is conducted in terms of price changes and not in terms of rates of return. The fact that the margin does not really represent capital invested in futures contracts, even in those markets where margin is required, might perhaps have been appreciated earlier by analysis of futures markets trading if brokers paid interest on the escrowed funds (or, what amounts to the same thing, if they allowed all traders to deposit or to hypothecate income-earning assets rather than cash). In practice, of course, the brokers presumably do pay interest on the escrowed funds, but only in the hard-to-see form of lower commissions or higher levels of "free" services than would otherwise be the case.

But we can interpret it as essentially the risk premium, $\tilde{R}_i - R_f$, on the spot commodity.[6]

What corresponds to the full return $\tilde{R}_i$ is the return (net of storage costs) that would accrue to the holder of an unhedged spot commodity.[7] That return consists of interest on the capital invested in the commodity plus any return, positive or negative, over and above pure interest due to the unanticipated change in the price of the commodity. If the spot holder chooses to hedge his holding, he thereby converts it to a riskless asset on which he earns only the riskless rate, R_f. The purchaser of the futures contract who takes over the risk has no capital of his own invested and hence earns no interest or pure time return on capital. He receives only the return over and above interest, which is to say, $\tilde{R}_i - R_f$.

This argument can be formalized by restating the Sharpe equilibrium conditions in present-value form. We say that the expected return on any asset i can be expressed as

$$E(\tilde{R}_i) = (1 - \beta_i)R_f + \beta_i E(\tilde{R}_w) \tag{4}$$

where $\beta_i = \text{Cov}\,(\tilde{R}_i, \tilde{R}_w)/\sigma^2(\tilde{R}_w)$. Equivalently, since we can represent $E(\tilde{R}_i)$ in terms of period 0 and period 1 prices for the asset as $[E(\tilde{P}_{i,1}) - P_{i,0}]/P_{i,0}$, the equilibrium risk-return relation on asset i can be expressed as

$$P_{i,0} = \frac{E(\tilde{P}_{i,1}) - [E(\tilde{R}_w) - R_f]P_{i,0}\beta_i}{(1 + R_f)} \tag{5}$$

Expression (5) says that the current price of any asset i is the discounted value (at the riskless rate) of its expected period 1 price, adjusted downward for risk by the factor $[E(\tilde{R}_w) - R_f]P_{i,0}\beta_i$.

Now suppose one were interested in knowing the price of asset i under a contractual agreement to purchase the asset at time 0 but with payment deferred a period to time 1. Clearly the current price for the asset under such an agree-

---

[6]I abstract from such complications as transaction costs, basis risk, the business risk of the storage and processing industries, limitations on borrowing, and so on. Or, what amounts to the same thing, I assume that differences in the returns on spot and futures market assets from these sources are so small and so unsystematic relative to the variations in returns on both assets as a consequence of price fluctuations that they can safely be ignored in a first approximation. Some of the main second-order qualifications are indicated at various points in the text and in footnotes in the course of the discussion.

[7]Actually total return to the spot commodity holder can be decomposed into three components: a pure time return to capital, a risk premium, and remuneration for storage costs, defined in this context as insurance charges, spoilage, and warehousing and administrative costs. Since we are concerned only with the return to capital embodied in the spot commodity, $\tilde{R}_i$, the "full" return on the spot commodity is to be understood as net of storage costs.

ment must be given by $P_{i,0}(1 + R_f)$. That is, since the transaction is made at time 0 but consummated at time 1, the purchaser must pay a one-period credit, or borrowing charge of $P_{i,0}R_f$ in addition to the current price $P_{i,0}$. Multiplying both sides of equation (5) by $(1 + R_f)$ we see that

$$P_{i,0}(1 + R_f) = E(\tilde{P}_{i,1}) - [E(\tilde{R}_w) - R_f]P_{i,0}\beta_i \qquad (6)$$

But the contractual agreement just described is a futures contract where asset i refers to the spot commodity. Hence the expression $P_{i,0}(1 + R_f)$ can be interpreted as the current futures price for delivery and payment of the spot commodity one period later, and $E(\tilde{P}_{i,1})$ can be interpreted as the spot price expected to prevail at time 1. The essential point is that buying a futures contract is like buying a capital asset on credit where the capital asset in this case happens to be the spot commodity.[8] The only issue is what is the "discount for cash" or, equivalently, the financing charge. Since the financing is assumed to be riskless, the correct charge is clearly R_f. That is, if $P_{i,0}$ is the current price for immediate payment, $P_{i,0}(1 + R_f)$ must be the price if the buyer buys on one-period credit terms.

Setting $P_{f,0} = P_{i,0}(1 + R_f)$ and rearranging terms, we get

$$\frac{E(\tilde{P}_{i,1}) - P_{f,0}}{P_{i,0}} = \beta_i[E(\tilde{R}_w) - R_f] \qquad (7)$$

Equation (7) can be interpreted as expressing the risk premium on the spot commodity as the change in the futures price divided by the period 0 spot price. Thus once again we see that futures contracts, properly interpreted, pose no problem for capital market theory.

One implication of this analysis is that there are two essentially equivalent ways of calculating the risk premium. On the one hand, we can try to measure the risk premium by taking the percentage change in spot prices (net of storage) over a given interval minus the riskless rate. Alternatively, we can approximate the risk premium as the percentage change in the futures price over the same interval.[9] Of these two approaches, it is the latter that will be adopted here.

---

[8] It does not really matter whether there is a spot commodity in existence yet. That is, just as I can order a car not yet produced, so I can agree to accept delivery next period at a specified price of a commodity still unproduced. The "implicit" spot price, which always exists, is then simply the futures price minus a discount for payment in advance, i.e., $P_i = P_f(1 + R_f)$. Note also that the seller need not actually contemplate producing the spot commodity; i.e., he can be a pure short speculator. He merely offers to make delivery to you next period, intending, if necessary to go out and buy the spot commodity then, if you insist on delivery rather than settlement.

[9] I have argued that in equilibrium $P_{f,t} = P_{i,t}(1 + R_f)$, where i refers to the spot commodity. Thus the percentage change in the futures price underestimates the risk premium on the

Data on futures prices are more accessible than spot price data and, of course, use of futures prices also avoids the necessity of having to estimate the storage costs directly. It is important to remember, however, that this choice of measurement is essentially a matter of computational convenience; and that the relevant risk from the general-equilibrium point of view remains the risk inherent in the ownership of the spot commodity itself, regardless of who actually chooses to bear it or what measurement strategy we choose to employ.[10]

IV. The Empirical Properties of Futures Market Returns

Tests of the risk-return relationship in the futures market are based on a sample of three heavily traded agricultural commodities: wheat, corn, and soybeans. There are five different contracts per year for wheat and corn and six for soybeans. For all contracts, semimonthly price quotations were obtained for a 15-year period from May 15, 1952 through November 15, 1967—resulting in an approximate sample size of 300 observations per contract.[11] In all cases returns were computed as a simple 2-week holding period yield with no allowance made for transaction costs. Following universal practice, returns have been computed separately for each commodity contract (e.g., May wheat or September corn).[12] It should be noted that the return series computed in this way

---

spot commodity by the factor $1/(1 + R_f)$. Given the intervals over which I will be computing returns, the factor $1/(1 + R_f)$ is likely to be very small. Hence for simplicity of exposition I shall refer (somewhat loosely) to the percentage change in the futures price as representing the risk premium on the spot commodity.

[10]I have assumed that unanticipated changes in the spot and futures prices are perfectly correlated. (For some evidence on the high degree of correlation between spot and futures prices, see Houthakker [1968].) Where this correlation is not perfect, the spot commodity holder will bear some risk even though hedged, and some compensation for this risk may be impounded in his return. Working (1953) has made this type of risk central to his analysis of futures markets. He regards spot commodity holders not as passive short hedgers but as speculators on the movement of the spot-future price differential, or basis, over time. He argues that professional commodity dealers are better able to predict differentials or relative prices than price levels. Thus they assume a position in both the spot and futures markets in response to expected changes in the basis. Since Working's hypothesis appears to have no testable implications with respect to the risk-return relation in futures markets of the kind that are of mean concern in this paper, I will not pursue it further here.

[11]Price quotations were taken from U.S., Department of Agriculture (1952–67). Lester Telser kindly supplied price data for 1952–64. The rest were collected independently from the same source. The terminal date of 1967 was the last year for which price data were available at the time this study was started. The initial date of 1952 was chosen to minimize wartime and postwar controls on commodity prices and futures trading.

[12]Another possible principle for computing returns would be on the basis of time to contract expiration (e.g., wheat contracts with exactly 4 months to run or corn contracts with 2½ months to run). In a later paper I shall show that the theoretical and empirical justification for looking at returns in this way is weaker than certain treatments of the matter, notably Samuelson's (1965), would suggest.

is discontinuous, since published price quotations on any one contract are typically available over a 9- or 10-month span.

Since the procedures for computing all subsequent statistical measures assume serial independence of returns, serial correlation coefficients of orders 1–10 have been computed for each contract return series.[13] The results are presented in table 1. As can be seen, the coefficients fluctuate about zero. Out of a total of 160 correlation coefficients, 132 are less than .10, and only 11 coefficients are more than two standard deviations away from zero. Even the largest in absolute value, moreover, is only .22 and hence accounts for only a trivial portion of the variation in returns on the particular contract. There are about the same number of negative as positive coefficients, with no particular pattern in the signs.[14]

V. Construction and Interpretation of a Keynesian Risk Measure

There is nothing in Keynes's essentially heuristic discussion of futures market risk to suggest the use of any one measure of simple variability over another. Subsequent writers have adapted the Keynesian argument to the Markowitz mean-variance framework (e.g., Johnson 1960; Schrock 1971). The use of sample variances to measure risk is open to objection, however, if the distribution of returns is stable non-Gaussian, as some have suspected may be true for futures market returns. For such distributions the second and higher-order moments of the distributions do not exist. The variances and standard deviations in any particular sample are always finite, but their behavior will be erratic and affected by outliers.[15]

Evidence of nonnormality is indicated by the normal probability plots of

---

[13] The sample serial correlation coefficient is defined as $\hat{r}_t = \text{cov}\,(\tilde{u}_t, \tilde{u}_{t-\tau})/\text{var}\,\tilde{u}_t$, where in this case $\tau = 1, \ldots, 10$ and u_t is the 2-week rate of return. Even in the case where $\tilde{u}_t$ belongs to the family of distributions for which variance does not exist, it has been shown that $\hat{r}_\tau$ is an adequate descriptive measure of the serial correlation in the population in the sense that it behaves much the same as its counterpart from a normally distributed sample of observations (see Fama and Babiak 1968, p. 1146). Under the hypothesis that the true serial correlation is zero, the standard error of the sample serial correlation coefficient is given by $\sigma(\hat{r}_t) = \sqrt{1/(N - \tau)}$, where N is the sample size and $\tau = 1, \ldots, 10$.

[14] These results are consistent with previous studies of the time series properties of futures prices. Studies by Larson (1960), Houthakker (1961), Smidt (1965), and Stevenson and Bear (1970) tend to show that although there are occasions when futures prices appear to have exhibited some degree of dependence, there have been no striking cases of large and pervasive price trends or patterns. Computed measures of statistical dependence have usually been small, and the profitability of trading rules has typically been less than that obtained by following a policy of buy and hold.

[15] See Fama and Roll (1971, p. 332) for evidence on the sampling variability of the standard deviation when the sample values come from a non-Gaussian distribution.

Table 1
Semimonthly Serial Correlation Coefficients for Wheat, Corn, Soybeans ($\tau = 1, 10$)

Contract	$\tau =$									
	1	2	3	4	5	6	7	8	9	10
Wheat:										
July	.14*	.01	-.15*	-.07	.10	-.07	-.02	.03	.12	-.03
Mar.	.07	-.07	-.03	.05	.03	.11	.12	-.11	.06	-.22*
May	.17*	.03	-.09	-.11	.06	.10	.10	.06	-.05	-.18*
Sept.	.15*	.07	-.02	-.03	.07	-.01	-.10	.09	.15	.05
Dec.	.14*	.10	.04	-.01	.04	-.14*	-.08	-.01	.03	-.11
$\bar{\rho}$	.13	.03	-.05	-.03	.06	-.00	.00	.01	.06	-.10
Corn:										
July	-.02	-.04	.03	.03	-.05	-.02	.01	-.03	.08	-.06
Mar.	.01	.08	-.09	-.00	-.03	.10	.04	.17*	-.07	-.03
May	.02	.08	.00	-.03	-.04	-.02	.00	.05	.05	.05
Sept.	.10	.10	.02	-.02	-.04	.03	.08	-.04	.03	-.03
Dec.	.02	.06	.02	-.04	-.07	.05	-.07	-.06	-.01	-.04
$\bar{\rho}$	.03	.06	-.00	-.01	-.05	.03	.01	.02	.02	-.02
Soybeans:										
Jan.	.02	.05	-.04	-.04	-.11	.09	.03	-.10	-.03	.01
Mar.	.03	.18*	.02	.07	-.05	.13	-.05	.05	-.07	.10
May	.09	.17*	.16*	.11	.06	.10	.09	.19*	.06	.10
July	.09	.15*	-.07	.16*	.02	.06	-.02	-.01	.07	-.05
Sept.	.06	-.03	.07	.00	-.03	.04	.20*	-.11	-.08	.09
Nov.	.03	.06	-.07	-.08	-.09	.01	.13	-.09	.04	-.03
$\bar{\rho}$	.05	.10	.01	.04	-.03	.07	.06	-.03	-.00	-.04
SE($\hat{\rho}_\tau$) for $N = 300$	.058	.058	.058	.058	.058	.058	.058	.059	.059	.059

*Coefficient is twice its computed standard error.

the cumulative distributions of sample returns in figures 1–3. To facilitate comparisons among the distributions of contract returns, the normal probability plots have been grouped by commodity. Five observations in the critical upper and lower tails of the distributions have been plotted and every twenty-fifth observation in the less revealing middle range. If the distributions were normal, the plots would closely approximate a straight line with slope $1/s$ and intercept $\bar{x}/s$, where s is the sample standard deviation and $\bar{x}$ is the sample mean (Roberts 1964, chap. 7, p. 13). As can be seen, there are substantial departures from linearity, not only in the tail areas but in the middle range as well, in every graph. The departure from normality in the tails is particularly marked in the case of the six soybean contracts.[16]

It can be shown that any symmetric stable distribution is characterized by three parameters: a shape parameter, α; a location parameter; and a scale or dispersion parameter. For the normal distribution α has the value 2; the first moment or mean serves as a measure of the location parameter, and the standard deviation (divided by $\sqrt{2}$) defines the scale. The fat-tailed distributions encountered in studies of asset pricing have shape parameter α less than 2. For such distributions, the mean can still serve as the location parameter, provided α is greater than one (the case of $\alpha = 1$ being the Cauchy distribution), although it has been shown that a truncated mean has smaller sampling dispersion than the sample mean and thus is a better estimator of the location parameter.[17] But, as noted above, the second and higher-order moments, and hence also the standard deviation, are not finite. Interfractile ranges do exist, however, and have been found to serve quite adequately as measures of scale or dispersion.

Estimates of α, the scale factor, the .5 truncated mean, and standard errors for the last two estimators are presented in table 2.[18] Following Fama and Roll (1968, 1971) the .28–.72 interfractile range was used to estimate the scale factor, and a fractile matching procedure (in this case the .95) was used to estimate α.

From column 1 of table 2, it would seem safe to conclude that the distribu-

---

[16]The phenomenon of fat tails (i.e., more probability in the tail area of the distribution than in the Gaussian distribution) for distributions of futures returns has previously been noted, but not rigorously investigated, by Smidt (1965), Stevenson and Bear (1970), and Houthakker (1961).

[17]"The g truncated sample mean is the average of the middle 100g percent of the ordered observations in the sample. That is, in computing the mean, $100(1 - g)/2$ percent of the observations in each tail of the data distribution are discarded" (Fama and Roll 1968, p. 826). The optimum degree of truncation depends on the size of α. The lower the value of α, the greater the optimum degree of truncation, reflecting the fact that the more outliers there are in a sample, the greater the number of observations that must be deleted before an efficient estimate of location is obtained. Fama and Roll (1968, p. 832) conclude that "an estimator which performs very well for most values of alpha and N (sample size) is the .5 truncated mean."

[18]The procedure for estimating α assumes that successive returns are independent—a hypothesis that has already been tested.

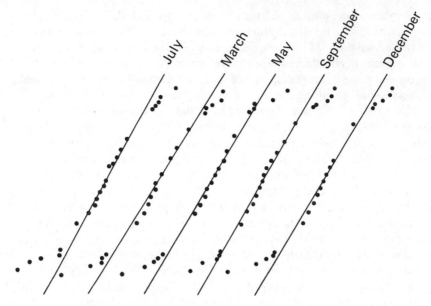

Figure 1. Normal probability plots: wheat contracts.

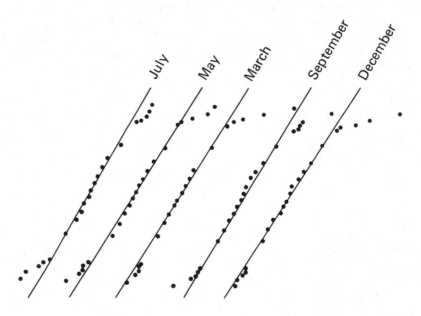

Figure 2. Normal probability plots: corn contracts.

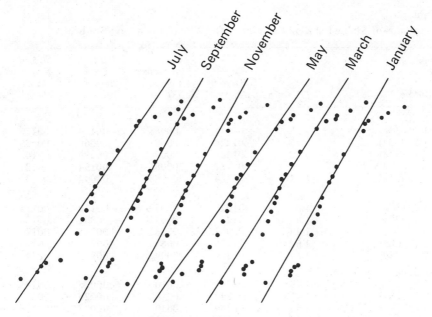

Figure 3. Normal probability plots: soybean contracts.

tions of returns on futures contracts conform better to the stable non-Gaussian family than to the normal distribution. The values of α range from 1.44 to 1.84, with half of the estimates below 1.56.

The scale factors, which I shall interpret as measures of Keynesian risk, and their standard errors of estimate are shown in columns 2 and 3 of table 2.[19] To judge how large these scale factors are, we can compare them to the corresponding dispersion parameter for some other more familiar capital asset such as common stock. The most convenient measure of common stock returns for our purposes is the Standard and Poor Composite Index of 500 industrial common stocks. The estimated dispersion parameter for that index taken semimonthly over the sample period 1952–67 is .0170, which is the same order of magnitude as the scale factors for the commodities. Since the Standard and Poor Index is in effect a well-diversified portfolio, we know that the variability of the average stock return will be two or three times as large (see King 1966; Blume 1968) and hence also two or three times that of returns on futures market assets.

These comparisons may surprise those accustomed to thinking of futures markets as especially volatile, and the futures contract as one of the riskiest of

---

[19]In principle, any number of interfractile ranges might serve as a measure of risk. For reasons of simplicity and economy we have chosen the same interfractile range used to estimate the dispersion parameter of the distribution.

Table 2

Estimates of Stable Paretian Parameters for Wheat, Corn, and Soybeans

Contract*	α† (1)	Scale Factor (2)	SE‡ of Scale Factor (3)	Truncated Mean Return (4)	SE§ of Truncated Mean (5)
Wheat:					
July (302)	1.55	.01111	.00085	-.00164	.00126
Mar. (302)	1.75	.01228	.00091	.00060	.00139
May (302)	1.70	.01259	.00094	.00096	.00142
Sept. (319)	1.56	.01127	.00086	-.00194	.00127
Dec. (319)	1.74	.01184	.00088	.00044	.00134
Corn:					
July (301)	1.52	.01027	.00079	-.00158	.00116
Mar. (301)	1.65	.01222	.00092	-.00381	.00138
May (301)	1.49	.01062	.00082	-.00268	.00120
Sept. (320)	1.65	.01136	.00086	-.00243	.00128
Dec. (320)	1.84	.01304	.00092	-.00212	.00147
Soybeans:					
Jan. (287)	1.49	.01293	.00100	-.00025	.00146
Mar. (287)	1.47	.01347	.00105	-.00029	.00152
May (287)	1.44	.01309	.00102	.00038	.00148
July (287)	1.44	.01399	.00109	.00006	.00158
Sept. (287)	1.66	.01391	.00105	-.00105	.00157
Nov. (287)	1.50	.01212	.00093	-.00071	.00137

*Numbers of observations are given in parentheses.

†No exact methods have been derived for computing the standard error of $\alpha_{.95}$ or its bias. Using Monte Carlo techniques, Fama and Roll (1971), p. 333) report that for samples of 299 observations the standard deviation of the values of $\hat{\alpha}_{.95}$ in 199 separate replications was about 0.13 when the true value of α was 1.5, about 0.15 when the true value of α was 1.7, and about 0.12 when the true value was 2.0. The mean value of $\hat{\alpha}_{.95}$ was slightly less than true of α when that value was very close to two; the apparent bias was only 0.04 when α was 1.9 and was beyond detection at a value for α of 1.7.

‡An expression for the variance of the scale factor is given in Fama and Roll (1971, p. 331). Standard errors have been computed from estimates of $\sigma(s)$ for standardized symmetric stable distributions. See Fama and Roll (1971, table 1, p. 332).

§The standard error of the truncated mean has been computed as: $s\sigma(\bar{x}_{5},_{N})$ where s is the scale factor from the underlying distribution of returns and $s\sigma(\bar{x}_{5},_{N})$ is the standard deviation of the .5 truncated mean from a standardized normal distribution. For a discussion of this estimator see Roll (1968, chap. 6, p. 30).

capital assets.[20] The impression of substantial return volatility probably arises from the practice of calculating percentage returns on the margin. It should be remembered, though, that the margin is not a capital asset within the economic

---

[20]Some indirect evidence on this point is afforded by the refusal of Merrill Lynch, Pierce, Fenner, and Smith to sell futures contracts to women on the grounds that they do not have the psychological stamina to withstand futures market price fluctuations.

meaning of that term. Hence in the general-equilibrium context the variability of rates of return on the margin is not a relevant measure of risk.

Since the variability of futures returns is about as great as that of a diversified portfolio of common stock, we should expect that if Keynes was correct in identifying asset risk with simple variability, then the mean return over and above the riskless rate should be about the same for both assets. The mean rate of return (over and above the riskless rate) on the Standard and Poor Index over the period 1952–67 on a semimonthly basis was approximately .0029 (with a standard error of .0012) without allowing for dividends.[21] Had dividends been included, they would probably have added another .0017 to bring the total return to .0046. This figure is in striking contrast to the point estimates of the truncated means for the commodity returns (table 2, col. 4). All of the truncated means for corn returns are negative and of roughly the same magnitude. In the case of soybeans, four of the six truncated means are negative but the range between the smallest and largest values is only .00143, which is the same order of magnitude as the standard errors of the estimates. The truncated means for wheat returns exhibit somewhat greater variation. The mean returns for the July and September contracts are large and negative whereas the mean returns for the March, May, and December contracts are slightly positive. For all but two of the 16 contracts, however, the mean returns are within two standard errors of zero.

These results are a serious blow to the theory of normal backwardation. Using Keynes's definition of asset risk, anyone who invested (i.e., sold insurance) in wheat, corn, and soybean futures in the period 1952–67 incurred risk for which he received on average a return very close to zero, if not actually negative. What is even more damaging to the Keynesian theory is the fact that for the same amount of risk (defined as simple return variability) an investment in a diversified portfolio of common stocks over the same period would have yielded a substantial positive return over and above the riskless rate.[22]

---

[21] An ordinary sample mean has been computed for the return on the Standard and Poor Index, since the distribution of stock returns more closely approaches normality than do the distributions of commodity returns (Officer 1971).

[22] Note that the evidence presented in table 2 does not constitute 16 different tests of the Keynesian hypothesis. The similarity in the distribution parameters (and indeed, of the entire distributions, as a glance at figs. 1–3 will testify) suggests that within any commodity group the distribution of returns has the same parameters and that such slight differences as do exist represent only sampling fluctuations. Correlation coefficients between the returns on different contracts of the same commodity have been computed. Out of 35 coefficients, 12 were .90 or higher; another 17 were between .80 and .89; and only six were below .79, the lowest being .72. In some cases, as, for example, the adjacent July and September wheat contracts or the adjacent March and May contracts for corn, the correlation was virtually perfect. As a group, wheat contracts seemed to exhibit the most interdependence, and soybeans the least. This high correlation between returns on different contracts is especially striking in light of the insistence on contract uniqueness in much of the traditional literature on futures markets. The contemporaneous coefficients

VI. Construction and Interpretation of the Risk Measures for the Capital Market Interpretation

The Sharpe model of capital asset pricing defines asset risk as the contribution the asset makes to the variability of return on a well-diversified portfolio containing, in principle, all assets in the proportions in which they are outstanding. An estimate of the relative risk can be obtained from the linear regression:

$$\tilde{R}_i = \alpha_i + \beta_i \tilde{R}_w + \tilde{\epsilon}_i \tag{8}$$

where the usual assumptions of the linear regression model are assumed to hold.

Although equation (8) implies that the independent variable is the return on total wealth, such a variable is virtually impossible to construct, and instead some proxy measure must be utilized. In this study the return on the value-weighted Standard and Poor Index of 500 Common Stocks is used as a proxy for the return on total wealth. Common stocks, after all, represent an important fraction of total wealth, so that even in a more comprehensive index they would be heavily weighted. This has been, moreover, the standard approach followed in most studies of the asset pricing model.

The selection of the Standard and Poor Index to represent common stocks was dictated by the fact that the leading alternative, the Fisher index (1966), is available on a monthly basis, whereas the futures market returns are computed on a semimonthly basis. The main drawback of the Standard and Poor index is that it does not include the dividend component of returns on common stock. Dividends, however, are not highly variable in the short run, and their omission is not likely to have any noticeable effects on the regression coefficients that I will be using as measures of risk.[23]

Consistent with the interpretation of the futures return as a risk premium, that is, as a return over and above interest, the market index variable is also stated in risk premium form. As a measure of the riskless rate of interest, I used the 15-day Treasury bill rate.[24]

---

of correlation between returns for the same contract but different commodities have also been computed. Out of 13 correlation coefficients only two are even as high as .5, and even the highest of these coefficients (.67) is lower than the lowest correlation for returns on the same commodity (.72). Under these circumstances, then, there would appear to be little objection to maintaining a distinction among the three commodities.

[23]There are problems posed by the fact that the underlying distributions conform better to stable non-Gaussian than to normal distributions. It can be shown, however, that the ordinary least-squares coefficients are consistent estimators of the corresponding population parameters, but not necessarily efficient ones; particularly as α departs further from two. However, the loss of efficiency is not likely to be of much import for samples as large as we will be using (300 observations). See Blattberg and Sargent (1971).

[24]Since the variability of the bill rate was small relative to that of the Standard and Poor Index or to that of futures returns during my sample period, the estimates turned out to be virtually identical with those obtained when the index was used in regular return form.

Table 3
Regression Parameters for Wheat, Corn, and Soybeans

Commodity*	$\hat{\alpha}'_i$	$SE(\alpha'_i)$	β_i	$SE(\beta_i)$	R^2	Auto-correlation Coefficient of Residuals
Wheat:						
July (302)	−.020	.001	.048	.051	.003	.148
March (302)	.000	.001	.098	.049	.013	.080
May (302)	−.000	.001	.028	.051	.001	.163
Sept. (319)	−.002	.001	.068	.051	.006	.149
Dec. (319)	−.000	.001	.059	.048	.005	.163
Corn:						
July (301)	−.001	.001	.038	.046	.002	−.041
March (301)	−.003	.001	−.009	.050	.000	.015
May (301)	−.002	.001	−.027	.048	.001	.032
Sept. (320)	−.002	.001	.032	.048	.001	.100
Dec. (320)	−.001	.001	.007	.047	.000	.017
Soybeans (287 all contracts):						
Jan.	.002	.001	.019	.058	.000	.015
March	.003	.002	.100	.065	.008	.018
May	.003	.002	.119	.068	.011	.071
July	.002	.002	.080	.076	.004	.083
Sept.	.001	.001	.077	.065	.005	.060
Nov.	.002	.001	.043	.058	.002	.023

*Numbers of observations are given in parentheses.

The estimates of α'_i (where α' denotes regression variables expressed in risk premium form) and β_i from equation (8), their standard errors, the R^2s, and the first-order serial correlation coefficients of the residuals for the sample period 1952–67 are presented in table 3 for each of the 16 commodity contracts. The most striking feature of table 3 is the small size of the regression coefficients, which range from .007 to .119. With few exceptions the standard errors are approximately the same size, if not somewhat larger, than the regression co-efficients. Furthermore, the standard errors in table 3 may be understated because ordinary least squares is not efficient if the underlying returns are non-Gaussian (see Fama and Babiak [1968] for a discussion of this point). Thus the smallness of the regression coefficients relative to their standard errors is on balance even more pronounced than the figures in the table indicate. In the case of the intercept term, the standard errors are also large (in only two, possibly three, cases are they as small as half the value of the coefficient), which is

---

Other specifications of the regression equation were also tested, such as the use of log-arithms of the price relative, rather than percentage rates of return. There was little differ-ence in explanatory power and no noteworthy change in the absolute or relative sizes of the coefficients.

consistent with expression (3) and a value of the intercept of zero. The low serial correlation of the residuals suggests that the assumption of independence upon which the calculation of the standard error is predicted is a tenable one.

It is clear from table 3 that relative risk for wheat, corn, and soybeans is very close to zero.[25] To judge how low a level of systematic risk these regression coefficients represent, it is worthwhile, perhaps, to compare them to the regression coefficients for some well-known common stocks. By construction, of course, the average stock has $\beta = 1$. For American Telephone and Telegraph, considered to be a safe "widows and orphans stock," β was .34 over our sample interval. The average regression coefficient for the electric utility industry was .41, and the corresponding figure for the gas utility industry was .45.[26] Clearly, then, compared to common stocks, the systematic risk measures for wheat, corn, and soybeans are low indeed.

Since the mean returns (which are actually risk premiums) are also very close to zero, we may conclude that the data on commodity future returns during our sample period conform better to the capital markets model than to the Keynesian model. In fact, the contest is not even close.[27]

VII. Some Concluding Observations on Hardy and Keynes

Because both mean returns and systematic risk were zero, the sample evidence permits no direct confrontation between the capital market approach and the Hardy gambling casino theory, which also predicts a mean return of zero. Had we found a commodity for which the β's were substantially and unambiguously positive while the means were zero or negative (or found a commodity with

---

[25]It may strike some readers as paradoxical that there could exist an asset whose return is a random variable and whose β is zero. Remember, however, that a zero β asset has only zero covariance with other assets on *average*. With some assets its return will be positively correlated, and with others, negatively correlated. In fact, since the zero β assets will themselves be part of total wealth, they must be negatively correlated, on balance, with all other assets in the market portfolio. Because of this covariance with other assets, the zero β asset does make a sufficient contribution to the diversification and hence the risk reduction of the total portfolio to justify its inclusion even at a mean return (over and above interest) of zero. For a general treatment of zero β assets within the context of the Sharpe model, see Black (1972).

[26]Information supplied by Merton H. Miller and Myron Scholes, from an unpublished manuscript. The regression coefficients have been estimated using annual rates of return over the period 1947–66.

[27]Estimates of the Keynesian risk measure, or scale factor, the truncated means, and the regression coefficients have been computed by 5-year subperiod intervals. Although there is some tendency for both the scale factor and the regression coefficient to be higher in the first 5-year period (especially for wheat), there is no systematic pattern between risk and return. More often than not, high risk, in terms of either simple variability or systematic risk, is associated with negative means, and low risk with positive means.

significant negative intercept terms in expression [8]), we could have concluded that for such a case the evidence was more consistent with the gambling than with the portfolio interpretation. We would also have had to conclude that risk-averse investors are apparently not shrewd enough to recognize a bargain. For the existence of a futures asset with a positive value of β when regressed on a stock index and a zero (or negative) mean would make it attractive for risk averters to become "short speculators" in that market. Seeling futures short under such conditions would create an asset that was negatively correlated with the rest of the investor's portfolio and yet not reduce the mean return on the portfolio as a whole.

The possibility that other commodities besides these I studied may turn out to have nonzero β's also suggests a way of reconciling Keynesian and capital market views of risk and returns in futures markets. When Keynes wrote *The Treatise on Money* in the late 1920s, the variability that he identified with asset risk may in fact have included a sizable systematic risk component. In the late 1920s commodity prices were not subject to effective price support.[28] Thus prices could be expected to be more variable and also to be more strongly associated than at present with cyclical swings in the economy. It may well also have been the case that the particular commodities Keynes used as examples of futures market risk—cotton and copper—were strongly associated with the level of activity in British manufacturing in the early 1930s. If such a connection existed, share prices and the prices of raw commodities, including futures, would be related to each other. With cotton as the major input to a large sector of British manufacturers, it would hardly be surprising to observe a high correlation between the returns on cotton futures and the returns on British industrial stocks.

This reinterpretation of Keynes suggests that if my sample were broadened to include commodities more intimately associated with American manufacture, there might perhaps be cases of commodity futures having high positive β's and positive means as well. But such interesting prospects must await future research.

References

Black, Fischer. "Capital Market Equilibrium with Restricted Borrowing."
   J. Bus. 45 (July 1972): 444–55.
Black, Fischer; Jensen, Michael; and Scholes, Myron. "The Capital Asset Pricing
   Model: Some Empirical Results." In *Studies in the Theory of Capital Markets,*
   edited by Michael Jensen. New York: Praeger, 1972.
Blattberg, Robert, and Sargent, Thomas. "Regression with Non-Gaussian

---

[28]There were, of course, a number of price or output stabilization schemes in operation during this period, few of which were successful for any length of time.

Disturbances: Some Sampling Results." *Econometrica* 39 (May 1971): 501-10.

Blume, Marshall E. "The Assessment of Portfolio Performance: An Application of Portfolio Theory." Ph.D. dissertation, Univ. Chicago, 1968.

Cootner, Paul. "Returns to Speculators: Telser versus Keynes." *J.P.E.* 68 (August 1960): 396-404. (*a*)

——. "Rejoinder." *J.P.E.* 68 (August 1960): 415-18. (*b*)

Fama, Eugene. "Risk, Return, and Equilibrium." *J.P.E.* 79 (January/February 1971): 30-55.

Fama, Eugene, and Babiak, Harvey. "Dividend Policy: An Empirical Analysis." *J. American Statis. Assoc.* 63 (December 1968): 1132-61.

Fama, Eugene, and MacBeth, James. "Risk, Return, and Equilibrium: Empirical Tests." Manuscript, Univ. Chicago, 1972.

Fama, Eugene, and Miller, Merton H. *The Theory of Finance.* New York: Holt, Rinehart & Winston, 1972.

Fama, Eugene, and Roll, Richard. "Some Properties of Symmetric Stable Distributions." *J. American Statis. Assoc.* 63 (September 1968): 817-36.

——. "Parameter Estimates for Symmetric Stable Distributions." *J. American Statis. Assoc.* 66 (June 1971): 331-38.

Fisher, Lawrence. "Some New Stock Market Indexes." *J. Bus.* 39 (suppl.; January 1966): 191-225.

Gray, R.W. "The Search for a Risk Premium." *J.P.E.* 69 (June 1961): 250-60.

Hardy, Charles O. *Risk and Risk Bearing.* Chicago: Univ. Chicago Press, 1940.

Houthakker, H.S. "Can Speculators Forecast Prices?" *Rev. Econ. and Statis.* 39 (May 1957): 143-51.

——. "Systematic and Random Elements in Short-Term Price Movements." *A.E.R.* 51 (May 1961): 164-72.

——. "Normal Backwardation." In *Value, Capital, and Growth: Papers in Honour of Sir John R. Hicks*, edited by J.N. Wolfe. Chicago: Aldine, 1968.

Johnson, Leland. "The Theory of Hedging and Speculation in Commodity Futures." *Rev. Econ. Studies* 27 (June 1960): 139-51.

Keynes, J.M. *A Treatise on Money.* Vol. 2. London: Macmillan, 1930.

King, Benjamin F. "Market and Industry Factors in Stock Price Behavior." *J. Bus.* 39 (January 1966): 139-90.

Larsen, Arnold. "Measurement of a Random Process in Future Prices." *Food Res. Inst. Studies* (Stanford Univ.) 1 (November 1960): 313-24.

Leland, Hayne F. "Optimal Forward Exchange Positions." *J.P.E.* 89 (March/April 1971): 257-69.

Lintner, John. "Security Prices, Risk, and Maximal Gains from Diversification." *J. Finance* 20 (December 1965): 587-615.

Markowitz, Harry M. *Portfolio Selection: Efficient Diversifications of Investments.* New York: Wiley, 1959.

Miller, Merton H., and Scholes, Myron S. "Rates of Return in Relation to Risk: A Reexamination of Some Recent Findings." In *Studies in the Theory of Capital Markets,* edited by Michael Jensen. New York: Praeger, 1972.

Mossin, Jan. "Equilibrium in a Capital Asset Market." *Econometrica* 37 (October 1966): 763–68.

Officer, Robert R. "A Time Series Examination of the Market Factor of the New York Stock Exchange." Ph.D. dissertation, Univ. Chicago, 1971.

Roberts, Harry V. *Statistical Inference and Decision.* Lithographed. Univ. Chicago, 1964.

Rockwell, Charles S. "Normal Backwardation, Forecasting, and the Returns to Commodity Futures Traders." *Food Res. Inst. Studies* (Stanford Univ.) 8 (suppl.; 1967): 107–30.

Roll, Richard. "The Efficient Market Model Applied to U.S. Treasury Bill Rates." Ph.D. dissertation, Graduate School Bus., Univ. Chicago, 1968.

Samuelson, P.A. "Proof that Properly Anticipated Prices Fluctuate Randomly." *Indus. Management Rev.* 8 (Spring 1965): 41–49.

Schrock, Nichols W. "The Theory of Asset Choice: Simultaneous Holding of Short and Long Positions in the Futures Market." *J.P.E.* 79 (March/April 1971): 270–93.

Sharpe, William. "Capital Asset Prices: A Theory of Market Equilibrium under Conditions of Risk." *J. Finance* 19 (September 1964): 425–42.

Smidt, Seymour. "A Test of Serial Independence of Price Changes in Soybean Futures." *Food Res. Inst. Studies* (Stanford Univ.) 5 (1965): 117–36.

Stevenson, Richard A., and Bear, Robert M. "Commodity Futures: Trends or Random Walks?" *J. Finance* 25 (March 1970): 65–81.

Telser, Lester. "Futures Trading and the Storage of Cotton and Wheat." *J.P.E.* 66 (June 1958): 233–55.

———. "Returns to Speculators: Telser versus Keynes: Reply." *J.P.E.* 67 (August 1960): 404–15.

———. "The Supply of Speculative Services in Wheat, Corn and Soybeans." *Food Res. Inst. Studies* (Stanford Univ.) 7 (suppl.; 1967): 131–76.

U.S., Department of Agriculture, Commodity Exchange Authority. *Commodity Futures Statistics.* Washington: Government Printing Office, 1952–67.

Working, Holbrook. "Futures Trading and Hedging." *A.E.R.* 18 (June 1953): 314–43.

16 Special Information and Insider Trading

Jeffrey F. Jaffee

I. Introduction

Trading by corporate officers, directors, and large stockholders, who are commonly called insiders, commands widespread attention in the financial community. Academicians are interested in the amount of special information insiders possess, as well as in the profit they earn from such knowledge. The average investor seeks out useful information in the *Official Summary of Insider Trading,*[1] the monthly report listing the transactions of corporate officials.

Previous research on corporate insiders has focused on the profitability of their trading. Some researchers, examining months of intensive insider activity, have concluded that insiders can predict stock price movement up to 6 months subsequent to trading. Rogoff for example, examines 45 companies in which, within a single month, three or more insiders buy their company's stock and no insiders sell the stock.[2] He finds that the returns to the insiders of these companies in the following 6 months are on average 9½ percent greater than the return to the stock market as a whole.

Glass examiens 14 different calendar months and selects the eight securities with the greatest excess of buyers to sellers among insiders within a month.[3] He finds that the average return on these securities is 10 percent above the return on the stock market as a whole in the 7 months following the individual months of intensive buying.

Lorie and Niederhoffer investigate stock performance following months in which there are at least two more buyers than sellers or at least two more

Reprinted with permission of the author and University of Chicago Press from *The Journal of Business,* Vol. 47, July 1974, pp. 410–428. © 1974 by University of Chicago Press. I wish to thank my dissertation committee: Merton Miller (chairman), Fischer Black, and Eugene Fama, who guided me in this area of research. I also wish to thank the members of the Finance Workshop at the University of Chicago, especially G. Mandelker and R. Ibbotson.

[1]U.S., Securities and Exchange Commission, *Official Summary of Security Transactions and Holdings* (Washington, D.C.: Government Printing Office).

[2]Donald L. Rogoff, "The Forecasting Properties of Insider Transactions" (D.B.A. thesis, Michigan State University, 1964).

[3]Gary S. Glass, "Extensive Insider Accumulation as an Indicator of Near Term Stock Price Performance" (Ph.D. diss., Ohio State University, 1966).

sellers than buyers among the insiders of a company.[4] They find that a security experiencing an intensive buying month is more likely to advance than to decline relative to the market in the 6 months subsequent to the event. Conversely, a security experiencing an intensive selling month is more likely to decline than to advance relative to the market in the 6 months subsequent to the event.

Driscoll examines the trading by insiders prior to dividend changes and finds that insiders actually buy more stock than they sell in the 6 months prior to dividend decreases.[5] He concludes that the evidence does not suggest any noticeable speculative interest of insiders with respect to unfavorable dividend action.

Wu classifies months of insider trading in specific securities as either net buying or net selling months.[6] Studying the price movement of these securities in the month following the month of trading, he concludes that there is no relationship between insider trading and subsequent stock price movement.

Scholes investigates secondary offerings, many of which are issued by insiders,[7] and finds that the residuals of securities decline an average of 1 percent on the days of these offerings.[8] He rejects the hypothesis that the residuals fall because of selling pressure and concludes that the drop in residuals is due to the market's belief that the issuer possesses inside information of an adverse nature.

In summary, the evidence with respect to the profitability of insider trading is not clear-cut. On the one hand, Rogoff, Glass, and Lorie-Niederhoffer find evidence that insiders can predict price movements in their own securities as much as 6 months in the future. On the other hand, Scholes's results suggest that residuals drop on the day of the secondary distribution with no further systematic changes. Both Wu and Driscoll find no evidence of successful forecasting by insiders. Furthermore, some of the studies are outdated. A few of the studies employ small samples, while others ignore transaction costs, the relative risk of different securities, and general market conditions. This paper attempts to improve on the older and less efficient techniques, and, in the process, to resolve the existing differences of opinion.

---

[4]James H. Lorie and Victor Niederhoffer, "Predictive and Statistical Properties of Insider Trading," *Journal of Law and Economics* 11 (April 1968): 35–51.

[5]Thomas E. Driscoll, "Some Aspects of Corporate Insider Stock Holdings and Trading under Section 16b of Securities and Exchange Act of 1934" (M.B.A. thesis, University of Pennsylvania, 1956).

[6]Hsiu K. Wu, "Corporate Insider Trading Profitability and Stock Price Movement" (Ph.D. diss., University of Pennsylvania, 1963).

[7]Myron S. Scholes, "The Market for Securities: Substitution versus Price Pressure and the Effects of Information on Share Price," *Journal of Business* 45 (April 1972): 179–211.

[8]The calculation of residuals is explained later in this study. For the present, residuals can be viewed as the changes in a stock price not explained by the movement of stock prices in the market as a whole.

Another objective of this paper is to test the information content of the *Official Summary*. Though the publication was established in 1934, little research has been conducted on it. Of the research summarized above, only the Lorie-Niederhoffer study examines the returns to securities following publication of the *Official Summary*. As noted earlier, they conclude that a security experiencing an intensive buying event is more likely to advance than to decline relative to the market following publication of the event in the *Official Summary*. Conversely, a security experiencing an intensive selling event is more likely to decline than to advance relative to the market following publication of the event. The authors state: "This study indicates that proper and prompt analysis of data on insider trading can be profitable."[9]

This conclusion conflicts with the considerable body of research suggesting that stock prices fully reflect all publicly available information.[10] To resolve this issue, the present study reexamines the information content of the publication.

II. Insider Trading Characteristics and Problems of Measurement

As part of this study, a random sample of trading months was drawn covering 200 large firms in the period 1962–68. This will be referred to as the "initial sample," and methods of drawing it will be described in more detail in Section IV. Based on this sample and the *Official Summary of Insider Trading*, descriptive statistics of the size, direction, etc., of insider trades are presented in tables 1 and 2.

The sample covers trades in approximately 1,000 firm-months. In some of these, there were no insider transactions. In some others, there were more than one purchase, sale, or a combination of these.

The tables show that the number of purchases is slightly greater than the number of sales, and the average purchase size is slightly greater than the average sale size. The variability in the size of transactions is large.

The distribution is skewed to the right. While approximately 40 percent

---

[9] Lorie and Niederhoffer, p. 52.

[10] For a general review of the literature, see Eugene F. Fama, "Efficient Capital Markets: A Review of Theory and Empirical Work," *Journal of Finance* 25 (May 1970): 383–417. The following are individual studies dealing with publicly available information: Eugene F. Fama et al., "Adjustment of Stock Prices," *International Economic Review* 10 (February 1969): 1–21; Ray Ball and Philip Brown, "An Empirical Evaluation of Accounting Income Numbers," *Journal of Accountancy Research* 6 (Autumn 1968): 159–78; Gershon Mandelker, "Returns to Stockholders from Mergers" (Ph.D. diss., University of Chicago, 1973); Roger Ibbotson, "The Performance of New Issues" (unpublished manuscript, University of Chicago, 1973).

Table 1

Frequency Distribution of Size of Insider Trades (Based on Initial Sample)

Size*	Frequency	
	Purchases	Sales
Below 0.1	0	1
0.1–1	13	0
1–10	222	165
11–20	84	97
21–30	46	62
31–40	29	25
41–50	17	26
51–60	11	23
61–70	10	22
71–80	4	11
81–90	4	6
91–100	3	4
101–200	9	32
201–300	6	4
301–1,000	6	8
1,001 and over	2	0
Total	466	486

*In thousands of dollars.

of the transactions involve less than $10,000, many transactions involve over $100,000, and a few outliers involve over $1 million.

Of the three main groups of insiders, officers trade most frequently, though their average size of trade is the smallest. The differences among the trading patterns of the three groups is slight relative to the variability in the sample as a whole.

The price behavior of stocks of firms traded by insiders, like that of stocks in general, reflects a variety of market-wide, industry-wide, special, and "random" influences which must somehow be recognized in any effort at isolating the relationship between price and insider trading activity. Beyond this, the

Table 2

Breakdown of Insider Trades by Type of Transaction (Based on Initial Sample)

Type of Transactor	Total Number of Trades	Number of Purchases	Number of Sales	Average Size of Purchase (in $)	Average Size of Sale (in $)
All transactors	952	466	486	32,905	38,517
Directors	306	174	132	47,346	37,019
Officers	391	167	224	22,013	37,350
Officer-Directors	255	125	130	27,306	42,063

phenomenon of insider trading raises certain special problems of which a researcher must be aware.

Since brokerage commissions are approximately 1 percent per transaction
on a round lot sale, an insider must expect the return on his company's security
to be at least 2 percent greater than the return on securities of comparable risk
before it will be worthwhile for the insider to undertake a "round-trip" transaction in his company's security. As a result, insiders may not trade on special
information that leads only to stock price movement on the order of transaction
costs.

Recent developments in security regulation which have increased the
probability that an insider will be prosecuted for trading on inside information
may deter insiders from trading. In addition, under Section 16(b) of the
Securities and Exchange Act of 1933–34, insiders must return all profits from
a purchase and subsequent sale (or a sale and a subsequent purchase) occurring
within 6 months of each other. Therefore, an insider must be prepared to retain
his new acquisitions for at least 6 months in order to profit from his inside
information.

Statistical noise may increase the difficulty of detecting successful exploitation of special information. Many insiders presumably transact for reasons
other than to profit from special information. Residuals following their trades
should be distributed randomly about zero. In addition, insiders may purposely
trade without information to camouflage trading based on special information.

Insider gains may also be masked by "gamesmanship." When rational
investors learn of a purchase by a knowledgeable insider, they should bid up
the price of the stock to reflect this fact. A shrewd insider without information
can capitalize on the market's belief in the special knowledge of all insiders by
buying shares in his company at any time. Outsiders, learning of this transaction,
should bid up the stock price, allowing the insider to sell what he bought at
the now higher price. The reverse can occur for selling. Hence, if the market
cannot differentiate an insider with information from an insider without
information, in the limit shrewd but not otherwise knowledgeable insiders can
transact until they force the average price change after all insiders' trades to
zero. This will also camouflage trading with information.[11]

While transaction costs and regulatory restraints tend to reduce the
profitability of trading by nonknowledgeable insiders, they may not eliminate
it entirely. For example, if transaction costs are 1 percent per transaction,
nonknowlegeable insiders can confine the average price change after purchases
to not more than 2 percent. Insiders can avoid Section 16(b) by allowing friends,
relatives, or insiders of other firms—all of whom are free to sell within 6 months
without penalty—to purchase at the same time that insiders purchase.

---

[11]The argument assumes that all insiders can trade with anonymity. For example, this
method of profiting could not be applied to secondary issues where, as suggested in
Scholes, the price is depressed during, as well as after, the transaction.

Some of these phenomena may act to camouflage the gains from trading on inside information. To see if this is so, and in an effort to minimize their effect, this study makes use of additional samples limited to large trades or to months where there is an especially great preponderance of trades in a single direction. These circumstances, it is hoped, are most likely to be free of the effects of noise, gamesmanship, etc.

III. Methodology

Calculation of Residual

In order to estimate the profitability of insider trades, this study examines the performance of a security subsequent to specific types of insider trades in that security, which we call insider trading events.[12]

Sharpe and Lintner have developed a model of equilibrium pricing of risky capital assets.[13] This model postulates a linear relationship between the expected return on a security and the covariance of the security's return with the return on a portfolio composed of all securities in the market (commonly called the "market portfolio").

The following is a model of stochastic process generating period-by-period returns that is consistent with the two-parameter model of Sharpe and Lintner and that has empirically been found to provide a good representation of actual returns:[14]

$$R_{jt} = \tilde{\gamma}_{0t} + \tilde{\gamma}_{1t}\beta_j + \tilde{e}_{jt} \tag{1}$$

where $\tilde{R}_{jt}$ = rate of return on security j during period t; $\tilde{R}_{m,t}$ = rate of return on the portfolio of all assets in period t; β_j = the ratio of the covariance between $\tilde{R}_{jt}$ and $\tilde{R}_{mt}$ to the variance of $\tilde{R}_{mt}$ (β_j is proportional to the contribution of the jth security to the risk of the market portfolio; it is a measure of the relative

---

[12]Three types of insider trading events are examined: (1) a transaction of an insider, (2) a large transaction of an insider, (3) a month in which many insiders of a company transact. Precise specification of these events are presented later.

[13]William F. Sharpe, "Capital Asset Prices: A Theory of Market Equilibrium under Conditions of Risk," *Journal of Finance* 19 (September 1964): 425–42; John Lintner, "Security Prices, Risk, and Maximal Gains from Diversification," *Journal of Finance* 20 (December 1965): 587–615.

[14]See Fischer Black, Michael Jensen, and Myron Scholes, "The Capital Asset Pricing Model: Some Empirical Results," in *Studies in the Theory of Capital Markets,* ed. Michael Jensen (New York: Praeger Publishers, 1972); and Eugene Fama and James MacBeth, "Risk, Return, and Equilibrium: Some Empirical Tests," *Journal of Political Economy* 81 (May/June 1973): 607–36.

risk of the jth security, as compared to the risk of the market portfolio); $\tilde{\gamma}_{0t}, \tilde{\gamma}_{1t}$ = market-determined parameters showing the ex post relationship between risk and return in different time periods; $\tilde{e}_{jt}$ = the disturbance of the jth security at time t.

Equation (1) indicates that the return on a security in period t is a function of the disturbance, $\tilde{e}_{jt}$, which is specific to an individual security, as well as the market-wide variables, $\tilde{\gamma}_{0t}$, and γ_{1t}. The disturbance in equation (1) can serve as a measure of the abnormal performance of a security, since the effects of $\tilde{\gamma}_{0t}, \tilde{\gamma}_{1t}$, and β_j are netted out. Since it is assumed that insiders possess more special information concerning their own security than concerning the market as a whole, this study examines the residuals of securities subsequent to insider trading events. As the estimation of $\tilde{\gamma}_{0t}$ and $\tilde{\gamma}_{1t}$ for each month is needed to measure a security's disturbance in equation (1), this study uses the estimates of $\tilde{\gamma}_{0t}$ and $\tilde{\gamma}_{1t}$ derived in the Fama and MacBeth paper.[15]

Statistical Measurements

Based on information gathered from the *Official Summary of Insider Trading*, samples are chosen consisting of securities undergoing a specific insider trading event. Examples of events are listed above. To estimate and interpret the gains from insider trading, residuals subsequent to events are examined. This section presents methods for estimating both the magnitudes of the residuals, and the likelihood that residuals of that magnitude might have arisen purely by chance.

Procedure for Estimating Magnitude of Residuals

Assume that a sample is chosen consisting of securities with trading events occurring over a certain period of time. We define U_m, the mean residual over all securities in the sample for month m, as:

$$U_m = \frac{\sum_{j=1}^{N} \hat{U}_{j,m}}{N} H_j \tag{2}$$

where N = number of securities in the sample; $\hat{U}_{j,m}$ = estimated residual for security j in month m (month 0 in eq. [2] is the month of the event, while month 1 is the following month, and so on); H_j = 1, if the event of the ith

---

[15]Fama and MacBeth.

security is a purchase or set of purchases; and = –1, if the event is a sale or set of sales.

Next, define the cumulative average residual, CU_m, as:

$$CU_m = \sum_{k=-15}^{m} U_k \tag{2'}$$

Tests of Significance

Again, we assume that a sample is chosen consisting of companies with insider trading events over a certain period of time. We want to form a test statistic indicating whether residuals subsequent to trading events are statistically larger than zero. The following six steps describe a method of forming such a one-sided test statistic.

1. *Formation of portfolios.*   Let X represent a specified integer. A portfolio corresponding to month t is formed by including the securities of all companies with events between and including month t-X and month t. As there is one and only one portfolio per calendar month for each value of X, the portfolio corresponding to month t is called portfolio t.[16] If a company has events in c different months during the period from month $(t$-$X)$ to month t, it is included c times in portfolio t.

For example, if X equals one, the portfolio of June 1962 includes all companies with events in either May or June 1962. If a company has events in both May and June 1962, it is included twice in the portfolio of June 1962. Similarly, when X equals two, the portfolio of May 1962 includes all companies with events in either March, April, or May 1962. If a company has events in both April and May 1962, it is included twice in the portfolio of May 1962.

In this study X assumes the values of zero, one, and seven. These correspond to periods of 1, 2, and 8 months within which occurrence of an insider trading event will lead to the inclusion of corresponding security in a portfolio.

2. *Measurement of performance of a portfolio.*   Next, the performance of portfolio t in the month from t to $t + 1$, which we call month $t + 1$, is defined as follows:

$$\hat{e}_{t,t+1} = \frac{\sum_{i=1}^{S} (\hat{e}_{i,t+1} H_i)}{S} \tag{3}$$

---

[16]If there are no events between month $(t$-$X)$ and month t, portfolio t will contain no securities. As will be seen later, portfolios that contain no securities are ignored in statistical tests.

where $\hat{e}_{t,t+1}$ = residual of portfolio t in month $t + 1$; $\hat{e}_{i,t+1}$ = residual of the ith security of portfolio t in month $t + 1$ (as opposed to notation in [2], month $t + 1$ is a calendar month and not a period of time relative to the date of a trading event); S = number of securities in portfolio t; H_i = 1, if the event of the ith security is a purchase or set of purchases; = -1, if the event is a sale or set of sales.

3. *Measurement of variability of a portfolio's performance.* A measure of the variability of the performance of portfolio t, called $\hat{SD}_t$, is defined as the computed standard deviation of the residual of portfolio t, using data during the period from month $(t - 49)$ to month t. This can be written as:

$$\hat{SD}_t = \frac{1}{49} \sum_{j=1}^{50} (\hat{e}_{t,t-j+1} - \frac{1}{50} \sum_{i=1}^{50} \hat{e}_{t,t-i+1})^2$$

4. *Standardization of a portfolio's performance.* We define $se_{t,t+1}$ to be the standardized residual for portfolio t at time $t + 1$. It is expressed as:

$$\hat{se}_{t,t+1} = \frac{\hat{e}_{t,t+1}}{\hat{SD}_t} \tag{4}$$

5. *Measurement of standardized performance across all portfolios.* As a different portfolio is formed for each calendar month, for a given value of X, portfolio t is just one of many portfolios. The average standardized residual across all of these portfolios, called $\overline{sr}$, is defined as:

$$\overline{sr} = \frac{1}{n} \sum_{t=51}^{401} \hat{se}_{t,t+1} D_t \tag{5}$$

where D_t = 1, when there is at least one security in portfolio t, = 0, when there are no securities in portfolio t; n = number of months in which the portfolio corresponding to the month has at least one security

$$n = \sum_{t=51}^{401} D_t \tag{6}$$

As $\tilde{\gamma}_{0t}$ and $\tilde{\gamma}_{1t}$ are calculated from January 1935 to June 1968, month 1 is January 1935, and month 402 is June 1968. In equations (5) and (6), t begins at 51 because 50 months of past data are required to estimate a portfolio's residual variance. Similarly, month 402 is omitted in equations (5) and (6) as 1 month of future data is required to calculate $\hat{se}_{t,t+1}$.

    6. *Calculation of t-test.* The following equation tests whether $\overline{sr}$ is significantly different from zero:[17]

$$t = \frac{\overline{sr}}{s/\sqrt{n}} \tag{7}$$

where s = estimate of standard deviation of each standardized portfolio. This value is constrained to be one due to the standardization process. Since in this study, X assumes the values of zero, one, and seven, there are three sets of portfolios, one for each value of X. The six steps outlined above are repeated for each value of X, yielding three t-statistics. This approach is referred to henceforth as the "portfolio method."

Rationale for Methodology

Though the two-factor model of equation (1) removes much residual correlation, other phenomena, such as common industry effects, can cause residuals across securities in a given month to be correlated. Consequently, a test statistic should not assume independence of residuals across securities in a given month. The test statistic of equation (7) measures a portfolio's residual variance directly, thus taking account of the correlation between residuals of different securities in a given month.

    For samples of insider trading to be presented later, the serial correlation of standardized residuals across portfolios was measured. As the null hypothesis that the serial correlation is zero could not be rejected, the individual standardized residuals can be treated as independent observations in equation (7).

IV. The Samples

Initial Sample

The 200 largest securities on the Chicago Research in Security Prices (CRSP) tape constitute the initial sample. Insiders' transactions for each of the 200

---

[17]If the residuals of individual securities are normally distributed, the standardized residuals of eq. (4) will behave as if drawn from a t-distribution with 49 df. Equation (7), a weighted sum of these t-distributed variables, is t-distributed with degrees of freedom approximately equal to 49 n (see Kermit A. Brownlee, *Statistical Methods in Science and*

securities are observed in 5 separate months during the period from 1962 to 1968. The individual months of observation for a particular security are chosen in the following manner.

Five random numbers are selected, where each random number is a drawing from the set of integers from 12 to 18. The first month of observation on a security is designated by the first random numbers. Month 1 is defined as August 1961. As each random number ranges from 12 to 18, the first month of observation for a company is one of the months from July 1962 to January 1963. The second month of observation is designated by the sum of the first two random numbers, and the third month of observation is designated by the sum of the first three random numbers. The fourth and fifth months of observation are selected in a similar manner. Random numbers from 12 to 18 are chosen to separate the individual observations of a company by at least a year.

For example, if the five random integers of XYZ company are, respectively 13, 12, 14, 18, 14, insider trading of XYZ would be observed in month 13 (August 1962), month 25 (August 1963), month 39 (October 1964), month 57 (April 1966), and month 71 (June 1967). As the last month on the CRSP tape is June 1968, any observations beyond August 1967 are ignored.

In any month an individual trader is classified as a purchaser if the number of days during the month in which he buys stock is greater than the number of days in which he sells stock. Conversely, he is classified as a seller if the number of days in which he buys stock is less than the number of days in which he sells stock. If he purchases stock just as many times as he sells it, he is not included in the sample. Exercises of options are excluded from this and all other samples in this study because it is felt that options are exercised due to institutional factors rather than as a result of special information.

For each company in the initial sample, a month is classified as a month of net purchasers or a month of net sellers depending on whether the number of purchasers is greater or less than the number of sellers. Months during which the number of purchasers equals the number of sellers are excluded. Months of net purchasers and months of net sellers are defined as insider trading events. In this and all other samples in the study, events are excluded if companies are not listed on the CRSP tape for 50 months before the event and 10 months after the event. This restriction assures sufficient data to form portfolios and to calculate residual variances. There are 952 trades in the initial sample. Many companies have more than one trade in a month, so that the number of months of net purchasers plus the number of months of net sellers is only 362.

Engineering [New York: John A. Wiley & Sons, 1965], pp. 297–304). The degrees of freedom are very large and a normal distribution will suffice. Plots of standardized residuals from samples to be presented later suggest that the individual residuals are indeed *t*-distributed with a variance of one.

Sample of Large Transactions

While insiders may transact without special information, one might expect that their large transactions would more likely be based on inside information. Thus, a sample of large transactions may contain less statistical noise than the original sample.

All transactions from the initial sample whose values are greater than $20,000 are assembled into a subsample. This subsample contains 370 trades, representing 39 percent of the original sample of 952. The previous classification scheme is employed to separate months of net purchasers from months of net sellers.

Samples of Months of Intensive Trading

Since special information may lead to simultaneous purchases or to simultaneous sales by many insiders of the same company,[18] the percentage of traders with information might be higher in these intensive trading periods than in other periods. In order to reduce statistical noise, samples of intensive trading firms are chosen.

Any company with at least Y more purchasers than sellers in a month is classified as an intensive buying company for that month. Conversely, any company with at least Y more sellers than purchasers in a month is classified as an intensive selling company for the month. In the following sample, Y will assume the value of three.

This sample includes all intensive trading companies listed on the CRSP tape during the months from April to October 1961; from December 1961 to November 1962; from January 1964 to March 1965; from May to December 1965; and from September 1966 to March 1967.[19]

V. Results and Analysis

For each sample, table 3 presents the cumulative average residuals for the 1-, 2-, and 8-month holding periods following trading events. These three time

---

[18] It is also possible that the monthly transactions of insiders are drawings from an underlying distribution of a process unrelated to future stock price movements, so that the unusual months arise from chance rather than from special information.

[19] This sample is composed of the five samples used in Jeffrey F. Jaffe, "The Effect of Changes in Security Regulation on Insider Trading" (unpublished manuscript, Indiana University, 1973). In order to examine insider trading during periods with varying degrees of governmental regulation, the sample chosen is discontinuous.

Table 3
Cumulative Average Residuals and Significance Tests for Samples of Insider Trading, with Time Measured from Month of Trading Event

Length of Time Period (in Months)	Cumulative Average Residuals	t-value	One-tailed Significance Level
Initial Sample (362 Observations)			
1	.0060	1.93	.026
2	.0118	2.24	.012
8	.0136	1.32	.010
Sample of Large Transactions (204 Observations)			
1	.0062	1.99	.023
2	.0134	2.09	.018
8	.0184	1.14	.126
Intensive Trading Sample of the 1960s (Y = 3, 861 Observations)			
1	.0098	3.65	.0001
2	.0209	4.73	< .00001
8	.0507	5.23	< .00001
Intensive Trading Sample of the 1950s (Y = 4, 293 Observations)			
1	.0094	3.06	.001
2	.0174	3.16	.0008
8	.0514	4.69	< .00001
Intensive Trading Sample of the 1950s (Y = 5, 157 Observations)			
1	.0112	2.97	.001
2	.0174	2.76	.003
8	.0448	3.18	.007
Intensive Trading Sample of the 1950s (Y = 6, 80 Observations)			
1	.0125	1.60	.055
2	.0078	0.77	.227
8	.036	1.05	.147

intervals are chosen in order to study both the short-term and long-term predictive power of insiders. It also shows t-values and significance levels of these for the hypothesis that the expected values of the standardized residuals in equation (7) are zero. As an aid to understanding these findings, the following presentation for the initial sample gives additional detail.

Initial Sample

Figure 1 presents the cumulative average residuals from month –15 to month +15 for the initial sample. The procedure for estimating individual and cumulative average residuals is given in Section III, above. Under those procedures, data for sales are added, with their signs changed, to data for purchases. Thus, the residuals shown in figure 1 rise when purchased stocks rise and when sold stocks decline.

The cumulative average residuals actually fall by approximately 2 percent in the 15 months prior to events. Cumulative average residuals rise approximately one-half of 1 percent in the 15 months following trading. The most rapid rise occurs in the first few months after trading, suggesting that insiders can forecast residuals in the near future better than residuals in the distant future.

In addition to estimating the magnitudes of residuals, this study employs the portfolio method to test whether these residuals differ significantly from zero at three different periods of time. The first part of table 3 gives the results from the portfolio method for the initial sample. The t-value corresponding to the hypothesis that the expected value of the standardized residuals in equation (7) equals zero, and the one-tailed significance level of that t-value, are shown for each value of X.[20] The t-values are statistically large; the smallest, 1.32 and the largest, 2.24. Though these results suggest that insiders do possess and exploit special information, other samples must be examined before more definite conclusions are formed.

Sample of Large Transactions

This subsample of the initial sample was designed to be less subject to various kinds of noise, etc. As the cumulative average residuals are nearly identical with those of the initial sample, the results do not suggest that large transactions contain more information than small transactions.

The second part of table 3 presents the t-values associated with the portfolio method for this subsample. The associated t-values remain statistically large and indicative of successful prediction.

Intensive Trading Samples

The first and largest of these samples is for the 1960s and uses only months in which there are at least three more sellers than purchasers ($Y = 3$). Average

---

[20] As each t-statistic has a large number of degrees of freedom (see n 18), the one-tailed significance levels are taken from a normal probability table.

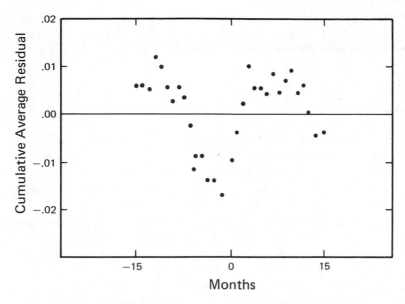

Figure 1. Cumulative average residuals for initial sample.

residuals are large, rising .0507 in 8 months. Similarly, the high *t*-values suggest that insiders trade successfully.

As a check on these results, a sample of intensive trading companies from a different time period is selected. For this sample *Y* assumes the values of four, five, and six. All intensive trading months occurring during the period from January 1953 to December 1955 and January 1958 to December 1959 for companies listed on the CRSP tape are included in the sample.[21] Where *Y* equals four, the cumulative average residuals again rise over 5 percent in 8 months, suggesting that insiders possess special information. The *t*-values are large: each of the three is greater than 3.0. For the samples where *Y* equals four and where *Y* equals five, the cumulative average residuals are of similar magnitude. The small sample size in the latter sample can explain the slightly lower *t*-values. When *Y* equals six, both the cumulative average residuals and the *t*-values are smaller. As this sample contains only 80 observations, the results are not as decisive as the results of the total sample.

The findings indicate successful trading by insiders. However, as the cumulative average residuals do not increase as *Y* increases, the results do not suggest that profit to insiders is an increasing function of the intensity of the

---

[21]This sample was collected for use in a preliminary draft of Jaffe. This sample is discontinuous as insider trading was observed in different periods with varying degrees of regulation.

trading. One might speculate that, as the number of insider traders increases, the nature of their information becomes increasingly similar to that of outsiders, either through leaks or from a common assessment of generally available information.

Inclusion of Transaction Costs

In order to determine the profits that insiders earn, transaction costs must be subtracted. This study assumes that transaction costs are 2 percent—1 percent brokerage charge for both a purchase and a subsequent sale (or a sale and a subsequent purchase). This is only approximate, as there are other costs and benefits. On the one hand, an insider must pay the specialist spread on his transaction. In addition, by concentrating his holdings in the stock of his own company, he may suffer a loss of utility due to underdiversification of his portfolio. On the other hand, since this study uses only monthly price data, insiders may reap undetectable profits from intramonth price movements. Finally, an insider who used his information to determine the timing of an appropriate one-way transaction would incur only a 1 percent transaction cost.

Measuring the magnitude of profit after transaction costs as defined above is simple in principle. Each cumulative average residual gross of transaction costs is 2.0 percent greater than the cumulative average residual net of transaction costs. Determining the proper t-statistic is more difficult, however. For any single trading event for a security, the portfolio method places that security into the portfolios associated with $X + 1$ successive months. This is equivalent to an insider buying a security in period t and selling it in period $t + X + 1$. Thus, for each event of a security, the 2.0 percent transaction costs must be allocated over $(X + 1)$ months. For example, when X equals seven, the transaction costs for each event are charged off at a rate of 0.25 percent for a period of 8 months.

Of the many combinations of sampling period, holding period, and trading intensity covered in table 3, only the four intensive trading samples have any cumulative average residuals greater than 2.0 percent transaction costs. Thus, only these samples are investigated after the addition of transaction costs.

For this set of tests we ignore results where the time period is 1 or 2 months, as transaction costs overwhelm the gains from holding securities for a short length of time. Table 4 presents the results net of transaction costs. The t-values for 8-month periods are statistically large. Insiders earned approximately 3 percent profits in the 8 months after transactions, indicating that transaction costs have diminished profits by 40 percent.

Summary

This study has examined three different samples. Together, the data suggest that insiders possess special information. This conclusion follows not only from

Table 4
Statistics on Profitability of Insider Trading after Transaction Costs

Y	8-Month Cumulative Average Residual after Transaction Costs	t-Value (Y = 7)	One-tailed Significance Level
3	.0307	3.26	.0006
4	.0304	2.92	.002
5	.0248	1.84	.032

the significance of the results from the first intensive trading sample, but also from the similarity of results from the different samples. It reinforces the results of previous researchers who uncovered evidence of special information (see above). However, only the intensive trading samples yield profits greater than commissions.

The results tell nothing about the profitability of transactions not required to appear in the *Official Summary*. For example, leakage of information to friends and relatives who need not report their transactions to the Securities and Exchange Commission (SEC) and reciprocal passage of information between insiders of different companies may escape the detection of government regulators. There is little doubt that arrangement such as these occur. Henry Manne even suggests that the primary purpose of board-of-directors meetings is to abet this reciprocal passage of information.[22] In addition, insiders may profit from information indirectly related to other companies, for example, if the insider learns that his own company won an unexpected contract from a competitor, the insider might sell short the competitor's stock.

New developments in security regulation outlaw trading based on this passage of information. However, since only corporate insiders are required to report their transactions to the SEC, the detection of the trades of noninsiders can be expected to be difficult.

VI. Information Content of the Official Summary

Introduction

The previous results, indicating that insiders earn profits on their own account, imply that the trades of insiders contain information. Unless the information is discounted prior to the distribution of the *Official Summary*, investors will be able to profit from the publication. This section deals with the information content of the *Official Summary*.

[22]Manne, p. 65.

The information content of the publication is investigated by examining the residuals of securities subsequent to the publication in the *Official Summary* of insider trading events in these securities. Lorie and Niederhoffer state: "The Summary is compiled from month-end reports of insiders and is in print approximately five weeks after the last transaction. The basic data, however, are frequently filed by the insiders with the stock exchanges within a few days of the transaction. Regulations require that information be filed with the exchanges within ten days of the end of the month in which the trading takes place."[23] This study assumes that the *Official Summary* always publishes an insider trading event 2 months after the event occurred. For example, if a company has an event in June 1962, we assume that the event is published in August 1962. Consequently, residuals of the company are examined beginning in September 1962.

Profits Gross of Transaction Costs

Figure 1 presents the cumulative average residuals for the initial sample. Residuals after month +2 occur subsequent to the publication of insider trades. Cumulative average residuals do not rise between month +2 and month +15 in the initial sample, suggesting little if any long-term informational effect. As the average residual for month +3 is large, it appears that any information from the publication is discounted rapidly.

Other samples are investigated as well. For the samples described in Section IV, table 5 presents the *t*-values and the cumulative average residuals on data subsequent to the *Official Summary's* publication dates. In each of the six samples, at least one of the three *t*-values is above 2.00, and all *t*-values are positive. In the first intensive trading sample, the *t*-values are extremely large, running from 2.53 to 4.77. There appears to be much informational content in the data; in the intensive trading samples where *Y* equals three and four, cumulative average residuals rise between 0.04 and 0.05 in the 8 months after publication of an event. As other samples show a less dramatic rise, the data suggest that the best trading schemes involve an examination of intensive trading companies. The cumulative average residuals after publication are only slightly lower than the cumulative average residuals presented in the first two sections of the paper. Thus, a large portion of the information contained in the trades of insiders is not discounted by the month of the publication of the trades.

Net of Transaction Costs

Since one must consider transaction costs in determining the value of the *Official Summary* to outsiders, this section examines the profitability of trading rules

---

[23]Lorie and Niederhoffer, p. 36.

Table 5
Cumulative Average Residuals and Significance Tests for Samples of Insider Trading, with Time Measured from Month of Publication of *Official Summary*

Length of Period (in Months)	Cumulative Average Residual	t-Value	One-tailed Significance Level
Initial Sample (362 Observations)			
1	.0087	2.55	.005
2	.0027	0.91	.184
8	.0070	0.98	.164
Sample of Large Transactions (204 Observations)			
1	.0098	2.23	.013
2	.0134	1.67	.047
8	.0184	1.36	.088
Intensive Trading Sample of 1960s (Y = 3, 861 Observations)			
1	.00741	2.53	.006
2	.01238	3.96	.00002
8	.04936	4.77	< .00001
Intensive Trading Sample (Y = 4, 293 Observations)			
1	.0010	0.281	.390
2	.0065	1.80	.036
8	.0412	3.71	.0001
Intensive Trading Sample (Y = 5, 157 Observations)			
1	.00095	0.00045	.50
2	.0098	1.307	.096
8	.0408	2.47	.007
Intensive Trading Sample (Y = 6, 80 Observations)			
1	.017	2.26	.012
2	.0212	1.45	.073
8	.0464	1.00	.159

based on the *Official Summary* net of transaction costs. Transaction costs are allocated to portfolios in the manner described in Section IV and are again set at 2 percent.

Table 6 presents the results of the portfolio method with the inclusion of transaction costs. Only the samples where Y equals three, Y equals four, and Y equals five are included, as commission charges are greater than cumulative average residuals in all other samples. Profits to outsiders after transaction costs are approximately 2–3 percent in these samples. Thus, transaction costs account for less than 50 percent of profits. The *t*-values for the samples where Y equals three and Y equals four are statistically large. As the sample where Y equals

Table 6

Statistics on Net Profitability after Transaction Costs of Insider Trades Subsequent to Their Publication in the *Official Summary*

Sample	8-Month Cumulative Average Residual after Transaction Costs	t-Value $(X = 7)$	One-tailed Significance Level of t-Value
$Y = 3$ (from sample of 1960s)	.0294	2.78	.003
$Y = 4$ (from sample of 1950s)	.0208	1.92	.027
$Y = 5$ (from sample of 1950s)	.0208	1.09	.137

four is independent of the sample where Y equals three, the above suggests that investors can profit by prompt use of the *Official Summary*'s information on intensive trading companies. Since transaction costs erased profits in all other samples, the results do not indicate any other profitable trading schemes.

Individuals desiring to invest excess funds would be interested in the informational content of the *Official Summary* gross of transaction costs, as they must pay these costs whether or not they use the publication. Thus they can use the publication's information on many different types of insider trading events profitably.

VII. Concluding Remarks

The present study attempts to resolve the conflicts in the results of previous papers by employing more powerful techniques and data sets. For all of the samples in the study, it was concluded that insiders do possess special information. However, after adjustment for transactions cost, only the intensive trading samples with 8-month holding periods were earning statistically large returns, with transaction costs accounting for approximately 40 percent of the gross profits in these samples. Results also indicate that much information contained in the trades remains undiscounted by the publication date in the *Official Summary*. Including transactions costs eliminated profits for outsiders in all but the intensive trading samples, where profits on the order of 2.5 percent could be earned.

Suggestions that corporate officials earn profits by trading on their own accounts are of interest to the public officials and legal profession. First, the results indicating that trading on inside information is widespread suggest that insiders actually do violate security regulations. Second, the evidence of information in the intensive trading samples indicates where the law enforcers should search for violators.[24]

The results of Section VI, as well as the Lorie and Niederhoffer study, indicate that the *Official Summary* contains information on future stock prices, a finding inconsistent with much of the research on efficient capital markets. Future research might investigate the causes behind the market's gradual adjustment to information contained in the publication.

The data suggest that the best of the trading rules based on information in the *Official Summary* involve an examination of intensive trading companies, as only these samples possessed residuals greater than the costs of transaction. Future research might further examine whether strategies based on intensive trading companies, as well as entirely new strategies, can consistently outperform a naive buy-and-hold strategy.

---

[24] The effectiveness of security regulation is investigated in detail in Jaffe.

17 Money and Stock Prices

Michael S. Rozeff

1. Introduction

The relation of money to stock prices has been a subject of academic research for many years. Past studies have made use of the *Monetary Portfolio* (MP) model developed by Brunner (1961), Friedman (1961), Friedman and Schwartz (1963), and Cagan (1972) among modern economists.[1] In this model, an investor reaches an equilibrium position in which, in general, he holds a number of assets including money in his portfolio of assets. A monetary disturbance such as an unexpected increase (or decrease) in the growth rate of the money supply causes disequilibrium in asset portfolios by making actual money balances depart from desired money balances. The attempt by investors as a group to attain their desired money positions then transmits the monetary change to markets at large. Investors respond to the wealth effect of increased money growth by exchanging money for a variety of assets in asset markets: short- and long-term bonds, stocks, real estate, durable goods, capital goods and human capital. The time response of investors has been viewed as sufficiently delayed that asset prices respond to the monetary disturbance with a *lag* usually characterized as long, variable and positive, on average. In addition, increased money growth in the MP model increases prices of durable goods relative to non-durable goods and makes the latter relatively more desirable. When prices

Reprinted with permission of the author and North-Holland Publishing Company from *Journal of Financial Economics,* Vol. 1, no. 3, September 1974, pp. 245–302. This research was done at the Graduate School of Management, University of Rochester. Many members of the Graduate School of Management of the University of Rochester have generously offered critical comment and enlightenment which have improved this study. In particular I wish to thank Professors Leon Courville, Marshall Freimer, Ronald Hansen, John Long, Ronald Schmidt and Dean William Meckling. I wish to acknowledge the excellent support given me at all stages of this study by my Dissertation Committee composed of Professors Michael C. Jensen, Kenneth Gaver and Ross Watts. I especially thank Professor Jensen who first suggested the possibility of the research topic. His continuously stimulating comments on many aspects of earlier drafts have benefited this study and my own education to an extent that I must always be in his debt. The content of the present work is, of course, solely my responsibility.

[1]The advance of this model over the quantity theory of money seems great enough that I prefer to use the descriptive title 'Monetary Portfolio' model rather than 'Simple Quantity' model which Cooper (1972) uses. Burger (1971, p. 1) independently calls the model 'The Portfolio Theory of Monetary Policy'. The MP model is reviewed by Patinkin (1972) and by Rozeff (1974, pp. 176–181).

of non-durables rise (also with a lag), the current production of goods and services is affected.

Tests of the MP model applied to stock prices have concluded (1) that changes in monetary variables do result in stock price changes and (2) that changes in monetary variables, on average, do lead changes in stock prices [see Sprinkel (1964), Palmer (1970), Homa and Jaffee (1971), Keran (1971), Reilly and Lewis (1971), Hamburger and Kochin (1972), and Meigs (1972)]. For example, Reilly and Lewis (1971, p. 64) 'expected that there would be a strong relationship between changes in the rate of growth of the money supply and stock price movements' and agreed with Sprinkel that this hypothesis was confirmed by the evidence.[2] They also concluded, based on both graphical and regression analysis, that monetary changes *led* stock price changes. The 'lag' is a prominent feature of the Sprinkel (1964) and Homa and Jaffee (1971) studies which report lagged relationships of stock prices to money variables and present trading rules (based on the lag) which earn returns in excess of a naive buy-and-hold (B&H) policy. Lagged relationships of money and stock prices are reported in the remaining studies and could, in principle, also be used to formulate trading rules.[3] The empirical work on stock prices using the MP model has therefore nurtured the widespread view that monetary policy has a lagged effect on the stock market and that astute investors can use the lag in trading rules. In general, this body of evidence has also increased the acceptance of the view that monetary policy has a long lagged effect on other markets in the economy as well.

By contrast, the *Efficient Market* (EM) hypothesis implies that in an efficient stock market, the lag (if any) of stock price change behind monetary change cannot on average be positive and cannot allow the formulation of trading rules which earn excess profits. Competition among profit-maximizing investors in an efficient market will ensure that current and past information is fully reflected in current security prices so that investors will *not* be able to develop profitable trading rules with this information. The time sequence of prices conditioned upon current and past information will consist of competitively determined equilibrium prices which fully reflect available information and leave investors able to earn only normal rates of return, on average. Monetary policy will not have a systematic lagged effect of any economic importance in an efficient market.

The profitable trading rules of Sprinkel and Homa and Jaffee use past

---

[2]Keran (1971) and Homa and Jaffee (1971) express this relationship in terms of *levels* of the variables rather than changes, i.e., the expected relationship is between stock price levels and rates of growth of the money supply.

[3]Hamburger and Kochin (1972, p. 236) recognize this possibility: 'It seems unlikely that the results presented above will help one to earn excess profits in the stock market (which is one reason why they are being published).'

available monetary data to predict stock returns and seem to contradict the
EM model. Furthermore, the remaining studies that have found significant lags
in the reaction of stock market prices to monetary data are inconsistent with
the EM model insofar as these lagged rleationships provide *potentially* profitable
trading rules. Compelling evidence consistent with the efficient market model
exists in volume.[4] Since monetary data is published in a similar manner to other
data available to the stock market, past studies of money and stock prices pose
a problem: is the stock market in fact inefficient with respect to monetary data?
The EM model and past studies using the MP model give conflicting answers.
This paper resolves the conflict.

Cooper (1972) has recognized the conflict between the monetary and
efficient market models. He attempts to demonstrate that the observed features
of the cross and lead/lag spectra of stock returns and money growth rates are
consistent with an efficient market which anticipates monetary growth rates at
some frequencies and lags at other frequencies. However, he relies on several
faulty algebraic approximations (see section 5 below), and he interprets (1972,
p. 46) the lead/lag spectrum as possibly being consistent with *either* a lead or
a lag of stock returns. His spectral analysis therefore does not provide clearcut
tests of either the EM model or the MP model. Despite its shortcomings,
Cooper's study provides an important new approach to the problem of money
and stock prices which I follow up in this paper.

Part of the conflict between the EM and MP models arises from a failure
by previous authors to distinguish two distinct hypotheses: (1) that monetary
change affects stock returns and (2) that monetary change affects stock returns
with a lag. The EM model does not conflict with (1) but it does conflict with
(2). Monetary variables may have a consistent effect on stock returns in an
efficient market without opportunities for excess profit arising. If monetary
data is reflected in stock prices *as it is published*, opportunities for excess returns
will be lacking and any relationship will be entirely *contemporaneous.* If stock
returns anticipate monetary change, a *negative* lag will arise. These hypotheses
are distinct from the hypothesis that stock price changes lag behind changes in
monetary variables. Neglect of the EM model has led to regression tests in the
past which seem to contradict the EM model and which improperly indicate
the sign and extent of the lag in effect of monetary policy on stock returns.
Prior studies overlook the possibility of a negative lag and do not distinguish
contemporaneous and lagged effects.

It is useful for further discussion and testing to define *two forms* of the
monetary portfolio model. The typical MP hypothesis states that monetary
variables affect stock returns with a lag. Some versions allow a contemporaneous
effect as well. Since, in an efficient market, *lagged* monetary variables cannot
affect *current* stock returns, the hypothesis that investors can use the depen-

---

[4]See Fama (1970) for a complete review; also see Brealey (1971) and Cootner (1964).

dence of stock returns on past (lagged) monetary variables in profitable trading rules conflicts with the EM model. To distinguish this conflict clearly, define first the *predictive* MP model: this form of the MP model is characterized by the statement that stock returns are materially affected *by only lagged* monetary variables. Equations which express stock returns as a function of past available money data are forms of this model. The predictive MP model therefore implies the existence of profitable trading rules that use past monetary data. So defined, the *predictive MP model is inconsistent with the EM model.*

However, the MP hypothesis need not be restricted to a lagged relationship only since monetary effects on stock prices may be contemporaneous. Since *current* data cannot be used to predict *current* stock returns, a purely contemporaneous relationship does not conflict with the EM model. We may go further than this. In an efficient market in which prices fully reflect available information, the market extracts from current data any implications it has for future stock returns and current stock returns reflect these implications. That is, if current data provides information about *future* monetary variables with implications for *future* prices, *current* prices will incorporate or 'discount' the information—otherwise information is underutilized and there are opportunities for trading rule profits. The hypothesis that money affects stock returns and the hypothesis that the stock market is efficient together imply that stock returns will be related to contemporaneous and possibly future monetary variables (if anticipations are accurate). This combined efficient market and monetary portfolio hypothesis I call the *non-predictive* MP model. It does *not* imply that stock returns can be predicted by profitable trading rules using lagged monetary data. It simply asserts that current stock returns are related to current monetary data or to current and future monetary data.

The rest of this paper is organized as follows: Section 2 briefly reviews the EM model emphasizing (1) its empirical implications and (2) its economic interpretation. Section 3 develops in detail testable forms of the predictive and non-predictive models, and section 4 presents the results of regression tests and trading rule tests of the models. Prior studies are analyzed in section 5, and section 6 presents the major conclusions of the study.

2. The Efficient Market Model

2.1. Trading Rules in an Efficient Market

A market is *efficient* with respect to a data subset B_t if price at time t 'fully reflects' B_t. 'Data subset B_t' refers to a subset of any data at time t that can possibly be used to provide relevant information about market value. 'Price' refers either to the price of a single asset or a price index of several assets. 'Fully reflects' means that investors have used the data subset (possibly in various ways) to arrive at information respecting asset values and that current market price has been determined conditional upon this information. Therefore if price fully reflects B_t, investors cannot earn excess profits using B_t. In defining data in B_t, *availability* is a relevant characteristic. Data available to a broad segment of the investing public is termed *publicly* available data. 'Weak' and 'semi-strong' form tests of the EM model employ publicly available data (weak-form tests limit the data to past security price data) while 'strong-form' tests of the model employ data that is not publicly available. In this study, money supply data appearing in the Federal Reserve Bulletin (FRB) is considered publicly available. Prior to 1943, however, no aggregate money supply series seems to have been publicly available on a timely basis. Friedman and Schwartz (1970) provide a reconstruction of money supply data prior to 1943.

Fama's (1970, p. 383) statement that an efficient market is 'a market in which prices always *fully reflect* available information' is, as he notes, too general to test since no one can test the hypothesis with respect to *all* information. When a *particular* data set is specified, the EM model can be tested with respect to that data and the information obtained from it. Tests take the form of examining the profitability of specific trading rules or testing specific models which could be used to earn excess profits. The existence of profitable trading rules refutes the EM hypothesis.

Consider a simplified version of the efficient market hypothesis [see Samuelson (1965, 1973) and Mandelbrot (1966)]. Define the investor group as the 'market'. Assume that the market formulates a probability distribution of future price and that the mathematical expectation of this distribution determines current market price. Assume that the market is efficient, that is, current price fully reflects the data subset B_t. Assume a zero rate of interest. These assumptions combined with the assumption that current price is determined conditional upon B_t give the following (tildes indicate random variables):

$$E(\tilde{P}_{t+1}|B_t) = P_t \tag{1}$$

That is, the expected value of the probability distribution of future price, $\tilde{P}_{t+1}$, conditional upon B_t is current price, P_t. Define the change in price from time t to time $t + 1$ as

$$\Delta \tilde{P}_{t+1} \equiv \tilde{P}_{t+1} - P_t \tag{2}$$

Then the expected price change conditional upon B_t is given by

$$E(\Delta \tilde{P}_{t+1}|B_t) = 0 \tag{3}$$

Eq. (3) is an implication of the EM model and the additional assumptions.

It follows directly from (3) that a trading rule producing information from B_t cannot be used to increase expected gain, since the expectation of the distribution of price already incorporates B_t [see Fama (1970, p. 385)]. Eqs. (1) – (3) can be summed up by the statement that the price sequence is a 'fair game' or 'martingale' variable with respect to B_t.[5] A 'submartingale' arises when the assumption of a zero rate of interest is relaxed and investors earn a 'normal' rate of return.[6] In the latter case, the implication is that trading rules using B_t cannot have greater expected gains than the alternative policy of B&H (buy-and-hold).

The Samuelson (1973) proof assumes that the random variables are generated according to a known stochastic process. If current price is interpreted as an estimate of future price, (3) states that the estimate is unbiased. In this case there can be no excess profits, on average, unless the mean of the distribution of future price shifts in such a way that market estimates become consistently biased. Gordon and Hynes (1970, pp. 388–389) point out that the fiscal-monetary authority is in a position to create biased estimates by the market but that the market will learn 'if the authorities follow a consistent

------

[5] A sequence of random variables (prices), $\ldots, p_{t-1}, p_t, p_{t+1}, \ldots$, is a martingale if the, mathematical expectation of p_{t+1}, conditional upon the sequence of past price, is current price, or

$$E(\tilde{p}_{t+1}|p_t, p_{t-1}, \ldots) = p_t$$

It follows that

$$E(\Delta \tilde{p}_{t+1}|p_t, p_{t-1}, \ldots) = 0$$

B_t can include the sequence of past prices as a special case. Fama (1970, p. 385) refers to the sequence of unexpected price *changes*, $\tilde{p}_{t+1} - E(\tilde{p}_{t+1}|B_t)$ (or in the case of a submartingale the sequence of unexpected returns) as the 'fair game' variable.

[6] In a submartingale with respect to B_t,

$$E(\tilde{p}_{t+1}|B_t) \geqslant p_t$$

and

$$E(\Delta \tilde{p}_{t+1}|B_t) \geqslant 0$$

Let

$$\tilde{r}_{t+1} = (\tilde{p}_{t+1} - p_t)/p_t = \text{one-period percentage return in period } t + 1$$

It is customary to express the submartingale as an equality,

$$E(\tilde{p}_{t+1}|B_t) = [1 + E(\tilde{r}_{t+1}|B_t)]p_t$$

where

$$E(\tilde{r}_{t+1}|B_t) \geqslant 0$$

policy of creating market *mistakes*' when increasing the acceleration of prices. The same argument—that the market will learn—applies to any *systematic* past mistakes the market may make in estimating returns. Systematic mistakes provide data that enters B_t. Therefore, in principle, market forecasts can take into account a non-stationary mean and the trading rule implication continues to hold. That is, eq. (3) holds even if the expectation expressed by (1) alters through time.

A further implication of the martingale property of (3) is that the fair game sequence (in Fama's terminology) of *excess returns, $\tilde{z}_{t+1}$*, where

$$\tilde{z}_{t+1} = \tilde{R}_{t+1} - E(\tilde{R}_{t+1}|B_t) \tag{4}$$

and

$$\tilde{R}_{t+1} = \text{one-period percentage return in period } t + 1$$

has zero serial covariances with respect to all elements of B_t [see Fama (1970, p. 391)]. With the additional assumption that the expected return is stationary through time, it follows that *returns themselves* are serially uncorrelated. However, if there is non-stationarity in the mean, zero expected *excess returns* do not necessarily imply serial independence of *returns*. For stocks, the variance of the return distribution appears to be so large relative to the mean and any non-stationarity of the mean that near-zero serial covariances of returns are in fact observed; that is, current stock returns are virtually unrelated to lagged stock returns. Nevertheless, there is an important theoretical difference between the trading rule implication and that of zero serial correlations which can be important empirically. If the mean returns are non-stationary and the data set is defined as past monetary data (a semi-strong-form test), the analogous test of serial covariance of stock returns with past monetary data need not *necessarily* indicate independence even if the market is efficient. Therefore it is desirable to use the trading rule test since it provides a natural measure of the degree of inefficiency implied by any observed non-independence of stock returns with past monetary data.

2.2. Specialized Resources, Competition and Efficient Markets

The existence of specialized resources is possibly inconsistent with an efficient market and may result in market inefficiency. One type of special resource occurs when an investor possesses a consistently superior predictive model not available to others. He may, for example, be endowed with special ability which enables him to use a publicly available data on subset B_t to develop new, private information. As a result, this investor may have higher expected trading profits than other investors. If his transactions are too small to affect market price, current price will not fully reflect B_t and there will be market inefficiency. Unless economists either have access to the 'system' and can test it or have access to the series of portfolio returns, such special ability will not be discovered. A second type of specialized resource occurs when an investor has consistent monopolistic access to data that is relevant to security values, such as new data (and therefore new information) which is obtained before it reaches the market as a whole. Even without a superior evaluation method, an investor who consistently obtains data ahead of others might have higher expected trading profits than others and again current price may not reflect the private data.[7]

An efficient market will arise under conditions that rule out specialized resources; namely, when transactions costs are zero, when all relevant data bearing on asset values reaches all investors simultaneously and costlessly and when all market participants agree on the implications of the data. (These conditions are clearly sufficient but not necessary.) An efficient market defined in this way is an *ideal* concept, analogous to an ideal competitive market in which transactions are costless, all participants have free and equal information about goods and no market participant (consumer or firm) affects prices. In fact, the EM model generalizes the concept of competitive equilibrium to describe in part the dynamic nature of the stochastic equilibria *through time* as market prices alter to reflect new information. It thereby avoids the inconsistency with the profit-maximization assumption which is characteristic of the dynamic models frequently used to describe the disequilibrium behavior of market prices.[8]

The hypothesis that prices fully reflect available information derives from profit-maximizing behavior by investors. If relevant publicly available data arises, investors have a profit incentive to trade upon it if it is not yet reflected in market price. For example, the Dow-Jones Ticker often provides information to investors one day before its appearance in the Wall Street Journal. With competition some investors will devote time and resources in order to exploit this data source by such means as renting tickers, spending time in broker's

---

[7] Specialized resources are not *necessarily* inconsistent with an efficient market since it is conceivable that investors can bring into existence new equilibrium prices by their own actions. That is, rents or excess profits are not necessarily inconsistent with a market in which at any time investors can expect to earn competitive rates of return. Inefficiency arises when information, public or private, is not reflected in market price. In an efficient market in which price fully reflects available information, the marginal investor can co-exist with the investor with special ability or information who earns rent on his special resources and, if price reflects all information, it will not pay the marginal investor to seek further information.

[8] See Gordon and Hynes (1970, p. 371) for a discussion of these models. The EM model is, as they point out, analogous to Muth's (1961) rational expectations model of dynamic price change.

offices which have tickers, calling their brokers frequently to check the news, etc.[9] Entry into such a 'data-exploitation' business is relatively easy and therefore we do not expect systematic lags in investor use of the data. Publicly available data can also be used to develop private trading rules. Here again competition will occur. Any investor can seek a trading rule; no investor can patent any rule he finds and therefore finding a profitable trading rule based on publicly available data is likely to be a difficult task.

Consider also monopolistic access to new data, that is, 'inside' information. Sole possession of new data promising excess profits provides incentives for activities designed to secure the information. The barriers are not insuperable. Resources may be expended to monitor new developments, to 'spy' on physical activities and on such persons as corporation officers and government officials who may have access to inside information. These activities, of course, will tend to cause market prices to reflect more quickly the 'inside' information.

Profit incentives to exploit information exist for markets other than capital markets so long as goods can be stored. The actions of profit-maximizing investors as they search out and use information contribute to market-efficiency. Therefore the efficient market hypothesis (and martingale price behavior) may apply to many markets. By contrast, models of price change with determinate price paths that allow profit possibilities net of transactions costs are inconsistent with profit-maximization and inconsistent with efficient markets. The EM model is highly descriptive of capital markets and there is reason to expect that its applicability extends to many other markets as well. Roll (1971), for example, examines the dynamic behavior of several price indexes in *goods* markets and finds evidence of martingale price behavior. In addition, Laffer and Ranson's (1971) results on an aggregate level also seem to be consistent with efficient markets in goods.

2.3. Empirical Caveats

Numerous tests of the EM model on a wide variety of data subsets with possible economic relevance to security pricing have been carried out. For publicly available data, very little evidence has been found that is inconsistent with the EM model. Most trading rules have not outperformed a B&H policy, including some which used powerful regression techniques that would have been unavailable and/or very costly to operate much before 1960. Careful analysis has usually demonstrated the failure of supposedly profitable trading rules to better B&H [see Fama and Blume (1966), Jensen and Bennington (1970)].

A number of incorrect procedures can cause a trading rule to outperform B&H including: (1) Defective treatment of dividends. Trading rules with short

---

[9]Individuals or firms that sell information also contribute to market efficiency.

selling must correct the returns for dividends which the short seller pays the lender. Omission biases the comparison in favor of the trading rule [see Fama and Blume (1966, p. 235)]. To omit dividends entirely from both the B&H policy and the trading rule (without short selling) also is incorrect. If the trading rule selects periods when stock price change is a relatively large component of the overall return, it can outperform the price performance of B&H even though the overall return with dividends may be the same for both. (2) Neglect of brokerage costs. Returns from a trading rule should be measured net of the costs of data search, model building and model operation. In practice this has meant subtracting brokerage costs from the gross returns of a trading rule although in principle other costs should be netted out before comparison with the B&H returns. Investors are free to engage in costly attempts to increase returns using available data. If successful in producing new information from available data, they should show returns, after deduction of the costs of their efforts, which are greater than B&H returns. On the other hand, if building and using a trading rule does not even cover its costs, i.e., is unprofitable, then the net returns from the trading rule will fall short of the B&H returns. Trading rules that outperform B&H do not automatically indicate market inefficiency since part of the total returns must cover the costs of using the rule. Therefore the costs of operating a trading rule must be subtracted from the gross returns before comparing them to the B&H returns. (3) Various forms of ex post selection bias such as finding a profitable trading rule that applies to one particular period after all the data and stock prices are available and failing to demonstrate that the rule is profitable outside the sample period. (4) Failure to adjust for risk. Since, given risk aversion, higher risk assets have higher expected returns, comparisons of a trading rule to a B&H policy should use assets of comparable risk—otherwise the trading rule can conceivably earn higher returns by operating on a higher risk portfolio. (5) Use of prices at which transactions could not have been executed in calculating the returns from the trading rule. (6) Allowing the use of data (at decision time) that is not available to the investor until after he makes his investment decision.

Some studies do not specifically give trading rules but nonetheless can be viewed in this context. For example, a regression model of the form

$$R_t = c_0 + \sum_{i=1}^{N} a_i \cdot \text{Data}_{t-i} + e_t \qquad (5)$$

(where R_t is stock returns) is consistent with the EM model if the explanatory power of the data (all past available data) is nil. [Recall that zero serial covariances of returns with past elements of the data set B_t is implied by (4) given stationarity.] If (5) has significant explanatory power, it can be interpreted as a *potential* trading rule, for if the model holds outside the sample period it may be a source of profits above B&H. Fama (1970, p. 394) has noted the ambiguity

in relating the degree of explanatory power of a regression to the expected
profitability of a trading rule. However, elsewhere Fama and Blume (1966,
pp. 240-241) present evidence showing a 'rather strong' degree of correspondence between the statistical test and the trading rule test. Therefore, significant
regressions as in (5) provide *potential* refutations of the EM model.

Other models requiring careful interpretation have the form

$$R_t = c_0 + \sum_{i=0}^{N} a_i \cdot \text{Data}_{t-1} + e_t \tag{6}$$

which includes the data term at time t. If the contemporaneous term in t, Data_t,
is *estimated* at time $t - 1$ from data available through time $t - 1$ and the equation
is used to predict stock returns in period t [cf. Homa and Jaffee (1971)],
(6) reduces to (5) which views returns as dependent on past data. If Data_t is
just the value of the independent variable that applies to period t, no predictive
value can be associated with Data_t since it becomes available contemporaneously
with R_t. Therefore, even if Data_t has significant explanatory power, no conflict
with the EM model arises as with Data_{t-1} and earlier terms. The presence of the
lagged terms in (5) or (6) is inconsistent with the EM model and must be treated
carefully if included.

For both (5) and (6), Data_t refers to data *published* in period t. When there
is a *lag in publishing data*, the index 't' will refer to different dates for R_t and
Data_t.[10] For example, with a one-month publication lag, R_t might refer to
November while Data_t for November will be October's figure. Previous studies
of money and stock prices neglect this point which is crucial in testing the EM
model. Neglect of the publication lag may produce significant regression equations which appear to be potential trading rules but, in fact, could not be so
used because the data is unavailable at the times when investment decisions
are made. In addition, all studies which use *revised* money supply data introduce
another source of unavailable information. FRB money supply revisions correct
earlier published money supply figures. Since revised data appears after the
fact, it should not be used in a trading rule that tests for efficiency with respect
to available data.

3. Models of the Money–Stock Return Relation

3.1. Basic Models

Friedman and Schwartz' (F&S) (1963) MP model assumes a growing economy
characterized by equilibrium rates of growth of such variables as prices, money

---

[10]Publication lag is discussed more fully in section 3.5 below.

stock and real income. In equilibrium, expected growth rates equal realized growth rates. An unexpected change in the rate of change (growth) of the money supply is the disturbance that produces portfolio adjustment.[11] Suppose that a report is published periodically which coincides with a realized rate of change of the money stock.[12] According to the non-predictive MP model, any unexpected change in the money growth rate occurring in a given period produces an effect on asset prices (as portfolio rearrangements occur) that is confined to the same period in which the disturbance occurs. In the predictive MP model, adjustment of asset prices to the disturbance takes place with a lag. The expected rate of return from holding securities consists of an expected percentage price change plus an expected dividend return. The monetary disturbance produces a temporary departure from equilibrium in the form of a once-and-for-all price change. Therefore, in the period(s) when stock prices incorporate the unexpected information, realized stock returns will differ from those expected by the amount of the unanticipated price change.

Define the following variables:

$$\tilde{R}_t = \text{stock return in period } t$$

$$\tilde{g}_t = \text{rate of growth of money stock in period } t$$

$E(\tilde{R}_t | B_{t-1}) = \text{expected stock return in period } t \text{ conditional upon informa-}$
tion set B_{t-1} at time $t - 1$

$E(\tilde{g}_t | B_{t-1}) = \text{expected rate of growth of money stock in period } t \text{ condi-}$
tional upon information set B_{t-1} at time $t - 1$

Also define

$$\tilde{R}_t = (\tilde{p}_t + \tilde{d}_t)/p_{t-1}$$
$$\tilde{g}_t = \tilde{M}_t/M_{t-1}$$

---

[11] Friedman and Schwartz and Sprinkel limit the monetary disturbance to unexpected changes in the equilibrium rate of growth of the money supply as does Meigs (1972). Changes in the money supply or simply levels of the money supply appear in some empirical interpretations of the MP model. Other studies of the 'lag in effect of monetary policy' [cf. Friedman (1961), Gibson (1970) and Cagan (1972)] tend to measure changes in 'monetary policy' by changes in money growth rates. This view omits consideration of control over margin requirements, credit controls, interest rate ceiling controls, innovations in reserve requirements such as on overseas' deposits, statements by Federal Reserve Officials, action in the Federal Funds market, etc. All of these items could influence stock returns. However, this study following the prior usage limits 'monetary policy' to policy with respect to the money supply, recognizing the narrowness of the definition.

[12] If there is no lag in collecting and publishing the data, the report will provide information as of the same period as the report. If there is a publication lag, the report in period t will refer to data occurring as of an earlier period (cf. section 3.5 below).

where

$$\tilde{p}_t = \text{stock price at end of period } t$$

$$\tilde{d}_t = \text{dividend on stock in period } t$$

$$\tilde{M}_t = \text{money stock at end of period } t$$

Finally, define

$$\tilde{R}_t^u = \tilde{R}_t - E(\tilde{R}_t | B_{t-1}) \quad \text{unexpected stock return in period } t$$

$$\tilde{g}_t^u = \tilde{g}_t - E(\tilde{g}_t | B_{t-1}) \quad \text{unexpected rate of growth of money stock in period } t$$

Consider a non-zero g_t^u. In the non-predictive MP model (and consistent with the EM model), the non-zero g_t^u is accompanied by a contemporaneous adjustment of stock prices, that is,

$$\tilde{R}_t^u = f(\tilde{g}_t^u) + \tilde{e}_t \tag{7}$$

$\tilde{e}_t$ is a random disturbance for all variables affecting stock returns in t other than $\tilde{g}_t^u$. The predictive version of the MP model implies a lag in the adjustment of stock prices, that is, the effect of g_t^u will be felt on $R_{t+1}^u, R_{t+2}^u, \ldots$ (as well as on R_t^u). By the same token, g_{t-1}^u will affect R_{t-1}^u, R_t^u, etc. It follows that in any time period t unexpected stock returns reflect in addition to g_t^u, the current error in predicting $E(\tilde{g}_t)$, the effects of past prediction errors as well, i.e.,

$$\tilde{R}_t^u = f(\tilde{g}_t^u, \tilde{g}_{t-1}^u, \tilde{g}_{t-2}^u, \ldots) + \tilde{e}_t \tag{8}$$

To specify (8) further, write

$$\tilde{R}_t^u = \tilde{R}_t - E(\tilde{R}_t | B_{t-1}) = f(\tilde{g}_t^u, \tilde{g}_{t-1}^u, \ldots) + \tilde{e}_t$$

or

$$\tilde{R}_t = E(\tilde{R}_t | B_{t-1}) + f(\tilde{g}_t^u, \tilde{g}_{t-1}^u, \ldots) + \tilde{e}_t \tag{9}$$

Take $\tilde{R}_t$ as the dependent variable and assume that the distribution of stock returns has a constant mean, that is,

$$E(\tilde{R}_t | B_{t-1}) = E(\tilde{R})^{13}$$

---

[13] $E(\tilde{R})$ can be estimated separately as Waud (1970) has done and subtracted from $\tilde{R}_t$ in measuring $\tilde{R}_t^u$. As noted above, the variability in the distribution of stock returns is so large relative to shifts in the mean that this refinement is not necessary.

One specific form of (9) is a linear form:

$$\widetilde{R}_t = c_0 + a_0(\widetilde{g}_t - E(\widetilde{g}_t|B_{t-1})) + a_1(\widetilde{g}_{t-1} - E(\widetilde{g}_{t-1}|B_{t-2})) + \ldots + \widetilde{e}_t \quad (10)$$

where $c_0 = E(\widetilde{R})$.

As a first specific model, estimate $E(\widetilde{g}_{t-i}|B_{t-i-1})$, which is the expected growth rate of the money supply in period $t - i$ at time $t - i - 1$, by a naive 'inertia' expectations model: assume that the growth rate expected in period $t - i$ is the most recent growth rate, g_{t-i-1}. Since g_{t-i-1} measures the expectation with error, the error term $\widetilde{e}_t$ now absorbs all the errors in estimating the lagged terms.[14] Thus we obtain

$$R_t = c_0 + a_0(g_t - g_{t-1}) + a_1(g_{t-1} - g_{t-2}) + \ldots + e_t \quad (11)$$

Eq. (11), which expresses stock returns as a linear function of contemporaneous and lagged changes in the rate of change of the money supply, is one specification of both the non-predictive and predictive forms of the MP model. The contribution of the predictive MP model to (11) consists of the lagged terms, the hypothesis being that they will contribute significantly to explaining the variation in current stock returns. Zero explanatory power of the lagged variables is consistent with the EM model and the EM model implies that the explanatory power of the lagged terms will be small enough that they cannot generate excess profits when used in a trading rule. The contribution of the non-predictive MP model to (11) is the current or contemporaneous term which should be significant according to the non-predictive MP model. It is consistent with the EM model if this is the case since the current term should be reflected in current stock prices and, in any event, cannot be used in a trading rule that seeks to predict R_t.[15] The non-predictive MP model can be tested with (11) containing both current and lagged terms and can use unavailable data (since the EM model is not an issue in this case), but if lagged terms are included, care should be taken in interpreting the significance of *individual* lagged terms (cf. section 4.5) since first differences in growth ratea are not serially independent.

Eq. (11) is very close to Hamburger and Kochin's (1972) regression—their dependent variable being changes in stock prices rather than stock returns.[16]

---

[14]There is also attenuation bias since the true regression variables are necessarily measured with error. Those attempting to use the lagged terms for prediction purposes must also use the data as measured.

[15]It is also consistent with the EM model if the contemporaneous term *lacks* significance.

[16]Their use of changes in stock prices does not appear to make a substantial difference. However, since the variability of stock price changes increases with the level of price of the stock, use of a stock price relative or stock return variable will avoid heteroscedasticity. Also their estimation procedure uses the Almon lag technique which is inappropriate for testing the predictive MP model (cf. section 5). Cagan (1972) has also derived (11) in the context of a dynamic form of the MP model.

Regressions such as those of Cooper (1972) and Meigs (1972) in which the independent variables are simply rates of growth of the money supply can be obtained as follows. Assume in (10) that

$$E(\widetilde{g}_{t-i}|B_{t-i-1}) = E(\widetilde{g}) \qquad \text{for all } i$$

that is, that the growth rate series has a stationary mean.[17] Then the mean values weighted by the coefficients can be absorbed into the constant term of the equation and stock returns can be considered a function of growth rates alone.

The approach of (7)–(10) can also be used to obtain models like those of Sprinkel and Reilly and Lewis which use moving averages of the monetary variables. Define

$$\widetilde{g}_{t,\text{ma}} = (\widetilde{g}_t + \widetilde{g}_{t-1} + \ldots + \widetilde{g}_{t-5})/6$$

$$\widetilde{g}^{\,u}_{t,\text{ma}} = \widetilde{g}_{t,\text{ma}} - E(\widetilde{g}_{t,\text{ma}}|B_{t-1})$$

To arrive at a predictive formulation using only lagged moving averages requires rewriting the basic model in (8) as

$$\widetilde{R}^{u}_{t} = f(\widetilde{g}^{\,u}_{t-1,\text{ma}}, \widetilde{g}^{\,u}_{t-2,\text{ma}}, \ldots) + \widetilde{e}_t \qquad (12)$$

The idea here is that the basic unit of observation to investors is the moving average of growth rates, presumably because of too much noise in one-period growth rates. A change in rate of change now means a change in the moving average of growth rates. These changes are what Sprinkel examined (cf. section 5). The model becomes

$$R_t = c_0 + a_0(g_{t-1,\text{ma}} - g_{t-2,\text{ma}}) + \ldots + e_t \qquad (13)$$

making the analogous naive expectations assumption that

$$E(\widetilde{g}_{t-i,\text{ma}}|B_{t-i-1}) = g_{t-i-1,\text{ma}} \qquad \text{for all } i$$

3.2. Comparison of Basic Models to Models Using Rates of Inflation

In section 3.1 the MP model of F&S provides a justification for expressing stock returns as a function of money growth rates or first differences in growth

---

[17]The correlogram of the growth rate series over 1947–70 indicates that the growth rate series is a stationary 3rd-order autoregressive process. Cooper (1972) and Booth and Ibbotson (1970) find the same result. Thus although the mean is stationary, the autoregressiveness in

rates.[18] Fama (1973) approaches the question of efficiency in the bond market by considering inflation rates. This section compares the Fama approach to the models of section 3.1.

Define:

$\tilde{c}_t$ = % change in purchasing power from $t - 1$ to t

$\tilde{r}_t$ = real return from $t - 1$ to t

$\tilde{R}_t$ = nominal return from $t - 1$ to t

Fama's equations, (14), (16) and (19), are compared to the equations that are relevant for stocks. For bonds, neglecting a second-order term,

$$\tilde{r}_t = R_t + \tilde{c}_t \tag{14}$$

This is a definition of real return; the one-period bond return from $t - 1$ to t, R_t, is observable at time $t - 1$ and is not written as a random variable. For stocks:

$$\tilde{r}_t = \tilde{R}_t + \tilde{c}_t \tag{15}$$

The change here is that nominal stock returns from $t - 1$ to t are also a random variable at time $t - 1$. Next, take conditional expectations of (14) and (15),

$$E(\tilde{r}_t|B_{t-1}) = R_t + E(\tilde{c}_t|B_{t-1}) \qquad \text{for bonds} \tag{16}$$

$$E(\tilde{r}_t|B_{t-1}) = E(\tilde{R}_t|B_{t-1}) + E(\tilde{c}_t|B_{t-1}) \qquad \text{for stocks} \tag{17}$$

For both stocks and bonds, it is necessary to assume a stationary mean real return through time:

$$E(\tilde{r}_t|B_{t-1}) = E(\tilde{r}) \tag{18}$$

Then for bonds, (16) becomes

$$E(\tilde{c}_t|B_{t-1}) = E(\tilde{r}) - R_t \tag{19}$$

---

the series implies that better predictions of $E(\tilde{g}_t|B_{t-1})$ are possible than simply the mean value of a sample of past observations. All models, using growth rates, changes in growth rates and autoregressive estimates of growth rates as independent variables, are tested below.

[18]A more sophisticated expectations model for monetary growth is considered below in section 3.4.

Notice that the information set at time $t - 1$, B_{t-1}, is absent from the right-hand side of (19). This is crucial to Fama's important result that the expected change in purchasing power given information at time $t - 1$ is not directly dependent on past changes in purchasing power. However, for stocks, (17) becomes

$$E(\tilde{c}_t|B_{t-1}) = E(\tilde{r}) - E(\tilde{R}_t|B_{t-1}) \tag{20}$$

The difference here is that the information set remains on the right-hand side of the equation. Since B_{t-1} is on both sides, (20) can be written equivalently:

$$E(\tilde{R}_t|B_{t-1}) = E(\tilde{r}) - E(\tilde{c}_t|B_{t-1}) \tag{21}$$

The justification for using money supply variables rests in this model on their relation to changes in purchasing power. Thus the anticipated change in purchasing power at time $t - 1$ may possibly be viewed as a function $h[\ ]$ of the anticipated money supply growth rate,

$$E(\tilde{c}_t|B_{t-1}) = h[E(\tilde{g}_t|B_{t-1})] \tag{22}$$

Since B_{t-1} includes such data subsets as money growth rates and errors in predicting money growth rates, h can be written as a function of this (or other) data. Substituting (22) into (21) gives a model for conditional nominal expected returns:

$$E(\tilde{R}_t|B_{t-1}) = E(\tilde{r}) + h[E(\tilde{g}_t|B_{t-1})] \tag{23}$$

(absorbing the minus sign into h). Recall that from (9) the non-predictive MP model could be written:

$$\tilde{R}_t = E(\tilde{R}_t|B_{t-1}) + f(\tilde{g}_t^u) + \tilde{e}_t \tag{24}$$

Substituting (23) into (24) gives:

$$\tilde{R}_t = E(\tilde{r}) + h[E(\tilde{g}_t|B_{t-1})] + f(\tilde{g}_t^u) + \tilde{e}_t \tag{25}$$

Eq. (25) is a more detailed specification of the basic model than (24). Although the implications of both are much the same, there are several differences. In (25) the intercept term assumed constant is $E(\tilde{r})$, the expected real return. Also in (25) lagged error terms in g^u are not explicitly present. However, past elements of B_{t-1} such as past growth rates or prediction errors for growth rates may be viewed as possibly entering the right-hand side through the arguments of the h function. Eq. (25) thus allows for the introduction of the possibly significant lagged terms in a manner different from the predictive MP model:

lagged terms in this case might influence the dynamic behavior of $E(\tilde{R}_t|B_{t-1})$ but at any time expected *excess* returns, conditional upon B_{t-1}, will still be zero and trading rules will be unprofitable.

3.3. Efficient Market Contribution to the Basic Model

In the predictive MP model stock returns are viewed as a function of *past* monetary growth rates or changes in growth rates (which represent deviations from anticipations). The EM model suggests that the market will extract information from the current data set B_t to form expectations of *future* growth rates or growth rate changes. These estimates will affect current stock returns $\tilde{R}_t$ in an efficient market if the MP model also holds (i.e., money supply growth rates are indeed relevant to stock returns). If the market is correct on average in its expectations, then actual realized future growth rates or growth rate changes provide measures of the anticipated variables. A test of the hypothesis that stock returns use information in B_t to anticipate future monetary variables can therefore be obtained by examining the relationship of $\tilde{R}_t$ to variables such as g_{t+i} and $g_{t+i} - g_{t+i-1}$ for $i > 0$. These terms are future monetary variables.

To be more precise, recall that in an efficient market $E(\tilde{p}_{t+1}|B_t) = p_t$. Current price can be viewed as dependent upon current data B_t via the effect of B_t in influencing expectations of future price. Since $\tilde{R}_t$ is directly related to $\tilde{p}_t$, B_t can be viewed as contributing to the random error term in (25). Among other things, B_t may provide data concerning future economic variables that can influence future stock prices; we expect $\tilde{R}_t$ to be influenced by such data in an efficient market. The MP model suggests that monetary data is of particular importance, so that future growth rates of the money supply (or changes in growth rates) may provide excellent proxy variables for any of the unspecified data in B_t which affects $\tilde{R}_t$. $\tilde{R}_t$ will be related to future monetary variables if (1) returns *are* affected by the expected future monetary variables and (2) there *is* data in B_t that results in correct anticipations of future variables. This conclusion follows from the fact that at time t the market does not yet know the future monetary variables. Thus, to sum up, if the future terms prove significant, it is evidence consistent with the dual hypothesis that monetary variables affect stock returns and stock returns anticipate these variables on the basis of information available in the present. Such anticipations are consistent with an efficient market in which price fully reflects available information.

Sims' (1972) test for 'unidirectional causality' provides another reason for testing a model with future terms. His test for whether or not causality runs one-way from a set of variables such as $[g_{t-1}, g_{t-2}, \ldots]$ to $\tilde{R}_t$ is to include future terms g_{t+i} in the regression and test the coefficients of the future terms for significance. If the future money terms are insignificant as a group, the test concludes that causality runs from money to stock returns only. Sims has also argued for a converse interpretation of this test. In this case, should the future terms prove significant, the converse interpretation would be that causality runs from stock returns to money. Note that if the EM and non-predictive MP models hold, we *expect future money terms to be significant,* providing a conflict with the interpretation that causality runs from stock returns to money.[19]

3.4. A Refined Expectations Model

The models of (24) or (25) express stock returns as a function of current and possibly lagged unanticipated rates of monetary growth where the monetary disturbances are measured by first differences in growth rates of the money supply [cf. (11)]. This use of first differences is a method of removing trend from the time series to obtain the unanticipated components. In another sense it is a method of making forecasts using the time series itself with $g_t - g_{t-1}$ having the interpretation of a prediction error. However, using g_{t-1} to forecast $E(\tilde{g}_t|B_{t-1})$ has the major failing that successive prediction errors are correlated since first differences of monetary growth rates are strongly autocorrelated. This implies failure to use all the information in the time series [see Nelson (1973, p. 207)].

An efficient market does not underutilize information and would not fail to use at least the predictive information inherent in the autoregressiveness of the money supply growth rate series—otherwise, if stock returns were contemporaneously related to growth rates, a profitable trading rule could be based on predicting next period's growth rate given current and past growth rates. Denote by g_t^* an estimate of $E(\tilde{g}_t|B_{t-1})$ obtained by taking into account the autoregressiveness in the growth rate of the money supply time series. (A regression model is used in section 4 to obtain these estimates.) Variables such as $g_t - g_t^*$ can be interpreted as the 'unpredictable' portion of the growth rate series based on the autoregressive relation. They are forecast errors which *do* largely take into account information about future growth rates contained in the time series itself. The manner in which the series $[g_t - g_t^*]$ is obtained ensures a nearly serially uncorrelated, or 'whitened', time series which provides measures of the monetary disturbances of each period.

Since stock returns can conceivably anticipate future components of even the $[g_t - g_t^*]$ series, it may appear paradoxical that stock returns can anticipate these 'unpredictable' variables. The paradox is explained by the fact that the market's expectations model for future growth rate changes need not be based solely on the time series of growth rates. The prediction errors, $[g_t - g_t^*]$, arise

---

[19]See section 4.5 and footnote 37 for further discussion.

contingent upon the autoregressive expectations model. If $\tilde{R}_t$ anticipates these errors, it means effectively that the market in forming anticipations is using information from B_t in addition to the past growth rates of the money supply.[20]

Cooper (1972, p. 51) suggests that the autocorrelation in money growth rates is enough to make it appear that stock returns anticipate money growth rates, since if $\tilde{R}_t$ is related to g_t it may also be related to g_{t+1}. By removing from the growth rate series the growth rate dependencies, it will be possible to tell whether stock returns anticipate money growth rates over and above this autoregressiveness. In addition, when the regressors are independent (or nearly so) individual t-values and simple correlation coefficients should be useful in determining clearly which individual regressors are important.

3.5. Data Availability in Testing the Models

Investors cannot use unavailable information to make decisions. Published reports usually give the money supply of an earlier date—1–2 months earlier in the case of monthly FRB reports. Therefore, regression models testing the predictive MP model must take care to match stock returns in period t to data *available* in period t. If the *non-predictive* model holds and publication lag is neglected, a regression may show stock returns in period t related to the money variable in $t - 1$ or $t - 2$ but there will be no inconsistency with the EM model due to the unavailability of the data in time for predictive use. For example, assume that on October 31 data for the money supply as of September 30 is the latest available that can be used before buying or selling on November 1. In this case, to confer upon the trading rule knowledge of the October 31 money supply gives it an advantage that can spell the difference between an unprofitable and a profitable trading rule.[21]

A similar data issue occurs with revised and unrevised money supply data. The FRB money supply revisions attempt to correct earlier omissions and widen the sampling of banks. They presumably move the revised money supply closer to the actual money supply which prevailed in the past but they appear long after the fact and are not publicly available in the time periods to which the revisions apply. Therefore, to test the *predictive* MP model against the EM model, or to test trading rules, *unrevised* data should be used.

On the other hand, in testing the non-predictive MP model the actual money supply known ex post can be used since, according to the MP model,

---

[20] In the event that stock returns anticipate the errors, $g_t - g_t^*$, the economist can improve his prediction model for growth rates by incorporating stock returns as an independent variable.

[21] In fact, knowledge of data with no lag provided a distinct advantage until the late 1960's when the advent of weekly data reports apparently erased it by providing most of the month's money supply data by the end of the month (cf. section 4.8).

portfolio adjustments depend upon the actual money supply whether investors receive this number in published form or not. In this case there is no possible conflict with the EM model since the hypothesis being tested is whether monetary variables have any relation at all to stock returns. $\tilde{R}_t$ may be affected by a wide variety of variables, including published reports of the unrevised money supply and, for example, securities dealers' unpublished knowledge of the money portion of their portfolios. Since either unrevised or revised data can be used, it is essentially an empirical question which to use. However, revised data is likely to reflect more economic information than unrevised data since it encompasses a broader sampling of banks. Therefore, it may better measure elements of B_t and be more closely related to $\tilde{R}_t$. Publication lag can also be neglected in testing the non-predictive model. The money supply as of its date of occurrence can be used since the EM model is not being tested. The same arguments as for revised data suggest that $\tilde{R}_t$ is likely to be more strongly related to the actually occurring money supply than to data published in t.

4. Major Empirical Results

4.1. Description of Data

The narrowly-defined money supply, M_1, is the primary monetary aggregate used in this study to compute growth rates of the money supply and changes in growth rates.[22] Monthly *revised* data was obtained from tabulations appearing in the December 1970 and February 1973 issues of the Federal Reserve Bulletin. The revised data in the FRB tabulations is itself based upon data appearing monthly in the FRB in the Table entitled 'Measures of the money stock'.[23] The revised money stock measures employ averages of daily figures. All monthly *unrevised* data was obtained from individual issues of the FRB in its original form as published for the first time in the Table entitled 'Details of deposits and currency'. This series, published continuously since 1946, contains money data as of the last Wednesday of the month.[24] The FRB provides (revised and unrevised) data that is either adjusted or unadjusted for seasonal factors. Quarterly growth rates of the money supply are derived from

---

[22] M_1 consists of demand deposits of commercial banks corrected for interbank deposits and float plus currency.

[23] See, for example, the November 1971 issue of the FRB 'Measures of the money stock', p. A-17, provides data for the revision appearing on pp. 884–955. The October 27, 1971 seasonally adjusted M_1 figure is $227.7 billion.

[24] For October 27, 1971, the unrevised and seasonally adjusted money supply is $215.4 billion.

these monthly data series. Weekly data was obtained from the revised and adjusted data appearing in the December 1970 FRB.

F&S (1970) is the source for most other monetary data used below, providing data for M_1 prior to 1947, M_2 and M_3 over 1947-70; this was also Sprinkel's data source.[25] All of this data is revised and adjusted. The FRB Table 'Measures of the money stock' is used to extend the F&S series beyond 1970.

The monthly stock return variable is the Fisher Link Relative Series and was drawn from the University of Chicago Center for Research in Security Prices Monthly Price Relative File for the period 2/26-6/70. Months outside this period use price relatives based on the Standard & Poor 500 Index of stock prices. Quarterly returns are computed from the monthly returns by multiplication of three consecutive monthly relatives. Weekly stock returns are price relatives computed from Standard & Poor's 500 Weekly Index. Commercial paper rates are drawn from a series of dealer commercial paper rates prepared by Black, Jensen and Scholes (1972).[26]

4.2. Regression Tests of Efficient Market Model versus Predictive MP Model

Table 1 reports summary statistics for monthly regressions of stock returns on past *available* monetary data based on M_1. The variable p_{t-1} is defined as the growth rate of the money supply *published* at time $t - 1$ and available to investors at $t - 1$. For example, suppose t refers to November 30, 1971, and R_t is stock returns for November 1971. The data published at time $t - 1$ (i.e., October 31, 1971) is available for use by investors in making investment decisions for November. This data would consist of the unrevised money supply figure as of September 30, 1971 due to the lag in reporting data. p_{t-1} would be the growth rate of the money supply from August 31, 1971 to September 30, 1971. (It is assumed that investment decisions for November are made November 1.) The statistics shown in the table are R^2 and $\bar{R}^2$, the multiple coefficients of determination, unadjusted and adjusted, respectively; $D.W.$, The Durbin-Watson statistic; $s(e)$, the adjusted standard deviation of the residuals; and the F-statistic for the regression. The regressions contain 17 lagged months of data. A 17-month period was chosen to encompass the Sprinkel 15-month lead (see section 5) and most other reported lagged reactions for the MP model. Preliminary tests indicated that an additional 8–13 months data

---

[25]M_2 consists of M_1 plus time deposits adjusted of commercial banks. M_3 consists of M_2 plus deposits at mutual savings banks plus deposits at the postal savings system.

[26]The dealer commercial paper rates were obtained from Banking and Monetary Statistics, Board of Governors of the Federal Reserve System, Washington, D.C.

Table 1
Summary Statistics from the Monthly Regression Models[a]

$$R_t = c_0 + \sum_{t=1}^{17} a_{t-i}(p_{t-i} - p_{t-i-1}) + e_t.$$

Line	Period	R^2	$\bar{R}^2$	D.W.	s(e)	F-statistic[b]
(1)	8/48–3/70	0.082	0.018	1.87	0.0399	1.278
(2)	8/48–5/60	0.208	0.100	1.97	0.0377	1.919*
(3)	6/60–3/70	0.146	0.001	1.78	0.0453	1.008
(4)	7/48–3/70[c]	0.099	0.036	1.89	0.0396	1.574
(5)	7/48–5/60[c]	0.213	0.106	1.97	0.0339	1.986*
(6)	6/60–3/70	0.145	0.000	1.80	0.0454	0.998
(7)	8/48–3/70	0.090	0.026	1.86	0.0397	1.403

[a]R_t = stock returns and p_t = growth rate of the money supply published in t. Regressions 4–6 use growth rates of the money supply, p_t, as independent variables. All data is M_1 unrevised and unadjusted except for line 7 which uses adjusted data.
[b]Asterisk indicates significance at 5% level.
[c]Use of growth rates allows an additional month of data at start of period.

did not greatly affect $\bar{R}^2$; conversely, reducinb the number of lagged terms to 9 affects $\bar{R}^2$ only slightly.

Recall that consistency with the EM model requires that the explanatory power of past available data be nil, in direct contradiction to the predictive form of the monetary model which stresses the importance of lagged money growth rates in influencing stock returns. The regression results over the entire period, 8/48–3/70, are entirely consistent with the efficient market model, whether changes in money growth rates or money growth rates alone are the lagged variables (table 1, lines 1, 4 and 7). Based on the F-statistics, the hypothesis cannot be rejected that the set of lagged coefficients is insignificantly different from zero over this period.[27] Over the entire period, adjusted R^2's vary from 0.018 to 0.036, depending on the monetary variable used. Correlations this order of magnitude and smaller are expected in efficient markets in which current returns are essentially independent of past information [cf. Kendall (1953), Alexander (1961), Moore (1962) and Fama (1965)]. The positive lag of stock returns behind changes in monetary policy as measured by changes in monetary growth appears to be virtually negligible in these regressions over 1948–70.

While such small $\bar{R}^2$'s are consistent with an efficient market, it bears

---

[27]Specifically, the hypothesis is that

$$a_{t-1} = a_{t-2} = \ldots = a_{t-17} = 0$$

repeating that regression tests of the EM model which use returns rather than excess returns should if possible be supplemented by tests of trading rules (see section 4.6 below) since the EM hypothesis implies the absence of excess trading profits. The significance (in terms of trading profits) of a regression model using returns as the dependent variable cannot be unequivocally related to its statistical significance. Lack of statistical significance is consistent with the EM model but statistical significance does not necessarily imply trading rule profits. Conversely, trading rule profits may occur in periods when statistical significance is absent. This may happen by change or it may possibly occur if the power of the two tests in testing the EM hypothesis differs.

When 1948–70 is split into two subperiods, the regression results over the earlier subperiod, 1948–60, are inconsistent with the EM model since the lagged coefficients are significant at a 5% level (table 1, lines 2 and 5). However, over 1960–70 the results are consistent with the EM model, the F-statistic being only 1.008 (table 1, lines 3 and 6). The regression model over 1948–60 with $\bar{R}^2$ of 0.10 does not appear to imply a profitable trading rule (cf. sections 4.6–4.7 below). However, this difference in behavior over the subperiods is noticeable and raises the question of whether the stock market was inefficient with respect to monetary data prior to 1960. To examine this issue, the behavior of the model was further examined over other subperiods with the F&S data. The independent variables in these tests, reported in table 2, use g_{t-i}, the growth of the money supply *occurring* during period $t - i$, as contrasted with p_{t-i}, the growth rate *published* at time $t - i$. For example, if R_t is dated November 30,

Table 2
Summary Statistics from the Monthly Regression Models[a]

$$R_t = c_0 + \sum_{t=1}^{N} a_{t-i}(g_{t-i} - g_{t-i-1}) + e_t$$

Line	Period	R^2	$\bar{R}^2$	D.W.	s(e)	F-statistic[b]	Data
(1)	8/16–4/71	0.043	0.013	1.60	0.0769	1.424	M_1
(2)	8/16–2/46	0.049	−0.009	1.58	0.0994	0.840	M_1
(3)	11/48–2/72	0.084	0.010	1.67	0.0405	1.141	M_1
(4)	8/18–2/60	0.056	0.023	1.43	–	1.689*	M_1
(5)	8/18–4/39	0.085	0.022	1.34	–	1.262	M_1
(6)	5/39–1/60	0.053	−0.013	1.63	–	0.760	M_1
(7)	8/48–4/68	0.109	0.040	1.87	0.0383	1.576	M_2
(8)	8/48–4/72	0.072	0.013	1.73	0.0407	1.222	M_2
(9)	8/48–4/68	0.096	0.026	1.88	0.0385	1.375	M_3

[a]R_t = stock returns and g_t = growth rate of the money supply occurring in period t. N, the number of lagged terms in the regression, is 20 in lines 1–3 and 17 in lines 4–9. All data is revised and adjusted.
[b]Asterisk indicates significance at 5% level.

1971, g_{t-i} is the growth rate of the money supply from September 30, 1971 to October 31, 1971. From approximately 1916–39, no money supply series was published at all; from about 1939–43, publication was with a lengthy and irregular lag of about six months; from 1943–46, data was published in the FRB with a three-month lag. By using g_{t-i} and by examining periods prior to 1939, revised money data is used (with no publication lag) that was collected and published long after its occurrence. This raises the possibility that a dependence may be observed which could not have in fact been used in a trading rule. Nevertheless, the evidence is largely consistent with the efficient market model. Over the subperiods 8/16–2/46, 8/18–4/39 and 5/39–1/60, the F-values of the regressions are very small, the largest being 1.257. The regression for 8/18–2/60 with an F-value of 1.69 does pass the 5% critical value of 1.63. The largest $\bar{R}^2$ of these regressions is 0.023. Over the entire period, 8/16–4/71, the lagged terms are not significant, and when the 1948–60 period is extended back to 1939, they are not significant. The latter result (as well as the other subperiod results) seems to indicate that the significance during the 1948–60 period arises from statistical variability, since the money data over 1939–60 is primarily Federal Reserve data of the same type as the 1948–60 data.

Sprinkel's (1964) graphical comparisons of money changes and stock price changes used 6-month moving averages of money growth rates. When these are used in the 1918–60 regression, $\bar{R}^2$ falls to 0.0104 and the F-value to 1.308, statistically insignificant.[28] Sprinkel (1971, p. 226) argues for a 'noticeable positive relation' not only in the years 1920-50 but also in the 1950's and 1960's. By and large, the statistical tests indicate the near total unimportance of the lagged money terms, and where statistical significance does occur (1948-60), the magnitude of the relationship appears to be so small as likely to be of no trading rule significance whatever.

Table 3 (lines 1 and 4) presents tests of the EM model using weekly and quarterly M_1 data and table 2 includes several tests using monthly data on M_2 and M_3. In these regression tests as in those using the F&S data, monetary growth rates which *occurred* during lagged periods are used. Even assuming zero publication lag, the lagged terms using M_2 and M_3 are not significantly different from zero (5% level)(cf. table 2, lines 7, 8 and 9). The lagged quarterly results (table 3, line 4) are in marked contrast to the apparent significance of

---

[28]The regression is

$$R_t = c_0 + \sum_{i=1}^{17} a_{t-1}(g_{t-i\,\mathrm{ma}} - g_{t-i-1\,\mathrm{ma}}) + e_t$$

where

$$g_{t,\mathrm{ma}} = (g_t + \ldots + g_{t-5})/6$$

Table 3

Summary Statistics from Regression Models Using Weekly and Quarterly Data, M_1, Revised and Adjusted[a]

$$R_t = c_0 + \sum_{t=j}^{s} a_{t-i}(g_{t-i} - g_{t-i-1}) + e_t$$

Line	Period	R^2	$\bar{R}^2$	F-statistic[b]	j^c	s^c	
(1)	7/1/60–11/26/69	0.044	−0.006	0.888	1	24	
(2)	7/1/60–11/26/69	0.059	−0.009	0.862	0	24	Weekly
(3)	7/1/60–11/26/69	0.099	0.033	1.511*	−8	24	
(4)	III/49–II/72	0.156	0.075	1.923	1	8	
(5)	III/49–II/72	0.305	0.209	3.189**	0	8	Quarterly
(6)	III/49–II/72	0.377	0.292	4.404**	−2	8	

[a]R_t = stock returns and g_t = growth rate of the money supply occurring in period t. Lines 1–3 are weekly models; lines 4–6 are quarterly models.

[b]Asterisk indicates significance at 5% level; two asterisks indicate significance at 1% level.

[c]Indices to sum in regression model: j = 1 gives all lagged terms; j = 0 adds current term; j negative adds future terms.

lagged terms in the similar Hamburger and Kochin (1972) regression which uses the Almon lag technique with the current term in the regression (see section 5). Eight lagged quarters of money data are not significant (5% level). The results with lagged weekly data (table 3, line 1) use a data series that was not publicly available until 1967 and also assume no lag in publication; yet the F-statistic for lagged terms is less than 1.0 and the $\bar{R}^2$ negative. The quarterly and weekly results are convincing evidence for market efficiency.[29]

In summary, the predictive MP model finds next to no support in these linear models while the data almost without exception appear to favor the EM model. If monetary policy is taken to mean money growth rates or changes in growth rates, there is virtually no evidence here to support the hypothesis that it operates with a lag upon the stock market. In this case at least, the lag in effect of monetary policy is essentially zero.

4.3. Tests of the Non-predictive MP Model

Tests of the EM model versus the predictive MP model leave unanswered the question: are stock returns in period t related to monetary growth rates occurring in period t, as the non-predictive MP model suggests? To test this hypothesis,

---

[29]Those who may question the quality of the weekly money supply data (as an explanation for these results) must explain the significant dependence of weekly stock returns on *future* weekly money data (cf. section 4.4 below).

Table 4
Summary Statistics from the Monthly Regression Models[a]

$$R_t = c_0 + \sum_{t=0}^{17} a_{t-i}(g_{t-i} - g_{t-i-1}) + e_t$$

Line	Period	R^2	$\bar{R}^2$	F-statstic[b]	Data
(1)	8/48–3/70	0.115	0.049	1.741*	M_1; revised, adjusted
(2)	8/48–3/70	0.107	0.040	1.597	M_1; unrevised, unadjusted
(3)	8/48–3/70	0.166	0.104	2.668*	M_1; revised, unadjusted
(4)	8/48–3/70	0.120	0.054	1.818*	M_1; unrevised, unadjusted
(5)	8/48–5/60	0.219	0.105	1.918*	M_1; revised, adjusted
(6)	8/48–5/60	0.240	0.128	2.127**	M_1; revised, unadjusted
(7)	8/48–5/60	0.308	0.207	3.045**	M_1; unrevised, unadjusted
(8)	6/60–3/70	0.176	0.026	1.176	M_1; revised, adjusted
(9)	6/60–3/70	0.264	0.130	1.975*	M_1; revised, unadjusted
(10)	6/60–3/70	0.139	−0.018	0.886	M_1; unrevised, unadjusted
(11)	8/16–2/46	0.052	−0.009	0.849	M_1; revised, adjusted[c]
(12)	8/18–2/60	0.082	0.047	2.375**	M_1; revised, adjusted
(13)	8/16–4/71	0.046	0.015	1.473	M_1; revised, adjusted
(14)	8/48–4/72	0.079	0.016	1.261	M_2; revised, adjusted
(15)	8/48–4/68	0.102	0.028	1.380	M_3; revised, adjusted

[a]R_t = stock returns and g_t = growth rate of the money supply occurring in period t.
[b]Asterisk indicates significance at 5% level; two asterisks indicate significance at 1% level.
[c]Regression over 8/16–2/46 has 20 lagged terms.

the regression models are enlarged to include the contemporaneously occurring growth rates. These models do not test the EM model since monetary data for period t is ordinarily unavailable until after period t.

Table 4 reports regression results for models with current terms for a number of time periods (monthly data). Over 1948–70 (lines 1–4), there does seem to have been a significant (although weak) relationship of stock returns to currently occurring monetary variables, with $\bar{R}^2$'s ranging from 0.040 to 0.104. The relationships are more marked when revised data is used.[30] Removal of the publication lag also contributes to these improved results. For example, if the line 4 regression in table 4 using unrevised and unadjusted data with $\bar{R}^2$ of 0.054 is run imposing the lag in publication, $\bar{R}^2$ falls to 0.033 and F-value to 1.490, not significant.[31]

---

[30]In all models over 1948–70, $\bar{R}^2$'s are higher when data from the FRB 1970 revision is substituted for unrevised data, holding constant the seasonal adjustment factor. However, the FRB 1973 revision gives slightly lower $\bar{R}^2$'s using unadjusted data than the 1970 revision, and slightly higher $\bar{R}^2$'s using adjusted data [cf. Rozeff (1974, pp. 98–99)].

[31]Similar results occur in regressions using lagged terms only: for unrevised and unadjusted data, removal of the publication lag improves $\bar{R}^2$ from 0.018 to a significant 0.045. This

Examining subperiods (lines 5–10), the relationship appears stronger in the period 1948–60 than 1960–70, as in table 1. Using the F&S data over 8/16–2/46 (line 11), the relation is insignificant. Similarly, the monthly data using M_2 or M_3 do not support the non-predictive model over 1948–72 (lines 14 and 15). Results on the non-predictive model using weekly and quarterly data appear in table 3. The weekly data with an $\bar{R}^2$ of –0.009 (line 2) provides no support for the model. On the other hand, a quite strong relationship emerges using quarterly data; $\bar{R}^2$ is 0.209 and there is significance at a 1% level (table 3, line 5), providing a marked contrast to the same model with lagged terms only (line 4). The result with quarterly data is consistent with the Hamburger and Kochin result over 1956–70 which finds an $\bar{R}^2$ of 0.26.

Thus, the post-1948 tests of the non-predictive MP model using monthly data on M_1 tend to support the model, although not strongly. The test with quarterly data provides a substantial $\bar{R}^2$ and indicates an important contemporaneous relationship of stock returns to monetary growth rates. Weekly correlations are probably much lower because of the measurement error in weekly money supply data.[32] The pre-1948 test of the non-predictive MP model using the F&S data provides a marked contrast with an $\bar{R}^2$ of but –0.009. A possible explanation of this difference in behavior is that the nature of the relation altered after 1946. However, tests of the equality of coefficients between the two relations do not seem to support this view. The relationship appears to be a stable one.[33] An alternative explanation is that the pre-1948 F&S money supply series has a greater measurement error than the post-1948 data. This could weaken the observed relationship.

4.4. Non-predictive MP Model with Anticipations

I noted above that in an efficient market, current stock returns might be partly explained by anticipations of future monetary variables based on infor-

---

aspect of the results is further examined in section 4.8 by examining trading rules which are allowed use of the $t - 1$ term with no publication lag.

[32] The quarterly regressions have higher R^2's than the monthly regressions and these have higher R^2's than the weekly regressions. This behavior appears to be explainable in familiar terms as arising from the greater random or transitory or measurement error component in the shorter term data. Suppose, taking an analogous case, that weekly incomes were paid according to a constant mean amount plus a random amount with mean zero. We would expect weekly expenditures to be less highly correlated with (the more variable) weekly incomes than monthly expenditures with monthly incomes, in which the random elements would tend to cancel. If portfolio adjustments and the stock returns which reflect them also are based on a 'permanent' expected rate of growth of the money supply, a strong relation of stock returns to weekly money movements containing a relatively large component is not to be expected.

[33] The F-test suggested by Johnston (1963, p. 136) gives F-values of 0.89 to 1.17 for various models and the 5% critical value is 1.45. Similarly, the hypothesis of equality of the coefficients in the split post-1948 period cannot be rejected.

Table 5
Summary Statistics from the Monthly Regression Models[a]

$$R_t = c_0 + \sum_{i=-8}^{17} a_{t-i}(g_{t-i} - g_{t-i-1}) + e_t$$

Line	Period	R^2	$\bar{R}^2$	F-statistic[b]	Data
(1)	8/48–3/70	0.247	0.163	2.937**	M_1; revised, adjusted
(2)	8/48–3/70	0.239	0.154	2.808**	M_1; revised, unadjusted
(3)	7/48–3/70	0.246	0.163	2.944**	M_1; revised, adjusted[c]
(4)	8/48–5/60	0.285	0.123	1.760*	M_1; revised, adjusted
(5)	8/48–5/60	0.344	0.196	2.323**	M_1; revised, unadjusted
(6)	6/60–3/70	0.378	0.200	2.124**	M_1; revised, adjusted
(7)	6/60–3/70	0.353	0.168	1.910*	M_1; revised, unadjusted
(8)	8/16–2/46	0.093	0.003	1.038	M_1; revised, adjusted
(9)	8/16–4/71	0.092	0.047	2.036**	M_1; revised, adjusted
(10)	8/48–4/72	0.234	0.156	3.026**	M_1; revised, adjusted[d]
(11)	8/48–4/72	0.179	0.096	2.157**	M_2; revised, adjusted
(12)	8/48–4/68	0.189	0.089	1.886**	M_3; revised, adjusted

[a]R_t = stock returns and g_t = growth rate of the money supply occurring in period t.
[b]Asterisk indicates significance at 5% level; two asterisks indicate significance at 1% level.
[c]Regression in line 3 uses growth rates only as independent variables.
[d]Uses February, 1973 FRB money supply revision.

mation in B_t. If anticipations are realized, on average, actual future variables provide suitable measures of the anticipated variables and are proxy variables for the unknown data in B_t used by the stock market. Thus, in an efficient market, we expect to find that R_t will be significantly related to the future money terms so long as anticipations are realized and money variables are important to stock returns.

Some results from testing models of this type are presented in table 5. (Results using unrevised data are quite close to those shown although somewhat weaker.) In the regressions over the period 8/48–3/70 (lines 1–3), a striking improvement results from inclusion of the future terms. The relationships are significant at the 1% level and $\bar{R}^2$ is 0.163 for both changes in growth rates (line 1) and growth rates (line 3). This improvement and significance occurs whether one uses adjusted or unadjusted data; the $\bar{R}^2$'s of the relationships do not appear to be systematically higher using adjusted (or unadjusted) data.[34]

---

[34]Evidence is presented in Rozeff (1974, p. 149) which indicates that in models with no future terms, returns are more closely related to the *unadjusted* data, holding constant the revision factor. Models with future terms given mixed results. On balance, the evidence is that Federal Reserve seasonal adjustment procedures do not add to the information investors gain from the unadjusted data. If the stock market has a model to adjust the unadjusted data, it appears to be a different model than the Federal Reserve model.

When the post-1948 period is split, the improvement and significance persists. Especially interesting is the statistical significance of the model over 6/60–3/70 (lines 6 and 7), in contrast to the rather weak relationships when only current and lagged terms are included. In fact, this decade provides a particularly clear illustration of the relationship of stock returns to monetary policy: returns reflect anticipated monetary policy as well as concurrent monetary policy, while at the same time remaining independent of past monetary variables. This apparently diverse behavior is entirely understandable within the framework of the efficient market model.

In the slightly longer period, 8/48–4/72 (line 10), which includes what to many is a turbulent period in monetary and stock market history (1966–72), the relationship continues significant. In lines 11 and 12, results using M_2 and M_3 are shown; the improvement in each is similar to that using M_1, although $\bar{R}^2$'s remain smaller. The only period using monthly data in which no significant relation emerges is 8/16–2/46 using the F&S data (line 8).

Recall again that table 3 gives results with weekly and quarterly data. The weekly model achieves significance for the first time when the future terms are included (line 3). The $\bar{R}^2$ of the quarterly regression becomes 0.292 (line 6), an improvement over the same model without the future quarters ($\bar{R}^2 = 0.209$).

All in all, these results strongly support the non-predictive MP model in the form which takes into account anticipations. There is little doubt that stock returns are strongly related to monetary growth rates as the MP model suggests. Stock returns do not, however, lag in adjusting to monetary policy. Instead the relationship appears to be contemporaneous and anticipatory as the EM model suggests it should be. Since a *linear* model with future terms finds the kind of relationship that the non-predictive MP model suggests will occur, we may infer that the tests of the EM model versus the *predictive* MP model are not unduly restrictive by being *linear* tests. It is also encouraging that the restricted identification of monetary policy with monetary growth rates is adequate in providing the kind of relationship suggested by the monetary portfolio model.

4.5. Models with Regression Prediction of Growth Rates

The first differences in money supply growth rates are autocorrelated as are growth rates themselves. If t-values of individual terms of the regressions of stock returns on these variables are examined, one will obtain a seriously distorted picture of the importance of individual money terms. Cagan's (1971) study, for example, appears to show important cumulative lagged effects of money supply growth changes on interest rate changes. The results using stock returns give a similar picture. Even though the statistical significance of lagged terms as a group is lacking, individual t-values may be high enough to suggest significance. See, for example, the comparison t-values in column 5 of table 6, for a model using first differences in growth rates (with future terms). Many of the individual lagged terms appear to be highly significant. To obtain an undistorted view of the significance of individual terms, a refined expectations model was suggested above. We now explore this model.

Table 6
Regression Coefficients, Whitened Growth Growth Rate Series[a]

$$R_t = c_0 + \sum_{i=-8}^{17} a_{t-i}(g_{t-i} - g_{t-i}^*) + e_t$$

$-i$	Coeff.	t-value	Simple Corr. Coeff. with R_t	Comparison t-values[b]
8	−0.6544	−0.75	−0.070	−0.32
7	−0.3093	−0.35	0.005	−0.36
6	−0.1932	−0.22	−0.011	−0.35
5	0.8091	0.93	0.057	0.84
4	−1.4200	−1.64	−0.082	−0.38
3	0.8658	1.01	0.044	0.51
2	3.4859	4.05	0.252	3.45
1	3.3836	3.94	0.244	5.62
0	1.4263	1.67	0.116	5.36
−1	1.0122	1.19	0.093	4.80
−2	0.5847	0.68	0.048	4.19
−3	−1.1020	−1.25	−0.038	2.55
−4	1.2689	1.43	0.089	3.40
−5	−0.0672	−0.08	0.000	3.27
−6	1.2789	1.46	0.076	4.14
−7	0.4006	0.46	0.037	4.10
−8	−1.9648	−2.26	−0.094	2.24
−9	0.9320	1.05	0.066	2.84
−10	0.5085	0.58	0.054	3.41
−11	0.1883	0.21	0.000	3.79
−12	−1.8498	−2.11	−0.092	1.83
−13	−0.7477	−0.86	−0.064	1.24
−14	−0.0707	−0.08	−0.014	1.63
−15	−0.5061	−0.57	0.014	1.45
−16	0.2489	0.28	−0.008	1.72
−17	−0.6578	−0.73	−0.067	0.76

R^2	$\bar{R}^2$	F-statistic	Period	Type of Model
0.204	0.123	2.519	5/47–12/72	Future, current and lagged terms.
0.077	0.014	1.228	5/47–12/72	Current and lagged terms
0.065	0.005	1.075	5/47–12/72	Lagged terms only

[a]R_t = stock returns and g_t = growth rate of money supply occurring in period t. g_t^* is a regression prediction of g_t as of time $t - 1$.

[b]These t-values are for the comparable coefficients of the model using first differences in growth rates as the independent variables.

Cooper (1972) finds that a 3rd-order autoregressive model describes the behavior of growth rates of the money supply. The data in this study confirm his result. Thus, regression predictions of $E(\tilde{g}_t | B_{t-1})$ were obtained as follows: Using data through time $t - 1$, the autoregressive relation

$$g_{t-1} = \alpha_0 + a_1 g_{t-2} + a_2 g_{t-3} + a_3 g_{t-4} + e_t \tag{26}$$

was computed. Using the estimated coefficients of this relation, the most recent values, $g_{t-1}, \ldots,$ were substituted to find a prediction, g_t^*, of $E(\tilde{g}_t | B_{t-1})$. In period t the additional realization, g_t, was used in re-estimating the coefficients, and a prediction of g_{t+1} was obtained. This method produces a set of variables, $[g_t - g_t^*]$, which are nearly independent. Of 325 elements in the simple correlation matrix of these regressors, 237 are less than 0.10 and only three are greater than 0.20, the largest being 0.21.

With the autoregressiveness in the independent variables removed, a very different picture emerges of the importance of individual terms (table 6, column 3). The two terms with the highest t-values, 4.05 and 3.94, are the first two *future* terms. Fifteen of the seventeen lagged terms have t-values that are insignificant. The binomial probability of 2 or more 'successes' (i.e., statistical significance) in 17 trials, given that the probability of success is 0.05, is 0.2077. Thus there is quite a large probability of observing several cases of significance even under the null hypothesis. This regression with future terms is significant at the 1% level; the lagged terms as a group have an $\bar{R}^2$ of only 0.005, and even with the current term, $\bar{R}^2$ is but 0.014. The simple correlation coefficients (column 4) are also revealing. The largest of these are for the first two future months and the current month, 0.252, 0.244 and 0.116 respectively. The lead of stock returns over future changes in money growth rates observed in earlier models persists even after the autoregressiveness is removed from the money supply series. Therefore, this lead cannot be explained by the fact that money growth rates are predictable (to an extent) from dependencies in the time series of past money growth rates.[35] The market seems to use all the information about future money growth rates inherent in the money series and in fact appears to use information over and above that contained in the subset of data $[g_t, g_{t-1}, \ldots]$. Since the data set B_t no doubt contains other information (than past growth rates) that is relevant to future monetary growth rates, we expect an efficient market to use it in making forecasts. In terms of the MP model, current stock returns do not depend on prior monetary disturbances but do anticipate part of future disturbances. This behaviour is expected if the

---

[35] In independent, unpublished research which came to my attention after this research was completed, Booth and Ibbotson, using data over 1947–62 and whitened time series, conclude that first differences in stock prices precede first differences in money supply by 4 months. The simple correlations range from 0.187 to 0.271. Lagged correlations are insignificant. This evidence is consistent with the results using regression estimates, g_t^*.

market uses any information in addition to the time series of growth rates to predict future monetary disturbances.[36]

The relationship of stock returns to future money growth rates is related to the problem of causality of money and income examined by Sims. Sims (1972, p. 545) develops from Granger's *definition* of causal ordering a

'practical statistical test for unidirectional causality: Regress Y on past and future values of X . . . Then if causality runs from X to Y only, future values of X in the regression should have coefficients insignificantly different from zero, as a group.'

Sims is concerned primarily with whether causality runs from money (X) to income (Y). Therefore he regresses income (Y) on past, current and future values of X and examines the coefficients of the future money (X) terms, concluding (1972, p. 546) that '. . . future values of M [money] were not significant in explaining the GNP variable.'

The Granger-Sims definition and test of causality reasons that past Y should not influence current X if X causes Y solely. Thus if money 'causes' income, current income should be unrelated to future money terms, unless there is a bidirectional relation. But what if X causes Y *and forecasts of future X are reflected in current* Y? If the forecasts are accurate on average, current Y *will* be related to future terms in X even though X is causing Y. The test for unidirectional causality will fail. Sims finds it 'difficult to imagine' that X can cause Y, that current Y will be related to future X without past Y appearing to affect current X (i.e., without bidirectional structure).

Money and stock returns provide just such a case as Sims thought implausible. Let X represent money growth rates and Y stock returns. In a regression of stock returns (Y) on future, current and past values of growth rates (X), current and past coefficients of X are insignificant as a group while the coefficients of the future money terms are significant. Significant coefficients of the *future* money terms are *exactly* what the efficient market hypothesis predicts, so long as the market has available to it *any* information (in addition to past growth rates) regarding future growth rates and uses it to form accurate anticipations. Footnote 11 has listed a number of plausible *monetary* variables that may provide indications of the future course of the money supply: changes

---

[36]Several alternative growth rates of the money supply models are investigated in Rozeff [1974, pp. 93–98] and this research is continuing. One possibility is that growth rates of the monetary base in prior periods help to predict future money growth rates. Inclusion of lagged monetary base terms in the autoregressive money growth model does improve its explanatory power slightly. A second possibility is to use current data to predict the money multiplier and then growth rates [cf. Burger (1972)]. In this case, the autoregressive model produces implicit money supply forecasts with a smaller forecast error than the Burger model over 1964–71, perhaps because the Burger model limits the sample size to 36 past observations at any one time while the autoregressive model has a sample size of about 300 [cf. Rozeff (1974, pp. 96–98)].

in margin requirements, credit ceilings, reserve requirements, etc. In addition, it is possible [cf. Homa and Jaffee (1972)] to develop models of Federal Reserve behavior that take into account politically important variables such as rates of inflation, interest rate levels, the unemployment rate, the balance of payments and threatened bankruptcies. Sprinkel, for example, when he is not insisting on the importance of trends in monetary aggregates, mentions a large number of other events that enter his analysis of changes in monetary policy [cf. Sprinkel (1971, p. 95 ff.)].

According to Sims' definition of causality, a minimal conclusion for stocks is that causality does not run one-way from current and past values of money growth rates to stock returns. One might even conclude [cf. Sims' discussion (1972, p. 542)] that regressions of money growth rates upon stock returns did have a causal interpretation, namely, that stock returns caused money growth rates. A different interpretation seems more plausible. The 'reversed-causation-with-accurate-anticipations' model (that Sims mentions and dismisses) seems entirely consistent with both the monetary view of portfolio adjustment and the view that capital markets are efficient. The hypothesis that stock returns are a causal variable cannot be ruled out, of course, without testing its implications. Nevertheless, the alternative view that the Fed signals its intentions about money supply growth prior to execution of its policy, and that stock market returns (efficiently) reflect this information prior to actual monetary growth, can explain the observed relation without rejecting either the monetary hypothesis, that causality runs from the monetary variable to stock prices, or the EM hypothesis that prices fully reflect available information.[37]

4.6. Trading Rules—Methodology

Even weak linear relationships of stock returns to the money supply might result in profitable trading rules. Therefore, to test the EM model, trading

---

[37] If stock returns are related to *future* monetary variables, the combined EM-MP models provide *one* possible explanation. A second hypothesis is that both stock price changes and money supply changes are determined jointly by *other* variables but with different reaction speeds. For example, Brunner and Meltzer (1972) provide a general equilibrium model in which the money supply and the price of real capital are endogenous. In the model, a change in real output can disturb asset-market equilibrium, tax collections and the size and financing of the government budget. While implications as to reaction speeds are not drawn, it appears to be consistent with this model if asset prices change more quickly than any deficit financing which changes the money supply. It is consistent with the EM model if the market uses information on prospective debt and tax financing to forecast money supply growth rates. Thus the EM model is consistent with an endogenous money (and stock price) model.

It is difficult to see how a definitional criterion of causality like the Sims' test can help to distinguish between the hypotheses since, in the case of an efficient market, it seems arbitrarily to select stock returns as a 'causal' variable.

rules should be compared to equivalent risk B&H policies if possible. A number of trading rules are examined in this section.

The prediction models begin by computing a linear regression of stock returns on a set of monetary growth rate changes (or monetary growth rates). For example, a rule based on available data proceeds as follows: On 9/56, all data available through 9/56 dating from 1/47 is used to compute a regression of stock returns on past changes in growth rates. The estimated coefficients are then employed with current data to obtain a predicted stock return for 10/56 (a procedure similar to that used to obtain money growth rate predictions). This predicted stock return is compared to this month's commercial paper rate. If it is less than this rate, a 'sell' signal is given (or a signal to remain out of the market if we previously have sold). If the predicted stock return exceeds the paper rate, a 'buy' signal is given (or a signal to remain in stocks if we previously had bought). Buying and selling orders are assumed to be executed at the beginning of the month. In all these trading rules, the stock portfolio is the 'market'. In the next period, 10/56, another observation is added to the linear regression; it is recomputed and another prediction obtained, this time for 11/56. In this way 170 predictions are generated through the month of November 1970. It is then possible to compute the returns from the trading rule by employing actual realized stock returns and realized returns from commercial paper during the months when the rule placed us in stocks and in commercial paper, respectively.

The trading rules tested differ according to the linear prediction model and data allowed. They are also executed over several subperiods of the total 170 month testing period. Table 7 gives the intervals over which the rules were tested; there are three non-overlapping intervals from 1956–70 as well as several overlapping intervals within this period. Table 8 describes the six types of trading rules that were tested. The major distinction here is between *predictive* and *non-predictive* rules, with rules 1–3 of the former type and rules 4–6 of the latter type. Predictive rules could have been used by an investor. They rely solely upon data available in time to make a prediction and act upon it— unrevised data received with a publication lag. These rules (1–3) therefore provide tests of the EM model against the predictive MP model. Rules 4–6 are

Table 7
Trading Rule Intervals and Dates

Months–dates	Months–numbered	# Months in rule
10/56–10/62	1–73	73
10/56–4/67	1–127	127
10/56–11/70	1–170	170
11/62–4/67	74–127	54
5/67–11/70	128–170	43

Table 8
Descriptions of Six Trading Rules Tested

Number	Type	Description
(1)	Predictive	Lagged growth rates; unrevised and unadjusted data.
(2)	Predictive	Lagged first differences in growth rates; unrevised and adjusted data.
(3)	Predictive	Lagged first differences in growth rates; unrevised and unadjusted data.
(4)	Non-predictive	Lagged first differences in growth rates with zero publication lag assumed; unrevised and unadjusted data.
(5)	Non-predictive	Future, current and lagged first differences in growth rates with zero publication lag assumed; unrevised and unadjusted data.
(6)	Non-predictive	Future, current and lagged first differences in growth rates with zero publication lag assumed; revised and adjusted data.

'trading rules' which use *unavailable* data. Rule 4 uses data with no publication lag as of month $t - 1$ in making predictions for month t. Rules 5 and 6 in addition make money data for month t and several future months available in predicting returns for month t.

The definitions of the variables are as follows:

$$T = \text{number of months in trading rule}$$

$$R_i = 1 + \text{rate of return for } i\text{th month of trading rule}$$

$$\prod_{i=1}^{T} R_i = \$ \text{ return of trading rule}$$

$$\left(\prod_{i=1}^{T} R_i \right)^{1/T} - 1 = \text{monthly return}$$

$$\left(\prod_{i=1}^{T} R_i \right)^{12/T} - 1 = \text{annual return}$$

With transactions costs of CT percent per transaction and NT transactions per trading rule,

$$\left(\prod_{i=1}^{T} R_i \right) (1 - CT/100)^{NT} = \$ \text{ return}$$

'Round trip' transactions costs to sell stocks, buy and sell commercial paper and buy stocks are taken as 1% for the entire round trip.

Let

$R_{s,i}$ = monthly stock return, ith month

$R_{f,i}$ = monthly commercial paper return, ith month

Then B&H returns over a T-period interval are

$$R_s = \prod_{i=1}^{T} R_{s,i} \quad \text{for stocks} \quad R_f = \prod_{i=1}^{T} R_{f,i} \quad \text{for commercial paper}$$

Equivalent risk B&H returns for a trading rule are then defined as follows: Let

NM = number of months trading rule is not in stocks

DD = T – NM = number of months in stocks

then

B&H \$ return = $(\text{NM}/T)(R_f) + (\text{DD}/T)(R_s)$

This equivalent risk B&H return represents the following policy: at the start of the T-period interval, divide \$1 between an investment in the stock portfolio and an investment in commercial paper, this portfolio to be held without revision until the end of the period. The original \$1 is divided proportionately between stocks and commercial paper according to the fraction of the T-period interval that the trading rule placed the investor in stocks and in commercial paper respectively. The variability of this B&H policy should approximate the variability of a trading rule which is in stocks DD/T percent of the period unless the trading rule selects a distribution of months with a different standard deviation of return (as well as a different mean return), but this is not likely since both B&H and the trading rule operate on the market portfolio.

4.7. Trading Rule Tests of EM Model versus Predictive MP Model

Recall that the regression results over 1948–60 indicated a possibly profitable trading rule might exist. Table 9 includes tests of trading rules over this period slightly extended to 1962 (panel 1). The extended period maximizes sample

Table 9

Summary Statistics for Six Trading Rules and B&H for Various Time Periods, Monthly Returns[a]

(1) Period	(2) Rule	(3) Net of 1% Trans. Costs	(4) Gross of Trans. Costs	(5) B&H Returns	(6) Std. Dev. Rule[b]	(7) Std. Dev. Mean[c]	(8) Std. Dev. B&H	(9) F-value[d]	(10) t-value[e]
(1) 10/56–10/62	1	0.00221	0.00428	0.00577	0.033	0.00385	0.031	1.13	−0.39
	2	0.00300	0.00479	0.00554	0.033	0.00382	0.029	1.29	−0.20
	3	0.00229	0.00464	0.00536	0.032	0.00378	0.027	1.40	−0.19
	4	0.00758	0.00994	0.00522	0.031	0.00367	0.025	1.54*	+1.29
	5	0.00966	0.01133	0.00531	0.030	0.00357	0.026	1.33	+1.69
	6	0.01026	0.01179	0.00536	0.029	0.00343	0.027	1.15	+1.87
(2) 10/56–4/67	1	0.00619	0.00818	0.00944	0.035	0.00308	0.033	1.12	−0.41
	2	0.00760	0.00975	0.00911	0.034	0.00301	0.032	1.13	+0.21
	3	0.00779	0.01011	0.00916	0.035	0.00313	0.032	1.20	+0.30
	4	0.01005	0.01253	0.00857	0.033	0.00292	0.029	1.30	+1.36
	5	0.00890	0.01082	0.00882	0.028	0.00253	0.030	0.87	+0.79
	6	0.00963	0.01147	0.00902	0.030	0.00268	0.031	0.94	+0.91
(3) 10/56–11/70	1	0.00356	0.00564	0.00714	0.038	0.00290	0.036	1.12	−0.52
	2	0.00664	0.00884	0.00706	0.037	0.00283	0.035	1.12	+0.63
	3	0.00452	0.00678	0.00706	0.039	0.00300	0.035	1.24	−0.09
	4	0.00654	0.00893	0.00672	0.036	0.00273	0.031	1.35*	+0.81
	5	0.00847	0.01050	0.00676	0.030	0.00227	0.032	0.88	+1.65
	6	0.00875	0.01054	0.00691	0.034	0.00259	0.033	1.06	+1.40
	1	0.01160	0.01348	0.01351	0.037	0.00498	0.032	1.31	−0.01
	2	0.01386	0.01650	0.01309	0.035	0.00472	0.031	1.25	+0.72
	3	0.01528	0.01755	0.01411	0.038	0.00516	0.034	1.24	+0.67

(4) 11/62–4/67	4	0.01339	0.01604	0.01223	0.035	0.00473	0.028	1.54	+0.81
	5	0.00770	0.01014	0.01288	0.025	0.00346	0.030	0.72	−0.79
	6	0.00878	0.01103	0.01351	0.032	0.00430	0.032	0.98	−0.58
	1	−0.00416	−0.00183	0.00241	0.046	0.00695	0.043	1.12	−0.61
	2	0.00382	0.00617	0.00196	0.045	0.00688	0.045	1.00	+0.61
	3	−0.00507	−0.00297	0.00211	0.048	0.00730	0.044	1.19	−0.70
(5) 5/67–11/70	4	−0.00374	−0.00164	0.00270	0.041	0.00629	0.042	0.96	−0.69
	5	0.00721	0.00956	0.00313	0.033	0.00505	0.040	0.69	+1.27
	6	0.00618	0.00783	0.00270	0.043	0.00653	0.042	1.04	+0.79

[a]Trading rules 1–3 are *predictive* rules and rules 4–6 are *non-predictive* rules. See table 8 for description.
[b]Standard deviation of gross trading rule returns.
[c]Standard deviation of trading rule returns divided by square root of length of rule in months.
[d]Ratio of variance of trading rule returns to variance of B&H returns; asterisk indicates a significant difference at 5% level.
[e][(4)−(5)]/(7).

size and coincides with the period over which Sprinkel (1964, p. 127) has indicated money leads stock prices. Data from 1948–56 is used to generate model coefficients. B&H outperforms the trading rule whether adjusted (rule 2) or unadjusted (rules 1 and 3) data is used and whether one uses growth rates (rule 1) or changes in growth rates (rules 2 and 3) over this period. Compounded annual B&H returns are about 7% while trading rule returns net of 1% transactions costs are about 3%. (B&H returns are adjusted for risk as described above.) On the other hand, the same type of trading rules given *unavailable* data (rules 4–6) outperform B&H by a wide margin, about 12% versus 7% on an annual basis. Also notice (rule 4) that with the current month's data allowed (that is, assuming data for period $t - 1$ is known at time $t - 1$ in making predictions for t), the trading rule outperforms B&H. The profitability arising from this seemingly minor change underscores the importance of careful dating of data availability.

Thus over 10/56–10/62, a period of 73 months, several types of trading rules relying on different past available monetary data sets show no signs of profitability in predictive tests. This lack of profitability cannot be attributed to the simplicity of the trading rule or to the fact that it uses a linear equation, since over the same period similar rules outperform B&H by wide margins when given knowledge of the current month's money supply with no publication lag, or knowledge of the current and future months' data.

In panels 2 and 3 of table 9, over months 1–127 and months 1–170, the same results are observed in comparing B&H to trading rules *net* of 1% transactions costs. For trading rules that use past available data, B&H consistently outperforms the trading rule. By contrast, when given unavailable data the trading rule outperforms the trading rule. By contrast, when given unavailable data the trading rule outperforms the B&H policy in all cases but one (rule 4 of panel 3). In the shorter time periods (panels 4 and 5) there are some exceptions but no systematic change in the trading rule behavior.

Table 10 contains significance tests on the differences in B&H and trading rule returns. Differences are taken for predictive and non-predictive rules operating in consecutive non-overlapping time periods. In these t-tests the random variable is the difference between a trading rule mean return and the corresponding B&H return. The sample size is 9 for each type of rule (predictive or nonpredictive) and the t-statistic tests whether the mean difference is significantly different from zero. Although the time periods are independent, the trading rules within each period are not strictly independent (although they do use different data sets) so that these t-tests to some extent are likely to overstate the significance of the differences as compared with t-tests of individual rules appearing in table 9 and discussed below.

The mean return of the gross predictive trading rules is very slightly less than the mean B&H return, –0.00019 on a monthly basis or –0.25% on an annual percentage basis. The low t-value of –0.17 for the 9 differences is con-

Table 10
Differences between Trading Rule and Buy-and-Hold Returns

Period (Months)		Trading Rule Returns–Buy-and-Hold Returns					
		Predictive Rules[a]			Non-predictive Rules[b]		
		Net of 1% Trans. Cost	Gross of Trans. Cost		Net of 1% Trans. Cost	Gross of Trans. Cost	
1–73	1	−0.00356	−0.00149	4	+0.00236	+0.00472	
	2	−0.00254	−0.00075	5	+0.00435	+0.00602	
	3	−0.00307	−0.00090	6	+0.00490	+0.00643	
	1	−0.00191	−0.00030	4	+0.00148	+0.00396	
74–127	2	+0.00077	+0.00341	5	+0.00008	+0.00200	
	3	+0.00117	+0.00344	6	+0.00061	+0.00245	
	1	−0.00657	−0.00424	4	−0.00018	+0.00221	
128–170	2	+0.00186	+0.00421	5	+0.00171	+0.00374	
	3	−0.00718	−0.00508	6	+0.00184	+0.00363	
Mean diff., d		−0.00234	−0.00019		+0.00191	+0.00391	
Std. dev., $s(d)$		0.00322	0.00332		0.00176	0.00159	
$t(d) = \bar{d}/[s(d)/\sqrt{9}]$		−2.17	−0.17		+3.25	+7.37	
Number (−)		6	6		1	0	
Number (+)		3	3		8	9	

[a]Differences are for trading rules 1–3 from panels 1, 4 and 5 of table 9.
[b]Differences are for trading rules 4–6 from panels 1, 4 and 5 of table 9.

sistent with the view that the mean return of these rules is insignificantly different from B&H returns. Net of transactions costs the predictive rules seem to
perform significantly worse than B&H. On an annual percentage basis, the mean
difference is about −3.09%. Standard deviations of trading rule and B&H returns
are shown in table 9 (columns 6 and 8). The predictive rules are generally somewhat more risky than B&H using standard deviation of return as a risk measure
but the differences are not generally significant (5% level) using F-tests for
the ratios of variances (column 9). (Again there is probably not strict independence of the samples.) Since the mean returns of B&H and the predictive rules
(gross) are nearly the same and their risks are nearly the same, the behavior
of the predictive rules (gross) approximates B&H. With transactions costs, B&H
dominates the predictive rules.

On the other hand, the non-predictive rules (net and gross) have returns
that are on average greater than B&H returns. Net of 1% transactions costs, the
mean difference is +0.00191 or 2.51% on an annual basis. The gross difference
is 5.20% annually. The *signs* of the differences in table 10 which are consistently
positive with one exception also indicate the superiority of the non-predictive
rules over B&H. Standard deviations of the non-predictive rules are also quite
close to those of B&H. F-tests for the ratios of variances (table 9, column 9)

indicate mostly insignificant differences. Thus, as a rule the non-predictive rules seem to earn significantly higher returns without significant increases in risk.

The t-tests of individual trading rules are also presented in table 9 in column 10. The trading rule is considered as a sample of T months, and the hypothesis tested is whether the mean *gross* monthly return of the rule differs significantly from the value achieved by the corresponding B&H policy. Notice that the standard deviations of *monthly* returns are of the order of 0.03 compared to mean returns of 0.01 and smaller, reflecting the high variability always observed for stock returns. The estimated standard deviations of the sampling distributions of the mean (column 7) are of course much smaller but in most cases there is no significant difference (5% level) of the trading rule mean return from B&H in either direction. There *is* a noticeable difference in the size of the t-statistics between the predictive and non-predictive rules; t-values range from 0.01 to 0.72 (absolute values) for the predictive rules and from 0.58 to 1.87 for the non-predictive rules. In the cases where there are exceptions, i.e., a predictive rule doing better than B&H or a non-predictive rule failing to do better than B&H, t-values range from 0.21 to 0.79, in the lower part of the observed range of t-values. Despite their statistical insignificance, these t-values thus tend to agree with t-values obtained by examining the sample of differences in table 10. The predictive rules gross of transactions costs appear to behave about as well as B&H; the non-predictive rules have a majority of larger positive t-values with several significant at the 10% level, indicating the superiority of these rules to B&H.

By and large, the evidence obtained by examining the trading rules corroborates the regression tests: the stock market appears to be efficient with respect to money data since trading rules using available money data fail to outperform naive B&H strategies. When transactions costs are included, the B&H policy is superior on average to the trading rules which use the predictive MP model. From the point of view of trading profits as well as regression R^2, the lag in effect of monetary policy therefore appears to be negligible with respect to stock prices. The profitability of the non-predictive rules even after transactions costs demonstrates that linear trading rules of the type used to test the predictive MP model can become profitable but that it is necessary that they be allowed unavailable data before profitability occurs. The profitability of the non-predictive rules also tends to confirm the conclusion that stock returns are related to *future*, not past, monetary data.

4.8. Weekly Data Availability

In an efficient market, data is reflected in stock prices as it becomes available. The changing availability of monetary data over 1956–70 makes possible a test of the efficient market model that differs from previous tests. The EM model implies that knowledge (with no lag) of the current month's monetary data may be profitable if no alternative sources (such as weekly data) are available, but if weekly data (during the current month) is available and if current stock returns reflect the weekly data, knowledge of the current monthly data may no longer remain profitable. Current month refers here to month $t - 1$ when predictions are made for month t.

To derive the trading rule implications of infra-monthly data availability in an efficient market, assume two time periods, 1 and 2. In period 1 assume data is published monthly. In period 2 data is published infra-monthly. For simplicity assume data is published semi-monthly, midmonth and end-of-month. (The weekly case of interest can be obtained with no difficulty.) Let

$p_{m,t}$ = midmonth biweekly growth rate of the money supply *published* at middle of month t

$p_{e,t}$ = end-of-month biweekly growth rate of the money supply *published* at end of month t

Assume that these growth rates are measured such that the published growth rate for the entire month t is $p_t = p_{e,t} p_{m,t}$. Assume stock returns in period 1 are generated by the model

$$\tilde{R}_t = E(\tilde{R}_t | p_{t-1}, p_{t-2}, \ldots) + f(\tilde{p}_t) + \tilde{e}_t$$

or

$$\tilde{R}_t = v(\tilde{p}_t, p_{t-1}, p_{t-2}, \ldots) + \tilde{e}_t \qquad (27)$$

Past realizations of p are not random at t. No midmonthly data is available in period 1 to influence expectations. In this model, stock returns depart from those expected as of $t - 1$ by some function f of monetary data published in time t and a random error term. In an efficient market, $\tilde{R}_t$ will not depend on the arguments $p_{t-1}, \ldots$ of the function v (given stationarity). In period 1 assume a one-month publication lag. Let g_t stand as before for the growth rate of the money supply *occurring* in period t, $p_t = g_{t-1}$, etc. Thus:

$$\tilde{R}_t = v(\tilde{g}_{t-1}, g_{t-2}, \ldots) + \tilde{e}_t \qquad (28)$$

Now $g_{t-2}, \ldots$ do not influence $\tilde{R}_t$ in an efficient market.

In period 2 data is available at more frequent intervals and assume the *publication lag is also shortened*. Weekly data, for example, provides money supply data with an 11-day lag, not data on the month-ago week. It does not harm to assume for simplicity that the midmonth data, $p_{m,t}$, gives $g_{m,t}$, i.e., the publication lag disappears. (For the weekly data of interest published since

1967, the important fact is that even with an 11-day lag, several readings on the month's money supply are available before the end of the month.) Period 2 returns are given by

$$\tilde{R}_t = E(\tilde{R}_t | p_{e,t-1}, p_{m,t-1}, \ldots) + f(\tilde{p}_{e,t}, \tilde{p}_{m,t}) + \tilde{e}_t$$

$$= w(\tilde{p}_{e,t}, \tilde{p}_{m,t}, p_{e,t-1}, p_{m,t-1}, \ldots) + \tilde{e}_t \tag{29}$$

and with zero publication lag,

$$\tilde{R}_t = w(\tilde{g}_{e,t}, \tilde{g}_{m,t}, g_{e,t-1}, \ldots) + e_t \tag{30}$$

Eq. (28) in period 1 shows $\tilde{R}_t$ is a function of $\tilde{g}_{t-1}$. If in period 1 a trading rule is given the datum g_{t-1}, it should prove useful in 'predicting' R_t since $\tilde{R}_t$ depends on $\tilde{g}_{t-1}$ and g_{t-1} is unknown at time $t-1$ due to period 1's publication lag. If the procedure of giving the trading rule the datum g_{t-1} is carried over to period 2, it should prove of no benefit in predicting R_t, according to (30), for in this case $\tilde{R}_t$ doesn't depend on $\tilde{g}_{t-1}$ *in an efficient market.* At time $t-1$, knowledge of g_{t-1} is no longer useful in period 2 since it is no longer future information: by the end of month $t-1$, the infra-monthly reports have already provided the information g_{t-1} can provide.

The non-predictive trading rules numbered 4 can be used to carry out the hypothesis test. These rules use a predictive equation of the form:

$$R_{t-1} = c_0 + \sum_{i=1}^{17} a_i(g_{t-i-1} - g_{t-i-2}) + e_t$$

That is, coefficients are estimated using a regression that uses at time $t-1$ data up to time $t-2$. Then *given* g_{t-1} (i.e., zero lag in publication), 'predictions' of R_t can be made. Over months 1–73 the publication lag was one month in the FRB and no infra-monthly data was available; over months 74–127 semi-monthly data was available but was not reported in *Barron's* until month's end; over months 128–170 the lag was vastly reduced with the advent of weekly data which provides data with an 11-day reporting lag. For trading rules of type 4, the EM model therefore implies profitability for months 1–73 (if the data is useful), a strong likelihood of profitability for months 74–127 and probably performance approximating B&H in months 128–170.[38]

---

[38]Public availability of data on a regular basis should not be confused with the first appearance of weekly data in the 8/62 FRB. From 8/62 to 6/66, weekly data was published in the FRB at *month's end* but the weekly release did not begin until 6/66. *Barron's* first reporting of weekly data began slightly later in 4/67.

The following are the annual returns:

Months	Gross	Net	B&H
1–73	0.126	0.095	0.064
74–127	0.210	0.173	0.157
128–170	–0.020	–0.044	0.033

These results are exactly what we expect if weekly data is rapidly reflected in stock returns. The trading rule given the current month's data outperforms B&H for the first two subperiods. But in months 128–170, when weekly data was available, B&H returns exceed those from the trading rule, given current data with no lag. In this subperiod (unlike months 74–127), the trading rules with several months of future data continue to outperform B&H so that the lack of profitability of Rule 4 is not likely to be a chance event. The difference in behavior of the trading rule over 1956–70 as data availability changed is a subtle consequence of market efficiency and provides evidence that stock market prices reflect weekly monetary data with no lag, further contradicting the predictive MP model.

4.9. Past Studies

Except for the summary in section 6, the rest of this paper analyzes past studies of money and stock prices. My aim is to point out and resolve (where possible) the conflicts of past studies with the efficient market model and the evidence of this paper. The analysis also clarifies a number of theoretical and empirical issues. Due to the wide acceptance and influence of some of these studies as well as their number, I believe such a review is of value to the reader.

5. Past Studies of Money and Stock Prices

5.1. Sprinkel's Study

Sprinkel's study is the first to apply the MP model to stock prices systematically and thoroughly. His most important conclusion, based upon graphical analysis of peaks and troughs, is that changes in stock prices lag behind changes in growth rates of the money supply (measured as a 6-month moving average). He uses this lag in investment timing rules and compares their returns to B&H. The first statement of the basic trading rule given by Sprinkel (1964, p. 126) is:

'Table 12 gives specifics on sales and purchases of stocks from 1918 to 1960 based on monetary change, assuming stocks were sold 15 months after monetary growth peaked, and stocks were bought two months after the monetary trough.'

Later the rule is stated as follows [Sprinkel (1964, p. 149)]:

'All funds were invested in stocks until monetary growth had declined 15 months, and then all funds were invested in bonds until monetary growth had risen two months.'

This procedure, assuming switches into cash and neglecting dividends and brokerage cost, is used by Sprinkel to produce an average annual compound yield of 12.5% while a B&H all stock policy (also neglecting dividends) averages 5.8% [cf. Sprinkel (1964, p. 151)].[39] A common interpretation of Sprinkel's procedure is that it provides an empirical test of the *predictive* power of his trading rule [cf. Reilly and Lewis (1971, p. 9)]:

'. . . in order to test the predictive power of the monetary growth series, Sprinkel assumed that a bear market in stock prices was predicted 15 months after each peak [etc.] . . .'

If applied as stated above, the trading rule generates buy signals different from Sprinkel's (1964, p. 150). For example, monetary growth rose for two months ending January 1924 while Sprinkel's buy signal is June 1924; and monetary growth rose for two months ending June 1930 while the buy signal is given as May 1932. If the trading rule is executed literally by selling 15 months after each peak in monetary growth and buying after two months of rising monetary growth over the period 1918–1960, the average annual compound yield is 5.0% (again excluding brokerage and dividends), *lower* than the 5.8% B&H yield. The details of the Sprinkel rule *when executed literally* are given in table 11. Monetary and stock price data are those used by Sprinkel (1964, appendix). The dates when stocks are bought and sold as Sprinkel uses his rule are far fewer.

The explanation for the discrepancies is that Sprinkel *selects* peaks and troughs from the sample. Locating a National Bureau of Economic Research (NBER) business cycle reference peak, he proceeds back to find the first peak in the money series, defined as a high point not exceeded for 15 consecutive months. Proceeding back from an NBER reference trough, he finds the first trough in the money series, defined as a low point not exceeded (in a downward direction) for 2 consecutive months. This procedure is not a matter of investing in stocks 'until monetary growth had declined 15 months'. Instead, monetary peaks and troughs are chosen ex post by selecting particular

---

[39]The omissions of dividends and brokerage costs are in principle incorrect but unlikely to account for the large difference in yields of 6.7% per year.

Table 11
Sprinkel Trading Rule—Literal Execution[a]

Buy	Sell	S&P 425 Index	
Aug. 1918	March 1920	5.66	7.31
Aug. 1921	Sept. 1923	4.57	6.11
*Jan. 1924	Feb. 1926	6.84	10.10
*June 1926	Jan. 1929	9.59	21.22
*July 1929	*Jan. 1931	22.95	12.34
*March 1931	*June 1932	13.45	3.80
*Aug. 1932	Sept. 1936	5.94	15.17
*March 1937	*July 1938	17.52	12.12
*Sept. 1938	*Feb. 1941	11.81	9.64
*Jan. 1942	*June 1944	8.95	12.58
*Aug. 1944	April 1946	12.67	18.02
*July 1946	*Oct. 1947	17.42	15.19
*Sept. 1948	April 1953	15.53	24.84
*Feb. 1954	May 1956	26.12	49.64
*Dec. 1956	*April 1958	49.79	45.09
*June 1958	Feb . 1960	47.62	59.60

[a]Starred transactions are those not occurring in Sprinkel's reported transactions.

peaks and troughs associated with NBER business cycle reference peaks and troughs. [Sprinkel (1964, p. 134) briefly notes that the procedure is ex post.]

Since NBER reference points are not known for at least several quarters after the turning points, it is impossible ex ante for an investor to implement the Sprinkel trading rule as he has executed it. By providing the hypothetical investor with unavailable data, the Sprinkel rule does not provide a correct trading rule test of the EM model and, by its ex post nature, it does not provide the investor with a usable investment rule.

However, it does appear to be Sprinkel's view that his trading rule has predictive power and can be profitably employed by future investors.[40] Sprinkel (1964, p. 120) suggests that 'both theoretical arguments and empirical evidence strongly suggest that future liquidity change will provide some useful guidance to future investment timing decisions', and cites correct signals given by the rule in 1960 and 1962. He concludes (1964, p. 127) that 'by either test [foresight or hindsight], the monetary approach remains reasonably well intact, albeit not completely unscathed'. Such statements are not convincing since the Sprinkel trading rule cannot possibly serve as a guide to investment timing decisions.

---

[40]He also emphasizes that investors will have to employ other available information such as total reserves, free reserves, gold flows, employment, industrial production, etc., but no attempt is made to indicate how these are systematically related to stock price changes as is done with monetary growth. The primary emphasis remains the relation of changes in monetary growth to stock price changes.

Much of the widespread impact of Sprinkel's study stems from the graphical analysis, even among those who place little or no credence in the trading rule [cf. Lorie and Hamilton (1973, p. 23)]. That is, some have interpreted the graphical evidence as supporting the *non-predictive* MP model. This evidence is subject to serious criticism.

First, in comparison with inferences based on statistical methods of analysis, visual examination of graphs is more likely to be misleading or wrong. The selection of peaks and troughs is subject to error. Second, it is difficult to identify *changes* by looking at graphs of *levels*. Third, monetary peaks and troughs are chosen by Sprinkel with reference to NBER turning points using the method described above. This method neglects a great deal of information contained in the time series. Consider, for example, Sprinkel's (1971, pp. 225–227) identification of turning points in money and stock prices. The change in the rate of change of the money supply in 1922–23 represents a peak and trough according to Sprinkel but changes of apparently similar magnitude in 1929, 1930, 1935, 1940 and 1944 are ignored. Fourth and finally, a reasonable interpretation of the MP model is that smaller changes in the money supply should have smaller effects on stock returns and conversely. To weight equally a 5% decline in monetary growth with a 25% decline (in finding 'average' leads) seems an unreasonable method of testing the model and yet this is the outcome of selection of monetary peaks and troughs according to business cycles.[41]

5.2. Palmer's Study

Palmer (1970) extends Sprinkel's graphical method to the years 1960–69. His stock price variable is a 6-month moving average of monthly percentage changes in stock prices. If the MP model is specified as a linear regression, this dependent variable will have *simple* correlations with lagged data terms even if the true relation is actually only contemporaneous.[42] The effect on R^2 may

---

[41]William Meckling brought this criticism to my attention.

[42]Let

$$\tilde{R}_{t,\text{ma}} = (1/6) \sum_{i=0}^{5} \tilde{R}_{t-i}$$

$$\tilde{R}_t = c_0 + c_1 \tilde{g}_t + \tilde{e}_t$$

Consider

$$\text{cov}\,(\tilde{R}_{t,\text{ma}}, \tilde{g}_{t-j}) = (1/6) \sum_{i=0}^{5} [\text{cov}\,(\tilde{R}_{t-i}, \tilde{g}_{t-j})] \qquad j = 1, \ldots, 5$$

not be noticeable but the moving average stock return variable will be correlated with lagged variables even if only the *non-predictive* model holds. Therefore, the Palmer method provides a biased test of the predictive MP model.
This point is somewhat academic since although Palmer asserts that his smoothed
money supply series leads the smoothed stock price series, no clear evidence
in the paper supports this conclusion. The graphical series are depicted with
respect to time periods of 'favorable' and 'unfavorable liquidity for stocks'
which are undefined and Palmer's footnote 7 which presents a number of
correlation coefficients does not define the regression variables. Palmer's (1970,
p. 22) conclusion that 'there still appears to be sufficient time for the investor
to gauge the future course of the market' is inconsistent with the EM model but
is unsupported by evidence.

5.3. Reilly and Lewis Study

Reilly and Lewis (R&L) (1971) explore the money–stock price relationship
graphically and by regression analysis over 1960–70. Monetary variables are
revised monthly data smoothed by moving averages. Typically they find *weak*
relationships. Monthly changes in stock prices regressed on current and give
lagged changes in the money variable, for example, give low R^2's ranging from
0.01 to 0.11. R&L (1971, p. 66), noting the statistical significance of the first
two lagged terms, conclude that the regression analysis is consistent with
Sprinkel's graphical analysis as well as their own but that the lag has become
shorter. In their graphs they observe (1971, p. 20) that 'major and sustained
declines in the growth rate of the money supply are followed by stock price
declines but false signals are possible'. They attribute the low R^2's to the
occasional failure of stock prices to respond to changes in monetary growth.
In the face of evidence of the *un*importance of the current and lagged terms,
R&L continue to accept the Sprinkel results and implicitly reject the EM model.

5.4. Keran's Model

Keran's study (1971) provides another example of a well-known model which
is inconsistent with the EM model. His stock price equation expresses the
quarterly *level* of stock prices (quarterly averages of daily stock prices) as a
linear function of current and lagged *changes* in the money supply, real GNP,
GNP Deflator and current and lagged levels of real corporate earnings. An

---

For each j, $j = 1, \ldots, 5$, a term cov $(\bar{R}_{t-j}, \bar{g}_{t-j})$ appears in the sum and is non-zero if $\bar{R}_t$ is related to $\bar{g}_t$ as the non-predictive model implies. Therefore $\bar{R}_{t,\text{ma}}$ will be related to the
lagged growth rate terms.

Almon (1965) lag is used to estimate the regression. Despite its complexity, the model is logically equivalent to eq. (6), that is, a stock price variable written as a function of current and past data. The high R^2 of the model, 0.98, is probably explained by the common trend of stock prices and earnings and other variables over the period, 1956–70 [see Miller's (1972) discussion].

From the standpoint of the EM model, Keran's graph (1971, p. 26) showing a very close fit of actual and 'predicted' stock prices is misleading since these predictions use contemporaneous and ex post data. The impression given is that stock prices can usefully be predicted from past monetary and other economic data by an equation that uses a stock price lag.

While Keran does not give a trading rule, he does use an 'ex ante simulation' which (1971, pp. 29–30) 'predicts values of the stock price index beyond the time period in which the model was statistically estimated . . .' and he concludes that 'these ex ante simulations tend to perform well in the first four to eight quarters after they are started. . .'.

These simulations are performed by using values of the independent variables in the stock price equation estimated from the St. Louis Econometric Model. In that model the key exogenous variables are the corporate tax rate, changes in Government spending and changes in the money stock. Thus the *predictive* ability of the stock price equation ultimately depends in part upon the predictions made of the exogenous variables. Keran assumes that the tax rate remains unchanged; Government spending is estimated from the Government budget. As for changes in the money stock, 'the most significant policy variable in the model' (1971, p. 30), there is no predictive model. Instead, simulations are executed at *several* growth rates, assumed constant over the simulation period of IV/1970 to IV/1972.

Underlying Keran's use of his model as a predictive device is the assumption that the model can improve upon the efficient market price prediction which is current price plus an expected rate of return. To improve upon the efficient market prediction of future stock price by predicting exogenous variables requires predictions (of the variables) superior to those implicit in current market price. Keran's model cannot produce superior predictions if the market is efficient with respect to the data used in the model and predicts the exogenous variables of the St. Louis model at least as well as Keran can. To be successful his procedure would have to imply a profitable trading rule and refute the EM model.[43]

Keran forecasts the quarterly level of Standard & Poor's 500 Index, quarterly averages of daily prices, for IV/1970–IV/1972, under alternative money growth rate assumptions of 0% to 9%. A comparison to efficient market predictions can be made using his forecasts. Assume that Keran's prediction

---

[43]Similar statements apply to the stock price sector of the Federal Reserve-MIT-Penn (FMP) model [cf. Modigliani (1971)].

Table 12
Keran Stock Price Index Simulations Compared to Martingale Predictions[a]

Quarter	Keran Predictions[b]			Martingale Predictions		
	Pre-diction	Actual[c]	Error[d]	Pre-diction	Actual	Error[e]
1970/IV	89.1	86.23	+2.87	78.74	86.23	−7.49
1971/I	91.9	96.73	−4.83	86.23	96.73	−10.50
II	92.6	101.44	−8.84	96.73	101.44	−4.71
III	90.3	98.55	−8.25	101.44	98.55	+2.89
IV	90.5	96.41	−5.91	98.55	96.41	+2.14
1972/I	92.7	105.41	−12.71	96.41	105.41	−9.00
II	93.4	108.16	−14.76	105.41	108.16	−2.75
III	94.0	109.20	−15.20	108.16	109.20	−1.04
IV	93.5	114.04	−20.54	109.20	114.04	−4.84

[a]Source of Keran predictions is Keran (1971, p. 30).
[b]At Keran's assumed monetary growth rate of 9%.
[c]Standard & Poor's 500 Index of Stock Prices; 1941–43 = 10.
[d]Absolute mean error = 10.43; root mean square error = 11.76.
[e]Absolute mean error = 5.04; root mean square error = 5.91.

model for money growth rates produces perfect forecasts. M_1 revised and adjusted (1973) grew at a rate of approximately 6.9% from IV/1970 to IV/1971 and 7.4% from IV/1971 to IV/1972, calculating growth rates as the ratio of the quarterly average money supply in the later quarter to that in the earlier quarter. I examine his 9% predictions (which have a smaller mean square error than the 6% predictions). Table 12 contains the Keran predictions along with the actual stock price indexes and the prediction errors. For comparison assume a stock price model

$$\tilde{p}_t = E(\tilde{p}_t | B_{t-1}) + \tilde{e}_t \tag{31}$$

and a martingale in stock prices

$$E(\tilde{p}_t | B_{t-1}) = p_{t-1} \tag{32}$$

so that

$$\tilde{p}_t = p_{t-1} + \tilde{e}_t \tag{33}$$

Since the error term, $\tilde{e}_t$, has expected value zero, this period's price index is a best linear unbiased estimator of next period's price index. Table 12 also records these forecasts and errors. The errors of the martingale predictions are far smaller than the Keran predictions; the absolute mean error of the martingale model is about 40% that of the sophisticated model.

This comparison, despite its simplicity, underscores the logical connection of predictive models like Keran's to the efficient market model. If current price fully reflects data in B_t, attempts to use data in B_t to produce price predictions are attempts to find profitable trading rules which refute the EM model.

5.5. Hamburger and Kochin Study

Hamburger and Kochin (H&K) (1972) introduce and test another stock price equation of interest. Earlier, Cagan and Gandolphi (1969), Cagan (1972) and Gibson (1970) regressed changes in interest rates on current and lagged changes in money growth rates in order to test the influence of changes in money supply growth rates on bond interest rates. H&K employ a similar procedure for stocks with changes in stock prices as the dependent variable. The adjusted R^2's, 0.26–0.31, for several periods over 1956–70 indicate a substantial relationship between stock price changes and changes in money growth rates, an important result. While H&K recognize the potential use of the equation as a trading rule and discount its value in this direction, the lagged terms are not unimportant if the t-values are taken at face value. The first and second lagged quarters have t-values of 3.55 and 2.64 respectively, compared to 2.75 for the contemporaneous term. The appearance and apparent significance of lagged terms in the stock price equation is disturbing from the standpoint of the EM model and requires explanation.

To estimate their regressions, both Keran and H&K impose an Almon lag, a technique which constrains the regression coefficients along a polynomial. Both models have the form of eq. (6). As previously pointed out, the coefficient a_0 of the contemporaneous term may be positive if the *non-predictive* MP model holds and the remaining coefficients, $a_1 = a_2 = \ldots = a_N = 0$, if the EM model holds. Schmidt and Waud (1973, pp. 6–7) point out (in another context) that any choice of a constraining polynomial of order $p < n$ must involve a specification error in just the above situation, since a polynomial of order p can equal zero in only p places, unless it is identically zero:

'. . . it is simply impossible for the data to indicate the absence of a lag as long as $p < n$ . . . The presence or absence of a lag is not a testable proposition when the Almon lag technique is used.'

To illustrate, Schmidt and Waud impose a polynomial lag scheme for a case where *only the contemporaneous terms are correlated* (perfectly) and conclude (1973, p. 7) that the 'effect of the polynomial estimation procedure is to *smear* the contemporaneous influence back over preceding time periods . . .'

Since a test of the *predictive* MP model against the EM model requires examining the set of lagged coefficients, Keran's and H&K's regressions using the Almon technique do not provide unequivocal tests of these hypotheses, and significant t-values for individual lagged coefficients tell us nothing about the presence or absence of lags. If the EM model holds, regressions imposing an Almon lag obscure the true relative importance of the contemporaneous and lagged independent variables. The reason is that if the non-predictive MP model holds and the contemporaneous relationship is significant, the Almon technique may make the lagged terms also appear to be significant. (Recall that even with no Almon lag, lack of independence among regressors may also obscure the true importance of individual terms.)

5.6. Homa and Jaffee Study

Homa and Jaffee (H&J) (1971, p. 1045) seek to forecast 'movements in aggregate indices of common stock prices' with still another stock price equation, citing their work as an attempt to improve upon Sprinkel's methods. In their equation, stock price levels depend upon the current level of the money supply and growth rates of the money supply for the current and preceding quarters, a formulation similar to Keran's but far simpler. The high R^2 of this model, 0.97, is in large part due to the common trend over the period in levels of stock prices and money supply. High cross-sectional dependence of stock price levels and money supply levels provides no indication of the predictive ability of the equation, since to predict stock prices a prediction of the future money supply is required that is superior to that implicit in current market price.

H&J (1972, p. 1049) selected the regression variables after 'a number of regressions were fitted with alternative lag structures on the money supply and monetary growth rate', and the entire body of data was used to select the variables 'which yielded the best fit', a procedure which is a source of selection bias that disqualifies the use of the equation as a trading rule on the same body of data.

Several occasions for the introduction of unavailable information arise in this study; it is unclear from the text whether or not these pitfalls have been avoided. First, there is no indication of whether the money data was collected issue by issue from the FRB or whether it is revised data published later. Second, the stock price equation seems to use current and lagged monetary data neglecting publication lag. Third, to use the equation as a predictive device, forecasts of money growth are required. H&J use a prediction model for money growth in which the independent variables include data on unemployment, balance of payments data, a price index and a lagged money growth rate term, all dated as of the time of prediction. The question is whether or not this equation could be used to predict money growth rates since the balance of payments data is published with a two-month lag and the remaining data with a one-month lag.

The selection bias or the introduction of unavailable data may explain why the H&J trading rule outperforms B&H by 1.2% per year. Malkiel and Quandt (1972) find that by extending the time period to 1970 and employing revised data, the H&J rule performs no better than B&H. Their result and the likelihood of selection bias and/or use of unavailable data in the rule indicate that the H&J trading rule can be regarded as highly tenuous evidence, at best, against the EM model.

5.7. Cooper's Study

The Cooper study (1972) differs greatly from prior studies of money and stock prices since it introduces the efficient market model and sets out the contradiction between Sprinkel's model and the EM model. The simple quantity, or SQ, model (comparable to the MP model) is characterized by Cooper by an equation which represents stock returns as a function of current and past money supply *growth* rates, g,

$$\tilde{R}_t = f(g_t, g_{t-1}, \ldots) + \tilde{u}_t \tag{34}$$

Cooper also develops another model in which unanticipated stock returns are a function of current and past unanticipated money supply growth rates, g^u,

$$\tilde{R}_t - E(\tilde{R}_t) = \tilde{R}_t^u = k(g_t^u, g_{t-1}^u, \ldots) + \tilde{v}_t \tag{35}$$

Expected returns, $E(\tilde{R}_t)$, are given as a function of current and lagged prediction terms, g_t^a, where it appears that g_t^a is a prediction of g_{t+1}, g_{t-1}^a is a prediction of g_t, etc.,

$$E(\tilde{R}_t) = h(g_t^a, g_{t-1}^a, \ldots) + \tilde{v}_t' \tag{36}$$

Combining (35) and (36) gives

$$\tilde{R}_t = f(g_t^u, g_{t-1}^u, \ldots) + h(g_t^a, g_{t-1}^a, \ldots) + \tilde{w}_t \tag{37}$$

(37) is Cooper's combined SQ-EM model. Cooper (1972, p. 15) identifies the arguments of h as the 'efficient markets hypothesis portion of the model'. To test the efficient market model, however, it is unclear why past anticipations $(g_{t-1}^a, \ldots)$ should be identified as the EM hypothesis. Also the current term g_t^u *could* be significant (or not) in an efficient market. Although the approach taken by (35) is in the right direction, the hypotheses to be tested are not clearly stated by Cooper. Thus when testing is undertaken, Cooper (1972, p. 32) states that in the SQ model (34) 'current and lagged values of money supply changes should be the determinants of returns' while the SQ-EM model (37)

'would have returns both leading and lagging money supply changes'. There are two logical difficulties in these statements of the hypotheses: (1) both the EM model and the SQ model are consistent with a world in which current money supply changes determine returns; (2) the EM model is inconsistent with a world in which returns lag money supply changes.

Cooper presents regressions that correspond to (34) modified to include future monetary terms. The relationship to (37) is unclear. $\bar{R}^2$ using monthly data is 0.069 for (34) with 12 lagged terms and 6 future terms. An F-test for the significance of the regression is not reported nor are other details such as the definitions of the variables and the period the test covers.[44] Of particular interest in testing the EM model against the predictive MP model would have been an F-test for the significance of the lagged money terms, even though publication lag was ignored. There is some evidence in the regression that stock returns anticipate future monetary growth, since months 2 and 3 *after* the current month are individually significant at a 90% level, but these highly suggestive results were not followed up.

In Cooper's spectral analysis, it is unclear whether any future terms are used; he refers to coherence spectra which employ 48 (and 96) lagged terms, so that future terms may be omitted. The coherence spectra of returns and money growth rates using monthly and weekly data indicate very weak relationships overall, but Cooper has provided no joint tests across all frequencies. Had he done so, it is quite possible that the weekly data would not have supported any money–stock price relationship since only a few bands are significant at the 90% level. Similarly, the monthly coherence spectrum does not seem to show much of a relation except for a few bands which pass 90% confidence tests at low frequencies. It appears to be a prime concern of Cooper to explain this spectrum feature.

Lead/lag spectra are also presented. According to Cooper (1972, p. 46), these are in principle ambiguous on the crucial question of the sign and length of any lags:

'However . . . there is some difficulty in interpreting the phase spectrum: namely, the phase is only unique in the range 0 to 2π. For example, for a phase shift of one-quarter cycle for a frequency corresponding to eight months, the phase may be interpreted as money lagging returns by two months, or lagging by ten months (two plus eight), etc., or even leading by six months. Therefore, a priori information must be incorporated in order to uniquely represent the lead/lag spectrum.'

Cooper presents two versions for interpretation. In one, returns lead money growth rates over many low frequencies by a fairly constant 0–3 months and lag over high frequencies by 0–1 month; in the other, money growth rates consistently load returns but with greater variation: 0–5 months for approxi-

---

[44] At this time after several inquiries I have been unable to obtain this information.

mately ¾ of the frequencies and 5–80 months as the frequencies grow smaller. Cooper favors the former interpretation because of the constancy of the lag over the low frequencies, although even in this case the lead of returns over money does vary to as much as 16 months at the lowest frequency. There does seem to be a fundamental ambiguity in choosing a spectrum that is 'preferable'.

In summary, Cooper recognizes the conflict between the EM and MP models but does not test the different hypotheses. His regression evidence provides some support for the hypothesis that monetary variables affect stock returns but is silent on the sign and length of any lag or its usefulness in prediction if it exists. The coherence spectra do not appear to provide very much support for the non-predictive model. The lead/lag spectra are ambiguous on the question of whether money leads stock returns or vice versa. They do not provide hypothesis tests that allow us to choose between the EM model and the predictive MP model.

Cooper attempts to show that two features of the spectra are consistent with his SQ–EM model (37). These features are the larger coherence at lower frequencies and, for the preferred lead/lag spectrum, the observed lead of returns at lower frequencies and lead of money growth rates at high frequencies. Cooper's presentation contains several crucial errors of interpretation which undermine his conclusions.[45]

Cooper employs a function $G_4(f)$ which is essentially the ratio of the cross spectrum of his variables g and g_t^a to the spectrum of g. He does not provide definitions for the cross spectra, Fourier transforms or cross covariance functions that he uses. Using Fishman's definitions (1969, pp. 90–93) and letting $y_t = g_t^a$ and $x_t = g_t$, $G_4(f)$ can be written:

$$G_4(f) = (R_{y,0}^{\frac{1}{2}} \cdot \sum_{s=-\infty}^{+\infty} C_{xy,s} e^{-ifs}) / (R_{x,0}^{\frac{1}{2}} \cdot \sum_{s=-\infty}^{+\infty} C_{x,s} e^{-ifs}) \qquad (38)$$

where

$$R_{x,s} = E[(x_t - u_x)(x_{t+s} - u_x)] \qquad \text{autocovariance}$$

$$u_x = E(x_t) \text{ and } u_y = E(y_t) \qquad \text{stationary means}$$

$$R_{xy,s} = E[(x_t - u_x)(y_{t+s} - u_y)] \qquad \text{cross-covariance}$$

$$C_{x,s} = R_{x,s}/R_{x,0} \qquad \text{autocorrelation}$$

$$C_{xy,s} = R_{xy,s}/(R_{x,0}R_{y,0})^{\frac{1}{2}} \qquad \text{cross-correlation}$$

Cooper states that when y_t (i.e., g_t^a) is a perfect predictor of x_{t+s} (i.e., g_t),

---

[45] Discussions with Professor Marshall Freimer contributed to the formulation of these criticisms.

$G_4(f)$ will equal one. This is not necessarily the case since $G_4(f)$ is a ratio of *covariances,* not correlations, and is therefore uncorrected for scale. Even if $C_{x,s} = C_{xy,s}$ for every s and y is a perfect predictor of x, the ratio can be ½ or 2 or any other number due to the presence of the scaling factors $R_{x,0}$ and $R_{y,0}$ whose magnitudes are unknown. Thus the contention that $G_4(f)$ equals one when g_t^a is a perfect predictor of g_t is erroneous.

Cooper then states that no predictive content for y_t implies that $G_4(f)$ is zero. Written out, the numerator of the ratio contains such terms as

$$\ldots + E[(x_t - u_x)(y_{t-2} - u_y)] e^{2if} + E[(x_t - u_x)(y_{t-1} - u_y)] e^{if}$$

$$+ E[(x_t - u_x)(y_t - u_y)] + E[(x_t - u_x)(y_{t+1} - u_y)] e^{-if} + \ldots$$

'No predictive content' can mean that x_t is unrelated to the predictors y_{t-1}, y_{t-2}, etc., and that all these cross covariances are zero. But why should the terms in y_{t+1} not be allowed to have positive covariances with x_t? In particular, suppose that the predictions y_{t+i} are based on past values of x_t. These predictions could prove to be wrong and yet these covariances would not necessarily vanish. Cooper's conclusion in his equation (2.25) that $G_4(f)$ lies between zero and one appears to be faulty. But it is this numerical simplification which is crucial to his remaining interpretations of the spectra.

5.8. Conclusions

Past studies of money and stock prices (except Cooper's) differ in detail but agree that stock returns lag behind changes in monetary policy. Sprinkel, Palmer, Reilly and Lewis and Homa and Jaffee explicitly reach this conclusion with Sprinkel and Homa and Jaffee attempting to develop profitable trading rules using the lag. Keran implicitly assumes market inefficiency when he predicts stock prices from available data and Hamburger and Kochin present a regression model in which lagged money terms appear to be highly significant. All of these studies are therefore inconsistent with the EM model.

As section 4 shows, the lag of stock price changes behind changes in monetary policy is for all practical purposes non-existent in regression tests and of no use in trading rules. Stock returns in fact seem to *anticipate* future monetary change. This evidence is consistent with the EM model.

The conflicts between prior studies and the efficient market model can be resolved in favor of the EM model. For a variety of reasons, past studies have reached the opposite conclusion. Sprinkel's conclusions depend upon tenuous graphical analysis and an ex post selection procedure which is not in fact a valid trading rule. Palmer's evidence for a lag is non-existent. Reilly and Lewis' conclusions are at odds with the evidence they themselves present which shows weak relationships of money and stock returns even including current monetary terms. Keran's model does not produce better predictions of stock prices than a simple martingale model which assumes that next period's price will be equal to this period's price. The significance of lagged terms in Hamburger and Kochin's model seems to be a result of imposition of the Almon lag as well as non-independence in the regressors. Finally, in the Homa and Jaffee trading rule there is some degree of selection bias and probably the introduction of unavailable information in the trading rule.

6. Summary

The purpose of this study was to elucidate and resolve the apparent conflict between two widely known and accepted economic models, the monetary portfolio (MP) model (as applied to the stock market) and the efficient market (EM) model. The monetary portfolio model seeks to explain how changes in monetary policy, particularly changes in money growth rates, transmit their effects to market prices via portfolio rearrangements of market participants. As applied in many studies, the MP model implies a positive average lag of stock price changes (or returns) behind changes in the growth rates of monetary aggregates. This raises the possibility of the existence of profitable trading rules based on the lag. In an efficient market, however, available information concerning changes in monetary policy is fully reflected in *current* stock prices. Profit-maximizing investors who utilize available information about current and prospective changes in monetary policy produce a competitive equilibrium in which all available information is reflected in current prices. The efficient market model thus denies the positive lag and profitable trading rules based on it.

Section 2 reviewed the efficient market model and elucidated the areas of conflict (and agreement) of the two models. While the efficient market model conflicts with the *predictive* form of the monetary model, which states that stock returns can profitably be predicted using lagged money data, it is consistent with the *non-predictive* form of the monetary model, in that stock returns can be related to current or future money data. Section 3 developed models which were used to test the hypotheses in section 4. Section 5 analyzed past studies of money and stock prices. The major conclusions reached in section 5 can be summarized as follows:

(1) Sprinkel's graphical analysis is insufficient to demonstrate any lag of stock price changes behind monetary growth and, in fact, presents no convincing evidence of any relationship at all between money and stock prices. His 'trading rule' is entirely ex post in nature not only in application but also logically, i.e., it could not possibly be used by any investor in an attempt to generate extranormal profits since it relies on a knowledge of NBER business cycle turning points that is unavailable when investment decisions must be made.

(2) The Keran and Hamburger and Kochin models demonstrate statistically that stock returns are related to current and lagged monetary variables as a group. However, the coefficients of lagged variables are constrained by an Almon lag which involves a specification error if the lagged coefficients are zero (which is consistent with the efficient market model). The effect of the constraint is to smear a contemporaneous relation back over the lagged coefficients and bias a test of the significance of the lagged coefficients against the EM model. Keran attempts to use his model to predict stock prices and concludes that the model is successful. The comparisons that we made using his predictions indicate failure to out-predict a martingale model.

(3) Cooper outlines for the first time in a major published study the efficient market model's disagreement with the monetary portfolio model and suggests that stock returns may be related to future monetary terms; but in his use of spectral techniques, he fails to distinguish lagged, current and future terms. Hypothesis tests are lacking and his algebraic interpretation of the spectra appears to be faulty.

(4) All of the studies appear to be insufficient for testing the efficient market model since they employ ex post data in the form of revised measures of the money supply and data is assumed to be available with zero lag in publication.

The findings of section 4 are as follows:

(1) Stock returns are virtually unrelated to *past available* data on growth rates of the money supply and first differences in growth rates. We expect this result in a market that is efficient with respect to monetary information. *There are no meaningful positive lags.* Trading rules based on any relations that do exist are unprofitable compared to equivalent risk buy-and-hold policies. Past money supply data carries no information about future changes in stock prices.

(2) Current stock returns bear a significant relationship to current monetary growth rates, but excess profits cannot be earned on the basis of the relation unless one has advance knowledge of growth rates of the money supply. This evidence is consistent with the *non-predictive* form of the monetary portfolio model. All relationships of stock returns to monetary variables are significantly improved when current stock returns are related to *future* monetary data. The improvement is consistent with a world in which changes in the rate of growth of the money supply affect stock prices and there exists an efficient market which uses available information to form accurate anticipations of future monetary growth rates.

(3) Using refined measures of unexpected changes in money growth rates based on dependencies in the time series of money growth rates, the relationship of stock returns to past monetary disturbances is shown to be vanishingly small. By contrast, stock returns anticipate even some part of the money growth rate series that cannot be predicted from the time series of past growth rates. The market thus appears to make use of all information contained in the serial

dependence of money growth rates and, in addition, other information such that stock returns anticipate elements of the 'whitened' growth rate series.

(4) Sims' test for one-way causality cannot be used with what he calls a 'reversed-causation-with-accurate-anticipations' model. In an efficient market, this model is exactly what we would expect. Thus, stock returns are unrelated to the lagged values of the money variable but *are* related to future values. A model with both stock returns and money endogenous is also consistent with the evidence but, given an efficient stock market, Sims' test for unidirectional causality seems arbitrarily to assign causality to the stock variable.

(5) The stock market appears to process weekly monetary data efficiently. Prior to 1967, money data was published 1–2 months after its occurrence, implying excess profits for anyone learning of monetary information without publication lag. Since 1967, weekly data has greatly reduced this publication lag and, despite the larger measurement error in weekly data, has apparently erased any previous advantage of having the current data. This evidence is also inconsistent with the hypothesis that stock returns lag behind monetary policy.

In conclusion, the evidence is inconsistent with the predictive form of the monetary portfolio model and consistent with the efficient market model. *For the stock market, the lag in effect of monetary policy is essentially zero.* Stock returns do not lag behind growth rates of the money supply, nor would we expect them to do so in an efficient market. Still, changes in stock prices *are* related to monetary variables as the non-predictive form of the monetary portfolio model suggests. A substantial fraction of current stock price change can be linked to current monetary policy. In addition, an important part of current stock price change appears to reflect stock market anticipations of future monetary growth, a result we would expect in an efficient market.

References

Alexander, S.S., 1964, Price movements in speculative markets: Trends or random walks, in: P. Cootner, ed., The random character of stock prices (M.I.T. Press, Cambridge) 199–218.

Almon, S., 1965, The distributed lag between capital appropriations and expenditures, Econometrica, Jan., 178–96.

Black, F., M.C. Jensen and M. Scholes, 1972, The capital asset pricing model: Some empirical tests, in: M.C. Jensen, ed., Studies in the theory of capital markets (Praeger, New York).

Booth, D.G. and R.G. Ibbotson, 1970, The relationship between the money supply and stock prices, Preliminary draft of unpublished paper, March.

Brealey, R.A., 1971, Security prices in a competitive market (M.I.T. Press, Cambridge).

Brunner, K., 1961, Some major problems in monetary theory, American Economic Review Proceedings, May, 47–56.

Brunner, K. and A. Meltzer, 1972, Money, debt, and economic activity, Journal of Political Economy, July, 951–977.

Burger, A.E., 1971, The money supply process (Wadsworth, Belmont, Calif.).

Burger, A.E., 1972, Money stock control, Federal Reserve Bank of St. Louis Review, Oct., 10–16.

Cagan, P., 1972, The channels of monetary effects on interest rates (Columbia University Press, New York).

Cagan, P. and A. Gandolphi, 1969, The lag in monetary policy as implied by the pattern of monetary effects on interest rates, American Economic Review, May, 277–284.

Cooper, R.V.L., 1972, Efficient capital markets and the quantity theory of money (The Rand Corporation, Santa Monica) forthcoming in the Journal of Finance.

Cootner, P., 1964, The random character of stock prices (M.I.T. Press, Cambridge).

Fama, E.T., 1970, Efficient capital markets: A review of theory and empirical work, Journal of Finance, May, 383–417.

Fama, E.F., 1973, Short-term interest rates as predictors of inflation, First draft of unpublished paper, July.

Fama, E.F. and M. Blume, 1966, Filter rules and stock market trading profits, Journal of Business, Jan., 226–241.

Fishman, G., 1969, Spectral methods in econometrics (Harvard University Press, Cambridge).

Friedman, M., 1961, The lag in effect of monetary policy, Journal of Political Economy, Oct., 447–466.

Friedman, M. and A.J. Schwartz, 1963, Money and business cycles, Review of Economics and Statistics, Supplement, Feb., 32–64.

Friedman, M. and A.J. Schwartz, 1970, Monetary statistics of the United States (Columbia University Press, New York).

Gibson, W.E., 1970, The lag in the effect of monetary policy on income and interest rates, Quarterly Journal of Economics, May, 288–300.

Gordon, D.F. and A. Hynes, 1970, On the theory of price dynamics, in: E.S. Phelps, ed., Microeconomic foundations of employment and inflation theory (Norton, New York).

Hamburger, M.J. and L.A. Kochin, 1972, Money and stock prices: The channels of influence, Journal of Finance, May, 231–249.

Homa, K.E. and D.M. Jaffee, 1971, The supply of money and common stock prices, Journal of Finance, Dec., 1056–1066.

Jensen, M.C. and G.A. Bennington, 1970, Random walks and technical theories: Some additional evidence, Journal of Finance, May, 469–482.

Johnston, J., 1963, Econometric methods (McGraw-Hill, New York).

Kendall, M.G., 1964, The analysis of economic time-series, Part I: Prices, in: P. Cootner, ed., The random character of stock prices (M.I.T. Press, Cambridge), 85–99.

Keran, M.W., 1971, Expectations, money and the stock market, Federal Reserve Bank of St. Louis Review, Jan., 16–31.

Laffer, A.B. and R.D. Ranson, 1971, A formal model of the economy, Journal of Business, July, 247–270.

Lorie, J.H. and M.T. Hamilton, 1973, The stock market, theories and evidence (Richard D. Irwin, Homewood, Ill.).

Malkiel, B.G. and R.E. Quandt, 1972, The supply of money and common stock prices: Comment, Journal of Finance, Sept., 921–926.

Mandelbrot, B., 1966, Forecasts of future prices, unbiased markets, and 'Martingale' models, Journal of Business, Jan., 242–255.

Meigs, J.A., 1972 Money matters (Harper & Row, New York).

Miller, M.H., 1972, Discussion, Journal of Finance, May, 294–298.

Modigliani, F., 1971, Monetary policy and consumption: Linkages via interest rate and wealth effects in the FMP model, in: Consumer spending and monetary policy, The linkages, Conf. Ser. no. 5 (The Federal Reserve Bank of Boston, Boston).

Moore, A.B., 1964, Some characteristics of changes in stock prices, in: P. Cootner, ed., The random character of stock prices (M.I.T. Press, Cambridge) 139–161.

Muth, J.F., 1961, Rational expectations and the theory of price movements, Econometrica, July, 315–335.

Nelson, C.R., 1973, Applied time series analysis for managerial forecasting (Holdern-Day, San Francisco).

Palmer, M., 1970, Money supply, portfolio adjustments and stock prices. Financial Analysts Journal, July–Aug., 19–22.

Patinkin, D., 1972, Studies in monetary economics (Harper & Row, New York).

Reilly, F.K. and J.E. Lewis, 1971, Monetary variables and stock prices, Working Paper no. 38, March (School of Business, University of Kansas, Lawrence).

Roll, R., 1971, Interest rates on monetary assets and commodity price index changes, Preliminary draft, Oct.

Rozeff, M.S., 1974, Money and stock prices: Market efficiency and the lag in effect of monetary policy, Unpublished doctoral dissertation (Graduate School of Management, University of Rochester).

Samuelson, P.A., 1965, Proof that properly anticipated prices fluctuate randomly, Industrial management review, Spring, 41–49.

Samuelson, P.A., 1973, Proof that properly discounted present values of assets vibrate randomly, The Bell Journal of Economics and Management Science, Autumn, 369–374.

Schmidt, P. and R.N. Waud, 1973, The Almon lag technique and the monetary versus fiscal policy debate, Unpublished paper, Oct.

Sims, C.A., 1972, Money, income, and causality, American Economic Review, Sept., 277–284.

Sprinkel, B.W., 1964, Money and stock prices (Richard D. Irwin, Homewood, Ill.).

Sprinkel, B.W., 1971, Money and markets: A monetarist view (Richard D. Irwin, Homewood, Ill.).

Waud, R.N., 1970, Public interpretation of Federal Reserve discount rate changes: Evidence on the 'announcement effect', March, 231–250.

18

How to Use Security Analysis to Improve Portfolio Selection

Jack L. Treynor and Fischer Black

It has been argued convincingly in a series of papers on the Capital Asset Pricing Model that, in the absence of insight generating expectations different from the market consensus, the investor should hold a replica of the market portfolio.[1] A number of empirical papers have demonstrated that portfolios of more than 50-100 randomly selected securities tend to correlate very highly with the market portfolio, so that, as a practical matter, replicas are relatively easy to obtain. If the investor has no special insights, therefore, he has no need of the elaborate balancing algorithms of Markowitz and Sharpe.[2] On the other hand if he has special insights, he will get little, if any, help from the portfolio-balancing literature on how to translate these insights into the expected returns, variances, and covariances the algorithms require as inputs.

What was needed, it seemed to us, was exploration of the link between conventional subjective, judgmental, work of the security analyst, on one hand—rough cut and not very quantitative—and the essentially objective, statistical approach to portfolio selection of Markowitz and his successors, on the other.

The void between these two bodies of ideas was made manifest by our inability to answer to our own satisfaction the following kinds of questions: Where practical is it desirable to so balance a portfolio between long positions in securities considered underpriced and short positions in securities considered overpriced that market risk is completely eliminated (i.e., hedged)? Or should one strive to diversify a portfolio so completely that only market risk remains? As this implies, in the highly diversified portfolio market sensitivity in individual securities seems to contribute directly to market sensitivity in the overall portfolio, whereas other sources of return variability in individual securities seem

---

[1] William F. Sharpe, "CApital Asset Prices: A Theory of Market Equilibrium under Conditions of Risk," *Journal of Finance* 19, no. 3 (September 1964): 425–42; John Lintner, "The Valuation of Risk Assets and the Selection of Risky Investments in Stock Portfolios and Capital Budgets," *Review of Economics and Statistics* 57, no. 1 (February 1954): 13–37; and Jack L. Treynor's paper, "Toward a Theory of the Market Values of Risky Assets" (unpublished, 1961).

[2] Harry Markowitz, *Portfolio Selection: Efficient Diversification of Investments* (New York: John Wiley and Sons, 1959; New Haven, Conn.: Yale University Press, 1970); and William Sharpe, "A Simplified Model for Portfolio Analysis," *Management Science* 9 (January 1963): 277–93.

to average out. Does this mean that the latter sources of variability are unimportant in portfolio selection? When balancing risk against expected return in selection of individual securities, what risk and what return are relevant? Will increasing the number of securities analyzed improve the diversification of the optimal portfolio? Is any measure of the contribution of security analysis to portfolio performance invariant with respect to both levering and turnover? How do analysts' opinions enter in security selection? Is there any simple way to characterize the quality of security analysis that will tell us when one analyst can be expected to make a greater contribution to a portfolio than another? What role, if any, does confidence in an analyst's forecasts have in portfolio selection? This paper offers answers to these questions.

The paper has a normative flavor. We offer no apologies for this. In some cases, institutional practice and, in some cases, law are shortsighted; in all cases they reflect what is by anybody's standard an old-fashioned idea of what the investment management business is all about. If we tried to develop a body of theory which reflected some of the constraints imposed institutionally and legally, it would inevitably be a theory with a very short life expectancy. Our model is based on an idealized world in which there are no restrictions on borrowing, or on selling securities short; in which the interest rate on loans is equal to the interest rate on short-term assets such as savings accounts; and in which there are no taxes. We expect that the major conclusions derived from the model will largely be valid, however, even with the constraints and frictions of the real world. Those that are not valid can usually be modified to fit the constraints that actually exist.

Certain recent research has suggested that professional investment managers really have not been very successful,[3] but we make the assumption that security analysis, properly used, can improve portfolio performance. This paper is directed toward finding a way to make the best possible use of the information provided by security analysts.

The basic fact from which we build is one that a number of writers have recognized—namely, that there is a high degree of comovement among security prices. Perhaps the simplest model of covariability among securities is Sharpe's Diagonal Model. As Sharpe sees it, "The major characteristic of the Diagonal Model is the assumption that the returns of various securities are related only through common relationships with some basic underlying factor. . . . This model has two virtues: it is one of the simplest which can be constructed without assuming away the existence of interrelationships among securities and there is considerable evidence that it can capture a large part of such interrelationships."[4] This paper takes Sharpe's Diagonal Model as its starting point;

---

[3]Michael Jensen, "The Performance of Mutual Funds in the Period 1945–1964," *Journal of Finance* 23 (May 1968): 389–416.

[4]See Sharpe, n. 2.

we accept without change the form of the Diagonal Model and most of Sharpe's assumptions.

Use of the Diagonal Model for portfolio selection implies departure from equilibrium in the sense of all investors having the same information (and appraising it similarly)—as, for example, is assumed in some versions of the Capital Asset Pricing Model. The viewpoint in this paper is that of an individual investor who is attempting to trade profitably on the difference between his expectations and those of a monolithic market so large in relation to his own trading that market prices are unaffected by it. Throughout, we ignore the costs of buying and selling. This makes it possible for us to treat the portfolio-selection problem as a single-period problem (implicitly assuming a one-period utility function as given), in the tradition of Markowitz, Sharpe, et al. We believe that these costs are often substantial and, if incorporated into this analysis, would modify certain of our results substantially.

Definitions

Following Lintner, we define the excess return on a security for a given time interval as the actual return on the security less the interest paid on short-term risk-free assets over that interval.

A regression of the excess return on a security against the market's excess return gives two regression factors. The first is the market sensitivity, or "beta," of the security; and, except for sample error, the second should be zero. We define the explained return on the security over a given time interval to be its market sensitivity times the market's excess return over the interval.

We define the independent return to be the excess return minus the explained return. The independent return, because of the properties of regression, is statistically independent of the market's excess return. Our model assumes that the "independent" returns of different securities are almost, but not quite, statistically independent. The "risk premium" on the ith security is equal to the security's market sensitivity times the market's expected excess return. Symbols for these concepts are defined as:

r = riskless rate of return

x_i = return on the ith security

y_i = excess return on the ith security

y_m = excess return on the market

b_i = market sensitivity of the ith security

$b_i y_m$ = explained, or systematic, return on ith security

z_i = independent return on ith security

Let E [ ] and var [ ] represent the expectation and variance, respectively, of the variable in brackets. Then define

$$\bar{z}_i = E[z_i]$$

$$\bar{y}_m = E[y_m]$$

We call the first the "appraisal premium" for the ith security, and the second, the "market premium."

$$\sigma_i^2 = \text{var}[z_i - \bar{z}_i]$$

$$\sigma_m^2 = \text{var}[y_m - \bar{y}_m]$$

and

$$b_i E[y_m] = \text{market premium on the } i\text{th security}$$

If one defines the "explained error" in a security's return as the explained return minus the risk premium, and the "residual error" as the independent return minus the appraisal premium, the structure of the model described above can be summarized in the following way:

Actual return
    Riskless rate, $r\Delta t$
Excess return
  Explained return
    Market premium, $b_i \bar{y}_m$
    Explained error, $b_i(y_m - \bar{y}_m)$
  Independent return
    Appraisal premium, $\bar{z}_i$
    Residual error, $z_i - \bar{z}_i$

We can arrange this structure to group together the components of the total return as follows:

Actual return
  Expected return
    Riskless rate, $r\Delta t$
    Market premium, $b_i \bar{y}_m$
    Appraisal premium, $\bar{z}_i$

Actual minus expected return
  Explained error, $b_i(y_m - \bar{y}_m)$
  Residual error, $z_i - \bar{z}_i$

Using our definitions we can write the one-period return on the ith security as

$$x_i = r\Delta t + y_i = r + b_i y_m + z_i \tag{1}$$

Sharpe's Diagonal Model stipulates that

$$E[(z_i - \bar{z}_i)(z_j - \bar{z}_j)] = 0, E[(z_i - \bar{z}_i)(y_m - \bar{y}_m)] = 0 \tag{2}$$

for all i, j. As noted above, these relationships can hold only approximately.

The return on a security over a future interval is uncertain. This paper shares with Markowitz the mean-variance approach, implying normal return distributions. There is fairly conclusive evidence that the distribution is not normal, but that its behavior is similar to that of a normal distribution, so the model assumes a normal distribution as an approximation to the actual distribution. The qualitative results of the model should not be affected by this approximation, but the quantitative results should be modified somewhat to reflect the actual distribution.

However one defines "risk" in terms of the probability distribution of portfolio return, the distribution, being approximately normal, is virtually determined by its mean and variance. But under the assumptions noted here (finite variances and independence) the mean and variance of portfolio return depend only on the means and variances of independent returns for specific securities and on the explained return (and, of course, on the portfolio weights). On the other hand, risk in the specific security is significant to the investor only as it affects portfolio risk. Hence it is tempting to identify risk in the ith security with the elements in the security that contribute to portfolio variance— the variance of the independent return σ_i^2 ("specific risk") and the variance of explained return $b_i^2 \sigma_m^2$ ("market risk"). In what follows, we will occasionally yield to this temptation.

Let the fraction of the investor's capital devoted to the ith security be h_i. Using symbols defined above, the one-period return on his portfolio is

$$\sum_{i=1}^{n} h_i x_i - r\Delta t \left(\sum_{i=1}^{n} h_i - 1 \right) = \sum_{i=1}^{n} h_i(y_i + r\Delta t) - r\Delta t \left(\sum_{i=1}^{n} h_i - 1 \right)$$

$$= r\Delta t + \sum_{i=1}^{n} h_i y_i \tag{3}$$

We note that, although there are three sources of return on the individual security—the riskless return, the explained return, and the independent return—only two of these are at stake in portfolio selection. Henceforth we shall ignore the first term in equation (3).

Understanding the way in which portfolio mean and variance are influenced by selection decisions requires expansion of security return into all its elements. Excess return on the portfolio, expressed in terms of the individual securities held, is

$$\sum_{i=1}^{n} h_i b_i y_m + \sum_{i=1}^{n} h_i z_i \tag{4}$$

Evidently we have only n degrees of freedom—the portfolio weights h_i, with $i = 1, \ldots, n$—in selecting among $n + 1$ sources of return. Since the market asset can always be freely bought or sold to acquire an explicit position h_m in the market asset, when we take this into account we have for the excess portfolio return the expression

$$\left(h_m + \sum_{i=1}^{n} h_i b_i \right) y_m + \sum_{i=1}^{n} h_i z_i \tag{5}$$

It is obvious that availability of the market asset makes it possible to achieve any desired exposure to market risk, approximately independently of any decisions regarding desired exposure to independent returns on individual securities. In effect, we then have $n + 1$ mutually independent securities, where

$$h_{n+1} = h_m + \sum_{i=1}^{n} h_i b_i, \mu_i = E(z_i) \quad i = 1, \ldots, n, \mu_{n+1} = E[y_m] \tag{6}$$

If we apply these conventions and run our summations from 1 to $n + 1$, we have for the mean and variance of the portfolio return, respectively,

$$\mu_p = \sum_{i=1}^{n+1} h_i \mu_i, \sigma_p^2 = \sum_{i=1}^{n+1} h_i^2 \sigma_i^2 \tag{7}$$

We take as our objective minimizing σ_p^2 while holding μ_p fixed. We form the Lagrangian

$$\sum_{i=1}^{n+1} h_i^2 \sigma_i^2 - 2\lambda \left(\sum_{i=1}^{n+1} h_i \mu_i - \mu_p \right) \tag{8}$$

introducing the undetermined multiplier λ, differentiate with respect to h_i, and set the result equal to zero:

$$2h_i \sigma_i^2 - 2\lambda \mu_i = 0 \tag{9}$$

Solving for h_i we have

$$h_i = \lambda \mu_i / \sigma_i^2 \tag{10}$$

Substituting this result in equation (7) we have

$$\mu_p = \lambda \sum_{i=1}^{n+1} \mu_i^2 / \sigma_i^2, \sigma_p^2 = \lambda^2 \sum_{i=1}^{n+1} \mu_i^2 / \sigma_i^2 \tag{11}$$

We see from (11) that the value of the multiplier λ is given by

$$\lambda = \sigma_p^2 / \mu_p \tag{12}$$

The optimum position h_i in the ith security ($i = 1, \ldots, n$) is given by equation (13):

$$h_i = \frac{\mu_i}{\mu_p} \frac{\sigma_p^2}{\sigma_i^2} \qquad i = 1, \ldots, n^- \tag{13}$$

In order to obtain an expression for the optimal position h_m in the market portfolio, we recall that

$$\mu_{n+1} = E[y_m] = \mu_m$$

$$\sigma_{n+1}^2 = \text{var}[y_m] = \sigma_m^2$$

and substitute these expressions together with the definitions of h_{n+1} from equation (5) in (11) to obtain

$$\sum_{i=1}^{n} h_i b_i + h_m = \lambda \mu_m / \sigma_m^2 \tag{14}$$

Multiplying both members of (10) by b_i and summing we have

$$\sum_{i=1}^{n} h_i b_i = \lambda \sum_{i=1}^{n} b_i \mu_i / \sigma_i^2 \tag{15}$$

which can be substituted in (14) to give

$$h_m = \lambda \left(\mu_m / \sigma_m^2 - \sum_{i=1}^{n} \mu_m / \sigma_m^2 \right) \tag{16}$$

It was apparent in equation (5) that market risk enters the portfolio both in the form of an explicit investment in the market portfolio and implicitly in the selection of individual securities, the returns from which covary with the market. Equation (13) says "take positions in securities $1, \ldots, n$ purely on the basis of expected independent return and variance." The resulting exposure to market risk is disregarded.

Equation (16) provides us with an expression for the optimal investment in an explicit market portfolio. This investment is designed to complement the market position accumulated in the course of taking positions in individual securities solely with regard to their independent returns. Under the assumptions of the Diagonal Model, position in the market follows the same rule as position in individual securities; but because market position is accumulated as a by-product of positions in individual securities, explicit investment in the market as a whole is limited to making up the difference between the optimal market position and the by-product accumulation (which may, of course, be negative, requiring an explicit position in the market that is short, rather than long).

Equation (16) suggests that the optimal portfolio can usefully be thought of as two portfolios: (1) a portfolio assembled purely with regard for the means and variances of independent returns of specific securities and possessing an aggregate exposure to market risk quite incidental to this regard; and (2) an approximation to the market portfolio. Positions in the first portfolio are zero when appraisal premiums are zero. Since the special information on which expected independent returns are based typically propagates rapidly, becoming fully discounted by the market and eliminating the justification for positions based on this information, the first portfolio will tend to experience a significant amount of trading. Accordingly, we call it the "active portfolio."

It is clear from equation (10) that changes in the investor's attitude toward risk bearing (λ), or in his market expectations (μ_m), or in the degree of market risk (σ_m^2)—which, as we shall see, depends on how well he can forecast the market—have no effect on the proportions of the active portfolio.

The Capital Asset Pricing Model suggests that any premium for risk bearing will be associated with market, rather than specific risk. If investors in the aggregate are risk averse, then an investment in the market asset—explicit or implicit—offers a premium. We call this particular source of market premium "risk premium"—as opposed to "market premium" deriving from the investor's attempts to forecast fluctuations in the general market level. When all the appraisal premiums are zero, the optimal portfolio is therefore the market portfolio—even if the investor has no power to forecast the market. We shall call a portfolio devoid of specific risk "perfectly diversified." In other words, in our usage "perfect diversification" does not mean the absence of risk, nor does it mean an optimally balanced portfolio, except in the case of zero appraisal premiums.

In general, a given security may play two different roles simultaneously: (1) A temporary position based entirely on expected independent return (appraisal premium) and appraisal risk. As price fluctuates and the investor's information changes, the optimum position changes. (2) A position resulting purely from the fact that the security in question constitutes part of the market portfolio. The latter position changes as market expectations change but is virtually independent of expectations regarding independent return on the security. Hence we call the approximation to the market portfolio employed to achieve the desired level of systematic risk the "passive portfolio." The literal interpretation of equation (16) is that a desired explicit market position h_m would be achieved by adding positions in individual securities in the proportions in which they are represented in the market as a whole. For example, let the fraction of the market as a whole comprised by the ith security be h_{mi}. Then an explicit market position h_m can be achieved by taking positions $h_m h_{mi}$ in the individual securities. These positions are, of course, in addition to positions taken with regard to specific return. Overall positions are then given by combining positions desired for fulfilling the two functions of bearing appraisal and market risk:

$$h_i = \lambda h_{mi} \left(\mu_m / m^2 - \sum_{i=1}^{n} b_i \mu_i / \sigma_i^2 \right) + \mu_i \sigma_i^2 \tag{17}$$

This is the result one would get by solving the Markowitz formulation, under the assumptions of the Diagonal Model, in the absence of constraints. But it is not a solution of much practical interest, because approximations to the market portfolio add very little additional specific risk while being vastly cheaper to acquire than an exact pro rata replica of the market.

A practical interpretation of equation (16) is that portfolio selection can be thought of as a three-stage process, in which the first stage is selection of an active portfolio to maximize the appraisal ratio, the second is blending the active portfolio with a suitable replica of the market portfolio to maximize the Sharpe ratio, and the third entails scaling positions in the combined portfolio up or down through lending or borrowing while preserving their proportions. Becuase the investor's attitude toward risk bearing comes into play at the third stage, and only at the third stage, a second-stage definition of "goodness" that disregards differences in attitude toward risk bearing from one investor to another is possible.[5]

The Sharpe and Appraisal Ratios

From equation (10) we have, for the optimal holdings, $h_i = \lambda \mu_i / \sigma_i^2$, where, for the optimal second-stage portfolio, we have

$$\mu_p = \lambda \sum_{i=1}^{n+1} \mu_i^2 / \sigma_i^2$$

$$\sigma_p^2 = \lambda^2 \sum_{i=1}^{n+1} \mu_i^2 / \sigma_i^2 \tag{18}$$

How good is the resulting portfolio? A relationship between expected excess return and variance of return is obtained by forming

$$\frac{\mu_p^2}{\sigma_p^2} = \frac{\lambda^2 \left(\sum\limits_{i=1}^{n+1} \mu_i^2 / \sigma_i^2 \right)^2}{\lambda^2 \sum\limits_{i=1}^{n+1} \mu_i^2 / \sigma_i^2} = \sum_{i=1}^{n+1} \mu_i^2 / \sigma_i^2 \tag{19}$$

The resulting ratio is essentially the square of a measure of goodness proposed by William Sharpe;[6] we shall call it the Sharpe ratio. It is obviously independent of scale. The right hand expression readily partitions into two

---

[5]See, for example, William Sharpe, "Mutual Fund Performance," *Journal of Business* 39 (January 1966): 119–38.

[6]Ibid.

terms, one of which depends only on market forecasting and the other of which depends only on forecasting independent returns for specific securities:

$$\frac{\mu_p^2}{\sigma_p^2} = \mu_{n+1}^2/\sigma_{n+1}^2 + \sum_{i=1}^{n} \mu_i^2/\sigma_i^2$$

It is easily shown by writing out the numerator and denominator, and then simplifying as in equation (19), that the second term of (19) is the ratio of appraisal premium, squared, to appraisal variance. This number is obviously invariant with respect to changes in the holdings in the active portfolio by a scale factor, hence of shifts in emphasis between the active and passive portfolios. It measures how far one has to depart from perfect diversification to obtain a given level of expected independent return. Because it summarizes the potential contribution of security appraisal to the portfolio, we call it the appraisal ratio.

Consider, for example, two portfolio managers with the same information about specific securities and the same skill in balancing exposure to specific returns. One can generate a larger appraisal premium than the other simply by taking large positions in specific securities (relative to the market). Hence appraisal premium (as, for example, measured by the Jensen performance measure)[7] is not invariant with respect to such arbitrary changes in portfolio balance. The fact that the appraisal ratio *is* invariant with respect to such changes commends it as a measure of a portfolio manager's skill in gathering and using information specific to individual securities. If, in addition to the same information specific to individual securities, two portfolio managers have the same market expectations, then their scale of exposure to specific returns (relative to their market exposure) should, of course, also be the same, as implied by equation (16). But in performance measurement, it is not safe to assume that the optimal balance will be struck by every portfolio manager. (How well he adheres to the optimal balance between market and specific risk is certainly one aspect of performance. But it is an aspect quite distinct from how well he uses security analysis.)

The appraisal ratio has much to recommend it as a measure of potential fund performance, although it does not directly measure the utility of the overall portfolio to investors. If "aggressiveness" refers to the amount of market risk borne by a diversified fund, and "activity" refers to the amount of trading undertaken in optimizing the active portfolio, then the second stage (at which the active portfolio is balanced against the passive portfolio) determines the

---

[7] See n. 3.

degree of activity in the risky portion of the fund, and the third stage (at which the active portion is mixed or levered to obtain the balance between expected return and risk which meets the investor's personal objectives) determines the aggressiveness of the overall fund.

What happens to the degree of portfolio diversification as (1) the number of securities considered is increased? (2) the number of securities considered is kept constant while the contribution to the appraisal ratio of the average security is increased? Does the former improve the degree of diversification while the latter degrades it? We demonstrate below that the degree of diversification in an optimally balanced portfolio depends on these factors only as they influence the appraisal ratio. (It also depends on market ratio, but the latter is obviously independent of both the contribution to the appraisal ratio of the average security and the number of securities considered.) We also demonstrate that the higher the appraisal ratio (for a given market ratio) the less well diversified the resulting portfolio will be. In short, the more attractive incurring specific risk is relative to incurring market risk, the less well diversified an optimally balanced portfolio will be. Indeed, it is easily shown that at optimal balance we have

$$\frac{\text{appraisal premium}}{\text{market premium}} = \frac{\text{appraisal variance}}{\text{market variance}} = \frac{\text{appraisal ratio}}{\text{market ratio}} \tag{20}$$

where market ratio is defined, analogously with appraisal ratio, as

$$\text{market ratio} = \frac{(\text{market premium})^2}{\text{market variance}} \tag{21}$$

The demonstration below actually applies to optimal (relative) holdings of any two assets whose specific returns are statistically independent. In particular, the "assets" consisting of the market, on one hand, and a weighted combination of independent returns, on the other, are statistically independent for any set of weights, including the optimal set. On the one hand, we have the contribution to the optimally balanced portfolio of market return, y_m, with expectation μ_m and variance σ_m^2. On the other hand, we have the contribution from optimally balanced returns $z, \ldots, z_n$,

$$\sum_{i=1}^{n} h_i z_i$$

with expectation μ_a defined by

$$\mu_a = \sum_{i=1}^{n} h_i \mu_i$$

and variance σ_a^2 defined by

$$\sigma_a^2 = \sum_{i=1}^{n} h_i^2 \sigma_i^2$$

This contribution is, of course, the essential part of the active portfolio, since the contribution of market risk to the overall portfolio is independent of the market risk in the active portfolio (see eq. [16]). It is also statistically independent of the market portfolio, since we have

$$E\left[y_m \sum_{i=1}^{n} h_i z_i\right] = \sum_{i=1}^{n} h_i E[z_i y_m] = 0$$

Let optimal holdings for the market and active portfolios, respectively, be represented by h_m and h_a. Then from equation (10) we have

$$\frac{h_a}{h_m} = \frac{\mu_a/\sigma_a^2}{\mu_m/\sigma_m^2}$$

$$\frac{h_a \mu_a}{h_m \mu_m} = \frac{\mu_a^2/\sigma_a^2}{\mu_m^2/\sigma_m^2} \qquad (22)$$

which demonstrates the equality between the first and third fractions in (20). Squaring and then multiplying both sides by $(\mu_n^2/\sigma_n^2)/(\mu_a^2/\sigma_a^2)$ we have

$$\frac{h_a^2 \sigma_a^2}{h_m^2 \sigma_m^2} = \frac{\mu_a^2/\sigma_a^2}{\mu_m^2/\sigma_m^2} \qquad (23)$$

which demonstrates the equality between the second and third fractions of (20). In an optimally balanced portfolio, total portfolio variance is given by

$$\sigma_p^2 = \sum_{i=0}^{n} h_i^2 \sigma_i^2 = \sum_{i=0}^{n} \left(\lambda \frac{\mu_i}{\sigma_i^2}\right)^2 \sigma_i^2$$

$$= \lambda^2 \sum_{i=0}^{n} \frac{\mu_i^2}{\sigma_i^2} = \lambda^2 \frac{\mu_0^2}{\sigma_0^2} + \sum_{i=1}^{n} \frac{\mu_i^2}{\sigma_i^2} \tag{24}$$

where the first term is the contribution of market variance and the second is the contribution of the combined variance of the independent returns (i.e., the unique variance). Partitioning total variance into these two terms enables us to write the coefficient of determination ρ_p^2 expressing the fraction of total variance accounted for by systematic, or market, effect as

$$p_p^2 = \frac{\lambda^2 \dfrac{\mu_0^2}{\sigma_0^2}}{\lambda^2 \dfrac{\mu_0^2}{\sigma_0^2} + \lambda^2 \displaystyle\sum_{i=1}^{n} \dfrac{\mu_i^2}{\sigma_i^2}}$$

$$= \frac{1}{1 + \dfrac{\displaystyle\sum_{i=1}^{n} \dfrac{\mu_i^2}{\sigma_i^2}}{\dfrac{\mu_0^2}{\sigma_0^2}}}$$

$$= \frac{1}{1 + \dfrac{\text{appraisal ratio}}{\text{market ratio}}} \tag{25}$$

In this form it is clear that any improvement in the quality of security analysis, or in the number of securities analyzed at a given level of quality, can only cause an optimally balanced portfolio to become less well diversified.

Consider again the expression for appraisal ratio

$$\text{appraisal ratio} = \sum_{i=1}^{n} \frac{\mu_i^2}{\sigma_i^2} \tag{26}$$

On the average, half the securities analyzed will be overpriced and half under-priced. Thus if short selling is permitted, on the average half the positions in an ideal active portfolio will be long positions and half short. Since the degree of market risk will generally be distributed among securities randomly with respect to the sign of the current price discrepancy, hence the sign of positions in the active portfolio,[8] the expected level of market risk in an ideal active portfolio is zero. In the ideal case, therefore, the second-stage blending between active and passive portfolios is particularly simple: All the appraisal risk is in the active portfolio, and all the market risk is in the passive portfolio. When short selling is not permitted, however, the expected level of market risk in the active portfolio is the average level for the universe from which active securities are selected. Half the terms in (26) are suppressed, thus on average reducing the appraisal ratio by half.

Deriving Forecasts of Independent Returns from Security Analysis

How are the appraisal premiums and variances for individual securities generated by the security analysis process? There are doubtless many ways of answering this question. The one that follows, which assumes a bivariate normal for the joint distribution of the analyst's opinion and the subsequent independent return, is certainly one of the simplest.

Presumably the analyst begins by appraising the security in question. We have shown that the composition of the active portfolio should be independent of expectations regarding the level of the market as a whole. It follows that, in order to be useful in selection of the active portfolio, the analyst's findings should be expressed in such a way that they are invariant with respect to his overall market expectations. Perhaps the easiest way for the analyst to generate opinions with the desired invariance property (under the independence assumptions of the Diagonal Model) is to estimate the value of the security (i.e., what the equilibrium price would be if all investors had his information) consistent with the consensus macroeconomic forecast implicit in the general level of security prices obtaining at the time of the estimate. The value an analyst assigns to a security may be either greater or less than its present price. (Some analysts may be unwilling to assign a value to the security; they may be more comfortable giving a "buy" price and "sell" price, and we can take the point halfway between as their estimated value.)

The analyst then compares his appraisal with the current market price of the security. It is not important how discrepancies between the analyst's

---

[8]See eq. (27).

estimate and the market price are expressed. The important thing is that there be a significant correlation between the discrepancies and the subsequent actual returns. A portfolio manager can show good results consistently only if his analysts as a group are able to identify discrepancies that are significantly related to the subsequent actual independent return. If data are available for a series of time intervals one can regress independent returns on various securities for various time intervals against the discrepancies for those time intervals in order to determine the relation between the discrepancies and the actual returns.

The familiar two-variable regression model can be used to relate the expected independent return for the ith security to the analyst's current estimate e_i of the discrepancy between market value and his own appraisal as follows:

$$\bar{z}_i = f_i(e_i + g_i) \tag{27}$$

It is possible for an analyst to be persistently bullish or bearish about the independent returns for his stocks. Or the analyst may be free from bias, but consistently overstate (or understate) independent returns, regardless of sign. The term g_i corrects for any persistent upward or downward bias in the analyst's estimate, and the factor f_i corrects for any tendency on the part of the analyst to be too "excitable"; that is, to estimate too high when his appraisal exceeds the current market value and too low when current market value exceeds his appraisal. The same factor can also serve to provide the necessary adjustment when the analyst is not "excitable" enough.

The expression $f_i(e_i + g_i)$ translates an estimate e_i expressed as a percentage of current market value into μ_i. It is worth noting that a forecast of the independent return necessarily implies something about the expected rate at which the market price will adjust to eliminate the alleged discrepancy. Thus the forecast of independent return contains the time dimension, whereas the analyst's estimate of the discrepancy between his appraisal and the current market price does not.

The expected independent rate of return z_i and the estimated discrepancy e_i are assumed to be distributed according to a bivariate normal distribution. The analyst's confidence that he rather than the market is right may vary from one point in time to another; nevertheless, in what follows, the parameters of the distribution are assumed to be stationary. (Since we are discussing an individual security we drop the subscript.) The variables z and e are characterized by variances, or their respective square roots s_z and s_e. A third parameter is necessary to complete the specification of this distribution, namely the correlation coefficient ρ between the variables z and e. In composing the active portfolio we are interested in the conditional distribution of z given e, or $z|e$. Unless an analyst is able to anticipate *all* the events affecting the price, hence the return, on a security, some portion of the independent return variance remains unexplained by his forecasts.

In terms of the parameters characterizing the joint normal distribution of e and z, equation (27) can be rewritten

$$z = \rho \left(\frac{S_z}{S_e} \right) (e + g) \tag{28}$$

Regressing z against e, we get estimates of the slope coefficient $\rho(S_z/S_e)$ and the constant term $\rho(S_z/S_e)g$. It is important to look at the significance of the regression factors found. Normally data covering a number of intervals will be needed to show that any of the regression factors is significantly different from zero. Some of the deviations of the regression coefficients from zero will be due to sample error rather than an actual relation between analysts' estimates and independent returns.

We are also interested in the residual variance (i.e., that part of the total variance in the independent returns on a security not explained by the analyst's estimate). The amount of a security that should be held in the active portfolio depends not only on the independent return expected on the security but also on the residual variance of the independent return around its expected value. The variance σ^2 of forecast errors between $\bar{z}$ and actual z is

$$\sigma^2 = \mathrm{var}\,[z|e] - (1 - \rho^2)s_z^2 \tag{29}$$

We saw in equation (26) that the value of the appraisal ratio for an optimally diversified portfolio depends only on the value of the ratio $\bar{z}^2/\sigma_z^2$ for individual securities. Given the analyst's current appraisal (e), the conditional value of this ratio is

$$\frac{\bar{z}^2}{\sigma^2} = \frac{\rho^2}{1 - \rho^2} \frac{(e + g)^2}{s_e^2} \,_9 \tag{30}$$

The right-hand factor in equation (30) is, of course, merely the square of the analyst's estimate, corrected for bias and normalized to unit variance. The current contribution of the security in question to the appraisal ratio of the active portfolio also depends on the analyst's ability to forecast fluctuations in independent return successfully (ρ).

To say that one analyst is "better" than another implies something about the expected value of the contributions of their respective securities to an active portfolio averaged over a series of holding periods and without specific reference to the forecasts obtaining at the beginning of each holding period. At the begin-

---

[9] See, for example, Harald Cramer, *The Elements of Probability Theory* (Princeton, N.J.: Princeton University Press, 1946), pp. 141 and 142.

ning of each holding period, expectations of independent returns are formed as described above. We continue to denote these expectations by a bar over the appropriate symbol: $\bar{z}$. But now consider a longer-run expectation, based purely on the joint distribution of estimated and actual return, denoting the latter kind of expectations by $E[\ldots]$: We note that, since the expected value over time of $(e + g)$ is zero (with g correcting for any bias in e), the expected value of $(e + g)^2$ is given by

$$E[(e + g)^2] = \text{var}[e] = s_e^2 \tag{31}$$

Thus if the expectation of equation (30) is taken with respect to the distribution of the analyst's forecasts, we have

$$E\left[\frac{\bar{z}^2}{2}\right] = \frac{\rho^2}{1 - \rho^2} \tag{32}$$

In the absence of prior knowledge concerning the analyst's current forecast, therefore, the potential contribution of the security in question to the optimum active portfolio depends solely on ρ. The larger ρ is, the more the security contributes to the optimal active portfolio. The expression in equation (32) can be thought of as the ratio of the variance in residual price changes explained by the analyst's estimates to the variance left unexplained.

In any forecasting problem, there are three kinds of variables: (1) the dependent variable (in this case, independent return); (2) one or more independent explanatory variables (in this case, the analyst's opinion, etc.); and (3) the expected value, or maximum-likelihood forecast of the dependent variable, based on knowledge of the independent variables. In the case considered in this section, the explanatory variable was the difference between the analyst's estimate of value and current price.

When (e) is treated as the discrepancy between current price and appraised value, then, however long a discrepancy has been outstanding, the fraction expected to be resolved in the next holding period is the same (or, equivalently, the probability of complete resolution in the next period is the same). The fraction to be resolved (or the probability of resolution) is independent of the scale of the discrepancy. No allowance is made for the possibility that the rate of resolution may depend in part on the kind of insight leading to identification of the discrepancy or on the source of the insight.

For any or all these reasons, the portfolio manager may prefer to supply his own approach to formulating forecasts of independent return. If (e) is interpreted as representing the explanatory variable upon which the forecast is based—whether derived by fundamental, technical, or other means—the regression model in which (e) appears (eq. [27]) is reduced to the less ambitious role of relating the explanatory variable, forecast, and actual return, without linking the forecasting process directly to the determinations of the security analyst. The price of this decision is, of course, that the process by which the explanatory variable is generated then becomes a black box, determination of whose contents is outside the scope of the model presented here.

The fact that (e) is susceptible of the more general interpretation means, however, that the results regarding the role of the coefficient of determination ρ^2 in portfolio selection are not limited to the model presented here, in which price discrepancy is itself the explanatory variable, but are in fact as general as the application to the forecasting problem of the regression model itself.

All the preceding comments on forecasting the independent return apply to forecasting the market return y_m.

Summary

1. It is useful in balancing portfolios to distinguish between two sources of risk: market, or systematic risk on the one hand, and appraisal, or insurable risk on the other. In general it is not correct to assume that optimal balancing leads either to negligible levels of appraisal risk or to negligible levels of market risk.

2. Without any loss in generality, any portfolio can be thought of as having three parts: a riskless part, a highly diversified part (that is, virtually devoid of specific risk and market risk. The amount of market risk in the active portfolio is unimportant, so long as one has the option of increasing or reducing market risk via the passive portfolio. The overall portfolio can usually be improved by taking a long or short position in the market as a whole.

3. The rate at which a portfolio earns riskless interest is independent of how the portfolio is invested or whether or not the portfolio is levered and depends only on the current market value of the investor's equity.

4. The rate at which the portfolio earns risk premium depends only on the total amount of market risk undertaken and is independent of the size of the investor's equity and of the composition of his active portfolio.

5. Optimal selection in the active portfolio depends only on appraisal risk and appraisal premiums and not at all on market risk or market premium; nor on investor objectives as regards the relative importance to him of expected return versus risk; nor on the investment manager's expectations regarding the general market. Two managers with radically different expectations regarding the general market but the same specific information regarding individual securities will select active portfolios with the same relative proportions. (Here, as elsewhere in this paper, we ignore possible differences in the tax objective, liquidity considerations, etc.)

6. The appraisal ratio depends only on (a) the quality of security analysis and (b) how efficiently the active portfolio is balanced. It is independent of the

relative emphasis between active and passive portfolios and of the degree to which the risky portfolio is levered or mixed with debt. It is also independent of the market premium. Obviously, it is not necessary for a professionally managed fund to be optimal in terms of all three stages in order to be socially (or economically) successful: An individual investor may choose to perform the third-stage balancing himself, with the appropriate amount of personal borrowing or lending. He may even perform the second-stage balancing himself, determining the appropriate emphasis between a brokerage account or "go-go" fund on the one hand and a virtually passive old-line mutual fund or living trust on the other. On the other hand, any attempt to compare the skill with which professional investment managers select securities (i.e., performs the first-stage balancing) using historical rates of return must be designed invariant with respect to second- and third-stage balancing policies.

7. The security analyst's potential contribution to overall portfolio performance over time depends only on how well his forecasts of future independent returns correlate with actual independent returns, and not on the magnitude of these returns.

Appendix

In his paper, "Simplified Model for Portfolio Analysis,"[10] William Sharpe proposes the following model of the return from a risky security:

$$R_i = A_i + B_i I + C_i$$

$$I = A_{n+1} + C_{n+1}$$

(A1)

where A_{n+1} and the A_i are constants, and C_{n+1} and the C_i are random variables with expected values of zero and variances Q_i and Q_{n+1}, respectively. Sharpe postulates that the covariances between C_i and C_j are zero for all values of i and j $(i \neq j)$.

As Sharpe sees it "the major characteristic of the Diagonal Model is the assumption that the returns of various securities are related only through common relationships with some basic underlying factor. . . . This model has two virtues: it is one of the simplest which can be constructed without assuming away the existence of interrelationships among securities and there is considerable evidence that it can capture a large part of such interrelationships."[11] Regarding the way the model is intended to be used, Sharpe says, "The Diagonal

----

[10]See Sharpe, n. 2.

[11]Ibid.

Model requires the following predictions from a security analyst: (1) the values of A_i, B_i, and Q_i for each of n securities, (2) values of A_{n+1} and Q_{n+1} for the Index."[12] In order to give the best possible results, the analyst's estimates of the A_i should be free from bias, consistent from one security to the next, and reflect both the analyst's current appraisal of the securities and his knowledge of current market prices. It is, of course, also necessary that he have a rational basis for estimating the Q_i. If there is indeed a significant degree of comovement among securities, then his estimates must recognize this fact.

In the equations which follow, r is the risk-free interest rate. Let $E[\ ]$ represent the expectation of the random variable in the brackets, var$[\ ]$ the variance, and cov$[\ ,\ ]$ the covariance of the two variables within the brackets. If Sharpe's market index $I(= A_{n+1} + C_{n+1})$ can be identified with the return on market as a whole, then, according to the Sharpe-Lintner-Treynor theory, expected return on the ith security in equilibrium must satisfy

$$E[R_i - r] = k \, \text{cov}[R_i, I]$$

$$= k \, \text{cov}[A_i + B_i(A_{n+1} + C_{n+1}) + C_i, A_{n+1} + C_{n+1}]$$

Eliminating constant terms and terms in C_i, which by definition have zero covariance with I, we have

$$E[R_i] = B_i k \, \text{var} \, C_{n+1} = B_i k Q_{n+1}$$

In equilibrium, therefore, we have

$$E[R_i] = r + B_i k Q_{n+1} \tag{A2}$$

On the other hand, the Sharpe Diagonal Model stipulates that

$$E[R_i] = A_i + B_i A_{n+1}$$

The only way both equations can hold for all values of B_i is if

$$A_i = r$$

$$A_{n+1} = \tag{A3}$$

It is clear that, in a dynamic equilibrium in which all investors evaluate new information simultaneously, A_i is the sirkless rate and $A_{n+1} B_i$ is the expected excess return on the ith security.

---

[12]Ibid.

Once we abandon the assumption that all investors have the same information, it is no longer true that expected excess return on the ith security is proportional to B_i. It is apparent that the values of $A_i, i = 1, \ldots, n, A_{n+1}$ leading to a given set of expectations of the R_i are not uniquely determined by specifying expected returns for a set of securities. A set of values that implies that half the universe of securities are overpriced relative to the current market and half are underpriced, that is, the set for which

$$\sum_i M_i(A_i - r) = 0 \qquad\qquad (A4)$$

we call market neutral.

In order to eliminate the ambiguity, we shall assume henceforth the A_i are implicitly defined to be market neutral. Then A_i is the sum of the pure rate and expectation of a disequilibrium price movement, and A_{n+1} is the expected excess return on the market. In the case in which an investor has special information on the ith security, A_i will differ from the equilibrium value by an amount which we will call the appraisal premium, in deference to the source of the premium:

$$\text{appraisal premium} = A_i - r$$

$$A_i = \text{appraisal premium} + \text{riskless rate} \qquad\qquad (A5)$$

We can now summarize our interpretations of the symbols in Sharpe's Diagonal Model (modified slightly as noted above):

1. A_i = the sum of the risk-free rate and the appraisal premium on the ith security.
2. A_{n+1} = the investor's expectation of excess return for the market as a whole. If he is not trying to outguess the overall market, it is the premium offered to investors generally for bearing market, or systematic, risk.
3. B_i = the volatility of the ith security—that is, its degree of sensitivity to market fluctuations.
4. C_{n+1} = the difference between actual return on the market and expected return on the market. Its variance is Q_{n+1}. If an analyst has no power to forecast market fluctuations, Q_{n+1} is the variance of the market return.
5. C_i = the difference between actual return on the ith security and the return explained by the actual market return (plus the prime interest rate). Its variance is Q_i. If an analyst has no power to forecast the independent return, Q_i is the residual variance of return of the ith security regressed against the market.

Now consider again Sharpe's expression for return on the ith security: $R_i = A_i + B_i(A_{n+1} + C_{n+1}) + C_i$. Can we define $I = A_{n+1} + C_{n+1}$ in terms of the R_i? If not, then I is not truly an "index" in the sense of return on a market average. Let M_i be the total market value of the ith security. Then define

$$I = A_{n+1} + C_{n+1} + \Sigma M_i(R_i - r) \tag{A6}$$

When the so-called market index I is defined in this way, one of the assumptions in Sharpe's model no longer holds exactly. Forming the sums of each term in equation (A1) over the whole set of securities, weighted by respective market values, and rearranging we have

$$\Sigma M_i(R_i - A_i) = (A_{n+1} + C_{n+1})M_i B_i + \Sigma M_i C_i \tag{A7}$$

Substituting from equation (A6) and invoking equation (A4) we have

$$(A_{n+1} + C_{n+1})(\Sigma M - \Sigma MB) = \Sigma MC$$

This expression can hold in general only if

$$\sum_i M_i C_i = 0$$

$$\frac{\sum_i M_i B_i}{\sum_i M_i} = 1 \tag{A8}$$

The second equation merely requires that the weights sum to 100 percent. The first, however, is a constraint on the independence of the C_i. The constraint conflicts slightly with Sharpe's own model, which postulated $E[C_i C_j] = 0$ for all $i \neq j$, and $E[C_i C_{n+1}] = 0$ for all i. The conflict arises from a confusion— possibly unintended or possibly intended—in the Diagonal Model between an underlying explanatory variable to which all securities are sensitive in greater or lesser degree, and a Market Index such as $I = \sum_i M_i(R_i - r)$.

19

Optimal Utilization of Market Forecasts and the Evaluation of Investment Performance

Michael C. Jensen

1. Introduction

A numbers of authors in the recent past[1] have considered the problem of evaluating the performance of the managers of investment portfolios. The purpose of this paper is to examine the problem faced by the portfolio manager attempting to optimally incorporate forecasts of future market returns into his portfolio. Given the solution to this problem we then shall focus our attention on the problem involved in measuring a portfolio manager's ability when he is explicitly engaged in forecasting the prices on individual securities (i.e., security analysis) and in forecasting the future course of market prices (i.e., 'timing activities'). We shall consider these problems here in the context of the Sharpe [11]-Lintner [8] mean-variance general equilibrium model of the pricing of capital assets, and in the context of the expanded two factor version of the Sharpe model suggested by Black et al. [2]. In addition we shall concentrate our attention here on an investigation of just what can and cannot be said about portfolio performance solely on the basis of data on the time series of portfolio and market returns.

In section 2 we outline the foundations of the analysis and its relationship to the general equilibrium structure of security prices given by the Sharpe-Lintner model. In section 3 we briefly summarize the measure of security selection ability suggested by Jensen [6]. Section 4 contains a solution to the problem of the optimal incorporation of market forecasts into portfolio policy and provides the structure for the analysis in section 5 of the measurement problems introduced into the evaluation of portflio performance by market forecasting activities by the portfolio manager. Section 6 presents the complete development of the model within the two factor equilibrium model of the pricing of capital assets suggested by Black [1] and Black et al. [2]. Section 7 contains a brief summary of the conclusions of the analysis.

Reprinted with permission of the author and publisher from *Mathematical Methods in Investment and Finance,* G. P. Szegö and K. Shell (Eds.), Amsterdam: North-Holland Publishing Company, 1972, pp. 310–335. I am indebted to Fischer Black, Jack Treynor, John Long, and the members of the Finance Workshop at the University of Rochester for helpful comments and to the Ford and National Science Foundations for financial support.

[1] Cf. Treynor [13], Treynor and Mazuy [12], Sharpe [10], Jensen [5,6], and Friend and Blume [4].

2. Foundations of the Model[2]

Let

$$\tilde{R}_{jt} = \tilde{r}_{jt} - r_{Ft} = \text{excess return on the } j\text{th asset in time } t; r_{jt} = \text{the}$$
total returns (dividends plus capital gains) on the
jth asset in time t, and r_{Ft} = the riskless rate of
interest for time t (1a)

$$\tilde{R}_{Mt} = r_{Mt} - r_{Ft} = \text{excess returns on the market portfolio in}$$
time t (1b)

$$E(\tilde{R}_M) = E(\tilde{r}_{Mt}) - r_{Ft}: \text{that is we assume the expected excess return}$$
on the market portfolio is constant through
time (2)

$$\tilde{R}_{jt} = E(\tilde{R}_{jt}) + b_j \tilde{\pi}_t + \tilde{e}_{jt}: \text{the 'market model' formulation}$$ (3)

where b_j is a parameter which may vary from security to security and $\tilde{\pi}_t$ is an unobservable 'market factor' which to some extent affects the returns on all securities. We also assume

$$E(\tilde{\pi}_t) = 0 \tag{4a}$$

$$E(\tilde{e}_{jt}) = 0 \qquad\qquad j = 1, 2, \ldots, N \tag{4b}$$

$$\text{cov}(\tilde{\pi}_t, \tilde{e}_{jt}) = 0 \qquad\qquad j = 1, 2, \ldots, N \tag{4c}$$

$$\text{cov}(\tilde{e}_{jt}, \tilde{e}_{it}) = \begin{cases} 0 & j \neq i \\ \sigma^2(\tilde{e}_j) & j = i \end{cases} \qquad j = 1, 2, \ldots, N \tag{4d}$$

Now using arguments similar to those of Jensen [5] it can be shown that to a close approximation the excess returns on the market portfolio can be expressed as:

$$\tilde{R}_{Mt} \cong E(\tilde{R}_M) + \tilde{\pi}_t \tag{5}$$

The Sharpe [11], Lintner [8], Mossin [9] models of the pricing of capital assets under uncertainty imply that

$$E(\tilde{R}_{jt}) = \beta_j E(\tilde{R}_M) \tag{6}$$

[2] Sections 2–5 are a reformulation and extension of some of the material which appears in Jensen [6, pp. 395–96]. I am indebted to John Lintner for pointing out the existence of an error there. The reformulation which appears here corrects that error and makes clear some assumptions which were only implicit in the previous paper.

where

$$\beta_j = \frac{\text{cov}(\tilde{R}_{jt}, \tilde{R}_{Mt})}{\sigma^2(\tilde{R}_{Mt})}$$

and as shown by Fama [3] and Jensen [5] $\beta_j \cong b_j$. Using this result and substituting from (5) into (6) for $E(\tilde{R}_M)$ and adding $\beta_j \tilde{\pi}_t + \tilde{e}_{jt}$ to both sides of (6), we have

$$E(\tilde{R}_{jt}) + \beta_j \tilde{\pi}_t + \tilde{e}_{jt} \cong \beta_j [\tilde{R}_{Mt} - \tilde{n}_t] + \beta_j \tilde{\pi}_t + \tilde{e}_{jt} \tag{7}$$

Using (3) and the fact that $\beta_j \cong b_j$ the LHS of (7) is just $\tilde{R}_{jt}$. Hence (7) reduces to

$$\tilde{R}_{jt} = \beta_j \tilde{R}_{Mt} + \tilde{e}_{jt} \tag{8}$$

Thus, if the asset pricing model given by (6) and the market model given by (3) are valid, (8) says that the *realized* excess returns on any security or portfolio can be expressed as a linear function of its systematic risk, the *realized* excess returns on the market portfolio and a random error, $\tilde{e}_{jt}$, which has an expected value of zero.

3. A Measure of a Portfolio Manager's Ability to Forecast the Prices of Individual Securities

Eq. (8) can be estimated for a managed portfolio. However, if the manager is able to forecast individual security prices he will tend to systematically select securities which realize $\tilde{e}_{jt} > 0$. Hence his portfolio will earn more than the 'normal' risk premium for its level of risk. We allow for this possibility by not constraining the estimating regression to pass through the origin. That is, we allow for the existence of a non-zero constant in (8) by using (9) as the estimating equation:

$$\tilde{R}_{jt} = \alpha_j + \beta_j \tilde{R}_{Mt} + \tilde{u}_{jt} \tag{9}$$

where $\tilde{u}_{jt}$ is assumed to have zero expectation and to be independent of $\tilde{R}_{Mt}$. The intercept α_j measures the increment in average returns due to the manager's security selection abilities (assuming for now that he does not attempt to forecast general movements in market prices). As such it represents a measure of the manager's ability to forecast individual security prices (cf. Jensen [6] for a detailed discussion of these issues).

4. Optimal Portfolio Adjustment to Market Forecasts

Assume for the moment that all investors with an interest in a given portfolio have identical perference functions[3], $U[E(\tilde{R}_j), V(\tilde{R}_j)]$, involving only the single period mean, $E(\tilde{R}_j)$, and variance, $V(\tilde{R}_j)$, of portfolio excess return. The portfolio manager should incorporate his forecasts, $\tilde{\pi}^*$, of the market factor, $\tilde{\pi}_t$, into his portfolio in a manner which will result in maximum expected utility for the portfolio shareholders. The forecast, π^*, of the market value of the market factor $\tilde{\pi}_t$ for period t based on the information set $\phi_{j,t-1}$ available to the manager j at time $t - 1$.

$$\tilde{\pi}_t^* = E(\tilde{\pi}_t | \phi_{j,t-1}) \tag{10}$$

Thus, the market excess return expected by the manager of portfolio j is $E_j(\tilde{R}_{Mt}) = E(\tilde{R}_M) + \tilde{\pi}_t^*$. We shall represent the variance of this conditional distribution by $\sigma_j^2(\tilde{\pi}_t)$, where

$$\sigma_j^2(\tilde{\pi}_t) = \text{Var}(\tilde{\pi}_t | \phi_{j,t-1}) \tag{11}$$

Assuming that the manager has no special information about the future returns on individual securities his problem is to decide upon the division of the portfolio's assets between the market portfolio and the riskless asset. Let γ_t be the fraction invested in the market portfolio at time t and $1 - \gamma_t$ the fraction invested in the riskless asset. Under the assumptions that there are no transactions costs, and no restrictions on borrowing, lending, and short selling the expected excess return and variance of return on the portfolio are

$$E(\tilde{R}_{jt}) = \gamma_t[E(\tilde{R}_M) + \tilde{\pi}_t^*] \tag{12a}$$

$$V(\tilde{R}_{jt}) = \gamma_t^2 \sigma_j^2(\tilde{\pi}_t) \tag{12b}$$

The manager's problem is to

$$\max_{\gamma_t} U[E(\tilde{R}_{jt}), V(\tilde{R}_{jt})] = \max_{\gamma_t} U[\gamma_t(E(\tilde{R}_M) + \tilde{\pi}_t^*), \gamma_t^2 \sigma_j^2(\tilde{\pi}_t^*)] \tag{13}$$

and the solution to this yields

---

[3]In reality this assumption is not as restrictive as it seems since many portfolios have only one investor and when we consider mutual funds it can still be approximately valid if the funds announce investment policies in advance and then investors distribute themselves across funds according to the matching of preferences and policies.

$$\gamma_t = \frac{1}{2\sigma_j^2(\tilde{\pi}_t)} \frac{dV(R_j)}{dE(R_j)} [E(\tilde{R}_M) + \tilde{\pi}_t^*] \tag{14}$$

where

$$\frac{dV(R_j)}{dE(R_j)} = -\frac{\partial U}{\partial E(R_j)} \bigg/ \frac{\partial U}{\partial V(R_j)} > 0 \text{ is minus the marginal rate of substitution}$$
of variance for expected excess return for each of the portfolio's investors (or the slope of the indifference curve between variance and excess return)

Now since $\beta_M = 1$ and $\beta_{jt} = \gamma_t \beta_M$ we see that $\beta_{jt} = \gamma_t$. Thus, at each point in time the managers optimal choice of systematic risk for the portfolio, β_{jt}, is given by

$$\beta_{jt} = \theta_{jt} E(\tilde{R}_M) + \theta_{jt} \tilde{\pi}_t^* \tag{15}$$

where

$$\theta_{jt} = \frac{1}{2\sigma_j^2(\tilde{\pi}_t)} \frac{dV(R_j)}{dE(R_j)}$$

Thus, the size of θ_{jt} determines the degree to which he allows his forecasts to affect the portfolio risk level, and it in turn depends on his uncertainty regarding his forecast, $\sigma_j^2(\tilde{\pi}_t)$, and his investor's willingness to bet on his forecasts as summarized by $dV(R_j)/dE(R_j)$ (the slope of their indifference curves between mean and variance). The larger is the uncertainty of his forecast as measured by $\sigma_j^2(\tilde{\pi}_t)$, the smaller will be the amount by which he changes the risk level to incorporate his forecasts. In addition the more averse to marginal increments of risk are his investors the lower is $dV(R_j)/dE(R_j)$ and the smaller will be the amount by which he changes the risk level.

Let us assume that the manager's forecasts and the market factor follow a bivariate normal distribution. Then, in general

$$\tilde{\pi}_t = d_0 + d_1 \tilde{\pi}_t^* + \tilde{v}_{jt} \tag{16}$$

where d_0 and d_1 are constants which correct for any systematic biases in the manager's forecasts, $\tilde{v}_{jt}$ is normal with $E(\tilde{v}_{jt}) = 0$, and we assume $\text{cov}(\pi_t^*, \tilde{v}_{jt}) = 0$. If d_0 and d_1 are zero and unity respectively the manager's forecasting technique tends neither to produce estimates which are systematically high or low ($d_0 = 0$), nor does he systematically under- or over-estimate the magnitude of any market movement ($d_1 = 1$). The manager could estimate d_0 and d_1 by regression techniques given a file of past forecasts and if $d_0 \neq 0$ or $d_1 \neq 1.0$ the optimal utilization of the forecasts requires adjustment of the forecasts π_t^*. Let $\tilde{\pi}_t'$ be the adjusted forecast defined by

$$\pi_t' = d_0 + d_1 \pi_t^*$$

$$= \tilde{\pi}_t - \tilde{v}_{jt} \tag{17}$$

where we assume here that the manager knows the true coefficients d_0 and d_1. Substituting π_t' given by (17) for π_t^* in (15) we have

$$\beta_{jt} = \theta_{jt} E(\tilde{R}_M) + \theta_{jt} \pi_t' \tag{18}$$

and now using (16) and (17) we see that $\sigma_j^2(\tilde{\pi}_t) = \sigma^2(\tilde{v}_{jt})$; and if we assume that $\sigma^2(\tilde{v}_{jt}) = \sigma^2(\tilde{v}_j)$ for all t, θ_{jt} is given by

$$\theta_{jt} = \frac{1}{2\sigma^2(\tilde{v}_j)} \frac{dV(R_j)}{dE(R_j)} \tag{19}$$

and if $dV(R_j)/dE(R_j)$ is a constant independent of $V(R_j)$ or $E(R_j)$ (or approximately so)[4], we can write (18) as

$$\beta_{jt} = \beta_j + \theta_j \tilde{\pi}_t' \tag{20}$$

and $\beta_j = \theta_j E(R_M)$ can thus be considered his 'target' risk level—that risk level which on the average the manager wishes to maintain given the unconditional expected returns on the market portfolio and the preferences of his shareholders.

If the manager, in addition to forecasting market returns, also believes he has information about individual securities he will not simply lever the market portfolio up or down. He can construct a portfolio he views as optimal given his information set, call it P, and this will not be the market portfolio. He might then speculate on his market forecasts by levering the portfolio P up or down.[5]

---

[4] $dV(R_j)/dE(R_j)$ is, of course, literally constant for the special case of constant absolute risk aversion on the part of investors. For other utility functions, to the extent that we ignore changes in the value of $dV(R_j)/dE(R_j)$ associated with changes in $E(R_j)$ and $V(R_j)$ we are ignoring only the second order effects, so for small changes in $E(R_j)$ and $V(R_j)$ this approximation is probably not bad.

[5] However, this procedure is not likely to be an optimal one (cf. F. Black and J. Treynor, 'How to use security analysis to improve portfolio selection', in proceedings: *Seminar on the analysis of security prices,* University of Chicago Graduate School of Business, November, 1967), but in order to obtain tractable results we shall assume that this procedure is approximately descriptive of the manager's policies.

The analysis is analogous to that performed above. However, since β_P need not equal unity, we find that

$$\beta_{jt} = \gamma_t \beta_{Pt}$$

and again assuming that $\sigma^2(\tilde{v}_{jt})$, $dV(R_j)/dE(R_j)$, and β_{Pt} are constant through time we get an expression for β_{jt}, which is identical to (20) except that

$$\theta_j = \frac{\beta_P}{2\sigma^2(\tilde{v}_j)} \frac{dV(R_j)}{dE(R_j)} \tag{21}$$

Thus, if the manager levers the portfolio P instead of the market portfolio there is little difference in the analysis. Henceforth we shall assume that the manager is engaged in both security analysis and market forecasting activities and we leave the definition of θ_j to be whichever is relevant for a given situation.

5. Effects of a Manager's Ability to Predict the Market Factor π

5.1. Effects on Portfolio Returns

Utilizing the results obtained above we find that the process generating the returns on a portfolio whose manager is engaged in both security analysis and market forecasting activities can be represented by

$$\tilde{R}_{jt} = \alpha_j + \tilde{\beta}_{jt}\tilde{R}_{Mt} + \tilde{u}_{jt} = \alpha_j + (\beta_j + \theta_j \pi'_t)\tilde{R}_{Mt} + u_{jt} \tag{22}$$

If the manager can forecast the market factor $\tilde{\pi}$ and acts upon his forecast in a rational manner, he will, of course, be able to increase the returns on his portfolio. To see the effects of his forecasting ability on the expected returns of the portfolio we take the expected value of (22) to obtain

$$E(\tilde{R}_{jt}) = \alpha_j + \beta_j E(\tilde{R}_M) + \theta_j E[\tilde{\pi}'_t(E(\tilde{R}_M) + \tilde{\pi}_t)]$$

$$= \alpha_j + \beta_j E(\tilde{R}_M) + \theta_j \rho^2 \sigma^2(\tilde{\pi}) \tag{23}$$

where ρ is the correlation between the manager's unadjusted forecasts $\tilde{\pi}^*_t$ and $\tilde{\pi}_t$. Eq. (23) follows from the fact that $E(\tilde{\pi}'_t) = 0$ and

$$E(\tilde{\pi}'_t\tilde{\pi}_t) = \text{cov}(\tilde{\pi}', \tilde{\pi})$$

$$= d_1 \text{cov}(\tilde{\pi}^*, \tilde{\pi})$$

$$= \rho^2 \sigma^2(\tilde{\pi})$$

$$\text{cov}(\tilde{\pi}^*, \tilde{\pi}) = \rho\sigma(\tilde{\pi}^*)\sigma(\tilde{\pi})$$

$$d_1 = \rho\sigma(\tilde{\pi})/\sigma(\tilde{\pi}^*)$$

Now by (6) we know that $\beta_j E(R_M)$ represents the expected compensation for the average risk level of the portfolio. Furthermore, as we saw above, α_j represents the amount by which the portfolio returns are increased as a result of the manager's ability to select undervalued securities. Thus, the last term in (23), $\theta_j \rho^2 \sigma^2(\tilde{\pi})$, represents the expected increment in the portfolio returns which is due solely to the manager's ability to forecast the unexpected market returns, $\tilde{\pi}$. Given that the manager can forecast to some extent, his profit opportunities are proportional to $\sigma^2(\tilde{\pi})$, the variance of the market factor. In addition to $\sigma^2(\tilde{\pi})$ the profits depend on θ_j (which involves the residual uncertainty $\sigma^2(\tilde{v}_j)$ and the shareholders risk-return trade off $dV(R_j)/dE(R_j)$) and ρ, the correlation between his forecasts and the actual market returns. Since $\sigma^2(\pi)$ and θ_j are given exogeneously to the manager, we see that the profits from his forecasting ability are directly related to ρ, and thus his forecasting ability is totally summarized by ρ.[6]

5.2. Effects on the Estimated Risk Coefficient

The large sample least squares estimate of β_j for a time series of returns, $t = 1, 2, \ldots, T$ is

$$Plim\beta_j = Plim \frac{\hat{\text{cov}}[\tilde{R}_{jt}, \tilde{R}_{Mt}]}{\hat{\sigma}^2(\tilde{R}_{Mt})}$$

$$= Plim \frac{\sum_{t=1}^{T} [\tilde{R}_{jt}(\tilde{R}_{Mt} - \bar{R}_M)]}{\sum_{t=1}^{T} [\tilde{R}_{Mt} - \bar{R}_M]^2}$$

---

[6]Black and Treynor [∴] have also obtained this result.

$$= \mathrm{Plim} \frac{\sum_{t=1}^{T} [\{\alpha_j + \beta_j(E(\widetilde{R}_M) + \widetilde{\pi}_t) + \theta_j\widetilde{\pi}_t'(E(\widetilde{R}_M) + \widetilde{\pi}_t) + \widetilde{u}_{jt}\}\{\widetilde{R}_{Mt} - \bar{R}_M\}]}{\sum_{t=1}^{T} [\widetilde{R}_{Mt} - \bar{R}_M]^2}$$

$$= \beta_j + \theta_j \left[\frac{\mathrm{cov}(\widetilde{\pi}', \widetilde{\pi})E(\widetilde{R}_M) + E(\widetilde{\pi}'\widetilde{\pi}^2)}{\sigma^2(\widetilde{\pi})} \right]$$

$$= \beta_j + \theta_j \left[\rho^2 E(\widetilde{R}_M) + \frac{E(\widetilde{\pi}'^3)}{\sigma^2(\widetilde{\pi})} \right] \tag{24}$$

since $\mathrm{Plim}\,\widetilde{R}_{Mt} - \bar{R}_M = E(R_M) + \widetilde{\pi}_t - E(R_M) = \widetilde{\pi}_t$. Thus, the estimate of β_j will be unbiased only if the manager cannot forecast market movements. If he has no forecasting ability ρ will be zero, and in addition $E(\widetilde{\pi}'^3)$ will also be zero since by eq. (17) $\widetilde{\pi}'$ will always be equal to $E(\widetilde{\pi}) = 0$, a constant when $d_1 = 0$. Since we have assumed he optimally adjusts his forecasts by d_0 and d_1, this is not surprising since he is assumed then to know he cannot forecast, and in fact under these conditions $\beta_{jt} = \beta_j$ is a constant for all t. Somewhat more surprising is the fact that if we assume the manager does not go through the forecast adjustment process discussed in section 4, but instead acts upon his forecasts according to (15) even when $\rho = 0$ this same result holds.

If the manager simply uses his unadjusted forecast π_t^* then by the bivariate normality of π_t^* and π_t we can use the other regression

$$\widetilde{\pi}_t^* = d_0' + d_1'\widetilde{\pi}_t + \widetilde{v}_{jt}' \tag{25}$$

to obtain the portfolio return generating process, in (25) d_0' and d_1' are regression coefficients, and $\widetilde{v}_{jt}'$ is a normally distributed random error with $E(\widetilde{v}_{jt}) = 0$ and $\mathrm{cov}(\widetilde{v}_{jt}, \widetilde{\pi}_t) = 0$. Again, if d_0' and d_1' are zero and unity respectively the estimates are unbiased. Substituting for $\widetilde{\pi}_t^*$ from (25) into (15) (and again assuming that θ_{jt} is constant for all t, $V(R_j)$ and $E(R_j)$) we find the riskiness of the portfolio to be given by

$$\widetilde{\beta}_{jt} = \beta_j + a_j\widetilde{\pi}_t + \widetilde{w}_{jt} \tag{26}$$

where $a_j = \theta_j d_1'$, $\widetilde{w}_{jt} = \theta_j\widetilde{v}_{jt}'$ and $\beta_j = \theta_j(E(\widetilde{R}_M) + d_0')$ can now be considered his 'target' risk level. Under these conditions the portfolio return generating process is given by

$$\widetilde{R}_{jt} = \alpha_j + (\beta_j + a_j\widetilde{\pi}_t + \widetilde{w}_{jt})\widetilde{R}_{Mt} + \widetilde{u}_{jt} \tag{27}$$

and since $\tilde{v}'_{jt}$ in (25) is independent of $\tilde{\pi}_t$ the error $\tilde{w}_{jt}$ in (27) is uncorrelated with $\tilde{\pi}_t$ (which is certainly reasonable since if it were correlated, the forecast could be improved). The large sample least squares estimate of β_j for a time series of returns, $t = 1, 2, \ldots, T$ is

$$P \lim_{T \to \infty} \hat{\beta}_j$$

$$= P \lim_{T \to \infty} \frac{\sum_t [\{\alpha_j + \beta_j(E(R_M) + \tilde{\pi}_t) + (a_j\tilde{\pi}_t + \tilde{w}_{jt})(E(R_M) + \tilde{\pi}_t) + \tilde{u}_{jt}\}\{\tilde{R}_{Mt} - \bar{R}_M\}]}{\sum_t [\tilde{R}_{Mt} - \bar{R}_M]^2}$$

$$= \beta_j + a_j \left[E(R_M) + \frac{E(\tilde{\pi}^3)}{\sigma^2(\tilde{\pi})} \right] \tag{28}$$

Thus, we see that if the manager acts on his estimates even when he cannot forecast (i.e., $d'_1 = 0$ or $\rho = 0$) we see that our estimate of β_j is unbiased since $a_j = \theta_j d'_1$ will be zero in this case.

Note, however, that if the manager can forecast the market factor to some extent that $\hat{\beta}_j$ will be a positively biased estimate of β_j under either set of assumptions if ρ and d'_1 are positive since $E(\tilde{R}_M) > 0$ always, and if $E(\tilde{\pi}'^3)$ and $E(\tilde{\pi}^3)$ are not zero they are most likely to be positive due to the lower bound of -100% on the returns. These biases are serious since they will affect our estimates of α_j. We shall consider this issue below. For completeness we note here that the mean portfolio returns for the case in which the manager simply uses his unadjusted raw forecasts is given by the expected value of (27)

$$E(\tilde{R}_{jt}) = \alpha_j + \beta_j E(\tilde{R}_M) + a_j\sigma^2(\tilde{\pi}) \tag{29}$$

Again the last term, $a_j\sigma^2(\tilde{\pi})$, represents the expected increment in returns which is due solely to the manager's ability to forecast the unexpected market returns.

5.3. Effects on the Measurement of the Manager's Stock Selection Ability

The large sample estimate of α_j obtained from applying traditional least squares procedures to (22) (which assumes optimal forecast adjustment) is

$$\text{Plim } \hat{\alpha} = E(R_j) - \hat{\beta}_j E(R_M) = \alpha_j + \theta_j \rho^2 \sigma^2(\tilde{\pi}) - \theta_j \left[\rho^2 E(\tilde{R}_M)^2 + \frac{E(\tilde{\pi}'^3)}{\sigma^2(\tilde{\pi})} E(\tilde{R}_M) \right] \tag{30}$$

by substitution from (23) and (24). Now, by our previous arguments, if the manager cannot successfully forecast future market returns, the last two terms on the RHS of (30) will be zero and hence our estimate of the increment in portfolio returns due to the manager's stock selection ability, α_j, will be unbiased. This also holds true in the non-forecast adjustment case (which henceforth we shall refer to as the naive forecast model) where

$$\text{Plim } \hat{\alpha} = E(R_j) - \hat{\beta}_j E(\tilde{R}_M) = \alpha_j + a_j \sigma^2(\tilde{\pi}) - a_j \ E(\tilde{R}_M)^2 + \frac{E(\tilde{\pi}^3)}{\sigma^2(\pi)} E(\tilde{R}_M)$$

$$(31)$$

is the estimate obtained from applying least squares to (27) (by substitution from (28) and (29)). In this case if the manager cannot forecast a_j will equal 0 and $\hat{\alpha}$ is therefore unbiased for this case as well.

However, if in either case the manager can forecast future market returns to some extent the simple time series regression technique will not allow us to separate the incremental returns due to his stock selection ability from the incremental returns due to his ability to forecast the market (the first two terms in (30) or (31)). This follows from the fact that ρ^2 in (30) and a_j in (31) will both be non-zero (and for the relevant case a_j in (31) will be positive). Furthermore, we will in general not even be able to obtain an unbiased estimate of the sum of the two components if the manager can successfully forecast the market. By using short time intervals for our time series observations (say weekly or monthly data), or by using continuously compounded rates, we can probably eliminate the negative bias due to the term involving $E(\tilde{\pi}'^3)$ in (30) or $E(\tilde{\pi}^3)$ in (31), since either procedure will tend to yield symmetric return distributions for which $E(\tilde{\pi}'^3)$ and $E(\tilde{\pi}^3)$ will be zero. However, since $E(R_M)^2$ will always be positive, we will still underestimate the *total* increment in returns from the managers ability by an amount equal to $\theta_j \rho^2 E(\tilde{R}_M)^2$ for the optimal forecast adjustment case and by $a_j E(\tilde{R}_M)^2$ for the naive forecast case.

It is worthwhile to reiterate the point that these bias problems arise only when we are considering a manager who can actually forecast the market. The mere fact that a manager attempts to forecast future market returns and shifts his portfolio's risk level in an attempt to capitalize on these forecasts does not hinder the measurement of his stock selection ability if his forecasts are in fact worthless.

5.4. An 'Unbiased' Measure of Stock Selection Ability[7]

If the manager's forecasting and decision periods are coincident with the periods over which we measure his portfolio returns and if the manager follows the

---

[7] The essence of the approach suggested here is similar to that first suggested by Treynor and Mazuy [12].

naive forecasting model we can separate and obtain unbiased measures of his stock selection and market forecasting abilities. Rewriting (27) in terms of $\tilde{\pi}$ we have

$$\tilde{R}_{jt} = \alpha_j + (\beta_j + \tilde{w}_{jt})E(\tilde{R}_M) + [\beta_j + \tilde{w}_{jt} + a_j E(\tilde{R}_M)]\tilde{\pi}_t + a_j\tilde{\pi}_t^2 + \tilde{u}_{jt} \quad (32)$$

Assuming we know $E(\tilde{R}_M)$ and can thus measure $\tilde{\pi}_t$, we can run the quadratic regression[8]

$$\tilde{R}_{jt} = \eta_0 + \eta_1\tilde{\pi}_t + \eta_2\tilde{\pi}_t^2 + \tilde{v}_{jt} \quad (33)$$

If $\tilde{\pi}_t$ is symmetrically distributed about zero $\tilde{\pi}_t$ and $\tilde{\pi}_t^2$ are uncorrelated and the large sample estimates of the coefficients in (33) are

$$Plim \; \hat{\eta}_0 = \alpha_j + \beta_j E(\tilde{R}_M) \quad (34a)$$

$$Plim \; \hat{\eta}_1 = \beta_j + a_j E(\tilde{R}_M) \quad (34b)$$

$$Plim \; \hat{\eta}_2 = a_j \quad (34c)$$

Given these estimates our estimate of the manager's contribution to the portfolio return through his stock selection ability is

$$\hat{\alpha}_j = \hat{\eta}_0 - [\hat{\eta}_1 - \hat{\eta}_2\bar{R}_M]\bar{R}_M \quad (35)$$

From (14) we can see that the estimate of the manager's contribution to the portfolio returns through his market forecasting activities is given by

$$\hat{\eta}_2\hat{\sigma}^2(\tilde{\pi}) \quad (36)$$

However, if the manager follows the optimal forecast adjustment model estimation of the quadratic equation (33) will not enable us to separate the returns due to market forecasting from the returns due to security analysis or to obtain an unbiased measure of the sum of the two components. Rewriting (22) in terms of $\tilde{\pi}_t$ and $\tilde{\pi}_t^2$ we obtain

$$\tilde{R}_{jt} = \alpha_j + \beta_j E(\tilde{R}_M) + (\beta_j + \theta_j E(\tilde{R}_M) - \theta_j\tilde{v}_j)\tilde{\pi}_t + \theta_j\tilde{\pi}_t^2 - \theta_j E(\tilde{R}_M)\tilde{v}_j + \tilde{u}_{jt} \quad (37)$$

Now, if we run the quadratic regression given by eq. (33) (assuming still that $\tilde{\pi}$ and $\tilde{v}$ are symmetrically distributed) the large sample coefficient estimates are:

---

[8]For large samples, of course, $\tilde{\pi}_t = R_{Mt} - \bar{R}_M$ and hence as long as the distributions are stationary there are few problems with measuring $\tilde{\pi}_t$.

$$Plim \; \hat{\eta}_0 = \alpha_j + \beta_j E(\tilde{R}_M) + \theta_j(\rho^2 - 1)\sigma^2(\tilde{\pi}) \qquad (38a)$$

$$Plim \; \hat{\eta}_1 = \rho^2 \theta_j E(\tilde{R}_M) + \beta_j \qquad (38b)$$

$$Plim \; \hat{\eta}_2 = \theta_j \qquad (38c)$$

and since we now have four unknowns and only three equations we cannot solve for the parameters of interest. In this situation we need to have exogeneous knowledge of ρ in order to provide a complete breakdown of the manager's performance. This, of course, will require more data than just the time series of portfolio and market returns. If we had data on the time series of the manager's forecasts, π_t^*, then we could estimate ρ directly and we could then solve the performance measurement problem in a fairly straight forward way. However, in general, this type of information will probably be extremely difficult if not impossible to obtain.

5.5. A Temporal Aggregation Problem

In the previous analysis we have implicitly assumed that the manager forecasts future market movements over the next unit time interval and then suitably adjusts his portfolio—all at the beginning of the time interval. More importantly we also implicitly assumed that the time interval used by the manager in these activities is identical to the observation interval from which our return data is obtained. Of course it is unlikely that these conditions will ever be met exactly, and the question arises as to what difficulties this introduces into the performance estimation procedure. Let us assume that the manager forecasts market changes over each period (and thus eq. (32) applies to single period intervals), but we measure returns over an interval of n periods. Adding a subscript τ to refer to the period within the tth observation interval and summing[9] over τ to obtain $\tilde{R}_{jt}$ for the naive forecast model we have

$$\tilde{R}_{jt} = \sum_{\tau=1}^{n} \tilde{R}_{jt\tau}$$

$$= n\alpha_j + \sum_\tau (\beta_j + \tilde{w}_{jt\tau})E(\tilde{R}_{Mt\tau}) + \sum_\tau [\beta_j + \tilde{w}_{jt\tau} + a_j E(\tilde{R}_{Mt\tau})]\tilde{\pi}_{t\tau} + \sum_\tau a_j \tilde{\pi}_{t\tau}^2 + \sum_\tau \tilde{u}_{jt\tau}$$

$$= n\alpha_j + (\beta_j + \frac{1}{n}\tilde{w}_{jt})E(\tilde{R}_{Mt}) + [\beta_j + a_j \frac{1}{n}E(\tilde{R}_{Mt})]\tilde{\pi}_t + a_j \sum_\tau \tilde{\pi}_{t\tau}^2 + \sum_\tau \tilde{w}_{jt\tau}\tilde{\pi}_{t\tau} + \tilde{u}_{jt}$$

$$(39)$$

---

[9] Assuming we are dealing with continuously compounded rates or short periods so that summation is appropriate.

where $E(\tilde{R}_{Mt}) = nE(\tilde{R}_{Mt\tau})$ since $E(\tilde{R}_{Mt\tau})$ is assumed constant for all τ, $\tilde{\pi}_t = \Sigma_\tau \tilde{\pi}_{t\tau}$, and $\tilde{w}_{jt} = \Sigma_\tau \tilde{w}_{jt\tau}$. Taking expectations of (39) we have

$$E(\tilde{R}_{jt}) = n\alpha_j + \beta_j E(\tilde{R}_{Mt}) + a_j n\sigma^2(\tilde{\pi}_\tau) \tag{40}$$

where $n\alpha_j$ is the increment in portfolio returns per n-unit time interval (i.e. the observation interval) due to the manager's stock selection ability, $\beta_j E(\tilde{R}_{Mt})$ is the return due to the average riskiness of the portfolio and $a_j n\sigma^2(\tilde{\pi}_\tau) = a_j\sigma^2(\tilde{\pi})$ is the return due to the manager's market forecasting abilities (all these returns being per n-unit time interval).

Note now that we cannot estimate (39) directly since $\Sigma_\tau \tilde{\pi}_{t\tau}^2$ is not observable if we can obtain measurements only over intervals of n periods or if we do not know n (i.e. if we do not know the length of the manager's forecasting interval). However, assuming $\tilde{\pi}_t$ is symmetric, if we estimate the single variable regression given by (9) the large sample estimate of α_j is

$$\text{Plim } \hat{\alpha}_j = n\alpha_j + a_j n\sigma^2(\tilde{\pi}_{t\tau}) - a_j \frac{1}{n} E(\tilde{R}_{Mt})^2 \tag{41}$$

where as before $\sigma^2(\tilde{\pi}_{t\tau})$ is the variance of the market returns over the manager's forecasting interval. If n is large, as it will be if the manager's forecasting period is very short relative to our measurement interval, the term $a_j 1/nE(\tilde{R}_{Mt})^2$ will be negligible. Thus, the intercept in (9) will be an approximately unbiased estimate of the average *total* increment in portfolio returns per n-unit time interval due to the security selection and market forecasting abilities of the manager. Hence if we know the forecasting interval is small relative to our measurement interval we can obtain an approximately unbiased estimate of the total increment in portfolio returns due to the manager's ability but we cannot break this total down into its two components. Of course, for this case if the forecasting interval is longer than our measurement interval and we know what it is we can use the quadratic estimation procedure given by eqs. (33)–(36) as long as the ratio of the two intervals is integer.[10]

Now, for the case of optimal adjustment of market forecasts if $\tilde{\pi}_{t\tau}$ is symmetrically distributed the large sample estimate of α_j obtained from running the single variable regression (9) on the data for which the observation interval spans n forecasting periods is

$$\text{Plim } \hat{\alpha}_j = n\alpha_j + \theta_j \rho^2 n\sigma^2(\tilde{\pi}_{t\tau}) - \theta_j \frac{1}{n} E(\tilde{R}_{Mt})^2 \rho^2 \tag{42}$$

---

[10]Under these conditions we should ordinarily be able to adjust the measurement interval to accomplish this.

And, as was the case for the naive forecast model, if n is fairly large this estimate provides us with an approximately unbiased estimate of the average *total* increment in portfolio returns per n-unit time interval due to the security selection and market forecasting activities of the manager.

5.6. Effects of the Length of Forecasting Interval on Profit Opportunities

It is interesting to note that if the manager can shorten his market forecasting horizon (i.e., increase n) his potential profits increase enormously. Let us consider first the optimal forecast adjustment model and let θ_j^n refer to the coefficient in (19) for a manager forecasting over an n-unit time interval. As we have demonstrated his expected profits, P^n, *per n-unit time interval* from these activities will be

$$P^n = \theta_j^n \rho^2 \sigma^2(\tilde{\pi}_t) \tag{43}$$

where

$$\theta_j^n = \frac{1}{2\sigma^2(\tilde{v}_j)} \frac{dV(R_j)}{dE(R_j)} \tag{44}$$

Now, if he could reduce his forecasting interval to a single period (without changing the correlation, ρ, between his forecasts and the actual market returns) his expected profits *per unit time interval* would be $\theta_j^1 \rho^2 \sigma^2(\tilde{\pi}_{t\tau})$. Thus, his total expected profits, P^1, over n such periods would be

$$P^1 = \theta_j^1 \rho^2 n\sigma^2(\tilde{\pi}_{t\tau}) = \theta_j^1 \rho^2 \sigma^2(\tilde{\pi}_t) \tag{45}$$

since $\sigma^2(\tilde{\pi}_t) = n\sigma^2(\tilde{\pi}_{t\tau})$. Note, however, that

$$\theta_j^1 = \frac{1}{2\sigma^2(\tilde{v}_{j\tau})} \frac{dV(R_j)}{dE(R_j)}$$

$$= n\theta_j^n$$

since $\sigma^2(\tilde{v}_j) = n\sigma^2(\tilde{v}_{j\tau})$. Thus, we can rewrite (45) in terms of θ_j^n for comparison with the profits of the n period forecast interval as:

$$P^1 = n\theta_j^n \rho^2 \sigma^2(\tilde{\pi}_t)$$

$$= nP^n \tag{46}$$

Thus, for a given forecasting ability a manager's expected market forecasting profits over a given time interval increase in direct proportion to the number of forecasting periods in a given time interval. Identical conclusions hold for the naive forecast model as long as the coefficient d_1' does not change. Intuitively these results make sense since what is happening is that as the forecasting period is shortened the manager is able to profit from many more fluctuations in market prices. However, lest this seem too pat and simple let us note that it is probably extremely difficult to forecast over shorter and shorter periods with the same degree of success (i.e. constant ρ).

6. Evaluation of Portfolio Management under the Two Factor Asset Pricing Model

6.1. The Two Factor Asset Pricing Model

Black [1] has derived the equilibrium structure of security prices in a market in which no riskless borrowing or lending opportunities exist. He has shown that the expected return on any asset j will be given by

$$E(\tilde{r_j}) = E(\tilde{r}_Z)(1 - \beta_j) + E(\tilde{r}_M)\beta_j \tag{47}$$

where the lower case r's represent total returns, $\beta_j = \text{cov}(\tilde{r}_j, \tilde{r}_M)/\sigma^2(\tilde{r}_M)$, $E(\tilde{r}_M)$ = the expected total returns on the market portfolio and $E(\tilde{r}_Z)$ represents the expected total returns on a portfolio which has a zero covariance with $\tilde{r}_M$. Vasicek [14] has also demonstrated that (47) holds when there exist riskless lending opportunities but no riskless borrowing opportunities.

In addition Black et al. [2] have demonstrated that the *ex post* returns on all securities on the New York Stock Exchange in the interval 1931–65 appear to be generated by a process given by

$$\tilde{r}_{jt} = \tilde{r}_{Zt}(1 - \beta_j) + \tilde{r}_{Mt}\beta_j + \tilde{u}_{jt} \tag{48}$$

where $\text{cov}(\tilde{r}_Z, \tilde{r}_M) = \text{cov}(\tilde{r}_Z, \tilde{u}_j) = \text{cov}(\tilde{r}_M, \tilde{u}_j) = E(\tilde{u}_j) = 0$. We now shall consider the optimal incorporation of forecasts of the zero beta portfolio, $\tilde{r}_{Zt}$, and the market portfolio, $\tilde{r}_{Mt}$, into a portfolio and then go on to consider the problems involved in measuring a manager's ability in the context of the two factor model. This expanded model appears to incorporate the inconsistencies of the observed risk-return relationship with the simple form of the model (6) which have been documented by Miller and Scholes [7], Friend and Blume [4] and Black et al. [2].

6.2. Optimal Incorporation of Forecasts of $\tilde{r}_Z$ and $\tilde{r}_M$ into a Portfolio

Assume again for simplicity that the investors in the manager's portfolio all have the same preference function $U[E(\tilde{r}_j), V(\tilde{r}_j)]$, on the single period return and variance of the portfolio and that the manager engages only in trading activities designed to profit from his forecasts of next period's expected return on the market and beta factors. Given his forecasts his problem then consists of determining the fraction γ_t to invest in the market portfolio and the fraction $(1 - \gamma_t)$ to invest in the zero beta portfolio.[11] The expected return and variance on his portfolio are given by

$$E(\tilde{r}_{jt}) = \gamma_t [E(\tilde{r}_M) + \pi^*_{Mt}] + (1 - \gamma_t)[E(\tilde{r}_Z) + \pi^*_{Zt}]$$

$$V(\tilde{r}_j) = \gamma_t^2 \sigma_j^2(\tilde{\pi}_M) + (1 - \gamma_t)^2 \sigma_j^2(\tilde{\pi}_Z)$$

where π^*_{Mt} and π^*_{Zt} are the manager's forecast of the 'unexpected' returns on the market and zero beta portfolios based on his information set $\phi_{j,t-1}$ at time $t - 1$.

$$\pi^*_{Mt} = E[\tilde{\pi}_{Mt} | \phi_{j,t-1}]$$

$$\pi^*_{Zt} = E[\tilde{\pi}_{Zt} | \phi_{j,t-1}]$$

and $\sigma_j^2(\tilde{\pi}_M)$ and $\sigma_j^2(\tilde{\pi}_Z)$ are the variances of these conditional distributions (assumed constant for all t)

$$\sigma_j^2(\tilde{\pi}_M) = \mathrm{Var}(\tilde{\pi}_M | \phi_{j,t-1})$$

$$\sigma_j^2(\tilde{\pi}_Z) = \mathrm{Var}(\tilde{\pi}_Z | \phi_{j,t-1})$$

The manager's problem is to choose γ_t so as to

$$\max_{\gamma_t} U[E(\tilde{r}_{jt}), V(\tilde{r}_{jt})] \tag{49}$$

Differentiation with respect to γ_t yields the optimal value

$$\gamma_t = \frac{\sigma^2(\tilde{\pi}_Z)}{\sigma^2(\tilde{\pi}_M) + \sigma^2(\tilde{\pi}_Z)} + \frac{1}{2[\sigma^2(\tilde{\pi}_M) + \sigma^2(\tilde{\pi}_Z)]} \frac{dV(r_j)}{dE(r_j)} [E(\tilde{r}_M) - E(\tilde{r}_Z)]$$

---

[11] The particular zero beta portfolio in which he is interested is, of course, the one with minimum variance.

$$+ \frac{1}{2[\sigma^2(\tilde{\pi}_M) + \sigma^2(\tilde{\pi}_Z)]} \frac{dV(r_j)}{dE(r_j)} [\pi^*_{Mt} - \pi^*_{Zt}] \tag{50}$$

where $dV(r_j)/dE(r_j)$ is as defined in section 4, $E(\tilde{r}_M)$ and $E(\tilde{r}_Z)$ are the unconditional expected returns on the market and zero beta portfolios (again assumed constant through time).

Again since $\beta_M = 1$ and $\beta_Z = 0$, we see that $\beta_{jt} = \gamma_t$, and since we have assumed his anticipations regarding $\sigma_j^2(\tilde{\pi}_M)$ and $\sigma_j^2(\tilde{\pi}_Z)$ are constant through time, we can rewrite (27) as

$$\beta_{jt} = \beta_j + \theta_j(\pi^*_{Mt} - \pi^*_{Zt}) \tag{51}$$

where

$$\theta_j = \frac{1}{2[\sigma_j^2(\tilde{\pi}_M) + \sigma_j^2(\tilde{\pi}_Z)]} \frac{dV(r_j)}{dE(r_j)}$$

and

$$\beta_j = \frac{\sigma^2(\tilde{\pi}_Z)}{\sigma^2(\tilde{\pi}_M) + \sigma^2(\tilde{\pi}_Z)} + \theta_j[E(\tilde{r}_M) - E(\tilde{r}_Z)]$$

can be thought of as the 'target' risk level of the portfolio. Let the manager's forecasts and the realized values of the market and beta factors be bivariate normal so that

$$\tilde{\pi}_{Mt} = d_{M0} + d_{M1}\tilde{\pi}^*_{Mt} + \tilde{v}_{jt} \tag{52a}$$

$$\tilde{\pi}_{Zt} = d_{Z0} + d_{Z1}\tilde{\pi}^*_{Zt} + \tilde{s}_{jt} \tag{52b}$$

where $\tilde{v}_{jt}$ and $\tilde{s}_{jt}$ are normally distributed forecast errors, $\tilde{\pi}_{Zt} = \tilde{r}_{Zt} - E(\tilde{r}_Z)$ and $E(\tilde{v}_{jt}) = E(\tilde{\pi}^*_{Mt}\tilde{v}_{jt}) = E(\tilde{s}_{jt}) = E(\tilde{\pi}^*_{Zt}\tilde{s}_{jt}) = 0$. Now as in the earlier single variable model if the manager is to make optimal use of his forecast π^*_{Mt} and π^*_{Zt} he will adjust them to remove any systematic biases by forming the adjusted forecasts π'_{Mt} and π'_{Zt}:

$$\pi'_{Mt} = d_{M0} + d_{M1}\pi^*_{Mt} \tag{53a}$$

$$\pi'_{Zt} = d_{Z0} + d_{Z1}\pi^*_{Zt} \tag{53b}$$

Thus substituting these adjusted forecasts into (51) the systematic risk of the portfolio is

$$\tilde{\beta}_{jt} = \beta_j + \theta_j(\pi'_{Mt} - \pi'_{Zt}) \tag{54}$$

and again β_j can be thought of as the manager's 'target' risk level. We note in passing that given our assumption of bivariate normality between the forecasts and outcomes of the two factors the conditional variances $\sigma_j^2(\tilde{\pi}_M)$ and $\sigma_j^2(\tilde{\pi}_Z)$ in the definition of θ_j are respectively given by:

$$\sigma_j^2(\tilde{\pi}_M) = \sigma^2(\tilde{v}_j)$$

$$\sigma_j^2(\tilde{\pi}_Z) = \sigma^2(\tilde{s}_j)$$

If the manager simply uses his raw forecasts $\tilde{\pi}_{Mt}^*$ and $\tilde{\pi}_{Zt}^*$ we can use the relations

$$\tilde{\pi}_{Mt}^* = d'_{M0} + d'_{M1}\tilde{\pi}_{Mt} + \tilde{v}'_{jt} \tag{55a}$$

$$\tilde{\pi}_{Zt}^* = d'_{Z0} + d'_{Z1}\tilde{\pi}_{Zt} + \tilde{s}'_{jt} \tag{55b}$$

(where $E(\tilde{v}'_{jt}) = E(\tilde{s}'_{jt}) = E(\tilde{\pi}_{Mt}\tilde{v}'_{jt}) = E(\tilde{\pi}_{Zt}\tilde{s}'_{jt}) = 0$) to obtain the systematic risk of the portfolio for the naive forecast model as:

$$\tilde{\beta}_{jt} = \beta_j + a_{Mj}\tilde{\pi}_{Mt} + a_{Zj}\tilde{\pi}_{Zt} + \tilde{w}_{jt} \tag{56}$$

where β_j is now defined so as to incorporate the effects of d'_{M0} and d'_{Z0}, $a_{Mj} = \theta_j d'_{M1}, a_{Zj} = \theta_j d'_{Z1}$, and $\tilde{w}_{jt} = \theta_j(\tilde{v}'_{jt} - \tilde{s}'_{jt})$

6.3. Measurement of the Manager's Abilities to Increase Portfolio Returns

We obtain the equation which describes the process generating the portfolio returns for the optimal forecast adjustment model by substituting from (54) into (48) and adding a constant, α_j:

$$\tilde{r}_{jt} = \alpha_j + [E(\tilde{r}_Z) + \tilde{\pi}_{Zt}][1 - \beta_j - \theta_j(\tilde{\pi}'_{Mt} - \tilde{\pi}'_{Zt})]$$

$$+ [E(\tilde{r}_M) + \tilde{\pi}_{Mt}][\beta_j + \theta_j(\tilde{\pi}'_{Mt} - \tilde{\pi}'_{Zt})] + \tilde{u}_{jt} \tag{57}$$

The expected returns on the portfolio are[12]

$$E(\tilde{r}_{jt}) = \alpha_j + (1 - \beta_j)E(\tilde{r}_Z) + \beta_j E(\tilde{r}_M) + \theta_j \rho_Z^2 \sigma^2(\tilde{\pi}_Z) + \theta_j \rho_M^2 \sigma^2(\tilde{\pi}_M) \tag{58}$$

---

[12]Note that by definition that π'_M is independent of π_Z and π'_Z is independent of π_M.

where ρ_Z is the correlation between the manager's forecast, $\tilde{\pi}_Z^*$, of the unexpected return on the zero beta portfolio and the actual unexpected return, $\tilde{\pi}_Z$ and ρ_M is similarly defined as the correlation between $\tilde{\pi}_M^*$ and $\tilde{\pi}_M$, the forecast and unexpected returns on the market portfolio. As in the single variable model discussed earlier we can identify the source of each of the terms contributing to the expected returns on the manager's portfolio. The first term, α_j, is the per period expected increment in portfolio returns due to the manager's security selection activities. The second and third terms involving $E(\tilde{r}_Z)$ and $E(\tilde{r}_M)$ are the returns due to the average riskiness of the portfolio, and the last two terms are the returns due to the manager's forecasting activities. Again we see that the returns due to the managers forecasting activities are directly proportional to the variance of the two factors and, given the variances, directly proportional to the coefficients of determination between his forecasts and the outcomes of the factors.

The large sample estimate of the portfolio's systematic risk, β_j, is

$$\text{Plim } \hat{\beta}_j = \frac{\text{cov}(\tilde{r}_j, \tilde{r}_M)}{\sigma^2(\tilde{r}_M)} = \beta_j + \theta_j \left[\rho_M^2 [E(\tilde{r}_M) - E(\tilde{r}_Z)] + \frac{E(\tilde{\pi}_M^3) - E(\tilde{v}_j^3)}{\sigma^2(\tilde{\pi})} \right] \quad (59)$$

and as before we see that this estimate is upward biased if $\rho_M^2 > 0$ (since $E(\tilde{r}_M)$ and $E(\tilde{r}_Z)$ are always positive (cf. Vasicek [14]) and the third moments of $\tilde{\pi}_M$ and $\tilde{v}_j$ will be either zero or positive). If we are dealing with continuously compounded rates or with sufficiently small differencing intervals we can probably eliminate the term involving the third moments of $\tilde{\pi}_M$ and $\tilde{v}_j$. Hence we shall in the later analysis assume the distributions to be symmetric about zero and ignore these terms.

For the naive forecasting case we can obtain the portfolio return generating process by substitution from (56) into (48) and the addition of the constant α_j:

$$\tilde{r}_{jt} = \alpha_j + [E(\tilde{r}_Z) + \tilde{\pi}_{Zt}](1 - \beta_j - a_{Mj}\tilde{\pi}_{Mt} + a_{Zj}\tilde{\pi}_{Zt} - \tilde{w}_{jt})$$

$$+ [E(\tilde{r}_M) + \tilde{\pi}_{Mt}](\beta_j + a_{Mj}\tilde{\pi}_{Mt} - a_{Zj}\tilde{\pi}_{Zt} + \tilde{w}_{jt}) + \tilde{u}_{jt} \quad (60)$$

The large sample estimate of the portfolio's systematic risk is

$$\text{Plim } \hat{\beta}_j = \frac{\text{cov}(\tilde{r}_j, \tilde{r}_M)}{\sigma^2(\tilde{r}_M)} = \beta_j + a_{Mj} \left[E(\tilde{r}_M) - E(\tilde{r}_Z) + \frac{E(\tilde{\pi}_M^3)}{\sigma^2(\tilde{\pi}_M)} \right] \quad (61)$$

and the expected returns on the portfolio are

$$E(\tilde{r}_{jt}) = \alpha_j + E(\tilde{r}_Z)(1 - \beta_j) + E(\tilde{r}_M)\beta_j + a_{Zj}\sigma^2(\tilde{\pi}_Z) + a_{Mj}\sigma^2(\tilde{\pi}_M) \quad (62)$$

and the interpretation of these equations is similar to that discussed above.

If we simply run a revised version of (9)

$$\tilde{r}_{jt} = \lambda_j + \beta_j \tilde{r}_{Mt} + \tilde{e}_{jt} \tag{63}$$

in an attempt to obtain an overall estimate of the manager's contribution to portfolio returns the large sample estimate of λ_j for the optimal forecast adjustment case will be

$$Plim \; \lambda_j = \alpha_j + E(\tilde{r}_Z)(1 - \beta_j) + \theta_j \rho_Z^2 \sigma^2(\tilde{\pi}_Z) + \theta_j \rho_M^2 \sigma^2(\tilde{\pi}_M)$$

$$- \theta_j \rho_M^2 E(\tilde{r}_M)[E(\tilde{r}_M) - E(\tilde{r}_Z)] \tag{64}$$

As we can readily see, λ_j does not provide a direct estimate of the managers contribution to portfolio returns since it includes returns due to the beta factor, $E(\tilde{r}_Z)(1 - \beta_j)$, and the last term (similar to that in the earlier simple formulation) will cause a negative bias if the manager can forecast the returns on the market portfolio to any extent ($\rho_M^2 > 0$).

Similarly the estimate of λ in (64) for the naive forecast model is

$$Plim \; \lambda_j = \alpha_j + E(\tilde{r}_Z)(1 - \beta_j) + a_{Zj}\sigma^2(\tilde{\pi}_Z) + a_{Mj}\sigma^2(\tilde{\pi}_M) - a_{Mj}E(\tilde{r}_M)[E(\tilde{r}_M) - E(\tilde{r}_Z)] \tag{65}$$

and we have identical problems here if the manager can forecast $\tilde{\pi}_{Mt}$ to some extent.

The key to solving many of the problems we have here is to obtain an unbiased estimate of β_j. For large samples we can obtain such an unbiased estimate for the naive forecasting model (as long as our return measurement interval is identical to the manager's forecasting interval) by estimating

$$\tilde{r}_{jt} = \eta_0 + \eta_1 \tilde{\pi}_{Mt} + \eta_2 \tilde{\pi}_{Mt}^2 + \eta_3 \tilde{\pi}_{Zt} + \eta_4 \tilde{\pi}_{Zt}^2 + \tilde{u}_{jt} \tag{66}$$

Examination of (60) indicates the coefficients will be

(a) $\quad \hat{\eta}_0 = \alpha_j + (1 - \beta_j)E(\tilde{r}_Z) + \beta_j E(\tilde{r}_M)$

(b) $\quad \hat{\eta}_1 = \beta_j + a_{Mj}[E(\tilde{r}_M) - E(\tilde{r}_Z)]$

(c) $\quad \hat{\eta}_2 = a_{Mj}$

(d) $\quad \hat{\eta}_3 = 1 - \beta_j - a_{Zj}[E(\tilde{r}_M) - E(\tilde{r}_Z)]$

(e) $\quad \hat{\eta}_4 = a_{Zj} \tag{67}$

and from this we can obtain[13] two estimates of β_j

(a) $\quad \hat{\beta}_j = -\hat{\eta}_3 + 1 - \hat{\eta}_4 [\bar{r}_M - \bar{r}_Z]$

or

(b) $\quad \hat{\beta}_j = \eta_1 - \eta_2 [\bar{r}_M - \bar{r}_Z]$ $\hfill (68)$

and using either one of these estimates our estimate of α_j is given by

$$\hat{\alpha}_j = \hat{\eta}_0 - (1 - \beta_j)\bar{r}_Z - \beta_j \bar{r}_M \qquad (69)$$

and our estimate of the increment in portfolio returns due to his forecasting ability is given by

$$\hat{\eta}_2 \hat{\sigma}^2(\tilde{\pi}_M) + \hat{\eta}_4 \hat{\sigma}^2(\tilde{\pi}_Z) \qquad (70)$$

Unfortunately, as in the simple model of section 4 we cannot obtain equivalent solutions for the case where the manager follows an optimal adjustment procedure for his forecasts π_M^* and π_Z^* without having exogenous knowledge of the parameter ρ_M^2. In the interest of brevity we omit the proof here.

6.4. Performance Measurement with Unknown (but Small) Forecasting Intervals

As in the simple model discussed earlier the procedures outlined above apply only if we can measure the portfolio returns over intervals identical to the manager's forecasting interval. As before let us take the forecasting interval as unity and assume that we measure returns over a number of such intervals n. Then $\tilde{r}_{jt} = \Sigma_\tau^n \tilde{r}_{jt\tau}$ and using this we find that the estimated risk coefficient β_j for the optimal forecast adjustment model is

$$\text{Plim } \hat{\beta}_j = \beta_j + \theta_j \frac{1}{n} [E(\tilde{r}_M) - E(\tilde{r}_Z)] \rho_M^2 \qquad (71)$$

---

[13]We obviously need estimates of the mean values of the returns on the market and zero beta portfolios. The market portfolio poses no problem and procedures for obtaining efficient estimates of the mean returns on the zero beta portfolio are given in Black et al. [2].

and for the naive forecast model is

$$\text{Plim } \hat{\beta}_j = \beta_j + a_{Mj} \frac{1}{n} [E(\tilde{r}_{Mt}) - E(\tilde{r}_{Zt})] \tag{72}$$

where $E(\tilde{r}_{Mt})$ and $E(\tilde{r}_{Zt})$ are the expected returns of the market and zero beta portfolios over the n-unit measurement time interval. (We are continuing to assume all third moments are zero.) We can see that the large sample estimate $\hat{\beta}_j \cong \beta_j$ if n, the number of forecasting periods in our measurement interval is large.

If we estimate (63) the intercept λ_j for the optimal forecast adjustment case is

$$\text{Plim } \hat{\lambda}_j = n\alpha_j + E(\tilde{r}_Z)(1 - \beta_j) + \theta_j \rho_Z^2 \sigma^2(\tilde{\pi}_Z) + \theta_j \rho_M^2 \sigma^2(\tilde{\pi}_M)$$

$$- \theta_j \rho^2 \frac{1}{n} E(\tilde{r}_M)[E(\tilde{r}_M) - E(\tilde{r}_Z)] \tag{73}$$

and for the naive forecast model it is

$$\text{Plim } \hat{\lambda}_j = n\alpha_j + E(\tilde{r}_{Zt})(1 - \beta_j) + a_{Zj} n\sigma^2(\tilde{\pi}_{Zr}) + a_{Mj} n\sigma^2(\tilde{\pi}_{M\tau})$$

$$- a_{Mj} E(\tilde{r}_{Mt}) \frac{1}{n} [E(\tilde{r}_m) - E(\tilde{r}_Z)] \tag{74}$$

Thus, if n is large we can to a close approximation for large samples estimate the *total* increment in portfolio returns due to the manager under either forecast model by:

$$\hat{\lambda}_j - \bar{r}_Z(1 - \hat{\beta}_j) \cong n\alpha_j + \theta_j \rho_Z^2 \sigma^2(\tilde{\pi}_Z) + \theta_j \rho_M^2 \sigma^2(\tilde{\pi}_M) \tag{75}$$

for the optimal forecast adjustment case, and

$$\hat{\lambda}_j - \bar{r}_Z(1 - \beta_j) \cong n\alpha_j + a_{Zj} \sigma^2(\tilde{\pi}_Z) + a_{Mj} \sigma^2(\tilde{\pi}_M) \tag{76}$$

for the naive forecasting model. We could also run the equivalent of (9) defining $\tilde{R}_{jt} = \tilde{r}_{jt} - \tilde{r}_{Zt}$ and $\tilde{R}_{Mt} = \tilde{r}_{Mt} - \tilde{r}_{Zt}$ and then $\hat{a}$ would provide us with an approximately unbiased estimate of the RHS of (75) or (76). Thus, again, if the forecasting interval is small relative to our return measurement interval we can obtain an estimate of the total increment in portfolio returns due to the manager's ability under either forecast model even if we don't know the forecasting interval. We cannot, however, obtain separate estimates of the returns due to his security selection and forecasting abilities under these conditions.

7. Conclusions

In considering the evaluation of a manager's ability we have examined four major questions:

(1) How should the manager optimally incorporate his market forecasts into his portfolio policy?

(2) If the manager engages in market forecasting activities, under what conditions can we evaluate his performance in his market forecasting and security selection activities separately?

(3) Does it make any difference if he does or does not optimally adjust his forecasts?

(4) Under those conditions where we cannot separately evaluate his performance in these two dimensions can we obtain unbiased measurements of the sum of the incremental portfolio returns due to both activities?

Based on our solution for the optimal utilization of market forecasts we demonstrated that if the manager's forecasts are valueless (but he nevertheless engages in trading activities designed to capitalize on his forecasts) we can still obtain unbiased estimates of his security selection ability. We also demonstrated for the naive forecasting model that if the manager can forecast market returns and if the interval over which we measure portfolio returns is identical to the manager's forecasting interval we can evaluate the manager's performance in both dimensions separately. However, if the return measurement and forecasting intervals differ we cannot accomplish this separate evaluation. In this situation we can, however, obtain to a very close approximation an estimate of the total incremental portfolio returns due to the manager's talents if his forecasting interval is small relative to the return measurement interval. This it seems is as far as we can get in measuring performance utilizing only the time series of portfolio returns and the market and zero beta portfolio returns. If we desire any more detailed measurements it appears we shall have to have much more detailed information, such as the manager's forecasts and the portfolio composition at each point in time. We also demonstrated that these same qualitative results hold under the two factor capital asset pricing model which seems to be a solution to many of the problems of performance measurement which have been encountered in the utilization of the single factor model (cf. Friend and Blume [4] and Black et al. [2]).

References

[1] F. Black, 'Capital market equilibrium with no riskless borrowing or lending'. Unpublished manuscript, August, 1970.

[2] F. Black, M.C. Jensen and M. Scholes, 'The capital asset pricing model:

some empirical tests', in: *Studies in the theory of capital markets* (ed. by M.C. Jensen), New York, Praeger, forthcoming, 1972.

[3]   E.F. Fama, 'Risk, return and equilibrium: some clarifying comments', *Journal of Finance* 23 (March, 1968) pp. 29–40.

[4]   I. Friend and M. Blume, 'Measurement of portfolio performance under uncertainty', *American Economic Review* 60 (September, 1970) pp. 561–575.

[5]   M.C. Jensen, 'Risk, the pricing of capital assets, and the evaluation of investment portfolios', *Journal of Business* 42 (April, 1969) pp. 167–247.

[6]   M.C. Jensen, 'The performance of mutual funds in the period 1945–1964', *The Journal of Finance* 23, No. 2 (May, 1968) pp. 389–416.

[7]   M.H. Miller and M. Scholes, 'Rates of return in relation to risk: a reexamination of some recent findings', in: *Studies in the theory of capital markets,* (ed. by M.C. Jensen), New York, Praeger, forthcoming, 1972.

[8]   J. Lintner, 'Security prices, risk, and maximal gains from diversification', *Journal of Finance* 20 (December, 1965) pp. 587–616.

[9]   J. Mossin, 'Equilibrium in a capital asset market', *Econometrica* 34 (October, 1966) pp. 768–783.

[10]   W.F. Sharpe, 'Mutual fund performance', *Journal of Business* 39, Part 2 (January, 1966) pp. 119–138.

[11]   W.F. Sharpe, 'Capital asset prices: a theory of market equilibrium under conditions of risk', *Journal of Finance* 19 (September, 1964) pp. 425–442.

[12]   J.L. Treynor and K.K. Mazuy, 'Can mutual funds outguess the market?', *Harvard Business Review* (July–August, 1966), pp. 131–136.

[13]   J.L. Treynor, 'How to rate management of investment funds', *Harvard Business Review* 43 (January–February, 1965) pp. 63–75.

[14]   O.A. Vasicek, 'Capital asset pricing model with no riskless borrowing'. Unpublished manuscript, Wells Fargo Bank, March, 1971.

About the Editor

James L. Bicksler received the B.A. from Beloit College (1959), the M.B.A. and the Ph.D. from New York University in 1960 and 1967. He is professor of finance and director of research at Rutgers University, Graduate School of Business, where his current research is in micro capital theory and financial issues in regulation.